1975
1

Barron's
How to Prepare for
College Board
Achievement Tests

SOCIAL STUDIES
AMERICAN HISTORY

By David A. Midgley

Head of History Department, The Albany Academy
Lecturer in History and Government, Russell Sage College

BARRON'S EDUCATIONAL SERIES, INC.
WOODBURY, NEW YORK

FOREWORD

This book provides a basic core of material which is specific and which has to be studied in order to be fully grasped. It is this knowledge which distinguishes the sound, well-grounded student from those who are uncertain and superficial.

It is selective. Most cultural background content has been omitted in favor of concentrating on the material usually asked on examinations. Double and single asterisks throughout the text designate material that deserves special emphasis.

There is more factual detail than usually found in review books or outline texts. The factual accounts are enriched by interpretative treatment intended to enhance interest, aid understanding, and provoke thought. The author is convinced that when a student is presented with substantial factual material to hold a story together and give it meaning, the painful problem of memorizing by rote is nearly eliminated, while appreciation increases so as to make history interesting and comparatively easy to learn.

The "Articles of Confederation" are given a thoughtful and different treatment; the section on "Knowing the Constitution of the United States" is unusually complete and appropriate to our times.

The "List of Presidents" adds several appropriate facts to the standard "name and date" list. Using them as a framework, the student should learn them cumulatively throughout the year and relate his broader summaries of historical development to them. Combining the facts from the "List of Presidents" provides material for difficult essay-type answers on special topics.

The amply detailed table of contents is a convenient way to find important topics. The student should read a section of his standard text, then find the same area through the table of contents and read the interpretation in this book for a better understanding and amplification of his knowledge.

Granted, there is much to memorize in history, but when the facts are understood in relation to the broader movements of history they are easier to remember.

Good luck to all of you and a good appreciation of what America is!

DAVID A. MIDGLEY

Contents

America and Americans

Our Country's Name

A reasonable beginning for the study of American history is an inquiry into the meaning of America and Americans. From the Rio Grande and the Gulf of Mexico to the Canadian border about 200,000,000 people think of the United States as being America. Some people of Central and South America are mildly irritated when citizens of the United States call themselves Americans; it suggests to them that the United States is considered by its own people to be the only nation of importance in the Americas. Of course we Americans have no such idea in mind; we have merely fallen into a pattern of terminology. Two of our best loved patriotic songs, "America" and "God Bless America," are about the United States. To us American history begins in 1492 when Columbus landed at San Salvador (Watling Island) in the Bahamas. In 1499 and 1501 Amerigo Vespucci, an Italian explorer (he would have called himself a merchant of Florence), sailed along the north and east coasts of South America and discovered it to be a continent. This Florentine merchant was employed by the king of Portugal. A professor in Lorraine, Martin Waldseemüller, helped make a map of the New World. This German professor put the name, America, on the map. Now we have a North, a South, and a Central America. The origin of the name of our country is mixed enough to make it "typically American." The exact meaning of America can be determined only in the context in which it is used.

Migrations from Asia

Now, how about Americans? Some 30,000 years ago, give or take a few thousand, people from Asia crossed from Siberia to Alaska. On a clear day, land is continuously visible as one crosses the Bering Strait. Today's maps show Uelen in Siberia, and Wales in Alaska, on opposite sides of the strait. Just about midway between them is Diomede Island which rises over 1,500 feet above the sea. Primitive savages with crude rafts could have made the crossing. Alaska, where they would land, offered abundant supplies of salmon and seal. We can guess why these Asiatics left Siberia for Alaska. It is almost certain that all the guesses we make

are true. Hunger due to a prolonged period of poor hunting, pressure from hostile tribes, changes in climate, or just the restless meanderings of a primitive people could have been the reasons. From Alaska these people from Asia spread in all directions. When Columbus arrived, the "American Indians" were distributed throughout the Americas. We think the first Asians to cross to Alaska were Mongols, but the migrations covered so long a period of time and the types of Indians and Eskimos are so varied that it is probable that several types of Asians crossed the Bering Strait. These savages soon lost all sense of contact with their past.

Today's scholars most interested in the origins of human life in the Americas and most curious about these very early settlers are the ethnologists, the anthropologists, and the archaeologists. They are the experts. Ethnologists study races and groups of people to determine their distinctive characteristics and their relationships to one another. Anthropologists study mankind as an animal; they delve into his physical and psychological characteristics. The archaeologists uncover history by seeking buried relics of the remote past. These authorities support the conclusion that nowhere in the Americas did civilization begin. The Americas have no true natives. All the people who ever lived in the Western Hemisphere have been descended from people whose origin goes back to one of the "cradles of civilization" such as the Nile Valley, the Tigris-Euphrates Valley, the Ganges-Indus Valley, and the Hwang Ho Valley—or possibly other cradles yet to be found. From the historical view this makes Columbus a recent arrival. He started a new stream of people to America, this time primarily from Europe. That Columbus started such a continuous movement of peoples gives him undisputed rank as first among the explorers, and justly the most renowned.

The American Indians

The Indians of the Americas have been classified more according to their language than any other single factor. However, many considerations determined their groupings into families and tribes. The Indian family contains several tribes. The Indian culture is the oldest in America; but it is, in a sense, also the newest, because only recently archaeologists have added substantially to our knowledge concerning them. Today's schoolboy (or girl) has every opportunity to live a full and fascinating life tracking the Indians. The first step toward such a goal is the hard work, and probably also the fun, of becoming a competent scientist.

The following Indian families lived in areas now part of the United States. Most of us know of them through reading and the T.V. "Westerns."

A] The Iroquois were warlike. They displayed a quality most unusual among Indians, the ability to organize along political lines. Iroquois tribes formed the "Five Nations" of central New York State. Its members were the Cayuga, Mohawk, Onandaga, Oneida, and Seneca tribes. Hiawatha is probably the most widely known Iroquois chief.

B] The Algonquin family spread itself all over North America. Their tribal names were Arapaho, Blackfoot, Cheyenne, Fox, and Shawnee. The familiar Algonquin chiefs were Massasoit, King Philip, Pocohontas, Pontiac, Tammany, and Tecumseh. Evidently the General Motors Corporation and the New York City Democrats favor the Algonquin family.

C] The Muskogean family was comparatively peaceful. They lived in the south-eastern part of the United States. Their more familiar tribe names were Cherokee, Chickasaw, Choctaw, Creek, and Seminole. Osceola was one of their well-known chiefs.

D] The Siouan family occupied the Great Plains. They were nomads who followed the Buffalo. Their familiar tribe names were Crow, Dakotas, Iowa, Kansas, and Omaha.

E] The Pueblo Indians were really not a family as were the previously mentioned groups. Pueblo means town and is a Spanish word used to describe the Indians who lived in towns. These town-dwelling Indians lived in New Mexico and Arizona. They were the only North American Indians to depend primarily upon agriculture; hence they had settled communities. Their housing and crafts were more fully developed than those of any other Indians within the limits of the United States.

Indian families much more exciting to the scientists lived in the Yucatan peninsula of Mexico and in Honduras. They were the Maya and the Toltec Indians. The Mayans developed a civilization vastly superior to that of the North American Indians. Their buildings were of tremendous size. They worked in wood, stone, and metal. They developed an accurate calendar. Their many settlements were united into a league of city-states. This remarkable Indian civilization was at its peak about 1100. In 1191 the Mayan federation was conquered by the Toltec Indians who maintained the civilization and perhaps advanced it a bit. For reasons still obscure, this Mayan-Toltec civilization faded out in the middle of the 1400's. No other Indian civilization reached the high level of this Mayan-Toltec era.

Not too many years before Columbus arrived at the Bahamas, the Aztec Indians took over the Mayan-Toltec area, but never revived its culture. Under the leadership of their king, Montezuma, the Aztecs were tricked and conquered by Cortez and his well-disciplined soldiers. This Spanish conquest took place in 1519-1521. About a decade later, 1531-1535, the Inca Indians of Peru were conquered by Pizarro for Spain. Both the Aztecs of Mexico and the Incas of Peru reached a higher level in the crafts and in building than most of the North American Indians. Their society was dominated by the priests, and some of their religious rites would appear to us to be grotesque, cruel, and horrible. Chiefs and priests formed a combined dictatorship over the tribes.

The Age of Exploration

Factors Favoring Exploration

It is difficult to explain with certainty why the period of exploration occurred when it did. We can be sure that certain facts were common knowledge among the navigators and map makers who gathered around and worked with Prince Henry, "The Navigator," of Portugal during the first half of the 1400's. These facts were as follows.

1] Aristotle had concluded that the earth was a sphere and another Greek, Eratosthenes, had calculated the circumference to be 28,000 miles, an over-estimate of about one-seventh. This speculation, while not commonly known, had been kept alive by scholars throughout the centuries between Aristotle (350 B.C.) and Prince Henry, the navigator (1450).

2] Marco Polo had lived in China (Cathay) for seventeen years. He had taken four years to go from Constantinople to Peking.

3] John Gutenberg's printing press, 1450, made Marco Polo's book of truth and tall tales common knowledge among navigators.

4] The magnetic compass had made navigation beyond the sight of land and without the sight of the stars a more certain art.

5] The astrolabe was a new device for determining latitude.

6] The caravel (such as the Santa Maria, Niña, and Pinta) was a new Portuguese invention. Its sails were a great improvement for sailing against the wind. It was the fastest large ship of its day.

7] More important perhaps than all other facts, but less easy to explain, was the ferment in men's minds during the 1400's. The dull re-hash of ancient learning and the preoccupation of scholars with religious thought had given way to a fresh looking-forward. A vital curiosity about man, nature, and things scientific had developed.

THE EXPLORERS

The following list of explorers has many dates. It is suggested that you learn those that are underlined. Develop the habit of noticing dates for the purpose they are intended to serve; namely, to place the event in its proper relation to other events. Some students are irritated by dates, others find them helpful; it's all a matter of your mental approach.

The explorers are grouped according to the nation sponsoring the expedition. Within each national group the listings are in chronological order.

Explorers often worked for nations other than their own. For example, Amerigo Vespucci we may call an Italian. He thought of himself as a citizen of Florence. His first exploration was in the service of Spain and his second in the service of Portugal. Henry Hudson was English but he worked for the Netherlands. Both Cabots, father and son, were citizens of Venice but they explored for England.

DATE	EXPLORER	NATION	ACCOMPLISHMENT
1000	Leif Ericson	Norway	Atlantic coast from Nova Scotia to R.I. First European to land in America. Unimportant because there was no chain of events as a result.
1488	Bartholomeu Dias	Portugal	Rounded southern tip of Africa, the Cape of Good Hope. Turned back.

DATE	EXPLORER	NATION	ACCOMPLISHMENT
1498	Vasco da Gama	*Portugal*	Rounded the Cape of Good Hope. Crossed Indian Ocean to India. Started continuous trade by sea between Europe and the Far East.
1501	Amerigo Vespucci	*Portugal*	Second trip. Sailed along much of the eastern coast of South America. On his first trip in 1499, working for Spain, he had sailed along much of the northern coast. Both trips together gave geographers a good idea of the size of the continent from north to south.
1492	Christopher Columbus	*Spain*	Aug. 3, 1492 the Santa Maria, Pinta, and Nina sailed from Palos. On Oct. 12th they arrived at the Bahama Islands. Columbus called the island San Salvador (probably Watling Island). He explored the islands of Cuba and Haiti (Hispaniola).
1493	Christopher Columbus	*Spain*	Explored the Leeward Islands and Puerto Rico. Made the settlement of Santo Domingo on the island of Haiti headquarters for further explorations.
1498	Christopher Columbus	*Spain*	Explored the Island of Trinidad and the nearby coast of South America.
1502	Christopher Columbus	*Spain*	Coast of Central America from Panama to Honduras.
1499	Amerigo Vespucci	*Spain*	See above—1501—Vespucci.
1513	Ponce de Leon	*Spain*	Explored Florida searching for the "fountain of youth."
1513	Vasco Núñez de Balboa	*Spain*	Saw the Pacific Ocean from the Isthmus of Panama on Sept. 25, 1513. This led to the idea that North and South America might be about as wide as Panama.
1519-1521	Hernando Cortez	*Spain*	Conquered the Aztec Indians of Mexico under their king, Montezuma. Great wealth in gold and silver shipped to Spain.
1519-1522	Ferdinand Magellan	*Spain*	First circumnavigation of the world. Left Spain Sept. 20, 1519; killed in the Philippines April 27, 1521. Expedition returned to Spain Sept. 6, 1522. Claimed Philippines for Spain.
1530-1536	Francisco Pizarro	*Spain*	Conquered the Inca Indians of Peru and founded a settlement at Lima.
1539-1542	Hernando de Soto	*Spain*	Explored the Gulf coast from Florida to the Mississippi River. Went into what is now Georgia, Alabama, Mississippi, Arkansas and Oklahoma. Died of fever and buried in the Mississippi River.

DATE	EXPLORER	NATION	ACCOMPLISHMENT
1540-1542	Francisco Vásquez de Coronado	Spain	Discovered the Grand Canyon of Arizona. Also explored New Mexico, the Panhandle area of Texas, and Kansas.
1524	Giovanni da Verrazano	France	Explored the coast from Carolina to Nova Scotia. Also entered New York Harbor and Narragansett Bay.
1534	Jacques Cartier	France	Explored the St. Lawrence Gulf and River to Montreal.
1608-1615	Samuel de Champlain	France	Went up the St. Lawrence and through the Great Lakes to Lake Huron. Discovered Lake Oneida and Lake Champlain. Made eleven trips. Established fur trade with the Indians. The "Father of New France."
1673	Père Marquette & Louis Joliet	France	Explored Mackinac Strait, Lake Michigan, Green Bay, Wisconsin River and Mississippi River to the Arkansas River.
1682	Robert, Sieur de La Salle	France	Went from the Great Lakes to the Mississippi River and down to its mouth.
1497	John Cabot	England	Sailed along the coast from Newfoundland to Maine.
1498	John Cabot	England	Sailed from Newfoundland to Chesapeake Bay.
1509	Sebastian Cabot	England	Explored northeast coast.
1577-1580	Sir Francis Drake	England	Second circumnavigation of the world.
1609-1611	Henry Hudson	Netherlands	Explored the Hudson River and Hudson Bay. A mutinous crew set him adrift in Hudson Bay in June 1611.

In the very early period of these explorations, the Spanish government urged the pope, Alexander VI, who was himself a Spaniard, to issue an edict or "papal bull" concerning the New World. In 1493 the pope declared that all lands west of a line of longitude 100 leagues (about 300 miles) west of the Azores and the Cape Verde Islands should belong to Spain. This, of course, brought a reaction from Portugal and the original papal bull was modified by a treaty. In its modified form the agreement set the "demarcation line" at 320 leagues west of the Cape Verde Islands (about 1110 miles). This line cut off a part of the hump of Brazil east of the line for Portugal, and left all the rest of the western hemisphere to Spain. In 1493 no one knew how such a line would in fact divide the New World. But line or no line, the period of exploration was destined to be followed by a struggle for empire. The big question was not who found it, but who could settle it and hang on to it.

Viewing the list of explorers not merely as something to remember but as a factual record to be interpreted, we can form certain conclusions.

1] Portugal was early but did more navigating than exploring of land areas.

2] Spain was almost as early as Portugal and much more active in supporting expeditions.

3] England was early but made only a weak effort.

4] France was a bit late but put forth a substantial effort.

5] The Netherlands was late and apparently disinterested. (The East Indies and the "spice trade" were more attractive to her.)

6] Spain explored the Bahamas, West Indies, Central America, Florida, Mexico, Peru, Philippines, Georgia, Alabama, Mississippi, Arkansas, Oklahoma, Texas, Kansas, and Arizona.

7] The French went into the St. Lawrence River, through the Great Lakes, into Green Bay, down the Wisconsin River and down the Mississippi River to the Gulf of Mexico. They went down into New York State to Lake Oneida and to Lake Champlain close to the Mohawk and Hudson Rivers.

8] The English hired two Italian navigators who sailed along the North Atlantic Coast of North America no farther south than Chesapeake Bay.

The Spanish, French, and English were to be the nations to build empires based on the explorations. This pattern of exploration was roughly repeated in the settlements made by these contenders for empire in the New World. Spain dominated the south and west. France dominated the great waterways entering North America at the St. Lawrence River and proceeding by way of the Great Lakes into the heart of the continent and out southward by way of the Mississippi River. Henry VIII (1509-1547), Queen Elizabeth (1558-1603), the Spanish Armada (1588), the first two Stuart kings, James I and Charles I—1603-1649), combined to supply England with national power, hatred of Spain and France, and a constant flow of Englishmen willing, and often eager, to leave their homeland. And there was the eastern seaboard of North America waiting for them.

*Some European Influences and Rivalries in Colonial America

When settlements were made in North America, the people who came here brought with them their points of view about government and religion; they brought with them their homeland customs. For the French, Spanish, and Dutch, this meant a natural acceptance of autocratic, absolute government with all power centered in the sovereign or his representative. It would not occur to them to have a legislature made up of settlers. The French and Spanish would be Roman Catholics. They would easily accept both church and king as authorities generally to be obeyed and certainly not to be questioned. Although church and government had their rivalries and jealousies, nevertheless they worked reasonably well together. Their joint supervision of the people was accepted as a matter of course. The position of the Dutch settlers in these respects was not very different even though there was no official church. Their government was absolute. Almost all of the Dutch settlers were Protestants whose church affiliation was a dominant factor in their lives.

The English were different. Magna Carta (the Great Charter) of 1215 and the Model Parliament of 1295 had sown seeds of liberty that could not be completely killed. Popular monarchs (Henry VIII and Queen Elizabeth) could ignore Parliament and rule as dictators, but unpopular kings ran into difficulties. Charles I had managed to get his head cut off in 1649. By 1600 the "divine right of kings" theory either was dead or dying as far as the English were concerned. Having had representative government in England, they had assemblies in the English colonies. The "Tree of Liberty" found more favorable soil in the New World even though it took a deal of cultivating and required time to develop. The English settlers were accustomed to private ownership of land by ordinary people as well as by the landed aristocracy. The French, Dutch, and Spanish were much closer to feudalism in the distribution of land; the Patroon system of the Hudson Valley with its tenant-farmers illustrates the point. The Dutch and Spanish had a "land problem" not too different from that of the present "distribution of land problem" throughout the Latin American Republics.

The French settlements were strung so thinly along the major waterways (St. Lawrence, Great Lakes, Mississippi) that land ownership was not a problem. The French were fur-traders, hence nomads, circulating from Indian tribe to Indian tribe. There were comparatively few French women in America. Towns were few, forts and trading posts were many. Little wonder that the successful French fur trader was a man who had learned to live, act, and perhaps think, as an Indian. By and large, the French and the Indians liked one another; the Frenchman didn't want the Indian's land and the trading supplied both with what they wanted.

The Spanish explorers struck it rich in Mexico and Peru. This was, in spite of its initial appearance, a misfortune for them and their nation. This taste of success kept later Spanish expeditions intent upon fruitless searches for more treasure. The English "sea-dogs" such as Drake, Cavendish, Davis, and Frobisher harassed the Spanish treasure-laden ships on their homeward journey. The Spanish took in so much treasure that they spent it importing merchandise, most of it from England. Spanish arts and crafts languished while England's flourished. Spain poured her treasure into the greatest armament program of the day, the building of the Great Armada. In 1588 this was a complete loss when it was defeated by a picked-up English merchant-marine with a few cannon aboard (England had no navy), the superior seamanship of the English sea-dogs, the comparative clumsiness of the large Spanish ships, and stormy seas. This catastrophe was Spain's quick start on a prolonged decline as a world power. Thus the real struggle for North America was left to England and France.

In comparison with today's rapid pace, events moved slowly in the sixteen and seventeen hundreds. Then, as now, international politics, economics, and religious turmoil in Europe had their repercussions in North America. Without attempting any detail, we can get an appreciation of this intermingling of European and American affairs by listing a series of wars between France and England. Many other nations were involved, but the primary opponents were England and France. Notice the dates. Figure out the intervals between the wars. What chance did a generation of English or French boys have to escape war between 1689 and 1815?

THE WARS IN EUROPE		THE SAME WARS IN AMERICA	
1]	War of the League of Augsburg (also called War of the Palatinate)	1689-1697	King William's War
2]	War of the Spanish Succession	1701-1713	Queen Anne's War
3]	War of the Austrian Succession	1740-1748	King George's War
4]	Seven Years War	1756-1763	French & Indian War
5]	France, Holland and Spain at war with England during the American Revolution	1775-1783	American Revolution
6]	Napoleonic Wars (Intermittent)	1798-1815	War of 1812 (1812-1815)

By the end of the first four of these six wars the French had been driven out of North America, and the Spanish had lost Florida. The last two wars were unsuccessful attempts by France to re-establish herself in North America. At the end of the American Revolution, Spain did make a slight recovery by regaining Florida.

The English Colonies

Two of the earliest permanent English colonies to be established in America were Virginia in the south and Massachusetts in the north; one in sympathy with England both as to politics and religion, and the other at odds with England in these respects. Each represented the economic and social structure typical of its area. By 1775 both had wealth, population, and more than their share of men destined to greatness in the formative period of the history of our nation. For these two colonies a rather detailed account was recorded of their early days—about the first hundred years.

* Virginia at Jamestown, 1607—The Bare Facts

1] Three vessels arrived at Virginia April 26, 1607. One hundred five settlers established themselves at Jamestown on May 24th.

2] Captain John Smith, according to his own account in "A True Relation" (relation of events), led the colony through the first eight months.

3] The winter of 1609-1610 was the terrible starving time.

4] Lord De La Warre rescued the colony in the spring of 1610. Governor Thomas Dale's harsh but wise rule maintained the colony. Governors Gates and Yeardley succeeded Dale and continued a similar tough, practical policy.

5] John Rolfe introduced West Indian tobacco to Virginia.

6] Sir Edwin Sandys, treasurer of the London Company, formed Virginia's first General Assembly, the House of Burgesses, in 1619.

7] Misfortune from many directions drove the London Company into bankruptcy in 1622. Virginia became a royal colony in 1624.

8] In 1675 Nathaniel Bacon led a rebellion against Governor Berkeley.

Some of the Virginia Story

The London Company was a private stock company. Shares were sold for £12 10s (a very rough estimate, $60.). This sum would then pay for about eighteen weeks' labor. Money raised by selling shares of stock financed the venture. Very few shareholders were also settlers. To the owners of stock, the London Company was an investment— or was it a speculation? To the British government the London Company was a device for building empire. As a business venture the colony was a failure; as a factor in establishing an empire it was a success.

The Virginia story is a harsh one. One hundred twenty men (no women) were on three vessels that set sail for Virginia. Sixteen died during the crossing. Some accounts say only thirty-two survived to see Christmas of 1607; some say fifty-three survived to see the spring of 1608. It seems safe to accept as fact that about fifty percent or less of those who left England for Virginia survived the first year.

Although instructed by the officers of the London Company to select a high, dry site on a river, the settlement was made on low ground in a swampy region about thirty miles up the James River. This group of about one hundred men have been described as "decayed gentlemen," released prisoners, and a few craftsmen. They were the wrong kind of persons and they did the wrong things. The ideal settlers would have been tough young farmers and laborers intent upon wresting a living from virgin land. The actual settlers were intent upon finding treasure or upon following every stream with the hope that it would bring them within sight of Cipango (Japan) or Cathay (China).

The first crude houses they built let in rain and cold. The long trip over had exhausted the ships' food supplies. Hunger, disease (especially malaria), bickering among themselves, and fighting with the Indians made life miserable. What food was raised was put into a common storehouse to be given out as needed in the winter. Such a plan might have been necessary for the first season. But, as time went on, the fact that how much food one received had no relation to how much one had done to maintain the colony would result in less food produced. Basically, this is the same problem the tremendous collective farms of present-day Red China and the U.S.S.R. have been unable to solve. Any scheme which separates a man's effort from the reward he may expect encourages declining effort and smaller production.

During the first year Captain John Smith managed to keep food production to at least the minimum required. He was captured by the Indians, but his life was spared through the intercession of the Indian maiden, Pocohontas, daughter of the chief. At any rate his influence was lost to the colony which slacked off in its one important task, the raising of food.

More ships had arrived in Virginia in 1608 and 1609, so that about nine hundred had come to the colony by Christmas of 1609. Yet the next spring only sixty people were alive. These were the few who survived the terrible "starving time" of the winter of 1609-1610. These miserable, half-starved men were ready to leave Jamestown when Lord De La Warre arrived with new settlers and more supplies. Had De La Warre been one or two days later the colony of Virginia might have been, as Roanoke Island was, a lost colony.

Lord De La Warre was ill and soon returned to England. He left Governor Thomas Dale in charge. The London Company was re-organized with governors Thomas Gates and George Yeardley succeeding Dale. Under all three governors much the same policy was followed. The colony became a virtual concentration camp. Men were marched under armed guard to work in the fields twice a day. The basic rule was: those who don't work, don't eat. The common storehouse could be kept reasonably well supplied if enough force could be applied to keep the men at work. Treasure hunting and searching for Cathay ceased. Another re-organization of the London Company brought Sir Edwin Sandys in as treasurer in 1619. Reforms were instituted. The common storehouse had given way to individual farms. A general assembly was formed. Twenty-two members represented groups of settlers (two from each group). This is the famous House of Burgesses, the first representative government in the New World. The two delegates represented a *Hundred* or a *town* or a *plantation*. These three terms meant an area where enough men lived to warrant two delegates.

Tobacco gave a great economic lift to Virginia. John Rolfe introduced West Indian tobacco plants, a great improvement over the local variety. From 1616 to 1619, the tobacco exported from Jamestown rose from under 3,000 pounds to over 50,000 pounds.

The year 1619 not only found Virginia eating well, enjoying a thriving tobacco trade, and inaugurating the House of Burgesses, it also witnessed the arrival at Jamestown of the first slaves, twenty of them, and of the first women, ninety of them. The women were described as "respectable maidens." They may have remained respectable for the rest of their lives, but they soon ceased to be maidens. It takes both men and women to give stability to a community. One of Virginia's great weaknesses during its first dozen years was the lack of family life and the very many civilizing influences it brings. The slaves were a curiosity of no real economic value. Who then could have foreseen the horror and tragedy which the introduction of slavery foreshadowed? We are still paying for that wickedness.

The year 1622 might be called Virginia's year of misfortunes. Disease, especially malaria, poor crops, a slump in the tobacco trade, and increased Indian troubles combined to drive the colony into a desperate situation and the London Company into financial collapse. When the London Company gave up the king took over. The privy Council of James I supported the colony with soldiers and supplies. It held Virginia in a virtual receivership. The colony was valuable to the British government as an outpost of empire. National pride, if nothing else, demanded its continuance. So in 1624 Virginia became a royal colony directly under the authority of the king.

The House of Burgesses continued under the royal governors. Virginia grew in strength. Small farms worked by their owners lined the James, York, and Rappahannock rivers. Life was still simple and hard. Among these middle-class farmers were the grandfathers and fathers of the Virginia "Greats" of the late 1700's and the early 1800's— Washington, Patrick Henry, Jefferson, Madison, and Monroe.

Just a century before the thirteen colonies had their revolution against England, the colony of Virginia had its rebellion against a royal governor. In 1675 Nathaniel Bacon led a rebellion against Governor Berkeley. By this date Jamestown had spread out. The poorer farmers lived on the outer fringes of the colony and were from time to time the victims of Indian outrages. The governor's militia was adequate to control this situation provided the governor was determined to use it. In 1675 a series of Indian raids on isolated farms accounted for over thirty deaths. Families left their homes in fear of further attacks. Governor Berkeley made no move to handle the problem. It was charged that the reason behind the governor's lack of action was to be found in his private fur trade with the Indians. He could control the Indians and thereby impair his fur business, or he could overlook the occasional massacres and maintain the fur business at its peak. Berkeley was suspected of placing a higher value on his private business interests than on the lives of a few not-so-important

Virginians. He was faced with a conflict of interests; his interests as a businessman and his duty as a public official. The mere fact of being a public official invites this conflict of interest. President Cleveland expressed it another way in the words, "A public office is a public trust." Putting monetary gain ahead of human life is the twisted sense of values which forms the heart of many of today's "rackets" and of organized crime. Many present-day problems are old ones in new wrappings.

Nathaniel Bacon led an unofficial armed force of about five hundred men against the Indians to do what the governor should have done. Governor Berkeley branded him an outlaw. Bacon's answer was to march his men into Jamestown where he drove the governor and his militia from the town. Much of Jamestown was burned during this fight. With everything going in his favor Bacon died suddenly. The rebellion collapsed. Berkeley re-established his authority, rounded up some of Bacon's most prominent supporters and executed twenty-three of them. King Charles II was disgusted with Berkeley and called him back to England. The American colonials in the colony most in harmony with their motherland had thus shown, a century before the American Revolution, that royal authority was not secure when it earned the intense displeasure of the people. Like many a lesson, it wasn't learned.

* Massachusetts Bay Colony at Boston, 1630— The Bare Facts

1] John Winthrop was elected governor before the colonists embarked from Southampton, England.

2] In 1630 eleven ships sailed from Southampton and others from Bristol and Plymouth. Over one thousand colonists, some in family groups, settled at and near Boston.

3] By October 1630 a representative government was organized. It was made up of Governor Winthrop, a governor's council (which was also a court and the upper house of the legislature), and an assembly.

4] For about thirty-five years the right to vote and to hold office was restricted to church members in good standing. (Theocratic government)

5] Harvard College was founded. Its main purpose was to maintain a well-educated clergy for the Puritan church. (Later the Congregational denomination)

6] In 1636 Roger Williams, a minister in Salem, was tried and ordered banished to England. He

escaped to Narragansett Bay where he started the Rhode Island colony at Providence. Here *complete* religious freedom was established.

7] In 1636 Ann Hutchinson persuaded some clergymen and many others to accept unorthodox religious ideas. She was excommunicated. With her family she went to Providence. She established a settlement at Portsmouth, R.I. and soon thereafter started another settlement on Long Island.

8] In 1636 the Rev. Thomas Hooker was at odds with Boston's theology. He and some of his congregation settled at Hartford. In 1639 they drew up the Fundamental Orders, the first written constitution in the New World.

9] In 1638 the Rev. John Davenport was also unhappy about the religious set-up in Boston. He founded a colony at New Haven.

10] In 1643 the New England Confederation was formed to give more effective defense against the Indians and to guard against encroachment by the Dutch from the Hudson Valley. The four members were Massachusetts Bay, Plymouth, New Haven, and Connecticut (Hartford).

11] In 1665 four commissioners from King Charles II came to New England. Their reception by Boston officials led three of them to advise the king to revoke the Massachusetts charter.

12] King Philip's War in 1675-1676 spread all over New England. It was the Indians' last great effort in New England to stop the spreading white settlements. About half of the towns were attacked and twelve were wiped out. But New England manpower was too great; the Indians really had no chance to succeed.

13] In 1684 King James II made Massachusetts a royal colony. (See below the list of items under *Massachusetts Irritates the King*.)

14] Sir Edmund Andros arrived at Boston in December 1686 as the appointed royal governor of New England. He was to unite New England, New York, New Jersey and Pennsylvania under his command as a precaution against war with France. (See *Rule of Andros*—following page.)

15] In 1689 news of the expulsion of James II and the coming to power of William and Mary (William III) led to the arrest of Andros and his being shipped back to England. This was the Bloodless or Glorious Revolution as it was known in England.

16] In 1691 the friendly king, William III, granted a new charter which kept Massachusetts a royal colony, rescinded all punitive acts taken against it, forbade religious qualification for political rights, and made Maine and Plymouth part of Massachusetts Bay Colony.

* Massachusetts Irritates the King

1] In 1630 the first settlers and Governor Winthrop brought the charter of the colony to Boston with them. This put the charter beyond easy reach of the king, his privy council, and his judges. It gave Massachusetts a sense of independence she could not otherwise have had.

2] In the 1640's and 1650's Massachusetts annexed New Hampshire towns, Nashua, Exeter, Dover, Hampton; also the Maine towns of Kittery and York. Massachusetts aided these nearby towns against the Indians and perhaps she figured that what she was called upon to protect she might as well possess. Nevertheless, she acted without the king's permission and in violation of charter rights.

3] In 1643 the New England Confederation was formed. It was a defense against Indians and a precaution against encroachment by the Dutch. Massachusetts organized and dominated it. This union was made without the king's permission and against his wishes. Any union of colonies could be turned against the king.

4] In 1653 Massachusetts refused to aid England in her conflict with Holland. Every colony's first duty was to come to the aid of the mother country in time of war.

5] In 1665 the king's commissioners were rudely treated and their demands rejected. Massachusetts refused to
   a. allow all orthodox churches freedom to observe their religion,
   b. have all heads of families take an oath of allegiance to the king,
   c. repeal all local laws repugnant to the king.

The Rule of Andros (Dec. 1686 to Jan. 1689)

1] Rhode Island and Connecticut were declared to be royal colonies. Connecticut hid its charter in an oak tree. (Charter Oak) In 1691 King William III declared this change in the status of Rhode Island and Connecticut to have been illegal and of no effect.

2] New England, New Jersey, New York, and Pennsylvania were united under Andros in anticipation of war with France.

3] The Old South Meeting House was changed to an Anglican Church.

4] All land titles were to be re-examined. Any quitrents still due must be paid if the landholder was to keep his property.

5] The only town meetings permitted without the special consent of Andros were the annual meetings for the election of officers.

6] Andros levied taxes without any action by the legislature.

All of these measures were resisted. The president of Harvard College, Rev. Increase Mather, stole off to England to lodge a protest. The hostile climate of opinion greatly hindered Andros in getting his program actually established. He had created bitterness and chaos before the Glorious Revolution ended this episode.

* Some of the Massachusetts Story

Much of this story has been covered by *The Bare Facts.* (*Massachusetts Irritates the King* and *The Rule of Andros.* In addition the atmosphere, character, and spirit of Massachusetts, as well as New England in general, deserves attention.

The Pilgrims of Plymouth had deep religious convictions as their reason for leaving England. First they went to Leyden, Holland. Because their children were becoming little Dutchmen, they made arrangements to return to England in preparation for the trip to America. They were Separatists, so-called because they wished to separate entirely from the Anglican Church. The Mayflower with its 101 colonists, 35 of them from the Leyden group, arrived at Cape Cod in early November in 1620. Before landing, forty-one men representing themselves and their families signed the Mayflower Compact. This was an agreement to make "just and equal laws" to which they promised "all due submission and obedience." Hence this Compact is often called the first example of self-government in the New World. About half of those who arrived in the Mayflower died during the first winter, yet none of the survivors decided to return to England in the spring. William Bradford was their governor for thirty of the first thirty-six years. For toughness of fiber, for unshakable faith in God, and for noble living, this band of Pilgrims presents one of the most inspiring examples in our history.

The Puritans who settled in Boston and nearby areas also had a religious difference with the Anglican Church. They did not wish to separate from it. They wished to purify it; hence the name, Puritans.

When Henry VIII started the Protestant Reformation in England, he merely replaced the Pope as head of the Church of England (Anglican Church). To Henry VIII the move was the result of a personal quarrel with the Pope which also gave Henry an opportunity to grab more power. Hence, when the Anglican Church separated from the Roman Catholic Church, the immediate change was a shift of power from a pope to a king. The rituals, ceremonies, architecture, vestments, statuary, stained glass windows, and other ecclesiastical symbols remained as before. As time went on the similarity of the Anglican and the Roman Catholic churches irked those English people who had become Catholic-haters and pope-haters. The Stuart Kings were unpopular in England, largely because they were suspected of being friendly toward Catholicism or even being Catholics themselves. With the Stuarts as head of the Anglican Church, there was some fear that a reunion with the Roman Catholic Church was in the making. The first two Stuarts ruled from 1603 to 1649, just the period within which Pilgrims and Puritans settled in America. "If the Catholics had it, we don't want it; if the Catholics did it this way, we'll do it some other way" expressed the Puritan attitude. This may be a bit over-simplified, but it has substantial truth. The Puritans did not believe in religious tolerance, let alone religious freedom. They demanded that the church be run their way and that everyone conform. Not to be a member of the Puritan church was to be a person of questionable desirability. Non-church members could live in Boston only if they were careful to stay mute (keep their mouths shut) on religious matters. And to the "mutes" in a Puritan community the doors of opportunity, socially and economically, were pretty well closed. Some Quakers were hanged. Ministers who failed to subdue differences of religious belief found it wise to found other colonies. The Puritan church restricted political rights to its own members. With all this narrowness and its attendant cruelties, the Puritan communities had great strength and many virtues. Puritan clergymen and Puritan public officials set a high standard of personal and official conduct which was reflected by, or may have been the result of, a similar level of conduct by the populace. Integrity, simplicity, and industry characterized this society more than most. The word *Puritan* today may be used to mean narrow and harsh; it may be used to mean strong and noble. The real Puritans were both.

List of Colonies

COLONY	*DATE PLACE FOUNDER	TYPE a) When founded b) In 1775	PERTINENT BITS OF INFORMATION
Virginia	**1607** Jamestown London Co.	a) Charter to stock company b) Royal	See pp. 9-10
Plymouth	**1620** Plymouth Pilgrims	a) Self-governing b) Royal	Leyden, Holland Wm. Brewster—first leader Separatists Miles Standish—military leader Wm. Bradford—early governor See p. 12
New Hampshire	1623 Portsmouth John Mason	a) Mass. claimed it, the title was obscure. Charles II made it royal in 1679. b) Royal	Very weak settlement Southern towns taken over by Mass. See p. 12
Maine	1623 Portland Sir Ferdinando Gorges	a) Proprietary Claimed by Mass. b) Royal	Became part of Mass. in 1691
New York	1624 Albany and New Amsterdam Dutch	a) Proprietary in 1664 when the Duke of York took it for England. b) Royal	N.Y. harbor and the Hudson River separated the English colonies. This was an intolerable situation to the empire-minded British.

COLONY	DATE PLACE FOUNDER	TYPE a) When founded b) In 1775	PERTINENT BITS OF INFORMATION
New Jersey	1624 Part of New Netherlands with N.Y. Dutch	a) Same as N.Y. b) Royal	For a period it was divided into East and West Jersey. For several years New York's governor also governed N.J. although the courts and the legislature were separate. Not until 1738 was N.J. definitely a separate, unified colony.
Massachusetts	<u>1630</u> Boston Mass. Bay Co.	a) Charter to stock company b) Royal	See pp. 11-12
Maryland	1634 St. Mary's Province Cecilius Calvert the 2nd Lord Baltimore	a) Proprietary b) Proprietary	Started as a Catholic colony. The Toleration Act of 1649 gave freedom of religion to all who believed in the Trinity. Granted to protect Catholics from interference by other Christians.
Rhode Island	<u>1636</u> Providence Roger Williams	a) Self-governing b) Self-governing	Freedom for all religions and for non-believers. Ann Hutchinson See p. 11
Connecticut	<u>1636</u> Hartford Thomas Hooker	a) Self-governing b) Self-governing	Fundamental Orders in 1639 was the first written constitution in the New World. Davenport's colony at New Haven became part of Conn. in 1662. See p. 11.
Delaware	1638 Wilmington Swedes	a) Proprietary after conquest by England in 1664. b) Proprietary	First settled by Swedes
North and South Carolina	1665 Albemarle Eight Noble Lords	a) Proprietary b) Royal	Albemarle Sound and Charleston Harbor where the earliest settlements were made are 300 miles apart. They had little contact with each other. Started with an impractical government based on John Locke's ideas. There was almost continual political strife. North and South Carolina became separate colonies in 1711.
Pennsylvania	<u>1683</u> Philadelphia Wm. Penn	a) Proprietary b) Proprietary	Quaker settlement Also many Germans (Pennsylvania Dutch) In the buying of the land from the Indians and allowing complete religious freedom Pa. followed the good example of R.I. Penn's colony was called "The Holy Experiment." After 1700 it had a unicameral (one-house) legislature.

COLONY	* DATE PLACE FOUNDER	TYPE a) When founded b) In 1775	PERTINENT BITS OF INFORMATION
Georgia	**1733** Savannah James Oglethorpe	a) Proprietary b) Royal	A mismanaged attempt at human rehabilitation. Many debtors and other unfortunates were among the first settlers. The prohibition of the rum trade and slavery during the first decade was an economic mistake. It had the unenviable location to serve as a buffer between Spanish Florida and the Carolinas.

* Do not be confused by different dates in different books. The year a charter is granted and the year an actual settlement is made are often different. There were many conflicting claims where grants by the king overlapped. In such cases the selection of a particular date is necessarily arbitrary.

The dates underlined are selected as those best to remember.

*Colonial Governments

As noted in the preceding list of colonies there were three types of government: proprietary, royal, and self-governing. The colonies that were to become the original thirteen states represented all three types. Rhode Island and Connecticut started out as self-governing and remained that way right up to the American Revolution in 1775. Pennsylvania, Maryland, and Delaware began as proprietary and so remained. The other eight: Massachusetts, New Hampshire, New York, New Jersey, Virginia, North Carolina, South Carolina and Georgia had become royal colonies by 1775 even though they had not all started as such.

All three types had a governor and a legislature. Pennsylvania had a unicameral (one-house) legislative body, which was unusual. The typical colonial legislature was bicameral (two-house). The council, a small group of advisors to the governor, was the upper house. It was sometimes, if it was a royal colony, appointed by the king. Sometimes the governor or the proprietor appointed the members of the council. In some cases the lower house, the assembly, elected the council. Besides being an upper house of the legislature, the council was usually also a court. A not uncommon provision in the charter of a colony was that the king's privy council in England could, within a specified time, veto an act of the colonial legislature. Governors could veto laws. The trump card held by the colonial legislatures was the power of the assemblies to appropriate money; they held the "power of the purse." Even the governors of royal colonies, except for Virginia, depended upon the assembly for their salaries. This often put the royal governor in a difficult position. When the king's policy ran counter to colonial wishes, what would the gover-nor do? Ignore the king and lose his job or ignore the colonists and lose his salary? Royal governors got directives from the king which they simply could not carry out; they had the legal authority but lacked the actual means necessary in the situation. In short, a royal governor had responsibility without adequate power. This knotty problem occurs again and again in government, business, and the professions.

The right to vote was restricted to those who met the property qualifications. It is difficult to be confident about how liberal or how restrictive colonial regulations were. Property qualifications differed from colony to colony, and over periods of time there were changes within each colony. The significant fact is that nowhere else in the world except in England was there a comparable degree of popular, representative government. As the New England colonies grew to contain several towns within a single colony, the famous town meeting developed. This political device was direct democracy which permitted tax payers to go to meeting and vote their local ordinances into effect.

The significant point to be learned from the several colonial governments is that they were wonderful training schools for those who were to become revolutionists in 1775. This experience in political know-how accompanied by the belief in the "Immemorial Rights of Englishmen" prepared our people to set up and operate a government of their own. With the end of World War II we entered a period of many revolutions. But the people who have won their independence, and those who may do so in the future, have had no such training ground for self-government as the founders of The United States had as English colonials.

Mercantilism in the English Colonies 1650-1763

To understand this period keep two facts constantly in mind:

1] The *Mercantile Theory of Trade* was accepted as the guide for building the strength of a nation.

2] *North America* was a *Battleground for Empire* between *England* and *France*.

Mercantile Theory of Trade

A basic concept of this theory of trade was that a nation must sell abroad (export) goods of greater money value than she buys from abroad (imports). In this way a nation will have a *favorable balance of trade* because she will collect more in payments from foreigners than she will pay to foreigners. When we say a *nation* buys and sells we mean the total bought and sold by the people of that nation; it is the sum total of all imports and exports, visible and invisible. A cargo of tobacco would be a visible export or import. An English ship carrying a cargo of wine from France to Sweden would be an invisible export from England because an English ship owner would be paid by a French wine company for transportation. England exported a service (invisible) for which she was paid.

The mercantile theory of trade meant that something had to be done to bring about and maintain an excess of exports, in terms of money value, over imports. Individual businessmen could make no such plans. Whatever was done had to be done by government. Laws had to be passed that would give encouragement to exports from England and discouragement to imports. However, England needed many goods that she herself could not produce. To buy such goods from France, Holland, Sweden, Spain, etc. would have increased their exports and strengthen those nations. Such a result was to be avoided. The mercantilists thought one nation's prosperity had to be gained at the expense of some other nation or nations. To them international trade was a perpetual "cold war."

Any goods obtained from one's own colonies would make the colonies prosper, keep the trade away from other nations, and supply England with goods she herself could not produce. Any goods commonly produced in England must not be produced in the colonies. Colonies were naturally sources of raw materials: forest products, minerals, fish, and whatever agricultural products were best suited to them. Mercantilism dictated that the colonies be encouraged in these commercial pursuits and restricted to them. For example: skin the beavers in Albany, N.Y., sell the skins to a London furrier, sell the beaver caps and capes wherever there is a market for them. But don't allow manufacturing of beaver caps and capes in the colonies. Was this a ruinous policy for the colonies? Not at all. As long as the supply of beaver skins held out, the beaver trade could grow and grow provided the English furrier could find purchasers for caps and capes. Of course, if the supply of beavers was exhausted that would be quite another story. But during this period of over one hundred years the colonial supplies of raw materials did not run out; in fact, the tremendous wealth of the American colonies was hardly more than scratched on the surface. This sort of regulation could be applied to many products. Lumber and iron ore from the colonies must be sent to England only in a crude state. The processing must be reserved for the craftsmen and manufacturers in England.

Invisible items of international trade must be regulated. All ships owned by British subjects and engaged in the business of transportation constituted the British merchant marine. Whenever these ships were hired by foreigners, the transaction was a British export. Under mercantilism this transportation service by ship was so important a business that it must be closely controlled by laws. Every effort must be made to favor the British ships and discourage the foreign ships. Notice the *British* included the people throughout the empire, not only the people of England.

If the examples of beaver skins, lumber, and iron ore have been understood, the basis for the many Acts of Trade is clear. Similarly, the regulation of invisible items of commerce explains many of the Acts of Navigation. Before discussing how these regulations affected commerce and how great a factor they were in building up to the American Revolution, several trade and navigation acts are worth consideration.

List of the Provisions of Some of the Trade and Navigation Acts 1650-1764

Think of each provision in terms of how it serves to carry out the mercantile theory of trade. The provisions with an asterisk (*) are suggested as worth special attention.

*1] 1650 No foreign ships can trade in a British colony without a license.

2] 1651 Ships entering English ports with goods from Asia, Africa, or America must be owned by British subjects, captained by a British subject, and manned by a crew most of whose members are British.

3] 1651 No foreigners can import fish into England, Ireland, or any British colony.

4] 1651 No foreign ship can carry cargo from one English port to another; that is, no coastal trade.

*5] 1660 No goods, no matter where from, can enter or leave a British colony except in a British ship with a British captain and a crew that is at least three-fifths British.

*6] 1660 Certain enumerated (listed) products from the colonies must be shipped only to England or to other British colonies. (sugar, indigo, tobacco,† and a few others)

7] 1696 All colonial laws in opposition to English navigation laws are void.

† Laws forbade the growing of tobacco in England, required the American tobacco colonies (Virginia and Maryland) to export tobacco only to England, and forbade the importation into England of tobacco from Spain and Portugal.

8] 1699 No wool products can be exported from the colonies.

*9] No beaver hats can be exported from one colony to another. Making beaver hats was put under severe restrictions.
  a. Only those who have served a seven-years apprenticeship can make beaver hats.
  b. No more than two apprentices can be employed in each establishment.

*10] 1733 Rum, spirits, sugar, and molasses from foreign West Indies to America are taxed.
  9 pence per gallon on rum and spirits
  6 pence per gallon on molasses
  5 shillings per hundred pounds on sugar
  (These were heavy duties.)

*11] Several times throughout the 1700's, bounties were granted on certain colonial products. A bounty was a sum of money paid to the colonial shipper by the English government to encourage the flow of certain goods into England. From time to time there were bounties paid on tar, pitch, turpentine, masts, rice, indigo, and a few other items. Total bounties paid over seventy years are estimated at about one and one-half million pounds.

*12] 1750's Smelting furnaces, rolling mills, and forges were prohibited in the colonies. Pig and bar iron could be sent to England duty free.

*13] 1764 The duties on sugar and molasses were lowered from the levels set by the law of 1733. The importation from the foreign West Indies of rum and spirits was prohibited.

The Triangular Trade

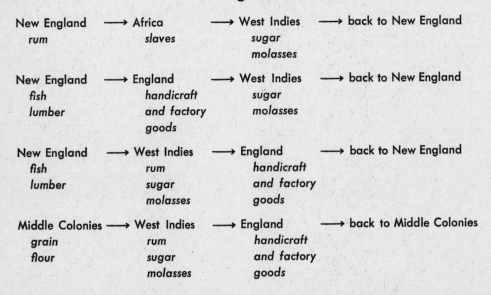

| New England | → Africa | → West Indies | → back to New England |
| rum | slaves | sugar molasses | |

| New England | → England | → West Indies | → back to New England |
| fish lumber | handicraft and factory goods | sugar molasses | |

| New England | → West Indies | → England | → back to New England |
| fish lumber | rum sugar molasses | handicraft and factory goods | |

| Middle Colonies | → West Indies | → England | → back to Middle Colonies |
| grain flour | rum sugar molasses | handicraft and factory goods | |

These triangular trips with a pay-load on each leg of the triangle were lucrative.

* How English Legal Restrictions Affected American Colonial Commerce up to 1764

Colonial trade was aided by some of the trade and navigation laws. It would have been hurt by other laws had they been enforced. The provision that a foreign ship must have a license in order to enter a British port usually helped the colonies by cutting foreign competition. But occasionally the British so needed the cargoes foreign ships carried that it was a hardship to go without. Licenses were neither freely nor quickly granted. The laws of foreign nations kept British ships out of their ports, for all countries followed the mercantile theory of trade. Thus, in an effort to preserve trade for themselves and their own colonies, the nations sometimes prevented commerce which they really wanted. The laws restricting shipping to British ships, captains, and crews helped New England ship yards and enabled many a New Bedford, Providence, or Boston lad to "follow the sea." Restrictions on manufacturing in the colonies undoubtedly prevented the formation of many enterprises, even though a few smelting furnaces operated illegally. The tobacco laws guaranteed American colonies a monopoly in selling to the British Isles, but did not allow the colonies to sell tobacco to Europe. Much American tobacco got to Europe, the English merchant being the middleman. The duties on sugar and molasses from foreign West Indies, had they been enforced, would have severely hurt the distilleries in Massachusetts, Connecticut, and Rhode Island. Making rum in New England had grown to such proportions that the manufacturers needed more sugar and molasses than the British West Indies could supply. Without foreign supplies, production would have been curtailed. These duties were well-nigh prohibitive and were intended to give the British sugar planters a monopoly in the American market. The payment of bounties on naval stores, rice, and indigo was a cash bonus based on the quantity delivered in England. As does everyone, the colonials liked to get something extra beyond the market price for the goods they sold.

Such trite remarks as "government is a necessary evil" and "that government governs best that governs least" may not be the epitome of wisdom, yet they do direct attention to the very natural, if not always reasonable, resentment individuals feel against government regulations. Those trade and navigation acts that helped the colonists were obeyed; those that made their businesses less profitable were violated more often than not.

* Salutary Neglect

Salutary means beneficial. One perceptive school boy defined neglect as what usually happens to home work. The salutary neglect with which we are concerned was beneficial to England and to her colonies. By and large the trade and navigation acts which were harmful to colonial trade were not enforced. The government was aware of the situation but made no appreciable effort to correct it. Official graft accounted for some of the laxness. A political favorite in London would be appointed customs officer for a colonial port. He wished to live in England so he hired someone in the colonies to do the job. To this local "deputy" he paid part of his salary, gave no thought to his official duties but kept a good share of the salary. The local "deputy" was naturally sympathetic with his friends and neighbors who might well be his business associates and members of his church. London was many weeks and three thousand miles away. It became customary not to notice smuggling and equally customary for the local customs official to receive a keg of rum occasionally as a friendly token of esteem and appreciation from a grateful shipper. The navigation law requiring a ship with a cargo from Europe to America to stop at England to have the cargo transferred to an English vessel was also commonly evaded. It is easy to see why the colonists evaded these laws, but why did England permit such evasion?

The presence of the French in North America is the best single answer. England needed the manpower of the seaboard colonies for the final showdown that was certain to come. The King and Parliament would not wish to create a hostile spirit in America toward England. It worked both ways. The colonists were very conscious of the presence of the French along the Great Lakes and the Mississippi River. They were anti-French and generally anti-Catholic. They were aware of how important the British navy was to their safety. When the final test of strength arrived, they would need the leadership, wealth, and power of England. So the colonists accepted the many trade and navigation laws without organized protests and with little grumbling. The regulations irked them, but were rated more as a nuisance than a grievance, especially in view of the policy of salutary neglect. Another point should be noted: trade within the

British empire was less thoroughly regulated than that of the French, Dutch, and Spanish empires. Had the British colonials looked about them, they would have seen that under the control of England they enjoyed more freedom of commerce than did the colonists of their rival nations.

The French and Indian War 1754-1763

The Indians Helped the French

In Europe this was called the Seven Years War (1756-1763). It was the fourth in a series of six wars with France and England opposing one another (see p. 8). Most of the Indian tribes from Canada to Florida were allied with the French; hence, to the English colonists in America, this was a war against the French and Indians. The Iroquois of central New York were anti-French so they gave some support to the English. This war was decisive. By it the French were forced off the continent of North America.

Instead of a running review of the war, we list below dates, people, places and events which an adequate account would contain.

1753 Governor Dinwiddie and George Washington

Governor Dinwiddie of Virginia sent George Washington, twenty-one year old major in the Virginia militia, to tell the French to get out of the Allegheny-Monongahela rivers area. Washington delivered the message and returned to Richmond.

1754 Washington Led Troops Against the French

The French had erected Fort Duquesne at the junction of the Allegheny and Monongahela rivers. Washington built Fort Necessity nearby. The ensuing battle at Great Meadows opened the war with a victory for France. Fort Necessity was surrendered to the French on July 4th.

* 1754 Albany Plan of Union (The Albany Congress) Benjamin Franklin

In early summer, delegates from the colonies and Iroquois Indians gathered at Albany, N.Y. For months Indians had made raids all along the line from Florida to Canada. The colonists figured this was white man's planning (French). It was correctly judged to be the opening of the final struggle for North America. The Albany meeting was called to deal with this situation. Benjamin Franklin from Pennsylvania submitted a plan to centralize and unify the handling of defense problems and Indian affairs. The plan called for a Grand Council elected by the colonial assemblies. Each colony could have from two to seven delegates. The more dues a colony paid to the organization the more delegates it could have. A President General appointed by and paid by the king would preside over the Grand Council. Taxes would be levied to pay for a single armed force to represent all the colonies, to regulate trade agreements with the Indians, to handle treaty-making with the Indians, to settle boundary disputes with them, and to take care of those matters which were obviously of common concern to the colonies as a group.

The plan was rejected by the Albany Congress, which was not ready for this much cooperation. Each colony was reluctant to place its armed men in a force which it could not control and under the command of someone who would be from another colony. At this point, 1754, the individual colonies were more fearful of losing the power of independent action than they were fearful of being wiped out by the French and Indians. The king of England, George II, rejected the plan for a different reason. He felt that such a union with an armed force representing the several colonies constituted at least a potential threat against the crown. If the union were formed, who could tell to what purpose it might be turned? Franklin's plan was a good idea, but the time was not ripe. Some of its features reappeared when the Articles of Confederation were drawn up.

* 1755 General Braddock and Washington

General Braddock with about 2,000 men, 1,400 British regulars and some Virginia militia, made a second attack upon Fort Duquesne. Lt. Colonel Washington was second in command. They were badly defeated at the Battle of the Wilderness within ten miles of Fort Duquesne. Braddock was killed. Washington led the retreat to Fort Cumberland, Md.

1756 The War Spread to Europe

Prussia lined up with England; Austria sided with France.

1757   General Montcalm Took Fort William Henry at Lake George, N.Y.

* 1757   William Pitt (Pitt the Elder), Earl of Chatham, Headed a New Ministry

The war in Europe and in America was going badly for England. War loans were raised, new taxes levied, men and supplies were thrown into the struggle. New commanders of outstanding ability, Lord Jeffrey Amherst and James Wolfe, replaced those who had failed.

1758   Amherst and Wolf Took Fort Louisbourg, Cape Breton Island

1758   The English Captured Forts Frontenac and Duquesne

Fort Duquesne was renamed Fort Pitt. It is now Pittsburgh, Pa.

1759   The English Captured Fort Niagara

General Amherst's superior manpower led to French withdrawal from Ticonderogo and Crown Point.

* 1759   General Wolfe Defeated General Montcalm on the Plains of Abraham to Take the Great Fortress of Quebec

Both generals were mortally wounded. This was the decisive battle; England had won the war. Today the Hotel Frontenac towers above a small park where a unique monument stands. The monument honors both the victor, General Wolfe, and the loser, General Montcalm.

1760   General Amherst Took Montreal

A few days later Detroit fell to the English and thereafter other French forts on the Great Lakes were deserted.

1762   The Treaty of San Ildefonso

France transferred to Spain all French territory west of the Mississippi River and New Orleans. Spain had been drawn into the war as an ally of France. She had lost to the English some of her possessions in the Far East and in the West Indies. To compensate Spain for these losses, France ceded to her the lands in North America that England had not yet taken from her.

* 1763   Treaty of Paris

1]   France gave up all of Canada to England. (By the Treaty of Utrecht, 1713, England had taken much of northern Canada.)

2]   France and Spain gave all lands east of the Mississippi River except New Orleans to England. (Spain had owned Florida.)

3]   The West Indies were unscrambled and redivided much as they had been before the war.

4]   France got two small islands, St. Pierre and Miquelon, off the south coast of Newfoundland. They were not to be fortified. The French needed them as a base for fishing fleets. France was guaranteed fishing rights off Newfoundland.

5]   Spain's title to New Orleans and lands west of the Mississippi River as arranged in the Treaty of San Ildefonso was recognized.

* Significance of the French and Indian War

As far as the American colonists were concerned, the war was over with the fall of Montreal. The colonies had contributed very substantially of their manpower and wealth. England and the colonists rejoiced together. The French had been driven from North America; no need to wait for the peace treaty to know that. This initial burst of pride in empire and good-will among Englishmen was a frothy, surface reaction without roots. The changed circumstances brought about by this victory rather clearly foreshadowed separation of the American colonies from England.

With the French out of North America, the colonists had no need of the British fleet, of British soldiers, or of British wealth to preserve their way of life. To the government in England this victory seemed to be the final defeat of France after four exhausting wars. England was victorious and broke. No foreign power threatened her empire. She needed no longer to humor the colonials with "salutary neglect." It was time to put the imperial house in order, to collect taxes, and to levy new taxes. The American colonies had benefited greatly by the late war; they should carry much of the tax load to pay for it. This English official view seemed reasonable in London at the time; it sounds so even now.

True historical insight pointed in another direction. There were about 3,000,000 people in the American colonies. Philadelphia, Boston, New York City, and Charleston ranged in population from about 10,000 to 25,000. Still, ninety per-cent or more of the people lived in rural areas and hence were widely scattered. London was too far away in both time and distance to enforce unpopular laws, whether just or not. England had one wise choice, which was to let go of the American colonies under terms that would keep them in the empire with strong ties of friendship and with no more authority from London than the colonists themselves would easily tolerate. Neither George III nor Parliament could think in terms of "dominion status" or of a "commonwealth of equals" within the empire. One hundred years later England displayed this kind of statesmanship with Canada. When the facts of history at any given time and place will no longer accept imperial control, then the control will disintegrate, either by explosion or by some more gradual form of release. England has done rather well in permitting parts of her empire to melt away while she, for the most part, retained their friendship, cooperation, and trade. France apparently did not learn from England's experience.

Heading Into the American Revolution 1763-1775

1763 The Proclamation Line

The western edge for colonial settlement was set at the Alleghenies. West of the Alleghenies was reserved for the Indians.

When the Great Lakes strong points held by the French collapsed after the fall of Detroit, the British tried in vain to make agreements about trading with the Indians. Negotiations broke down. Pontiac, chief of the Ottawas, destroyed most of the English forts in the Ohio Valley area. About the only posts the English saved were Duquesne and Detroit. By midsummer Pontiac made peace terms with Sir William Johnson. This uprising by the Indians explains, in part at least, why the Proclamation Line made sense to King George III and his ministers. To keep peace with the Indians by a chain of forts adequately manned would have taken thousands of soldiers, tremendous expenditures, and probably wouldn't have worked.

To the colonists the problem seemed quite different. Thousands of settlers were already west of the Alleghenies in the Ohio region. The Proclamation directed such settlers "forthwith to remove themselves." When would word get to the frontiersmen thinly scattered over thousands of square miles? When they did hear of it, how much attention would these truly rugged individuals pay to such an order? The colonists east of the Alleghenies complained that the Proclamation Line "hemmed them in" and there is every reason to think they believed it even though, two centuries later, scores of hunters still get lost every fall in the woods east of the Alleghenies. The real trouble with the Proclamation Line was that it simply could not be enforced. This fact should have been obvious to the English ministry. It could and did irritate the colonials with no compensating advantage to England.

1764-1765 The Grenville Program
1764 Sugar Act

This act was proposed by the Chancellor of the Exchequer (treasurer), George Grenville, in the British ministry (see p. 18).

1764 Ending the Policy of "Salutary Neglect"

Grenville noted that England was collecting about one-fourth as much money from the American colonies as she was spending to collect it. To reverse this financial idiocy certain measures were taken.

1] A vice-admiralty court was established in Halifax where tax cases could be taken for trial without a jury. Local colonial courts had a history of being sympathetic toward tax evaders.

2] Shippers were required to post heavier bond (larger sums of money) so that, when found guilty of tax evasion, the money to pay the fine would be readily available.

3] Tax collectors could no longer live in England and have a deputy in America do their work. The local "deputies" gave way to tax officials from England (see p. 19).

4] Soon after the new tax officials arrived in America, an increase in the number of soldiers was evident. About 10,000 came allegedly to strengthen the defenses of the colonies against the Indians. As most of the soldiers were stationed in the cities and towns along the coast, the colonists got the idea that their real purpose was to back up the tax collectors.

5] Tax officials were given writs of assistance (blanket search warrants).

1764 The Stamp Tax was Proposed

That this tax was proposed a year before it was to go into effect reflected both Grenville's fairness and his lack of political wisdom. No one likes to pay taxes, so there would be no expression of support from the colonies in favor of *any* tax. On the other hand, the delay of a year gave all opponents of the tax, all who feared they might have to pay stamp taxes, a chance to organize opposition and marshal arguments against it. Benjamin Franklin was in London at the time. He expressed the opinion that the American colonists would not like the tax, a sure-fire prediction about any tax. However, he used his influence to get a job for one of his friends as a tax-stamp distributer. He did not foresee the strong reaction that greeted the passage of the law in 1765.

1765   The Stamp Act Passed

Stamps had to be affixed to about fifty items such as legal documents, insurance policies, playing cards, newspapers, pamphlets, and licenses. These stamps varied in cost from a half-penny to two pounds (1¢ to $10).

American colonials were to be given the jobs as tax-stamp distributers and the income from the tax was to be used to pay the expense of defending the colonies.

1765   The Stamp Act Congress

James Otis persuaded the Massachusetts legislature to call a protest meeting. Letters were sent to all the colonies suggesting the meeting be held in New York City. In October the Stamp Act Congress met. Nine colonies were represented (Massachusetts, South Carolina, Rhode Island, Connecticut, New Jersey, Delaware, New York, Pennsylvania, Maryland). Their petition to the king and Parliament brought up the issue of taxation without representation and stated their conviction that only their own assemblies could levy taxes *for revenue* purposes.

1765   Boycott—Sons of Liberty—Stamp Tax Repealed

Just days after the Stamp Act Congress adjourned, merchants in New York City, Boston, Philadelphia, and Charleston signed pledges not to buy anything shipped from England. In many towns, groups calling themselves "Sons of Liberty" organized to use violent means, if need be, to punish merchants found violating the boycott. They attacked the colonials who had been appointed tax distributers. In Boston the vice-admiralty court records were burned; homes of unpopular officials were entered and ransacked. In New York City the royal governor's coach was overturned in the street and burned. These Sons of Liberty were a strange mixture. Some of their members were responsible business and professional men. Many were from the rowdy element bent upon exercising power and enjoying the fun of playing the bully in a popular cause. Merchants suspected of violating the boycott found the manners and methods of the Sons of Liberty rougher than the inspections by British officials with their hated writs of assistance.

The boycott so damaged the business of merchants in England that they petitioned Parliament for a repeal of the Stamp Tax. They cited their losses and claimed that a wave of bankruptcies had resulted from the enactment of the tax. This protest alone probably was enough to convince Parliament; added to the furor in America it resulted in the repeal of the Stamp Tax, May 1st 1765.

* Evaluating Grenville and His Program

Lord Grenville was a conscientious treasurer. His job was to raise money. Had the enforcement of the program presented no problems, the plan itself was reasonable and quite as equitable as many a successful tax program before and since. Grenville was thinking in terms of bookkeeping and economics; not in terms of people. The big difficulty was a political one. The question was not *what* to tax nor *how* to tax; it was how could taxes be levied in such a manner that the colonists would accept them? Perhaps there was no effective answer. Grenville seemed not to appreciate the problem, so with a good conscience, a desire to be reasonable, and no suspicion of what was to come, he blundered right into a hornet's nest. The Grenville program explained its purpose to be the improvement *"of the revenue* of this Kingdom." The Stamp Tax was on items originating wholly within each colony and not intended to go out of the colonies. It openly proposed *to raise revenue* for a stated purpose. Colonial assemblies were loaded with legal minds which quickly seized upon this new direction the Grenville program had taken. Up to 1764 the laws of Parliament regulating the colonies had been for the control of intercolonial and foreign trade. This was a natural part of building and maintaining an empire, this was a normal implementation of the mercantile theory of trade, and this was obviously a proper area of control by King and Parliament. If such regulations *incidentally* created revenue, that too was acceptable. But the Grenville program was openly a *revenue* raising scheme. If accepted it would expand; and if it expanded, it would take the "power of the purse" from the colonial assemblies. This "lawyer's argument" had time to develop and grow while the Stamp Tax was delayed for a year during 1764; it was ready to explode when the Stamp Tax was passed in 1765.

1766   Declaratory Act

At the same time the Stamp Act was repealed, Parliament passed the Declaratory Act. It stated that Parliament did have the right to make any laws which held the colonies and the British government together. This was a flat rejection of the colonial argument about taxation without representation, about taxation for revenue, and about any distinction between internal and external taxes. In celebrating the repeal of the Stamp Tax, the colonists gave scant heed to the Declaratory Act. But, to those who would look, it was apparent that a cleavage of opinion, probably an irreconcilable one, was in the making.

1766   Quartering Act

General Gage had more troops stationed in New York City than barracks to house them. At his request Parliament had passed a Quartering Act which required the colony in which troops were stationed to supply living quarters for those troops not accommodated by the military authorities. Inns, any vacant public buildings, and private homes could be used. New York resented the presence of the soldiers, as did all the coastal cities and towns. They also resented the expense. The populace erected liberty poles (a mast or staff with a liberty-cap on top) as a symbol of derision and defiance toward the soldiers. The red-coats pulled them down. The Sons of Liberty were leaders in such disorders.

The New York assembly belatedly and grudgingly appropriated money for use under the Quartering Act but, in the meantime, Parliament had declared the New York assembly suspended. Upon hearing that funds had been voted, the suspension was lifted.

1767   The Townshend Acts (Charles Townshend, Chancellor of the Exchequer)

While Townshend denied there was any legal distinction between internal and external taxes, he was smart enough to make all the new taxes external ones. This would irritate the colonials less and provide them with less on which to base objections. His tax plans appealed to the English landed aristocracy and the country gentlemen. British land taxes were reduced by almost half a million pounds. The new taxes on imports into America were to make up this loss, to pay salaries of officials stationed in America, to pay for operating new vice-admiralty courts, and to establish an American Board of Commissioners of Customs. The new customs commissioners at Boston would be colonials but they would be responsible directly to the British treasury. The new import taxes were on glass, tea, lead, paint, and paper.

* 1767   John Dickinson's "Farmer's Letters"

These letters appeared in the Pennsylvania Chronicle. They were an attack on the Townshend duties, their main point being that import duties levied for the purpose of *raising revenue* could not legally be levied by Parliament. Only duties levied to control trade or to regulate the affairs of empire were within the proper sphere of King and Parliament. Dickinson then pointed out that the Townshend duties were, as the laws themselves plainly stated, revenue taxes. This may have been good legal argument; it was widely circulated throughout the colonies and favorably received. But Franklin said something at this time which had more the flavor of insight and the tang of common sense. He expressed doubt about being able to split hairs and agree upon a line somewhere between the views of Parliament and the views of the colonies. He said, "Either Parliament has the power to make *all laws* for us, or Parliament has the power to make *no laws* for us; and I think the arguments for the latter more numerous and weighty than those of the former."

* 1768   Circular Letters—Samuel Adams—Boston

Sam Adams drew up a series of statements protesting the Townshend Acts and reiterating the slogan, "taxation without representation is tyranny," and also calling for united action by the several colonies. The Massachusetts House of Representatives adopted this document and provided that it be sent to the other colonial assemblies. The royal governor declared the Circular Letter seditious. The ministry in England approved the governor's attitude and suggested that any assemblies adopting any such measures be dissolved. But the idea had caught on. Within three months Connecticut, New Hampshire, New Jersey, and Virginia had passed similar resolutions. Here we have colonial assemblies formally asserting what they consider to be their rights and acting together in so doing. We also have the British ministry asserting that colonial assemblies may be dissolved by action taken in England. It was a natural step from this Circular Letter by Sam Adams to the much more effective Committees of Correspondence, also started by Sam Adams only four years later.

1768 The Second Boycott

Items on the Townshend list were not to be bought by the colonial merchants. The plan was initiated in Boston and after a few months had spread to most of the colonies. It reduced appreciably the volume of trade, much as had the boycott of 1763, but there was no petition this time to Parliament by English merchants for relief. It so happened that trade with Europe was unusually brisk and made up to the English merchant what he lost from the declining American trade. Nevertheless, by the spring of 1769 word had been sent to the colonial governors that a modification of the Townshend duties was imminent.

1770 Townshend Duties Repealed, Except on Tea

About the middle of April the new prime minister, Lord North, came into power. He called the Townshend duties "preposterous" and he accomplished the repeal of all of them except the tax on tea. The tea tax was retained to emphasize the point that Parliament had the *right* to levy such taxes. No new taxes were levied. The Quartering Act, which had a two-year time limit written in it, expired and was not renewed. These moves so eased tensions that colonial merchants dropped the boycott. Only in Boston was there an organized attempt to continue the boycott, but it failed. In New York City a house to house canvass was made to sound out the people. The poll favored dropping the boycott on all items except tea.

* 1770 The Boston Massacre (March 5th) Five Killed

Soldiers and Bostonians frequently exchanged other than complimentary greetings. Sons of Liberty and Red-coats (Lobster-backs) carried large-sized chips on their shoulders. A fist fight occurred between a soldier and a civilian on March 5th. The onlookers participated in a small-sized riot before order was restored. Throughout the day civilians and soldiers in small groups walked the streets alert for trouble. They found it. That evening in King Street near the state house, an altercation started between a sentry and some civilians. People gathered; the sentry was joined by Captain Preston and a squad of soldiers. Stones and snowballs flew, the crowd pressed closer, the soldiers with fixed bayonets raised their guns, and someone shouted, "Fire!" Five civilians were killed. Who gave the command to fire? Certainly not Captain Preston, probably not the more or less disciplined soldiers. We don't know. This was not a wanton or callous firing into a crowd. But it was immediately called a massacre. The people of Boston were dangerously angry. Every grown boy, every man, and many women could handle guns, a common household possession. The British "bloody-backs" had better be off the streets of Boston come daylight. Sam Adams would play to the hilt the propaganda advantages against England that this "massacre" presented, but he feared a general uprising of the civilians in a clash with the soldiers. He went to Lt. Governor Hutchinson and pointed out the certain dangers the next day would present. He proposed getting the soldiers out of reach of the civilians for a few days until the situation cooled off. Hutchinson agreed. The troops were sent during the night to islands in Boston harbor. This sensible cooperation between a leader of the Sons of Liberty, Sam Adams, and the British Lt. Governor Hutchinson averted what could have developed into a real massacre. King George III had another view of the incident. That a civilian of Boston could tell the king's official what to do with the king's troops, and have the official do it, was beyond understanding. The angry ministers began to ask whether the soldiers were the "king's troops or were they Sam Adams' regiments?" From this moment King George III wished to meet Sam Adams of Boston. The British soldiers on the march to Lexington and Concord five years later were searching for stores of arms and also keeping a sharp eye out for Sam Adams.

Seven months later Captain Preston and four of his soldiers were tried. Two were convicted of manslaughter and given a rather mild penalty. They were branded on the hand and allowed to go free. The others were acquitted. John Adams, cousin of Sam Adams, and Josiah Quincy were the defense lawyers for Captain Preston and his men. Both lawyers were unsympathetic with the British authorities; hence their action displayed both professional integrity and personal courage.

1770 (April) to 1773 (December) The Quiet Period

For over three years business was good. The import duties, even the tea tax, were being collected. The amount collected was about three times the cost of collection, a considerable improvement over the situation faced by Grenville. Leading men in all walks of life throughout the colonies as well as the royal governors welcomed both the prosperity and the quiet. Benjamin Franklin resorted to verse in his expression of good will toward England.

"Know too, ye bad neighbors, who aim to divide
    The sons from the mother, that still she's our
            pride,
And if ye attack her, we're all on her side,
        Which nobody can deny, deny,
            Which nobody can deny.

A few sour notes marred this three-year period of comparative quiet. In Rhode Island the British revenue ship *Gaspee* pursued a suspected smuggler in Narragansett Bay. The smaller local ship led the *Gaspee* onto a sandbar. That evening, June 9, 1772, several small boats attacked the stranded *Gaspee,* forced its crew ashore, and burned it. Today this sand-bar is Gaspee Point. A reward of 500 pounds for the identification of these Rhode Islanders failed to uncover a single person. Public sentiment approved their action and the Sons of Liberty would know how to deal with anyone showing undue interest in the reward.

Much less exciting but nevertheless disturbing was the news, a few days after the burning of the *Gaspee*, that Governor Hutchinson at Boston was henceforth to be paid by the king, not by the Massachusetts assembly. The colonials were quite aware that, "he who pays the fiddler calls the tune."

There were at least three very important people in the colonies who were not at all pleased with peace and quiet. Samuel Adams, Patrick Henry, and Thomas Jefferson were quite sure that they preferred a revolution. The decision to have the king pay Governor Hutchinson's salary set Sam Adams to work. He persuaded a Boston town meeting to set up a committee of twenty-one men to form committees of correspondence in every Massachusetts town. James Otis was chairman of the Boston committee. From Boston, Sam Adams sent a rehash of every complaint and violated right of the past eight years throughout the colony. It was a propaganda campaign to fan the fires of rebellion. The idea spread. Thomas Jefferson and Patrick Henry took hold of it in Virginia. Early in 1774 the Committees of Correspondence were in high gear in all the colonies except North Carolina and Pennsylvania. The inflammatory material circulated by these committees was a confused mixture of fact and fancy; it was deadly serious in being anti-English. However, it was just propaganda and in itself probably unable to create real trouble. It required an act by England which would so offend the colonists that the sober, conservative merchants and other men of property would join the radical leaders and the Sons of Liberty. England, through the British East India Company, performed that act.

* 1773   The Boston Tea Party (Dec. 16th)

The British East India Tea Company was almost bankrupt. It had to pay a shilling tax per pound as tea was imported into England. To help the company, Lord North's ministry permitted the tea to be shipped directly from the British East Indies to America and thus not have to pay the shilling import tax. With this tax relief the company could afford to pay the low three-penny tax as the tea entered the American ports. It could even reduce the price of the tea and still make a good profit. In addition England had given the British East India Tea Company a monopoly of the tea trade within the empire. The arrangements permitted legal British tea to be sold in America at prices below that of tea smuggled in from the Dutch East Indies. So far a large business enterprise had been rescued from failure and the colonists were able to buy tea at a lower price.

Then the British East India Tea Company announced that all tea sold in America would be handled exclusively by agents of the company. This was the intolerable blow! England had given a monopoly to a company. The company had restricted marketing of the product to its own agents. Profits from an extensive tea trade had been set beyond the reach of colonial merchants. If this could be done with tea, why not with other items? Where might it lead? The Sons of Liberty denounced everyone who handled tea. Many were afraid to become agents for the company. Any pilot who guided a tea ship into Boston harbor would answer to the Sons of Liberty. While Boston was more violent in its reactions, a similar sentiment was evident in all the sea ports from Massachusetts to Virginia. The distinction between radicals and conservatives was beginning to fade; they were all becoming patriots.

Three tea ships had been in the harbor for days. The law provided that a cargo is subject to seizure by the government twenty days after its arrival if the proper duties have not been been paid. Mass meetings in Boston demanded that the ships be sent back still unloaded. Governor Hutchinson refused to permit the ships to leave the harbor. The Sons of Liberty were more popular and hence stronger than ever. Any attempt to unload the tea and store it in warehouses would almost certainly result in broken heads and burned warehouses. Captain Rotch of the *Dartmouth* faced a dilemma. His first concern was the property of the East India Tea Company—the cargo of tea and the ship. The twenty-day period was running out. He must pay the duties or have the tea subject to seizure for non-payment; but it would be foolish to pay the duty before he unloaded the tea. Governor Hutchinson would not give clearance (permission for the ship to leave the harbor). A mass meeting had been called by Sam Adams in front of Old South Church the evening of December 16th. Adams wanted to know if and when the governor would permit the tea ships to sail from the harbor. Captain Rotch came to the meeting, where there were about 8,000 people, to inform Adams that Governor Hutchinson still refused to let the ships leave. Adams, who was chairman of this meeting, gave a signal. Several men disguised as Indians withdrew from the crowd. They boarded the three tea ships tied up at Griffin's wharf and three hundred forty-two chests of tea, valued at about $70,000, were dumped into the harbor. There was no vandalism, no destruction of other property. It was a well executed commando raid in native costume.

Reaction among the people of Boston differed. John Adams had been out of sympathy with the extreme position frequently taken by his more radical cousin, Sam; but in this instance he wrote of the Tea Party, "Many persons wish that as many dead carcasses were floating in the harbor as there are chests of tea." Presumably the carcasses he had in mind would have worn red coats or royal insignia. On the other hand, some merchants were so shocked with the great destruction of property that they suggested a collection be taken among them to pay for the tea. No other port had a tea party such as Boston's; but tea met with difficulties in several places. At New York City and Philadelphia tea ships were turned back before they entered the harbor. At Charleston a cargo of tea was forfeited for non-payment of duties within the twenty-day period. It was stored in a warehouse. In July of 1776 it was sold to raise money for the emerging new nation, the United States of America. During 1774 a few scattered attempts to land English tea were made by small shippers, not the British East India Tea Company. One such ship had its cargo dumped into

New York harbor, another was burned at Annapolis, Maryland, and a shipment of tea discovered in a warehouse in New Jersey was burned. Handling British tea in the American colonies after the Boston Tea Party was risky business.

* 1774 The Intolerable Acts

During March, April, and May, Parliament followed King George III's lead. He had a bloc of members known as "the king's friends" who would cast their votes and use their very considerable influence as he wished. The king had built this political machine by granting lucrative favors. George III resented the fact that Parliament had grown in prestige and power during the reigns of his father and grandfather, George II and George I. He was determined to "rule as well as reign" a bit of advice his mother had persistently urged upon a receptive mind. In 1774 George III was bent upon two objectives; to make the colonies accept the tea tax even if it took force to do it, and to show Parliament that his program must be passed, that the king did rule. There were wiser heads in Parliament, William Pitt, the elder, and Edmund Burke; but the king's friends had the votes.

The king's program resulted in the passage of the following laws. Not only in Massachusetts, but throughout the colonies, they were so strongly resented that they have become known as the Intolerable Acts.

1] The Boston Port Bill: No ships can enter or leave Boston harbor except those with military supplies and whatever food ships the customs officials at Salem permit. These restrictions may be lifted by the king after the East India Tea Company has been paid for the tea.

2] Any official of the king charged with a capital crime in connection with enforcing his official duties will be tried in England.

3] The upper house (Council) of the Massachusetts Assembly will be appointed by the king instead of continuing to be elected by the lower house (House of Representatives).

4] There will be no town meetings without the Governor's consent, and even such meetings will confine themselves to an agenda approved by the governor.

5] Quebec province shall extend southward to the Ohio River.

6] The Quartering Act shall again be put into effect.

7] General Gage shall replace Governor Hutchinson. (George III probably made it clear to Gage that the king's troops were not to be ordered about by Samuel Adams.)

All of these changes took effect within three months, March, April, and May of 1774. Blocking Boston by sea was compared with the action of Rome's spreading salt over the site of destroyed Carthage. The Virginia House of Burgesses declared a "day for fasting, humiliation, and prayer" as a protest against closing the port of Boston. Other measures of the king's program changed the government of Massachusetts and thus were threats to all the American colonies. If it could happen to Massachusetts it could happen to them. Before this series of "intolerable acts," there were two opinions in the colonies about those "Mohawk Indians" who dumped the tea into Boston harbor, but afterward there was no doubt about it; they were patriots.

When the Virginia House of Burgesses called for "a day of fasting, humiliation, and prayer" the royal governor dissolved the Assembly. Many of the members held a "rump session" at Raleigh's Tavern, Williamsburg. There on May 27, 1774 action was taken calling for a meeting of all the colonies at Philadelphia. Ten days earlier, the Rhode Island Assembly had urged an intercolonial meeting. Pennsylvania and New York had also suggested joint consideration of the situation by all of the colonies. Thus, before the call came from Virginia, the New England and the Middle colonies had expressed the same thought. Now the most important of the Southern colonies had spoken. This action by Virginia at Raleigh's Tavern crystalized the idea into a definite plan of action. Arrangements were made for a meeting at Philadelphia in 1774. As usual, Massachusetts, sparked by Sam Adams, was most active in stirring up resistance. As soon as the order closing its port was made, Boston used the Committees of Correspondence to the utmost and urged a complete boycott against England. The answer of the colonies to this plea was the counter suggestion of calling a meeting where all colonies would be represented. There had been two boycotts before. They had hurt England, but also hurt the colonies. They had resulted in adjustments in England's strategy in handling American affairs but not to any real change in policy. It was now time to attempt a review of the whole problem of English-American relations. This could best be done by a meeting which could speak for all the colonies with one voice; not necessarily a voice of defiance, but rather a voice seeking a solution while protesting the whole pattern of controls exercised by George III and Parliament since the Treaty of Paris in 1763.

* 1774 First Continental Congress (Sept. 5th to Oct. 26th)

There were fifty-six delegates who attended the Congress held in Carpenters Hall, Philadelphia. Georgia was the only colony not represented. Delegates were chosen in a variety of ways. It was an extra-legal body; those who took part in it believed they were exercising their rights even though there was no legal provision for such an organization. Extra-legal devices are always open to the charge of being illegal, and whether they are or not can best be measured by the acceptance or the rejection of their acts. The extreme radicals would be represented at such a congress, but the extreme conservatives would reject the meetings as illegal. The bloc of delegates looked upon as the conservatives shared with the radicals the belief that revenue taxes and the control of internal affairs were outside of the proper area of authority of King and Parliament.

The Congress, each colony having one vote, adopted the Suffolk Resolves. Suffolk County, Massachusetts, reflected the opinion of its largest city, Boston. Paul Revere was the messenger who brought these resolutions from Boston to Carpenters Hall, Philadelphia. The contents were such that King George III could have detected in them an obstinacy equal to his own. They resolved to

1] Keep trade with England at a minimum by a boycott on imports, by a drastic curtailment of exports, and by refusal to wear, use, or consume English products.

2] Consider null and void all of the punitive measures taken against Boston and Massachusetts since the Tea Party.

3] Approve the efforts of Massachusetts to operate a colonial government separate from royal control until the punitive measures had been repealed.

4] Urge all colonies to raise and train a militia of their own.

To enforce these resolutions an Association was organized with a committee in each colony. These committees working under the Association were more closely knit and under better control than was the case with the Sons of Liberty, but their function was pretty much the same. The trade restrictions were most effectively carried out. Drilling in uniforms as colorful as local imagination could devise and drilling in no uniforms at all became common practice in most of the colonies. In Philadelphia, the city of brotherly love, a militia unit was formed with the incongruous name, "The Quaker Blues." Young men who could afford it would join a company outfitted in resplendent uniforms. In some instances a wealthy individual would pay for the uniforms for a company. Usually, however, men and boys drilled without uniforms and with whatever firearms they happened to have.

The adoption of the Suffolk Resolves can best be understood if viewed as an angry reaction to the outrageously severe measures taken against Massachusetts. To the colonists the punishment did *not* fit the crime. After showing that it stood firmly behind Massachusetts, the First Continental Congress voted upon the Galloway Plan of Union. This plan set up a Grand Council for all the colonies much as had the Albany Plan of 1754. This council would act as an adjunct to the British Parliament. Measures dealing with the colonies would have to pass both Parliament and the Grand Council. The king was to appoint a president-general with authority to veto acts of the Grand Council. This plan recognized the right of the King and Parliament to regulate external trade and any matters that were clearly affairs of empire; it also denied the right of King and Parliament to levy revenue taxes or interfere with the internal affairs of the colonies. By a one vote margin the Galloway Plan failed to pass. Compared with the Suffolk Resolves this plan was conciliatory. Even though it failed to pass and even though it was later stricken from the records of the meetings, it did reflect an opinion far short of readiness for revolution. It was an opinion shared by a substantial minority throughout the colonies, perhaps by a majority of the more prosperous segment of the population.

The First Continental Congress sent a petition to the king requesting the repeal of all regulatory acts since 1763 and informing him of the economic restrictions that were being taken against England. Before they adjourned, the Congress set May 10, 1775 for another meeting. In the meantime King George III would have ample time to reply or perhaps to modify British policy so as to make another meeting unnecessary.

* 1775   The King's Reply, Lexington and Concord (April 19th)

While the boycott and other economic moves against England were very effective in reducing trade, they had no effect upon the determination of George III and Parliament to make the colonies pay the tea tax and force them to abide by the coercive regulations which followed the Tea Party.

General Gage was ordered to enforce the laws. His first move was to send troops to Concord to seize stores of arms from which the rapidly forming companies of militia were being supplied. On the night of April 18th the British started from Boston. Paul Revere and William Dawes, riding by different routes, aroused the whole countryside along the fifteen miles to Lexington. From Lexington they proceeded toward Concord about six miles away, but both were prevented by British patrols from getting through. However, a third rider, Dr. Samuel Prescott, did get the warning to Concord so that when the British arrived the colonials were expecting them.

At dawn, on the 19th of April, Captain John Parker had seventy Minute Men in formation on the village green at Lexington. Major Pitcairn, in command of a much larger British force, ordered the colonials to disarm and disperse. After several such commands a few Minute Men broke formation and started to walk off. They did not drop their rifles. At this point a shot was fired; no one knows from which side. There then followed a quick burst of shots from the British and a few scattered shots from the colonials. One British soldier was wounded, eight colonials were killed and ten wounded. This was the Battle of Lexington. The British marched on to Concord.

At the North Bridge in Concord a small group of colonial militiamen fired a volley into the British troops. ("The shot heard 'round the world.") The British destroyed military stores and food supplies and at about noon were ready to march back to Charlestown and Boston. By this time the countryside was swarming with militiamen and they were angry. From Concord back to Lexington the British red-coats were easy targets for the colonial soldiers shooting from behind trees and stone walls. The British were saved from utter rout by the arrival of reinforcements at Lexington. April 19th cost the British about three times the casualties suffered by the colonials; about 275 to 93 killed, wounded, and missing. British troops involved in this day's fighting numbered about 700 while more than 3,000 colonials had reported for duty.

1775 Ticonderoga Captured by Ethan Allen (May 10th)

On the very day that the Second Continental Congress met, Ethan Allen and his Green Mountain Boys took Fort Ticonderoga, which was taken by surprise so that the only casualty was one British soldier wounded. Allen demanded the surrender, "in the name of the great Jehovah and the Continental Congress." The cannons captured here were dragged to Boston where they became a decisive factor in persuading the British to leave Boston harbor in March of the next year.

* 1775 Second Continental Congress

The meetings were held in Independence Hall, Philadelphia. Again the radicals were in control. John Hancock was president. Thomas Jefferson, who had developed the theory that England had no right to make any laws affecting the American colonies, was present. Benjamin Franklin, who had experienced some embarrassment because of his versifying (see p. 28), was a delegate. But now he was for complete independence, a decision he had not reached quickly nor easily. John Dickinson was an effective spokesman for the conservative faction among the delegates who wished to send more petitions and appeals to the king. The decision in favor of a war for independence was made outside of the Congress by the events of 1775 and Thomas Paine's "Common Sense" pamphlet of January 1776.

Lexington and Concord were before the Second Continental Congress convened. Bunker Hill was five weeks after the opening meeting of the Congress. This battle, actually fought on Breed's Hill, cost the British over a thousand casualties and the colonials about four hundred. The news of the capture of Ticonderoga and Crown Point arrived in Boston about the same time the Battle of Bunker Hill took place. In the summer of 1775, colonial troops under General Philip Schuyler and later under General Richard Montgomery were in Canada.

In September they had occupied Montreal, which the British had evacuated, and were forming an expedition to attack Quebec. In short, by the end of 1775 war was well under way. Colonial attempts to persuade Canada to become the fourteenth colony and the colonial invasion of Canada could be interpreted in England in no other way than a direct attack upon the empire. Even the leader of the conservatives in the Congress, John Dickinson, had stated that if war came the colonies could look with confidence for foreign aid. While Dickinson was expressing these sentiments in America, King George III in England said (August 1775) in a formal proclamation that the colonies in America were in a state of rebellion. Nevertheless, it was still true that in January 1776 colonial officers and General Washington were continuing the custom of drinking to the king's health. There was still a rather heavy haze of indecision concerning the exact state of the American-English relationship.

1775 Washington Appointed Commander-in-Chief June 15th)

Events from the 19th of April through May pushed the Second Continental Congress into acts which transformed it from an organization of protest to one of revolution. After Lexington and Concord the Massachusetts militia, several thousands strong, hemmed in the British on the land sides of Boston. The Congress called for more militia from Virginia, Pennsylvania, and Maryland. A full week before Bunker Hill the Congress was considering uniting all colonial forces into a Continental Army under a unified command. John Adams had suggested George Washington as the man to head this army.

Perhaps no single act begins to compare in importance with the choice of Washington as *the factor* in the war which contributed most to victory. Not only was the choice a superb one because it selected a man with the right character and abilities; it also displayed political know-how. Boston and Massachusetts had been so much the area of violent incidents, so much the victim of British retaliation, so much the instigator of boycotts and anti-English propaganda that there was some danger that the revolution would appear to be a Massachusetts rather than an American revolution. In 1775 Samuel Adams and John Hancock, both Bostonians, seemed to be rated by George III as public enemies numbers one and two. It was therefore politically important to give prominence early in the war to some colony other than Massachusetts. Virginia had Patrick Henry, a flaming revolutionist, and Thomas Jefferson, the most effective spokesman for self-government in the colonies. It was strong in wealth and manpower. Its social and economic structure differed from that of New England; it represented the southern area much as Massachusetts represented the northern. It was a political necessity that Virginia be brought into as prominent a position as possible at the very beginning of the war. Hence, the Congress unanimously voted Washington as head of the Continental Army. Once having recognized the political wisdom in going to Virginia for the man, the Congress selected Washington.

The Ideology of the American Revolution

* 1776 *Common Sense* by Thomas Paine (January)

This pamphlet was a political catalyst. A catalyst, a term used frequently in chemistry, is a substance which greatly speeds up a reaction. The American colonies were, with hesitancy and with troublesome doubts, moving toward independence. Paine's *Common Sense* was definite, tough, clear, uncomplicated common sense to the people. If anything was read by every literate person in the colonies, it was *Common Sense*. Not only did it say with vigor and sharpness what people wanted to hear, it lifted them above themselves with its plea to make of America the one place in the world where freedom and love of mankind could flourish. Through Paine's pamphlet popular opinion caught up with and further stimulated the radical leadership in the Second Continental Congress. The political catalyst had worked the change. Six months later the Congress would adopt the Declaration of Independence signed by representatives of each of the thirteen colonies.

1776 Declaration of Independence (July 4th)

On June 7th Richard Henry Lee of Virginia made a motion which was seconded by John Adams of Massachusetts. Lee was acting in accordance with instructions from his state. The motion contained three parts: that the American colonies are independent states, that foreign aid should be sought, and that a confederate form of government be prepared for submission to the several states. The motion was discussed for four days and then it was decided to postpone a vote until July 1st. In the meantime, a committee was appointed to draw up a declaration of independence and another committee to work on a constitution for a confederation. The members of the committee on the declaration of independence were Thomas Jefferson (Virginia), Benjamin Franklin (Pennsylvania), John Adams (Massachusetts), Robert Livingston (New York), and Roger Sherman (Connecticut). The committee asked Jefferson to write the first draft of the Declaration. With very few changes, Jef-

ferson's work was presented to the Congress. From July 1st to the 4th consideration was given to Lee's motion and to the proposed Declaration of Independence. Some changes were made in Jefferson's work by the Congress, and then on July 4th by a vote of 12 to 0 the Declaration of Independence was adopted. New York abstained from voting. John Hancock, president of the Congress, signed in such large clear letters that, ever since, the phrase "put your John Hancock" has meant, sign your name. On July 9th the New York Provincial Congress formally approved the Declaration.

** The Nature and Content of the Declaration of Independence

Jefferson set out to express effectively ideas commonly held. In the American colonies the "natural rights of man" concept was just the obvious common sense of the day. If the document could justify rebellion, arouse enthusiasm, instill determination, and inspire nobleness of purpose, so much the better. The job was so well done that it not only served the occasion for which it was written, the American Revolution, but has continued to be a source of inspiration throughout the world. Wherever freedom through independence is sought, our Declaration of Independence is a guiding star. Since 1945 it has been a vital influence in the struggle of several peoples for freedom and self-government in Asia and Africa; it may speak yet again to the peoples of eastern Europe.

The Declaration falls into three main divisions. First there is a statement of the "natural rights" of man. This is packed into four not very long sentences. Next is a long list of complaints about the king and a statement or two about the humble patience of the American colonies under such treatment; and finally, there is the declaration that the colonies are now independent states.

For all the generations since the establishment of our nation, the statement of belief in "natural rights" and unalienable rights is the heart of the Declaration. One may speculate interestingly on just what "all men are created equal" meant to the fifty-five signers. Possibly not one of them considered slaves as "men." Yet certain it is that, at the time of our Civil War, this statement of the Declaration was a clarion call to the Abolitionists. No doubt Eugene V. Debs drew strength from "all men are created equal" when he battled for the cause of labor unions in the late 1800's. No doubt Ghandi appreciated the nobility of these words when he fought the battle for the untouchables of India. Even those who fought valiantly and long for women's rights were encouraged by "all men are created equal." And so it will continue to the end of time. Whenever a society recognizes that certain of its members are subjected to unequal treatment that a sizeable minority think unjust, there will be people drawing inspiration from our Declaration of Independence. This political expression of faith in the sacred and unalienable rights of individuals is shared in common with the two great religions that have most persistently influenced our nation, Christianity and Judaism. Not only is there recognition of, but there is insistence upon, belief in the dignity and importance of the individual. There is no such thing as an unimportant person. "All men are created equal" is not a statement of fact revealing truth; it is a statement of faith displaying wisdom.

The second part of the Declaration is much less impressive. The list of compaints is long and not completely convincing. It is repetitious. It blames George III for almost everything in spite of the fact that much of our quarrel was with Parliament. But it is a good lawyer's list; it builds an impressive case with the material at hand. Certainly it was effective in convincing most of its readers of the wickedness and obstinacy of the king; it served well the cause of revolution.

For its time, July 1776, the high point of the Declaration which put into shade every other sentence in the document was the ringing statement, "We, therefore, the representatives of the United States of America, in General Congress assembled, appealing to the Supreme Judge of the world for the rectitude of our intentions, do, in the name and by the authority of the good people of these colonies, solemnly publish and declare, that these united states are, and of right ought to be, free and independent colonies; . . . And, for the support of this declaration, with a firm reliance on the protection of Divine Providence, we mutually pledge to each other our lives, our fortune, and our sacred honor."

The American Revolution 1775-1783

** The Great Experiment in Self-government

In one sense this was not much of a revolution; in another, and much more significant sense, it was the greatest revolution of history. The social and economic status of the people of America did not change markedly as a result of the war. The families that were in positions of leadership in social, economic, and political affairs before the war were also in such positions after the war. Of course, the King's agents and their appointees were thrown out of power; but the colonials prominent in the local governments of 1763 were, by and large, still the leaders in 1784. Loyalists lost their property in many instances. But compared to the immediate results of the French Revolution of 1789 and the apparently lasting results of the Russian Revolution of 1917, the changes produced by the American Revolution were much less extensive and much less extreme.

In the more significant sense the American Revolution was an experiment in the field of political economy that shook and frightened the rulers of the western world of its day and has continuously kept alive in people of many places a determination to govern themselves. This experiment had a great laboratory in the remote continent of North America. A whole people were to govern themselves through a representative framework of office holders chosen by the sovereign people. Could a large republic be established? Could it live if established? Did people really have "natural rights" just because they were human beings? Could a people govern themselves? Would not freedom breed chaos, and chaos necessitate dictatorship to restore order? What if the experiment in republican government did work, would American success then mark the beginning of the disintegration of monarchies? Put yourself in imagination back to 1770 and try to answer each of the preceding questions. It might give you a fuller appreciation of how great a faith our founding fathers had in mankind; it might put meaning in Thomas Paine's, "These are times that try men's souls." It would be ridiculous to think that all of the soldiers in the Continental Army were inspired by this noble concept; it would be more ridiculous not to know that many of the leaders were so inspired. What was so well stated by Jefferson, Paine, Henry, and Otis was reiterated by hundreds of men of lesser fame. The ideology emphasizing the "natural rights of man" and the right of a people to govern themselves through their chosen officials had permeated colonial America. Men with a cause fight with tenacity; the more noble the cause, the greater the tenacity.

Because our cause was great, we were able to recruit several notable personages with special military skills. The Marquis de Lafayette helped America before his country became our ally. Later he was a leader in the French Revolution. The famous French *Declaration of the Rights of Man* was Lafayette's adaptation of Jefferson's Declaration of Independence. Major General Johann de Kalb died fighting for the American cause, so did Count Casimir Pulaski. Colonel Thaddeus Kosciusko and Inspector General Baron von Steuben also joined the American forces because they deemed the cause worth the risk of life itself.

Strengths and Weaknesses of England and America

England's Strong Points
She had a great navy, a well equipped army, and money.
There was considerable loyalist support in America.

England's Weak Points
Her supply line included 3,000 miles of ocean requiring four to six weeks to cross.
Pitt, Burke, and Fox opposed in Parliament the war policy of King George III.
A large segment of English opinion (Whig Party members) were more pleased with the failure of the King's policies than distressed by failure in war.
The English were slow to develop techniques of fighting to suit conditions in America.

America's Strong Points
George Washington's leadership was superb (see p. 36).
American rifles were superior to those of the English.
American soldiers had gained experience in the French and Indian War.
To hasten victory, they were determined to avoid capture and continue resistance.

Defensive tactics served the American cause; attack could be reserved for favorable circumstances.

America's Weak Points

Discipline was often poor.

Enlistments were for short terms.

"Desertions" were frequent. (Soldiers would be temporarily "A.W.O.L." during planting and harvesting seasons).

The Americans lacked military supplies, money, and an adequate navy.

It had a poorly organized government.

* What Made Washington "First in War"?

Persistence in rebellion, no matter what the outlook, and avoidance of capture were the two *musts* for American success. Time and again Washington slipped away when the British expected a fight under circumstances favorable to them. From the British point of view the exasperating thing about Washington was that, even though he could be beaten, he couldn't be caught. He would not give up. The following list of only a few of the trials and troubles Washington experienced makes the tenacity of the man apparent. He must have had his mind and heart riveted to the main purpose: a people's government such as the world had never known, a goal so great that any discouragement was, in comparison, a petty matter.

1] The Continental Army totaled less than 10,000 ready for duty at any one time. (There were probably a quarter of a million men in the colonies, widely scattered, of course.)

2] The militas of the states totaled about 20,000. They fought well in defense of their own towns. Discipline was usually poor. They "deserted" and returned to service as they saw fit.

3] Much of the time soldiers had no uniforms. Lack of proper footwear was a major problem.

4] Pay was seldom on time for the soldiers, and when it arrived the Continental currency was of little value. The soldiers were not too far wrong when they said that their pay was $20 a month in worthless money.

5] Political intrigue was aimed at displacing Washington. The Conway Cabal in 1778 revealed letters by General Gates attacking him.

6] Generals Charles Lee and Benedict Arnold were traitors.

7] Shortages that caused the intense suffering at Valley Forge were more the result of mismanagement than of genuine shortages.

8] In 1780 two Connecticut regiments at Morristown paraded under arms demanding full rations (they had been on one-eighth rations) and back pay. Pennsylvania troops held them in check.

9] In 1781 over a thousand Pennsylvania troops broke away from the encampment at Morristown. Several officers were wounded. The men were bent upon marching to Congress to demand back pay. About half of these soldiers returned.

10] The Newburg Letters attempted to stir up rebellion against Congress over back pay, short rations, etc. Major John Armstrong, General Gates, and Assistant Attorney General Barber were instigators of this conspiracy.

This list could be expanded to many times this length. Only the dedication of a great man to a great cause can explain why Washington did not resign in disgust. But he didn't. A few years later he was again ready to be the leader of this same great cause when he assumed the office of president.

* Campaigns of the American Revolution
(See also chronological list pp. 39-42.)

Two campaigns were clearly discernible as such. One was the plan to converge upon Albany, N.Y. from the north, south, and west. This would separate New England from the other colonies. Once isolated, rambunctious New England might be subdued. With New England under control, the spirit of rebellion might simmer down in the middle and southern colonies where Loyalist sentiment was stronger. On paper the plan was sound. One who knew the distances and the terrain, especially the approach to Albany from the north, might have recognized how difficult its execution would be. Each of the three British forces would try to do its own job and hope, that upon arrival in Albany, the other two also would be there, or thereabouts. Effective communication during the operation would be impractical. This campaign has been called the "British Blunder of 1777." The blunder was not in the plan, but in its execution. Lord George Germain, head of the British war office, failed to send instructions to Sir William Howe at New York City. As a result, Howe left New York for Chesapeake Bay and Philadelphia at the very time he should have been starting up the Hudson for Albany. General Burgoyne found the forests of northeastern New York State very difficult terrain for his overburdened troops. He carried much unnecessary equipment; he had not learned that what an army might reasonably carry along roads and fields in Europe from battle to battle could not be lugged from place to place in America. He was trapped at Saratoga and surrendered October 17, 1777. This led to an alliance with France. Saratoga is considered above all other battles to be the turning point of the war.

Colonel St. Leger came up the St. Lawrence River and across Lake Ontario to Fort Oswego. From there he marched along the Oswego River and Oneida Lake route to lay siege to Fort Stanwix on the Mohawk River. At nearby Oriskany the American General Herkimer repulsed an attack, and General Benedict Arnold arrived in the vicinity to help raise the siege of Fort Stanwix. By trickery Arnold persuaded the Indians to desert the British, and St. Leger to give up the attack on Fort Stanwix. So a military plan that looked very good on a map was turned into a complete failure by mismanagement, difficult terrain, long distances, plus Arnold, Morgan, Gates, Herkimer, Stark and several thousands of sharp-shooting Americans.

The other campaign was the setting of the trap to capture Cornwallis at Yorktown. Washington received word that the French fleet under Admiral DeGrasse was leaving the West Indies for Chesapeake Bay. Here too, distances were great and effective communication impossible. Cornwallis was on the York peninsula, a perfectly good position so long as the British fleet controlled Chesapeake Bay. The arrival of DeGrasse could not be closely timed and it must be kept secret from the large British fleet units available in the New York harbor area. Washington had to pretend to be preparing for action along a semi-circular line around New York City. While maintaining this pretense, he slipped away with most of the troops and went south to combine with French troops under Lafayette and Rochambeau. The combined French-American forces held Cornwallis at Yorktown while DeGrasse entered Chesapeake Bay. With retreat by sea cut off, Cornwallis was under siege and his position soon became untenable. The surrender which ended the war took place on October 19, 1781.

In addition to the above two campaigns, the activities of General Washington should have our attention. In 1776 and into January of 1777 he led a masterly retreat from Long Island, up the Hudson, across to New Jersey, and south to Trenton where he suddenly stopped retreating and made his surprise attacks at Trenton and Princeton. In these maneuvers Cornwallis was determined, in his own words, "to bag the fox" but the "fox" slipped from the British time after time. Washington set up winter quarters in northern New Jersey at Morristown in January 1777. The following September and October he tried unsuccessfully to prevent the British from taking up quarters at Philadelphia (Brandywine and Germantown). In December, 1777, and the rest of the winter, the troops were half-starved and half-frozen at Valley Forge. The following June, 1778, the treachery of General Charles Lee allowed Clinton's army to escape capture at Monmouth, N.J. For the rest of the war until Yorktown the main winter quarters were at Morristown, N.J. Washington had his forces around New York while the British enjoyed the comforts in the city with the fleet insuring their safety. DeGrasse's plan to come to Chesapeake Bay set up the Yorktown campaign.

CHRONOLOGICAL LIST OF BATTLES AND A FEW OTHER EVENTS DURING THE WAR

The symbol (GW) indicates a battle involving forces where George Washington was in direct command, or other forces in the immediate area acting in conjunction with him.

The symbol (HM) indicates battles that were part of the Hudson-Mohawk rivers "Blunder of 1777."

There are more items listed than you will care to remember. They are for easy reference. However, if you decide to learn about a battle, find it on a map and get an idea of distances and type of terrain; otherwise a battle is pretty much a name without substance. Automobile road maps can be very useful and interesting for location and distance; they are an excellent supplement to text-book maps.

1775 (April 19th)—Lexington and Concord

Major John Pitcairn was sent by Governor Gage of Massachusetts to seize military supplies at Concord. Paul Revere, William Dawes, and Dr. Samuel Prescott aroused the countryside. Skirmishes at Lexington (Capt. John Parker in command of the colonials) and at Concord (see pp. 31-32).

1775 (May 10th)—Fort Ticonderoga taken by Ethan Allen (See p. 32.)

1775 (May 12th)—Crown Point taken by Ethan Allen

Crown Point and Ticonderoga were important control points on the southern end of Lake Champlain.

1775 (June 15th)

The Second Continental Congress voted unanimously to appoint George Washington commander-in-chief of the Continental Army. Washington accepted the commission on the 16th (see pp. 32-33).

1775 (June 17th)—Bunker Hill (fought on Breed's Hill)

To prevent the British from occupying Dorchester Heights, 1,200 colonial troops under Colonel William Prescott secretly took positions the night of the 16th on Breed's Hill. They worked all night throwing up fortifications. Sir William Howe was astonished at the sight easily visible from the British ships in the harbor. Because of the tide, landing of British troops was delayed until noon. By that time the colonials had 1,600 men on the hill. The attacking force numbered 2,400. Two frontal attacks failed. The third one succeeded only because the defenders' ammunition gave out. The retreat was precipitous, not quite a rout. British casualties included many officers and totaled about 1,050, over three times the colonial losses. This defeat was immediately a source of pride. Raw colonial militia had met the best soldiers the British had. The word around Boston was that they wished they had more hills to sell at that price.

1775 (Aug. through Dec.) Expedition Against Quebec

General Richard Montgomery invaded Canada. He took St. John's and forced the British to leave Montreal which he then occupied. His forces were strengthened by joining with a second invading force led by Benedict Arnold. The combined attack on Quebec on the last day of the year was a complete failure. Montgomery was killed, Arnold wounded, and about one-third of the colonial troops were killed or captured.

1776 (Mar. 17th) Howe Evacuates Boston

Cannon and other artillery captured at Ticonderoga were mounted on Dorchester Heights bringing most of the town and harbor within effective range. The British decided to evacuate. About 1,000 Loyalists of the Boston area went with the fleet to Halifax.

1776 (July 4th) Declaration of Independence (See pp. 34-35.)

1776 (Aug. 27th) Long Island (Brooklyn Heights)

Having left Boston, General William Howe went to New York City to set up headquarters.

Washington knew of this move and went to Long Island to interfere with these plans. On the island Howe took possession of Brooklyn Heights and apparently had Washington trapped. This cost the Americans casualties of *GW about one-fourth of their force of 5,000 men. Here the war might have ended in favor of the British had Howe pressed his advantage without delay. But Howe took the cautious path by regrouping his forces. During the night Washington got his troops onto Manhattan Island so that by daylight General Howe had no one to fight.

* A situation in which Washington was a major factor.

1776 (Sept. 16th) Harlem Heights

The British had occupied the city and Washington slowed them down as best he could. His forces were being pressed northward. At Harlem Heights he made a successful temporary stand and was allowed to stay behind fortified positions GW in the area for about three weeks. During this interval a great fire destroyed hundreds of buildings in the city. Also during this period, on September 22nd, Nathan Hale was hanged as a spy. His last statement: "I only regret that I have but one life to lose for my country."

1776 (Oct. 28th) White Plains

Retreating north along the east side of the Hudson, Washington left a substantial force to guard Fort Washington (near the Manhattan end of the present George Washington Bridge). As General Howe was attempting to encircle GW him, Washington hastened north to White Plains (about 25 miles north of present Times Square). Again Howe managed to gain a superior position on high ground. Again he delayed, awaiting reinforcements; and again, while Howe waited, Washington slipped away.

1776 (Nov. 15th) Fort Washington fell to the British

Howe sent a force of about 13,000 to take Fort GW Washington. They did. About 2,800 Americans were taken prisoner.

1776 (Nov. 18th) Fort Lee fell to the British

Cornwallis forced General Greene to evacuate Fort Lee. While Greene saved his men, he gave GW up a large amount of sorely needed military supplies.

1776 (Dec. 26th) Trenton

Washington crossed the Hudson into New Jersey to join forces with General Greene. They proceeded southward not too far ahead of the pursuing Cornwallis. After a few days the British gave up the chase. By mid-December they went into winter quarters but left defense forces at Trenton, Princeton and a few other places. Washington had crossed the Delaware River going south, but he surprised the British by turning north, recrossing the Delaware about ten miles north of Trenton, splitting his 2,400 force GW into two divisions and entering Trenton from two directions early in the morning the day after Christmas. The Hessians, mercenary troops from the German state of Hesse, had celebrated Christmas. The Americans celebrated the day after. At about breakfast time there was an hour's street-fighting from house to house and then it was over. The Americans' casualties totaled 5 and Hessians about 30. However, 900 Hessians were taken prisoner. This sudden victory after a string of defeats was a tonic to the depressed spirits of the army and of Congress.

1777   (Jan. 3rd) Princeton

The British were stung by the surprise at Trenton. They reacted quickly. Cornwallis caught up with Washington a few miles east of Trenton on January 2nd. Both sides apparently prepared for battle, but the British attack did not come. Heavy reinforcements were nearby so Cornwallis chose to delay until the next morning. Again Washington kept enough activity going on in GW sight of the British to make them believe that he, too, awaited a battle at dawn. But by dawn Washington was several miles north. Here he ran into the British reinforcements just south of Princeton and defeated them. Three days later Washington was settling down in winter quarters in the hills of Morristown, New Jersey. After Trenton, this victory put the frosting on the cake.

1777   (June 14th) The United States Adopts a Flag

The Second Continental Congress voted to have an official flag for the United States of America, "thirteen stripes alternate red and white, that the Union be thirteen stars white in a blue field. . . ."

1777   (Aug. 6th) Oriskany

Oriskany is on the Mohawk River, southeast of Fort Stanwix. Genearl Herkimer was ambushed while going to the relief of Fort Stanwix. He fought off the British and their Indian allies. Word that General Benedict Arnold was coming *HM with reinforcements as numerous as "leaves on

the trees" frightened the Indians into deserting the British under St. Leger. This stopped St. Leger's attack on Fort Stanwix and put an end to his advance toward Albany.

* A situation which is part of the Hudson-Mohawk River campaign.

1777   (Aug. 16th) Bennington, Vt.

General Burgoyne, while on his way south from the St. Lawrence River to Albany, sent General Baum with about 700 troops to Bennington, Vt. to seize military supplies known to be stored there. General John Stark with superior numHM bers of raw recruits who were good shots captured almost the entire British force. Reinforcements arrived for both sides and in a second encounter the Americans again won. The remnants of the enemy found their way back to rejoin Burgoyne.

1777   (Sept. 11th) Brandywine

Brandywine is about 25 miles southwest of Philadelphia. Sir William Howe left New York City for Chesapeake Bay and Philadelphia (see p. 36) to establish winter quarters. Washington GW came south from Morristown to prevent him from entering Philadelphia. At Brandywine Washington suffered a severe defeat with casualties of about 1,000, twice those of the British.

1777   (Oct. 4th) Germantown

Germantown was a bit north of Philadelphia; it is now within the city limits. Howe had most of his troops encamped here. In an attempt to GW pry the British out of Philadelphia, Washington was again defeated. He then retired to winter quarters at Valley Forge about 20 miles to the west.

1777   (Oct. 16th) Kingston Burned by the British

Burgoyne had been having trouble for weeks as he headed south through the rough terrain of northeastern New York. General Clinton at New York City had received a call for reinforcements. Clinton started up the Hudson and got as far HM as Kingston, then called Esopus, and burned the town. Feeling that he was too far from his base with too few soldiers, he returned to New York City. He still had about 90 miles to go to get to Saratoga at the time he burned Kingston only one day before Burgoyne's surrender.

1777   (Oct. 17th) Saratoga

Burgoyne had suffered a series of set-backs in encounters throughout the ten days immediately

HM preceding the surrender at Saratoga. Before this, his situation had been desperate; supplies were low, reinforcements were not available, and progress through hostile wooded country was extremely slow and costly. He had already turned back when his forces were practically surrounded by American troops about three times as numerous as his own. There was some fierce fighting in which Arnold and Morgan distinguished themselves. Burgoyne surrendered his entire army of about 5,700 men (see p. 38).

1777   (Nov. 15th)

The Second Continental Congress voted to adopt the Articles of Confederation which had been submitted to them as early as July 12, 1776. The Articles would become the official government of the United States of America only when *all* of the thirteen states ratified them. This did not occur until March 1, 1781.

1777   (Dec.—On Through the Winter) Valley Forge

GW After defeats at Brandywine and Germantown, Washington retired to Valley Forge. Shortages of food, clothing, and blankets made the winter one of intense suffering. The shortages were due more to inefficient management, and poor logistics, than to genuine shortages. This situation did not help morale.

1778   (June 17th) France Becomes Our Ally

HM The victory at Saratoga set off negotiations in Paris toward a formal alliance. As early as February 1777, it was agreed that, if and when England and France were at war, the military alliance between America and France would automatically come into effect. A clash at sea between the British and French occurred on June 17th 1778. It was agreed that neither America nor France would make a truce or sign a peace until the other consented.

1778   (June 17th) England Offers Peace ("Extends the Olive Branch")

The catastrophe at Saratoga clearly invited an American-French alliance. Parliament and King George III realized it. In February they began arranging terms to offer America. The Earl of Carlisle headed a committee which arrived in Philadelphia on June 9th. Their terms were that Parliament would impose no revenue taxes upon the colonies, that the coersive acts and the tea tax would be repealed, and that all acts by Parliament affecting the colonies passed since 1763 would be suspended. These terms offered before Lexington and Concord would have been joyfully accepted. They might have been accepted after Bunker Hill, but not after Saratoga. On June 17th Congress announced that it would agree to no terms other than the complete withdrawal of British soldiers from American soil and the recognition by England of the complete independence of the United States of America.

1778   (June 28th) Monmouth (about 25 miles east of Trenton, N.J.)

GW Washington attempted to intercept General Clinton's forces which were going from Philadelphia to New York City. Through the treachery of General Charles Lee, a major American victory was prevented. Most of Clinton's army escaped. At the time Lee was disciplined for inefficiency and disobedience, but was later found to have been a traitor.

1778   (July 4th) Kaskaskia (Cahokia and Vincennes)

George Rogers Clark carried the war as far west as the Mississippi River. Starting out with 175 men, he went down the Ohio River to within a few miles of the Mississippi, then cut across to Kaskaskia. This cross-country march was extremely difficult. The men had to march through swamps holding their rifles high. It was a march fit to test the endurance of a well conditioned commando team of our day. Clark picked up a number of reinforcements among the Indians of the area. Surprise was the chief element in Clark's success. Kaskaskia was so remote and inaccessible that its defenders were not alert. During the following few months, Clark took the British forts at Cahokia and Vincennes. These operations are sometimes called the "war in the west."

1779   (June 21st) Spain Declared War on England

Within a week Congress sent John Jay to try to get money and supplies from Spain. He had very little success. Spain refused to recognize our independence and she refused to pledge herself to continue at war with England until our independence was, in fact, established. This circumstance became significant during the peace negotiations at the end of the war.

1780   (May 12th) Charleston Captured by the British

General Clinton with very small casualties of his own, about 500, took four American ships and about 5,000 prisoners when he occupied the city.

1780 (Aug. 16th) Camden

Camden is about 30 miles north east of Columbia, S. C. Washington advised Congress to send General Greene to oppose the British in the south, but Congress sent General Gates instead. Gates was thoroughly defeated, his retreat being a rout. Gates had been as much a hindrance as as a help at Saratoga even though he had been in command. He encouraged disaffection against Congress and Washington. He seemed to be a general of great personal ambition and small capacity. It was at this battle that Baron de Kalb lost his life.

1780 (Sept. 21st) Benedict Arnold's Treason

Arnold's treason can be traced back to May in 1779. He was given command of West Point on August 5th 1780. On September 21st he met the British officer Major John André and gave him the plans of West Point with suggestions as to its weak points. André was caught with these papers at Tarrytown before he got back to British lines. On September 25th Arnold fled to the British warship *Vulture* in the Hudson River. On September 30th André was hanged.

1780 (Oct. 7th) King's Mountain (Borderline of North and South Carolina)

The British Major Ferguson lost almost all of his force of about 1,100 men to a group of sharpshooting frontiersmen. This American victory lifted morale in the Carolinas and throughout the South.

1781 (March 1st) The Articles of Confederation went into effect.

Maryland finally ratified the Articles, the last of the thirteen states to do so.

1781 (Aug. 14th) News from Admiral De Grasse

The French admiral, De Grasse, sent word to Washington that he was bringing his fleet to Chesapeake Bay from the West Indies. He GW would be available for about three months. Washington then made plans to bottle up Cornwallis in Virginia on the York Peninsula.

1781 (Oct. 19th) Yorktown (The War is Virtually Ended)

Washington left troops around the land sides of New York City and maintained activity to deceive the British into expecting an offensive action against the city. Meanwhile, he went south with his main force to join with Lafayette, Rochambeau, and De Grasse to trap Cornwallis. The position of Cornwallis at Yorktown was a good one so long as the British fleet had control GW of Chesapeake Bay. Cornwallis had no inkling that the French fleet was about to hem him in. The siege began on October 9th. Colonel Alexander Hamilton gave distinguished service during this engagement. By the 18th the British position was hopeless. Cornwallis and his 8,000 men surrendered on the 19th. Casualties for the British were about 550, for the Americans about 260.

1782 (Mar. 5th) Parliament Acts to Bring the War to a Close

The House of Commons passed a bill against any further prosecution of the war against America. It further directed that peace terms be arranged.

1782 (Nov. 30th) Peace Terms Arranged

Our ministers, John Adams, Franklin, and Jay signed a separate treaty with England, not waiting for France to agree. France was not ready to make terms because she was allied with Spain who wished to continue the war until England would give her Gibraltar. We had no treaty obligations with Spain. In fact, Spain's attitude toward America had been less than friendly (see p. 41). France seemed inclined to think that the western border of the United States should be the Alleghenies rather than the Mississippi River. Our signing peace terms before France did was a source of irritation to that country, but Franklin was able to smooth things over. Although the terms were agreed upon between England and the United States, they were not to go into effect until France and England had come to terms. The agreements reached were as follows.

1] The independence of the United States of America was recognized.

2] The northern border would be the St. Croix River, the St. Lawrence-Atlantic water-shed divide (not easily determined), the 45th parallel to the St. Lawrence River, the Great Lakes, and from Lake Superior to the Mississippi River (not very definite).

3] The western border was the Mississippi River as far south as the 31st parallel.

4] The southern border was the 31st parallel to the St. Mary's River to the Atlantic Ocean. (This line was disputed by Spain.)

5] Debts existing between British subjects and Americans were valid.

6] Congress would recommend restoration of property and rights to the Loyalists.

7] The British would evacuate American soil "with all convenient speed."

1783 (Sept. 3rd) Peace Treaty Signed at Paris

The treaty was ratified by our Congress on January 14th 1784.

American Naval Operations During the War

The best brief account would be to state that America had no navy. But that would not be quite accurate. There was a Continental Navy, made up of ships built or bought by order of Congress and paid for by the United States. This navy had seven ships at the end of the war. Some of the states had navies of their own, but their services were un-coördinated and were of very little account. There were over a thousand privateers. Privateers were privately owned ships whose captains carried letters of marque and reprisal which certified that they were acting with the permission of their government against ships of an enemy nation. If captured, the possession of letters of marque and reprisal made the personnel of the ship prisoners of war, to be treated as such, rather than pirates to be hanged. Privateers got whatever they captured. Captured ships would be sold with their cargoes and the money would be divided among the crew. The officers got larger shares than the common seamen. Privateering often paid handsomely. This was a great hindrance to recruiting men for the Continental navy. In the regular navy a landsman (inexperienced sailor) got $6.66 per month, an able seaman $8.00, petty officers $9.00 to $15.00, lieutenants $20.00, surgeons $21.33, and captains $32.00. A ship in the Continental navy took prizes only incidentally; its main purpose was to engage enemy ships, to break a blockade, or to do a dozen other tasks, none of which involved prize money. If a regular navy ship captured a prize, most of the money went to the government, not to the crew. Serving in the navy was more dangerous than privateering as well as much less profitable. No privateer would attack a ship unless it appeared to be a rather easy victim. Most privateers could out-sail enemy warships. Discipline on a privateer was much more lax than on a naval ship. So, all told, a young man could have more fun, less work, more money, and a rather good chance to strike-it-rich on a privateer. The privateers raised havoc with British commerce. Insurance rates hit the sky. Frequently the prize cargoes contained military supplies that were sorely needed. Privateering not only had its compelling attractions, it was also a service to one's country; so why join the navy?

If we had no really effective navy, we did have a spectacular naval hero, John Paul Jones. He made raids on coastal towns near his boyhood home in Scotland, took a few prisoners and burned a few houses. It caused tremendous excitement throughout the British Isles which had known no raids from the sea since 1667. Consternation in England meant jubilation in America. His raids did keep many British ships roving the waters of the North and Irish seas when they might otherwise have been doing more important work. Jones took many prizes, outmaneuvered British warships too powerful for him to fight, and he defeated those he did engage. His most spectacular victory was at the battle between the *Bonhomme Richard* and *H.M.S. Serapis* (Se-ray'-pis).

The *Bonhomme Richard* had a crew of 380 men; 20 officers (mostly American), 43 petty officers (mostly British), 144 seamen (46 Americans-54 British-44 other nationalities), 137 French marines, and 36 French landsmen. She displaced 900 tons, had 40 cannon, and had been converted from a merchantman into a warship. The *Serapis* was a bit larger and had greater fire power, both in weight and number of cannon, than the *Bonhomme Richard*. She was a better ship.

The battle started September 25th 1779 in the North Sea off the Yorkshire coast. The *Bonhomme Richard* was flying a British flag in order to be able to approach the *Serapis*. When within hailing distance Jones lowered the Union Jack and raised the stars and stripes. At times the ships were only a few feet apart. Much of the time they were 80 to 100 yards apart. Jones rammed the *Serapis* and the two ships held fast. At this point Captain Pearson of the *Serapis* shouted, "Has your ship struck" (meaning surrendered) and Jones shouted back, "I have not yet begun to fight." The ships pulled apart, but Jones wanted them together so that small arms fire would be effective and boarding parties possible. If the battle became a short range cannon duel, the advantage would be with the *Serapis*. The *Bonhomme Richard* was maneuvered along-side the *Serapis* and the anchor chains became entangled. The two ships could swing at all sorts of angles to each other but they could not break apart. They fought thus for two hours. The *Bonhomme Richard* was on fire, it was sinking, only three of its cannon could fire. Jones' officers called upon him to surrender. The *Serapis* was badly damaged. The engagement had started at 6:45 P.M. on a beautiful moonlight night. People gathered on the Yorkshire coast had a good view of the battle. At 10:30 P.M. the mainmast of the *Serapis* creaked and trembled, it seemed about to crash. Captain Pearson surrendered. John Paul Jones had really been beaten but he didn't know it. Every one but Jones would have surrendered to the *Serapis* and in doing so they would have been judged to have fought gallantly. This was a victory of one man's courage, foolhardy and magnificent. Casualties were about 100 on each ship. The *Bonhomme Richard* could not be saved so Jones transferred to the *Serapis* and crawled across the North Sea to the safety of Dutch waters. Several duels between American and British warships were fought with victories overwhelmingly with the Americans. As a tonic for sustaining national morale these exploits did have value; otherwise they did not influence the course of the war.

*The Articles of Confederation
March 1, 1781-March 4, 1789

Confederation and Federation

The first constitution of the United States of America was the Articles of *Confederation.* In 1789 we became a *federation* under a new constitution; our central government became the *federal* government. The most serious challenge to the union of the states was the Civil War, and for that conflict the South became the *Confederate* States of America. Dictionary definitions of *confederation, federation, federal,* and *confederate* as terms applied to government give no clear distinctions or differences for these words. But within the context of American politics the difference between a confederate and a federal government is both distinct and important. Each has a different emphasis and points toward a different goal.

In a confederation each state retains the major powers of government; each state guards its sovereignty (the right in the last analysis to do as it pleases) to such an extent that the central government is unable to force any state to act against its own will. A confederation emphasizes the rights of states and holds to a minimum the power of the central government.

In a federation the central government exercises the major powers. While the rights and powers of states must be an important concern, the first consideration must be the establishment of effective central authority. A federation emphasizes the strength of the union. Its primary purpose is to maintain, and perhaps build, centralized power.

How strong the emphasis should be toward power for the states as against power for the central government was the major point of controversy during the campaign for the ratification of our Constitution; it was a basic issue of the Civil War; it is basic to the controversies over the United States Supreme Court decisions upon segregation in the schools (1954) and upon apportionment in state legislatures (1962).

Facts to Know About the Articles of Confederation

1] There was no chief executive.

There was a "Committee of States" made up of one delegate from each state. But, this committee existed only during the intervals between the sessions of the Congress. This committee could, in the absence of Congress, "mind the house" by performing routine governmental functions. It was specifically denied the power to make any policy decisions or to do anything which required a majority of nine of the thirteen states when the Congress was in session.

A committee of thirteen considered as an executive authority lacks responsibility; it invites split decisions and its members can disclaim individual responsibility. This committee of thirteen elected one of its members to preside over the meetings, but this presiding officer had no special powers and was in no sense the chief executive.

2] There was no judicial department.

There was no court to handle disputes between or among the states. If a dispute arose which could not be resolved by the states involved, then Congress was authorized to select three persons from each state (39 in all). From this panel each party to the dispute could in turn strike off one name at a time until the total number of potential judges left on the panel had been reduced to thirteen. At this point Congress would intervene and select by lot not fewer than seven nor more than nine names. Thus a court was established to judge the dispute. While the decision of this court was stated to be "final and conclusive" there was no provision for the enforcement of the verdict. The cumbersome procedure, plus the lack of authority to enforce the decision, gives substance to the statement that there was no judicial department.

Do not allow the above to lead you into the error of thinking that during the Articles of Confederation there were no courts. There was an adequate court system in each of the thirteen states. It is probably no exaggeration to say that the courts of our states at this early period were excellent in comparison with courts anywhere in the world.

3] A majority of nine votes was required to pass important laws.

A few routine matters of minor importance

could be settled by a simple majority vote, and it was these few and minor powers that were also possessed by the "executive department" previously described. Nine votes out of thirteen is a two-thirds majority. Passing laws was a slow and difficult process. The Congress was unicameral (one house) and each state had from two to seven delegates, but only one vote.

4] Congress could requisition taxes from the states, but could not force their collection.

Based upon the value of "all land within each state, granted to or surveyed for any person" the Congress told each state what it should pay in taxes toward the support of the United States of America. It was left to the states to collect this money and turn it over to the central government. As one might well guess, the states did not pay the amounts requisitioned. For example, in 1781 a total of $8,000,000 was requisitioned. Over two years later less than $1,500,000 had been paid. No doubt each state legislature was primarily interested in not paying into the common fund more in proportion to the other states than they were interested in meeting in full their own quota.

5] The Congress could requisition men into the armed forces but could not draft men into the service of the United States.

Based upon population "in proportion to the number of white inhabitants in each state" Congress told each state how many men to supply for the armed forces. It was up to the states to raise the quota "clothed, armed and equipped" and march them "to the place appointed." This worked about as ineffectively as did the raising of money.

6] The members of Congress were paid by the states and a state could recall any delegate at any time.

This arrangement made the members of Congress think and act as ambassadors for their states. They did not serve the United States nor, under this system, should they have done so. Their function was to protect and advance the interests of their own states and cooperate for the welfare of the United States only when such cooperation coincided with this objective.

7] Congress was not given exclusive power to regulate interstate and foreign commerce.

Each state set its own import duties and soon each state tried to protect its own internal trade by levying tariffs against goods from other states. Thus, effective trade agreements between the United States and any foreign nation were well nigh impossible, and internal trade across state borders reached a very low volume.

8] Congress was not given the exclusive power to issue paper money.

Congress did fix the value of coins by setting the weight and the alloy used regardless of whether the coins were "struck by their own authority, or by that of the respective states." But the paper money situation became utterly chaotic.

9] Treaties made by the United States could be nullified by the action of the states.

If any provision in a treaty required the cooperation of the states, there was no way the central government could guarantee such cooperation.

10] Amending the Articles of Confederation required the unanimous vote of the thirteen states.

This provision expresses the concern sovereign states have whenever they form a league or common government. The right to exercise a veto power at some critical point is each state's protection against being coerced by the combined will of several other states.

Some Worthwhile Sidelights on the Articles of Confederation

Soon after the Second Continental Congress appointed the committee to draw up a declaration of independence, it also formed another committee to draw up a constitution for the new nation. This second committee reported several days later by submitting to the Congress the Articles of Confederation. Several of the concepts written into the Articles of Confederation stemmed directly from Benjamin Franklin's "Albany Plan of Union" of 1754. From time to time the Second Continental Congress considered the original draft of the Articles and made revisions. By November in 1777 the Articles had been approved and submitted to each of the thirteen states for ratification. The Articles would become the official government of the United States of America when ratified by *all* of the thirteen states. All but one state ratified them rather quickly. Maryland held out until March in 1781, which is only about seven months before the Yorktown campaign that ended the Revolutionary War. So, for a war that lasted about five and one-half years as far as fighting was concerned, we had a make-shift government except for the last seven months. Much has been made of the mismanagement of the Revolutionary War by the Second Continental Congress, but perhaps the fact that is really surprising is that a loosely organized

Congress not intended for the purpose did prosecute a war and win it.

Maryland refused to ratify the Articles of Confederation because she was a small state. She feared union with so many large states which might yet become larger. Only Rhode Island, Delaware and New Jersey were smaller and all four of these small states had no claims to western lands. Their boundaries were fixed; they could become no larger. Maryland withheld ratification until she was assured that the states having claims to vast western areas lying roughly between the Allegheny Highland and the Mississippi River and from the Great Lakes to Spanish Florida would relinquish them. Perhaps more than could have been realized at the time, Maryland performed a service to our country. The war itself made desire for unity stronger than usual. The creation of a new central government, the Articles of Confederation, offered an acceptable solution of what to do with the western lands. Whatever the pulls and tugs of the politics of the time, the fact is that pressure from Maryland did induce the states to cede their western lands to the United States. The acquisition of these lands by the central government set the stage for the Northwest Ordinance of 1787, and greatly aided the solution of the financial problems during the first shaky years of our Republic under the present Constitution.

** Understanding and Appreciating the Articles of Confederation

The ten weaknesses of the Articles of Confederation previously listed were not mistakes; that is, not mistakes in the sense that they were not intended. Each protection of the sovereign power of the states and each limitation on the power of the United States was deliberately and carefully calculated. Had the power of the central government been made greater, the states would have refused to form the union. With the Declaration of Independence and the reforming of the colonial governments into state governments, each of the thirteen states became a republic, an independent sovereign power. Modifying sovereignty is perhaps the most difficult of all political necessities to bring into effect. And no sovereign power is induced to sacrifice sovereignty until the painful necessity to do so is less painful than the penalty for not doing so.

The American statesmen of the late 1700's were wrestling with the same problem that plagues the statesmen of the world today. It may be that an effective union of the states was a smaller and simpler problem, that fewer and not so great difficulties tended to hold the states apart. Nevertheless, a close study of our difficulties in developing from the Second Continental Congress to the Articles of Confederation to the present Constitution may point the direction for the nations of the world. Certainly our experience is not a pattern to be followed. Nations are not for the foreseeable future ready to jump from confederation to federation. But the confederation of nations, The United Nations, may be modified toward, if not to, federation; and nations may modify their exercise of sovereignty. One speculation seems obviously sound; the movement of nations toward more effective international controls will be difficult and slow. Nations will back into it reluctantly only because they fear the cost of not doing so. The European Common Market and the concern of the United States over international trade remind us of the foreign trade problems and the internal difficulties under the Articles of Confederation. Perhaps American history from 1781 to 1789 is worth serious contemplation by the world at large. Does it suggest the direction of things to come? Does it emit a ray of hope?

The Critical Period 1781-1789

or

The United States under the Articles of Confederation

The Crisis

The historian John Fiske gave the period between the American Revolution and the adoption of the Constitution the title "Critical Period." It fitted so well that its acceptance has been complete. The crisis that built up during these years was the issue of life or death for our republic. Washington, who could not be discouraged during the Revolution, was on the verge of despair over the prospects for its survival. In a letter referring to the multitude of disorders and difficulties of the time, Washington wrote, "They exhibit a melancholy proof of what our trans-Atlantic foe has predicted; and of another thing, perhaps, which is still more to be regretted, and is yet more unaccountable, that mankind, when left to themselves, are unfit for their own government. I am mortified beyond expression when I view the clouds that have spread over the brightest morn that ever dawned upon any country." Jefferson, then our ambassador at Paris, reported to Congress that the French government simply wouldn't take this country seriously; he concluded with "We are the lowest and most obscure of the whole diplomatic tribe." Washington again expressed himself, less philosophically but more explosively, "There are combustibles in every state which a spark might set fire to. I feel infinitely more than I can express for the disorders which have arisen. Good God! Who besides a Tory could have foreseen, or a Briton have predicted them?" During the year before the Philadelphia Convention was held, there were rumors that perhaps the son of George III would be invited to become our king, limited, of course, by a constitution. It was reported that Prince Henry of Prusia was under consideration also. When John Fiske called this "The Critical Period" he hit upon the proper title.

*A Sampling of Conditions During the Critical Period

Shays' rebellion in Massachusetts made plain the desperate condition of the debtors and the dangerous situation of the creditors. Captain Daniel Shays had seen service at Bunker Hill. He was a farmer from a small town near Worcester, which was truly a rural area in the 1780's. He and most farmers felt themselves to be different from, and antagonistic to, the city people of Boston, forty miles away, and the fishing and trading towns of the Massachusetts sea coast. Like most of his contemporaries, he was not a well informed man. But he did know that the farmers, many of them veterans of the Revolution, were unable to pay their debts, that their farms were being taken from them by court action so that creditors could be satisfied. Many of these farms had been family homes for years. Things were tragically wrong. Shays didn't know what to do, nor was he, and hundreds of others like him, to blame for the economic troubles that beset them. He thought it must be the government's fault, or, at least, that the government should do something about it.

Seen through Shays' eyes the Revolutionary War was fought for "liberty," for "independence," for a "republic." In Shays' mind these words meant non-payment of taxes, ignoring laws one doesn't like; in short, behaving much as patriots did in the early 1770's. Certainly, in their distress, the government should come to their aid. A stop should be put to the foreclosure of mortgages on farms and homes, more paper money should be printed and, even though it was worth about two cents on the dollar, creditors should be forced by law to accept it in payment of debts. Governor Bowdoin and the Massachusetts legislature refused to pass any such laws. Protest meetings were held in many rural towns throughout Massachusetts. In September mobs formed; violence broke out in the Worcester-Springfield-Berkshire areas of central and western Massachusetts. Shays led the largest and most persistent armed group. Mobs prevented judges from holding court. From early September 1786 to early February 1787 rural Massachusetts was in a turmoil. Militia from Boston finally rounded up the leaders, the resistance fell apart, and order was restored. The central government had played no part in restoring order.

In Rhode Island the situation was really worse, though less violent. The state legislature passed "stay" and "tender" laws. The stay laws postponed payment of debts without any accumulation of interest; the tender laws forced merchants and creditors to accept at face value the worthless paper money. The result was that businessmen closed their shops so they would not have to exchange valuable merchandise for worthless money. Creditors avoided their debtors so that they would not receive payment in worthless money of debts contracted in good money.

There was a depression. The mere adjustment from war to peace is upsetting to business, but it should have been a minor factor in the simple and overwhelmingly agricultural economy of the post-Revolutionary period. Tariff walls had been erected by each of the thirteen states against imports from any other state; all states trying by laws to confine trade to their own people had created a condition where there was precious little trade for anyone. The political and business leaders, often the same men, were aware of this. They had a meeting at Mt. Vernon in 1785 where Virginia and Maryland had representatives hoping to abolish or modify tariffs: Two states could do nothing effective, so they planned a meeting at Annapolis, Maryland, where more states might meet to do something about the depressed interstate commerce. Five states, Delaware, New Jersey, New York, Pennsylvania, and Virginia attended this second effort at planning to improve trade. But five states were too few to act effectively, so a third meeting was arranged where an effort would be made to get all the states represented. This turned out to be the Philadelphia Convention of 1787. All states but Rhode Island were there. At the Annapolis meeting, Alexander Hamilton suggested that the third meting consider *all* problems, not just commerce, that confronted the states. Congress acted upon Hamilton's idea late in February, 1787, by calling a convention "for the sole and express purpose of revising the Articles of Confederation." Unlike the violent methods and foolish demands of Captain Shays and those who supported his actions, this was a sensible approach to the problems facing the new nation. However, Shays displayed a characteristic that may be essential to the health of any democratic republic; he had the capacity for righteous indignation and the courage to channel it into action. Maybe it was Daniel Shays and his fellow farmers who really aroused the states and Congress to constructive action.

Neither did the representatives in the Congress under the Articles think highly of our government. Their attendance was so poor that it was frequently impossible to get the quorum necessary for doing business. A member of any state legislature held a position of prestige and dignity in the eyes of his fellow citizens; but not so with a member of Congress. Why would a man of caliber seek membership in a political body that could advise and ask, but never command? Of course, some of our leading statesmen did serve in the Congress, but they were fully aware of the impotence of that body and of the low opinion generally held of their office.

In the field of foreign relations our government was having its troubles. England would not get its subjects out of the Ohio River Valley where they continued their fur trading in competition with our own people. Spain had closed the Mississippi River to our commerce. As part of the British Empire, we had enjoyed certain protections and favors in trade, but these evaporated when we became an independent nation. Add to this the fact that all the major powers of the world were monarchies and that this new republic was, by its very existence, a threat to their system of government. We were in an unfriendly world. Under the best of conditions it would have been difficult for a new nation to break through the trade barriers which mercantilism established.

The infant United States did have one big advantage. The Atlantic and the Pacific oceans were vast. There was no threat to our safety from any quarter in the western hemisphere. As a nation we were dazed and staggering; but if we had within us the capacity to recover, we could do so. There was no close neighbor to give us the knock-out blow.

There was one glittering success story written by the Congress under the Articles. This stemmed from Maryland's refusal to ratify the Articles until the other states had agreed to abandon their claims to western lands and cede the areas to the central government. Roughly this was an extensive area east of the Mississippi River, west of the present boundaries of the original thirteen states, south of the Great Lakes, and north of Spanish Florida. This great national domain was a source of financial strength. But much more important in the long run was the foresight and wisdom shown by Congress when it passed the Land Ordinance of 1785 and the Northwest Ordinance of 1787. Both of these laws applied to the Northwest Territory, but they also served as a pattern for other public lands.

In 1785 the Northwest Territory was the northwest corner of the United States; now it is the states of Ohio, Indiana, Illinois, Michigan, Wisconsin, and an adjacent corner of Minnesota. It is within the area almost enclosed by the Mississippi River, the Ohio River, and the Greak Lakes. Before the Land Ordinance of 1785, confusion about boundary lines of property was very common. Trees, fences, stone walls, boulders, and other objects that time would move or destroy marked boundaries. Strangely irregular shapes in pieces of property were not uncommon. The Ordinance of 1785 brought order into a confused picture. The Northwest Territory was cut into square townships measuring six miles on each side. Each township was cut into 36 square miles. The government would sell no less than one square mile, 640 acres, at a price no less than one dollar per acre. An individual settler could rarely pay as much as $640.00, but Land Companies, states and banks could. Their purchases from the government supplied a ready revenue. When resold to settlers the one square mile, 640 acres, could be sold in plots no smaller than 40 acres. One square mile, called a section, in each township was reserved so that any income received therefrom could be used for public education. Here is the first United States law granting aid to education.

The Ordinance of 1787 made the Northwest Territory one political unit ruled by a governor and judges appointed by Congress. When 5,000 male adults lived in the territory it could organize a bicameral legislature and send a delegate to Congress. A territorial delegate could speak, but not vote in Congress. Three to five states could be formed in the Northwest Territory. The formation of a state required a population of 60,000. The Ordinance guaranteed trial by jury, freedom of worship, forbade slavery, and provided for support of public education. By far the most significant provision was that every state carved out of the Northwest Territory would enter the Union on an equal footing with the original thirteen. Thus a pattern was set which permitted us to grow into a strong unified nation of fifty states. Had the original thirteen been given political privileges as charter members of the Union, all other states would have been second-class states. The development of the United States into a great power rests largely on the concept that new states were extensions of the United States, with each new state having full rights and dignity with every other state.

**The Constitutional Convention

The Demi-gods

Congress had set May 14th as the date for the opening of the convention at Independence Hall, Philadelphia. By that date all except New Hampshire and Rhode Island had selected delegates. The New Hampshire delegates arrived late in July. Rhode Island was not represented. The precise timing of meetings, which are routine today, was impractical for 1787. Only two states had delegates on hand by the scheduled day of the opening. Eleven days later, May 25th, seven states were represented, so the convention got under way with a majority present. Each state, no matter how many delegates, was to have one vote. Within a few days delegates from four other states arrived and, finally, New Hampshire.

Fifty-five delegates in all attended the convention at one time or another. The average daily attendance was between thirty and thirty-five. Ages ranged from 81 to 26, the average was in the low forties. Twenty-nine had attended college, twenty-nine were lawyers, seventeen were prominent in business (banking, insurance, shipping, merchants), fifteen were slave owners (owning from 6 to 200 slaves), eleven were large land owners, and seven held high public office (governors, judges, legislators). These statistics differ with others available; but whatever the differences the outstanding conclusion is unmistakable; the delegates were men of superior talents, recognized leadership, and ample property.

Obviously a government that will pay its debts and maintain a stable currency system would serve the personal financial interests of the delegates. Charles A. Beard in his "Economic Interpretation of the Constitution of the United States" assembled an impressive array of facts about the economic status and interests of each of the fifty-five delegates, but he did not conclude that the private interests of the delegates were determining factors in the decisions they reached. Thomas Jefferson, much more inclined to protect liberty than property, gave these founding fathers too extravagant praise in one word; he called them demi-gods. Looking back upon the work of the Convention, Mr. Madison wrote, ". . . there never was an assembly of men, charged with a great and obvious trust, who were

more pure in their motives, or more exclusively and anxiously devoted to the object committed to them than were the members of the Federal Convention of 1787." Professors Morison and Commager, in writing of the founding fathers over 150 years after the event, expressed a judgment accepted with practical unanimity among historians; "Seldom has a class acted more wisely for the good of the whole, than . . . the property owners, publicists, and professional men that framed the Federal Constitution. . . ." The delegates appreciated the historical importance of the work of the Convention. Very early in the sessions, possibly before the formal sessions began, Washington remarked, "It is too probable that no plan we propose will be adopted. Perhaps another dreadful conflict is to be sustained. If to please the people, we offer what we ourselves disapprove, how can we afterwards defend our work? Let us raise a standard to which the wise and the honest can repair. The event is in the hands of God." Well along in the sessions when failure seemed very probable because the small and the large states could not come to terms over representation, Benjamin Franklin offered a proposal which was thereafter followed—that each session be opened with prayer.

Chosen unanimously because his prestige would help immeasurably to gain acceptance among the people for anything done by the Convention, Washington was the chairman of the Constitutional Convention. Just as surely as Washington was the first citizen of America to his countrymen, so too was Franklin the most renowned of Americans throughout the world. Franklin, at 81, wielded influence in informal conferences and in committees; he was able to subdue the sharpness of conflicting views, but he played only a minor part in the formal debate on the floor of the convention. James Madison made very fine and full notes of all the proceedings. At the close of each meeting he went to his boarding house and carefully recorded in detail the business accomplished and the views expressed. All delegates were instructed not to discuss the convention business except during the meetings. Secrecy was well kept. The notes written by Mr. Madison were not made public until 1840, four years after his death. These notes and The Federalist Papers by Hamilton, Madison, and Jay are invaluable for the light they shed upon the Constitution and the thinking of the men who made it. For purposes of secrecy Washington ordered that the official minutes kept by the secretary be merely a record of motions made and the vote taken. It was felt, and very wisely so, that had all the details of debate been made public, the members of the Convention would be unable to speak their minds as their best judgment directed. Honest, constructive deliberation can best be accomplished free from the pressures of public opinion.

The Convention Decides to Make a Constitution and Adopt Compromises

The big problem was one of representation, a serious divergence of opinion between the large and the small states. Edmund Randolph presented the Virginia Plan. Its most controversial point was that which set up a bicameral legislature with representation in both houses based on population. The people would elect the lower house. Members to the upper house would be elected by the lower house from nominees chosen by the state legislatures. William Patterson presented the New Jersey Plan. It provided for equal representation for each state in both houses of the legislature. The debate continued for about three weeks. It was then decided that building a new constitution was more practical than amending the Articles of Confederation. This decision of July 19th made the Constitutional Convention an extra-legal body; some claimed an illegal one. Congress had called it for the purpose of "amending the Articles of Confederation." Another month of meetings passed before Roger Sherman presented the Connecticut Plan. This compromise proved acceptable to both large and small states. It provided for a bicameral legislature with representation in the lower house (House of Representatives) according to population, and equal representation for each state in the upper house (Senate). Before this compromise was reached, there were days when the Convention seemed about to break up in failure. After this agreement, the rest of the convention's business presented difficulties, but eventual success was never in doubt. Hence, the formation of the House of Representatives and the Senate under the Constitution has been called The Great Compromise.

Another compromise was over economic matters. The southern states with their export of tobacco and naval stores led the agricultural interests in demanding that a two-thirds vote be required to pass laws regulating foreign commerce. Their principal fear was that there might be an export tax. The northern states with a strong commercial interest wished to have import taxes levied to stimulate the growth of manufacture, so they opposed the two-thirds vote requirement. The agricultural interests were placated by two provisions: export taxes were made illegal, and Congress could pass no law interfering with the importation of slaves until 1808, except for a tax, which was never levied, of $10 per head. In return for these two concessions the commercial states of the north were favored by a provision permitting import taxes, tariffs, to be levied by a simple majority vote.

Still a third important compromise was required to modify the differences between the slave and the free states. The slave states wanted slaves counted as part of the population when determining how many representatives they could have in the House of Representatives, but not counted when Congress levied direct taxes according to population. The free states wished just the opposite arrangement. The compromise reached was that for both purposes of representation and taxation the population of a state would be determined by counting all free people plus three-fifths of "all other persons," meaning slaves. While slavery was by no means a major concern, either economic or moral, in the minds of the delegates, it is interesting to note that the words *slave* and *slavery* do not appear in the Constitution until the 13th amendment, added after the Civil War. Could it be there was some uneasiness, some embarrassment, foreshadowing things to come?

Ratification of the Constitution

Article VII of the Constitution reads, "The ratification of the conventions of nine States, shall be sufficient for the establishment of this Constitution between the States so ratifying the same." It was the Congress that had called the meeting at Independence Hall, Philadelphia to "amend the Articles of Confederation." It was to the Congress that the Philadelphia Constitutional Convention submitted the Constitution on September 20th 1787. The Constitution was before the Congress about a week, during which time there was an attempt to have Congress censure the Philadelphia Convention for exceeding its authority. But, on the 28th of September, Congress sent copies of the Constitution to each state legislature with instructions that they submit the new government to the people through state-wide conventions. Article VII, quoted above, was attacked as a violation of the provision of the Articles of Confederation which required a unanimous vote for any changes in its constitution.

A bit of political meditation may be apropos here. There is no doubt that the Philadelphia Convention exceeded its authority. There is no doubt that changing from the Articles to the Constitution by action short of a unanimous vote violated the intent and purpose of the Articles. Can "extra-legal" devices, or, in plain language, illegal measures be taken whenever "circumstances warrant?" If an easy "yes" is the answer, then laws are a fraud and governments become a thin pretext, machines to be manipulated for the benefit of office holders. If the answer is an adamant "no," then people become victims of constitutions and laws; they discover that governments established to serve them have become their masters. To this ever-present dilemma there is no answer; yet every thoughtful citizen must make his own answer as occasions arise. History and government raise a multitude of questions which have no certain answers. If indifference permits too many "easy-yes" answers, there will be corruption ad nauseam; if there are too persistent "adamant-no" answers there will be armed clashes between civilians and officials, perhaps civil war. An informed citizenry, easily aroused to political activity and well disposed toward the common good can avoid both extremes. But the problem of what decision to make faces a people when there are differences of opinion on issues which they consider important.

On December 7, 1787 Delaware was the first state to ratify the Constitution. On June 21, 1788 New Hampshire was the ninth state to ratify, and therefore the Constitution, in accordance with Article VII, became the government of the United States for the nine states. A committee of Congress, under the Articles of Confederation, named New York City as the capital, made February 4th the date for the presidential electors to vote for president, and set March 4th as the opening of the first Congress under the Constitution. North Carolina and Rhode Island entered the Union in the late fall of 1789 and the spring of 1790, respectively, after Washington had been inaugurated.

Just what part the people played in the ratification of the Constitution has been pretty well determined. The state of New York was the only one that made a special arrangement for this occasion by allowing universal manhood suffrage for the election of delegates to the state convention. In the other states the usual qualifications for electing delegates were the same as required for voting for members of the lower house of the state legislature. Less than 5% of the population lived in towns of 8,000 or more. Rural America, with relatively few exceptions, was made up of small farmers, and such men met the property qualifications for voting. Professor Beard has estimated that between two-thirds, and four-fifths, of the male adults were enfranchised. But many qualified voters did not vote. Towns and cities organized rallies and parades which kept interest high and got out the vote. Newspapers and pamphlets circulated almost exclusively in urban areas and tended to keep interest alive. The towns, though much smaller in potential voting strength, were much greater in actual votes cast than the rural areas. The Federalist Party in supporting the Constitution worked much more effectively than the Anti-Federalists in working against it. Had every qualified voter cast his vote, there is little doubt that the Constitution would have failed of ratification. Nevertheless, this ratification campaign was a memorable, historical event. Citizens, not public officials, had gathered together and drawn up a framework of government which had then been submitted to a vote of the people in each of the thirteen states. To determine the will of the voters the most representative political machinery then known, the convention, was used. In accordance with this vote a new government was set in motion. For its day this was a tremendous political achievement; to the new nations of the middle 1900's it is still quite an example!

Vote of the States on Ratification of the Constitution

The states are listed in the order in which they ratified the Constitution.

	VOTE OF THE DELEGATES	
	FOR	AGAINST
Delaware	unanimous	
Pennsylvania	46	23
New Jersey	unanimous	
Georgia	unanimous	
Connecticut	128	40
*Massachusetts	187	168
Maryland	63	11
South Carolina	149	73
*New Hampshire	57	47
*Virginia	89	79
New York	30	27
*North Carolina	194	77
Rhode Island	34	32

* These states proposed amendments which, in each case, amounted to a bill of rights.

**The Constitution

An Approach to the Constitution

The Constitution should not be approached as if it were Holy Writ. It should not be approached casually as if it were an ordinary document. In learning about the Constitution there can be no tolerance of slovenliness; if one can't quote a provision therein or give an accurate paraphrase thereof, then he simply does not know it. *Almost* correct is wrong. The Constitution is a legal document, not just laws, but basic or fundamental law. It is the legal framework upon which all other laws rest.

William E. Gladstone, several times prime minister of England in the latter half of the 1800's, referred to our Constitution as, ". . . the most wonderful work ever struck off at a given time by the brain and purpose of man." When, in 1887, we celebrated the 100th anniversary of the adoption of the Constitution, Gladstone wrote to the committee in charge this more subdued statement, "I have always regarded that Constitution as the most remarkable work known to me in modern times to have been produced by the human intellect, at a single stroke (so to speak), in its application to political affairs." This Constitution has been in continuous operation longer than any other basic law written for the government of a people.

The Preamble

The preamble grants no power, neither to the government nor to anyone. It is a statement of purposes. One way to estimate the success of the Constitution would be to consider each of the six purposes listed, and form an opinion as to how well each purpose has been accomplished.

1] "to form a more perfect union"

Success here is 100%. The union formed is more perfect than that under the Articles of Confederation. The union was severely, but unsuccessfully, challenged by the Civil War.

2] "to establish justice"

Courts throughout the United States operate in a manner that approximates justice to a commendable degree. There is room for improvement. On this issue of justice, smug satisfaction is always dangerous.

3] "to insure domestic tranquility"

Violence between states, since the Civil War, seems outside the realm of the most remote possibility. Violence between the federal government and a state or states seems almost as unlikely. Violence associated with labor problems and organized crime are usually, though not always, state problems. In the minds of the founding fathers the words *domestic tranquility* may have had a reference to such situations as Shays' Rebellion. Note that we have just speculated about what may have been in the minds of the writers of the Constitution. Is that legitimate? Can domestic tranquility mean different things at different times?

4] "to provide for the common defense"

The United States has not been on the losing side in any war.

5] "to provide for the general welfare"

Measured by the standard of living of its people, the United States is among the very top few nations, possibly at the very top. Was standard of living what general welfare meant to those who wrote the Constitution? What does general welfare mean now?

6] "to secure the blessings of liberty to ourselves and our posterity"

That this is the "land of liberty" has not been an empty phrase. Our people do (and always have under the Constitution) possess religious, political, and economic liberty to a high degree. Liberty is as unstable and fragile as it is precious. No generation can guarantee it to its posterity. "Eternal vigilance is the price of liberty."

Did "we the people" ordain and establish this constitution? The people had no direct voice in sending the delegates to the Constitutional Convention. State legislatures chose most of them. The question of choosing delegates to the convention was not an issue in any state election. The meetings of the Constitutional Convention were secret. The people played no part in the framing of the Constitution.

In the ratification of the Constitution the issue was presented by each state to its people. Conventions in each state were formed by the vote of the people. The percentage of adult males who qualified as voters was high, far superior to any other place on earth then or ever before. The campaigning was on the one issue of ratification, publicity by both sides was unhindered, and voting was unimpaired. The ratification campaign was a major political achievement, a milestone along the hard road toward self-government. The people were as free to reject the Constitution as to accept. They accepted it.

A Bicameral Legislature

The Senate (upper house) and the House of Representatives (lower house) constitute Congress. Each state has two Senators. The number of members each state has in the House of Representatives is directly in proportion to its population (see p. 52).

The small states are protected in their equal representation in the Senate by the clause in Article V reading, ". . . no State, without its consent, shall be deprived of its equal suffrage in the Senate." This clause is the only one in the Constitution not subject to change unless every state agrees. There must be a federal census every ten years so that seats in the House of Representatives may be reapportioned according to population changes. The first census was in 1790, and each state was allowed one representative for every 30,000 people. To keep the House from becoming too large, Congress, in 1912, restricted the membership to 435. As each census is taken, the total population is divided by 435 to determine each state's quota in the House. According to the 1960 census, it requires about 400,000 population for each member in the House of Representatives. Any state has at least one representative in the House. Nevada has a total population of under 300,000. With fifty states there are 100 Senators; hence the total membership of Congress is 535 and will remain so unless more states are created.

Qualifications for Senators

AGE   30 years old or over
CITIZENSHIP   Must have been a citizen of the United States for at least nine years
RESIDENCE   Must reside in the state he represents

Qualifications of Members of the House of Representatives

AGE   25 years old or over
CITIZENSHIP   Must have been a citizen of the United States for at least seven years
RESIDENCE   Must reside in the state he represents

Powers of the Senate Not Possessed by the House of Representatives

1] May ratify treaties (requires a ⅔rds vote)

2] May elect the Vice-President if the Electoral College fails to do so (see p. 60)

3] May try officials who have been impeached and, by a ⅔rds vote, may dismiss them from office

4] May ratify presidential appointments to certain high offices as specified in the Constitution or by Congress. The approval by a simple majority vote is required for the appointment of ambassadors, consuls, judges of the Supreme Court, and cabinet officials

Powers of the House of Representatives Not Possessed by the Senate

1] May introduce revenue bills

2] May elect the President when the Electoral College fails to do so (see p. 60)

3] May impeach public officials

To impeach an official means to decide that he should be tried on charges that have been made against him. Only the House of Representatives can make such a decision; it requires a simple majority vote. Impeachment does not imply guilt; it does show that, in the opinion of the House, the charges made and the prevailing circumstances make trial before the Senate desirable.

How Bills Become Laws

In order to pass Congress and then get to the President, a bill must meet three conditions: pass *each house* of Congress in *identical form* by a *simple majority* vote.

Identical form means exactly what it states; any changes in punctuation, in spelling, in wording, no matter how minor, require the bill to be again submitted to the house which passed it before such alterations occurred. To prevent endless shuttling of bills between the House and Senate, bills are referred to joint committees made up of members of both houses. These committees iron out the form of a bill and then submit it to Congress. Most of the serious work of law-making is done in committees.

After a bill has passed each house of Congress in identical form by a simple majority vote, it then is submitted to the President. At this point four things may happen to it.

A] The President may sign it. It is then law.

B] The President may ignore it. If Congress continues in session for more than ten days after the bill has been sent to the President, the bill automatically becomes law on the eleventh day. Sundays are not counted.

C] The President may veto the bill. He does so by attaching in writing his objections to the bill and sending it back to the house in which it originated. If each house then passes the bill by a 2/3rds vote, taken by roll call, it becomes law. This is overriding a veto. Unless the vetoed bill is passed by the 2/3rds majority, it is dead.

D] If the President ignores the bill and Congress adjourns within the next ten days, not counting Sundays, the bill is dead. This is a pocket veto.

Special Privileges of Members of Congress

1] Except for a felony, treason, and breach of the peace a congressman can't be arrested during a session of Congress or on his way to or from Congress. Arresting legislators for picayune offenses, real or imagined, was once a device used to keep them away from the legislature for political advantage to the opposite party.

2] No action for libel, no charges, no official questioning is permitted against a Congressman concerning anything he may have said in Congress or in any committee of Congress. This permits Congressmen to voice suspicions which, if true, might uncover corruption; if false, might be libelous. This unusual completeness of freedom of speech is a substantial protection to Congressmen, as it enables them to seek the public good without fear of libel suits. Obviously this privilege is subject to abuse, and if abused, can result in serious injustice to the victims. The only protection against such abuse is the judgment and responsibility of the Congressmen. As always, great power can be properly exercised only when controlled by great restraint. The record of Congressmen in this respect throughout the years has been good, but not perfect.

Special Prohibitions on Members of Congress

1] No person may be a member of Congress and also hold any other federal office. This reflects a fundamental theory which runs through our Constitution, the theory of separation of powers. The powers to be kept as separate as is practical are the executive, legislative, and judicial. Any Congressman with two federal positions might find himself in two of these major departments. The interests of these divisions of government are frequently in conflict. A legislator with a second position in the executive department might find himself forced to serve one interest and betray the other.

2] No member of Congress can vote himself a raise in pay. Any law increasing salaries does not apply to any member of Congress at the time the law is passed. The increase applies only to Congressmen elected after the law was passed; hence, new members benefit immediately upon election and so do the old ones after they have served out their terms and won reelection.

Some of the Powers of Congress

Section 8 of Article I in the Constitution lists eighteen paragraphs of powers. It is easy to know almost all of them. In fact, people old enough to be likely to be reading this, already know most of them. The following powers of Congress are common knowledge. Congress has power:

*1] to *levy and collect* taxes

2] to borrow money

3] to coin money and regulate a currency system

4] to punish counterfeiters

5] to punish piracy

6] to establish post offices

7] to provide an army

8] to provide a navy

9] to issue patents

10] to issue copyrights

The following powers may not be common knowledge, but should be known:

*11] to regulate foreign and interstate commerce

12] to establish uniform rules of naturalization

13] to establish uniform rules of bankruptcies

14] to constitute courts inferior to the Supreme Court

*15] to declare war

16] to govern the District of Columbia

*17] to make all laws necessary and proper for carrying into execution the provisions of this Constitution. (a paraphrase of the Implied Powers or Elastic Clause)

* See further comment in the following paragraphs.

Brief Comment on Certain Powers of Congress

To levy and collect taxes

The Constitution restricts this power to three purposes. Every tax must be levied in order to pay the public debt of the United States, to provide for the common defense, or to promote the general welfare. A tax levied for any other purpose would be illegal.

If there is resistance to the collection of taxes, Congress is empowered by the Elastic Clause to pass any laws necessary and proper to force the collection of taxes.

To regulate foreign and interstate commerce

The Mt. Vernon and Annapolis meetings were attempts to do something about the confused state of commerce due to interstate tariffs and the varying regulations of the several states in regard to foreign commerce. This weakness of the Articles of Confederation was the one which led to the Philadelphia Constitutional Convention. Granting Congress exclusive authority in regulating interstate and foreign commerce solved the problem.

To declare war

Congress declares war only in response to a request by the President. He makes such a request by speaking to a joint meeting of both houses held in the chamber of the House of Representatives. After the President has requested a declaration of war, the members of the Senate go back to their own quarters. Both the House and the Senate vote separately. A simple majority vote in each house is required. Modern warfare has made the declaration of war a rather empty procedure. In World War I and World War II we were at war for some time before there was a declaration of war. That is, the declaration was not a decision; it was merely a recognition of what had already happened. Any future war may be over before it occurs to the President or Congress to go through the motions of declaring war. Or the next war may be some "limited" action which will not be called a war, and for which there will be no declaration.

"To make all laws which shall be necessary and proper for carrying into execution the foregoing powers, and all other powers vested by this Constitution in the government of the United States, or in any department or officer thereof."

Later we shall discuss the word *necessary* in this Implied Powers Clause, but at this juncture there are two other points to notice.

1] This provision is the last of the list of direct grants of powers to Congress. So listed, it appears as one more power added to those previously listed. Its purpose would then seem to be to assure Congress that it has ample power to carry out the provisions of the Constitution. Had this Implied Powers Clause been placed in Section 9 of Article I, a different interpretation would be in order. Then the clause would appear to be a caution to Congress not to exceed its powers, to be careful to do only what was necessary and no more. This clause taken away from its context could be telling Congress to do whatever is necessary, or it could be warning Congress to do only that which is necessary. The first interpretation tends to increase the powers of Congress, while the second tends to restrict them.

2] In Section 10 of Article I of the Constitution the following words occur, ". . . except what may be *absolutely necessary* for . . ." If in one part of the Constitution the words *absolutely necessary* are used, while in another the word *necessary* occurs, what difference is there, if any, in the meaning?

These small distinctions are helpful to a consideration of the formation of the first major parties under President Washington.

Miscellaneous Facts to Know About Congress

1] Except for the fact that the Vice-President is the presiding officer of the Senate, both the House and Senate choose their own officers and make their own rules.

2] If a President or Vice-President has been impeached by the House, the trial before the Senate will be presided over by the Chief Justice of the Supreme Court. In all other cases the Vice-President will preside.

3] Congress must meet at least once a year. This regular meeting begins on January 3rd as provided by the 20th amendment adopted in 1933.

4] A quorum is a simple majority of each house. Fewer than a quorum may adjourn from day to day and may take measures to compel other members to attend in order to achieve a quorum.

5] Each house must keep a journal containing a record of the proceedings. The record shall include all debates and speeches as well as a record of the voting. Anything which, in the judgment of Congress, requires secrecy may be omitted from the record. In accordance with this provision the Congress prints the Congressional Record in two sections, a Senate edition and a House edition.

6] A roll call vote with the yeas and nays of the

members individually recorded can be demanded by a vote of one-fifth of those present.

7] A member of either house may be expelled by a ⅔rds vote.

8] A member of either house may be refused his seat by a simple majority. Occasionally an election of a member to Congress comes under serious questioning due to irregularities during the campaign. A Congressman elected under such circumstances may find himself excluded.

9] A vote of censure in either house requires a simple majority. This is a way Congress has of severely reprimanding one of its members for conduct which they consider extremely distasteful, but for which they do not wish to invoke expulsion.

10] Both houses must agree on the same time for the adjournment of a session of Congress. However, adjournments within a session of Congress can be for not more than three days and in such cases the House and Senate may act independently.

Powers Forbidden to the United States

A writ of habeas corpus could be translated into "thou shalt have the body." It is a queer legal way of saying that a person who has been arrested has the right to be brought before a proper official to be told why he is being held, to be informed what law he is alleged to have broken. He must be so informed within a reasonable time after arrest, usually within forty-eight to seventy-two hours. A prisoner gains three protections from a writ of habeas corpus.

1] It practically eliminates intentional false arrest. In early English history some kings had a nasty habit of putting individuals in jail because they didn't like them, frequently because they had refused to lend money to them. Under a writ of habeas corpus a person arrested for no legal reason can get free again so quickly that it makes little sense to arrest him. Of course, now there are severe legal penalties against any person or officials guilty of causing a false arrest.

2] As soon as a prisoner knows the precise charges brought against him, he can then prepare for a defense.

3] Being charged with breaking a particular law puts a prisoner in a position where he can demand the right to be released on bail. In a very few extremely serious crimes, bail may be refused. Anyone released on bail is free until his trial. Bail is refunded when the trial begins, but if the defendant has "jumped bail," not returned for trial, he forfeits the bail and is subject to arrest for the offense of jumping bail in addition to the original charge.

No bill of attainder or ex-post-facto law shall be passed.

A bill of attainder is a special law made to apply in a particular instance. It treats this one case in a different manner than that prescribed by law. The unusual treatment contained in the bill of attainder denies trial by jury and other safeguards to a fair trial. The necessity for protection against a bill of attainder grew out of English history.

An ex-post-facto law is one which makes punishable an act which was legal when committed.

There shall be no export taxes.

In the regulation of interstate and foreign commerce there shall be no favoring of one state over another.

No money shall be drawn from the United States treasury unless an appropriation has been made by Congress.

No title of nobility shall be granted by the United States.

No direct tax shall be levied by the United States unless it is apportioned among the several states according to their population. While this prohibition is still in effect, there is one huge exception to it, the income tax, which became the 16th amendment in 1913.

Powers Forbidden to the States

States shall not make treaties, grant letters of marque and reprisal (see p. 43), coin money, issue paper money, make anything except gold and silver legal tender, pass a bill of attainder or an ex-post-facto law, pass a law impairing the obligation of a contract, or grant a title of nobility.

Qualifications for the President and His Term of Office

The President must be at least 35 years old, have lived in the United States for fourteen years, and be a citizen by birth. No President may be elected more than twice nor serve for more than ten years. The term of office is four years and shall begin at noon on January 20th. If a Vice-President becomes President after the middle of a presidential term, he serves out the last two years. He may then be elected for two full terms and, in this manner, achieve the maximum period of just under ten years. If a Vice-President becomes President before the middle of the term of office, he is then eligible to be elected only once. In this case his maximum period as President could be as little as just over six years.

How the President and Vice-President Are Elected by the Electoral College

The President is elected by a simple majority vote of the Electoral College. Each state has as many votes in the Electoral College as it has members in Congress. The District of Columbia has as many electoral votes as any state having the least number of such votes.

The day popularly known as election day is the first Tuesday after the first Monday in November. A presidential election occurs every fourth year, always falling on the years with a date evenly divisible by four. The political parties hold conventions in each state, usually in the spring, to nominate the members of the Electoral College. Whichever party polls the largest vote in the state has thereby elected its nominees to the Electoral College. The Electoral College members meet, usually in their state capitols, on the first Monday after the second Wednesday in December and cast their votes for President. By custom, not by Constitutional provision, the electors vote for the candidate of their party, which results in all the electoral votes of any state going to the candidate with the largest popular vote in that state. The list of votes is signed and sealed by the governor of the state and sent to the president of the United States Senate, the Vice-President. On January 6th a joint session of Congress is held at which the Vice-President presides and the ballots are counted. Technically, this is the election of the President. If January 6th is a Sunday the election is held the following day.

The Electoral College members vote for President and Vice-President on separate ballots. The President and Vice-President must come from different states. The procedures for election of President and Vice-President are identical unless the Electoral College fails to give a majority vote to any candidate. In that case the procedures differ from that point on.

How the President and the Vice-President Are Elected When the Electoral College Fails to Reach a Decision

If no candidate for President gets a majority of the electoral votes, the election goes to the House of Representatives. There each state has one vote. The members of the House from each state have to caucus, hold a meeting, and decide how to cast their one vote. Two-thirds of the total number of states must be present and it takes a majority of all the states to elect the President. The House is restricted in its choice to the *top three* candidates who received the most votes in the Electoral College.

If no candidate for Vice-President gets a majority of the electoral vote the election goes to the Senate. There each Senator has one vote. Two-thirds of the total number of Senators must be present, and it takes a majority of all the Senators to elect the Vice-President. The Senate is restricted in its choice to the *top two* candidates who received the most votes in the Electoral College.

No matter what the circumstances of the election, the President and the Vice-President must be from different states.

When circumstances arise during an election for which there is no provision in the Constitution or other law, it will be the duty of Congress to find some way out of the tangle.

Oath of Office for the President

When the President takes office on January 20th at noon, the following oath is taken as prescribed in the Constitution. "I do solemnly swear (or affirm) that I will faithfully execute the office of President of the United States, and will, to the best of my ability, preserve, protect, and defend the Constitution of the United States."

There is a choice here between an oath, "I do so solemnly swear," and an affirmation, "I do solemnly affirm." This may reflect the Quaker influence so strong in Pennsylvania at the time of the Constitutional Convention. It would be a violation of Quaker beliefs to "swear" to anything. It certainly reflects the concern shown by those who drew up the Constitution to avoid having in our framework of government anything that would set up a conflict between religious convictions and participation in government. Usually the oath or affirmation is administered by the Chief Justice of the Supreme Court.

Very similar oaths or affirmations are taken by members of state legislatures, by governors, by Congressmen, by judges and by many other office holders, both state and federal. Note that the oath or affirmation is not to support any person, such as a governor or a president, but is always to support laws: the state constitutions, the federal Constitution, the laws of the land. Loyalty is given to governments, not to officials as individuals.

Powers of the President

1] The President is commander-in-chief of the armed forces of the United States at all times. Any state militia automatically comes under his command whenever used in the service of the United States.

2] He may require written reports from "the principal officer in each of the executive departments."

This is an example of the brevity and effectiveness of the wording of the Constitution. Nothing else is said about "executive departments" and "the principal officer," but from these few words in conjunction with the Implied Powers clause the cabinet has been established. If the Constitution provides for the President's getting reports from heads of executive departments, Congress must pass laws "necessary and proper" in order to create such departments, each with a "principal officer." During the first year of Washington's presidency Congress created the departments of state, treasury, war, justice, and post office. There are now (1965) ten executive departments, each with a principal officer called a member of the President's cabinet. These cabinet heads, plus the Vice-President, are sometimes referred to as the President's official family.

3] He can "grant reprieves and pardons" to federal prisoners, "except in cases of impeachment."

4] He can make treaties which become effective only after ratification by a ⅔rds vote of the Senate.

5] He may make appointments (see p. 56) with or without the approval of the Senate as specified by the Constitution and the laws of Congress.

6] He may make recess appointments to executive positions. Such appointments will last through the recess and also to the end of the next session of Congress.

Duties of the President

1] He must, "from time to time," deliver to Congress a message on "the state of the Union."

This "State of the Union" message is given at the opening of each regular session of Congress. The President may read it to Congress or he may send it to be read to Congress. With the greatly increased complexity and scope of federal affairs the Congress has by law required the President to send two more messages to them each year. In 1921 Congress required a budget message each year from the President and since then a third message, one on the economic state of the Union, has been added. The State of the Union message required by the Constitution is usually the President's own thoughts on what should occupy the attention of Congress for the coming session. The budget message and the economic message are more technical in content and are largely the work of advisors to the President who are specialists in these fields.

2] He may call special sessions of Congress.

3] If the two houses of Congress cannot agree on a date for adjournment, he may set the date for them.

4] "He shall receive ambassadors and other public ministers."

5] He shall "commission all the officers of the United States."

6] "He shall take care that the laws be faithfully executed."

This, of course, is the chief responsibility of the President. It is so much the core of his office that he is often called the Chief Executive.

The Judicial Power of the United States

The Constitution directs Congress to establish "one Supreme Court" and "such inferior courts" as Congress sees fit.

In September of 1789 Congress passed the Federal Judiciary Act which established a Supreme Court with a Chief Justice and five Associate Justices. District and circuit courts were created. The pattern set by this rather voluminous law is still in effect. In February of 1790 John Jay was appointed as the first Chief Justice.

Term of Office and Pay for Federal Judges

Judges shall serve during "good behavior." For all practical purposes this means for life or until voluntary retirement. Judges can be impeached for cause.

The pay of a judge cannot be reduced during his term of office. The appointment, the term of office, and the pay of federal judges combine to make them independent, that is, free from pressures that could threaten their status and possibly influence their judgment. (See p. 66 under checks and balances.)

Jurisdiction of Federal Courts

Federal courts have jurisdiction in the following cases:

1] Arising under the Constitution and laws of Congress

2] "Affecting ambassadors, other public ministers, and consuls"

3] "Of admiralty and maritime jurisdiction"

4] "Of controversies to which the United States shall be a party"

5] "Between citizens of different States"

6] "Between a State, or a citizen thereof, and foreign states, citizens or subjects"

Original Jurisdiction of the Supreme Court

When a case is heard by the Supreme Court before it has been taken to any other court, it is said to be a case of original jurisdiction. Cases involving "ambassadors, other public ministers and consuls, and those in which a State shall be a party" are cases of original jurisdiction.

Ambassadors, ministers, and consuls on duty in the United States are most unlikely to become involved in court action. Trained diplomats are usually diplomatic enough to keep out of court. If such an official representative of another nation becomes entangled with the law in a manner that reflects unfavorably upon him, his usefulness to his own country ends. He will be recalled. If the United States finds such an official unwelcome to us, we will designate him "persona non grata," an unacceptable person, and then he will be recalled by his home government. We sometimes dismiss foreign representatives for flagrant violations of the diplomatic code of behavior. Sometimes we dismiss an ambassador, minister, or consul merely because his country has dismissed one of our officials, a tit-for-tat procedure. This dismissal and recalling of diplomats is most unusual except under conditions where there has been a long-standing unfriendliness between nations, a situation we have come to call a "cold war." The point here is that troubles involving diplomats practically never get into our courts; they are handled in some other manner. Hence, cases of original jurisdiction before the Supreme Court involving foreign officials are extremely rare.

There are cases involving states that come under the original jurisdiction of the Supreme Court, but by far the greater number of cases before the court are those that have been tried in lower courts and have been appealed. Whenever a case is retried, it must be by a court of higher jurisdiction than the court rendering the decision in question. All such cases are known as cases of appellate jurisdiction.

The appellate jurisdiction of the Supreme Court is subject to complete regulation by Congress (see p. 66). As the Constitution puts it, the Supreme Court's appellate jurisdiction may be modified "with such exceptions and under such regulations as the Congress shall make." (Article III, Section 2) If Congress and the Supreme Court ever develop a spirit of hostility toward one another resulting from decisions in which the Court has declared laws of Congress unconstitutional, the Congress could drastically modify the jurisdiction of the Court in all *appellate* cases. Many of the most important decisions in our history involving the constitutionality of laws of Congress have been made in cases of appellate jurisdiction. Congress has not used this

grant of power in any such manner; there seems very little likelihood that it will, but the power is available.

The Congress has no authority over the original jurisdiction of the Supreme Court.

There is absolutely no way in which a decision of the Supreme Court can be altered in any particular case. The Supreme Court is the final authority at any given time. The Supreme Court has given a decision one way at one time and reversed itself, changed its mind, some years later and given a very different answer to the same question. But each decision, when made, was final and authoritative. What the Supreme Court has declared illegal, such as an income tax law in 1894, may be made legal by a Constitutional amendment, the 16th amendment in 1913; but this does not qualify in the least the fact that, at any given time, the Supreme Court is the final authority.

Definition of Treason (Article III, Section 3)

"Treason against the United States shall consist only in levying war against them, or in adhering to their enemies, giving them aid and comfort." "No person shall be convicted of treason unless on the testimony of two witnesses to the same overt act, or on confession in open court."

States Should Recognize Each Other's Official Acts

Article IV states that "Full faith and credit shall be given in each State to the public acts, records, and judicial proceedings of every other State." It goes on to say that each state should aid other states in the recovery of fugitives from justice and of "persons held to service or labor in one State, under the laws thereof, escaping into another. . . ." (slaves) This is one part of the Constitution that has been repeatedly broken. Sometimes states have refused to honor divorces granted in other states. Governors of states have refused to return fugitives from justice at the request of other states. In the years before the Civil War several states passed laws designed to prevent the recapture of fugitive slaves. When a state deliberately violates the Constitution in these respects, it does so with the solid backing of public opinion within its own borders, and probably the public opinion of a much larger area. When a prisoner from state "X" escapes to state "Y" where he then lives for years as a good citizen, brings up a family, holds a job, and wins the respect of his community, there may then be a deliberate violation of the Constitution by the governor of state "Y." He may refuse the request of the governor of state "X" for the delivery of the escaped prisoner to officials sent to rearrest him. No attempt by the federal government is made to coerce the governor of state "Y" into obeying Article IV of the Constitution. The escaped convict should avoid traveling into the state from which he escaped, for he is still a "fugitive from justice."

The significance of this situation is that it poses a problem for which there is no quick and easy answer, and never will be. Are there circumstances when human rights, whatever they may be, should over-ride legal rights; when people are to be put above law? When laws conflict with conscience, there will be problems in the enforcement of law. If the conscience is the public opinion of a community, a state or a group of states, and the law is the Constitution, then there is a problem in government. Can acceptance of law violation be justified? Can it ever be a wise policy? In the abstract, these questions have no answers; when raised in relation to a particular instance, there will be conflicting answers.

Admission of States to the Union

The Constitution gives Congress the power to admit states to the Union. This became a political issue of major importance at the close of the Civil War. President Lincoln usually referred to the war as a rebellion; that is, an unsuccessful four-year attempt to leave the Union. Restoring the ex-rebellious states to their normal status in Congress would, in this case, be under the authority of the President. On the other hand, if the eleven Confederate states had really left the Union, it then became the responsibility of Congress to readmit them on such terms and in such manner as Congress decided.

No state can be divided into more than one state without the consent of the states concerned and of Congress. No states can combine into one state without the consent of the states concerned and of Congress. In 1820 Massachusetts was divided into Massachusetts and Maine with the consent of both states and of Congress. This was part of the Missouri Compromise.

Every State in the Union is Guaranteed a Republican Form of Government

The conditions that constitute a "republican form of government" as stated in the Constitution are that each state must have a legislature elected by the people under broad suffrage privileges which allow a large part of the adult citizens to vote.

Supremacy of the Constitution

Article VI contains the famous "Supreme Law of the Land Clause." It is a part of the Constitution that deserves close attention. The following is an acceptable paraphrase of this clause.

> This Constitution, the laws made in pursuance thereof, and treaties to which the United States is a party constitute the supreme law of the land; and the judges in every state shall be bound thereby. Any state laws and any provisions in any state constitution incompatible with the supreme law of the land are unconstitutional, null and void.

This makes three legal authorities supreme, the Constitution, the laws made in pursuance thereof, and treaties. There is no certain justification for assuming that there is any significance in the order in which these three legal authorities are listed. Plausible reasons can be advanced for placing the Constitution as first in importance; there are also plausible reasons for considering treaties first in importance.

The Constitution is our basic law, the very foundation of our government. Laws made in pursuance thereof are intended to carry out the provisions of the Constitution. Treaties are made and become binding upon the United States in accordance with procedures set forth in the Constitution. This may seem to support giving the Constitution precedence over a treaty in case there appears to be a conflict between them.

The terms of a treaty receive the approval of the President before he presents it to the Senate for ratification. The President has taken an oath to support the Constitution. Every Senator has taken an oath to support the Constitution. It takes a ⅔rds vote of the Senate to make a treaty binding upon the United States. Once made, it should be impossible to later decide that some provision in it is unconstitutional and hence not binding. Such an action would be equivalent to saying that the President and at least ⅔rds of the Senate either made a mistake or violated their oath of office. Other nations have a right to be sure that any treaty we make with them will not later be declared unconstitutional and therefore not binding upon the United States.

As federal laws are made only by Congress why does the Constitution state, "laws made in pursuance thereof" rather than simply stating *laws of Congress?* It strongly suggests that the founding fathers considered the possibility that Congress might pass a law that would not be in pursuance of the Constitution, and, if it did, such a law would not be part of the supreme law of the land. The Constitution still leaves a key question unanswered; namely, who is to decide whether a law of Congress is, or is not, in pursuance of the Constitution? The Supreme Court has, over the years, assumed this responsibility; but its doing so is not based upon any Constitutional provision. This assumption of power by the Supreme Court to pass upon the constitutionality of laws of Congress is part of what is called *judicial review*. The other part of judicial review is a power specifically given to the courts by the Supreme Law of the Land Clause, that is, the power to pass upon the constitutionality of state laws and state constitutions.

The practice of judicial review over laws of Congress is by now well established. It receives the well-nigh complete approval of the people. This is a unique feature of our government, as no other nation grants its courts the authority to nullify the acts of its legislature. It can hardly be considered a necessary feature of our government, as other nations get along without it, and prefer to do so. But judicial review of laws of Congress has worked well for us. We like it.

The judicial review written into the Constitution over state laws and state constitutions is absolutely essential. Without it we would soon have as many interpretations of the Constitution as we have states. Federal laws and the interpretation of the Constitution must be uniform throughout the fifty states in order to prevent intolerable chaos.

No Religious Test

Article VI states, ". . . no religious test shall ever be required as a qualification to any office or public trust under the United States."

This conviction, that a person's religion should have no bearing upon his eligibility for public office, is still far ahead of the thinking of many citizens of the United States today. The explanation may lie in the fact that the framers of the Constitution were aware of the part religious hatreds played in the wars of Europe and the British Isles. These men knew more history than their contemporaries, and knew it more clearly than our own generation does. The framers of the Constitution were men whose superiority of character, intellect, education, and experience in public affairs was so marked that the extravagant praise by Jefferson (see p. 51) for them as men, and by Gladstone for the Constitution they wrote (see p. 51) is still widely accepted as an essentially sound historical judgment. In short, the public opinion of today has a long way to go to catch up with the informed judgment of those who framed the Constitution. Do we improve slowly, school generation by school generation? Not until most voters resent the common practice of political parties in present-ing candidates selected to attract votes on the basis of religious affiliation, will the people of the United States attain the goal set by Article VI.

Methods of Amending the Constitution

Article V set forth four methods. Amendments must first be proposed and then ratified; there are two ways of doing each.

Amendments may be proposed by:

1] a ⅔rds vote of each house of Congress.

2] a convention of the states called by Congress whenever the legislatures of ⅔rds of the states request such a convention.

Amendments may be ratified by:

A] the legislatures of ¾ths of the states.

B] conventions in ¾ths of the states.

When an amendment is proposed Congress shall tell the states which method of ratification is to be used. The same method of ratification must be used by all the states for any given amendment. The four possible combinations of proposing and ratifying an amendment are as follows:

  * Proposal #1 and ratification "a"
  **   "   #1 "   "   "b"
  ***   "   #2 "   "   "a"
  ***   "   #2 "   "   "b"

    *Used for all amendments except the 21st.
    ** Used for the 21st amendment only. (repeal of prohibition)
  *** Never used

Article V also reiterates that, ". . . no state, without its consent, shall be deprived of its equal suffrage in the Senate" (see p. 56).

The Reasons for Checks and Balances

Our federal government operates according to the provisions of the Constitution, to laws "made in pursuance thereof," to procedures so well established that they have become "unwritten law," and to practices which have developed from a combination of circumstances and common sense.

When the Constitution was drawn up at Philadelphia, care was taken to achieve balance between the power of any one of the three major departments of government (executive, legislative, and judicial), and the other two. No one department was to be able to dominate the others. The problem of balance was important *within* the legislative department (see p. 67) between the House of Representatives and the Senate. The basic difference of approach among the delegates at the Convention was a matter of balance. All wanted a government stronger than the Articles of Confederation. Some were intent upon creating a new government very much stronger in order to make sure that it would have effective authority; others were intent upon creating a government that would have no more authority than absolutely necessary to maintain the union of states. With a good deal of sense, one might look upon the Constitution as an intricate, intellectual balancing act: federal power vs. states' rights, the interplay of executive, legislative, and judicial departments, the granting of powers to officials and the limiting of power of the officials. The ideal balance is one which grants to federal government effective power while reserving to the states and the people adequate freedom. Yet everything that is written into law as a power of government is a restriction on the freedom of the individual; everything that guarantees freedom to the individual is a restriction on the power of government. Emphasize freedom for the individual to a ridiculous extent and anarchy develops; emphasize power for the government to an extreme degree and tyranny develops. The history of the human race illustrates the development over thousands of generations from anarchy, absence of government, to national states and international organizations. This story is replete with tyrannies of individuals, absolute monarchs, and dictators. There are also the tyrannies of oligarchies where a very small group exercises all the powers of government in its own behalf. Much of the world is now living under such tyrannies. Tyrannies have one characteristic that is highly desirable in government, efficiency. Here we use the word *efficiency* in its strict meaning; able to act, able to make decisions, able to execute decisions, able to effect its purposes. But tyrannies have no balance; their efficiency works only on behalf of the tyrant; the people are victims of government. Tyrannies lack other characteristics that are highly desirable in government. Not only do they deliberately deny freedom for the people, they lack stability. Political intrigue, and frequently assassination, are their normal methods by which transfer of power occurs; armed forces not only suppress revolution, but also breed leaders ambitious to become the next tyrant. By great struggle and at tremendous cost peoples of western Europe, especially including the British Isles, created limited monarchies and republics which reduced the efficiency of government and increased its safety, decreased the power of government and increased the freedom of the people. The desired goal is a free people served by an efficient government. A workable balance of safety from tyranny (freedom for the people) and efficiency will necessarily differ according to a people's

historical background, their stage of political development, and their indigenous sense of values. No pattern of government which works well for one people is likely to fit another. The framers of the Constitution were struggling with an age-old problem in seeking safety for the states, safety for the people, and efficiency for the federal government, all in proper balance. They wrote certain devices into the Constitution to achieve this, and we have since developed political practices designed for the same end. We are throwing all of these laws and practices together and calling them checks and balances.

The Executive Department Can Check the Legislative Department

1] The president may veto a bill passed by Congress.

2] The president may pocket-veto a bill passed by Congress.

3] The power of patronage has created a "honeymoon period" for the President. There are a great many federal jobs that are filled by Presidential appointment with no confirmation by the Senate required. Members of Congress of the President's party submit names of persons they hope to have appointed to these many federal offices. When a Congressman can get appointments for those selected by the local party organization, the "political machine" is working well and will get out the vote on election day. If a Congressman fails to get the appointments, much of his usefulness to the local party has gone, and with it, the party's support in election years. Congressmen, being very sensitive to this situation, are inclined to cooperate with the President until the appointments have been made. The President will have bills he considers part of his program introduced early in the session. Those Congressmen who vote "right" will surely have the names on their appointment lists approved. A President can withhold making appointments for a few months, long enough to get quite a few major bills before Congress. It is this period which is called "the President's honeymoon," for it is then, if ever, that Congress will treat him with kindly consideration.

4] Direct appeals to the people enable the President to influence Congress. Radio and television have greatly enhanced the President's influence. If in news conferences by radio and T.V. and numerous other direct contacts with the people the President builds himself into a popular personality in whom the people have confidence, he has also greatly increased his influence with Congress.

5] If the President wanted a person for an office whose appointment required the approval of the Senate, he could have that person in the office in spite of any objections by the Senate. This could be done by recess appointment. Such appointments last not only during the recess, but also during the whole of the next session of Congress. So by repeated recess appointments the President could keep his candidate in office over the opposition of the Senate. Any President would be most unlikely to use this method of checking the Senate. There are too many ways in which the Senate can make a President's life miserable.

6] The President as head of his party has considerable influence with members of Congress in his party. He can always get legislation introduced. The leaders in the House of Representatives and the Senate of the President's party, whether they be majority or minority leaders, try to put through bills favored by the President. The Speaker of the House is often a member of this legislative team working for the President. The Vice-President, who presides over the Senate, can sometimes be used by the President in ways that build his importance and influence in the party and hence with the Senate. Through the party organization and the President's position as its head, the President of the United States is the most powerful lobby in Washington, even though he is just one man.

The Legislative Department, Congress, Can Check the Executive Department

1] Congress can refuse to pass bills favored by the President.

2] Congress can over-ride a Presidential veto by a ⅔rds vote.

3] Congress can make executive departments, commissions, committees, and programs ineffective by refusing sufficient appropriations for their operation.

4] The House of Representatives may impeach the President and the Senate may then try him.

5] The Senate may refuse to ratify a treaty presented to it by the President.

6] The Senate may refuse to approve appointments.

Checks Upon the Supreme Court Exist, but They Are Ineffective

1] The President appoints the members to the Supreme Court with the approval of the Senate. Almost always the President appoints a member of his own political party. He naturally appoints a man whose views are like his own, or at least with opinions on public issues that are acceptable to him. This gives the President much less influence on the Supreme Court than it would seem to. Experience has shown that appointees expected to give the Court a liberal tinge have turned out to emphasize its conservatism, and vice versa. Justices who have been close to the President for years before their appointment to the Supreme Court have frequently made decisions contrary to the views of the President. Once the appointment is made, of course, no influence results therefrom. Hence, this power of the President to select men for the Supreme Court has had no influence upon the Court that can be termed a check upon it.

2] If Congress dislikes a decision of the Supreme Court when it declares a federal law unconstitutional, it may propose an amendment to the Constitution that will permit such a law. For example, the Supreme Court in 1894 declared a federal income tax law to be unconstitutional, and Congress proposed the Income Tax Amendment in 1913. A check that takes nineteen years to operate is hardly any check at all.

3] The House of Representatives can impeach and the Senate can try a member of the Supreme Court. The occasions for impeachment are possibilities on paper, but, in reality, they are non-existent. Certainly the legal possibility of impeachment and dismissal from office does not influence the Supreme Court.

4] The very real check that could be used to cut drastically the power of the Supreme Court in its handling of all appellate cases has never been used. It is the clause in Article III, Section 2, Paragraph 2. Under this clause Congress could restrict the power of the Supreme Court to declare laws of Congress unconstitutional in cases of appellate jurisdiction; it could deny this power to the Court completely, or it could insist that the vote in appellate cases must be unanimous, or majorities of six, seven, or eight rather than the present five. In 1954 the anti-segregation in public schools decision (*Brown* v. *Board of Education of Topeka*), even though reached by a unanimous decision of the Supreme Court, aroused a small flurry of talk among southern Congressmen that the Court's wings should be clipped through this clause in the Constitution.

Checks Exercised by the Supreme Court Are Effective

The Court can declare a law of Congress unconstitutional and, in doing so, cancels the work of Congress and of the President if he signed it. The Court can declare an act of a President unconstitutional. In 1952, during the conflict in Korea, President Truman ordered government seizure of the steel companies in a strike situation which he claimed to be a national emergency of major proportions. The Supreme Court invalidated the Presidential order on the grounds that there are no such powers as *emergency powers* of a President, and that every power must originate in the Constitution itself, either by a clause therein or through a law of Congress made in pursuance thereof.

The Balance of Power Within the Legislative Department

The primary function of the Senate is to act as a check upon the House of Representatives. The colonial assemblies were bicameral with a governor's council as the upper house to check the popularly elected lower house. The upper house was appointed by the king or governor, or elected by the lower house. When the colonies became states, they kept the bicameral legislature with the upper house still being a check upon the lower. For many decades under the Constitution the members of the Senate were elected by state legislatures. The direct, or popular, election of Senators did not become a constitutional provision until the 17th amendment adopted in 1913.

The facts that the minimum age for the Senate is five years older than for the House of Representatives, that the term of a Senator is three times as long, and that at each Congressional election only one-third of the Senate seats are subject to change, instead of all of them as in the House of Representatives, were all designed to make the Senate the more permanent and stronger branch of Congress.

It is difficult to pressure the Senate into action which it is reluctant to take. Popular opinion back home has little effect upon a Senator with over two more years to serve. If he plans to run for another term, the last eighteen months should be long enough for "mending political fences." Being a United States Senator is usually the high point of a man's political career, so there is seldom any temptation to divide one's attention between the job at hand and the office he hopes to get. Many members of the Senate are financially able to retire; many could greatly increase their annual income in private employment, so there is no threat to a hoped-for political advancement or to financial security if a Senator fails to be re-elected. There are several circumstances that tend to make re-election a less compelling matter to a Senator than to a Representative. After six years in office a Senator is often well within the age range where retirement is attractive. Senators completing a second term are less apt to seek re-election. Senators seeking re-election usually turn in a large percentage of victories. As only one-third of the seats are open for election at any one time, only a slight change in the membership of the Senate can take place. The shift in the party strength in the Senate is apt to be somewhat less marked than the slight shift in personnel.

All of these factors combine to make it easy for Senators to vote their convictions with a minimum of modification due to any sort of pressure. As many Senators have served in the House of Representatives, or in state legislatures, or as governors, they represent a great deal of political experience. The senate is admirably suited to give considered judgment to public issues; it need not be swayed by popular clamor nor be set off course by a wave of emotionalism. Wisdom has a chance to survive and prevail in the United States Senate. Today's problems, both domestic and foreign, are much more complex than they were several decades ago. The first popular opinion on such matters is necessarily without substantial factual foundation; it represents a feeling rather than a judgment. Whether such a popular demand is sound is a matter of chance.

The House of Representatives is very sensitive to the public opinion of the states, sometimes of the congressional districts within the states. These varying opinions find expression and votes in the House of Representatives and in combination are as good a reflection of the opinion of the nation as is obtainable in a legislative body. A two-year term is very short. A "freshman" Representative spends about a year learning the ropes, and the second year preparing to get re-elected. Only when he has won re-election can he settle down to the serious business of being a Congressman. This could be a slight exaggeration, but only slight. Many members of the House are in mid-career in public service; they are aiming for several terms until they can climb another rung in the political ladder. Whenever there is an irreconcilable clash between the views of their constituents and their own judgment on a public issue, they must think more than twice before deciding which way to vote. There is real danger of becoming a well informed, courageous statesman who failed to be re-elected. It may be better to be a wise politician who goes along temporarily with his constituents and gets re-elected. A re-elected politician is still in a position of power where he may serve the public interests. Popular opinion does become better informed in time. Congressmen play an important part in this educational process, so that they frequently find themselves able to vote both their own convictions and the will of their constituents.

A Representative sometimes leans on the Senate for sound legislation. He must vote to include some unwise provision in a bill because the people back home favor it so strongly. However, the Representative knows that the Senate will change the House bill by excluding the provision. When the improved legislation comes back to the House, he votes for it. The Representative can claim that he served the will of his constituents. The chances are good that this technique will serve the Representative's immediate goal, to stay in office, and also his long-term purpose, the good of the nation.

The Senate and the House of Representatives combine to form a balanced legislature. It is remarkable that a plan made in 1789 is still suitable. The most difficult problem before the Constitutional Convention was well resolved in "The Great Compromise" (see p. 52).

AMENDMENTS TO THE CONSTITUTION

The Bill of Rights

The first ten amendments are called the Bill of Rights. During the campaign to ratify the Constitution the most telling argument against ratification was the absence of a Bill of Rights. The state constitutions had their individual bills of rights. The Federalists, who were campaigning for ratification, explained that the federal government could do only those things provided for in the Constitution and that there was no need to list what it could not do or to list the rights reserved to the states or the people. But the argument was not convincing. Some states ratified only with the proviso that a Bill of Rights be added; they even submitted such a Bill of Rights with their ratification (see p. 54).

The first ten amendments were added to protect the states against possible encroachment by the federal government. The first amendment begins, "Congress shall make no law . . ." The next seven amendments were interpreted to be prohibitions on Congress even though Congress is not mentioned. This acceptance of the Bill of Rights as restrictions on the federal government persisted until the 1870's. With the Slaughter House Cases of 1873 the *minority* opinion in a five to four decision held that provisions in the 14th amendment protected the individual from any encroachment by a state on any of the privileges and immunities listed in the Bill of Rights. This minority decision has, over the years, become the majority decision in a series of cases, so that today it is true that the Bill of Rights does protect the individual from all governments, federal, state, and sub-divisions of states. It is through the instrumentality of the 14th amendment that individuals get the protection of the Bill of Rights. The sentence of the 14th amendment that gives this protection reads, "No State shall make or enforce any law which shall abridge the privileges or immunities of citizens of the United States; nor shall any State deprive any person of life, liberty, or property, without due process of law, nor deny to any person within its jurisdiction the equal protection of the laws."

The 14th amendment, adopted in 1868, was part of the settlement of the Civil War. The attempts to give the Negro the benefit of its provisions by military occupation of the South through carpetbag-scalawag state governments has been aptly called the Crime of Reconstruction. The 1954 Supreme Court decision against segregation in public schools and the 1962 decision concerning apportionment of representatives in the lower house of state legislatures has brought the 14th amendment to the forefront in the protection of civil rights of the individual. With these recent decisions in mind it becomes well nigh impossible to consider the Bill of Rights without turning also to the 14th amendment.

The Bill of Rights might be considered an integral part of the Constitution, not an addition. The agreement that there would be such provisions added was made a condition to be met in order to secure ratification by the states. All ten amendments were ratified by 1791.

Privileges and Immunities in the Bill of Rights

Freedom of religion
Freedom of speech
Freedom of press
Freedom of assembly
Freedom of petition
Freedom of a state to have a militia and the people to bear arms
Freedom from having soldiers quartered in private homes in time of peace; or even in time of war

unless a special law to that effect has been passed

Freedom from unreasonable searches and seizures

Freedom from being held for an alleged criminal act unless a grand jury has brought an indictment (This does not apply to the armed forces where martial law prevails.)

Freedom from being tried again for the same offense when one has already been tried and found innocent

Freedom from being forced to testify against one's self

Freedom from being deprived of life, liberty, or property without due process of law

Freedom from having one's property taken for a public use without just compensation

Freedom, in all criminal cases, to have a speedy, public trial by jury; to have counsel for one's defense, to compel witnesses in one's behalf to testify, and to be confronted by witnesses against one's self

Freedom to demand a jury trial in any case where the value in controversy exceeds twenty dollars

Freedom from excessive bails, excessive fines, and cruel and unusual punishments

The preceding list of freedoms is contained in the first eight amendments. The ninth amendment gives a blanket protection for other individual rights. Read it, be sure that you appreciate exactly what it says, and then memorize it. "The enumeration in the Constitution of certain rights shall not be construed to deny or disparage others retained by the people."

The tenth amendment states in all-inclusive specific terms the purpose and intent of the Bill of Rights. It explains why the Bill of Rights was accepted as a defense for the states against possible encroachment by the federal government. It, too, should be read, understood, and then memorized. "The powers not delegated to the United States by the Constitution, nor prohibited by it to the States, are reserved to the States respectively, or to the people."

AMENDMENT XI *Modification of the Original Jurisdiction of the Supreme Court.*

It cancels the right previously given of federal courts to have original jurisdiction in cases where a state is involved in a case with a citizen of another state or with a subject of a foreign nation.

AMENDMENT XII *Election of President and Vice-President.*

(See p. 60.)

AMENDMENT XIII *Slavery Is Abolished.*

AMENDMENT XIV

This amendment contains several provisions. Along with amendments XIII and XV it might be looked upon as the peace settlement forced upon the defeated Confederate States.

1] It defines citizens as, "All persons born or naturalized in the United States, and subject to the jurisdiction thereof, are citizens of the United States and of the State wherein they reside."

2] "No State shall make or enforce any law which shall abridge the privileges or immunities of citizens of the United States; nor shall any State deprive any person of life, liberty, or property, without due process of law, nor deny to any person within its jurisdiction the equal protection of the laws."

3] Representation in the House of Representatives for each state shall be based upon the total population. If any state denies the right to vote to any of the male inhabitants, it shall have its representation in the House of Representatives reduced. This was a completely unsuccessful attempt to coerce the ex-Confederate states into allowing Negroes to vote. All states deny suffrage to thousands of male citizens for a variety of reasons, mostly legitimate. No state has ever lost representation in Congress in accordance with this clause of the 14th amendment. It has never been enforced; no one wants it enforced; it is too cumbersome to be enforced; it was a mistake in the first place.

4] Any person who held a public office which required an oath of allegiance to the Constitution and later joined the armed forces of the Confederate States is prevented from holding any such office again. The theory is that a person who broke his oath once should not be allowed to take another oath.

This provision was unfortunate for several reasons. It was punitive in purpose. The Southerners maintained with complete sincerity and with some substantial arguments (see p. 102) that they had a right to secede from the Union and that it was the North that violated the Constitution when it refused to permit them to leave the Union. Most unfortunate of all was the effect this provision had upon the recovery of the South. It denied positions of leadership to the men most capable of providing it. By force of arms the South had been thoroughly defeated. Then by Constitutional amendment, they were being severely retarded in rebuilding. Congress was empowered to remove this restriction as it affected any individual. It did vote exemption for General Robert E. Lee, but he retired to private life to become president of Washington College, later Washington and Lee.

5] The United States shall pay its Civil War debts, but the debts "incurred in aid of insurrection or rebellion against the United States . . . shall be held illegal and void."

AMENDMENT XV *Negroes Made* Potential *Voters.*

"The rights of citizens of the United States to vote shall not be denied or abridged by the United States, or by any State, on account of race, color, or previous condition of servitude."

This does not extend the right to vote to any person, although, of course, its intent was to make the ex-Confederate States extend suffrage to Negroes on the same basis as it did to whites. It does give three reasons which can not serve as a legal basis for denying the right to vote. The 13th amendment failed to achieve its purpose. Intimidation of the Negro and a variety of state laws have kept the Negro vote in much of the South to negligible proportions. There has been, since World War I, an increase in the Negro vote, due primarily to changes in the local climate of opinion. Literacy tests are the most effective current method used to hold down the Negro vote. The tests are administered so that Negroes who have been to college fail the tests, while whites whose schooling did not go beyond the primary grades pass them.

Since World War II and the establishment of the United Nations in New York City, the "second-class citizenship" of the Negro in the United States is a serious handicap to us in the "Cold War." The "equal protection of the laws" clause of the 14th amendment may be used to coerce the South on this issue of voting, just as it is being used in the abolition of segregation in public schools. The whole problem of the civil rights of the Negro is receiving more attention now than any time since the Reconstruction Era.

AMENDMENT XVI *Income Tax.*

Congress may levy a *direct* tax on incomes *from whatever source derived* without apportionment among the several states according to population. This tax is our single largest source of income. It is the only direct tax the federal government can levy without apportionment among the states according to population.

AMENDMENT XVII *Direct Election of Senators.*

The Constitutional provision that United States Senators be elected by state legislature had been under popular attack for at least three decades.

The direct election of Senators by the voters as granted by this amendment accomplished the demanded reform.

Notice that it is the states that determine who shall vote for a United States Senator. The state sets the qualifications required for voting for a member of the lower house of its own legislature; it is these same qualifications that must then allow one to vote for a United States Senator.

AMENDMENT XVIII *Prohibition of the Manufacture, Sale, and Transportation of Intoxicating Beverages.*

This proved an unsuccessful attempt to deal with the difficult and real problem presented to the nation by the intemperate use of alcoholic beverages. It was in effect from 1920 to 1933. (See pp. 193-194.)

AMENDMENT XIX *Suffrage for Women.*

No citizen can be denied the right to vote "on account of sex." As in the 15th amendment this does not guarantee to any individual the right to vote. It adds a fourth reason that can not be used to deny the right to vote.

AMENDMENT XX *Makes "Lame Duck" Sessions of Congress Most Unlikely.*

Before this amendment there were four months between election day in early November and inauguration day on March 4th. Between these dates there was a short session of Congress. The "Lame Ducks" were those Congressmen who had failed to win re-election but, nevertheless, were still in office during this session. There are now only two months between election day and the convening of the new Congress on January 3rd. The Christmas recess occurs during this two-month period, so there isn't time for a session of Congress until the new Congress takes over. The date of the inauguration of the President is January 20th. It is possible, but very unlikely, that a special session of Congress could be called between early November and January 3rd. Every effort would be made to avoid it.

AMENDMENT XXI *Repeal of Prohibition.*

The problems growing out of intemperate use of intoxicating beverages are more serious than ever. The great increase in the use of automobiles has added dimension and tragedy to the problem.

AMENDMENT XXII *The President Restricted to Two Terms.*

This amendment was ratified in 1951 to make into written law what had been unbroken tradition (unwritten law) for about 150 years. It prevents any one being elected president more than twice and prevents his holding that office more than 10 years. When the death of a president brings his successor into office during the first two years of a term, this amendment limits the new president to one election; thus restricting him to anywhere from 6 to 8 years in office. If the president dies within the last two years of a term, the new president will be eligible to be elected twice and thus may serve as long as 10 years. The election of Franklin Roosevelt in 1940 broke the only-two-terms tradition, which had been observed for about 150 years, and then he went on to win election for a fourth term in 1944. This amendment was a reaction to this situation.

It is not altogether certain that this is a wise amendment. It assumes that the voters cannot be trusted to decide how long a president may continue in office; it takes from them the freedom of choice they exercised in 1940 and 1944. The amendment is not restricted to consecutive terms and thus prevents a leader from going in and out of office over a 20 to 30 year period as did Gladstone and Disraeli in England in the late 1800's. With the minimum age for the presidency set at 35 and the instances of outstanding heads of state serving well into their 70's (Churchill and Adenauer) it is quite possible that the restrictions of the 22nd Amendment will prove regrettable.

AMENDMENT XXIII *District of Columbia Given Votes in the Electoral College.*

The District of Columbia is governed by Congress. Its residents had no suffrage rights. This amendment gives them a vote for President and Vice-President by giving to the District as many votes in the Electoral College as those states having the smallest number of electoral votes.

AMENDMENT XXIV *Non-payment of taxes can not be used as a reason for denying to any citizen the right to vote for President, Vice-President, or a member of Congress.*

This abolished the practice, common in a few states in the South, of using a poll tax as a device for cutting down the Negro vote. A poll tax due in the summer when interest in elections was at a low point, coupled with a minimum of publicity about its collection, plus the tendency not to pay taxes disenfranchised many negroes. In some states non-payment was accumulative so that after a few years the total of back taxes due was substantial enough to make the delinquent taxpayer a permanent non-voter. Where the political climate of opinion was such that the poll tax was a device to control voting rather than to raise revenue, it would also be true that enforcement of the law against Negroes would be rigid while enforcement against others would be much less than complete.

The 24th Amendment "The right of citizens of the United States to vote in any primary or other election for President or Vice President, for electors for President or Vice President, or for Senator or Representative in Congress, shall not be denied or abridged by the United States or any state by reason of failure to pay any poll tax or other tax."

The Constitution and Statute Law

Statute law refers to laws passed by legislatures as distinguished from the fundamental law, which is the Constitution itself. Good constitution writing is quite a different task from writing statutes. Statutes should be specific, so expressed as to be subject to only one reasonable interpretation, so clear as to leave no room for differing opinions as to its meaning. Constitutions, on the contrary, should make considerable use of general terms that defy exact interpretation. Our Constitution gives some splendid examples of the wise use of general terms and the wise avoidance of detail.

In the Bill of Rights we have such words as *excessive* bails, *cruel* and *unusual* punishments, and *unreasonable* searches. Had any attempt been made to write into the Constitution exactly what these words meant, the meanings suitable for 1800 would be unsuitable for 1900. As it is, each generation can, through its courts, give a reasonable, workable definition to such words. The phrase *due process of law* and the word *commerce* have been interpreted in importantly different ways to suit a changing environment with its shifting climate of public opinion. In 1789 the word *person* in the 5th amendment (no *person* shall be deprived of life, liberty, or property without *due process of law*) did not include slaves; in the 14th amendment it particularly meant ex-slaves, and since the middle 1880's it has come to mean all human beings plus corporations which are now considered to be "legal persons."

The wisdom of not going into detail in writing a Constitution is shown in Article III. "The judicial power of the United States shall be vested in one Supreme Court, and in such inferior courts as the Congress may from time to time ordain and establish." Not a word more about the structure of our federal court system. Let Congress construct the court system by statute law; it will need adjustments from time to time, and it is much easier to pass laws and repeal laws than to amend the Constitution.

The Constitution did not attempt to set up executive departments. It says that the President may get reports from heads of executive departments. Only time would tell what departments are necessary, how they might best be set up, and what their duties should be.

This use of general terms and avoidance of detail was skillfully done in the right places, so that our Constitution has adaptability; it is part of the reason it has lasted for well-nigh two centuries.

There are a few examples where the Constitution is too specific. In Amendment VII a trial by jury may be demanded if the value in controversy "shall exceed twenty dollars." Twenty dollars has varied from about a month's pay to a day's pay for comparable services. If all civil cases involving values in excess of twenty dollars were tried before a jury, the economic life of the United States would have to stop while we all served on juries.

Perhaps the tragic failure of the Prohibition Amendment is due to the mistake of too definite language. Congress was directed to "prohibit" the manufacture, sale, and transportation of intoxicating beverages. Suppose such a word as *control* had been used instead of "prohibit." By a series of laws Congress could have encouraged temperance at whatever rate and to whatever degree was palatable to public opinion. In its attempts toward temperance Congress would have had the good will of the great majority of the people. Over the years, surely by this time, we could have arrived at a control that would deny freedom only to individuals who had abused it, and permit freedom in the use of intoxicating beverages to others. Laws can not enforce reform ahead of public opinion, but they can gently persuade people toward reform. "Prohibit" gave Congress no lee-way; it was too definite; it left no room for interpretation to suit circumstances.

Knowing the Constitution

To know well all the information about the Constitution on the preceding pages is not equiva-

lent to knowing the Constitution. It is a good start, and a start is all that can be expected short of intensive study in the field of Constitutional law, a specialized field for lawyers. Do not feel that a little information is worse than none or that a little knowledge is dangerous; quite the contrary. A little knowledge about anything is dangerous only when it is mistaken to be complete information. It isn't what you know that is dangerous, but what you don't know. The following illustrations will give definite point to the thought that knowing what the Constitution says is not the same as knowing the Constitution.

Article I opens with, "All legislative powers herein granted shall be vested in a Congress. . . ." "All" is a difficult word to quibble about. It has only one meaning. Yet it is common knowledge that the President arranges and puts into effect changes in tariffs. This is clearly a legislative power exercised by the President.

The 13th amendment states there shall be no "involuntary servitude" except as a punishment for crime. For many years it was commonly believed that compulsory military service in time of peace was impossible in the United States, because it would involve "involuntary servitude." Yet in September of 1940, over a year before we entered World War II, Congress passed the first peace-time draft in our history.

Just what freedom of religion, speech, and press mean are issues that repeatedly come before the courts. In several decisions before 1954 segregated schools did not violate the 14th amendment, but since then they do. The extremely uneven representation of districts within a state in its legislature is now, 1965, a violation of the 14th amendment. This is a reversal of previous court decisions.

Obviously, then, to be able to read the Constitution and interpret it according to its literal sense is far from a safe guide to its legal interpretation. The Constitution is interwoven with the threads of our economic, political, and social history; it must be interpreted in that complex context.

George Washington

1789-1797

1732 - 1799

☆

Vice-President JOHN ADAMS

Secretary of State THOMAS JEFFERSON   *Secretary of Treasury* ALEXANDER HAMILTON

WASHINGTON'S PUBLIC SERVICE BEFORE HE BECAME PRESIDENT

Lt. Col. in the French and Indian War (1753-1756)
Virginia delegate to the 1st and 2nd Continental Congresses (1774 and 1775)
Head command of the Continental armies in the Revolution (1775-1783)
Virginia delegate to the Annapolis Convention (1786)
Chairman of the Constitutional Convention (1787)

MAJOR ITEMS OF WASHINGTON'S ADMINISTRATIONS

Judiciary Act (1789)   *Foreign Debt*
Tariff (1789)   *Assumption of State Debts*
Sale of Public Lands   *French Revolution (Citizen Genêt)*
Whiskey Rebellion   *Jay Treaty with England (1795)*
1st Bank of the United States *Pinckney Treaty with Spain (1795)*
Domestic Debt   *Farewell Address*

Election

Washington was elected by the unanimous vote of the Electoral College. He was inaugurated on April 30th, 1789 at Federal Hall on the corner of Wall and Broad Streets, New York City. Before leaving Mount Vernon for the ceremonies, he had written a letter expressing doubts about both his suitability for the position and the success of the Republic. But he did believe he possessed certain qualifications for the office, for he wrote, "Integrity and firmness are all I can promise."

Regardless of political affiliation, the Congress and the people had confidence in Washington. They had different ideas of what should be done, but there was no faction trying to wreck the Republic. Those who had opposed ratification of the Constitution were now working to establish the government. They hadn't changed their minds, even though they accepted the fact that the Con-

stitution was the government. They were willing that changes to make it more to their liking be achieved by peaceful, legal procedures, not by trying to destroy by violence what had been established by fair elections. This sort of political maturity was remarkable. How different from the experience of several new nations created since World War I!

Re-election

On December 5th, 1792 the Presidential Electors, members of the Electoral College, gave Washington 132 votes. Three did not vote. No one else got a vote. John Adams was re-elected to the Vice-Presidency with a vote of 77. An Antifederalist, George Clinton, received 50 votes. This again emphasized that, regardless of whether the Presidential Electors favored a much stronger central government (Federalists) or were intent upon preserving the power of the states (Antifederalists), they all put their confidence in George Washington. In this respect they faithfully reflected public opinion.

Judiciary Act of 1789

1] It established a Supreme Court of six judges, a chief justice, and five associate justices. (John Jay was the first Chief Justice.)

2] It provided for 13 District Courts and 3 Circuit Courts.

3] It established the office of Attorney General. (Edmund Randolph was the first Attorney General, head of the Justice Department.)

This was a very complete and detailed law setting forth procedures which, for the most part, are still in effect. Part of this law became an important factor in the Marbury v. Madison Case of 1803 (see p. 85).

* Tariff (1789)

This tariff, passed on the 4th of July, has been called Hamilton's 10% tariff. Duties on about ninety items ranged from 5% to 10% advalorem (according to their invoiced value). Most of the rates were below ten percent. Hamilton, as Secretary of the Treasury, was anxious to establish the tariff as a regular source of revenue and he was just as anxious to establish the principle of protection of domestic manufacture by tariffs. The revenue was an immediate necessity; the protection was of minor immediate importance, but was destined to develop into a persistent political issue throughout our history.

Even in the very simple agrarian economy of 1789 there were sectional differences over what imports to tax. The South, for example, wanted duties on hemp which it raised, but New England ship builders needed rope and wished to buy at the lowest possible price. New England distillers wanted import duties on rum, but other sections wished to buy rum at the lowest possible price. After a good deal of haggling in Congress over many such differences, the agreement was reached that all would give up their demands for protection. The result was a tariff that produced revenue, but provided practically no protection. As Hamilton's report on manufactures of 1791 made a strong plea for protection, there is no doubt that he was not fully pleased by the tariff of 1789. Congress would not go along with him.

Sale of Public Lands

Under the Articles of Confederation, the Land Ordinance of 1785 and the Northwest Ordinance of 1787 set the pattern followed under the Constitution (see pp. 49-50). In spite of minor adjustments such as raising the minimum price of land per acre to $2.00 and cutting the minimum acreage per purchase from 640 acres to 320 acres, a series of land laws encouraged purchase of huge areas by speculators rather than farms by settlers. It raised considerable revenue quickly and easily.

Excise Tax

An excise tax is one levied on something produced, sold, and used in the United States. Excise taxes were bound to cause trouble. Rural United States, and most of it was rural in Hamilton's time, still held to the views of Daniel Shays and his followers (see p. 48). To have to pay excise taxes was looked upon as a violation of the liberty for which the Revolution was fought. Hamilton recommended and Congress passed an excise tax on whiskey. This rubbed salt on a raw spot, for the corn farmers west of the Alleghenies had to change their corn into whiskey in order to transport it for miles without roads to market.

* Whiskey Rebellion (1794)

The western areas from Pennsylvania through North Carolina produced corn. Practically every farmer had his whiskey still. Bulky loads of corn could not be hauled to markets in the east; that simply wouldn't pay. But barrels of whiskey could be transported in the months between the times of mud and the snow on trails, through brush, and along wheel ruts. If a farmer couldn't get the whiskey to market this year, it became more valuable as it aged-in-the-wood. To a corn farmer the whiskey tax was a tax on a large part of his year's labor. He felt picked upon, and perhaps he was right. Hamilton was a city man who considered the more prominent merchants, shippers, and professional men to be the people who would build the nation. Their interests, he felt, should receive protection and advancement by the government. He was in favor of teaching the uneducated, often illiterate, farmers the necessity of paying taxes.

Throughout the western counties in Pennsylvania tax collectors were tarred and feathered. Along the Allegheny and Monongahela Rivers armed bands were formed to resist the tax. It was another Shays' Rebellion. The Governor of Pennsylvania was reluctant to quell the uprisings, but this time the central government did not stand aside. Hamilton led between 15,000 and 16,000 soldiers into western Pennsylvania. President Washington rode with the troops for a few miles to give the prestige of his person and office to the enforcement of the tax laws. As a cartoon of the day put it, such a large force sent against so few farmers for the collection of a small tax was like swatting a fly with a meat axe. It worked. The troops under federal command overawed the rebellious farmers. Their resistance crumbled without a clash of arms. The tax was paid. From the time of this episode the saying that "Nothing is sure but death and taxes" took on a ring of truth throughout the United States. This little rebellion was turned into a big victory for the United States Government.

* An Appreciation of the Tax Problems Faced by Hamilton

From the Sugar Act of 1733 to the Treaty of Paris 1763, non-payment of taxes and smuggling were so common-place as to be respectable. It was the period of Salutary Neglect. From 1763 to 1775 it became increasingly patriotic for the American colonials not to pay taxes to England. From 1781 to 1789 the Congress under the Articles of Confederation could not collect taxes. After over half a century of largely successful resistance to taxation, there is little wonder that an excise tax would run into trouble. Perhaps anyone willing to be the first treasurer of the United States under the Constitution deserved some sort of recognition for courage. The tariff, the sale of public lands, and the excise tax were the three major sources of revenue. The first two were comparatively painless, but the excise tax was obvious and painful. The lesson of taxation had to be learned and Hamilton taught it well.

** First Bank of the United States (1791-1811)

A Bank of the United States (B.U.S.) was proposed by Hamilton. President Washington received written statements from Hamilton and Jefferson on the Constitutionality of such a bank. Hamilton developed the theory of "loose" construction of the Constitution in support of the Bank, while Jefferson expounded the theory of "strict" construction in opposition to it. Washington accepted Hamilton's reasoning and Congress passed the law establishing the Bank.

Does the Implied Powers (Elastic) Clause give Congress the right to create a bank? Jefferson's answer was an emphatic, NO! "Congress shall have power to make all laws which shall be *necessary* and proper for carrying into execution the foregoing powers. . . ." If "necessary" means something less than absolutely necessary, it begins to mean highly convenient, or merely convenient, or perhaps just a bit helpful. If the word *necessary* is to have its strict meaning modified at all, how can there be any particular point beyond which no further modification is permissible? If the word *necessary* can have some elasticity in its meaning, it can have complete elasticity; and with complete elasticity it can be stretched to cover any grant of power Congress cares to seize. It would always be a simple matter to draw a plausible connection between one of the several powers specifically delegated to Congress and some additional power Congress might wish to assume. Any such loose interpretation clears the way for the United States Government to accumulate power and eventually overwhelm the states. "Loose" construction would destroy the protection the states believed they had in the 10th amendment. "The powers *not delegated* to the United States by the Constitution, nor prohibited by it to the States, are reserved to the States respectively, or to the people." Massachusetts had ratified the Constitution with the understanding that this particular provision would be incorporated into a Bill of Rights. Thus reasoned Jefferson.

Hamilton insisted that a sovereign government must have ample authority to carry out any specific grant of power in the Constitution. He pointed out that navigation aids, such as lighthouses, had been authorized by laws of Congress under the right to regulate commerce. Nowhere did the Constitution state, or need to, that Congress could erect lighthouses. He expressed his reasoning so well in one sentence of his defense of "loose" construction that it is worth close consideration. "If the end be clearly comprehended within any of the specific powers, and if the measure have an obvious relation to that end, and is not forbidden by any particular provision of the Constitution, it may safely be deemed to come within the compass of the national authority." From this view it became apparent that the creation of a United States Bank would be a measure with an obvious relation to the following powers granted in the Constitution:

1] to collect taxes

2] to borrow money

3] to pay the public debt

4] to regulate commerce

With this Hamilton (loose construction) versus Jefferson (strict construction) debate, the people split into two groups which soon became definite political parties. Loose constructionists were Federalists, strict constructionists were Republicans. (The Republicans were sometimes called Democratic Republicans.) The Federalists were pretty much the same people who had most ardently supported ratification of the Constitution. They were the more prominent business men, the people whose prosperity was closely associated with commerce and trade, and the professional men of the larger communities. The Republicans were those who had opposed the ratification of the Constitution and those who had supported it with some misgivings. These people were small farmers living away from the towns, and the more prosperous land owners of the coastal areas of the South; in short, the agrarian interests. While the differences that separated the two parties included education, wealth, and social position, the basic factor that outweighed all others was economic. How people made their living placed them in one party or the other; it was agriculture versus commerce and manufacturing. One important group of businessmen did oppose the Bank, even though they were Federalists. This was the bankers. To them the Bank of the United States was unfair competition to all other banks. It was a private bank which enjoyed exclusive advantages from the government.

Some of the following facts explain why the Secretary of the Treasury considered the establishment of the Bank of the United States the key point of his financial program.

1] The Bank was a private institution.
80% of its stock was owned by private individuals.
20% of its stock was owned by the United States.

2] Total capitalization was $10,000,000.

3] The Bank could issue paper money, that is, bank notes, so long as it was redeemable in gold.

4] Branches of the Bank in major cities could transfer credit easily from city to city by bank drafts and thus greatly aid business.

5] Taxes could be paid to the Bank.

6] The sale of United States bonds could be handled by the Bank.

7] Short term loans could be made by the Bank to the United States.

As it turned out the B.U.S. aided the Treasury Department in several of its functions; it had a stabilizing effect upon the currency system; it tended to make other banks adopt sound banking practices. It was an asset to the economy. It was a very prosperous private business. Its very prosperity seemed unfair to Jefferson.

In his opinion, the Bank not only dangerously increased federal power and used it for the benefit of commerce and manufacture, but it also used funds of the government for the advantage of the wealthy. Only comparatively wealthy people owned stock in the B.U.S. The government funds on deposit belonged to the people as a whole, but 80% of the profits of the Bank from the use of these funds went into the pockets of a handful of stockholders. However, supporters of the Bank might point out that the services of the Bank to the economy benefited everyone and were far more important.

The Bank issue, with the "loose" and "strict" interpretation of the Constitution which it developed, was the first great debate under the new government. Political affiliation often springs more from emotion than thought, more from immediate self-interest than considered judgment. It is a mark of superior and mature citizenship to think *before* forming a judgment.

The Domestic and Foreign Debts

The people of the United States held government bonds totaling, with accumulated interest, almost $45,000,000. The foreign debt was almost $12,000,000. Hamilton advocated combining these two debts by issuing new bonds in exchange for the original bonds which were greatly depreciated. This would form one new debt which had every prospect of being paid at the face value of the bonds, plus the interest. There was no organized opposition to paying the foreign debt which was owed chiefly to France and Holland. But there was strong opposition to handling the domestic debt in this manner. This combining of the domestic and foreign debts and refinancing them by a new issue of bonds is often called *funding* the debt.

The opposition stemmed from the fact that those who originally bought the bonds were no longer the owners. This was more true of small bondholders than of others. Almost all of the thousands of people of modest means who had bought government bonds during the Revolution had long since sold them at a small fraction of their face value. The depression of the middle 1780's had forced them to sell. By the time Hamilton proposed funding the debts, the owners of the bonds were wealthy people in the larger cities. The Republicans again charged that this was another scheme of Hamilton's to enrich the rich at the expense of the poor. Jefferson believed it to be part of a plot by the Federalists to make the government serve commercial interests much as King George III and "His Friends" in Parliament had tried to use the colonists to serve the commercial interests of the United Kingdom.

Hamilton got his way with Congress by insisting that the credit of the United States must be established. The infant nation could never get respect or make favorable trade agreements with other countries until it had earned the reputation that it paid its bills and that its currency was sound. Hamilton also stated that a government bond was a contract with the bondholder, that part of the value of a bond was the fact that it could be sold whenever the owner could find a purchaser at a price acceptable to both parties. Establishing credit and the integrity of a government contract were of fundamenal importance, not to be set aside because some people gained and others lost. Those who sold government bonds far below their face value expected them to become worth even less in time, those who bought them took a risk. Risk-taking, the chance for large gains and the possibility of large losses, are a normal, even desirable, aspect of business.

* The Assumption of State Debts

The passage of this legislation was more than Hamilton and the Federalists could do without the cooperation of Jefferson and the Republicans. The total debt of all the states was about $25,000,000. Of this over $21,000,000 had been spent by the states in conducting the Revolutionary War. Left to themselves, some of the states would certainly have failed to pay off their bonds at face value. Again Hamilton emphasized the necessity of establishing the credit of governments, state as well as federal. Congress passed the bill by which the United States assumed the debts contracted as part of their war effort, the $21,000,000. This money had been spent in a common cause.

It so happened that the Southern States had already paid off a much larger share of their bonds than had the New England States. So again, Hamilton's plan brought financial advantage to commercial interests at the expense of agrarian interests. The Assumption Bill meant that all of the states would pay off the total debt. So the South would pay again, while New England would benefit.

The Federalists needed some Republican support to get the Assumption Bill passed. Jefferson agreed to persuade a few Republicans to vote for the Bill if Hamilton would persuade a few New Englanders to vote to have the permanent capital of the United States located on the Potomac River. At this time Philadelphia, a Federalist stronghold, seemed the most likely city for the capital. Thus, the Assumption Bill was passed and the capital was located on the Potomac. This sort of

political deal whereby one bloc or party gives support for one measure in return for support for another, is called *logrolling*. The good aspect of logrolling is that it is a practical way of getting things done. The unfavorable aspect is that such political deals have no relation whatever to the merit of the legislation involved.

* French Revolution and Citizen Genêt

In the early spring of 1793 France was at war with England and Spain. In April we heard the news of the beheading of King Louis XVI in the previous January. The Girondist Party, the moderate revolutionary party, sent Citizen Genêt, who arrived April 8th, to seek aid under the Treaty of Alliance of 1778. Washington issued a Neutrality Proclamation.

There was a good deal of enthusiasm for the French Revolution among the people of the United States. "Liberty, equality, fraternity" and Lafayette's Declaration of the Rights of Man had a good sound to American ears so recently tuned to their own Revolution. Intense dislike of England was widespread because of the recent war and because there were constant sources of irritation left over from the Treaty of Paris, 1783. Comparatively few people in the United States were pro-English. England bought well over half of our exports and paid even a larger part of the duties collected on imports. Friendship with England was important to private commercial interests because of trade, and to our government because of revenue. Again we have the same line-up. Those who were pro-French were the same people who opposed the B.U.S., opposed the payment of the domestic debt, and opposed the government's assumption of the states' debts. Those who had favored these policies and had been able to get them put into effect were now the ones who favored England. It is difficult to say precisely when the Republicans and Federalists recognized themselves as political parties, but, when their differences included foreign policy as well as domestic fiscal policy, the division was well defined.

President Washington's Neutrality Proclamation set our official policy. Jefferson favored a sympathetic attitude toward France, but not to the extent of going to war as her ally. When Genêt realized he could get no help through our government he appealed directly to the people by recruiting men and outfitting privateers. His aim was to raise troops to take Florida and Louisiana from Spain to become French possessions, and to take Canada as an addition to the United States. The privateers were to prey upon British merchantmen in the Caribbean. Jefferson, whose followers had held banquets and parades in Genêt's honor when he first arrived, agreed with the President that he must demand Genêt's recall. By this time, August of 1793, the Girondists had been overthrown by the Jacobins in France. When the new French minister arrived to replace Genêt he had an order for Genêt's arrest. Return to France probably meant the guillotine. During the Reign of Terror the reward for failure was death. But Genêt had other ideas. President Washington graciously allowed him to remain in the United States so that he could carry out much pleasanter plans. He married Governor Clinton's daughter and settled in up-state New York across the Hudson River from Albany. He lived long and presumably happily in useful obscurity teaching school. An historical plaque marks the place of his burial on the side of highway U.S. 9 in East Greenbush, N.Y.

* Jay Treaty with England (1795)

In 1793 England made it clear that she would keep her subjects in the trading and military posts of our Great Lakes—Ohio River Valley area until British merchants had been paid the debts owed to them by American merchants. England also sought recompense for the Loyalists whose property had been seized during the Revolution. (See terms 5, 6, and 7—Treaty of Paris, pp. 42-43.)

In November of 1793 the British began a campaign against neutral shipping in the West Indian waters. Any ship carrying products from French colonies to any destination was seized. Its cargo was confiscated, some of the crew impressed into the British navy, and others put in jail. The enforcement of this policy was such that any American ship that the British could catch was seized, regardless of where it got its cargo or where it was going. The officers and crews of British warships shared in the prize money for these seizures, so they were energetic in their hunting. This was a serious blow to Yankee shipping. The Federalists began to think war with England was the only answer.

In the spring of 1794 Washington sent Chief Justice Jay to attempt a settlement of these difficulties. Jay did not do well. The problems of British interference with our shipping, the debts owed to the British merchants, and the Maine-Canadian border were left for settlement by British-American commissioners. The detail of working out the debts and the boundary could be hammered out more suitably by a mixed commission; but the seizure of American ships and especially the impressment of American sailors should have

been part of the treaty. Some understanding should have been reached about the British encroachments along the Canada-Northwest Territory border and their encouragement of Indian unrest in that area. The South, especially Virgina, resented the failure to get any payment for the slaves the British stole at the end of the Revolution.

The terms of the treaty were:

1] The British would get out of the Northwest trading and military posts by June of 1796.

2] American ships displacing not over 70 tons could trade with the British West Indies, but their cargoes must not include cotton, molasses, or sugar.

The treaty was so unsatisfactory that the Senate considered it in a secret session, but the terms leaked out. Genuine and bitter protests greeted the treaty and, to this sincere reaction, the Republicans added political ballyhoo in generous measure. Mr. Jay was burned in effigy at protest meetings and parades. Probably no one was more chagrined than President Washington, but he was not free to indulge in the expression of his emotions.

When Washington sent Jay to London he sent him to make arrangements that would permit this nation to remain at peace. If Jay's mission was not a "peace at any price" one, it was a peace-at-almost-any-price mission. After Jay came back with the treaty, Washington wrote that he was sure that twenty more years of peace would find this nation strong enough to, ". . . bid defiance in a just cause to any power whatever . . ." . Washington requested the Senate to ratify the treaty even though his Secretary of State, Edmund Randolph, opposed it. By a close vote the Senate gave the President the necessary ⅔rds majority. Washington's acceptance of the treaty was an act that was unpopular, wise, and courageous. We could survive humiliation, but not war.

* Pinckney Treaty with Spain (1795)

This treaty is also known as the San Lorenzo Treaty. Thomas Pinckney got better terms than he hoped for, much better than we might have accepted. Perhaps the Jay Treaty helped. Spain may have believed that the Jay Treaty was ushering in a period of Anglo-American friendship that could be a threat to Spanish possessions in America. Both Republicans and Federalists were pleased. The terms of the treaty were:

1] The United States had free navigation of the Mississippi River.

2] The 31st parallel was accepted as our southern boundary line.

3] The United States had the right of deposit at New Orleans. This gave us the use of the port of New Orleans on the same basis as the Spanish. It permitted Americans to ship goods down the river on flat boats for trans-shipment by sailing vessels to foreign ports. New Orleans was the only exit for foreign trade by Americans living west of the Alleghenies.

** Washington's Farewell Address

This address was printed in the American Daily Advertiser, September 17, 1796. It was Washington's statement that he would not run for a third term. He had been formulating the ideas since the end of his first term. During that period he consulted with Madison, Hamilton, and Jay; but the address was Washington's. It contained foresight rooted in experience and discerned by wisdom.

1] A Religious and Moral Note

"Of all the dispositions and habits which lead to political prosperity, religion and morality are indispensable supports. In vain would that man claim the tribute of patriotism who should labor to subvert these great pillars of human happiness—these firmest props to the duties of men and citizens. . . . reason and experience both forbid us to expect that national morality can prevail in exclusion of religious principle."

2] An Ethical Note

Here Washington cautions that good results must not be obtained by irregular means. Good ends do not justify evil means. "If in the opinion of the people the distribution or modification of constitutional powers be in any particular wrong, let it be corrected by an amendment in the way which the Constitution designates. But let there be no change by usurpation; for though this in one instance may be the instrument of good, it is the customary weapon by which free governments are destroyed. The precedent must always greatly overbalance in permanent evil any partial or transient benefit which the use can at any time yield."

3] On the Value of the Union

"The unity of government which constitutes you one people is . . . dear to you. It is justly so, for it is a main pillar in the edifice of your real independence, the support of your tranquility, your peace abroad, of your safety, of your prosperity, of that very liberty which you so highly prize." He goes on to urge the people to frown upon, ". . . the first dawning of every attempt to alienate any portion of our country from the rest or to enfeeble the sacred ties which now link together the various parts."

4] On Foreign Relations

"The great rule of conduct for us in regard to foreign nations is, in extending our commercial relations, to have with them as little *political* connection as possible. . . . Europe has a set of primary interests which to us have none or a very remote relation. . . . Taking care always to keep ourselves suitable establishments on a respectable defensive posture, we may safely trust to temporary alliances for extraordinary emergencies. . . . It is our true policy to steer clear of permanent alliances with any portion of the foreign world."

5] On Strife between Political Parties

"I have already intimated to you the danger of parties in the State, with particular reference to the founding of them on geographical discriminations. Let me . . . warn you in the most solemn manner against the baneful effects of the spirit of party generally. . . . It serves always to distract the public councils and enfeeble the public administration. It agitates the community with ill-founded jealousies and false alarms; kindles the animosity of one part against another; foments occasionally riot and insurrection. It opens the door to foreign influence and corruption, which find a facilitated access to the government itself through the channels of party passion. Thus the policy and the will of one country are subjected to the policy and will of another. . . . In governments purely elective, it is a spirit not to be encouraged. . . . it is certain there will always be enough of that spirit for every salutary purpose; and there being constant danger of excess, the effort ought to be by force of public opinion to mitigate and assuage it. A fire not to be quenched, it demands a uniform vigilance to prevent its bursting into a flame, lest, instead of warming, it should consume."

Do the five opinions quoted above express views that were wise for Washington's time, but not for ours? Or do they contain a wisdom fitting to all times? Try to form such a judgment for each point separately. Are any of the quotations particularly applicable to the present?

John Adams

1797-1801

1735 - 1826

FEDERALIST

☆

Vice-President THOMAS JEFFERSON

ADAMS' PUBLIC SERVICE BEFORE HE BECAME PRESIDENT

One of the most effective writers against the Stamp Act
Defended the British soldiers involved in the Boston "Massacre"
Massachusetts delegate to both the 1st and 2nd Continental Congresses
Helped to negotiate the Treaty of Paris, 1783
Vice-President under Washington

MAJOR ITEMS OF JOHN ADAMS' ADMINISTRATION

X.Y.Z Affair
Alien Act; Sedition Act; Naturalization Act; "Midnight Judges"
Kentucky and Virginia Resolutions

Election 1796

John Adams received 71 electoral votes. Thomas Jefferson, leader of the Republican Party, received 68 votes. This is the first presidential election under the Constitution determined along party lines. The issue of the campaign was the Jay Treaty. The election of the two rival candidates as President and Vice-President resulted from the original provisions of the Constitution. Members of the Electoral College voted for two persons with no designation as to whether they were intended as votes for President or for Vice-President. The votes were then totaled and the candidate receiving the most votes, provided it was a majority, became President; the candidate receiving the next largest vote became Vice-President. This unsatisfactory method was replaced in 1804 by the present method provided in Amendment XII (see p. 60).

* X.Y.Z. Affair (1797)

The American people were unhappy about the Jay Treaty; France was angry about it. France considered it a violation of the Treaty of Alliance of 1778. The French view was that when she was at war with England in 1794, the Treaty of Alliance required the United States to become an active ally with her against England. Instead we negotiated the Jay Treaty which was a tacit acceptance of Eng-

land's violation of our rights on the high seas (see p. 78).

In complete disregard of Washington's advice to avoid extreme party strife, the Republicans applauded the seizure by the French of hundreds of American merchantmen. So, in 1797, the French were attacking our shipping much as England had done in 1793. The very corrupt, five-man Directory was in charge of France. Talleyrand, foreign minister for the Directory, sought to take advantage of the weakness of our new nation and the public sympathy in the United States for the French Revolution.

President Adams was axious to avoid war. He appointed commissioners Charles C. Pinckney, Elbridge Gerry, and John Marshall to try to come to some acceptable terms with France. Three "unofficial" Frenchmen informed our commissioners that before formal talks could begin, they must be prepared to arrange a loan to France and a $240,000 payment for foreign minister Talleyrand. This proposition was offered on Oct. 18, 1797. Our commissioners expected to pay some sort of bribe, but not $240,000. The demand for a loan as another condition just to arrange for the opening of official talks between governments was outrageous. After weeks of haggling, Marshall refused to make any concessions. He and Pinckney returned to report to

President Adams. Gerry stayed in Paris to prevent a complete severance of diplomatic relations and thus make a formal declaration of war less likely.

When the President reported this story to Congress on March 19, 1798, the "unofficial" French envoys were referred to as X. Y. and Z. A wave of indignation swept through the United States. The Republican Party lost thousands of supporters. Jefferson had nothing to say. "Millions for defense, but not one cent for tribute," was the slogan of the day. President Adams enjoyed a brief spell of popularity. The Republican Party was flat on its back gasping for breath. It had been so wrong about the French!

The United States prepared for war. A Navy Department was established, Congress declared the Treaty of Alliance of 1778 at an end, Washington was named commanding general, and about two hundred merchantmen became privateers. France was expected to declare war, but instead Talleyrand pretended that the X.Y.Z. episode was all a misunderstanding. He claimed that the "unofficial" French envoys had no connection with the French government and acted without his knowledge. He said that the American commissioners had hurried home too soon and thus prevented an opportunity to straighten things out. Obviously France did not want war with America, and this suited President Adams. Negotiations dragged on through most of 1800 when it was agreed that the Treaty of Alliance of 1778 was not in effect. During the approximately two years that negotiations were taking place, there was a full-fledged naval war, though undeclared, between France and the United States. Several engagements between warships occurred and the Yankee privateers just about drove French commerce out of West Indian waters.

* Naturalization Act; Alien Act; Sedition Act; "Midnight Judges"

These items are listed together because they were all acts which contributed to the downfall of the Federalist Party

The Naturalization Act (June 18, 1798)

It provided that an alien could not become a citizen until he had lived in the United States fourteen years. The previous residence requirement had been five years.

The Alien Act (June 25, 1798)

It gave the President the power to deport any alien he considered dangerous to our peace and safety or inclined to be engaged in treason. No alien was ever deported under this law.

The Sedition Act (July 14, 1798)

1] A fine of not more than $2,000 and imprisonment for not more than two years for publishing, "any false, scandalous and malicious writing" about the government of the United States, Congress, or the President.

2] A fine of not more than $5,000 and imprisonment for not more than five years for persons unlawfully conspiring to oppose any law or official of the government.

3] The truth of statements published shall be accepted as a defense thereof.

4] This act shall continue in force until March 3, 1801.

"Midnight Judges" (Feb. 27, 1801—March 3, 1801)

Less than a week before Jefferson's inauguration, the "lame duck" Federalist Congress and the rejected President Adams passed and signed the Judiciary Act of 1801. It changed the Supreme Court from six to five judges, created 16 additional circuit court judgeships, and provided jobs for several marshalls, attorneys, and clerks. Some of the commissions for these judgeships and other jobs were signed the last night of Adams' term in an effort to fasten Federalist control on the judicial branch of the government. As Adams and the Federalist Congress might have foreseen, this law was futile and served only to hurt their party. The new President and the new Republican Congress repealed the Judiciary Act of 1801 two months after it had been passed. But the facts that the Federalist Party had defied public opinion as clearly expressed in the election of 1800, and had used the establishment of federal courts for purely political purposes were not forgotten. To many voters the "Midnight Judges" proved that the Federalist Party would grab power any way it could and that it had no respect for the opinion of the people.

The Naturalization Act, the Alien Act, and the Sedition Act all purported to defend the United States from dangerous subversives. The Reign of Terror of the French Revolution was followed by the X.Y.Z. Affair and two years of undeclared war with France. The Jacobins of the 1790's offered the Federalist Party a chance to whip up hysteria for partisan advantage. The Naturalization Act made it more difficult for Jacobins to become citizens; at least it would take them nine years longer than before. The Alien Act would permit the deportation of any Jacobin who seemed to the President to be undesirable. The Sedition Act could stop any organizing and publishing by Jacobins bent upon subversion. All Jacobin aliens would be French, Frenchmen were most unpopular in the United States after the X.Y.Z. Affair, and the Republican Party had been pro-French. The set-up made it easy for the Federalist Party to pose as the defender of the United States from a foreign menace. Perhaps some Federalists really believed in the Jacobin scare.

But it was equally true that naturalized citizens became Republicans. Almost all immigrants were rather poor people who earned their living as hired help in the towns or as farmers on the more remote and poorer farms. The overwhelming majority of them would eventually vote Republican, if they voted at all. The Sedition Act didn't bother any Jacobins, but it did put Republican newspaper editors in jail. As the scare over Jacobins subsided, the suspicion grew that the Naturalization, Alien, and Sedition laws were Federalist tricks to hurt the Republican Party. The Sedition Act especially aroused antagonism. It was the only one that put people in jail. It seemed a denial of the restriction put upon Congress by the 1st Amendment, "Congress shall make no law . . . abridging the freedom of the press; of the right to . . . assemble, and to petition . . ." To assemble might be considered a conspiracy, or to petition the government for a redress of grievances might be considered a malicious criticism of the government or its officers according to the Sedition Act. These restrictive laws boomeranged against the Federalists.

* Kentucky and Virginia Resolutions (Nov. and Dec. 1798)

Jefferson wrote the Kentucky Resolutions and Madison wrote the Virginia Resolutions. Each having been passed by a state legislature was an official pronouncement. Jefferson was, and many would say still is, the foremost spokesman for democratic principles: Madison was generally accepted as the best informed man in the field of government at the Constitutional Convention. These men were sincerely alarmed at the growing power of the central government under "loose construction." They were sure that the Sedition and the Alien Act were unconstitutional.

The Kentucky Resolutions made the following points

1] The states made a "compact," an agreement, known as the Constitution.

2] The Constitution set up a "general government," the federal government, for special purposes, gave it definite powers, and reserved to each state all other rights and powers.

3] Whenever the "general government assumes undelegated powers, its acts are unauthoritative, void, and of no force."

4] The government made by this compact, ". . . was not made the exclusive or final judge of the extent of the powers delegated to itself."

5] The limited power of the general government and the sovereignty of the states is made clear by the 10th Amendment, "that the powers not delegated to the United States by the Constitution, nor prohibited by it to the States, are reserved to the States respectively, or to the people."

6] The acts listed in the Sedition Act are punishable only by the states, ". . . the power to create, define, and punish such other crimes is reserved, and of right appertains solely and exclusively to the respective States, each within its own Territory."

7] ". . . no power over the freedom of religion, freedom of speech, or freedom of the press being delegated to the United States by the Constitution, nor prohibited by it to the States, all lawful powers respecting the same did of right remain, and were reserved to the States, or to the people: . . . that therefore (the Sedition Act) which does abridge freedom of the press, is not law, but is altogether void and of no effect."

8] Aliens, "are under the jurisdiction and protections of the laws of the State wherein they are; that no power over them has been delegated to the United States, nor prohibited to the individual States distinct from their power over citizens; . . . the (Alien Act), which assumes power over alien friends not delegated by the Constitution, is not law, but is altogether void and of no force.

9] Under the Alien Act the President may, without accusation, without jury, without public trial, without confrontation of the witnesses against him, without having witnesses in his favor, without defense counsel, . . . is therefore not law, but utterly void and of no force."

10] ". . . that the friendless alien has indeed been selected as the safest subject of a first experiment, but the citizen will soon follow, or rather has already followed; for, already has a sedition act marked him as its prey: that these and successive acts of the same character, unless arrested on the threshold, may tend to drive these States into revolution and blood, and will furnish new calumnies against Republican governments, and new pretexts for those who wish it believed, that man cannot be governed but by a rod of iron:"

** Significance of the Kentucky and Virginia Resolutions

At the time these resolutions were adopted by Kentucky and Virginia, there was no intent to claim, much less act upon, the right of a state to withdraw from the union. But it clearly followed, and this was noted at the time, that acceptance of the Jefferson-Madison reasoning would make both nullification of laws of Congress by states, and the withdrawal of states from the Union obviously lawful steps for any state to take. The Constitution says nothing about the power to nullify acts of Congress, it says nothing about a state withdrawing from the Union; it therefore follows that these powers or rights are residual, and thus belong to the states, or to the people. It is an interesting detail that the Articles of Confederation contained the words, "perpetual Union," but no such designation occurs in the Constitution. On the basis of the ideas expressed in the Kentucky and Virginia Resolutions the prophecy that the states would be driven, "into revolution and blood," became a tragic truth in 1861.

Thomas Jefferson

1801-1809

1743 - 1826

REPUBLICAN

☆

Vice-President AARON BURR

Secretary of State JAMES MADISON

JEFFERSON'S PUBLIC SERVICES BEFORE HE BECAME PRESIDENT

Member of the Virginia House of Burgesses
Wrote "A Summary View of the Rights of British America" in 1774
Virginia delegate to the Second Continental Congress, 1775-76
Wrote the Declaration of Independence
Governor of Virginia, 1779-'81
United States Minister to France, 1785-'89
Secretary of State, 1789-'93
Leader of the Republican Party (Democratic Republican)
Vice-President under Adams
Wrote the Kentucky Resolutions

MAJOR ITEMS OF JEFFERSON'S ADMINISTRATIONS

Marbury v. Madison (1803)
Louisiana Purchase (1803)
Lewis and Clark Expedition
12th Amendment (1804)
Embargo Act (1807)
Non-Intercourse Act (1809)

Election of 1800 and Re-election in 1804

In 1800 the campaign issues were:
The Alien and Sedition Acts
Relations with France and England
Trade with France had almost vanished; we were officially at peace and actually at war. Impressment and the Jay Treaty still created anti-English sentiment which hurt the Federalists.

President Adams and Hamilton had split the Federalist Party. Their disagreement over how to handle our relations with France grew into a bitter personal feud which had the Party fighting within itself more vigorously than it fought the Republicans. Although the legislatures of the states refused to accept the logic of the Kentucky and Virginia Resolutions, the voters were impressed by the prestige of Jefferson and Madison as leaders accusing the Federalists of contempt for the people and greed for power. After Washington left the presidency, it wasn't too difficult to paint the political picture with the Federalists as the party of "Privilege" and the Republicans as the "Peoples' Party."

Jefferson and Burr both received 73 electoral votes to 65 for John Adams. It was the intention of the Republican Electors to elect Jefferson as President and Burr as Vice-President. Legally, however, Burr had as good a claim to the office as did Jefferson. The election went to the House of Representatives with each state having one vote. It took 36 ballots to elect Jefferson. The Federalist Party had control of the House. They decided in a caucus to elect Burr, but Hamilton was able to persuade them to reverse this decision and vote for Jefferson. Hamilton knew Jefferson to be a man worthy of the office of President; he knew Burr was not. Perhaps this episode played a major part in Burr's challenging Hamilton to a duel about four years later.

The reelection of Jefferson in 1804 marked the first time the members of the Electoral College voted separately for President and Vice-President under the terms of the 12th Amendment. Jefferson got 162 electoral votes to 14 for the Federalist candidate, Charles C. Pinckney. Even the New England states, except for Connecticut, voted for Jefferson.

** *Marbury v. Madison* (1803)

President Adams had appointed William Marbury as a Justice of the Peace in the District of Columbia. The commission had been properly signed, but had not been delivered. Jefferson took office. He instructed his Secretary of State, James Madison, not to deliver any of the commissions to the "midnight" appointees who hadn't yet received them. William Marbury asked for an order from the Supreme Court directing the Secretary of State to deliver his commission to him. Such an affirmative order whereby the court tells someone to do something, is called a *mandamus*. President Jefferson instructed Madison to pay no attention to the mandamus. The Judiciary Act of 1789 provided that the Supreme Court could issue a writ of mandamus to any officer of the United States. The officer in this case was Secretary of State, Madison. At this point we have a President refusing to do, through the Secretary of State, what a law of Congress empowers the Supreme Court to order done.

The pertinent points in the decision delivered by Chief Justice Marshall, were:

1] Marbury was entitled to his commission.

2] It was the duty of the President to see that the commission was delivered to Marbury.

3] The Supreme Court could not issue an order (mandamus) that the commission be delivered, because the clause in the Judiciary Act of 1789 authorizing the Court to do so, was unconstitutional.
  a. This clause enlarged the *original* jurisdiction of the Supreme Court, a jurisdiction fixed by the Constitution and not subject to modification by Congress.
  b. This clause violated the fundamental principle of separation of powers. It provided that Congress reach over into the Judicial Department, the Supreme Court, to enlarge its powers beyond limits defined in the Constitution.

This case is to be understood as a political contest between a Federalist Chief Justice and a Republican President. Had Marshall ordered Jefferson to deliver the commission to Marbury, Jefferson would not have done so. The Chief Justice could not make the President obey a Court order. The Supreme Court would then invite public ridicule, its prestige would wither almost before it had sprouted, and a popular President would be a bit more popular. Had Marshall ruled that the President didn't have to obey the Judiciary Act, it would have been an abject surrender by the Court to the President. So the Chief Justice ruled that Marbury should get his commission, that Jefferson was wrong in not giving it to him, and that the Court's hands were tied because the mandamus clause of the Judiciary Act was unconstitutional. This decision did more than get the Chief Justice out of a debater's dilemma; it gave Jefferson a petty political victory by withholding commissions from Marbury and a few other "midnight" appointees, while it formed the entering wedge by which judicial review of laws of Congress became the established custom. It was a tremendous victory for "loose construction" of the Constitution and the tendency toward a stronger federal government. It was not until 1857, the Dred Scott Case, that the Supreme Court again ruled that a law of Congress was unconstitutional.

** Louisiana Purchase, 1803

The Louisiana Territory was bought from France for $15,000,000. Of this amount $11,000,000 was for land and the balance of $3,750,000 represented debts owed by France to United States citizens, which debts the United States agreed to pay. The area totaled about 830,000 square miles and just about doubled the size of our nation. The boundaries were indefinite. The Mississippi River was the eastern border. On the south the territory extended to the Gulf of Mexico, on the west to the Rocky Mountains, and on the north to Canada. Was Texas included? Did it include any of the Gulf coast which was then called Florida? Just what lines marked the Rocky Mountains or the Canadian border between the source of the Mississippi River and the Rockies? Complete answers to these questions were not reached until 1818 and 1846.

Our minister to France, who handled most of the negotiations, was Robert Livingston. James Monroe was sent over by President Jefferson as a special minister to help bring about a favorable deal. The day before Monroe arrived in Paris, Napoleon's foreign minister, Talleyrand, still refused to sell only the New Orleans' area; but he did suggest that the United States buy the whole Louisiana Territory. With Monroe's arrival both our ministers recognized this offer as not only too good to lose, but one to be concluded as quickly as possible. The agreement was made on May 2, 1803.

Livingston and Monroe had not been authorized to buy any such vast area nor to agree to a price over $10,000,000. Napoleon asked and got assurance that the French and Spanish subjects in the territory would become United States citizens with the transfer of the land, and that eventually Louisiana would become states in the Union.

The Senate ratified this treaty with France by a vote of 24 to 7 on Oct. 20, 1803.

** President Jefferson Had Compelling Reasons for This Purchase

1] The Pinckney Treaty of 1795 (see pp. 78-79) gave the United States freedom to use the Mississippi River and the port of New Orleans. In May, 1801, Jefferson learned that Napoleon had forced Spain to sign over Louisiana to France. This change caused Jefferson to write to Robert Livingston in Paris, "The day that France takes over New Orleans . . . we must marry ourselves to the British fleet and nation."

To one who appreciates the patriot, Thomas Jefferson, this is an astounding statement. It was the fiery three, Samuel Adams, Patrick Henry, and Thomas Jefferson, who were intent upon bringing about the Revolution. Certainly Jefferson's basic philosophical ideals and ideas about the "natural rights of man" and the republican form of government, combined with the long list of grievances against the English king (Declaration of Independence) made Jefferson an Anglophobe. By the Letters of Correspondence he played a leading part in keeping "the fires of revolution alive" during periods which favored a peaceful rapprochement for England and her American colonies. He strongly disliked pomp and ceremony, which could have been a reflection of his anti-English bias. He was pro-French and anti-English as the leader of the opposition party during both of Washington's terms as president. But in 1803 Jefferson was not a patriot working toward revolution, he was not the leader of the opposition party; he was President of the United States with the responsibility of that office. Whatever nation denied to the United States the free use of the Mississippi River and the port of New Orleans must be opposed, and that nation's major foe became our natural partner.

2] The situation in the southwestern area of the United States made the use of the Mississippi River an urgent matter. The volume of trade down the Mississippi totaled about $1,000,000 a year. The settlers of the Ohio valley area (what is now Ohio, Indiana, Illinois, and Kentucky) could get cash for goods shipped to New Orleans. The whole western area including the Ohio valley and what is now Tennessee, Mississippi, Louisiana, and Alabama looked with a jaundiced eye upon Congress and the eastern seaboard. To President Jefferson, this was a serious problem. These trans-Allegheny settlers could recall the Jay-Gardoqui proposal of 1785 and 1786, in which the Congress under the Articles of Confederation almost agreed to Spain's having exclusive use of the Mississippi River in exchange for some special trading privileges for Yankee shippers in Spanish ports in Europe. Congress refused to sell out the vital interests of the west for a not very important advantage for the New England shippers, but only by a vote of 7 to 5. It required only two more votes to sacrifice the West to the East. The climate of opinion in the southwest corner of the United States in 1803 was self-centered, strictly sectional. Their attitude toward the "original thirteen" ranged from indifference to unfriendliness. President Jefferson had reason for concern lest the Southwest fall away from the United States if it had to choose between loyalty and the use of the Mississippi River. The uncertainties in this area were emphasized a little later, in 1805 and 1806, when Aaron Burr and General Wilkinson were suspected of some sort of plot. We don't know what their plans were. Wilkinson betrayed Burr who was tried for treason and acquitted in 1807. The only factor one can get hold of here is that President Jefferson knew the situation was delicate and that loss of the use of the Mississippi could set off serious internal trouble.

3] It was clear that the United States must get all of the Louisiana Territory if the opportunity arose. The Napoleonic Wars were on. If England won, she would force France to give her Louisiana. England had Canada and she was mistress of the seas. In short, a British victory meant that the United States would be surrounded by British Canada, British Louisiana, and British naval power. If Napoleon won, France would force England to give back Canada which England had taken from France in 1713 and 1763 (Treaties of Utrecht and Paris). Canada and Louisiana would then be French, and France would also be mistress of the seas, for she could not win without first destroying British sea power. To President Jefferson the outlook was bleak indeed. As seen in 1803, the results of the Napoleonic Wars meant big trouble for the young United States. Little wonder that Talleyrand's offer was eagerly accepted!

** The Purchase of Louisiana Posed a Special Problem for President Jefferson

We have seen how Jefferson made a right-about-face in his attitude toward England and France, as soon as France threatened our use of the Mississippi River. Strange as it may have seemed to him to be pro-English and anti-French, he could see clearly where our national interests lay. Another problem bothered him deeply. He had built a political party and a national reputation on the "strict" interpretation of the Constitution. He believed that no officer of the federal government, no department, had the right to exercise any power or do anything as an agent of the government unless that power was expressly and clearly stated in the Constitution. But nowhere in the Constitution was there any provision about buying such a tremendous area of land. Certainly the president was not empowered to negotiate such a deal. Nor was there in the Constitution any provision allowing the promise made about making United State citizens of the people in the area, or the promise that the territory would eventually enter the Union as states. On the other hand, the Constitution did flatly say, in the 10th Amendment, that any power not given to the United States and not denied to the states did belong to the states or to the people. As Jefferson saw it, that which must be done for reasons of national interest (the acquisition of Louisiana) could not be done by him without violating the basic principle on which he had built a political party and career. His inclination was to take the issue to Congress. Had he done so, it almost certainly would have become an inter-party fight during which Napoleon might have withdrawn the offer, or England might have seized Louisiana. However, the suggestion that the purchase be viewed as a treaty, and handled as such, was acted upon. This restricted controversy to the Senate where national interests could prevail more easily over the temptation toward factional strife for party advantage. President Jefferson put national necessity above all else; above the Constitution as he saw it, above the political convictions of a life-time. It could not have been easy.

** Why Napoleon Was Willing to Sell the Louisiana Territory

Slave revolts on the island of Haiti (Santo Domingo) had been erupting intermittently since about 1795. Thinking to quell the disorder once and for all, Napoleon sent a sizeable expedition of ships and men to Haiti. When order had been restored to Haiti, this force was then to go to New Orleans and set up a military and naval garrison there. However, a native leader, Toussaint L'Ouverture, offered such effective leadership to slaves and such damaging resistance to the French, that Napoleon's naval and land forces were depleted to the point of uselessness. Napoleon's chance to build a base for his empire in the western hemisphere was lost. His problem became one of selling Louisiana before the British took it. At the crucial moment, April in 1803, Napoleon was as anxious to sell as Livingston and Monroe were to buy.

Wars were expensive, even in the early 1800's. Napoleon needed all the cash he could get. We also had a motive that is part of any expansion program. There are always many who favor bigness for its own sake. Napoleon's desire for money and our inclination toward expansion for its own sake were real, but not the compelling, factors.

Lewis and Clark Expedition

Meriwether Lewis and William Clark, younger brother of George Rogers Clark, were sent by President Jefferson to explore the Louisiana Territory. They started up the Missouri River in May of 1804 and reached the Pacific Ocean in November of 1805. They wrote reports on the plants, animals, Indians, soil, rivers, type of country, etc. It was a scientific, as well as an exploring, undertaking. On the return trip, completed in September of 1806, Lewis and Clark separated for part of the journey to take different routes. There were between forty and fifty men in the party. All but one returned safely. They had been instructed to avoid trouble with the Indians and to find a pass over the Rockies; both instructions were carried out. Clark's diary makes good reading and provides an easy and enjoyable way to take the trip over again.

Apparently Jefferson was not bothered by the fact that he had ordered the expedition to go across the Rockies beyond our western border. Captain Robert Gray had sailed into the mouth of the Columbia River in 1792; in fact, the river got its name from his ship. Then the Lewis and Clark expedition came down the Columbia to the Pacific (1805) and half a dozen years later the permanent settlement at Astoria, established by John Jacob Astor, was a fur trading post near the mouth of the river. These facts combined to give the United States its claim to the Oregon Territory which we acquired in 1846.

12th Amendment (1804)

This amendment provides for the election of President and Vice-President (see p. 60).

Embargo Act (1807) and Non-Intercourse Act (1809)

The Napoleonic War was raging in Europe and on the high seas. Recruiting in England for the British navy was accomplished, in some instances, by direct action. Any sailor who was alone when he left a water-front tavern a bit unsteadily might be shanghaied by a pair of recruiting officers. By the time the lone sailor recovered his wits, he might well be enlisted in the royal navy and already on board a British warship. Equally direct recruiting for the royal navy took place on the high seas. United States ships were stopped, boarded, and the crew lined up on deck. Any sailors who seemed physically fit and who spoke English were likely to be taken off as deserters from the British navy. This was impressment. In June of 1807 a flagrant violation of our rights occurred when the United States frigate, "Chesapeake," was stopped off the Virginia coast by the British frigate, "Leopard." Three Americans were killed, eighteen were wounded, and four men were impressed into the British navy. One of the four was a deserter; the other three had been impressed before and then escaped only to be impressed a second time. Scores of British sailors deserted to escape harsh discipline and poor food. They sought employment in the United States navy and merchant marine. It was not uncommon for one-quarter to one-half of the crew of an American naval vessel to be aliens, most of whom would be from the United Kingdom. The situation was chaotic. England claimed that "Once an Englishman, always an Englishman" was good law; but the United States had to have legal arrangements which could grant American citizenship to aliens. In 1807 the British and the Americans were violating each other's navigation laws and concepts of the rights of neutrals on the high seas. But, granting all the confusion about legal rights, the British had perpetrated an intolerable insult by the "Chesapeake" incident. Jefferson's answer was not war, but the Embargo Act.

The terms of the Embargo Act were:

1] No American ship can leave an American port for a foreign port.

2] No foreign vessel can load a cargo at an American port.

3] Coastwise shipping must post a bond equal to twice the value of the ship and cargo before leaving port. On delivery of the cargo the bond will be repaid.

Smuggling by ship and also over the Canadian border, especially through New York State, robbed the Embargo Act of whatever effect it might have had. Above all, Jefferson wished to avoid war. He faced a more difficult and provocative situation than Washington had at the time of the Jay Treaty. Both France and England were violating our rights as neutrals. While the Jay Treaty was humiliating, it had no new and substantial adverse economic

effect. The Embargo Act made no attempt to assert our rights; it was intended to keep our ships out of danger by keeping them home. Its adverse economic effects ruined the shipping business along the Atlantic coast. It hit New England with special force. State officials refused to support the enforcement of the embargo. There were not enough federal officials to do the job without local support. A New England convention was seriously considered, but not called, to protest the Embargo Act as an unconstitutional exercise of federal authority. The governor of Connecticut flatly branded the Embargo Act unconstitutional. The northeast now advanced the nullification theories of Jefferson and Madison. President Jefferson was convinced, and remained so throughout his life, that, had the Embargo Act been properly enforced, both England and France would have come to terms soon. He believed their need for goods was greater and more urgent than our need for their business. As it worked out, however, the regular shipping businesses were ruined, while smuggling flourished.

The Non-Intercourse Act of 1809 was passed a few days before the end of Jefferson's second term. It allowed American ships to trade everywhere except in ports controlled by England or by France. There followed a slight increase in trade, but no increase in the respect paid to our rights as a neutral nation. England and France continued to molest our commerce.

* Jefferson's Administrations Illustrate a Basic Pattern in American Politics

Presidential campaigns are carried on as if the nation would be saved or ruined, depending on which party won. Yet shifts from one party to the other have resulted in so little change in the direction of public affairs that a common criticism of our political set-up is that both parties are as alike as two peas in a pod. Whether this circumstance protects and advances the public welfare or whether it defeats and retards it, is a worthwhile topic for discussion. Right now, we are directing our attention to the fact itself, and the way Jefferson's election and administrations illustrate it.

During the campaign of 1800 dire prophecies were made. The Federalists claimed, and seemed to believe, that a Republican victory would be the beginning of a revolution. Jefferson's election would usher in the violence and immoralities of the French Reign of Terror. Yet what happened?

Jefferson did not disturb the Bank of the United States which he and his party had so bitterly opposed. He, as Washington and Adams had done, conducted foreign affairs with avoidance of war as the key aim. In trying to avoid war, the Federalists accepted the unpalatable Jay Treaty, much as Jefferson accepted the humiliation of continued violation of our rights on the high seas by France and England. Because the vital interests of this Republic demanded it, Jefferson cast aside his political theories of strict construction and states' rights. By what possible stretching of the Constitution did the President and the Senate have the right to pledge in a treaty that subjects of France and Spain in Louisiana would automatically become citizens without individual naturalization? By what right did they pledge that eventually the huge area would be admitted into the Union as states? Certainly, by Jefferson's thinking, no right whatever. Yet he did it. It is difficult to see what President Adams and the Federalists would have done, had they won in 1800, that would have been importantly different from the program of the Republicans. This was so true that a faction of Jefferson's party opposed the "Federalist policies" of President Jefferson. Their leader was John Randolph of Virginia and they were called Quids. Other Republicans who thought Jefferson had deserted Republican principles and measures called themselves "Old Republicans." All this reminds one of "Old Guard" Republicans calling "Teddy" Roosevelt a Socialist, of Al Smith breaking with "F.D.R." to help form the Liberty League in opposition to the "New Deal" Democrats, of Barry Goldwater offering to lead the Republican Party back to "sound conservatism" and away from the "progressive" Republican leadership represented by President Eisenhower and Governor Rockefeller. In brief, our two major parties frequently develop factions within themselves which contend that the party leadership has deserted sound principles and gone over to the unsound thinking of the opposition party. Just as Jefferson accepted the Bank of the United States, so the present-day Republican Party accepted T.V.A. which they long and strenuously opposed. This is typical of American politics. The reversal of an important program seldom results from a change in parties. Of course, the Senate is a powerful built-in stabilizer, but it is by no means a complete explanation.

As Washington established the "no third term" precedent, Jefferson also rooted it into our political "unwritten law" by refusing to run for a third term. It was 144 years before this precedent was broken, whereupon the "unwritten law" was made into Constitutional law by the 22nd Amendment.

James Madison

1809-1817

1751 - 1836

REPUBLICAN

☆

Secretary of State JAMES MONROE

MADISON'S PUBLIC SERVICE BEFORE HE BECAME PRESIDENT

Member of the 2nd Continental Congress from Virginia, 1780-'83
A leading force in arranging the Mount Vernon, Annapolis, and Philadelphia Constitutional
  Conventions
Author of several issues of the Federalist Papers
Secretary of State under Jefferson

MAJOR ITEMS OF MADISON'S ADMINISTRATIONS

Macon Act—Berlin and Milan Decrees —Orders in Council
"War Hawks"
War of 1812
Hartford Convention (1814)
First Protective Tariff (1816)

Election in 1808 and Re-election in 1812

The electoral vote was 122 for Madison and 47 for Charles C. Pinckney, the Federalist candidate. The loss of the shipping business and the continued violation of our neutral rights by France and England were the major points of attack on the Republicans. The Federalist Party revived in New England to make considerable gains in the House of Representatives, but not enough to get control.

The re-election of Madison took place five months after the start of the War of 1812. Some anti-war Republicans joined with the Federalists of the northeastern seaboard to oppose his re-election. But the electoral vote was Madison, 128; Clinton, 89. The Federalists made heavy gains in Congress. The South and West supported Madison, but the only state of the Northeast that Madison carried was Vermont, a state without a seacoast.

* Macon Act—Berlin and Milan Decrees—Orders in Council

These three items complete the story begun by the Embargo Act of 1807 and continued by the Non-Intercourse Act of 1809. Together they tell what our government did in its efforts to keep out of war and, at the same time, force belligerents to recognize our rights as neutrals.

The British Parliament by its Orders in Council and Napoleon by his Berlin and Milan Decrees had established the policy of seizing any neutral shipping headed for enemy ports. This had almost the same effect as making all neutral shipping bound for the British Isles or a European port subject to capture by either England or France. In enforcing their orders and decrees, neither England nor France was too careful about confining its attacks to ships carrying contraband or actually bound for an enemy port.

The Macon Act of 1810 made a third attack on this problem. It withdrew all restrictions on trade with England and France. It further provided that whichever nation ceased its attacks upon our commerce would be rewarded by having the United States cease trading with the other nation. The American hope was that both England and France would repeal the Orders in Council and Berlin and Milan Decrees respectively. Had they done so, we would then be trading with both belligerents in non-contraband goods and trading without molestation with other neutrals, as we had a right to do. Napoleon quickly announced the repeal of the Berlin and Milan Decrees, but actually continued to harass American shipping. Being a dictator, he could make quick decisions. The English had a

House of Commons, a House of Lords, a Ministry, and Afternoon Tea; they couldn't compete with Napoleon in quickness of decision and deception. Over a year went by before the Parliament repealed the Orders in Council. Meanwhile, we had renewed the embargo against England in accordance with the Macon Act, and England, in retaliation, stepped-up impressment of American sailors and other violations of our rights. The Macon Act had enabled Napoleon to maneuver the United States to the verge of war against England. In fact, some fighting occurred off the coast of Virginia. On May 16th, 1811 the U.S. frigate *President* attacked the British corvette *Little Belt* killing 9 and wounding 23 of her crew. This attack was our reaction to the continuing impressment and other interference with our shipping.

The Macon Act has been pictured as a very low point in American diplomacy. However, it seems right to recall that no diplomacy, weak or strong, has yet been able to persuade major powers at war to respect the rights of neutrals on the high seas. It may well be that the Embargo Act, the Non-Intercourse Act, and the Macon Act were clumsy diplomacy; but it is certain that they were attempting to achieve what today still seems to be impossible.

The War Hawks

Henry Clay was leader of the *War Hawks*. He made the most of his position as Speaker of the House to fan the war spirit. John C. Calhoun of South Carolina, Felix Grundy of Tennessee, Richard Johnson of Kentucky, and Langdon Cheves of South Carolina were other leading *War Hawks*. They were motivated by hatred of England or by ambition for expansion, or both. Clay thought a few Kentucky riflemen could capture Canada. There was talk of taking Florida and Mexico. The members of Congress clamoring for war represented the inland areas. They blamed the Indian wars upon the Canadians. It was in this period that William Henry Harrison, Governor of Indiana Territory, defeated the Indian confederacy of Tecumseh in the battle of Tippecanoe, November 6, 1811. A popular saying of the day was, "The only good Indian is a dead Indian." The breaking of treaties and the making of fraudulent treaties with the Indians caused more hostilities than anything the Canadians did or could have done. At any given moment in history, what a people believe can be more influential and important than what is true. The period preceding the War of 1812 was such a time. A real danger in the Cold War of the 1960's is the possibility that what each side believes about the other, even though it may be false, can become more important than the truth.

** The War of 1812

This was a very strange war. Neither side wished it to happen. Had there been a trans-Atlantic telegraph, there would have been no war. The new Republic of the United States fought on the side of a dictator, Napoleon, against England, the most democratic monarchy in the world. We had a very small navy, yet we won our most brilliant successes on the seas and on the lakes against the "Mistress of the Seas." The British burned Washington. Our failure to take Canada was about as complete as it could be. Madison proved a poor leader under war conditions. Peace was agreed upon even though no agreement on peace terms could be reached. The one point of agreement was that both sides were willing to quit. Impressment, boundaries, Indian problems, fishing rights, and right of neutrals on the high seas were discussed to no avail. The Treaty of Ghent was agreed upon December 24, 1814. It contained no indemnities, no penalties, no territorial adjustments. Everything was to be as it had been before the war started. The problems left unsolved were to be taken up later by commissioners from each nation. Fifteen days after peace had been arranged, but before the news had reached America, the battle of New Orleans took place. General Andrew Jackson's artillery and riflemen mowed down close formations of British infantry. In less than half an hour 2,000 British soldiers were killed or wounded. The Americans lost 13. Had there been no Napoleon there would have been no War of 1812. The United States became involved in a great European conflict in spite of the geographical isolation afforded by the Atlantic Ocean. Just as the Federalists in the United States were protesting "Mr. Madison's War," so, too, the merchants and manufacturers of England were petitioning Parliament to restore normal trade relations with America.

The results of the War of 1812 upon the United States were tremendous. The American people believed we had won the war. No one complained of a peace without victory. Perhaps the enthusiasm over the victory at New Orleans created the feeling of triumph. But there were other factors.

A] Twice within forty years the United States had been at war with the greatest power on earth. The first time we gained independence. The second time we suffered no penalties. This was not the usual pattern for the enemies of Great Britain.

B] The Treaty of Ghent convinced Europe that the

United States had established itself as a permanent government. It would not be reabsorbed into the British Empire. The financial responsibility built into our government by the Federalists, plus the demonstrated ability to maintain ourselves by force of arms, gave the United States standing among the nations of the world.

c] A wave of nationalism swept over America. Pride in the United States as a nation hit a very high point. Political leaders spoke of themselves as citizens of America. They urged the people to think in terms of the nation as a whole and not to confine their loyalties or narrow their interests to their state or even to their section of the country. The Federalist Party committed its final act of self-destruction at the Hartford Convention. This fact was doubly clear, even to them, with the news of Jackson's triumph at New Orleans and the Treaty of Ghent. Only one party in the field, a great victory at New Orleans, and a peace treaty, combined to form a tidal wave of pride and patriotism. It ushered in the Era of Good Feelings.

A Chronology of Events in the War of 1812

Note especially the series of brilliant naval victories, but realize that they did not break the British blockade of our major Atlantic ports. News of these naval exploits were great morale boosters. American forces couldn't penetrate Canada. British forces couldn't effectively invade the United States.

1] *June 18, 1812* War was declared. The vote in the House of Representatives was 79 to 49 and the vote in the Senate was 19 to 13. Compare this with World War I when the House vote was 373 to 50 and the Senate vote was 82 to 6; or with the declaration of war on Japan after Pearl Harbor when the vote in the House produced only one negative vote and the vote in the Senate was unanimous. The War of 1812 started with a dangerously divided Congress and people.

2] *August 16, 1812* General William Hull surrendered Detroit to the British without firing a shot. He was court-martialed and dismissed from the army.

3] *August 19, 1812* Capt. Isaac Hull of the frigate *Constitution* destroyed the British frigate *Guerrière* off Nova Scotia.

4] *October 17, 1812* Capt. John Jacobs of the sloop *Wasp* defeated the British brig *Frolic* off the Virginia coast.

5] *October 25, 1812* Capt. Stephen Decatur of the frigate *United States* brought the British frigate *Macedonian* into New London after forcing her surrender off the coast of Morocco.

6] *December 29, 1812* Capt. William Bainbridge of the frigate *Constitution* destroyed the British frigate *Java* off the coast of Brazil. This slugging match at close range earned the *Constitution* its popular name, "Old Ironsides."

7] *April 27, 1813* Gen. Henry Dearborn and Capt. Isaac Chauncey crossed Lake Ontario from Sackett's Harbor and took York, the capital of Ontario. York is now Toronto. The governor's house and the government buildings were burned. The British raid on Washington and the burning of government buildings was claimed to be retaliation for this event.

8] *May 28-29, 1813* Gen. Jacob J. Brown repulsed a strong British attack on Sackett's Harbor in an attempt to invade the United States in force.

9] *June 1, 1813* The British frigate *Shannon* captured the American frigate *Chesapeake,* with Capt. James Lawrence in command. Capt. Lawrence died during the battle. His last order, "Don't give up the ship," became a slogan of the U.S. navy. It was inscribed on the flag of the battleship *Lawrence,* from which Capt. Oliver H. Perry directed the battle of Lake Erie.

10] *September 10, 1813* The battle of Lake Erie was fought near Put in Bay. Capt. Oliver H. Perry commanded 10 ships mounting 55 guns. The British had 6 ships mounting 65 guns. Perry's flagship, the *Lawrence,* was cut to pieces and 80% of her crew were casualties. Perry announced his victory with the message, "We have met the enemy and they are ours."

11] *October 5, 1813* Perry's victory on Lake Erie persuaded the British to evacuate Detroit. Major General William H. Harrison reoccupied Detroit and pursued the British northward into Canada. At the Thames River, east of Lake St. Clair, he defeated the enemy. The great Indian leader, Tecumseh, was killed in this battle. His death brought an end to Indian support of the British.

12] *July 25, 1814* Lundy's Lane, a little west of Niagara Falls and a few miles into Canada, was the most evenly fought and hardest fought land battle of the war. Both sides claim to have won it. The Americans with 2,600 men under Gen. Jacob Brown fought a British force of 3,000. After the battle was over, the Americans withdrew from the area.

13] *August 24-25, 1814* The British entered Washington on August 24th. They left on the next day. The approaches to Washington were very weakly defended. When the British arrived, the city had been evacuated. The Secretary of the Navy had burned the Navy Yard to prevent supplies falling to the enemy. The British continued the burning by setting fire to the White House, several government offices, some private homes, and the newspaper office.

14] *September 11, 1814* Capt. Thomas Macdonough drove the British off Lake Champlain. This victory by Macdonough's squadron stopped another British attempt to penetrate the United States. The engagement had lasted over two hours with the issue in doubt until Macdonough's flagship, the *Saratoga,* forced the surrender of the British flagship.

15] *September 13-14, 1814* The British approached Baltimore by land and sea. They found the defenses too well guarded. The bombardment of Fort McHenry by British ships inspired Francis Scott Key, an eyewitness, to write the words of the first stanza of the *Star Spangled Banner* during the cannonading which lasted, intermittently, over 24 hours. On March 3, 1931 Congress made the *Star Spangled Banner* our National Anthem.

16] *December 24, 1814* The Treaty of Ghent (Belgium) was agreed upon by representatives of the United States and England (see p. 91).

17] *January 8, 1815* Jackson defeated the British at New Orleans (see p. 91).

* The Hartford Convention (Dec. 15, 1814—Jan. 5, 1815)

The legislatures of Massachusetts, Connecticut, and Rhode Island elected delegates to this convention. New Hampshire and Vermont chose delegates by Federalist Party conventions. Hence, the delegates from the first three states were official representatives of the states, while those from New Hampshire and Vermont represented the Federalist Party only. This difference held no significance to the people of 1815, but it does make the resolutions of the Hartford Convention the official acts of Massachusetts, Connecticut, and Rhode Island.

The Massachusetts legislature sent out the call for such a convention in October. George Cabot of Massachusetts presided over the Convention. It was his leadership that curbed the more extreme Federalists and kept the resolutions clearly within legal bounds. The Hartford Convention was an assembly of angry men preparing a petition for redress of grievances accompanied by recommendations for relief therefrom. In view of the climate of opinion prevailing in southern New England the Hartford Convention displayed self-restraint and moderation.

The extreme Federalists openly expressed pleasure over the burning of Washington. Timothy Pickering, who had been Secretary of State in President Washington's second term and also under President John Adams, was proposing secession of New England from the Union. New England states refused to allow their militia to fight beyond the boundaries of their own states. An attack on Montreal was frustrated when units of state militia refused to cross the border into Canada. New York State militia joined with New England in this attitude. Smuggling goods to the British army and navy from New England and New York was a lucrative and widespread practice. It was "Madison's war." This was the atmosphere in which the Hartford Convention met.

The issue of secession was debated. The Convention rejected secession as inexpedient, not as unconstitutional. The Convention judged it to be inexpedient because the troubles of New England at the moment were due to a war in which the United States should play no part; or, if it did, it should be on the side of England against France. We were in the wrong war on the wrong side. New England's troubles, so they felt, also sprang from a weak and inept President. Bad as they were, the Convention recognized these misfortunes as temporary. Secession was too drastic a cure for faults that time and a few adjustments to the Constitution could remedy.

The most significant resolutions adopted by the Convention were proposals for amendments to the Constitution. They were as follows:

1] No embargoes shall last for more than 60 days.

2] A ⅔rds vote of each House of Congress shall be required to

   a. declare war. (This would have prevented the War of 1812.)
   b. place restriction on foreign trade.
   c. admit new states to the Union. (New states would be western agricultural states and therefore Republican.)

3] No naturalized citizen shall hold any federal office. (Almost all naturalized citizens would be Republicans.)

4] Direct taxes and representation in the House of Representatives shall be apportioned among the states according to the number of free inhabitants therein. (This would abolish the counting of ⅗ths of the slaves and thus reduce Congressional delegations from the South where the states were Republican.)

5] No President shall have more than one term. (The only President elected on the Federalist ticket, John Adams, served only one term. The other three Presidents had served two terms.)

6] No two successive Presidents shall be from the same state. (Washington, Jefferson, and Madison were Virginians.) New England was fed up with the "Virginia Dynasty."

Every one of the proposed amendments reflected partisan party politics. Under the circumstances of the moment they would benefit the Federalists. The comments in parentheses are intended to make this clear. Where there is no parenthesis the explanation seems unnecessary.

A committee of three, who called themselves "ambassadors," headed by Harrison Otis of Massachusetts, set out for Washington to "negotiate" with the federal government. News of Jackson's victory at New Orleans and of the Treaty of Ghent hit Washington at the same time Otis and his colleagues reached Baltimore on their way from Hartford. The "ambassadors" went home. Public ridicule and contempt were heaped upon the Federalists and their proposals. Many labeled them traitorous. While the Federalist Party continued as an organization in local elections, the Hartford Convention may well be considered its last act as a major party. President Washington had warned of the danger of excessive factionalism, of seeking party advantage regardless of national interests. No sooner was the advice given than the Federalists began to flout it. The Naturalization Act, the Alien Act, the Sedition Act, the "Midnight Judges," and the Hartford Convention were partisan tactics which disregarded the rights of individuals and the welfare of the nation. After having served the new Republic superbly for most of its first decade, the Federalist Party fell in love with itself and deservedly died.

* First Protective Tariff (1816)

The time had arrived when the ideas expressed by Hamilton in favor of protection became popular (see p. 74). From the Embargo Act of 1807 to the end of the War of 1812 the policies of our own government and the Napoleonic Wars combined to depress imports. Hostility toward England had created ill will toward British products. The spirit of unity and nationalism following the war smothered the sectionalism so characteristic of tariff legislation. The victory over the Indians at Tippecanoe in 1811, soon followed by the death of Tecumseh, greatly lessened the Indian menace in the Northwest Territory. People were moving west. Indiana became a state in 1816 and Illinois in 1818. The southwest was also growing; Louisiana had become a state in 1812, and Mississippi and Alabama would become states in 1817 and 1819. Holding the spreading population together became a common concern. The protective tariff seemed a good start. American manufacturers would have the domestic market relatively free from British competition. Agricultural America could feed the towns and cities and supply many of the raw products for factories. If highways, turnpikes, and canals, extending east and west, could be combined with a protective tariff program, the outlook for prosperity and unity seemed promising.

There were sharper and more demanding factors that favored a protective tariff. At the end of the war British merchantmen were ready to flood our markets with superior merchandise at prices the new and comparatively inefficient American manufacturer could not meet. Hundreds of small enterprises had been formed, especially in the North, to supply the demand created by the prolonged dearth in imports. Much of the capital that would normally have been employed in shipping went into manufacturing. The Pittsburg area had developed smelting to fill the demand when supplies of iron from Sweden and England dwindled. More sheep were being raised to replace the wool we used to get from England. Where smelting, sheep raising, and dozens of other enterprises had not yet started, there was eager expectation that something soon would. Every section of the nation either had enterprises to protect or believed it soon would have.

The average rates were about 25% ad valorum. The votes in Congress in favor of the bill came from all sections of the nation. Calhoun, soon to be the great Southern leader against protective tariffs, was working hand in hand with Clay in favor of this first protective tariff. Even Jefferson, who also changed his mind later, favored it. It was a very rare occasion when Jefferson favored a government policy aimed to assist the manufacturer.

James Monroe

1817-1825

1758 - 1831

REPUBLICAN

☆

Secretary of State JOHN QUINCY ADAMS

MONROE'S PUBLIC SERVICE BEFORE HE BECAME PRESIDENT

Revolutionary War record
  Fought at White Plains, Trenton (wounded), Brandywine, Germantown,
  and Monmouth
  Made a major during the winter at Valley Forge
  Member of the Virginia legislature
United States Senator
United States Minister to France (1794-1796)
Governor of Virginia
Special envoy to France at the time of the Louisiana Purchase (1803)
United States Minister to England (1803-1806)
Secretary of State under Madison (1811-1817) and also Secretary of War (1814-1815)

MAJOR ITEMS OF MONROE'S ADMINISTRATIONS

Marshall's Decisions
  McCulloch v. Maryland
  Dartmouth College Case
  Gibbons v. Ogden
Acquisition of Florida from Spain (1819)
Missouri Compromise (1820)
Monroe Doctrine (1823)
Sectional Tariff (1824)
Favorite Sons Election (Jackson, J. Q. Adams, Crawford, Clay) (1824)

Election and Re-election of Monroe (1816 and 1820)

The unpopularity of the Federalist Party resulting from their opposition to the War of 1812 gave Monroe an easy victory. The electoral vote was Monroe, 183; Rufus King (N.Y.), 34.

The re-election of Monroe was unchallenged. He got 231 electoral votes. Three electors didn't vote and one voted for John Quincy Adams. This reserved to Washington the distiction of being the only presidential candidate to receive a unanimous vote of the Electoral College.

* Marshall's Decisions

These decisions built prestige for the Supreme Court and set a pattern that was followed for many years. The Republican Party controlled the Congress and the Executive Department. Most of the judges of the Supreme Court were Republican appointees, but they had accepted both the intellectual leadership and the personal persuasiveness of the Chief Justice. Marshall thought the nation ought to be run by a strong central government to which the states would play strictly second fiddle. As we noticed, the Federalist Party was dead; but, with Marshall on the Supreme Court for 34 years, Federalist principles were being woven into the fabric of our financial, business, and commercial life.

McCulloch v. Maryland

The State of Maryland passed a law to serve the interests of the local banks chartered by the state. These state banks had always resented the favored position of the Bank of the United States. Seven other states passed similar restrictive laws to embarrass the B.U.S. and its branches. The test case came when the cashier, McCulloch, of the Baltimore branch of the B.U.S., refused to comply with the Maryland law. The law required that any bank in Maryland not chartered by the state must print its bank notes on special stamped paper at excessive costs. This was, in effect, a stamp tax. As an alternative, the "foreign" bank could pay an annual fee of $15,000. There was a fine of $500 for each note printed improperly.

The attorneys for Maryland challenged the constitutionality of the B.U.S. All of the Hamilton-Jefferson arguments were re-aired (p. 75). The Court accepted the "loose construction" reasoning of Hamilton and declared constitutional the law of Congress which had established the Second Bank of the United States.

The Maryland law with its restrictions, fees and fines not only could have destroyed the Baltimore branch of the B.U.S., but was intended to do so. Here was a direct conflict between the state law of Maryland and the law of Congress, a state law which destroyed what a federal law had created. In such a conflict of legal authorities the *Supreme Law of the Land Clause* of the Constitution clearly directs that the state law shall be declared null and void. Marshall so declared with the unanimous approval of the associate justices.

The Dartmouth College Case

The trustees of Dartmouth College split into two factions. One wished to continue the college as a private institution; the other wished the State of New Hampshire to take it over. The latter faction won support in the legislature which passed a law changing Dartmouth College to Dartmouth University, a state institution. The highest court of New Hampshire declared this action legal. An appeal was made to the Supreme Court.

Marshall accepted the contention of the lawyers opposing the State of New Hampshire, one of whom was Daniel Webster, that the original charter granted by the king to the trustees of Dartmouth College in 1769 was a contract. This charter remained in force after the Revolution as a contract between the State of New Hampshire and the Dartmouth trustees. Under powers denied to the states, the Constitution provides that no state shall "pass any law impairing the obligation of contracts." Thus, a direct conflict was established between a clause in the Constitution and a law of New Hampshire. *The Supreme Law of the Land Clause* directs that state laws in conflict with the Constitution must be declared null and void. Dartmouth remained a private college.

Gibbons v. Ogden

The New York legislature granted a franchise to Fulton and Livingston allowing them a monopoly of steamboat transportation on New York waters. Every additional steamboat operated by Fulton and Livingston would extend the monopoly for five years, but such a monopoly could not exceed thirty years. There was a scramble for the ferry business between New York City and points in New Jersey. A rash of state laws broke out. New Jersey, Connecticut, Georgia, Massachusetts, New Hampshire, Tennessee, Pennsylvania, and Vermont passed laws granting special privileges to their citizens to operate steamboats and providing penalties against nonresidents. The new invention in water transport seemed about to become a force for disunity among the states.

Under their franchise from New York State, Fulton and Livingston could sell a license to others to operate steamboats. Ogden had bought a license from them to operate between New York City and New Jersey. Gibbons had a license from the United States to operate steamboats along the coast. Ogden got a New York court to enjoin Gibbons from operating his boats, whereupon Gibbons appealed to the United States Supreme Court.

Marshall ruled that the New York franchise affected interstate commerce and was "repugnant to the Constitution" because it violated the clause which allows Congress to regulate commerce among the several states. He also ruled that New York had violated the clause in the Constitution which authorizes Congress to promote the progress of science and the useful arts.

Acquisition of Florida from Spain (1819)

During the War of 1812 a fort had been built at the mouth of the Apalachicola River on the Gulf coast of Florida. It had become a hangout for escaped slaves, border ruffians, and hostile Indians. In 1816 United States forces, acting under official orders, penetrated Spanish Florida and destroyed the fort. The next year General Andrew Jackson was put in command of the Georgia border patrol forces with orders permitting him to penetrate Florida in pursuit of hostile elements. Jackson wrote to President Monroe saying that if the United States desired Florida, he could take it in sixty days. There was no response to this letter. Jackson apparently assumed that silence meant consent. In the spring of 1818 he pursued hostile Indians into Florida for about 175 miles and took Pensacola. On the way, two English traders, Ambrister and Arbuthnot, were captured and executed after Jackson had them court-martialed. They were charged with stirring up the Indians and "aiding the enemy." British newspapers expressed indignation, but the British ministry, after a formal inquiry, made no complaint. Public opinion in the United States, especially in the West, acclaimed Jackson a hero. Senate and House committees reported unfavorably on Jackson's action. Several members of the cabinet urged disciplinary action against him. But President Monroe and Secretary of State John Q. Adams realized that this strong action improved our position in pending negotiations with Spain. In February, 1819, the United States and Spain reached agreement. Florida (East and West) was to belong to the United States. We gave up our claim to Texas and accepted responsibility for claims by people in Florida against Spain up to $5,000,000. The Spanish Step Line was established. It marked a definite western boundary to the Louisiana Territory from the mouth of the Sabine River in a series of steps to the 42nd parallel. As of 1819 the area south of the Step Line was Spanish and the area north of it was the Louisiana Territory and the Oregon Territory. Oregon was then in dispute between England and the United States.

* The Missouri Compromise (1820)

In 1820 there were 11 free and 11 slave states in the Union. Because of the greater population in the North, the 11 free states had 105 seats in the House to 81 seats for the slave states. The South was determined to maintain equal voting power in the Senate. The people of Maine petitioned Congress for admission as a state. Massachusetts had agreed to such a separation. Missouri petitioned Congress for admission. Perhaps, as had happened several times in the past, a slave and a free state could have been admitted without any political explosions if Representative Tallmadge of New York had not introduced an amendment to the bill for the admission of Missouri.

The *Tallmadge Amendment* would have prohibited any additional slaves entering Missouri and would have declared free on their 25th birthday any slaves born in Missouri after it became a state. It passed the House by a close vote, but was easily defeated in the Senate. A furious political storm broke. The slave states held that Congress had no right to attach conditions upon a state applying for admission. It could admit or refuse to admit, but it could not dictate social and economic conditions. If Congress had any such power it could create a class of inferior states and utterly destroy the sovereign equality of the states so essential to a federal union. But the free states pointed to the Northwest Ordinance which had set a precedent by forbidding slavery in the territories, and states to be made therefrom, at the same time that it guaranteed their equality with the original states. It is to be noted here that the fight was over political power of the two blocs of states, free and slave. The Northeast was anxious to break the domination of Virginia in national affairs; the South was fearful that westward expansion and the more rapidly growing population in the North would swing the balance of political power against her. Feelings were high, but the debate did not concern itself with the moral aspects of slavery. So long as this was true, the fireworks could be confined to Congress, to governors, and to state legislatures. Jockeying for political power was not likely to stir deeply the emotions of the people, and politicians can usually manage a compromise.

The compromise reached was that Maine should be admitted to the Union as a free state and Missouri as a slave state. The political balance in the Senate was maintained. As Missouri was the first state completely west of the Mississippi River and wholly within the Louisiana Territory, a decision was made to set the pattern for the rest of the Territory. This decision was that south of the parallel 36°30' within the Louisiana Territory slavery would be legal, but that north of this parallel, except in Missouri, slavery would be prohibited. The southern border of the new State of Missouri was on the 36°30' parallel.

The portentious threat lurking in this controversy did not go unobserved. Jefferson wrote, "This momentous question, like a fire bell in the night, awakened and filled me with terror. I considered it at once as the knell of the Union." And John Quincy Adams wrote in his diary, "I take it for granted that the present question is a mere preamble—a title page to a great, tragic volume." Congressman Cobb of Georgia accused Tallmadge of starting "a fire that only seas of blood could extinguish."

** Monroe Doctrine (1823)

The Monroe Doctrine grew out of a European situation. After Napoleon's defeat, the Congress of Vienna, 1814 and 1815, rearranged Europe to suit England, Russia, Austria, and Prussia. Having undone the work of Napoleon as much as they could on the continent, the next order of business was to straighten out the chaos that had resulted in the Spanish Empire from Mexico to the tip of South America. Able revolutionary leaders such as Simón Bolívar, José San Martín, and Bernardo O'Higgins were changing colonies into republics. Revolutions were in progress when the Congress of Vienna adjourned.

England had established a very lucrative trade with the new republics. Englishmen had invested substantially in mining rights. There was great promise of expansion for English trade and investment. With all the other governments of Europe, England shared an intense dislike of republics. One in the world, the United States, was enough. But the commercial opportunities were so real and vast that England decided to go for the business and tolerate the new republics.

Russia, Austria, and Prussia, the Holy Alliance, wished England to join with them in a reconquest of the Spanish Empire in the Americas. England rejected the idea. Without the support of the British fleet the Holy Alliance would be unable to carry through such a project.

The United States was negotiating the acquisition of Florida and the Step Line Boundary was finally fixed in 1819. Until that was complete and its ratification by our Senate assured, Monroe and his Secretary of State, J. Q. Adams, made no move toward recognition of the new republics to the south. However, with ratification of the Spanish treaty, the United States promptly extended recognition and arranged to send ministers and consuls to their capitals.

George Canning, the British Foreign Secretary, suggested to our ambassador, Richard Rush, that the United States join with England in telling the Holy Alliance, and any other powers in Europe, to refrain from any attack upon the ex-Spanish Empire in the western hemisphere. When this idea got to President Monroe he submitted it to two elder statesmen, Jefferson and Madison. Monroe liked the idea and so stated to both men. Both of them were warm in their approval of this English idea. But the Yankee, J. Q. Adams, reckoned on it a bit. He wondered when Cuba would break away from Spanish control. It could fall into England's lap. Would it not be wiser to act independently of England and deliver to Europe, including England, the message that the United States would look with displeasure at any interference by them with the independence of any republic in the western hemisphere? At the moment, England would favor such a policy even though she might be surprised that we made the declaration alone instead of with her as she suggested. There was really very little danger of any attack by the con-

tinental powers of Europe. If such an attack did occur, England could squelch it. John Q. Adams pressed his point on the cabinet and President Monroe. He won. As he expressed it, "It would seem more candid, as well as more dignified, to avow our principles explicitly to Great Britain and France, than to come in as a cockboat in the wake of the British man-of-war." Thus was a guiding principle of our foreign policy adopted.

In his annual message to Congress, December 2, 1823, President Monroe included the Monroe Doctrine. It is still a live issue. Read the following quotations from it and form a judgment concerning its applicability to present situations.

". . . the American continents, by the free and independent condition which they have assumed and maintain, are henceforth not to be considered as subjects for future colonization by any European powers . . ."

"In the wars of the European powers in matters relating to themselves we have never taken any part, nor does it comport with our policy so to do."

"We owe it, therefore, to candor and to the amicable relations existing between the United States and those powers to declare that we should consider any attempt on their part to extend their system to any portion of this hemisphere as dangerous to our peace and safety."

"With the existing colonies or dependencies of any European powers we have not interfered and shall not interfere."

". . . we could not view any interposition for the purpose of oppressing them, or controlling in any other manner their destiny, by any European power in any other light than as the manifestation of an unfriendly disposition toward the United States."

"Our policy in regard to Europe is . . . not to interfere in the internal concerns of any of its powers."

"It is impossible that the allied powers should extend their political system to any portion of either continent without endangering our peace and happiness." (What allied powers? What continents?)

* Sectional Tariff (1824)

In the eight years separating the tariff of 1816 from that of 1824 the South, especially South Carolina, had discovered that textile mills were not going to locate next to the cotton fields. Cotton was moving away from the Atlantic seaboard because repeated cultivation of the same soil without crop rotation or proper use of fertilizers greatly reduced the yield per acre. The few attempts to establish cotton mills had failed. The slave labor force proved unsuitable for factory work. In the South neither the investment capital to establish the cotton mills nor the capable managers to run them were readily available.

Only in combination with a system of highways linking the East, South, and West could the protective tariff be effective in building the nation as a whole. Only then could the products of each section find markets in the other two areas; the prosperity of one would then tend to be reflected in the others. The effect on business of the tariff of 1816 was immediate, but no east-west highways could be built immediately. All the benefits of the tariff were felt in the Northeast while the South was learning that its hopes for industrial development were not to be fulfilled. So, by 1824, Calhoun, who earlier had gone along with Clay's advocacy of protective tariffs and roads, had become opposed to both. In another four years he would be bitterly opposed. Calhoun expressed the position of the South. He saw the protective tariff as a device which raised the cost of living by increasing the price of manufactured articles from bassinets to caskets. A program of turnpikes built at federal expense would mean a tax burden on the South out of proportion to any benefits received by the South. Worst of all, vast building projects planned and paid for by the federal government would concentrate in Washington legal authority and political power which properly belonged to the individual states. At just about the same time that the South was turning against protective tariffs, Clay was advocating his three-point "American System": internal improvements at federal expense, the Bank of the United States, and protective tariffs. The harmonious note of national unity reflected by the Tariff of 1816 had changed to the discordant note of sectional strife reflected by the Tariff of 1824.

The Tariff of 1824 passed Congress with the vote clearly emphasizing the sectional interests of the Northeast and the South. The political balance of power was held by the West. If the South or the Northeast could gain the support of the West, it could control Congress and put its program into law. That was essentially the situation brought clearly to view by the *Sectional Tariff of 1824*.

* Favorite Sons Elections (Jackson, J. Q. Adams, Crawford, Clay) (1824)

All the candidates were Republicans. William Crawford (Georgia) had been chosen in the usual manner, by Congressional caucus. The other candidates represented sections of the country. Jackson (Tennessee) and Clay (Kentucky) were spokesmen for the West. J. Q. Adams (Massachusetts) represented the Northeast. Crawford was stricken with a serious illness during the campaign. Jackson was the hero of New Orleans and Florida. He was the man of action, the fighter both for his country and for himself. He had fought several duels and had killed one opponent. Jackson was the most popular candidate. Clay had a distinguished career in Congress and possessed more personal charm than any of the others. Adams had the most impressive record of public service. The election results were as follows:

	Popular Vote	Electoral Vote
Jackson	155,872	99
Adams	105,321	84
Crawford	44,282	41
Clay	46,587	37

No candidate had received the necessary majority of electoral votes. As provided in the 12th Amendment, the election went to the House of Representatives where each state had one vote. Each state delegation in Congress had to caucus to decide how to cast its one vote. Clay was out of the race as only the top three candidates were eligible. Clay was Speaker of the House. His influence was considerable. Upon his advice Adams was elected. On the first ballot thirteen states voted for Adams, seven for Jackson, and four for Crawford. Calhoun had considered being a fifth candidate for the presidency but had changed his mind and campaigned for the vice-presidency. He won easily with 182 electoral votes.

Under the best of circumstances this outcome would have been hard to accept. Many felt that there was a moral obligation on the part of the House of Representatives to elect Jackson because he had received the largest vote, both electoral and popular. As it was, Clay had decided the election. When President Adams appointed Clay Secretary of State the *Era of Good Feelings* was blown to dust. When the dust settled there were two political parties, National Republicans and Democratic Republicans, ushering in an *Era of Hard Feelings*. The Jackson supporters and many thousands of others believed the charge of "corrupt bargain" justified. The charge was that Adams and Clay had plotted to bring about the result. There had been no evidence that such an understanding had been in effect. The verdict of history is that there was no bargain of any kind. Clay supported Adams instead of Jackson because the two men were in agreement on public policy. Adams was an ardent supporter of *Clay's American System*. In Clay's mind, Jackson was too much the military man and, for other reasons, unsuited to be President. Adams asked Clay to be Secretary of State because he con-sidered Clay best qualified for the post. It was as simple and politically inept as that! John Q. Adams had a term in office as President, but the people were just biding their time until 1828. It was an open secret that Jackson would be the next Presi-dent.

John Quincy Adams

1767 - 1848

NATIONAL REPUBLICAN

☆

Vice-President JOHN C. CALHOUN

Secretary of State HENRY CLAY

ADAMS' PUBLIC SERVICE BEFORE HE BECAME PRESIDENT

Minister to the Netherlands (1794-96)
Minister to Prussia (1797-1801)
Minister to Russia (1809-14)
Minister to Great Britain (1815-17)
Secretary of State under President Monroe

MAJOR ITEMS OF ADAMS' ADMINISTRATION

New York State's Erie Canal
Tariff of Abominations (1828)
Calhoun's Exposition and Protest

New York State's Erie Canal

The first great east-west highway in the United States was the Erie Canal. It was completed in 1825. It was wholly within the State of New York and was paid for by the state. Taxes and lotteries raised the $7,000,000 it cost to make a 363 mile ditch 4 feet deep and 40 feet wide. It had 82 locks to raise boats a total of 571 feet between the Hudson River and Buffalo. It was by far the most comfortable and quickest way for passenger travel over such a distance. Costs for freight were cut as much as 90 per cent. Passenger fares were about a cent and a half a mile. From New York City to Buffalo was a five-day trip as the barges were pulled along the canal by horses on the tow paths.

A look at the map shows that the Mississippi River and its great tributaries form a splendid transportation system converging on New Orleans. It was apparently Mother Nature's inclination to draw commerce from the Great Lakes regions and the Ohio Valley southward. That was the direction of trade before the Erie Canal. But with the new route from Buffalo to Albany the traffic turned eastward. The population was to the east, the best markets were to the east, and the best approach to Europe was to the east. The Erie Canal bound the West to the Northeast much more effectively than the Mississippi River tied the West to the South.

Before the Erie Canal the port of New Orleans held promise of being the busiest port in the United States. After the Erie Canal the city of New York was an easy winner. Boston, Philadelphia, Baltimore, Charleston, and New Orleans all grew more slowly as a result of Governor Clinton's ditch. But the economic pull of the Erie Canal was not the whole story. Commercial ties form political ties. The political struggle between the Northeast and the South for the support of the West in their increasingly bitter conflict over commercial *vs.* agrarian interests, over increasing federal power *vs.* states rights, over interpretation of the Constitution, and finally over slavery were also part of the Erie Canal story. The Northeast and the West were brought closer together while the South was slipping into isolation.

* Tariff of Abominations (1828)

The political lesson the South learned from the Tariff of 1824 was plain. It showed that the South would lose in both the House of Representatives and the Senate in any vote on the issue of protection. The pro-tariff Congressmen not only outnumbered the anti-tariff members in 1824 and 1828, but the number of protective tariff Congressmen would continue to increase. The Northeast and the West were growing closer together economically,

101

as compared with the South and the West. There was every prospect that several new states would be formed from the northern areas of the Northwest Territory and the Louisiana Territory. Michigan entered the Union in 1837, Iowa in 1846, and Minnesota in 1858. While, in 1828, it could not have been known that these states would enter the Union precisely when they actually did, it was impossible not to see that such additions were part of the near future. The political outlook for the South was bleak. Only Arkansas, and possibly Kansas, could have been recognized as potential new States to give political support to the Southern way of life.

There was one tactic that might bring victory to the South. That was trickery. To defeat a protective tariff they must outsmart the opposition. Their attempt to do this resulted in the Tariff of Abominations of 1828. As this tariff bill was whipped into shape by the several committees working on it, the Southern Congressmen supported ample protective rates for most manufactured products of the Northeast, and ridiculously high protective rates for raw products which were vital to manufacturing. The resulting high prices the manufactures would have to pay for raw materials would rob them of much, if not all, of the advantages they would receive from the protection afforded their own products. This tactic, the South hoped, would so disgust several Congressmen from the Northeast that they would vote against the bill. The Southerners would also vote against it. This combined vote might defeat this obviously abominable tariff. Before the bill came to a vote, it was widely recognized for what it was—a political scheme which made no economic sense from anyone's point of view. It failed. The House vote was 105 to 94; the Senate 26 to 21. Under Vice-President Calhoun's leadership the South had dug a hole, fallen into it, and pulled the dirt in over itself. In South Carolina flags were flown at half-mast. There was talk of boycotts against New England's manufactured goods. Refusal to obey the new tariff law was seriously considered. Some even began to question the value of remaining in the Union. Calhoun sensed a deeper rift between North and South than tariff. In 1830 Calhoun said that the basic cause of the growing friction was "the *peculiar domestic institutions* of the Southern States."

** Calhoun's Exposition and Protest (1828) and South Carolina's Nullification Act (1832)

Defeated by a straightforward vote in Congress in 1824, victimized by its own political trickery in 1828, there was one more tactic available to the

South, and that one Calhoun proceded to use. He discovered that protective tariffs were unconstitutional. The Kentucky and Virginia Resolutions framed by Jefferson and Madison gave him all the arguments he needed, although he did extend them a bit. The reasoning followed these lines.

1] The Constitution is a compact (an agreement) among several sovereign states.

This assertion could be defended by the following points. States sent delegates to the Constitutional Convention. Compromises were worked out between large and small states, agrarian and commercial states, free and slave states. The Constitution was ratified by states. It became effective when 9 states had accepted it. It was not the government of the other 4 states until they individually ratified it. Everything about its formation and adoption was done in terms of states.

2] The federal government has only those powers delegated to it by the Constitution. (10th Amendment)

3] The power to regulate foreign commerce was clearly intended to be a means "Of extending commerce, by coercing foreign nations to a fair reciprocity in their intercourse with us," and only "incidentally connected with the encouragement of agriculture and manufactures."

4] No mention is made in the Constitution about power to nullify a law of Congress, nor about the right of a state to withdraw from the Union. All powers not denied to the states and not granted to the federal government, belong to the states. (10th Amendment)

The above four points express the Calhoun, Hayne, Davis thinking on the nature of the Union. Calhoun's Exposition and Protest, Hayne's arguments in the Webster-Hayne debate, and South Carolina's Nullification Act were the vehicles which gave effective expression to them.

Calhoun's discovery that a protective tariff was unconstitutional rests on the fact that a tariff is a tax. The Constitution says that taxes may be levied for only three purposes: to pay the public debt, to provide for the common defense, and to promote the general welfare. A protective tariff is intended to keep goods from entering the country. If it accomplishes this purpose, it raises no revenue, or does so only incidentally and in small amounts. Hence a protective tariff obviously is not a tax for raising money to pay debts or to build defenses. It is equally clear that a protective tariff promotes sectional division, that it seriously threatens the harmony of the Union, and therefore it can not promote the general welfare. Being a tax for a purpose *not* in the Constitution, it is therefore unconstitutional. Acting on this theory South Carolina passed the Nullification Act in November 1832.

** An Answer to Calhoun, Hayne, and Davis

1] The Constitution is not a compact of sovereign states. "We the people . . . do ordain and establish this Constitution." (See pp. 55-56 for support of this point.)

2] Control over foreign commerce is granted in the Constitution to Congress. The word *commerce* was given a very broad interpretation by the Supreme Court in the *Gibbons* v. *Ogden Case*. It certainly included regulation of imports.

3] Acceptance of the right of a state to nullify a law of Congress would soon result in utter confusion. Federal laws recognized in one state would not be recognized in other states. Eventually there would be as many interpretations of the federal Constitution as there were states.

4] The right of a state to secede from the Union contradicts the very purpose of the Constitution. "To form a more perfect Union" was the historical reason for abandoning the Articles of Confederation and became the first aim of the Constitution as stated in the Preamble. As a pure debating point there may be something to be said for the secession argument. But the inevitable result of acting upon any such theory would be the destruction of the Union. As Webster put it, the Union would become "a rope of sand." With the possible exception of South Carolina, no Southern state in 1832 was willing to entertain any such extreme position. It was to be almost three decades before South Carolina could mislead some of her neighboring states out of the Union.

Andrew Jackson 1829-1837

1767 - 1845

DEMOCRAT

☆

Vice-President JOHN C. CALHOUN
MARTIN VAN BUREN

JACKSON'S PUBLIC SERVICE BEFORE HE BECAME PRESIDENT

U.S. Senator from Tennessee (1797)
Judge of the Tennessee Supreme Court
Major General and Hero at the Battle of New Orleans (1815)
Led the Conquest of Florida (1818)
Military Governor of Florida (1823)
U.S. Senator from Tennessee (1823-25)

MAJOR ITEMS OF JACKSON'S ADMINISTRATIONS

Jacksonian Democracy
Tariffs of 1832 and 1833
The Second Bank of the United States
Formation of the Whig Party

Jackson's Election (1828) and Re-election (1832)

The campaign of 1828 revived the "corrupt bargain" cry against President Adams who was running for re-election. Adams simply didn't have a chance. The hero of New Orleans and of Florida was clearly the people's favorite. As they saw it, he had been cheated in 1824 and now it was time for him to become President. The popular vote for Jackson was 647,231, for Adams 509,097; the electoral vote, Jackson 178, Adams 83.

The re-election of Jackson in 1832 was an even more crushing defeat of the National Republican Party led by Henry Clay. The popular vote for Jackson was 687,502, for Clay 530,189; the electoral vote, Jackson 219, Clay 49. The Second B.U.S. was the great issue on which Jackson and Clay campaigned. On this issue Clay made more sense and had much the better cause. It is doubtful that the voters registered any decision other than that they still liked Andrew Jackson very much.

** Jacksonian Democracy

Andrew Jackson was the first President that the people could feel was one of them. His parents had been immigrants from northern Ireland who had settled in a backwoods area of South Carolina where Jackson was born. At the age of 14 he had been a prisoner of the British during the Revolution. Story has it that at this fairly tender age he defied a British officer when told to polish shoes and received a blow with a sword which left a life-long scar on his head. He also carried two bullets in his body, one in his chest and one in his left arm. These were mementoes from duels. The scar and bullets suggest that Andrew Jackson grew up taking no nonsense nor indignities from anyone. This tough man was no bully. His ethical code in private life was above reproach. He was the victim of vicious slander because his marriage took place a few weeks before his wife had obtained a divorce from her first husband. It was a legal tangle resulting from misinformation under circumstances such as no blame, even of carelessness, could possibly be justly attached to either Jackson or his wife. His climb to prominence in law, in war, and in politics brought wealth, but he was still a frontiersman in outlook. His integrity was as real and obvious as his courage. *Old Hickory* was the affectionate name given him by the soldiers at New Orleans. It was a good description. Jackson couldn't bend and he wouldn't break. All preceding Presidents had been from what the voters of America considered the aristocracy of Virginia and Massachusetts. Now they had a man from west of the Alleghenies, a man whose boyhood and youth had been as devoid of gracious living as that of most families throughout rural America in the early 1800's. The elevation of such a man to the White House gave a new spirit to the nation which proved fertile soil for reform movements, political, economic, and social. One can't say that Jackson caused these developments. One, at least, he did not approve—the abolition movement. The total effect of these developments which were either instituted in the 1820's and 1830's, or became prominently active then, is what we mean by Jacksonian Democracy.

1] *King Caucus* was replaced by the nominating convention. Crawford was the last presidential candidate to be selected by a caucus of the leading members of his party in Congress. The nominating convention was organized by the political party. We are still not satisfied with the workings of presidential nominating conventions, but the change from caucus to convention did bring into use a political device capable of shifting the selection of candidates from a few party leaders to a substantial segment of the party membership.

2] States that were still choosing their Presidential electors by their legislatures changed to the democratic system of direct election by the voters.

3] The remnants of religious qualifications for voting which still prevailed in some states were dropped. In many states property qualifications were greatly reduced or eliminated.

4] The *Spoils System* was praised by Jackson. He thought that the party that won the election should have its members appointed to government jobs. He believed that the demands made upon public officials could be met adequately by almost any ordinary citizen. While such an opinion would be ridiculous if applied to the complexities of today, it was a tenable position for the 1830's. Jackson's contention that rotation in office achieved a superior quality of democracy by developing more citizens versed in the arts of government was a bit thin. But the fact is that Jackson did not practice rotation in office to any unusual degree. Professors Morison and Commager point out that Jackson, during the eight years he was in office, removed only one employee out of every six, a record much the same as under President Jeffer-

son. Certainly Jackson made no attempt to build a political machine through the spoils system. New jobs and vacancies were filled with loyal party workers. "To the victor belong the spoils" made sense to Jackson. That his name is so closely associated with the *Spoils System* stems from his open and direct praise of it as a desirable technique of democracy, rather than from any extraordinary extension of its use during his administrations.

5] Labor unions began to seek political power. The first labor group to organize as a political force was in Philadelphia. In the late 1820's they had representatives on the city council. Similar progress was made in Boston and New York. These early unions were in the northern states in the larger cities. They worked for reforms such as the abolition of imprisonment for debt, free education for all, abolition of prison contract labor, laws against taking a craftsman's tools in payment of debt, and for a 10 hour day to replace the usual 12 hour day. All of these labor activities were on the city and state levels. Laws varied widely from state to state. In 1842 a strike was illegal in New York State, but legal in Massachusetts. The panic of 1837, with its unemployment and severe wage cuts, put an abrupt end to organized labor. The Jacksonian Era witnessed a spurt of labor organization that made a lively little flare and then died down. The real struggle of labor for recognition and rights did not get under way until after the Civil War.

6] Social reform was part of Jacksonian Democracy.

Dorothea Dix made people realize that the insane needed hospitalization rather than imprisonment. She also started the movement for prison reform.

Emma Willard founded the Troy Female Seminary at Troy, N.Y. in 1821. It was the first women's college in the United States. It is now the Emma Willard School.

Oberlin College became the first co-educational college in 1834.

Mary Lyon founded Mount Holyoke Seminary in 1837. It is now Mount Holyoke College.

The *American Temperance Union* held its first national convention in 1836. The Washington Temperance Society, organized in 1840, was a group of reformed drunkards which spread the gospel of abstinence. Perhaps they could be considered the forerunner of the modern Alcoholics Anonymous.

The *Grimké Sisters,* Sarah and Angelina, freed their slaves and left their homes in South Carolina to preach the cause of abolition. Both sisters were

Quakers, a small sect which made a large contribution to the leadership of humanitarian reforms.

Frances (Fanny) Wright set up a colony of free negroes near Memphis, Tennessee. The pressure of public and official opinion forced its abandonment. The negroes were transferred to Haiti. Frances Wright lectured and wrote in support of women's rights, labor unions, free public education, and against slavery.

Lucretia Mott opposed slavery and supported equal rights for women. She, with Elizabeth Cady Stanton, wrote a *Declaration of Sentiments* which was closely modeled on the Declaration of Independence. It made as good a case for equal rights for women as Jefferson's masterpiece had done for independence of the colonies. Lucretia Mott had attended a Friends' (Quaker) school and married a prominent Quaker, James Mott.

William Lloyd Garrison was the most effective spokesman against slavery. His paper, the *Liberator,* first appeared in Boston in 1831 and continued for 35 years with Garrison as its editor. He described the Constitution as "a covenant with death and an agreement with hell." He observed the 4th of July in 1854 by publicly burning the Constitution. As he dropped it in the flames he said, "So perish all compromises with tyranny." From time to time mobs raided his printing establishment. His frequent public speeches sometimes set off riots. With the cause of abolition won by the Civil War, Garrison turned to temperance reform and votes for women. Although Garrison is a part of the story of Jacksonian Democracy, he is one reformer Jackson might well have preferred to meet in a duel than at the dinner table. Jackson owned slaves and believed thoroughly in slavery. In his retirement at the *Hermitage,* near Nashville, his relationship with his slaves was as fine a one as the inherently evil institution permitted.

7] Free Public Education was extended.

Horace Mann organized a public school system in Massachusetts in the late 1830's and middle 1840's that greatly influenced public education throughout the United States. The first high school in the nation was in Boston (1821). In 1827 every town of 500 families or over had to have a high school. The first normal school, a training school for teachers, was established at Lexington in 1839. While Massachusetts took the lead in free public education under the guidance of Horace Mann, New York State was a rather close second in following her example. Workingmen's organizations in the cities of the Northeast were the most active groups supporting the creation and extension of free public schools.

William Ladd played a leading part in the forming of the *American Peace Society* in 1828 which called for a congress of nations and an international court. The idea that there must be some way other than war as a last resort for settling disputes among nations is an old one, much older than the American Peace Society. It is also as recent as the League of Nations and as current as the United Nations. Does it illustrate the immortality of truth or merely the persistence of error?

8] The spirit of democracy in the Jacksonian Era accepted and especially included the mill hand and the factory wage earners, the men without roots in a community through lack of ownership of their home. Such wage earners were usually illiterate and usually so close to poverty that a few weeks without a pay envelope put their families among the destitute. Jefferson had foreseen that a time would come when a large part of our population would be such people. He believed they would become the dupes of demagogues and a danger to the state. The "common man" in whom Jefferson placed his faith was usually illiterate, but he was a land owning farmer who had to pay taxes. He valued government for the protection of his property and he favored an inexpensive government because he had to pay for it. When Jackson was President the "common man" was under neither the conservative influence of owning property nor the restraining influence of paying taxes. The dangers Jefferson saw seemed to Jackson not to exist. Democracy in the United States still left no group outside the pale except the slaves.

* Tariffs of 1832 and 1833

We noted that when the Tariff of 1828, the Tariff of Abominations, was passed, the South had become the victim of its own scheming (see pp. 101-102). It did, however, have one hope left. That was that the incoming President, Jackson, would reflect the tariff views common to most people of the South and Southwest. But President Jackson kept out of tariff-making. He was not impressed by the arguments either pro or con on the issue of protective tariffs. His position was that he, as President, would accept any tariff policy the Congress saw fit to enact into law and he would see to it that the law was enforced. Congress passed the Tariff of 1832 which was an unimportant modification of the Tariff of Abominations. Calhoun resigned from the Vice-Presidency and entered the United States Senate. The split between Jackson and Calhoun fed upon both public and personal issues. Calhoun's *Exposition* and South Carolina's Nullification Act were flatly rejected by Jackson.

Mrs. Calhoun seemed to be the leader among the wives of the President's official family in pointed and repeated refusals to accept socially Mrs. Eaton, (Peggy O'Neal Eaton) wife of the Secretary of War. Mrs. Eaton had been a friend of the late Mrs. Jackson, who had died a short time before her husband's inauguration in 1829. This social tempest swirling around the White House caught Jackson's attention and didn't help Calhoun. Jackson had believed that Calhoun had defended him at the time of the Florida episode (1818), but now Jackson was shown a letter written by Calhoun at the time, which condemned Jackson and had recommended disciplinary action against him. Jackson presented the letter to Calhoun who was unable to deny it. The Jackson-Calhoun break was not only a political difference of opinion, it was a bitter personal feud.

The Nullification Act was a threat by South Carolina that she would not permit import duties to be collected within her borders in accordance with the tariff law. Jackson was determined that she would. He asked Congress for a power which he already possessed, the power to use whatever force might be necessary in order to carry out the laws of the United States. In passing this *Force Bill* in March 1833 by overwhelming majorities (Senate 32-1; House 149-47), the Congress was telling South Carolina and Calhoun that they had no sympathy with nullification and the state's intention not to obey the tariff law. Passed at the same time was *Clay's Compromise Tariff of 1833.* This provided for automatic annual reductions of tariff rates for ten years, so that at the end of this period the rates would be approximately at the moderate protective level of 1816. This "saved face" for Calhoun and South Carolina and was quite satisfactory to the President whose whole point had been that the law would be enforced in South Carolina. The doctrine of nullification and the claim that protective tariffs were unconstitutional were dropped, at least for the time being.

* The Second Bank of the United States

This bank had been established in 1816 by the Republican Party, the same party which, under Jefferson, had so vigorously opposed the First B.U.S. and the same party now led by Jackson. It had functioned well as a stabilizer for business as well as a conservative check upon less responsible banks. Ownership of its stock was held in about equal amounts by wealthy families in the South, in the Middle States, and by Europeans. New Englanders held about 6% of the stock and the West less than 2%. Nicolas Biddle was a very able banker with great pride in the Philadelphia aristocracy to which his family belonged. To him democracy was nonsense, probably dangerous nonsense. President Jackson and Biddle, under the most favorable circumstances, might have maintained a cold atmosphere of mutual respect for each other as persons, while realizing how fundamentally antagonistic their convictions were. Biddle was president of the Second B.U.S. when Clay opposed Jackson's re-election in 1832. Clay persuaded Biddle, a National Republican, to agree to making the recharter of the B.U.S. the major issue of the campaign. As the bank's charter had over three years to run before it expired, there was no need to bring it up until many months after the election. Clay hoped and believed that Jackson would oppose the recharter of the Second B.U.S. Clay needed to be on the right side of a sound issue in order to make any headway against the re-election of the popular President. Clay led the political maneuvering in Congress that got the recharter bill passed in July 1832. As Biddle and Clay saw it, at the moment, President Jackson responded beautifully with a long veto message which displayed much more emotion than sense.

Jackson's veto message contained the following points—and some others.

1] The B.U.S. is unconstitutional.

2] It is a monopoly.

3] The shares of stock of the B.U.S. are owned by "opulent" citizens and foreigners who thereby benefit at the expense of the people.

4] The present stock-holders have no right to special favors.

5] The B.U.S. could influence foreign policy through the power of its foreign stock-holders and it is therefore dangerous.

6] The B.U.S. had used its funds in an irregular manner to further the political views of its president, Nicholas Biddle, views shared by Clay and his National Republican Party.

7] The Supreme Court's decision that the B.U.S. is constitutional carries no authority. It is equally the right of the President and of Congress to make such a judgment.

So the campaign became a debate about the bank. Had the debate been a sober searching for the truth, and had the audience paid attention to such dry, unexciting, and important facts, there could have been no other conclusion than that

Clay was right and Jackson was wrong. There were a few malpractices that could be charged fairly against Mr. Biddle's operations as president of the B.U.S., but who burns down the house because there is a faulty washer in the kitchen faucet?

The result was what might easily have been predicted. Those who liked Jackson believed, at least during the campaign, that the bank was unconstitutional, was corrupt, and was a wicked device to enrich the rich by letting them use the taxpayers' funds supplied largely by the people. Those who liked Clay, and especially those who hated Jackson, saw the soundness of the bank and its great usefulness in the economy. To them Jackson seemed a dangerous demagogue leading the ignorant people. Jackson won handily (see p. 104). Personal popularity is usually unbeatable at the polls.

Jackson's re-election meant the destruction of the Second B.U.S. No more government funds were deposited therein. As expenditures depleted the government's funds already in the bank, the B.U.S. limped to its death at the expiration of the charter in 1836. The government funds were deposited in about 80 state banks. Because all banks would have liked to have been chosen as depositories for government funds, those that were chosen were called Jackson's "Pet Banks." The "Pet Banks" were wisely selected as became apparent during the Panic of 1837. Very little government money was lost even though there were many bank failures throughout the nation.

Formation of the Whig Party

After his defeat in 1832, Clay pondered on how to beat Jackson's Democratic Party. There was a growing number of Democrats who thoroughly disliked Jackson's appeal to the "people" and his tendency to view unkindly the people of both wealth and social prestige. The eastern seaboard states of the South contained many families who were the political power of the area and who were unhappy in the fact that a westerner of humble origin led their party. He was not the type of person they would prefer in the White House. Such petty prejudice was then, and can be now, a big factor in politics. Add to these the anger of the extremists in the South who could never forgive Jackson's firm stand against nullification, and also the much larger number of Southerners who were bitterly disappointed that Jackson had not taken a definite stand against protective tariffs. Clay saw that these anti-Jackson people had no political home. It was too much to expect them to join the National Republican Party because that was, to them, the traditional opposition party. The device of dropping the name *National Republican* and adopting the name *Whig Party* was the magnet that drew thousands of anti-Jackson southerners into the same political fold as the National Republicans. The name *Whig* was well chosen. The Whigs of the Revolutionary War days were the enemies of the king. They had become the patriots and the minutemen. These glorious Whigs fought the tyranny of George III, and now Clay was gathering together true patriots of the late 1830's and early 1840's to oppose the tyranny of *King Andrew*. Or so it seemed to those who opposed the Democrats. There was one basic weakness in the Whig Party. It was founded on the dislike of Jackson. Jackson and his influence could not last very long, so the cement that at first held them firmly together would gradually disintegrate and lose its adhesive strength. The Southern wing of the Whig Party did not believe in Clay's American System as did most of the old National Republicans. The attitude of the Northern wing of the Whig Party on tariff and slavery was incompatible with the views of the Southern members. As long as the Whig Party lasted, it had to avoid major political issues, because any major issue would split the party. It may be interesting to see how the Whig Party survived quite a while and did rather well as an organization devoted to electing public officers while carefully taking no definite stand on the important issues of the day.

Martin Van Buren

1837-1841

1782 - 1862

DEMOCRAT

☆

VAN BUREN'S PUBLIC SERVICE BEFORE HE BECAME PRESIDENT

United States Senator from New York (1821-28)
Governor of New York (1829)
Secretary of State under Jackson (1829-32)
Vice-President under Jackson (1833-37)

MAJOR ITEMS OF VAN BUREN'S ADMINISTRATION

Panic of 1837
Independent Treasury or Sub-Treasuries (1840)
Gag Resolutions (1836-44)

Election of Van Buren (1836)

The Democratic convention nominated Van Buren by a unanimous vote. Because Jackson's influence in the party and his popularity with the people was still at a high level, his preference for Van Buren assured him of the candidacy. Sometimes Van Buren is referred to as the "Crown Prince" because he "inherited" the presidency from his predecessor. The same could be said of William H. Taft who was the choice in 1908 of President Theodore Roosevelt.

The Whig Party nominated two candidates, Daniel Webster of Massachusetts to represent the northern faction, and Hugh L. White of Tennessee to appeal to the anti-Jackson southerners. A third group, the Anti-Masons, nominated William Henry Harrison of Ohio. All three of these candidates knew they had no chance to win a majority of the electoral vote, but they did hope to split the vote enough to throw the election into the House of Representatives. If each could draw a solid vote in his own section, Van Buren might fall short of a majority vote in the Electoral College.

No party issued a platform. The Whigs couldn't afford to (see p. 108) and Van Buren didn't need to. As Jackson's choice, everyone took it for granted that he opposed any Bank of the United States, would not tolerate nullification, opposed internal improvements at federal expense, and favored political power being used in the interests of the common people. The election returns were as follows:

	Popular Vote	Electoral Vote
Van Buren	762,678	170
Harrison	548,007	73
White	145,396	26
Webster	41,287	14

(South Carolina's 11 votes went to W. Mangum who was not a candidate.) (Vice-President Richard Johnson was elected by the Senate.)

Panic of 1837

The panic resulted from a combination of factors: over-speculation in land, unsound financing by state governments, the disturbing effects of the absence of the B.U.S., and the Specie Circular. Other factors could be mentioned, and it would be difficult to determine how much weight should be given to any one of these causes. The Specie Circular was issued in mid-summer of 1836 by President Jackson. This prevented payment for public lands in any other money than gold and silver and certain paper money that was as sound as the gold and silver specie. As almost all sales had been paid for in bank notes of questionable soundness, this order from Jackson brought a sharp decline in the number of sales. Fraud and speculation in public lands had become a grave public issue. Something had to be done. The Specie Circular was Jackson's method of protecting the United States treasury from accumulating vast amounts of greatly depreciated paper money. The Specie Circular did precipitate the Panic of 1837, but it did not cause it.

A depression set in that lasted throughout Van Buren's term of office. This alone would have made his administration unpopular, but there were other factors that further aggravated an already hopeless situation. Van Buren was a city man of considerable polish and wealth. He had aristocratic tastes and was without the "common-touch" of Andrew Jackson. Any man in the President's office will be the victim of a depression that lasts throughout his term, but Van Buren might have become unpopular without a depression.

Independent Treasury System or Sub-Treasuries (1840)

Jackson had always favored a safety deposit vault for federal funds. He didn't like the government's being in the banking business. With the expiration of the charter of the Second B.U.S. in 1836 and the depositing of government monies in state banks, Van Buren pressed for the creation of sub-treasuries in a few cities for the safe-keeping of federal funds. When the panic and depression witnessed many bank failures and some loss of government funds, Congress went along with the President and established the Independent Treasury System; that is, independent of any banking system. As the law provided places in different cities for the safe-keeping of government funds, these safety deposit vaults were sometimes called sub-treasuries. This system had a major virtue; it kept government funds safe from loss through fraud and mismanagement, both of which had taken heavy toll in the past. Otherwise it wasn't much of a banking system. The law passed in 1840 was repealed in 1841, but passed again in 1846 to remain in effect until the Federal Reserve System replaced it in 1913. During this time the only substantial modification of the Independent Sub-Treasury System was the Chase National Banking Act of the Civil War days.

* Gag Resolutions (1836-44)

Debate over slavery was time consuming, temper provoking, and useless. Nothing new could be said. Opinions in Congress would not be swayed by more discussion. It seemed a good idea to adopt rules in the House and Senate to stop this acrimonious waste of time. In 1836 the House passed a Gag Resolution which read as follows:

> ". . . all petitions, memorials, resolutions, propositions or papers relating in any way or to any extent whatever to the subject of slavery or the abolition of slavery shall, without being printed or referred, be laid upon the table and that no further action whatever shall be had thereon."

Ex-President John Quincy Adams served in the House of Representatives from 1831 to 1848. Probably no other ex-President has served his nation so well. When it came his time to vote on a roll call he refused to cast a vote on the Gag Resolution. Instead, he said, "I hold the resolution to be a direct violation of the Constitution of the United States, of the rules of this House, and of the rights of my constituents." What good was the right of petition guaranteed in the First Amendment if the House or the Senate operated under a Gag Resolution? A *resolution,* being in the nature of a rule of procedure rather than a law, was reviewed each year. Each year John Q. Adams spoke vigorously against it and by 1844 he won his fight. Gag Resolutions were discontinued. This illustrates a basic point fundamental to moral standards and to government; namely, the *means* to an end must pass the test of decency and legality. Temptation to side-step this principle occurs often in both private and public affairs. The way it is met "separates the men from the boys."

William Henry Harrison

1773 - 1841

WHIG

☆

Vice-President JOHN TYLER

Secretary of State DANIEL WEBSTER

HARRISON'S PUBLIC SERVICE BEFORE HE BECAME PRESIDENT

Governor of the Indiana Territory (1801-12)
In command at the Battle of Tippecanoe (1811)
Defeated the British in Canada (Thames River 1813) (See p. 92)
United States Senator from Ohio (1825-28)

Election of Harrison (1840)

Van Buren was nominated by the Democrats to run for re-election. The party platform called for opposition to Clay's American System, favored strict construction of the Constitution, and opposed interference by Congress in the slavery issue. The Whigs nominated Harrison who had no known convictions on any of the public issues of the day. Harrison had what political parties call *availability* as a presidential candidate. This means that the chance to elect him seemed good, a fact that had no connection with his suitability for the position of President. Clay, who had organized the Whig Party, was obviously a man of real stature and capacity; but his nomination would almost certainly have split the Whigs into northern and southern factions. Clay recognized this political fact and stepped into the background. The Whig Party avoided taking a position on the issues of banking, tariff, internal improvements at federal expense, slavery, and *loose* v. *strict* construction of the Constitution. Harrison was just the man for the occasion. He had taken no position on these issues and therefore had made no enemies. He could be presented to the voters as a great Indian fighter and as a hero of the War of 1812. Four years of depression under Van Buren made Whig hopes run high. To insure unity between the northern and southern Whigs John Tyler of Virginia was put on the ticket as Harrison's running-mate. Tyler would hold the southern anti-Jackson ex-Democrats in the Whig Party. "Tippecanoe and Tyler too" and

"Van, Van, is a used up man" were slogans of the campaign. The Democrats attacked Harrison as a common, vulgar person of small vision. Someone said that if he had a barrel of hard cider and a log cabin he would be happy to idle his life away. This characterization back-fired on the Democrats when the Whigs made floats in parades showing a log cabin, a bench outside the door, and a barrel of cider. The Whigs had a song for their "Log Cabin-Hard Cider" candidate.

"Let Van from his coolers of silver drink wine,
    And lounge on his cushioned settee;
  Our man on his buckeye bench can recline,
    Content with hard cider is he!"

There was so much noise, excitement, fun, and foolishness that the women turned out as never before to take part in the political parades and the bonfire celebrations. The Philadelphia Public Ledger bemoaned this unseemly feminine conduct by asking, "Was this the proper sphere of women? Was this appropriate to her elevating influence? Did such things improve men? No! They merely degraded women, and made men still more degraded than they were before." The election turned out as expected.

	Popular Vote	Electoral Vote
Harrison	1,275,017	234
Van Buren	1,128,702	60

On April 4, 1841, just one month after his inauguration, Harrison died.

John Tyler

1841-1845

1790 - 1862

ANTI-JACKSON DEMOCRAT ran as Vice-President on the WHIG Ticket

☆

Secretary of State DANIEL WEBSTER

TYLER'S PUBLIC SERVICE BEFORE HE BECAME PRESIDENT

>*Governor of Virginia (1825-27)*
>*United States Senator from Virginia (1827-36)*

MAJOR ITEMS OF TYLER'S ADMINISTRATION

>*Veto of Clay's Bill for a Third B.U.S.*
>*Webster-Ashburton Treaty (1842)*

Veto of Clay's Bill for a Third Bank of the United States

President Harrison's sudden death changed the Whig victory into a defeat. Senator Clay took the lead in forming a legislative program which abolished the Independent Treasury and passed a bill to establish a third B.U.S. President Tyler vetoed the bank bill and thereby started a political war between the President and the Congress. The Whig cabinet members resigned with the exception of Secretary of State, Daniel Webster.

* Webster-Ashburton Treaty (1842)

Webster did not resign because he was in the midst of negotiations with Lord Ashburton over the Maine-Canadian border. This boundary dispute had been long and, at times, bitter. In 1838 and 1839 lumber-jacks of Maine and New Bruns-wick had threatened to "shoot-it-out." The situation was so tense during this winter that it was called the Aroostook "War" even though no lives were lost. By 1842 the Webster-Ashburton Treaty Line was fixed. It followed the St. Croix River to its source, then went straight north to the St. John's River, along the St. John's River westward in an irregular horseshoe bend toward the south. The line left the St. John's River and proceeded in an irregular southward line to the 45th parallel at a point almost on the Connecticut River. At the 45th parallel the boundary extended west on the parallel to the St. Lawrence River and along the St. Lawrence to Lake Ontario. At the same time the border between the Lake of the Woods and Lake Superior was fixed along the Rainy River and a chain of Lakes. This settlement left the Mesabi iron deposits within the United States.

112

James K. Polk

1845-1849

1795 - 1849

DEMOCRAT

☆

POLK'S PUBLIC SERVICE BEFORE HE BECAME PRESIDENT

> Member of the House of Representatives from Tennessee (1825-39)
> Speaker of the House (1835-39)
> Governor of Tennessee (1839-41)

MAJOR ITEMS OF POLK'S ADMINISTRATION

> Texas Became a State (1845)
> Oregon Boundary Settled (1846)
> Mexican War (1846-48)
> Guadalupe Hidalgo Treaty (1848)
> Wilmot Proviso v. Calhoun-Davis Theory

* Election of Polk (1844)

In this campaign the organizer of the Whig Party, Henry Clay, became its candidate. Tyler had offended the party too deeply to win the nomination and a chance for a second term (see p. 112). His only influence in the Whig Party was with the relatively small southern wing. The Whigs did write a platform, but it said as little as possible. On the crucial issues of Texas and slavery it said nothing; it even avoided saying anything about a national bank. One might well wonder why they wrote a platform. Their candidate, Henry Clay, seemed to be head and shoulders above any candidate the Democrats could put forward. In 1832 Clay had lost to Jackson because Jackson had overshadowed him in prominence and popularity; now Clay had his opportunity to win the presidency because he overshadowed all prospective opponents. It seemed to be Clay's year to become president.

Van Buren was expected to get the nomination of the Democratic Party. He did get the pledge of support from most of the Democratic state conventions and also a majority of the votes on the first ballot at the national presidential nominating convention, but he did not get the necessary two-thirds majority then required by the Democratic Party. On the 9th ballot James K. Polk was nominated and the news was carried over the new invention, the telegraph. This news was greeted with one question, "Who is Polk?" This was the first surprise nomination, the first "Dark Horse" selection, in our history.

Van Buren and Clay had discussed privately the issue of Texas and found that they agreed that Texas should not be annexed. This was when they both expected to be presidential candidates, but before the nominating conventions. In letters to the newspapers they made their views known. They agreed that admitting Texas would offend Mexico and almost certainly result in war because the United States would then inherit the boundary dispute that Texas was still having with Mexico. Admission of Texas would also necessarily stir up the slave controversy between the North and South. This decision to agree on the two most emotion-packed issues of the day suited Clay completely. In presenting the voters with no choice to make other than Mr. Clay or Mr. Van Buren, Mr. Clay was as good as elected. But Andrew Jackson was still alive at the Hermitage. He said the Democrats needed a candidate in favor of expansion, preferably a man from the Southwest. Polk, who wasn't in the balloting at all until the 7th roll call of the states at the nominating convention, came in to win on the 9th ballot. An expansionist from the Southwest had been chosen. Polk came out shouting. He not only favored annexing Texas, he wanted Oregon too. He was afire with manifest destiny and righteous indignation. Was it not obvious that the United States was destined to spread to the Pacific? Had we not purchased Texas once as part of the Louisiana Territory? Had not Lewis and Clark started a steady stream of Americans into Oregon, thereby establishing our claim? "Reannexation of Texas and Reoccupation of Oregon" became an effective slogan;

but an even better spine-tingler was the "Fifty-four forty or fight" claim to Oregon. Northerners who didn't want Texas because of its slaves would want Oregon. In this campaign we have an unusually clear example of a program that was both extremely effective politics and distressingly poor statesmanship.

Clay was thus put in a difficult situation. Should he stick to his guns by opposing the annexation of Texas and repudiating the extreme demands for Oregon? If he did, he would be right again, as he had been about the bank issue in 1832 (see pp. 107-108). He would probably lose because the popular ballyhoo of the slogans would be hard to dissipate in a five-months' campaign. Clay decided to shift his ground on the issues. By doing so he would be close enough to Polk in his program and, that being so, the voters should pass over a "nobody" and choose the very considerable "somebody." There is a saying that passes as a political axiom, "You can't beat somebody with nobody," but in 1844 it happened. Clay's shiftiness about Texas took the enthusiasm out of his supporters. Clay said that he didn't object to annexing Texas if it didn't cause war with Mexico, that he didn't think the question of slavery should be confused with the annexation of Texas, and that he would be quite willing to do whatever the people of the United States wished about expansion. Clay would still have won on this slippery approach had it not been for a new minor party which entered the field for the first time. The Liberty Party ran James G. Birney for president. They favored abolition of slavery and almost all of their members were Whigs who would have voted for Clay if the Liberty Party had not been organized. The Liberty Party took enough votes away from Clay in Michigan and New York to give both states to Polk. New York alone would have given Clay the election, and in New York Birney got almost 16,000 votes while Polk won the state from Clay by only 5,000 votes.

	Popular Vote	Electoral Vote
Polk	1,337,243	170
Clay	1,299,068	105
Birney	62,300	0

(New York State had 36 electoral votes.)

Texas Became a State (1845)

Apparently President Tyler desired for his administration whatever prestige history might give for the annexation of Texas. On March 1st, three days before Polk was inaugurated, Texas became a territory of the United States. The Americans who had lived almost ten years in the Lone Star Republic saw their cherished ambition realized when Texas became a state on December 29, 1845.

Oregon Boundary Settled (1846)

"Fifty-four forty or fight" and "All of Oregon or none" were emotionally satisfying slogans, especially during a presidential campaign; but going to war against England over 54°40′ was quite a different matter from going to war with Mexico over the Rio Grande. In December of 1845, when England suggested that she would give consideration to the extension of the 49th parallel to the Pacific Coast, a peaceful settlement was assured. During these final stages of the Oregon negotiations, we had assurances from England that she would not interfere with United States-Mexican relations. That is, we had taken the precaution of not risking two wars at once —with Mexico in the southwest and with England in the northwest. On June 15, 1846 the Senate ratified the Oregon settlement which made the boundary an extension of the 49th parallel from the Rocky Mountains to the Pacific Ocean.

* The Mexican War (1846-48)

Both Clay and Van Buren had said before the 1844 presidential campaign got under way that the annexation of Texas would involve the United States in a boundary dispute with Mexico that might bring on a war. It did. When Texas was a state within Mexico its boundary was the Nueces River, not the Rio Grande. But when Texans under Sam Houston (*The Raven*) defeated the Mexican general, Santa Anna, at the San Jacinto River in April 1836 it declared itself an independent republic. This new Republic of Texas claimed the Rio Grande River as its southwestern border. General Santa Anna had signed a "treaty" after his defeat at San Jacinto which accepted the Rio Grande as the boundary. The Mexican Congress had rejected this agreement as having no legal status because it was made under force by a person unauthorized to conclude a treaty.

Almost as soon as the United States annexed Texas, Mexico broke off diplomatic relations. On June 15, 1845 General Zachary Taylor was ordered to defend the "territory of Texas" along the Rio Grande. Sizeable United States forces were in the disputed area by late summer. Several months before fighting broke out the United States tried to buy from Mexico the area we were soon to take by force of arms. Mexico refused to sell. In April 1846 an American reconnoitering force of 63 men was captured. In the accompanying skirmish 11 Americans were killed. The war was on. President Polk appeared before Congress on May 11th to ask for a declaration of war because Mexico had "shed blood upon American soil." War was declared on May 13th.

The states south of the Ohio River and west of the Alleghenies were enthusiastically in favor of this war. Among the original thirteen states the Old South was content with the annexation of Texas, while the Middle Atlantic states and New England were hostile to the war. To the Northeast, the Mexican War was a plot to acquire more slave states. This was reflected in the make-up of our armed forces. While many of the officers were West Point men from all sections of the nation, the volunteers came principally from the West and South. James Russell Lowell penned some bitter doggerel which expressed well enough the sentiment of New England boys.

> "They may talk o' Freedom's airy
>   Tell they're pupple in the face;
> It's a grand gret cemetary
>   Fer the barthrights of our race;
> They just want this Californy
>   So's to lug new slave-states in
> To abuse ye, an' to scorn ye,
>   An' to plunder ye like sin."

Fighting during this war was often severe, but there was never any doubt about the final outcome. John C. Fremont, the "Pathfinder," took a leading part in the conquest of California. He had led scientific expeditions in the Rockies, Nevada, California, and Oregon regions before the Mexican War broke out. General Stephen Kearny carried the war into New Mexico from Fort Leavenworth on the Missouri River to Santa Fe, then westward along the Gila River and on to San Diego and Los Angeles. General Zachary Taylor's victory at Buena Vista ended the war in northern Mexico. General Winfield Scott's campaign from Vera Cruz to Mexico City brought the war to a close. On September 14, 1847 the Marines broke through the walls of the mountain capital, Mexico City, and took possession of the "Halls of Montezuma." The war had cost the United States about 1,700 killed in battle and 11,000 victims of disease. Mexican losses were greater.

* Guadalupe Hidalgo Treaty (1848)

The United States added New Mexico and California to its territory. Mexico recognized the Rio Grande River as the southwest border of Texas. Including Texas, this area was over 1,000,000 square miles. The United States paid $15,000,000 to Mexico and assumed claims against her amounting to about $3,250,000.

There was considerable objection to this treaty among the people of the United States. In the Senate 14 votes were cast against it (38-14). It is true that the Mexican War was one of deliberate conquest. It is equally true that several battles were fought after the war had obviously been won. Delay in making the peace seemed to result more from confusion and disorganization within the Mexican government than from any determination to resist to the bitter end. The needless casualties in the last weeks of the war and the completeness of our victory gave rise to the demand that the United States annex the whole of Mexico. Had the United States pressed the issue, there seems to have been nothing that could have prevented these harsher terms—and with no payment of money. The purchase of the Gasden area in 1853 for the very generous price of $10,000,000 may well be considered part of the peace settlement. The United States wanted this relatively small additional territory because it contained a pass through the mountains suitable for a railroad. In trying to assess the pros and cons of the Mexican War, one should judge the events in the light of the prevailing climate of opinion and the accepted, even expected, conduct of nations in the middle 1800's. In 1840-42 England had started the partitioning of China with the Opium War, a venture in aggression for trade and empire that, by comparison, made the Mexican War appear positively polite. If nations develop character, it seems that the United States had a deep-seated aversion to taking part in aggression and empire-building. The very few moves in this direction that have been made have raised a storm of criticism within the United States and, after the event, the United States has taken measures to soften the injustice and, sometimes, even to more than compensate for it.

The Wilmot Proviso v. the Calhoun-Davis Theory

David Wilmot was a Democrat from Pennsylvania in the House of Representatives. He, along with the rest of Congress, took it for granted that the United States would acquire a large area of land from Mexico. While the war was going on he introduced a resolution that said, ". . . neither slavery nor involuntary servitude shall ever exist in any part of said territory." The Proviso passed the House by a comfortable margin, but had no chance to get by in the Senate. The raising of this question started a political storm. Wilmot's supporters claimed that Congress had a right to legislate about slavery in the territories, while his opponents called the Proviso an attack upon states' rights. Calhoun reiterated the arguments for nullification, the compact-theory, secession, and what is sometimes called interposition. This political war was to prove much more difficult to bring to a conclusion than the Mexican War they were then fighting. The surprising fact is not that we had a Civil War, but that we didn't ride immediately from the Mexican War into the Civil War. As early as 1847 Calhoun was saying that the non-slaveholding states were "aggressive" and that the Southern states were on the "defensive." "All we ask," he said, "is to be let alone." When the Civil War came, the people of the South backed the Confederate States of America wholeheartedly, not to defend slavery, but because they were convinced that the North would not let them alone. In their minds the North had to be taught to mind its own business.

Zachary Taylor

1784 - 1850

WHIG

☆

Vice-President MILLARD FILLMORE

TAYLOR'S PUBLIC SERVICE BEFORE HE BECAME PRESIDENT

Forty Years in the United States Army (1808-48)
Defeated Santa Anna at Buena Vista (1847)

Election of Taylor (1848)

Both the Democrats and the Whigs were beginning to fall apart over the slavery issue. Northern Democrats who supported the Wilmot Proviso (p. 115) were called Barnburners. The name indicated that they were willing to destroy the Democratic Party over the single issue of slavery; that is, to burn the barn down in order to kill one rat. They withdrew from the Democratic Nominating Convention. Many northern Whigs were fed up with their party's careful avoidance of major issues. They wanted a strong stand against slavery, and were therefore called "Conscience Whigs." They left the Whig Party. The Liberty Party which had put up Birney and thus defeated Clay in 1844 was a third organized group against slavery. These three groups united to form the Free Soil Party with Martin Van Buren as their candidate. "Free soil, free speech, free labor, and free men" was its campaign slogan. The Free Soil Party's position can best be stated as being opposed to the *extension* of slavery into any new areas. They would tolerate slavery in the states where it already existed. This view had a strong appeal for those people who opposed slavery, but also recognized the insuperable complications and difficulties inherent in any attempt at abolition.

The Democrats nominated General Lewis Cass. Polk did not seek renomination. Cass had favored expansion and hence was popular in the West. The Democratic Platform dealt as gently with slavery as it could. It denied the right of Congress to interfere with slavery in the states, but said nothing about the real question of the day—did Congress have the right to legislate about slavery in the territories?

The Whigs nominated Zachary Taylor because he had been a recent hero at the battle of Buena Vista. As Taylor had taken no strong position on any real public issue, he had no enemies. This made him an extremely "available" candidate for a party that was trying desperately to hold together by offending no one.

The Barnburners, the Conscience Whigs, and the ex-Liberty Party united in the new Free Soil Party. They got enough support in New York State to throw its 36 electoral votes into the Whig column and the election to Taylor.

	Popular Vote	Electoral Vote
Taylor	1,360,101	163
Cass	1,220,544	127
Van Buren	291,263	0

(In New York State Van Buren received more votes than Cass.)

President Taylor died on July 9th 1850. The great issue before the nation was the problem of slavery in the land taken from Mexico. The Compromise of 1850, which was in the making, was completed under President Fillmore.

Millard Fillmore

1800 - 1874

1850-1853

WHIG

★

Secretary of State DANIEL WEBSTER

FILLMORE'S PUBLIC SERVICE BEFORE HE BECAME PRESIDENT

Member of the House of Representatives for 8 years
Vice-President under Taylor

MAJOR ITEMS OF FILLMORE'S ADMINISTRATION

Compromise of 1850 (The Omnibus Bill)
Clayton-Bulwer Treaty (1850)
Uncle Tom's Cabin

** Compromise of 1850 (Omnibus Bill)

This is not one law. It is a combination of laws passed by Congress between the 9th and 20th of September. Congress and the people knew that the nation faced a severe crisis. The life of the Union was threatened and Civil War was possible. Some solution to the question of slavery in our newly acquired territories must be found.

Clay was the man with a plan and with the political stature to command attention. There had to be a Northerner to give the plan national status. Daniel Webster, once from New Hampshire and now from Massachusetts, filled this necessary role. The debates on these measures rank among the best that have occurred in Congress. Webster's "7th of March" speech may well be declaimed so long as there are schoolboys in America. "I wish to speak today, not as a Massachusetts man, nor as a Northern man, but as an American . . . I speak today for the preservation of the Union."

The following provisions were finally passed by Congress after months of consideration:

1] California was admitted into the Union as a free state.

The gold rush of 1849 had brought to California free men from all over the United States and from all over the world. Very few slaves were there.

2] Texas accepted a reduction in area in exchange for $10,000,000.

Slavery was already established in Texas and nothing was done to disturb it.

3] The areas taken from Mexico between Texas and California were divided at the 37th parallel.

South of the parallel was the Territory of New Mexico and north of it was the Territory of Utah. In these two territories there were no restrictions on slavery. But when either territory or any part of either territory became a state, the people living there could then decide by popular vote (squatter sovereignty) whether they wanted a slave or a free state.

Had Congress and the people been less emotionally stirred-up over the moral aspects of the slavery controversy, they could have paid attention to Webster's statement that there really was no issue at all, because climate and soil in New Mexico and Utah made the areas wholly unsuited to the use of slaves. It can be a mistake to become so attached to a "principle" that one loses sight of extremely pertinent practical facts.

4] A fugitive slave law was passed which contained provisions to make recovery of fugitive slaves as certain as a law could make it.

a. All law enforcement officials who failed to cooperate in the apprehension of fugitive slaves were made liable up to the value of the slave, if the slave was not captured or escaped while being held in custody.

b. All "good citizens are hereby commanded to aid and assist in the prompt execution of this law."

c. No alleged fugitive was allowed to testify in his own behalf and no trial by jury was allowed.

d. Any person who hindered the recovery of a fugitive slave was subject to $1,000 fine, imprisonment for 6 months, and the payment of $1,000 to the owner.

e. If mob violence threatened to rescue a re-covered fugitive from his master's custody, it was the duty of local officials to provide for the delivery of the slave to the place from which he had escaped.

5] The buying and selling of slaves was prohibited within the District of Columbia. Otherwise the in-stitution of slavery within the District was not af-fected.

The South was willing to live with the Compro-mise. But many Northerners resented the fugitive slave law. They were beginning to share the view of William H. Seward of New York who had said, during the debates in Congress, that there was "a higher law" than laws of Congress and the Consti-tution. But a period of quiet set in as the early 1850's witnessed prosperity throughout the nation. Calhoun foresaw what was to happen more clearly than other leaders. He died in March 1850, but he had already said that the Compromise could settle nothing, that it could merely postpone a settlement, and that such postponement could help only the North. Clay died in June and Webster in October of 1852. These two men had postponed the Civil War for 10 years by their Compromise; perhaps they thought they had prevented it.

* Clayton-Bulwer Treaty (1850)

Our acquisition of California in 1848 and the Gold Rush in 1849 increased United States' interest in the possibility of a canal across Central America. During the Mexican War we had made a treaty with Colombia, then called New Granada, giving us permission to maintain by armed guards a peaceful passage across the Isthmus of Panama. This was an isolated area which New Granada could not be ex-pected to police, but it was the most practical cross-ing from ocean to ocean. If our citizens cared to use it they could, and our government could pro-vide for their safe passage by use of whatever armed force was necessary. This simple treaty of accom-modation was to receive an unexpected interpreta-tion over 50 years later (see p. 179). For about 15 years Great Britain had been making aggressive moves in Central America, using British Honduras as a base of operations. The United States had also dickered with Nicaragua for rights to fortify a canal using Lake Nicaragua and the San Juan River on its southern border. For about a decade Great Britain and the United States considered each other as rivals seeking special influence in Central Amer-ica, especially in the areas where a canal seemed feasible. Hostility was increasing. The Clayton-Bulwer Treaty cleared the air. Both nations discov-ered that each was more worried about the other's gaining control of Central America than either was anxious to dominate the area. It was not too diffi-cult to reach satisfactory terms. The terms agreed upon were as follows:

1] Neither Great Britain nor the United States will seek or acquire control over Central America or any special privileges therein.

2] If any canal through Central America is built, it must be open to the ships of all nations on the same terms in both peace and war. The approaches to each end of the canal shall be similarly open to the use of all nations.

3] If such a canal is built, it must be with the free consent of the nation through whose territory it passes. Both Great Britain and the United States guarantee its neutrality by protecting it and the areas adjacent to it, both during its construction and thereafter.

One might ask why Great Britain and the United States made such conditions concerning an area far removed from their own nations, and over which they had no legal authority. The only, and quite sufficient, answer is that both nations were great powers and each believed its national interest demanded such arrangements. National necessity covers any contingency, if the nation has the power to back up its demands. In this case, the British Em-pire was as wide-spread as the world itself, and the United States had stretched across the continent from the Atlantic to the Pacific. Any such short-cut as an interoceanic canal was of such vital interest to these two great powers that they could not let it exist, except under conditions that fully pro-tected their national interests.

Uncle Tom's Cabin

This novel by Harriet Beecher Stowe had a pro-found effect. As Tom Paine's *Common Sense* crys-talized public opinion in support of revolution, so *Uncle Tom's Cabin,* published in March 1852, changed the abolitionists from a small lunatic fringe of fanatics to a great company of righteous crusaders. Harriet Beecher Stowe had made it re-spectable to be an abolitionist. When she was intro-duced to President Lincoln, his response has been reported as, "So, you're the little lady who caused the Civil War." In recent decades *Uncle Tom's Cabin* has been pushed aside as a sentimental, mis-leading tear-jerker with very little literary merit. But it took the North and most of the world by storm. Letters of appreciation and praise came to Mrs. Stowe from England, Germany, Switzerland, Sweden, Italy and from many prominent persons. Over half a million English women signed a petition of protest against slavery and of praise for *Uncle Tom's Cabin*. Florence Nightingale, Jenny Lind, Charles Dickens, Madame George Sand, Lord Carlisle, and Lord Shaftesbury and other "greats" of the day wrote to the author of *Uncle Tom's Cabin* and put themselves on record as being profoundly moved by the book which they believed to be a work of historical importance. Reading it today can bring an appreciation of the way tens of thousands of people felt about slavery in the 1850's.

Franklin Pierce

1804 - 1869

DEMOCRAT

★

PIERCE'S PUBLIC SERVICE BEFORE HE BECAME PRESIDENT

Brigadier General under General Scott in the Mexican War

MAJOR ITEMS OF PIERCE'S ADMINISTRATION

Japan Opened to World Trade (1853)
Kansas-Nebraska Bill (1854)
Underground Railroad and Personal Liberty Laws
Strife in Kansas
Ostend Manifesto (1854)

Pierce's Election (1852)

This is certainly one of the campaigns where the two major parties were as alike as two peas in a pod. Franklin Pierce, Democrat, and Winfield Scott, Whig, got the nomination at their party conventions on the 49th and 53rd ballots respectively. Both party platforms pledged adherence to the Compromise of 1850 and both condemned any further agitation about slavery. The Whig Party began to break up because it had originated as an anti-Jackson party and had never been able to take a stand on an important public issue. The southern members of the Whig Party were going back to the Democrats. Jackson had been dead for seven years, so there had ceased to be any reason for anti-Jackson Democrats to remain in the Whig Party. They never had been comfortable in their association with the northern Whigs. The result of this shift was a land-slide victory for Pierce in 1852.

	Popular Vote	Electoral Vote
Pierce	1,601,474	254
Scott	1,386,578	42

Japan Opened to World Trade (1853)

Commodore Matthew C. Perry sailed into Tokyo Bay in July, 1853. His mission was to make a trade treaty with Japan and to bring to an end the unpleasant Japanese custom of murdering shipwrecked sailors instead of rescuing them. A miniature railroad and a telegraph, displayed by Perry, convinced the Japanese emperor that our civilization might have some merit. A trade treaty was concluded. Strangely enough, the historical significance of Perry's visit was not the value of the trade with the United States or with other nations; the real significance was that Japan shifted from a policy of isolation to a program of modernization. Japan began to copy western ways which were destined to make her the dominant Asiatic power in the Far East.

** Kansas-Nebraska Bill (1854)

Stephen A. Douglas reopened the slavery issue in January. From then to late in May an increasingly bitter debate over this bill split the major parties and re-organized the people of the United States into a dangerous political pattern. The break-up of the Whig Party became complete as the Southerners still in the party, now left it to join the Southern Democrats. Political alignment was dictated by one issue, slavery. The Republican Party of today was born during the debate over the Kansas-Nebraska Bill. It became the party which attracted anti-slavery Democrats, the Know-Nothings who were anti-Catholic and anti-immigrant bigots with their greatest numbers in northern cities, the abolitionists of the Liberty Party, and the Free Soilers. By the late 1850's political lines had been drawn to coincide with geographical areas. No longer were there two *national* parties; there were two *sectional* parties. The political realignments resulting from the Kansas-Nebraska Bill invited Civil War.

The provisions of the bill divided the Nebraska Territory at the 40th parallel into the Territory of Kansas south of the line, and the Territory of Nebraska north of the line. The settlers in each Territory were to decide the issue of slavery by popular vote as soon as they had organized a territorial government. All of this area was in the Louisiana Territory north of 36° 30′ and had been made free by the Missouri Compromise of 1820, which the Kansas-Nebraska Bill specifically repealed. The repeal of the Missouri Compromise and the introduction of squatter sovereignty (popular vote) was a victory for the South because it took the decision away from Congress and gave it to the people who lived in the area.

Why Douglas reopened the slavery controversy is not clear. Certainly there was no necessity for it. The Compromise of 1850 had established an uneasy peace that might have continued for some time. Perhaps Douglas sought favor with the southern wing of the Democratic Party and had no idea that northern Democrats would be violently offended. He saw no moral issue involved either in slavery itself or in the repudiation of the Missouri Compromise. He had no professional polls to consult, no nationwide news services to measure public sentiment; it was easier then to assume one's own views to be the same as those generally held by sensible people. Being insensitive to the moral values involved, he may not have realized that the Kansas-Nebraska Bill would inevitably light the fuse that must sputter and burn ever more violently until it shattered the Union. The South had gained squatter sovereignty in the once free Territory west of the Mississippi River and north of 36° 30′, but, from that moment on, the "higher law" took over throughout the North, whose answer to the Kansas-Nebraska Bill was the revival of the Underground Railroad and the passage of additional Personal Liberty Laws.

* Underground Railroad and Personal Liberty Laws

By 1830 an organized Underground Railroad existed in 14 northern states. Fugitive slaves were hidden in houses and barns, called stations, along escape routes extending into Canada. In the earlier years few slaves were aided, because only abolitionists operated this escape method. Comparatively few slaves tried to escape. With the publishing of *Uncle Tom's Cabin* and the passage of the Kansas-Nebraska Bill, the abolitionists ceased to be only a small "lunatic fringe" of extremists. About 50,000 slaves traveled this route to freedom over the 30 years before the Civil War. During the 1850's it is estimated that the total slave population was somewhat in excess of 3,500,000. These few statistics show clearly that fugitive slaves did not constitute a serious problem to slave owners, nor did the Underground Railroad threaten slavery as an institu-

tion. The hatred between North and South stimulated by the legal and moral conflicts inherent in the Underground Railroad operation was far more important than any property values involved.

The Personal Liberty Laws were direct violations of the fugitive slave provisions of the Compromise of 1850. As state laws clearly incompatible with a law of Congress, they were unconstitutional. As the South saw these Personal Liberty Laws, they were a denial by the North of the one provision in the Compromise of 1850 which, to them, was the most important. To the North, these laws were a justified defiance of a federal law that ought not to be obeyed. Ralph Waldo Emerson expressed the Northern view of the federal fugitive slave law when he wrote, "I will not obey it." The state Personal Liberty Laws varied, but provisions common to many were: jury trial for alleged fugitives, local jails not to be used to detain suspected fugitives, and alleged fugitives allowed to testify in their own behalf. In the face of these laws the recovery of fugitive slaves was extremely difficult. In the northern states the apprehension of a fugitive slave was likely to result in mob violence against the master.

* Strife in Kansas

If Douglas wanted to stimulate the settlement of the West, his Kansas-Nebraska Bill succeeded; but not in the manner he intended nor anyone wished. It was obvious that Kansas would soon be organized as a territory. Both Northerners and Southerners rushed into the area to win it for their cause. With the slave state of Missouri adjacent to Kansas, the Southerners got there first with the larger numbers. Kansas was not suited for cotton and slavery, but, with feelings aroused, this made no difference. Southerners were thinking in terms of running the areas they occupied according to their way of life, which, of course, included slavery. Most Southerners didn't own slaves, and slaves were not, and could not become, economically important in Kansas. Interference by Northerners, who just wouldn't mind their own business, was the intolerable irritant that united Southerners, whether slave owners or not. On the other hand, the Northerners who rushed into Kansas were bent upon a holy mission; they felt themselves to be pursuing the Lord's business. Neither side was in any mood to be reasonable. Massachusetts organized the New England Emigrant Aid Company to finance young men willing to settle in Kansas in order to make it a free territory. In Missouri, organizations were formed to recruit settlers bent upon establishing slavery in Kansas. By 1856 two rival governments claimed authority in Kansas. Congress, accepting the popular sovereignty principle, looked on, but did nothing. President Pierce warned both factions to stop fighting, but the frequent armed clashes continued. "Border Ruffians" from Missouri, and Northerners armed with "Beecher Bibles" (rifles) raided each others' settlements. About 200 were killed and property damage ran into the millions of dollars. One of the most senseless acts of violence was John Brown's raid at Pottawatomie Creek where he and his four sons murdered five pro-slavery settlers. It was an act of pure fanaticism, for all Brown knew about the victims was that they favored slavery. One can't question the sincerity of John Brown; he believed himself to be a special agent of the Almighty. Read "John Brown's Body" by Benet, or, better still, listen two or three times to the recording of this poem. It will add much to your *appreciation* of this conflict between North and South.

While Congress was unable to act, it was able to talk. And its talk was violent. Senator Charles Sumner of Massachusetts gave a speech in 1856 which was a bitter and coarse attack, not only upon slavery, but upon individual southern Senators. Senator Butler of South Carolina, who was not present at the time, was the target of much of Sumner's vituperation. Two days later, Representative Brooks of South Carolina, a nephew of Senator Butler, entered Sumner's office and beat him over the head with a cane. It was almost murder. Several months later Sumner was able to resume his seat in the Senate. Brooks resigned his seat in the House and was quickly re-elected by South Carolina. In his own state he was a hero.

Constitutional conventions and elections were held in Kansas amid violence, trickery, and corruption. During this chaos President Pierce's term closed and Buchanan became President. Buchanan's strategy, if it can be called a plan, was to avoid trouble. His decisions seemed motivated by a desire to preserve party harmony in a situation that clearly made such an outcome impossible. In 1857 the Lecompton Constitution was submitted to the people of Kansas. The original agreement was to allow a vote on the Constitution as a whole. It became evident that a proslavery constitution would be rejected. The Lecompton Convention was controlled by proslavery delegates who refused to submit the constitution to a vote, but, instead, submitted two propositions. One would accept the constitution with slavery. The other would accept it without slavery, but "without slavery" was defined to forbid any more slaves entering Kansas, but to permit all those already there to remain slaves. No matter which way the vote went, there would be slavery in Kansas. Naturally, the antislavery voters refused to take part in any such fraudulent election, and the proslavery voters won by a landslide. This "Lecompton Fraud" was sent to Washington and President Buchanan advised Congress to approve it. Congress refused. Douglas, who, perhaps unwittingly, had started all this trouble with his Kansas-Nebraska Bill, opposed Buchanan on this issue and thus created a split in the Democratic Party which made Breckenridge the leader of many southern Democrats. This split was to put the Republicans into the presidency in 1860.

* Ostend Manifesto (1854)

The historian, David S. Muzzey, has described this document as "the most disgraceful public paper in all our history." It was the culmination of the strong desire of certain southerners for Cuba. Under President Polk, the United States had offered Spain $100,000,000. for Cuba. Filibustering expeditions, which our government did very little to prevent, were organized in New Orleans for raids on Cuba. Spanish authorities seized the *Black Warrior*, a United States merchant ship, suspecting it to be on an illegal mission. This incident occurred when Pierre Soulé, an extreme annexationist and proslavery advocate from Louisiana, was our minister in Madrid. Soulé, without awaiting instruction from Washington, presented the Spanish government with claims for damages and was unduly aggressive in his attitude. His bluster came to naught as Spain soon apologized and released the *Black Warrior*. Our Secretary of State, Marcy, told Soulé to confer with our ministers to France and England, Mason and Buchanan respectively, in an attempt to reach a settlement with Spain about Cuba. Soulé called the meeting at Ostend, Belgium. He wrote the Manifesto and the three ministers signed it. The following quotations from the Ostend Manifesto explain Professor Muzzey's remark.

> "It must be clear to every reflecting mind that, from the peculiarity of its geographical position . . . Cuba is . . . necessary to the North American republic . . ."
>
> "Indeed, the Union can never enjoy repose, nor possess reliable security, as long as Cuba is not embraced within its boundaries."
>
> "Its immediate acquisition by our government is of paramount importance . . ."
>
> "But if Spain, dead to the voice of her own interest, and actuated by stubborn pride and a false sense of honor, should refuse to sell Cuba to the United States, then, by every law, human and divine, we shall be justified in wresting it from Spain . . ."

When Secretary of State Marcy repudiated this statement, Soulé resigned. Mason and Buchanan were called home. It was felt that President Pierce had weakly tolerated the development of this episode because he was too much influenced by his Secretary of War, Jefferson Davis, later to become president of the Confederate States of America. Presidents Fillmore (New York), Pierce (New Hampshire), and Buchanan (Pennsylvania) were all northerners who took a tolerant attitude toward slavery and thus gained for themselves the uncomplimentary sobriquet "Doughface."

James Buchanan   1857-1861

1791 - 1868

DEMOCRAT

☆

Vice-President JOHN C. BRECKENRIDGE

BUCHANAN'S PUBLIC SERVICE BEFORE HE BECAME PRESIDENT

United States Minister to Russia
Secretary of State under Polk
Minister to Great Britain

MAJOR ITEMS OF BUCHANAN'S ADMINISTRATION

** *Taney's Dred Scott Decision* (1857)
* *Lincoln-Douglas Debates* (1858)
The "Irrepressible Conflict"

Buchanan's Election (1856)

A third party, with ex-President Fillmore at its head, entered this campaign. It was a combination of the American Party (Know Nothings) and the remnants of the Whig Party. The Know Nothings began their deservedly short life under the name of the "Order of the Star-Spangled Banner." Buchanan was chosen to lead the Democrats because he had gained favor with the South through his association with the Ostend Manifesto, and he was expected to appeal to the North because he came from Pennsylvania. The fact that he had kept aloof from the Kansas-Nebraska issue made him "available." John Breckenridge of Kentucky was his running mate on the ticket. The new Republican Party put its first candidate for President into the race, John Frémont of California.

The Democrats supported the Compromise of 1850 and the Kansas-Nebraska Bill. The Republicans claimed that Congress had the right to legislate on slavery in the territories, attacked the Ostend Manifesto, and favored the admission of Kansas as a free state. For a new party, the Republicans showed surprising strength.

	Popular Vote	Electoral Vote
Buchanan	1,838,169	174
Frémont	1,335,264	114
Fillmore	874,534	8

Only five free states voted for Buchanan. The Democratic Party was becoming a slave-state party. The Republicans were so elated with winning 11 states that they set to work building the party for the election of 1860. The poet, John Greenleaf

Whittier, expressed their enthusiasm in a political verse.

"Then sound again the bugles,
  Call the muster-roll anew;
  If months have well-nigh won the field,
  What may not four years do?"

** Taney's Dred Scott Decision (1857)

When President Buchanan was sworn into office, the Dred Scott Case was before the Supreme Court. In his inauguration speech the President included the expectation that the legal status of slavery in the territories would soon be settled by judicial authority. The decision came two days later. Chief Justice Roger B. Taney who had succeeded John Marshall in 1836, gave the 7 to 2 decision of the Court. In view of the extended period of controversy over the Kansas-Nebraska Bill and "Bleeding Kansas," many northerners were convinced that the decision rendered was influenced by the fact that five justices were southerners and seven of them were Democrats.

Dred Scott had been taken by his master from the slave state of Missouri into the free state of Illinois, then into the free territory of Wisconsin, and back to Missouri. Scott claimed his freedom on the basis of his residence in Illinois and Wisconsin where he had lived for a considerable period of time. The Court reached the following decisions.

1] Dred Scott was not a citizen and, therefore had no right to sue in a federal court.

His parents had been brought to the United States from Africa as slaves. The fact that Dred was born in the United States did not make him a *citizen* within the meaning of that word as used in the Constitution. Any state could make him a citizen of the state, but such citizenship would not extend beyond the borders of that state and would not include citizenship of the United States.

2] The Missouri Compromise was unconstitutional.

The Territory of Wisconsin had no right to exclude slavery. Property in the form of slaves was precisely the same as any other property and Congress had no right to restrict its ownership. Hence, the action taken by Congress in 1820, when it declared the Louisiana Territory north of 36°30′ free, was illegal.

3] Only a state had the right to forbid slavery.

There was no legal way to exclude slavery from the territories.

Dred Scott was not fighting for his freedom; he had already been assured of that. His owner, Sandford, was opposed to slavery and was using Scott as a test case to get a decision from the Supreme Court on the legal status of slavery in the territories. As we have noted, the first opinion given was that Dred Scott was not a citizen and couldn't bring suit in a federal court. Here the case could have ended; but the Court chose to go on to expound upon the decisions that it would make if such a case were before it. In doing this the Court was no longer concerned with Dred Scott, but was determining the legal status of slavery in the territories. This gave opponents of the decision a chance to claim that the case was actually closed as soon as the Court denied citizenship to Scott. In this view, all additional points made by the Court were unnecessary and uncalled for, that is, unofficial statements suggested by, but not part of, the case. Such a meandering of judicial opinion is called an *obiter dictum*. Should we speak of the Dred Scott *decision* or of the Dred Scott *obiter dictum*? Today, so long as we understand the situation, it doesn't much matter; but in 1857 it was a vitally important fact that a strong public opinion in the North refused to accept Taney's pronouncements as anything other than *obiter dictum*. The Republican Party had gathered unto itself the support of all anti-slavery votes except those of the most ardent abolitionists. Its official stand on slavery was that Congress should, by law, prevent its extension into the territories. Had the Republican Party accepted Taney's decision as authoritative, it would have lost its reason for existence; but it rejected the Court's opinion and went on to win the next presidential election.

* Lincoln-Douglas Debates (1858)

During the summer and early fall of the midterm elections, Lincoln and Douglas met in a series of debates throughout Illinois. Douglas was seeking re-election to the United States Senate. Lincoln believed slavery to be wrong, the Republican Party believed slavery to be wrong, and slavery, being wrong, should be prevented from spreading. There was a legal obligation to recognize the rights of slave states. But Lincoln and the Republican Party rejected the Supreme Court's Dred Scott decision, or, as they preferred to think of it, the Court's *obiter dictum*. Douglas held to the view that whether slavery was right or wrong was a matter to be decided in each state separately, and that all that was needed was for each state to mind its own business. Douglas, a bit obtuse about the moral force which was gathering strength in the North, saw no reason why the Union could not go on indefinitely part free and part slave. Lincoln had said, "I believe this government cannot endure permanently half slave and half free. I do not expect the Union to be dissolved . . . but I do expect it will cease to be divided. It will become all one thing, or all the other."

In the Freeport debate, Lincoln tried to force Douglas to make a choice between the Kansas-Nebraska principle of squatter sovereignty and the Dred Scott case. The Supreme Court had said that slavery could not be kept out of the territories, yet the Kansas-Nebraska Bill permitted the settlers to make a choice. It seemed that Douglas must either repudiate the Supreme Court decision, which would ruin him in the eyes of southern Democrats, or he must admit the error of the Kansas-Nebraska Bill which was his work. Douglas refused to make a direct choice, but he did give an answer that was the truth. It was also satisfactory to the Illinois voters. He said, "Slavery cannot exist a day or an hour anywhere, unless it is supported by local police regulations." This truth, known as the Freeport Doctrine, pointed out that slavery, while legal in all territories, could not exist in northern areas. Everyone knew that no northern territory would pass laws to sustain slavery, let alone enforce them. So the good people of Illinois could go home and sleep peacefully in full confidence that slavery was not going to spread northward. Douglas won re-election to the Senate, and Lincoln, although he could not have known it, had only two years to wait for the presidency. Douglas had driven many more southern Democrats into the Breckenridge camp. To please them, Douglas would have had to urge strict adherence and support for the Dred Scott decision, regardless of one's personal views about slavery. Any such firm stand in support of the Supreme Court would have lost Douglas his Senate seat. He had to win in the Senate race in 1858 to be in a position in 1860 to get the Democratic presidential nomination. Lincoln had put Douglas in a political dilemma. The tactics Douglas had to use to win his Senate seat cost him the presidency.

The "Irrepressible Conflict"

Was the Civil War the "irrepressible conflict between opposing and enduring forces" as Seward said in 1858? Since the fugitive slave law of 1850, the North had increasingly accepted Seward's statement that there was a "higher law" than the laws of Congress and the Constitution of the United States. In 1859, at Harpers Ferry in Virginia, John Brown and 18 followers seized a federal arsenal. After two days, they surrendered to Colonel Robert E. Lee. Two of Brown's sons and eight others of his small band were dead or dying. About six weeks later, John Brown was hanged and, soon afterward, six others went to the gallows. The audacity of John Brown's plan to organize a slave revolt, and the fanaticism of the leader created concern throughout the South. Thousands of Northerners accepted Brown as a hero, a martyr in a righteous cause. New England's philosopher and poet Ralph Waldo Emerson called him "the rarest of heroes, a pure idealist."

Slavery was emphasized by what Seward said and what John Brown did. It was the issue on which many Union soldiers were willing to risk their lives. There was no burning desire on the part of Confederate soliders to die for slavery. Many Confederate soldiers were convinced that the law was on their side. Jefferson's Kentucky Resolutions and the resulting theories of Calhoun were persuasive. The Constitution recognized slavery and the Supreme Court supported it everywhere except in free states. The Underground Railroad and the Personal Liberty Laws gave proof of the lawlessness of the North and its refusal to let the South alone. "Let the South alone" and "Mind your own business" were the refrains repeated again and again, in one form or another, by the South. Did the "higher Law" of the North and the "let us alone" of the South have to develop to the point of war? The Kansas-Nebraska Bill was an unnecessary blunder and there need never have been a Dred Scott Case. While the horrible slaughter of the Civil War and its attendant tragedies incline one to want to believe it was an "irrespressible conflict," the truth may well be that such a conclusion deserves no higher rating than that of wishful thinking. The economic differences of the North and South have been emphasized as the basic cause of the Civil War. Agricultural interests and industrial interests do develop political differences. A degree of sectionalism occurs when one nation has areas within it where such differences are extreme, but such economic conflicts were, and still are, common to many nations. Our Civil War did not wipe out, nor appreciably lessen, the economic conflict of interests between North and South. Such differences are common today in many nations and prevail in several of our states, but they are resolved, and re-resolved continually, by political action, not by force; by ballots, not by bullets.

Early in 1860, Senator Jefferson Davis of Mississippi offered a series of resolutions that were adopted. They pushed the political alignment a bit closer to war.

1] No state has the right to interfere with the domestic institutions of the other states.

2] The Federal government must extend all needful protection to slavery in the territories.

3] All state laws interfering with the recovery of fugitive slaves are unconstitutional.

The political result of these resolutions was the increased concentration of northern Democrats in the Douglas camp, and the southern Democrats in the Breckinridge faction. This solidifying of the sectional division of Democrats broke up the presidential nominating convention soon to be held.

Abraham Lincoln

1809 - 1865

1861-1865

REPUBLICAN

☆

Vice-President ANDREW JOHNSON

Secretary of State W. H. SEWARD   Secretary of Treasury SALMON P. CHASE

LINCOLN'S PUBLIC SERVICE BEFORE HE BECAME PRESIDENT

Member of Illinois State Legislature (Whig)
Member of U.S. House of Representatives (1846-48)

MAJOR ITEMS DURING LINCOLN'S ADMINISTRATIONS

The Union and the Confederacy Compared
The Problems Facing Each Side
Raising Men and Money
Relations with Foreign Nations

A Few Major Military Engagements of the War
Lincoln v. Congress at the End of the Civil War
Homestead Act
Lincoln's Assassination

* Election and Re-election of Lincoln (1860 and 1864)

After 10 days and 57 ballots the Democrats adjourned their nominating convention at Charleston, South Carolina, without selecting a candidate. The following month they held two separate conventions in Baltimore, Maryland, where one faction nominated Douglas and the other, Breckinridge. The two platforms were similar, with Breckinridge's making a more aggressively stated demand for federal protection of slavery in the territories. President Buchanan had broken with Douglas over the Lecompton Constitution and used his influence in favor of his Vice-President, Breckinridge. After his Freeport Doctrine, the cotton states Democrats did not trust Douglas.

The Republican nominating convention met in Chicago. Seward led in the first two ballots, but Lincoln won the nomination on the third ballot. The previous December, three days after John Brown was hanged, Lincoln had spoken at Cooper Union, New York City, where he had impressed eastern Republican leaders by his firm stand for the right of Congress to legislate on slavery in the territories, yet had addressed no harsh remarks toward the South. He had vigorously denied that the Republican Party had any part whatsoever in the John Brown raids, acts which he condemned completely. Lincoln was chosen because he possessed "availability"; he really had a log cabin background,

he could carry Illinois and probably Indiana, and he had won quite a national reputation by the Lincoln-Douglas debates of 1858. No one had any inkling that a giant of history had been discovered. The Republican platform rejected the Dred Scott Decision, asserted the right of Congress to exclude slavery in the territories, condemned the Lecompton Constitution, and advocated a protective tariff.

The Constitutional Union Party nominated John Bell of Tennessee. Their platform stated, "We recognize no political principle other than the Constitution, the Union of the States, and the Enforcement of the Laws." If there is any meaning to this, it is obscure. The Constitutional Unionists feared a war was coming, they earnestly hoped it wouldn't, and they had no idea what to do about it.

	Popular Vote		Electoral Vote
Lincoln	1,866,352	180	(18 free states)
Douglas	1,375,157	12	(1 slave state—Mo.)
Breckinridge	847,953	72	(13 slave states)
Bell	589,581	39	(3 slave states)

Between election day in November, 1860 and inauguration day the following March 4th, seven states seceded from the Union: South Carolina, Mississippi, Florida, Alabama, Georgia, Louisiana, and Texas. President Buchanan seemed bewildered as he took the position that these states had no right to secede, but that he had no right to prevent secession. Before Lincoln's inauguration the Confederate States of America had been organized. Jefferson Davis had been elected its president; Montgomery, Alabama had become its capital; the Stars and Bars had been adopted as its flag; it had sent agents abroad to seek aid, and President Davis had been authorized to raise 100,000 troops. In view of these preparations, Lincoln's first inaugural address was temperate as well as firm; it invited reconsideration by the secessionists.

> "I have no purpose, directly or indirectly, . . . to interfere with the institution of slavery in the states where it exists. I believe I have no lawful right to do so, and I have no inclination to do so."

> "I . . . consider . . . the Union is unbroken . . . I shall take care . . . that the laws of the Union be faithfully executed in all States."

> ". . . there need be no blood-shed or violence; and there shall be none, unless it be forced upon the national authority."

> "The government will not assail you. You can have no conflict without yourselves being the aggressors. You have no oath registered in heaven to destroy the government, while I shall have the most solemn one to preserve, protect, and defend it."

Lincoln's Re-election in 1864

This campaign was a struggle between the "Copperheads" and the fortunes of war. Copperheads were the "fifth column" of the North during the Civil War. Lincoln supporters gave them the name, referring to the poisonous snake, and the Copperheads attempted to turn the name into a symbol for freedom and justice by wearing in the visor of their caps a picture of the head of Liberty which was on the one-cent coin, commonly referred to as a copper. The mayor of New York, Fernando Wood, published the *Daily News* which advocated that the city secede from the Union. Agitation by Confederate spies, genuine labor unrest, and anger over the unfairness of the draft were whipped into a flame by the *Daily News* and resulted in four terrible days, July 13-16, 1863, of rioting, stealing, burning, and killing. Horace Greeley, editor of the *Tribune*, demanded a negotiated peace and accused Lincoln of prolonging the war to satisfy his personal ambition. The national leader of the Copperheads was Representative Clement L. Vallandigham of Ohio, who claimed that Lincoln was waging a "wicked" and "unnecessary" war in order to free the blacks and enslave the whites. Vallandigham was arrested and sent into the South, which also

had no use for him. The anti-war Democrats nominated General George B. McClellan on a platform calling for immediate cessation of hostilities and the preservation of the Federal Union of States. In the mid-summer of 1864, many in the North believed such a peace was possible in spite of the fact that Jefferson Davis had consistently denied that he would accept such terms. The terrific casualty lists and over three long years of fighting had brought the morale of the North close to the breaking point. The Confederacy had banked heavily on their ability to out-last the North and this calculation missed by a narrow margin. From July to October, General Philip Sheridan drove Jubal Early out of the Shenandoah Valley, and in September Sherman took Atlanta. The lift to Northern morale from these victories turned the tide toward Lincoln. Because thousands of "war Democrats" supported Lincoln, the Republican Party changed its name, for this election, to the Union Party.

	Popular Vote	Electoral Vote
Lincoln	2,216,067	212
McClellan	1,808,725	21

In his second inaugural address, Lincoln gave his version of why the war had started, what it was about, and what he now proposed to do about it. The spirit of revenge simply did not exist in this man; his strength before men was superb and his humility before God was complete.

> "Both parties deprecated war, but one of them would *make* war rather than let the nation survive, and the other would *accept* war rather then let it perish, and war came."

> "One eighth of the whole population was colored slaves . . . localized in the southern part (of the Union). These slaves constituted a peculiar and powerful interest. All knew that this interest was somehow the cause of the war."

> "Both (North and South) read the same Bible and pray to the same God, and each invokes His aid against the other. . . . Fondly do we hope, fervently do we pray, that this mighty scourge of war may speedily pass away. Yet, if God wills that it continue until all the wealth piled by the bondman's two hundred and fifty years of unrequited toil shall be sunk, and every drop of blood drawn with the lash shall be paid by another drawn by the sword, . . . so still it must be said, 'The judgments of the Lord are true and righteous altogether.' "

"With malice toward none, with charity for all, with firmness in the right as God gives us to see the right, let us strive on to finish the work we are in, . . . to do all which may achieve and cherish a just and lasting peace among ourselves and with all nations."

* The Union and the Confederacy Compared at the Beginning of the Civil War

Counting West Virginia, there were 24 Union states with a population of about 22,000,000. They contained most of the industry, most of the banks, and most of the railroad mileage. Their farms supplied a diversity of products, including ample food stuffs. Almost all of the merchant marine was owned by northerners. The federal government was their government with its army and navy and the organization to prosecute a war.

The Confederacy contained 11 states with a population of about 5,500,000 free persons and 3,500,000 slaves. Its industrial development and financial resources were less than one-third as great as that of the Union. Much of its agricultural wealth was in cotton, tobacco, sugar, and naval stores, all of which could aid in the war effort only if sold and delivered by ship to foreign ports. It could raise food stuffs, but railroad mileage and water transport being grossly inadequate, it could not deliver them where needed. The Southerners had to organize a government, a task made doubly difficult because they were fighting for state sovereignty and were extremely reluctant to grant power to a central government, even their own Confederacy in time of war.

The Confederate States were fully aware of the political, economic, financial, and man-power advantages of the Union, but they thought other factors made military success for their side well within the bounds of probability:

1] Great Britain wanted Southern products. A tariff-free exchange of British manufactured products for the agricultural raw materials of the South made such an attractive trade picture that the Confederacy fully expected an early alliance with England.

2] For the same reasons, but to a less compelling extent, France might materially aid the Confederacy.

3] Southerners knew fire-arms, horses, and the outdoor life. They arrogantly believed that one Southern soldier would be worth four or five Northern clerks, shop-keepers, farmers, artisans, and mill hands.

4] The South had a military tradition. Many of its men were professional soldiers and officers. Southerners had taken a major part in the Mexican War, an excellent dress rehearsal for the Civil War.

5] The Confederacy could fight a defensive war. It had no need to conquer the Union, but had simply only to resist stoutly enough to make the North war-weary.

6] The Confederacy more than half believed that the Union would not fight, and, if it did, they expected the North would be divided and half-hearted about it.

* The Problems Facing Each Side in the Civil War

The Union considered that the defeat of the Confederacy would entail four major accomplishments: capture Richmond, the nerve center and capital, blockade Confederate ports, control the Mississippi River and thus divide the Confederacy as well as cut off its meat supply from Texas, and cut the Confederacy into sections and then round up its armies. Clearly, this was a large order.

The Confederacy faced a seemingly much less formidable task. It had no military conquests that it must make. Its problem can be stated as four tactics: fight a basically defensive war, keep the Union off balance by threatening or making stabs at its nerve center, Washington, create dissension in the North, and outlast the Union by a resistance so spirited that Northern morale would break.

* Raising Men and Money

Raising Men

Although troops were drafted from April 1863 to the end of the war, the great bulk of the Union army was always made up of volunteers. The states had their quotas to raise and each state assigned quotas to cities, towns, and counties within its borders. So much pressure was created by local opinion and the desire of each community to meet its quota, that many a man "volunteered" with something less than enthusiasm. The effort to keep enlistments up led to the offering of bounties by local governments to all who volunteered. This encouraged "bounty jumping," a practice which consisted of enlisting to collect the bounty and then deserting in order to enlist again at another place to collect another bounty. Some bounty jumpers made 20 to 30 jumps. Local authorities were so anxious to fill their quotas that they pointedly neglected to ask too many questions when a stranger volunteered. After all, a bounty jumper did count toward the quota, if he were not recognized as such, and meant that one less local boy would be needed. In March, 1863, the draft was started and was very poorly organized. A drafted man could pay the government $300 and thus avoid service, or he could provide a substitute. Providing a substitute meant paying something less than $300 to another person willing to take one's place, and this meant that sons of well-to-do families could stay home while the young men who couldn't raise the money had to answer the draft. So, between the draft and accepting pay as substitutes, the families in the poorer communities contributed much more than their fair share of manpower for the Union armies. The obvious injustice of the situation led to the saying that the conflict was a "rich man's war, but a poor man's fight." Many who could buy their way out of the draft could take advantage of the booming war economy in the North and perhaps achieve membership in the "shoddy aristocracy." "Shoddy aristocracy" came to mean anyone who made money by war profiteering, but it originated as a description of those who cheated the government by selling it blankets and uniforms made of woolen fibers reclaimed from old cloth and getting paid at premium prices commanded by virgin wool fiber. Boots made of cheap substitute materials were sold at prices paid for fine quality leather. Bribing government purchasing agents was common. No wonder there were draft riots! (See p. 129 for riots in N.Y.C.) The more one reads of the Civil War the more one becomes convinced that there was much mismanagement and corruption. In refreshing contrast, however, two aspects of the war stand out in clear relief: the magnificent fighting qualities of the opposing armies and the nobility of Abraham Lincoln. And if greatness as a soldier and as a man can be granted to a leader in a less than noble cause, such an award must go without reservation to General Robert E. Lee.

The Confederacy started drafting men into the service in April, 1862, but it was the volunteers who kept the ranks filled throughout the war. The slaves were loyal to the families that owned them and the southern women directed their work in turning cotton and tobacco fields into acres of food crops. There were no bounties in the Confederacy, but there was some disaffection over the draft which, like that of the Union, permitted a drafted man to buy a substitute.

Raising Money

The Union financed the war by a tariff, an income tax, the National Banking System, excise taxes, and *greenbacks*. The Morrill Tariff had high rates which were intended to encourage American manufacturing, but, at almost any import duty, an appreciable flow of goods would enter the country under the conditions of the war economy in the North. The result was that the Morrill Tariff produced considerable revenue. The income tax took about 5% on incomes between $600 and $5,000 and 10% on higher incomes. The National Banking System was established in 1863 and was aimed to attract large amounts of money quickly. Banks bought United States bonds to the amount of $30,000 or more and, to belong to the system, had to invest at least one-third of their capital in such bonds. The banks could issue bank notes up to 90% of the face value of the bonds they purchased and then loan these notes at interest. Interest on their bank notes and interest on the bonds they purchased gave the banks almost double interest on their money, a circumstance which created much criticism. As it took some time to get this National Banking System under way, its effect on Civil War financing was not great; but it remained the mainstay of our banking system until replaced by the Federal Reserve System in 1913. Excise taxes, taxes on goods originating in this country, were placed on a great number of items, even including some food products. *Greenbacks* were issued to the amount of about $400,000,000. This "printing press" money had no material backing and was therefore completely inflationary. It was made legal tender for all private debts, but its value fluctuated during the war between 35 cents and 78 cents on the dollar. While the printing of such fiat money is always a dangerous type of financing, the Federal government restricted the amount issued to less than 15% of the cost of the war. By 1879 Congress had passed legislation which provided for the redemption of greenbacks in specie at face value.

The Confederacy levied excise taxes, sold bonds to its people, borrowed from foreign bankers, and printed fiat money. Loans from abroad were far smaller than the Confederacy had expected and totaled not more than $15,000,000. Income from excise taxes and from the sale of bonds amounted to no more than 15% of the total cost of the war to the South. The printing presses made most of the money and with the fortunes of war against it, the Confederate paper dollar was worth about 1½ cents after the defeats at Vicksburg and Gettysburg in July, 1863.

** Relations with Foreign Nations During the Civil War

England

1] On May 13, 1861, just one month after the surrender of Fort Sumter, Queen Victoria recognized the belligerency of the Confederacy. This was not, in itself, an unfriendly act. Recognition of the Confederacy did not mean that England acknowledged the independence of the South, but only that she was ready to treat the Confederacy according to international laws usually observed between belligerents and neutrals. It was common knowledge that official England favored the Confederacy, and this alone made the United States look with suspicion on any move England made. Lincoln was insisting that the Southern states could not, under our Constitution, secede; that they were rebelling, and that he was using the power of the federal government to quell the rebellion. Queen Victoria's quick recognition of "certain states styling themselves the Confederate States of America" was hardly in harmony with Lincoln's view of the nature of the Civil War and caused strong resentment throughout the Union.

2] When Captain Wilkes of the U.S.S. *San Jacinto* stopped the British mail steamer *Trent* on the high seas and seized two Confederate agents, Mason and Slidell, the American press and people hailed the incident with joy while the English press demanded an apology and reparations. Mason and Slidell were on their way to England and France, respectively, to raise money on cotton and tobacco and to urge whatever support for the Confederacy they could persuade these nations to give. They had evaded the Union blockade and had reached Cuba where they boarded the *Trent* at Havana. When Captain Wilkes took Mason and Slidell off the *Trent* on the high seas, international waters, he committed an act legally very similar to the British seizures from our ships which were a major grievance leading to the War of 1812. Secretary of State Seward advised President Lincoln that Captain Wilkes' action was legally indefensible, and Lincoln very wisely accepted this view of the affair and not only released Mason and Slidell, but had Seward apologize to the British minister. The Confederacy had a few weeks of high hopes that England would soon be their ally, for they noted that about 8,000 British troops were sent to Canada during this flare-up. Knowing when to back down and knowing when to hold firm are equally important; a misjudgment by Lincoln in the *Trent* affair would have tipped the scales toward a Confederate victory.

3] Lincoln's announcement in September, 1862, that the following New Year's Day the Emancipation Proclamation would become operative was far more important for its reception in England than for any effect it had within the Union or upon the Confederacy. Horace Greeley's *Tribune* was crusading in favor of such a proclamation and had made an eloquent plea under the title "The Prayer of Twenty Millions." In August, 1862, Lincoln's answer to Greeley set the record straight about the President's position on slavery.

> "I would save the Union. . . . If there be those who would not save the Union unless they could at the same time destroy slavery, I do not agree with them. My paramount object . . . is not either to save or to destroy slavery. If I could save the Union without freeing any slave, I would do it; and if I could save it by freeing all the slaves I would do it; and if I could save it by freeing some and leaving others alone, I would also do that. . . . I have here stated my purpose according to my view of official duty; and I intend no modification of my oft expressed personal wish that all men everywhere could be free."

One month after expressing this official opinion, Lincoln announced the Emancipation Proclamation. He did it, not because he had shifted his position on slavery, but because he was convinced that such a proclamation would help preserve the Union. And he was right. As long as the people of Europe believed the war was over the legal right of states to secede from the Union, they were inclined to favor the seceding states. Why should states be forced to remain in a government against their will? There is a well-founded tendency for people to be sympathetic with revolutionists in distant lands, for people seldom reach the point of rebellion except after long-standing and substantial grievances. Our minister to Spain, Carl Schurz, informed President Lincoln that Europe would be sympathetic to the Union only when they realized that a Union victory meant the end of slavery, and a Southern victory the continuance of slavery. What was true of people in continental Europe was doubly true of the English. Lincoln's Emancipation Proclamation was a political master-stroke for the preservation of the Union. Mass meetings in England demanded that their government stop the construction of ships for the Confederacy; unemployed mill hands in English towns demonstrated in favor of the Union even though their loss of jobs was due to the Union blockade; and the Russian czar, who had recently freed the serfs, sent some of his warships to American waters in readiness to help the Union if England entered the war on the side of the Confederacy. The Emancipation Proclamation certainly had something to do with the presence of well over 50,000 negro troops in the Union forces and the aid given by an even larger number of negro laborers who worked with the army. Lincoln had not become an abolitionist; he was still preserving the Union. (For provisions of the Emancipation Proclamation see p. 138.)

4] In 1862 and 1863 several commerce raiders were built in English shipyards for the Confederacy. English law, as well as international law, forbade the building and equipping of fighting ships in a neutral nation for a belligerent. But a Confederate agent persuaded English ship builders that it was legal to build such ships if only they didn't quite complete them and sent them to a foreign yard for the finishing touches. This they did. The *Alabama, Florida*, and *Shenandoah* were such vessels. They destroyed over 250 Union ships and caused several hundred American merchantmen to be transferred to foreign registries in order to avoid attack. These commerce raiders, built in English shipyards and finished in France or elsewhere, became the subject of arbitration at Geneva in 1872 (see p. 147).

France

1] The French government made a substantial loan to the Confederacy.

2] Emperor Napoleon III of France permitted commerce raiders to be built in French shipyards and he had, in July of 1862, suggested to the British government that the time was ripe for the recognition of the independence of the Confederacy. Slidell was then in Paris, thousands of bales of cotton in the Confederacy were ready for shipment, the shortages of cotton for the mills of France and England had become acute, and McClellan had been driven back in his attempt to take Richmond. This combination of factors convinced Napoleon III that the time was approaching when open assistance to the Confederacy might be good policy for France. Suddenly in mid-September of 1862 the picture changed. The repulse of Lee by McClellan at Antietam was followed by Lincoln's announcement of the Emancipation Proclamation; a combination of events that put an end to any plans Napoleon had for more active support of the Confederacy.

3] The most ambitious action of Napoleon III against the United States was his challenge to the Monroe Doctrine. In 1861 England, Spain, and France sent warships to Mexico in a move to collect debts owed to them. Mexico was able to negotiate a settlement with England and Spain, but France used the situation as a pretext for colonization. Napoleon III sent troops into Mexico and took Mexico City. He then invited the Austrian archduke, Maximillian, to accept the position of Emperor of Mexico. Maximillian, with the support of French troops, maintained control of Mexico throughout the Civil War. But soon after Appomattox, Lincoln ordered General Sheridan to proceed to Mexico with 50,000 seasoned Union soldiers. Napoleon promptly ordered the withdrawal of the French forces supporting Maximillian, who unwisely stayed after losing French aid and was executed by the Mexican government.

A Few Major Military Engagements of the Civil War

Fort Sumter (Surrendered April 14, 1861)

Union Major Anderson surrendered to Confederate General Beauregard.

The battle of Fort Sumter was really more a political maneuver than an armed conflict. The Southern view of Federal forts was that the forts went with the states, that is, if a state seceded, the forts automatically belonged to the states. Of course, Lincoln could not accept any such view. Virginia had not yet committed herself, and it was feared that any direct military move from Washington in support of Fort Sumter, which was running short on supplies, would play into the hands of the Virginia secessionists. If Virginia seceded, she would surely take other states with her into the Confederacy. Lincoln's cabinet, including Secretary of State Seward, advised against any attempt to send supplies to Fort Sumter, but, after several days delay, Lincoln notified South Carolina, on April 6, 1861, that an expedition "with provisions only" was being dispatched to relieve Major Anderson and his garrison. On April 11th South Carolina ordered Major Anderson to surrender; this he was willing to do after his supplies ran out and he then could surrender with honor. But the next day, April 12th, Confederate General Beauregard opened fire on Fort Sumter and, after a bombardment of about 34 hours, forced the surrender of the Union garrison. There were no casualties. Professors Morison and Commager give the frightening information that the decision to open fire was made by two Confederate staff officers who had taken it upon themselves to reject Major Anderson's offer to surrender within two days when his supplies would have been exhausted. Had this offer been known by Jefferson Davis, the decision might well have been different. One of these staff officers later said that the order to fire was given because they feared that consulting with Davis would have led to a conference with Secretary of State Seward, and might have resulted in a peaceful settlement. The young staff officers wanted war! Is this the way World War III is to start?

On April 15th, the day after Major Anderson's surrender, President Lincoln called for 75,000 volunteers. On April 17th Virginia seceded and within a month Arkansas, Tennessee, and North Carolina had joined the Confederacy. Perhaps the greatest blow to follow from Fort Sumter was General Robert E. Lee's resignation from the United States army because, as he put it, "I have been unable to raise my hand against my native state, my relatives, my children, and my home."

First Bull Run (Manassas Junction) July 21, 1861

Union forces under General McDowell were routed by Generals Thomas J. Jackson ("Stonewall Jackson"), Beauregard, and Joseph E. Johnston.

This battle was fought by Union recruits with not more than three months training. This unmanageable mass, whose officers were just as "green," was sent into battle to satisfy the clamor of the press and the people. With cries of "On to Richmond" 30,000 men and boys marched south to Manassas where they attacked before dawn on July 21st. Until mid-afternoon the Union seemed to be winning, but when Confederate reinforcements arrived, the battle turned into a disorderly rout of the undisciplined raw recruits under McDowell. For over 24 hours Union soldiers straggled back to Washington and, in their retreat, passed civilians driving south in their carriages to see the "fun." The spirit of expectant celebration of an easy victory changed to fear for the safety of Washington. But the Confederates in victory were almost as stunned as the Union in defeat. Both sides had caught a glimpse of the long tough fight ahead; reality had replaced glamour, determination had replaced heroics, and, of much less significance, General McClellan had replaced General McDowell.

The Peninsular Campaign (March to July 1862)

McClellan had 110,000 well trained, well equipped soldiers ready for battle. By mid-May this Army of the Potomac was within 20 miles of Richmond and then McClellan waited for re-enforcements which he didn't need. He won battles, but failed to press his advantage. On June 26 McClellan found his army seriously threatened by a trap set by General Lee. There followed the *Seven Days' Battles* in which the Union forces fought superbly and accomplished a retreat from a disadvantageous position. McClellan had saved the Army of the Potomac from capture, a substantial achievement,

but hardly the task he had set out to do; namely, capture Richmond. Lincoln was impatient, perhaps disgusted, with McClellan's over cautious tactics, and McClellan was deeply dissatisfied with Lincoln's withholding re-enforcements he thought he should have had. McClellan's popularity with his soldiers, his ability to win battles, and his personal ambition for public position combined to make him a figure of some political importance, especially to those who looked upon President Lincoln with something less than enthusiasm.

Second Bull Run (Manassas Junction) Aug. 29-30, 1862

Union General John Pope, was defeated by Generals Lee and "Stonewall" Jackson.

This was a bad setback for the Union. It cancelled what success the Union had so far in Virginia and posed a serious threat to Washington. Lincoln, without consulting his cabinet, put McClellan back in command on the theory that, in spite of his faults he could win battles.

Antietam (Sharpsburg) Sept. 17, 1862

Union General McClellan defeated Lee.

Had the Confederates won this battle, its forces under Lee would have been in a good position to advance on Washington or Philadelphia. Napoleon III of France was conferring with England about recognizing the independence of the Confederate States of America and proposing an end to the war. Had Lee been the victor and the peace feelers by England and France been rejected, the active intervention by England on behalf of the Confederacy would have been a distinct possibility. In the bloodiest single day's fighting of the war, McClellan's men fought Lee to a draw. The Union forces could have poured in fresh troops to change the result into a decisive victory, but McClellan allowed Lee to withdraw his forces. Casualties were about even, over 2,000 killed and over 9,000 wounded on each side. The fact that McClellan had forced Lee to retreat was overshadowed by the fact that he had failed to capture or to defeat the enemy when the opportunity to do so was excellent. Nevertheless, the stopping of Lee at Antietam checked all immediate intention by France and England to propose a peace or to make any official moves toward support of the Confederacy. This repulse of Lee's army gave Lincoln the situation he needed to announce the Emancipation Proclamation which was to become effective on January 1st, 1863. This announcement, made on September 22nd, 1862, greatly lessened the likelihood of foreign intervention.

Vicksburg (July 4, 1863)

With the surrender of Vicksburg to Grant by the Confederate General, Pemberton, the Union had complete control of the Mississippi River.

Commodore Foote and General Grant started this campaign in the west by taking Forts Henry and Donelson on the Tennessee and Cumberland Rivers respectively. The Union occupied Cairo at the junction of the Ohio and Mississippi Rivers and from there General Pope and Commodore Foote went down the Mississippi and captured Island #10. Grant marched south from Fort Donelson to Shiloh (Pittsburg Landing) where, in a tough two-day battle on April 6-7, 1862, he turned a near defeat into a victory. Union forces held Memphis, Tennessee, from which Grant marched south along the Mississippi which he crossed to the west bank in order to get south of Vicksburg. He then recrossed the Mississippi to the east bank on April 30, 1863 and went northeast until he could approach the Confederate fortress from the rear. The march to Vicksburg from the land side entailed a series of battles over a period of three weeks. Grant's army of 20,000 outfought larger Confederate forces over a distance of about 200 miles in enemy territory, and, on May 22, 1863, the seige of Vicksburg began. The Confederate garrison under Pemberton held out under a brutal bombardment and two major assaults until July 4th when he surrendered with his 30,000 troops who were on the point of mutiny through lack of food. Aside from prisoners, the casualties were about equal, between 9,000 and 10,000. Lincoln had found a general who could win and stick at it until he ran the enemy right into the ground.

While Grant, Foote, and Pope were securing the upper Mississippi River, Admiral Farragut had successfully forced his way by Forts St. Philip and Jackson which guarded the approach to New Orleans. The next obstacle up the Mississippi, Port Hudson at the northern border of Louisiana, fell to the Union on July 9, 1863 after about a seven weeks' seige. Between Port Hudson and Vicksburg there were no defenses and the Mississippi was wholly under Union control. The Confederacy was cut; the meat supply from Texas was to be sorely missed as the months of war dragged on.

Gettysburg (July 1-4, 1863)

Union General Meade defeated Lee.

Lee's advance into Pennsylvania was a stab into a northern state to break the morale of the Union. A victory on Northern soil could greatly increase the influence of the Copperheads and multiply the dissension already breaking out in draft riots. A victory in Pennsylvania could revive the probability of foreign aid for the Confederacy; it could make the task of winning the war appear to the North to be too tough and too long delayed to be worth the sacrifice required. A Confederate victory at Gettysburg might have achieved these ends, but it was not to be. Meade took favorable positions and awaited attack. The battles raged for three days, for Gettysburg was a series of engagements on a large battlefield. On July 3rd, Confederate General Pickett led a massive charge up Cemetery Ridge and failed. Lee maintained his positions until the next day and then withdrew. Confederate killed totaled about 4,000 and the Union dead about 3,000. The following November 19th Lincoln gave his Gettysburg Address at the dedication of the cemetery on the battlefield. In three minutes, with ten sentences, President Lincoln had spoken his heart and given the world a treasure.

From Chattanooga to Savannah (May 7th to December 22nd 1864)

General Sherman took Atlanta and cut a 60 mile wide swath to Savannah.

In the march from Chattanooga to Atlanta, Sherman's army of about 60,000 was delayed by a series of skirmishes and some real battles, but it was evident that the Union forces were too strong to be stopped. On July 17 Sherman came within eight miles of Atlanta and, after a seige of six weeks, took the city on September 2. After destroying everything of use to the enemy, Sherman left Atlanta for his famous march to the sea. For 300 miles his troops cut a path 60 miles wide in which railroads, bridges, warehouses, many homes, factories, crops, livestock, and any other property that was useful, or took the fancy of the Union troops, was confiscated or destroyed. On December 10, Sherman reached Savannah which he captured on December 22 in time to present to President Lincoln for Christmas.

The Wilderness Campaign and Drive on Richmond (May and June 1864)

Grant forced Lee to surrender at Appomattox.

At Culpeper, about 70 miles southwest of Washington and 80 miles northwest of Richmond, Grant had the Army of the Potomac ready to hammer its way, foot by foot, to the Confederate capital. The Union had the men to do the job, cost what it may;

and, finally, they had the general with the fortitude to lead large numbers of men to both death and victory. Lee picked the battle sites along his route of retreat. He picked them well and forced Grant to pay dearly, but in numbers and equipment the Union was greatly superior. Grant taught the Confederates that Northern men were as fully determined to preserve the Union as Southern men were to protect their homes and preserve their way of life. The gruelling campaign lasted from early May until the middle of June in 1864. Some of the major battles were: The Wilderness (May 4-6), Spotsylvania (May 8-12), Cold Harbor (June 1-3), and the unsuccessful assault on Petersburg (June 15-18). Union losses were twice those of the Confederacy, but the Union could still go on while the Confederacy had spent its strength.

For nine more months Petersburg was under siege. On April 2, 1865, Lee evacuated Petersburg in an attempt to go to Lynchburg, a few miles to the west, but Grant forced his surrender at Appomattox on April 9, 1865.

John Brown's Body

It would be a shame to leave the Civil War without reading the poem, *John Brown's Body*, by Stephen Vincent Benét. Read it, then listen to the recording (Columbia Masterworks). Here is the thinking and feeling of Northern and Southern soldiers, the battle of Gettysburg, the humility and strength of Lincoln, and the love and respect inspired by the rapier-steel quality of a true gentleman, General Lee. It is the poets who delve deepest with the fewest words.

** Lincoln v. Congress at the End of the Civil War

Lincoln insisted that the Southern states were in rebellion, that they had attempted to secede from the Union, and that they had been prevented from doing so. In December 1863 when it was evident that the question was no longer which side would win, but only how long the war could last, Lincoln announced his reconstruction plan. The rebelling states must adopt constitutions which forbade slavery and, in addition, the voters in these states must take an oath of allegiance to the United States. The number of voters required to take the oath of allegiance was to be not less than 10% of the number of persons who voted in each state in the election of 1860. This was called Lincoln's 10% Plan. Months before the war ended, Tennessee, Arkansas, and Louisiana conformed to this presidential plan, but Congress refused to seat their representatives. Lincoln's convictions were well expressed by General Grant at Appomattox when Union troops started to cheer as General Lee rode away after signing the terms of surrender. Grant ordered the cheering stopped and said, "The war is over; the rebels are our countrymen again." To take the view that the Confederate states had seceded would be to give Congress authority to set the pattern for their re-admission, for the Constitution gives to Congress the power to admit states to the Union. But quelling any civil disorder, even a four-year rebellion, is an executive function and, when peace is restored, it is the chief executive's proper function to set things in order again. This Lincoln hoped to do. His best chance to overcome the opposition of Congress would be to get the Southern states operating under the 10% Plan during the summer of 1865 when Congress was not in session. Lincoln's prestige might have been enough, coupled with his persuasiveness and the inherent wisdom of his program, to have won the political battle; but to stifle the desire for revenge after such a grievous conflict, especially when the spirit of revenge was the obvious method to sustain power for the Republican Party may well have been too great a task for any leader. What turned out to be the Crime of Reconstruction may well have been more truly the Irrepressible Crime than that the Civil War had been the Irrepressible Conflict. An assassin's bullet killed Lincoln less than a week after Appomattox. He could have had no idea of the place he had won in the hearts of his contemporaries, much less any inkling of his place in history. The Congress was bent on regaining power after four years of subordination to a war-time President. It was almost a decade before the voters realized the political motives behind the "bloody shirt" tactics of the Radical Republicans and turned away from them.

* Homestead Act (1862)

Westward expansion of our population continued during the Civil War. Prospectors were seeking gold and silver, California and Oregon were attracting new settlers, and many were going west to escape the draft. The Homestead Act stimulated this westward movement by offering 160 acres to any head of a family. The land could be his if he lived on it for five years, or he could buy it at $1.25 an acre after he had lived on it for six months. A registration fee of about $30 was charged. The purpose of the act was frustrated to a degree by land companies and other speculators buying the better lands at $1.25 an acre for resale. The provisions of residence and of being the head of a family were so fraudulently administered that the effect of the law was to encourage speculation more than homesteading.

Lincoln's Assassination (April 14, 1865)

On April 11th, two days after Appomattox, President Lincoln addressed a crowd that had gathered on the White House lawn to hear what they expected to be a victory speech. They heard a brief reiteration of his ideas for a peace settlement. Lincoln again explained his 10% Plan (see p. 136) and expressed the hope that negroes whose abilities warranted it, would be allowed to vote and that those negroes who had fought in the Union forces might be given the vote, but that all such matters of course, would be left to the individual states. On the morning of April 14th there was a cabinet meeting at which talk turned to the treatment of the rebels. Lincoln opposed any attempt to designate certain rebels as criminals to be hanged. As he put it, "Enough lives have been sacrificed." That evening he went to Ford's Theater with his wife. To attract more patronage, the theater had advertised that the President planned to attend the play, so that it was common knowledge in Washington where he would be, and what box at the theater the presidential party would occupy. A Washington policeman was on duty to stand guard at the entrance of the presidential box during the play, but he left his post long enough to permit the assassin to enter unnoticed, stand directly behind the President and fire at very close range into the back of Lincoln's head. This murder was the act of John Wilkes Booth, an actor, whose compelling motive seems to have been an intense hatred based upon Lincoln's hopes for the gradual advancement of the negro. Booth was a monomaniac, and the one idea about which he was insane was the racial issue. After firing the shot, Booth stepped onto the front rail of the box and jumped, but, as he jumped, one foot caught in a flag and he fell to the stage. As he got up he yelled, "Sic semper tyrannis—Virginia is avenged." The Latin phrase ("ever thus to tyrants") was the motto of Virginia, but this pathetic actor, with one revolver bullet, had dealt Virginia and the South a tragic blow, comparable, perhaps, to the suffering caused by the Civil War itself. On July 7, 1865, three men and a woman were hanged. Mrs. Mary Surratt kept the boarding house where Booth and the other men had frequently met to plot the assassination of Lincoln, Secretary of State, Seward, and Vice President Johnson. Seward was attacked at his home, but recovered from a slashed throat, and the attack on Johnson never occurred. It may be that Lincoln would have lost the battle with the Radical Republicans in Congress over the policy of reconstruction; but, with Andrew Johnson in the White House, there was neither the prestige nor the tact required if the presidential 10% Plan was to prevail.

Andrew Johnson

1865-1869

1808 - 1875

REPUBLICAN

☆

Secretary of State W. H. SEWARD

JOHNSON'S PUBLIC SERVICE BEFORE HE BECAME PRESIDENT

Democratic Congressman from Tennessee (1843-53)
Democratic Senator from Tennessee (1857-62)
Military Governor of Tennessee (1862-64)
Vice-President in Lincoln's Second Term (43 days)

MAJOR ITEMS OF JOHNSON'S ADMINISTRATION

13th Amendment (1865)	*Reconstruction Act (1867)*
14th Amendment (1868)	*Ku Klux Klan*
15th Amendment (1870)	*Tenure of Office Act (1867)*
Black Codes	*Johnson's Trial*

* Unfortunate Political Facts about President Johnson

Andrew Johnson had always been a Democrat, but as a War Democrat who had been the only United States Senator from a Confederate state to remain loyal to the Union, he had been put on the "National Union" (Republican) ticket with Lincoln in 1864 to give the party a national flavor. He had separated himself from the Democratic Party and was never accepted by the Republican Party. Coming to power through succession never brings with it the prestige gained by winning an election. Lincoln's cabinet and the experienced Republican leaders in Congress looked upon Johnson as an outsider who was merely the *nominal* head of the party and a President by accident. If President Johnson tried to direct policy, they would follow only when it was their policy he advised. Congressmen were not looking for presidential leadership; they were hoping to find a president who would go along with them, or, at least, cause a minimum of trouble by keeping out of their way. Congress was determined to reconstruct the South and to run the country, and no man, especially Andrew Johnson, who wasn't really a Republican, was going to stop them. Unfortunately, one of Johnson's few weaknesses was an inability to win men to his views or to work well with others. He managed to alienate public men who wanted to go along with his program. It was a time that demanded in great abundance the very characteristics that Johnson lacked. Then again, it is always a difficult situation when one succeeds to an office immediately after a great man has left it.

13th Amendment (1865)

This amendment was necessary to abolish slavery. The Emancipation Proclamation of January 1, 1863 applied only to "all persons held as slaves within a state or designated part of a state . . . in rebellion against the United States. . . ." This left slavery unaffected in the four loyal slave states; Delaware, Maryland, Kentucky, and Missouri. It applied only to rebellious areas which were still beyond the control of the federal government and would, therefore, pay no attention to it. Only as Union armies occupied Confederate territory were slaves freed under the Emancipation Proclamation. Missouri and Maryland freed their slaves by state law before the 13th Amendment was adopted, but individual state action could not guarantee abolition throughout the nation.

"Neither slavery nor involuntary servitude, except as a punishment for crime whereof the party shall have been duly convicted, shall exist within the United States, or any place subject to their jurisdiction."

14th Amendment (1868)

This amendment marks the end of the presidential reconstruction plan and the beginning of congressional control. Its provisions make constitutional the penalties and restrictions the Radical Republicans wished to place upon the ex-Confederate states. Its major purpose was to force the South to give equal civil rights to the negro.

1] A citizen was defined so as to include negroes. The Dred Scott Case had pointed to the need of such a definition. "All persons born or naturalized in the United States, and subject to the jurisdiction thereof, are citizens of the United States and of the State wherein they reside."

2] "No State shall make or enforce any law which shall abridge the privileges or immunities of citizens of the United States; . . ."

3] "Nor shall any State deprive any person of life, liberty, or property, without due process of law; . . ."

4] ". . . nor (shall any state) deny to any person within its jurisdiction the equal protection of the laws."

5] If males over 21 were not allowed to vote, the state would lose representation in the House in the same proportion it had denied suffrage. This was to punish any state that withheld the vote from its negro adults.

6] Any persons who had held a public office requiring an oath of allegiance to the Constitution and then had "broken" that oath by joining the Confederate armed forces, was not permitted to hold any such public office again. This provision robbed the South of its best leadership. It was purely punitive and wholly unwise, but probably no more severe, unjust, and foolish than the treatment usually handed out by the victors in a war.

7] The Confederate debts shall not be paid. This was an innocuous provision, for the ex-Confederate states had neither the ability nor the inclination to pay, and those who had loaned money to a losing cause did not expect to get it back.

The provision (number 5) intended to punish a state for denying suffrage has never been enforced, and never should be. All states have laws limiting suffrage, and determining just how many males over 21 are affected in each state would be a task in itself. Every state would be suspicious of every other state in its anxiety to receive a proportionately fair representation in the House, and the check by federal officials would offer a perfect setting for a perpetual political wrangle. Now that we have more women voters than men, the provision is that much more ridiculous. While it is a sound principle that fundamental law, such as our Constitution, must be upheld; there are rare exceptions, such as this, when a provision of basic law is best ignored.

President Johnson was opposed to this 14th Amendment and advised the ex-Confederate states not to ratify it. Only Tennessee quickly ratified it and thus escaped the worst effects of the "Crime of Reconstruction." The legislatures set up in the other ten ex-Confederate states during the summer of 1865 under the presidential 10% Plan, rejected the amendment and were labeled the "Sinful Ten" by the Radical Republicans who refused recognition to these re-organized state governments and proceeded to draw up the Reconstruction Act of 1867. This act stated that there was no legal government in any ex-Confederate state except Tennessee. It then went on to set up the Congressional plan of reconstruction (see p. 140).

15th Amendment (1870)

"The right of citizens of the United States to vote shall not be denied or abridged by the United States or by any State on account of race, color, or previous condition of servitude."

This amendment was intended to force the states to permit negro suffrage, but it had an easy loophole. It does not make negroes voters, it makes them only *potential* voters. Negroes may legally be kept from voting so long as the reasons for depriving them of the vote is something other than race, color, or previous condition of servitude. The result has been that, until after World War I, the negro vote throughout the South remained so small as to be without power. Even after World War II this was still a reasonably accurate statement, but there had developed an important difference; organized groups throughout the United States and substantial numbers of Southern whites had begun crusading for the fulfillment of the promise of the 15th Amendment. It is interesting to note that the 19th Amendment made women *potential* voters only, but immediately suffrage was extended to women in all states where they did not already have the vote. This gives a good illustration of how great a difference public opinion makes in the enforcement and administration of law.

* Black Codes

Immediately after Appomattox, the Southern states began painfully to pick themselves up. The freedmen, or ex-slaves, were a major problem. Vagrancy and apprenticeship laws became common devices for keeping the negro at work and under control. By definition an ex-slave was a vagrant; he had no home, no visible means of support, and was therefore a danger to the community. A substantial fine could be worked off by six months' labor for some white man designated by the court. This system could put the freedman back on his old plantation, living in the same slave hut, and working for his old master. Or a freedman could be apprenticed to his old master to "learn" a skill which he had commonly practiced for years as a slave. When the vagrancy and apprenticeship terms ended, they could be re-imposed. To the Southerner this was a practical solution to an immediate problem of gigantic proportions. To the Northerner this was slavery again under another name. It may be that the Black Codes were a good temporary answer to the situation if wages gradually replaced the system as soon as the increased economic well-being of the South permitted. It is not difficult to see, however, that the first two years after Appomattox was hardly the time to expect either the South or the North to see this problem with any objectivity. The clash of views over the Black Codes was inevitable and bitter, both sides being certain of the rightness of their own view and equally sure of the other's vindictiveness.

* Reconstruction Act   (1867)

The first Reconstruction Act was passed over President Johnson's veto on March 2nd, 1867. It required each of ten ex-Confederate states, the "Sinful Ten," to replace its already functioning government, established under the 10% Plan, with another government to be established through a state constitutional convention to which delegates were to be chosen by universal manhood suffrage, except for those leading white citizens who would be disqualified by the terms of the 14th Amendment. When elections were held in accordance with these new state constitutions and representatives were elected to the federal legislature, Congress could then decide whether each candidate was to be allowed to take his seat. Because the state governments believed, as did President Johnson, the Reconstruction Act to be unconstitutional, they stalled and resisted by all means short of violence. The answer of Congress was a series of supplements to the original Reconstruction Act which were passed in March and July 1867, and July of 1868. President Johnson, although he did all he could to stop such laws, felt it his duty to enforce them after they had passed over his veto. Thus the South was nudged into line.

The ten states (not including Tennessee) were divided into five military districts with a general in charge of each district. Martial law prevailed, and when the state governments failed to call the required state constitutional conventions, the military made the necessary arrangements and supervised the elections. There were 20,000 troops, including some negro militia, to enforce orders. About 700,000 negroes and 625,000 whites were registered as legal voters throughout the ten states. In South Carolina, Florida, Alabama, Louisiana, and Mississippi there were more negro than white voters.

The state legislatures elected under these new constitutions were led by Scalawags and Carpetbaggers. Scalawags were white Southerners who cooperated fully with the Radical Republicans and sometimes used their superior knowledge and abilities to seize as much power and steal as much money as they could by gaining high office in the "reconstructed" state governments. An influx of Northerners, some of them unsavory characters, came into the "Sinful Ten" states to become political leaders of the ignorant blacks and the hapless whites. Many negro legislators were unable to sign their names. Most of them were pleased with the flattery of holding office and easily bribed with cigars, liquor, and small change. The big graft went to the Scalawags and Carpetbaggers. The state constitutions were well drafted and, in many cases, improvements upon the previous ones; but ignorance, motivated and led by corruption, gave us a disgraceful period of history. The worst that Lincoln had foreseen had happened.

It is sometimes pointed out that many Carpetbaggers were sincere reformers who went South to try to help in the orderly recovery of the "Sinful Ten." There were undoubtedly some Scalawags with similar decent motives. But three factors made their work largely ineffective and certain to be resented by the South. One was the overthrow of the 10% Plan state governments which were organized and in operation by the fall of 1866. Lincoln had originated the plan and Johnson had continued it. The South had accepted the 13th Amendment. The substitution of any other plan of reconstruction would be strongly resented, especially one whose main feature was the perpetuation in power of the Radical Republicans. That the Congressional Plan had some good features and that some worthy men from the North would play key roles in the administering of the Southern state governments was hardly a recommendation as seen through Southern eyes. A second factor was the presence of thousands of federal troops with more to come from

Washington at the call of any Carpetbag or Scala-wag governor. The inclusion of negro troops was not a soothing influence. And the third factor was the very liberal sprinkling of rogues among the Carpetbaggers and Scalawags. It is not surprising that the evils of the period, even though perpe-trated and kept alive by a relatively small minority, overshadowed whatever was constructive and good. One can easily understand the Southern view that the "Crime of Reconstruction," and not the Civil War, has been the basis of such long sustained ill feeling between the North and South. But there is another light to be thrown on this miserable pic-ture. History has yet to record a major war where a decisive victory has been followed by a wise and benevolent settlement, and the periods immediately after civil wars have been especially tragic.

Ku Klux Klan

The Klan started almost immediately after Ap-pomattox. In the two years between Appomattox and the Reconstruction Acts, its activities were pri-marily restricted to frightening freedmen away from political agitation or any conduct considered a threat to white supremacy. White robed men and horses arousing negroes in the dead of night from their beds to advise, scold, and threaten them in a voice resembling their master's who had been killed in the war, often kept the ignorant and supersti-tious ex-slaves "properly submissive" to the whites. The Klan was only one of the secret societies or-ganized to control the negro; others were the Knights of the White Camelia, and the Order of the White Rose. After the Reconstruction Acts were passed, the struggle between the Carpetbag-Scala-wag state governments, supported by federal troops, and the Ku Klux Klan became vicious. Negroes too active in public affairs were sometimes whipped, Scalawags were in danger of assassination, and Car-petbaggers were likely to be warned once before they were attacked. Some defense can be made, for whatever it may be worth, for the Klan and similar secret terrorist groups. For a few years there was no legal avenue by which the Southern whites could get justice, or any semblance of it. Most of the able whites of the South were prevented by law from taking part in the government of their communi-ties. Federal soldiers paraded the streets ready to sustain the authority of the Carpetbag-Scalawag regime. Two courses were open to the Southern whites: patient submission until the oppression wore itself out, or conspiracies to retaliate with a campaign of terror. The Ku Klux Klan of the 1860's and '70's was essentially the same as the under-ground resistance movements against the Nazi op-pression in World War II. Once a secret terrorist group is organized, it provides protection for crim-inals who use it as a shield behind which they may commit crimes of violence. The skills of sabotage, theft, torture, and killing are virtues of war and of such organizations as the K.K.K. In war thousands of men become skilled in violence and hardened to the sufferings of others; they have learned quick ways to achieve ends. When war stops, or when terrorist groups have no legitimate reason to con-tinue, there is a crime wave resulting from the con-tinued practice by experts of the "arts" of war and the underground.

** Tenure of Office Act (1867)

By the middle of 1866 it had become clear that President Johnson was very obstinate, even though not skillful, in his fight to maintain the 10% Plan of reconstruction. Many men in high places agreed with him and spoke for his program, but they did not organize any group to put up congressional can-didates pledged to their program. The result was that the voters had no real choice in the election of 1866. They could vote for a Democrat or for a Radical Republican. The Democrats were easily pictured as too closely associated with the late re-bellion. The Black Codes (see pp. 139-140) could be used effectively against them. The Radical Republi-cans advocated the measures soon to be the 14th and 15th Amendments and few voters could guess at the political knavery that would develop from the Congressional plans for reconstruction. With no choice but a Democrat *vs.* a Radical Republican, the only possible result was a new Congress over-whelmingly Radical Republican. This Congress overrode Johnson's vetoes, and Thaddeus Stevens, chairman of the House delegation on the Joint Committee on Reconstruction, became more power-ful than the President. The Tenure of Office Act was a deliberate attempt to get rid of Johnson and make the executive department of the government subservient to the Congress.

About the same time as this "frame-up," the Tenure of Office Act, was passed, the *bloody shirt* began to wave. This political tactic struck two notes: one pictured the necessity of having federal troops throughout the "Sinful Ten" in order to pre-vent atrocities by whites against negroes, and the other kept alive the spirit of vengeance against the Southern "traitors." This was a political tactic be-cause so long as the North believed the atrocity stories or demanded vengeance, it would favor the military occupation which alone could keep negro voters sending Republican Congressmen to Wash-ington from the South. This *bloody shirt* oratory persisted in some states through the Hayes-Tilden campaign of 1876. In that election Robert G. Ingersoll gave a good demonstration. "The white Democrats . . . were as relentless as fiends. They killed simply to kill. They murdered these helpless people (negroes), thinking in some blind way that they were getting their revenge upon the people of the North. . . . All the hands dipped in Union blood were in the Democratic Party. . . . Every man that endeavored to tear the old flag from the heaven it encircled was a Democrat. . . . The man that assassinated Abraham Lincoln was a Democrat. . . . Every man that raised bloodhounds to pursue human beings was a Democrat. Every man that clutched from shrinking, shuddering, crouching mothers babes from their breasts and sold them into slavery was a Democrat. . . . Every man that tried to spread smallpox and yellow fever in the North was a Democrat. . . . Every scar, every arm that is missing, every limb that is gone is the souvenir of a Democrat. . . . Shall the solid South, a unified South, unified by assassination and murder, a South solidified by the shotgun—shall the solid South with the aid of a divided North control this great and splendid country?" (Taken from *The Tragic Era* by Claude Bowers.)

The Tenure of Office Act provided that all officials appointed by the President with the advice and consent of the Senate were subject to dismissal only with the consent of the Senate. The first congressional reconstruction plan of March 2, 1867 included the Command of the Army Act, which directed the President to give all commands through the General of the Army, an official removable only with the consent of the Senate. The Tenure of Office Act deprived the President of his authority over civil affairs, and the Command of the Army Act deprived him of authority over military affairs. Congress intended to run the United States. President Johnson consulted with his cabinet, all of whom, including Secretary of War Stanton, considered the Tenure of Office Act to be unconstitutional. Johnson accepted this challenge by Congress by dismissing Stanton who was a staunch supporter of the Radical Republican program. In spite of his own view that the Tenure of Office Act was unconstitutional, Stanton refused to resign as Secretary of War. Johnson, nevertheless, appointed General Lorenzo Thomas to this cabinet post. Now Congress thought they had a case against President Johnson. He had deliberately violated a law of Congress which he was sworn to obey and to uphold. They drew up eleven charges against him and easily got the required simple majority vote in the House to bring him to trial before the Senate. Thus Johnson was impeached.

Johnson's Trial

By no stretch of the imagination had President Johnson been guilty of any "high Crimes and Misdemeanors," in the phraseology of the Constitution. His real "crime," in the eyes of Thaddeus Stevens and Congress, was his determination to put through the 10% Plan. The Tenure of Office Act was passed because the President would ignore it, as he must if he were to exercise the powers of his office. The whole episode was recognized at the time as a political plot to unseat the President; nevertheless it almost succeeded. At the trial before the Senate the vote was 35 to 19 against Johnson, just one vote shy of the required two-thirds majority. Seven Republican Senators refused to go along with the plot and saved the nation from a disgraceful political act and a dangerous precedent. The trial had kept the country on edge from March 30 to May 26, 1868. During the last ten months of Johnson's term, the feuding between Congress and the President subsided and the campaign to elect Grant began.

Ulysses S. Grant

1822 - 1885

REPUBLICAN

☆

Secretary of State HAMILTON FISH

GRANT'S PUBLIC SERVICE BEFORE HE BECAME PRESIDENT

Captain in the Mexican War
"Unconditional Surrender" Grant at Forts Henry and Donelson
After Vicksburg and Chattanooga in supreme command of Union Army
Forced Lee's Surrender at Appomattox

MAJOR ITEMS OF GRANT'S ADMINISTRATION

First Transcontinental Railroad
—U.P. & C.P. (1869)
Crédit Mobilier
Whiskey Ring

Tweed Ring
Panic of 1873
"Alabama" Claims (Geneva Tribunal)

Grant's Elections in 1868 and 1872

During the last week of Johnson's trial before the Senate, the Republican Party held its nominating convention in Chicago. The Radical Republicans were in full control and nominated Grant by unanimous vote. Thousands of "boys in blue" would follow their great commander at the polls. The Democrats nominated a colorless candidate, Horatio Seymour, who had been governor of New York. Reconstruction policy was the major issue and *bloody shirt* oratory paid off. Grant won 26 states out of 34. Three states, Virginia, Mississippi, and Texas, had no vote as they had not yet been readmitted to the Union. In six states under Carpet-bag-Scalawag governments supported by federal troops, Grant got about 700,000 negro votes. As his margin of victory in popular votes was less than half this number, Grant was impressed with the necessity of military control of the South if he and the Republican Party were to continue in power.

Grant's re-election in 1872 was assured by the vitality still left in the *bloody shirt* attack. The wild assertions that withdrawal of federal troops would result in the massacre of thousands of negroes throughout the South were less effective than they had been four years earlier, but the feeling that the Democratic Party was to blame for the Civil War was too powerful a political handicap. Grant still held the major part of the Union veterans'

votes, even though corruption in high places was already evident. The weakness of the Democrats, rather than the strength of Grant and the Republicans decided the election.

Anti-Grant Republicans organized as Liberal Republicans and nominated Horace Greeley who was also nominated several weeks later by the Democrats. The only chance the Democrats had of winning was to cut deeply into the Republican vote. The one common factor Greeley shared with the Democrats was his opposition to Grant on the basis of Grant's unsuitability for the presidency and the corruption of his associates. On the tariff issue Greeley was an extreme protectionist. He had been a Republican from the birth of that party; he had, in fact, named it. He had supported the Civil War as a crusade against slavery rather than as a struggle to preserve the Union. Thus, Greeley had little appeal to Democrats other than that anyone would be better than Grant. To make a bad situation worse, Greeley had joined and supported so many minority causes that there was a wide-spread opinion that he was somewhat of a crack-pot. He had espoused co-operative living in a socialist community (Fourierism), he had dabbled in spiritualism, supported temperance, and championed women's rights. His paper, the New York *Tribune,* was noted for its receptiveness to all sorts of fads; its pages were open to bizarre and eccentric social and political movements and ideas. These facts help to explain why Greeley was a great newspaperman and a poor candidate for the presidency. Thousands might agree that Greeley was brilliant, but few would think him dependable, steady, or predictable.

	Popular Vote	Electoral Vote
Grant	3,597,070	286
Greeley	2,834,079	66 *

* Greeley died Nov. 29, 1872 before the electoral votes were cast, so the six states that had supported him divided their votes among public figures who had not been candidates.

First Transcontinental Railroad—U.P. & C.P. 1869

Railroad building was big in many ways. The laying of tracks and building of bridges was a big job; the recruiting of a labor force from all over the United States, from western Europe, and from China was a big job; the feeding and housing of the labor force was a big job; the bringing in of supplies and construction materials was a big job; the difficulties presented by weather, mountains, rivers, deserts, and Indians were big; the grants of land and money by the government were big; and the bribery and stealing which marred the railroad building were big.

In 1865 a race began between the Central Pacific Railroad (cutting the Pacific coastal area about at the center) and the Union Pacific Railroad (forming a union with roads east of the Missouri River and the new road being built from the Pacific coast). The United States government granted both roads charters which loaned them $16,000, $32,000, or $48,000 per mile of construction depending upon the difficulty of the terrain. Along the alternate sides of the roadbed the government gave the railroads strips of land one mile wide and ten miles long. The money loaned was ample to pay the full *legitimate* costs of construction, and the value of the land when the railroads were completed was many times the amount required to repay the loans. Hence, with the loans and the land in prospect, each road had a powerful incentive to build as much as it could before they met at some point between Sacramento, California and Council Bluffs, Iowa. The Central Pacific, building from Sacramento, used thousands of Chinese coolies to cut the path through the Rockies and go out across the desert to the Great Salt Lake. This was a tough job with extremes of temperature from far below zero to well over 100 degrees. Blasting through mountains would sometimes keep daily progress measured in yards, while laying track over the prairie or on the salt flats went along at several miles a day. The Union Pacific, employing hordes of Irish labor-

ers, began at Council Bluffs, Iowa on the east side of the Missouri River directly across from Omaha, Nebraska. For about two years there was no bridge over the river, but after the building got well under way it became the practice to send crews ahead to construct bridges so that they would be ready by the time the tracks reached the crossings. This meant hauling supplies and construction materials, sometimes by pack animal, to isolated spots miles ahead of the main work force. On May 10, 1869 the Central Pacific and the Union Pacific met at Promontory Point, Utah and the occasion was marked by driving a gold spike with a silver sledge hammer as the finishing touch to a tremendous achievement.

The building of this first transcontinental railroad was early in the period of great industrial expansion that dominated our history between the Civil War and World War I. In the 1860's and 70's the maximum of individual freedom and the minimum of government control was the ideal generally accepted as the natural and proper way of life. Some called it *laissez faire,* but it wasn't. There was plenty of government "interference" in private enterprise, but it was in the form of subsidies and gifts of one kind or another. Even before the Civil War considerable land had been given for turnpikes, canals, and railroads. Any transportation routes that aid commerce are also actual or potential assets for postal and military uses. In the case of the Union Pacific and Central Pacific the land grants totaled about 44,000,000 acres and the loans about $64,000,000. In the desire to attract railroads to build through their states, legislatures offered tax concessions, land, and funds in an effort to outbid neighboring states. The simple fact is that railroads could not have been built without very substantial government aid. In the United States railroads were extended through vast areas of almost uninhabited land. There could be no profits from freight rates and passenger fares until towns and farm communities developed along the railroads, and that would take years. The early income for these pioneering railroads came from the sale of land at attractive rates to settlers. Occasionally a rich bed of mineral wealth would be found in railroad land and, much more often, there were good stands of timber. Where towns formed, the railroads could pretty much dominate their economy through the ownership of land, cattle pens, and grain storage elevators, along with the control of the one practical communication link with the outside world. The early railroads were in the real estate business, the cattle business, the grain business, and either controlled or sought to control the federal congress, state legislatures, and city councils. There was much more to running a railroad than operating trains; there is good sense in calling the Leland Stanfords and the James J. Hills "empire builders" rather than merely railroad men.

* Crédit Mobilier (krǎ de mŏ blē ā)

In 1864 some of the larger stockholders of the Union Pacific Railroad formed the Crédit Mobilier, a corporation to finance and construct the U.P. The Crédit Mobilier sold supplies and construction materials at exorbitant prices to the U.P. It took on contracts for a multitude of individual jobs as part of building the U.P. and received outrageously high fees. The graft, in a variety of forms, resulted in the Union Pacific's paying fraudulently excessive prices and fees, while the profits rolled into the coffers of the Crédit Mobilier. Dividends on Crédit Mobilier stock got as high as 625% and its usual dividend rate was over 300%. Congressman Oakes Ames of Massachusetts was the agent for Crédit Mobilier who sold, or gave, its lucrative stock to key Senators and Representatives who would use their influence to see that Congress extended favors to the U.P. Ames's double duty was to get all he could from Uncle Sam and to prevent any investigation of Crédit Mobilier. But investigation did begin after the New York *Sun* reported the scandal on September 4, 1872, and it continued through February of the next year. Vice-President Colfax resigned and Representative Ames received a vote of censure from the House.

* Whiskey Ring

The Whiskey Ring started in St. Louis and spread to other cities. General John McDonald, supervisor of the Internal Revenue Department in St. Louis, headed the conspiracy to defraud the government. The scheme was simple. Revenue officials allowed distillers to sell a portion of their output without paying the tax thereon. For example, a distiller was allowed to pay $5,000 less in taxes than the law required if he would pay $3,000 to the revenue officials. The distiller saved $2,000 while the tax collectors got $3,000; the United States Treasury lost $5,000. Those businessmen who were reluctant to enter into such a conspiracy were pressured into it by threats of harassment by revenue officials. Being on the "wrong side" of the tax collectors could result in many difficulties ranging from petty annoyances to costly lawsuits. The result was that, between the desire to dodge taxes and to avoid harassment, the whiskey fraud was widespread and involved huge sums of money. Some officials of the Treasury Department were part of the conspiracy and sought protection for their "racket" by

contributing handsomely to campaign funds for the re-election of Grant in 1872. Grant's private secretary, General O. E. Babcock, supervised the Ring's activities from Washington and the chief clerk of the Treasury Department was on the payroll of the gang to warn of any moves that might be made toward investigation. When Grant visited the World's Fair in St. Louis, General McDonald was his host. The Whiskey Ring gave Grant a pair of fine horses with sets of harness with gold breastplates on which Grant's name was engraved. In April of 1875 the Secretary of the Treasury, Benjamin H. Bristow, sent agents secretly to St. Louis and consternation hit the Whiskey Ring. Distillery records were seized which exposed the whole mess. Shortly before leading figures in the conspiracy came to trial, an order from the Attorney-General's office directed that no immunity was to be granted to any witnesses. President Grant was either willing or anxious that the mouths of possible informers be shut. General Babcock's defense included having President Grant testify in his behalf as a character witness. On this occasion the President's memory seemed a bit weak, but, nevertheless, the prestige of a great general and of the presidency gave his testimony weight. Babcock was found not guilty, but the verdict of history is quite the contrary.

* Tweed Ring

"Boss" William M. Tweed was the Grand Sachem of Tammany Hall, the Democratic Club of New York City. Since his day, any political organization referred to as a *machine* controlled by a *boss* brings forth a picture of corruption, and *Tammany Hall* forms in the minds of many an image of a ruthless Tammany Tiger clawing at a prostrate female figure representing the republic, or liberty, or justice. That Tweed so affected the public mind is explained by two factors: the effectiveness of the Tammany organization with the gigantic stealing it accomplished, and the cartoons drawn by Thomas Nast in *Harper's Weekly* picturing Tammany Hall as a tiger. It was Nast who created the "political zoo" by his cartoons of the Tammany Tiger, the Democratic Donkey, (Nast was a Republican) and the Republican Elephant; three animals that have probably achieved immortality. The loot collected by Tweed and his Ring came from contracts for goods and services purchased by the city, and from all types of organized vice and illegal activities by which money could be made. Companies selling goods or services to the city were told to add from 10% to 100%, and sometimes much more, to the legitimate price when they presented their bills. The companies would get a fair price and the Ring would get the extra 10% to 100%, or much more. No one got city business unless he went along with this system. The Tweed Ring flourished in the late 1860's and the early 1870's. It was Nast's cartoons that made the general public resent the Ring's activities. As Tweed put it, he didn't mind the editorials in the New York *Times* because so few people read them, and most of his supporters, who voted en masse to keep the Ring in office, couldn't read; but they could "look at the damn pictures" and get the point.

The total stolen by the Ring from New York City in about six years has been estimated at about $200,000,000. Bribery bought either assistance or acquiescence from the mayor of the city, the governor of the state, several state legislators, some judges, and some newspapers. Nast was offered $500,000 to go to Europe to study art, that is, to get out of the United States and stop drawing cartoons. After it got possession of incriminating documents supplied by a clerk in the city auditor's office, the *Times* was offered $5,000,000 to stop its attacks upon the Tweed Ring. Nast and the *Times* proved to be bribe-proof and the members of the Ring scattered to foreign shores. The Grand Sachem, William M. Tweed, fled to Spain where he was apprehended and returned for trial to New York City. The one-time millionaire and czar of Manhattan was without friends or funds and died in a city jail in 1878.

The "boss and the machine" in the tradition of William M. Tweed are still alive. The greed of a few thousand unprincipled men of strength and determination tolerated by the passiveness of millions of decent people may kill our representative form of democracy. Yet the value of the Tweed story to the student is simple and clear in its presentation of a few basic facts of political life. Whenever the funds of a political machine come from a "cut" of the income (or "take") of organized (operated as a business) vice and crime, it is certain that corruption is widespread, involving both political parties and touching persons prominent in the social, economic, and political life of the community. Illegal business depends for its profits upon thousands of customers. If customers know how and where they can patronize a numbers racket or a horse room (illegal gambling on horse races), etc., it is ridiculous to believe that the police department knows nothing of their existence. Such enterprises can exist only with official protection. An alert minority party will publicize the existence of organized crime unless it is "paid off" with a few lucrative political jobs in order to keep it quiet. Obviously the suppliers and contractors with whom any city deals include many established businesses and contrac-tors. The principal owners, managers, and directors of such enterprises include some of the same families which are usually prominent in the social, cultural, and philanthropic activities of the city. The temptation to sell to the city under the pressure of adding 10% to 100%, or even more, for graft, involves a great deal of money; and every businessman faced with such a decision knows that if his company refuses to "play ball" with the crooks, some competitor will. Many a person who has cultivated a generous measure of public spirit, of honesty, and decency finds the situation presented by a corrupt political machine exceedingly tempting and insidious. Tweed's appreciation of the effectiveness of cartoons, because they reached even those who were illiterate, emphasizes the connection between an ignorant electorate and a corrupt government. Ignorance and indifference are major allies of the "Tweeds." The "boss" and the "machine" are doing a job that must be done, that is, they are governing; they are arranging slates of nominees, they are organizing their party, they are electing candidates. In a republic, whether on the national, state, or city level, these political functions must be performed. They should be performed by voters who feel a sense of citizenship which impels them to an active part in public affairs. The duties of citizenship are usually part-time and voluntary; they vary from merely casting a vote to running for office. Whenever people feel too preoccupied with their own personal affairs to accept the obligations of citizenship, there will always be some "Tweeds" and "Rings" to fill the vacuum. The saying, "People get the kind of government they deserve," makes a little sense; but it would be better to remind ourselves that we must deserve a better government, and prove it by getting it. If we are to succeed in the art of self-government, the term *politician*, must come to be a title of dignity because our elected and appointed officials represent our aristocracy of character, ability and brains.

Panic of 1873

The Panic was precipitated by the failure in September, 1873, of Jay Cooke & Company of Philadelphia, the most famous and presumably the strongest financial institution in the United States. It had put too much of its funds in the development of the Northern Pacific Railroad. Over-extension of credit, the prevalence of fraud in both government and private business, and thousands of investors using money for speculative ventures rather than productive purposes combined to create an economic situation destined to collapse. Western agriculture had over-extended to supply a European market which faded away with the end of the Franco-Prussian War. European business was in the doldrums and increased the severity of the depression in the United States. From 20,000 to 25,000 enterprises failed in the three years following the bankruptcy of Jay Cooke & Co. Hundreds of thousands of workers became tramps; many of them roamed the country in search of non-existent jobs. Clashes between protest meetings of unemployed and police were common. No one thought of the situation as one calling for a government program of relief. Farmers and factory workers bore the brunt of the hardships. Under the pressure of the depression, organized labor fell from a membership of about 300,000 to about 50,000. The most violent event of the depression was the railroad strike of 1877 which tied up the main northern roads from the Atlantic seaboard to the Mississippi River. The scene of greatest violence was Chicago. This strike started when four railroads in the east cut wages at the same time. Management had cooperated to fight labor; labor answered by fighting back. The police, the state militia, and the newspapers backed the railroads and saw in the gun battles and the vast destruction of property nothing less, and nothing more, than a revolutionary attempt by "communists and vagabonds" to overthrow the American way of life. Officialdom and the people were frightened, and rightly so, by the breadlines, the unemployed, the mass meetings, and the armed clashes. In about six years the depression had run its course and economic recovery set in. There were no plans to prevent a recurrence of such a depression, but at least one measure of questionable wisdom was taken to deal with the next one when it developed. It might be interesting to check on the date when your city armory was built; if it was soon after 1877 it is very likely that it was erected to meet any repetition of the violence of the 1870's by providing training facilities for the state militia.

* "Alabama" Claims (Geneva Tribunal) (1869-72)

One of the last acts of Secretary of State, William H. Seward, was to start negotiations with England in an attempt to recover damages caused during the Civil War by the commerce raiders *Alabama, Florida,* and *Shenandoah.* By 1871, Secretary of State Hamilton Fish was able to reach an agreement with England to submit the issue to an international tribunal for arbitration. The tribunal consisted of representatives from Brazil, Italy, and Switzerland. Senator Charles Sumner of Massachusetts, who had led the Radical Republicans in the Senate during Johnson's administration, almost ruined the attempt at arbitration before it began. As chairman of the Foreign Relations Committee, he felt privileged to proclaim his ideas on what the United States should demand. In a speech before the Senate he proved to be as extreme in foreign policy as he had been about reconstruction. His list of claims included two *billion* dollars for "indirect damages." This was based on the theory that the commerce raiders had prolonged the Civil War for two years, and that England, therefore, owed us half the cost of the four-year war. Another item was $110,000,000 for the loss to United States shipping which was driven from the seas through fear of attack. Realizing this huge sum was more than England could conveniently pay, Sumner suggested that we might accept Canada instead of a money settlement. Maybe Sumner had his tongue in his cheek and was engaging in a little Yankee horse trading, or perhaps he was making a speech he knew would be popular. Whatever his motives, the effect was to make the American people expect an impossible settlement and to arouse a storm of ill-will throughout England. It was much to the credit of Hamilton Fish and his English counterpart that they rode out the storm of public opinion on both sides of the ocean and proceeded to a reasonable conclusion. They ruled out Sumner's "indirect damage" concept before they submitted the controversy to the arbitration board. The findings of the tribunal were that England had clearly violated international law by permitting the construction of the commerce raiders in British shipyards, even though they were sent elsewhere to be completed. The United States was awarded $15,500,000, a sum somewhat in excess of the actual property damage caused by the raiders. The most significant result of the diplomacy of Secretary of State, Hamilton Fish, was the signing of the Treaty of Washington in 1871 by which England and the United States agreed to settle disputes over fisheries, boundaries, and the *Alabama* by arbitration. When two major powers agreed upon a peaceful technique for the settlement of their disputes, a tremendous advance in international conduct had been made. If we ever achieve an international civilization which rejects war, the Washington Treaty of 1871 may gain stature as the Magna Carta of international peace and the *Alabama* arbitration at Geneva will be the first example of its success.

Rutherford B. Hayes

1877-1881

1822 - 1893

REPUBLICAN

☆

HAYES' PUBLIC SERVICE BEFORE HE BECAME PRESIDENT

Governor of Ohio for Three Terms

MAJOR ITEMS OF HAYES' ADMINISTRATION

Bland-Allison Act (1878)

** Election of Hayes (1876)

By 1876 the "bloody shirt" technique (see pp. 141-142) had lost most of its effectiveness and the corruption prevalent during the past ten years made Republican prospects seem dim. Their party was split between the Liberal Republicans who had supported Greeley in 1872 and the regulars who had re-elected Grant. Those who had backed Grant now wanted James G. Blaine, "The Plumed Knight," as their candidate. He was a clever politician, a dependable organization man, and a good campaigner with a magnetic personality. But he ridiculed civil service reform as "snivel service" and was under attack for the *Mulligan Letters.* James Mulligan was a bookkeeper who possessed correspondence which contained evidence that Blaine had received large sums of money and bonds in return for his influence in behalf of the Little Rock & Fort Smith Railroad. Rumors of this deal spoiled Blaine's chance to lead a united party. After the nominating convention had rejected him, Blaine read the *Mulligan Letters* before the House, but he read only selected portions. This performance satisfied his friends, but failed to convince others or to satisfy the judgment of history. Rutherford B. Hayes, three times governor of Ohio and a colorless candidate with nothing against him, got the nomination on the 7th ballot. With good conscience, even if without enthusiasm, all Republicans could vote for Hayes.

The Democrats nominated Samuel J. Tilden of New York who had won a reputation as a reform Democrat. As state chairman he forced the removal from office of corrupt judges in New York City and later, when elected governor of New York in 1874, he played a major role in destroying the Tweed Ring (see pp. 145-146). Tilden was a strong candidate well calculated to carry the Democratic Party

into the presidency for the first time since the Civil War. But it was not to be.

Tilden carried the northern states of New York, New Jersey, Connecticut, and Indiana. Having made this inroad into Republican territory, it was assumed that he had the election. But three southern states, Florida, Louisiana, and South Carolina sent in two sets of electoral votes. Widespread fraud by both parties was apparent in these states. Analysis of what happened strongly supports the conclusion that Florida and Louisiana had voted for Tilden and South Carolina for Hayes. One of the electors in the Oregon electoral college delegation was a postmaster and therefore ineligible, according to the Constitution, to serve as an elector. The Democratic governor of Oregon replaced him with a Democrat, an act that was also illegal, and thus there was a fourth state whose electoral vote was in dispute. Not counting the electoral votes of these four states, Tilden had 184 votes. The simple majority required for election was 185. The election really belonged to Tilden and the nothern Democrats were willing to contest the issue to the bitter end before accepting any other result. There were no Constitutional provisions for handling this situation, so Congress had to improvise a solution.

An Electoral Commission of 15 members was created. It was composed of five Senators (3 Republicans and 2 Democrats), five Representatives (3 Democrats and 2 Republicans) and five judges of the Supreme Court (2 Republicans and 2 Democrats with a 5th judge to be chosen by these four). Judge David Davis was the only independent member on the Supreme Court. He hastily resigned from the Court and was elected to the United States Senate by the Illinois legislature. No man would wish to be "put on the spot" as the person who chose the president. With Judge Davis unavailable, the only other choices were Republicans. The Electoral Commission was thus formed of eight Republicans and seven Democrats and, right down the line of the four disputed states, that is the way they voted. Hayes won by 185 to 184. In popular vote, Tilden won by over 250,000. That this politically rigged vote by the Electoral Commission was tolerated is explained by the bargaining the Southern Democrats were willing to make. They were more anxious to get rid of federal troops stationed in their states and to receive federal patronage than they were concerned about the presidency. In return for accepting the findings of the Electoral Commission, pledges were made and kept to withdraw federal troops from the South, to make substantial federal appropriations for railroads in the South, and to appoint a Southerner to a cabinet post. The decision of the Electoral Commission was not made until March 2nd, 1877, only two days before Hayes took office.

This exciting election marked the end of the "Crime of Reconstruction." It inaugurated another real, and perhaps unavoidable, crime. With federal troops out of the South, the negroes were soon frightened out of public affairs. The 14th and 15th amendments were largely ignored and the negroes, as a political factor, were reduced to helplessness. The slave problem had not been solved by the Civil War, it had been transformed into a race problem. In 1876 the negroes began at the very bottom to struggle slowly and painfully toward economic and political equality of opportunity, a struggle far from finished.

	Popular Vote	Electoral Vote
Hayes	4,033,950	185
Tilden	4,284,757	184

Bland-Allison Act (1878)

Ever since the Civil War the demand had been for more Greenbacks. The farmers as a class, and especially those of the South and West, were for cheap money because it raised the prices of farm products, resulted in easy credit, and favored debtors. During the early 1870's several European nations went off the bimetallic (gold & silver) standard onto the gold standard. The United States, by the coinage act of 1873, stopped coining silver dollars and thus went on the gold standard. During the 1860's and early 70's no one wished to sell silver to the government because the market price was higher than the 16 to 1 ratio the government paid for silver. But when the new deposits of silver found in Nevada, Colorado, and Utah hit the market in the middle 70's the increased supply drove the market price down and there was a rush to sell silver to the government at 16 to 1. Then the knowledge that the United States was no longer buying silver for coinage purposes resulted in an angry cry of "The crime of 73."

With silver now a political issue, it made sense for the Greenbackers to shift their support to a demand for the unlimited coinage of silver at the ratio of 16 to 1. By doing so, the farmers and labor would join with the silver mine interests and greatly increase their political power; they would add some numbers to their cause and a great deal of money to promote lobbying. It was much less frightening to the conservatives to contemplate free coinage of silver than the unlimited printing of greenbacks, for silver did have obvious substance and value and was more convincing than a government promise that might be broken. "Silver Dick," Richard Bland of Missouri, introduced a bill in the House providing for unlimited (free) coinage of silver at the ratio of 16 to 1. In the Senate the bill was amended by Allison of Iowa to limit the government's purchase of silver at the market price to not less than two million nor more than four million dollars worth per month. The bill passed over President Hayes' veto. The government purchased the minimum amount each month and the inflationary effect was unnoticeable. Agitation continued for more cheap money until a second silver purchase act was passed in 1890 (see p. 162).

James A. Garfield   1881 Mar. 4 to Sept. 19

1831 - 1881

REPUBLICAN

Vice-President CHESTER A. ARTHUR
Secretary of State JAMES G. BLAINE

GARFIELD'S PUBLIC SERVICE BEFORE HE BECAME PRESIDENT

Member of the Ohio Senate
General in Civil War
  Distinguished Service at Shiloh and Chickamauga
U.S. Senator from Ohio (1880)

Garfield's Election (1880)

The wing of the party known as Radical Republicans during the Reconstruction Era was pretty much the same group now known as "Stalwarts." In 1880 they wished to break the two-term tradition by running Grant for a third term. But, on the 36th ballot, the reform faction won out at the convention and nominated James A. Garfield, a Civil War General with a good military record. To keep party unity during the election, Chester Arthur, a Stalwart choice, was accepted as the Vice-Presidential candidate. The Democrats nominated General Winfield Hancock of Pennsylvania, whose Civil War record was excellent, and the Greenback Labor Party put up General James Weaver. Aside from the fact that the Republicans advocated a protective tariff and the Democrats favored a revenue tariff, there was no significant difference between the two major parties. The battle of the generals resulted in a close election according to the popu-

lar vote, but a comfortable margin of victory for Garfield in the electoral vote.

	Popular Vote	Electoral Vote
Garfield	4,449,053	214
Hancock	4,442,030	155
Weaver	308,578	0

On July 2, 1881, Garfield was shot by C. Julius Guiteau, a mentally unstable "Stalwart" supporter who wanted to make Chester Arthur President. The attack occurred at the Washington railway station. President Garfield suffered until his death on September 19th. Guiteau was hanged June 30, 1882. The assassination aroused the public to the fact that corrupt government, a rampant spoils system, and the easy tolerance of "Stalwart" tactics had created a favorable environment for this tragedy. "Snivel service," as a sneering jibe at civil service reform, seemed no longer funny.

Chester A. Arthur

1830 - 1886

REPUBLICAN

☆

ARTHUR'S PUBLIC SERVICE BEFORE HE BECAME PRESIDENT
Quartermaster General of New York during the Civil War
Collector of Customs Duties at the Port of New York

MAJOR ITEMS OF ARTHUR'S ADMINISTRATION

* Pendleton Act (1883)
A Steel Navy Started

* Pendleton Act (1883)

When Arthur took the oath of office, the prospects for good government seemed dim. Arthur had been a small wheel in "Boss" Roscoe Conkling's machine of New York State; he had been appointed to the Customs collecting job in New York City by President Grant and removed from it by President Hayes. The removal was on the grounds that Arthur was active in party organizing and campaigns, activities that were illegal for a customs official. It was not long, however, before Arthur proved to be an able administrator with a constructive program. Perhaps it was the responsibility of the presidency and the shock of Garfield's assassination that persuaded Arthur to sponsor civil service reform. For years a Civil Service Reform League had advocated a merit system for the selection of public employees, and when Senator George Pendleton of Ohio introduced a bill including this principle, it received full support from the President. Congress passed the Pendleton Act which set up a three-man Civil Service Commission to implement the act. Some of the provisions were:

1] Competitive examinations must be given to determine which candidates merited the government positions.

2] Federal office holders can not be forced to contribute to campaign funds nor dismissed from office for refusing to contribute.

3] A list of federal positions was drawn up to which the law would apply, and the President was empowered to add to this list at his discretion.

4] In the granting of government jobs, attention was to be given to apportioning them among the several states according to their population.

The Pendleton Act covered about 15,000 jobs, or about 12% of the civilian employees of the federal government. It was a good beginning, even though it made only a small dent in the total Spoils System. States were encouraged to create merit systems of their own and the lists of jobs under the merit systems, both state and federal, have been growing ever since.

A Steel Navy Started

The engagement of the *Monitor*, the "cheesebox on a raft," and the ironclad *Merrimac* (Virginia) had clearly announced that all wooden navies were obsolete. Yet this historic Civil War naval battle of 1862 off Hampton Roads had not stirred Congress, nor any President, to rebuild our navy. In 1882 we had a puny navy which ranked 12th among the nations. President Arthur pushed for a steel navy and Congress went along to the extent of starting construction on the steel cruisers, *Chicago* and *Boston*. The first step had been made toward bringing the United States into the position of a leading naval power. One very sensible provision of this legislation, which also made it more appealing to many Congressmen, was that the steel used in building the ships must be of domestic manufacture.

Grover Cleveland 1885-1889

1837 - 1908

DEMOCRAT

★

★ Cleveland's Election (1884)

This campaign was a noisy, nasty contest in personal abuse. One could say that civil service reform, tariff, and monopolies were issues of the day; but the oratory of the campaign and the interest of the voters were directed at the two candidates, Mr. Blaine ("The Plumed Knight") and Mr. Cleveland ("Grover the Good"). They were the real issue. To the rank and file of the Republicans, Blaine was the image created by the orator Robert Ingersoll who declaimed, "Like an armed warrior, like a plumed knight, James G. Blaine marched down the halls of the American Congress and threw his shining lance full and fair against the brazen foreheads of the defamers of his country and the maligners of her honor." Blaine personified loyalty to the Republican Party organization. He had been one of the first supporters of Lincoln. As early as 1854 he edited the Kennebunk (Maine) *Journal* which was the first paper in the East to declare itself to be Republican. He was charming in manner and very competent in performance. "Blaine of Maine" stood out more persistently from the middle 1850's through the 1880's than any other public figure. He had been Speaker of the House, and for over a dozen years his "bloody shirt" orations had served his party well. Under Garfield he had served a brief term as Secretary of State. President Arthur deserved the nomination for a second term as a reward for his sound leadership, but he had offended the party bosses who had put him on the ticket as Vice-President in 1880. Thus he had lost the support of his old cronies without winning the confidence of the reform faction of the party. Blaine was at last to get his political reward, the top spot on the Republican ticket. The convention at Chicago nominated him on the 4th ballot. But there were thoughtful Republicans among the leaders of the party and the nation who would not accept Blaine's leadership. They would not overlook scandals associated with his Speakership in the House, the Mulligan Letters, another letter with the notation "burn this letter," and his long-standing association with the unsavory leaders in the party throughout a 20-year period marked by corruption. Such staunchly Republican publications as the Springfield (Mass.) *Republican* and *Harper's Weekly* with its arch-Republican cartoonist, Nast, rejected Blaine. James Russell Lowell, the New England poet, and Henry Ward Beecher, the noted Brooklyn preacher, could not accept Blaine. Charles Francis Adams, our able ambassador to England during the Civil War and the son of President J. Q. Adams, along with Carl Schurz, who had persuaded Lincoln of the necessity of an emancipation proclamation, all came out against Blaine. A month separated the Democratic convention from the Republican, so that by the time the Democrats met in Chicago, the word was out that the Republican Party was split and that any decent Democrat might get support from anti-Blaine Republicans. In derision, the Stalwart Republicans backing Blaine called the reform Republicans "Mugwumps." The ridiculous sounding name has been explained seriously as an Indian word meaning "big chief" and less seriously as the name of an imaginary bird which stands with its mug on one side of the fence and its wump on the other. Whatever Mugwump meant, the anti-Blaine Republicans accepted the title good-naturedly and gained many adherents.

The Democrats nominated Grover Cleveland on the second ballot. He was fully acceptable to the Mugwumps and, with the split in the Republican Party, the Democrats were headed for the presidency. Cleveland's public life as District Attorney of Erie County, as Sheriff, as Mayor of Buffalo, and as Governor of New York had been marked by economy, honesty, courage, and common sense. He had no outstanding talent or ability, but he did have in good measure a combination of virtues which we have a right to expect public officials to possess. If there are not tens of thousands of Clevelands among us at all times, we are a pathetic people. From Jackson to Cleveland, Lincoln was the only one to give both dignity and stature to the presidency.

Although Cleveland's public life was above reproach, his private life during the days he built his law practice in Buffalo and was Sheriff of Erie County had its imperfections. With young lawyers and businessmen Cleveland infrequently enjoyed a drinking party which sometimes became noisy enough with "singing" and talking to attract unfriendly attention. In the early 1870's an illegitimate child was named Oscar Folsom Cleveland. Cleveland may have been the father, but so may have other men who were his friends. Being a bachelor, Cleveland felt that the disgrace would fall less heavily upon him than the others, so he supported the child and gave the mother financial help until the boy reached maturity and the mother had married. When the Buffalo *Evening Telegraph* exploded this news under the headline, "A Terrible Tale," it seemed that the bottom had fallen out of the Cleveland campaign. But when Cleveland displayed the common sense, honesty, and courage to tell the truth and, when interviewed by the press, said he hoped all who knew anything of the situation would also tell the truth, much of the resentment against him was dispelled. A committee of clergymen interviewed Cleveland and reported that, without condoning his misconduct, his actions had been "singularly honorable" after the fact. So now both parties had plausible reasons for wallowing in the mud. The favorite jingle of the Democrats was

"Blaine, Blaine, James G. Blaine,
The continental liar from the State of Maine.
Burn this letter!"

and the Republicans sang

"Ma! Ma! Where's my Pa?
Gone to the White House,
Ha! Ha! Ha!

	Popular Vote	Electoral Vote
Cleveland	4,911,017	219
Blaine	4,848,334	182

The returns showed clearly that the Mugwumps had put Cleveland in office. The New York State vote was so close that Cleveland won by less than 1,200 votes out of a total of about 1,250,000. This close victory in a key state was brought about late in the campaign by a prejudice-loaded remark at an interview Blaine held with a group of Republican clergymen. The Rev. Dr. Samuel Burchard described the Democratic Party as one "whose antecedents have been rum, Romanism, and rebellion." Blaine did not rebuke the clergyman, he may not have noticed the remark; but when "RUM, ROMANISM, AND REBELLION" was headlined in Democratic papers the Republican fat was in the fire. Blaine was convinced that Burchard's three "R's" had cost him the election.

* Mills Bill and the Surplus

Tariff reform was the one message in Cleveland's "State of the Union" speech to Congress in 1887. He pointed out that the government had been collecting more in taxes than was required to meet government expenses and that the largest single source of revenue was the tariff. An annual surplus of about $100,000,000 had piled up in the Treasury for about seven years and was still growing. This Cleveland considered intolerable. As he expressed it, "Our present tariff laws, the vicious, inequitable, and illogical source of unnecessary taxation, ought to be at once revised and amended." His message made the following points.

1] Excessive government income is overtaxation; it robs the citizen of the fruits of his industry and enterprise and tempts the government to be extravagant.

2] The tariff not only raises prices on imports which are taxed, but on domestic goods whose prices are raised to, or very close to, those of the taxed imports. Only a few buy the taxed imports, but millions pay the extra prices put on corresponding domestic goods.

3] ". . . relief from the hardships and dangers of our present tariff . . ." can be achieved without "imperiling the existence of our manufacturing interests."

4] We do not need protection from "what is called the pauper labor of Europe" as is made evident by the fact that census figures show that only 26 of every 174 industrial workers are employed in protected industries, yet, the other 148 survive.

5] There is grave doubt that protective tariffs result in higher wages, but it is certain that they had resulted in higher prices.

6] Competition should keep prices below the levels permitted by the tariff, "But it is notorious that this competition is too often strangled by combinations quite prevalent at this time, and frequently called trusts, . . ."

7] More than 4,000 articles are subject to duty. Many of these do not compete with our own manufactures and should be on the free list.

8] Import duties "on necessaries of life . . . should be greatly cheapened."

9] Lowering our tariffs will help the manufacturers by giving ". . . them a better chance in foreign markets . . . extending their sales beyond the limits of home consumption, . . . and affording their employees more certain and steady labor."

10] A theoretical discussion of free trade and protection will be futile. There is a surplus in the Treasury and it is growing. The people are overtaxed. "It is a condition that confronts us, not a theory."

Cleveland was not a theorist on tariff, or anything else. He merely used his common sense. The result of this approach, as he saw it, was that protective tariffs were good in some instances and the rates should then be only as high as needed. He felt that there was a strong tendency for manufacturers to exaggerate their need for protection and to combine to maintain excessive prices and profits. He considered a revenue tariff a legitimate tax, but when the government wished to decrease income from taxes, it was wise to put items on the free list and thus gain the added advantage of a lower cost of living through the resulting lower prices. Both parties agreed that a tax cut was called for in view of the surplus in the Treasury; their point of disagreement was how to do it. Cleveland took the position that lowering the tariff and putting some goods on the free list was the method that would best serve the nation, while the Republicans took the position that tariff revision was the one approach that they would not accept. The Mills Bill, incorporating Cleveland's ideas on tariff revision, passed the House but could not get through the Senate. While most Republicans opposed the Mills Bill and most Democrats favored it, the two parties were split on the issue. Cleveland had made his position clear and had fought to bring about his solution. But the Mills Bill failed to become law and the surplus was larger than ever as Cleveland's first administration ended.

The question naturally arises, why not pay the national debt with the surplus? Neither party wished to do this. Much of the government debt was in the form of National Bank bonds issued under the Chase National Banking Act of 1863. To pay these bonds off before they became due would cause disturbing complications in the bond market and force the government to retire from circulation large amounts of bank notes (paper money), two results which would have adverse effects upon business.

* Knights of Labor

The Knights of Labor reached their peak of power in 1886. In the previous year they had won a strike against the Southwest Railroad System when their Grand Master, Terence V. Powderly, met with the financier, Jay Gould and arranged terms of settlement favorable to the Knights. This marked labor's first collective bargaining. The prestige from this first instance of the representative of a union meeting with a representative of industry resulted in a mushroom growth in the membership of the Knights of Labor to a peak of about 700,000. The Knights were more like a poorly organized political party than a labor union. Skilled and unskilled workers, men and women, black and white, citizens and aliens, some professional people and some illiterates were members. There were about 6,000 locals. Farmers would dominate some locals; workers in heavy industry, workers in textile mills, workers in mercantile establishments, railroad workers, etc. would dominate other locals. Farmers' locals would have no interest in an eight-hour day and they would approve unrestricted immigration to supply them with cheap labor at harvest and planting times. Steel workers and mill hands would want an eight-hour day and look upon every immigrant as a potential threat to their jobs. Skilled workers looked down upon less skilled, whites resented the presence of blacks in their unions, those with grammar school education looked down upon those with less education, "Americans" whose families had been in this country a generation or more did not enjoy association with the "foreigners," etc. The program of the Knights of Labor was political as well as economic. Their demands included a graduated income tax, abolition of child labor, temperance, consumers' and producers' cooperatives, and an eight-hour day. To gain their aims they favored boycotts and arbitration in preference to strikes.

* Haymarket Riot

A general strike was planned for May 1, 1886, in which all workers were urged to quit their jobs and hold meetings demanding an eight-hour day, the demand that had been the heart of labor's program during the twenty years since the Civil War. Over 300,000 workers attended meetings throughout the United States, but after the first day the protest fizzled out. The revolutionary character of a general strike aroused fear and hostility which hurt labor's cause. At the time there was a prolonged strike going on at the McCormick Harvester Company in Chicago. On May 3rd, police fired into a group of strikers assembled for picket duty. One striker was killed and others were wounded. The next day, May 4th, a meeting was held at Haymarket Square to protest the police brutality of the previous day. Anarchists, socialists, strikers, indignant citizens, and the simply curious formed a crowd of about 3,000. The Mayor of Chicago, Carter Harrison, and 180 policemen were there. The meeting was orderly and uninteresting at first, so the Mayor went home. Later, speakers were violent in their opposition to "law and order" which they claimed was loaded against them. One said of the law, "Throttle it, kill it, stab it, do everything you can to wound it . . ." After some more of the same sort of verbal fireworks, the police decided to disperse the meeting. As they moved in from the fringe of the crowd, someone threw a dynamite bomb which killed 7 and wounded 66 policemen. Dynamite was a new explosive which had never before been used as a weapon. The police charged the crowd, police revolvers taking an even larger toll than the bomb. Public opinion went violently against the unions and created such a climate of opinion that the courts were swept along in the wave of hysteria.

A round-up of anarchists, socialists, and labor leaders followed. Eight men were convicted. Judge Joseph E. Gary of the Cook County Criminal Court of Chicago informed the jury that anyone who had said or written anything that might incite the throwing of a bomb was equally guilty with the person who actually threw it. The eight men found guilty were anarchists and labor organizers. Some of them had not been at the Haymarket meeting, but, under the Judge's ruling, that made no difference. On appeal to higher courts this strange procedure was confirmed and four men were hanged. One committed suicide in jail and the other three had the death sentence commuted to life imprisonment. Six years later the newly elected governor of Illinois, John P. Altgeld, pardoned these three men on the ground that their trial had been unfair because of the "malicious ferocity" with which Judge Gary had conducted the case. The verdict of history is that none of the eight men was guilty of throwing the bomb or planning to have it thrown. The historical significance of such a distressing miscarriage of justice is that the only defense against such a situation is an informed and educated citizenry which has a strong sense of the importance of individual civil rights. The survival of democratic government may depend upon the capacity of people to develop a government that will not degrade itself by joining, in times of stress, with the tyranny of the majority.

Although the Knights of Labor as an organization played no part in the May Day general strike, and its president, Powderly, called those responsible for the bomb throwing at Haymarket Square, "cowardly murderers," the first week in May of 1886 was a sorry one for organized labor. In the public mind, union members were anarchists, a view encouraged by the press and used by management to fight the organization of labor. The Knights of Labor declined rapidly and before 1890 had, for all practical purposes, ceased to exist.

** Granges and Granger Laws

The big post-Civil War depression hit in 1873, but the distress of the farmers was real as early as 1867. The pattern was similar to the hard times after World War I which hit the farm belt in 1920, although the panic that set off the great depression was not until 1929. In President Johnson's administration the Agricultural Department, following the advice of Oliver H. Kelley, helped the farmers organize the *Patrons of Husbandry*. The local units were called Granges and their program was social and economic. Women were encouraged to be members, and monthly meetings at which food, entertainment, lectures, and general sociability prevailed, helped mightily to dispel the effects of the loneliness and hard work of farm life. Of course, both farm women and farm men talked shop and shared their experiences concerning home and farm problems. Outside speakers would inform the Granges on handling mortgages, credit, crop rotation, seed selection, fertilizers, livestock, and hundreds of other practical matters. Some Grange programs were especially for the women and dealt with cooking, preserving food, sewing, and ways of adding to the comfort and attractiveness of the home. Practical and eagerly desired as were these programs, the real vitality of the Granges was in the pleasure the members got in being together for a good time.

With the Granges well established it was inevitable that local office-holders, especially the elected ones, would cultivate the Granges; and that the Granges would invite members of the State legislatures to address their meetings. In short, the Granges became political, as well as social and economic clubs. The way to get elected to office in a farm community was to be well known and well liked by the Grangers; they had the votes.

In the economic field the Granges organized co-operatives on the famous Rochdale Plan. Farmers bought shares of stock to establish a business. Each share-holder had one vote, regardless of the number of shares he held. If so voted by the board of directors, shares paid a small interest. Whatever profits (often called patronage refunds) there were, would be distributed among the members (shareholders) in accordance with how much each had bought from the business if it was a consumers' co-operative, or in accordance with how much he marketed through the business if it was a producers' co-operative. The Grangers sometimes bought live stock, fertilizer, farm tools and machines, and supplies collectively, and saved substantial amounts for the individual farmers. They formed insurance companies, creameries, general stores, warehouses, and even factories to build farm machinery. Most of the more specialized businesses, such as the factories, succeeded for a short time only, as inexpert management and inadequate financing often led to failure. But their partial success was effective in bringing down prices and their group consciousness as an economic force encouraged Montgomery Ward & Company to establish, in 1872, a new form of merchandising, the mail-order house, especially to serve the Patrons of Husbandry.

The political activity of the Granges in the 1870's and 1880's was concerned with railroads. While cities such as Chicago and New York were served by more than one railroad, almost all rural areas were completely dependent on one railroad. This monopoly situation led to many abuses. Railroad rate-fixing followed the principle of charging "all the traffic will bear." Where railroads competed, rates were low; where a railroad had a monopoly, rates were high. Rather than not market his crop a farmer would pay an exorbitant freight

rate. Railroads built storage bins, grain elevators, at the side of the tracks and the farmers could store their grain as they harvested it. The charges for the use of these elevators were often very high. These problems were taken to the state legislatures through the Granges. The Illinois legislature passed laws regulating rates and other charges made by the railroads. Several other states did the same during the 1870's. These state laws were challenged in the courts.

The first test case was *Munn* v. *Illinois* in 1876. The state law fixed a maximum rate for the storage of grain in warehouses and elevators. The law was challenged on the basis that it violated the clause in the 14th amendment which reads, ". . . no State shall deprive any person of life, liberty, or property, without due process of law. . . ." The Supreme Court ruled that whenever private property was used in a manner that clothed it with a public interest it ceased to be only private property and was therefore subject to regulation by government. The use of storage warehouses and elevators where hundreds of farmers store grain in order to market it clothed such storage facilities with an obvious public interest and brought them within the regulatory powers of the state. The Illinois law fixing a maximum charge for the storage of grain was constitutional and valid. The reasoning in this case applies with complete force to the similar clause in the 5th amendment, which is addressed to the federal government. This decision confirmed long-standing common law and it is still in effect. A second ruling in this case took notice of the fact that grain was sometimes part of interstate commerce and that the state law would, in some instances, have an indirect effect on interstate commerce. But as the effect was *indirect* and the federal government *was not exercising* its right to regulate interstate commerce, there was no interference with nor encroachment upon federal authority. This ruling by the Supreme Court was soon substantially modified by the *Wabash* v. *Illinois* decision in 1886.

In the Wabash case the Illinois law had fixed freight rates within the state for the purpose of preventing a common abuse which set higher rates for short hauls than were charged for much longer hauls. For example, the freight rate on corn shipped from Gilman, Illinois, to New York City was 25 cents per hundred pounds; the rate from Peoria, Illinois, to New York City was 15 cents per hundred pounds. Gilman was 86 miles nearer New York City than was Peoria, but Gilman was served by only one railroad and its rates were based on the monopoly principle of "all the traffic will bear," while Peoria was served by more than one railroad and the rates were determined by competition. The Supreme Court ruled that to regulate railroad rates within a state did in fact regulate rates throughout the continuous journey through the several states. If individual states could fix rates within their borders, they could create confusion that would make it utterly impossible to operate railroads. If they could regulate rates, they could regulate safety devices, size of railroad crews, construction of cars, and an infinite number of other matters that come under the police powers of any state dealing with purely *intra*state commerce. The Supreme Court declared unconstitutional and void the rate fixing laws of Illinois. This decision did not actually contradict the *Munn* v. *Illinois* case, but it did make it impossible for states to deal effectively with many real railroad abuses. This decision took the steam out of the political activities of the Granges. They had already failed in many of their economic projects, especially farm equipment factories. By the late 1880's the Granges had decreased substantially in membership and had settled back into social activities which softened the hardness of rural life and gave it some comfort and culture through mutual self-help.

One aspect of the *Wabash* v. *Illinois* case was unusual and deserves notice. The Supreme Court seemed uncomfortable in its awareness of the need of such laws as Illinois had passed, even while it was declaring that Illinois had no right to pass them. The Court said, "Of the justice or propriety of the principle which lies at the foundation of the Illinois statute it is not the province of this court to speak." ". . . within the limits of the State, it (the state law) may be very just and equitable . . ." ". . . the regulation can only appropriately exist by general rules and principles, which demand that it should be done by the Congress of the United States under the commerce clause of the Constitution." Without saying so directly, the Supreme Court created the impression that the abuses attacked by the Illinois law were real, that the state could not deal with them, and that Congress had better get busy. Congress passed the Interstate Commerce Act on February 4th, 1887.

** The Interstate Commerce Act (1887)

After several futile attempts to pass legislation dealing with the railroads, Congress passed the Interstate Commerce Act. Its passage was demanded by public resentment over railway abuses and by the Wabash decision which made state laws unable to cope with the situation. The Act set up an Interstate Commerce Commission (I.C.C.) to enforce the terms of the law.

1] The Interstate Commerce Commission (I.C.C.) had five members appointed by the President with the advice and consent of the Senate. Each commissioner served six years with the terms so arranged that only one commissioner's term expired in any one year. No more than three commissioners could belong to the same political party and they could have no other employment while serving on the I.C.C.

2] All charges by the railroads had to be reasonable and just.

3] No special preference or advantage could be extended by the railroads to any one using their services. Secret rebates, drawbacks, or other devices extending such special advantages were illegal.

4] Pooling was forbidden.

5] No more could be charged for a short haul than for a long haul over the same road in the same direction.

6] Schedules of rates, fares, and charges had to be published and posted. No changes could be made without ten days' notice.

7] Railroads had to use an accounting system which was uniform and met with the approval of the I.C.C.

Pooling was usually an agreement among two or more railroads to charge the same rates in an area, such as New York or Chicago, to avoid competition in passenger, freight, and other charges. Business would then go to the railroads on the basis of convenience to the passengers or shippers rather than on the basis of the cost of the service. Every month, or some other agreed-upon interval, the railroads involved would divide among themselves the revenue taken during the period. The division would be in accordance with the terms of the pooling arrangement and would be based on the volume of traffic each road had carried in that area in the past. Of course, the common rates set for such pools would be high. Such pooling schemes did prevent "cut-throat" competition among railroads, that is, selling services below cost in order to drive another road into bankruptcy. Sometimes a "cut-throat" rate war did ruin one railroad and leave the other almost bankrupt, but in a monopolistic position so that it could raise its rates and recover. "Cut-throat" competition was bad for both the bankrupt road and the consumer who had to pay eventually more in monopoly rates than he had saved temporarily in below-cost rates. If the rate set by a pooling agreement was a "fair and just" one, much could be said in its favor. But the almost certain result of pooling was excessive rates; hence the legal provision against it.

The I.C.C. was not a success. Its ineffectiveness was due to the Commission's lack of power to make the railroads obey its orders. Railroads could challenge the orders of the I.C.C. in the courts and, in the meantime, continue the abuses the I.C.C. was trying to correct. The burden of proof was on the I.C.C.; it had to show that its orders were just and reasonable. When it came to lawyers and legal talent, the railroad was usually the giant and the I.C.C. the pygmy. It paid the railroads to contest orders of the I.C.C. even though they were reasonable and just, because during the time the case was before the courts, sometimes years, the old rates continued in effect and the profit therefrom was greater than the expense of the litigation. Small wonder that the I.C.C., finding itself cleverly and strongly opposed at every move, lost enthusiasm. At times it was little more than an inactive commission representing five political plums, three for one party and two for the other. After almost 20 years of ineffectiveness the I.C.C. had life breathed into it by the Hepburn Bill of 1906 (see pp. 185-186).

The very real significance of the Interstate Commerce Act lies in the fact that it was the first federal law to regulate a major private business. It marked a shift from the conviction that government must not interfere with private business to the reluctant admission that some private business was unavoidably an important factor in the public welfare and that government must therefore exercise substantial regulation over it. The I.C.A. of 1887 was the first big step in this new direction. Three years later the Sherman Anti-trust Act was the second step.

Benjamin Harrison

1889-1893

1833 - 1901

REPUBLICAN

☆

Secretary of State   JAMES G. BLAINE

HARRISON'S PUBLIC SERVICE BEFORE HE BECAME PRESIDENT

Officer in the Civil War (Indiana Regiment)
United State Senator from Indiana 1881-87

MAJOR ITEMS OF HARRISON'S ADMINISTRATION

Foreign Policy under Blaine
"Czar" Reed
Six States Enter the Union
Sherman Anti-trust Act (1890)

McKinley Tariff and Sherman Silver Act
Civil War Pensions
Navy and Coast Defenses
Populist Party Platform of 1892

Harrison's Election (1888)

The Democrats nominated President Cleveland for a second term. The Republicans nominated Benjamin Harrison, grandson of President William Harrison. The major issue of the campaign was the tariff. The Republicans advocated a high protective tariff and Cleveland continued his fight for a tariff such as the Mills Bill he had tried to put through during the last two years (see pp. 153-154). Cleveland's political strength rested with the voters of the party who were not part of the "machine" vote. He had not "played ball" with the local bosses in the cities and they didn't work to get out the vote. Had Tammany Hall delivered the usual New York City Democratic vote, Cleveland would have won the state and the election; but Tammany had no love for "Grover the Good." Even Tammany's betrayal would not have been fatal, had it not been for a last minute episode. The British minister at Washington, Sackville-West, received a letter purporting to come from an Anglo-American citizen requesting advice on how to vote in the coming election. The minister foolishly replied and advised that the vote be cast for Cleveland. The letter was a hoax. It had been written by a Republican in the hope that the British minister would be stupid enough to answer it. The Republican papers published the letters and aroused indignation at the foreign interference in an American election. In New York alone the Irish-American citizens who

turned from Cleveland to Harrison as a result of this incident lost the election for the Democrats, much as the Rev. Burchard's "3 R's" had lost for Blaine in 1884. Harrison carried his home state of Indiana, which, with New York, was a key state in this election.

	Popular Vote	Electoral Vote
Harrison	5,444,337	233
Cleveland	5,540,050	168

Without winning the popular vote, Harrison had won the election by 65 electoral votes.

** Foreign Policy under Secretary of State Blaine

Blaine was an aggressive Secretary of State in his attitude toward other nations and, perhaps because of this, popular with the American people. With some unnecessary blustering and, at times, extreme demands, Blaine achieved satisfactory results for the United States in his handling of incidents with Germany, England, Italy, and Chile.

Samoan Islands

In the early 1870's the United States made an agreement with the native government of the Samoan Islands which gave us control of the harbor of Pago Pago on the island of Tutuila. Here we had a naval base and a coaling station. Germany and England had similar agreements in this island group. American whalers had stopped frequently at the Samoan Islands as early as the 1830's, and American missionaries had established themselves there. The three powers, U.S., England, and Germany suspected each other of seeking favor with the native government to the detriment of the other two. Finally, in 1889, Germany made a move to push the U.S. and England off the islands and a tense situation developed when warships of the three powers were anchored in the harbor at Apia at the island of Upolu. A hurricane settled the issue by wrecking all the ships in the harbor. After talking the problem over, England agreed to withdraw from the Samoan Islands in exchange for German territory in Africa, and the U.S. and Germany made a peaceful division of the islands between them. This was our first venture into international agreements about a place far from our shores involving a people of quite different culture. The initiative taken by Germany in the incident may have been a reflection of the recent accession to the throne of Kaiser Wilhelm II. The Samoan Islands affair, in retrospect, gives a hint of America's excursion into imperialism and of the German-British rivalry that piled up to World War I.

Bering Sea

The Bering Sea dispute between the United States and Great Britain began soon after we purchased Alaska from Russia in 1867. When Russia owned both Siberia and Alaska, the Bering Sea was considered a closed sea belonging to Russia. But when the Bering Sea had Russian Siberia on one side and American Alaska on the other, the status of the Bering Sea was less clear. We had made laws restricting the killing of seals along the Alaskan coast and had established the months of June to October as the only time of the year when hunting seals was legal. We maintained that the Bering Sea was still a *mare clausum* and that it belonged to us. Great Britain ignored our claims to the Bering Sea, and Canadian sealers were depleting the seals to a point threatening extermination. Blaine took decisive action by having several Canadian ships seized by our revenue cutters. Britain complained and we continued to seize Canadian ships. In 1891 it was agreed that the dispute would be submitted to arbitration. As a result, the Bering Sea was declared an open sea with the usual three mile limit for territorial waters adjacent to Alaska, including the Aleutian Islands. But, more important, an international agreement accepted the regulation of hunting seals so that the severe threat of their extermination was removed. Seals are again plentiful in the Bering Sea.

Italy

In October, 1890, the Chief of Police of New Orleans was murdered. The Mafia ("Black Hand"), an organization of Italian criminals, was suspected and several Italians were arrested. They were tried and acquitted of the murder charge, but before they were released a mob broke into the jail and lynched 11 of them. It turned out that three were Italian subjects. The Italian minister filed a formal protest demanding an indemnity and punishment for the members of the lynch mob. Blaine unnecessarily created a fuss over the incident by informing the Italian minister that the lynching, deplorable as it was, was no affair of the United States and that jurisdiction over the case rested with the State of Louisiana and the City of New Orleans. Obviously, Italy could not, without humiliation, make any move to deal with the governor of a state or the mayor of a city; even our own laws would not allow a state to deal with a foreign nation in such a situation. Italy recalled her minister. Blaine's childish display of bad manners was inexcusable, but probably popular and hence good domestic politics. President Harrison quickly smoothed things over by condemning the lynching and assuring Italy that we accepted our responsibility. Congress appropriated $25,000 for families of the three victims, a solution that should have been reached without the silly fireworks.

Chile

Civil war broke out in Chile in 1891. Our minister to Chile, Patrick Egan, with the approval of Secretary of State Blaine, was overzealous in opposing the rebels. A rebel ship carrying arms was seized by the U.S.S. *Charleston,* but then released for lack of legal reason to hold her. When the rebels won the civil war, our Minister, Egan, and our Secretary of State, Blaine, were extremely unpopular in Chile. A Valparaiso mob attacked U.S. sailors from the U.S.S. *Baltimore,* killing two and injuring seventeen. The Chilean minister of the new government rejected President Harrison's protest and his defense of the actions of our navy. Blaine quickly demanded an apology and Harrison sent a message to Congress that was virtually a request for a declaration of war. Chile apologized and paid an indemnity of $75,000.

Reciprocity with Latin America

Blaine achieved a high degree of statesmanship when he initiated and worked for closer trade relations between the United States and the nations of

Central and South America. While he was Secretary of State in 1881 for the few months that President Garfield was in office, he made arrangements for a Pan-American conference. But with the death of Garfield came changes in the State Department and no Pan-American meeting was held. Blaine's purpose was to expand the volume of trade between the United States and the nations to the south of us. Their products were, for the most part, foodstuffs and other raw materials unavailable in the United States. Latin American nations were buying almost all of their imports from European countries. We levied tariffs on a few of their products, but most of their non-competitive items came into the United States duty free. Blaine proposed that we tell them that we would levy tariffs on their products unless they removed the tariffs against our exports to them. While Blaine was a protective tariff advocate for the east-west trade in competitive items between the United States and Europe, he wanted free trade, or an approximation to it, for the north-south trade in non-competitive items between the United States and Latin America. Blaine did not call his program free trade, he called it reciprocity in tariffs; if Latin America would let United States' exports in with very low duties, or no duty at all, we would do the same for their products. It was Blaine's hope that the United States would replace Europe as the chief supplier of manufactured goods for Latin America; he thought geography invited such an economic community of interests and that our position as a great power demanded it. When Blaine again became Secretary of State under President Benjamin Harrison, 1889-93, he got his first Pan-American Congress at Washington. Eighteen nations had delegates at the conference, but little progress was made. The United States was so big and so advanced economically, compared to the Latin American republics, that they shied away from commitments. Blaine's idea was a sound one, but it would take some time for Latin America to get used to it. It was his influence that got the reciprocity principle written into the McKinley Tariff of 1890. Coffee, hides, molasses, and tea were allowed to enter the United States duty free, but the President had the right to put duties on these products if the nation importing them was levying "unreasonable" tariffs against products sent to them from the United States. Ten Latin American nations reduced import duties against our products in response to this reciprocal clause in the McKinley Tariff. While Blaine never saw the fruition of the most statesmanlike endeavor of his career, his policy of reducing tariffs through reciprocal action became the heart of world-wide tariff policy after World War II.

"Czar" Reed

Perhaps part of the reason Congress passed more than the usual quota of laws in the 1889-90 session was "Czar" Reed. While the Republicans did have a majority in each House of Congress, obstructionist tactics could still make the Congress extremely inefficient. Speaker Thomas B. Reed took it upon himself to count as present those members he saw in the House, even though they refused to respond to the roll call in order to prevent a quorum and thus delay a vote. He counted members present if he knew they were in the building, even though they might be in the corridors or the barber shop. When Democrats made motions which were intended to delay action, he declared them out of order. There were some amusing scenes, at least for the Republicans, when Democrats rushed down the aisles to shake their fists in angry protest as they called the Speaker "Tyrant" and "Czar." But the man from Maine got the work done. In 1890 the "Reed Rules" were formally adopted by the House and the next time the Democrats had control they paid "Czar" Reed the highest compliment; they kept the rules.

Six States Enter the Union

North Dakota, South Dakota, Montana, and Washington entered the Union in 1889 and Idaho and Wyoming in 1890. These "Omnibus States" with 12 Senators and 6 Representatives made a political prize worth a political price. The Republican Party paid the price; it gave support for silver legislation in return for support for the McKinley Tariff.

** Sherman Anti-trust Act 1890

In his first annual message President Harrison had suggested that Congress might determine whether "those combinations of capital called trusts" should come under federal jurisdiction. Several states had passed anti-monopoly legislation, and public opinion was aroused to the need for some controls far more effective than any yet available. The United States Senate was being referred to as a "millionaires' club." A cartoon of the day by Meppler showed the Senate in session with the rear gallery filled with towering fat figures with top hats, dress coats, dollar signs on their expansive vests, and obscenely obese stomachs on which were printed the titles, *salt trust, envelope trust, paper bag trust, tin trust, sugar trust, iron trust, Standard Oil Trust, copper trust, steel beam trust, nail trust,* and *steel plow trust.* The caption read, "Bosses of the Senate." Even though Harrison's administration was extremely friendly to business and its most influential spokesman, Blaine, asserted that business was an area in which the government should not meddle, it was crystal clear that the voters demanded anti-trust legislation. So, with more reluctance than enthusiasm, the Republican Congress formulated the Sherman Anti-trust Act. It was passed by an almost unanimous vote, for, in the election of 1888, both parties had promised some sort of federal action on the trust problem.

The key provision of the Sherman Act stated, "Every contract, combination in the form of trust or otherwise, or conspiracy, in restraint of trade or commerce among the several states, or with foreign nations, is hereby declared to be illegal." The key weakness of the law was the prevalence of "weasel" words which were not only ambiguous, but may have been intended to be so. What was a "trust?" Just when was an understanding an agreement, and when was it a "conspiracy?" Any contract or combination among businessmen intended to promote their business would, if successful, probably take away trade from some other business. Was it then a "conspiracy" which was "in restraint" of trade? If restraint was permissible to some degree, to what degree? If every agreement (*contract, combination, conspiracy*) which restrained interstate or foreign commerce was prohibited, the government's interference in trade would be intolerable. If the "weasel" words were interpreted loosely there would be varying court decisions in similar cases and hence an uneven and unjust enforcement of law. The situation was so confusing that the law was interpreted as though it meant almost nothing. The sugar "trust" which controlled over 95% of the refining process was declared not a trust because refining was manufacturing, not interstate trade. (*U.S.* v. *E. C. Knight & Co.* 1895.) The government lost cases so consistently under the Sherman Act that the Attorney General's office was reluctant to start cases. One Attorney General, Olney, thought the law impossible to enforce and saw no point in "prosecuting under a law I believe to be no good." The ten years after the Sherman Act was passed saw over seven times as many business combinations as there had been in the decade before the law. Not until the Northern Securities Case of 1904 was the government able to break up a trust. It was this case which breathed a spark of life into a Sherman Anti-trust Act which for fourteen years had been considered dead.

In spite of its shortcomings as an effective weapon against monopoly power in business, the Sherman Anti-trust Act was a very significant law. Over the three-quarters of a century since its pas-

sage it has been supplemented by further anti-trust legislation, and both Congress and the courts have long since viewed these laws in the same light that the great mass of voters viewed them before 1900— as laws really intended to curb the power of business combinations exercising monopoly power against the public interest. While the problems posed by organizations of commerce, industry, and labor are still with us, the basic fact today is the acceptance of the view that government has the right to protect the public welfare from abuses by aggregates of private economic power.

* McKinley Tariff and Sherman Silver Act (1890)

The Republicans may have taken no joy in the passage of the Sherman Anti-trust Act, but they did enthusiastically support the McKinley Tariff. William McKinley of Ohio, chairman of the Ways and Means Committee, introduced the bill. The average ad valorum (according to value) rate was 49.5% and about every American manufacturer who wanted protection got it. For the first time farmers' products, wheat, corn, and potatoes were on the protective list. This was a bit silly as the United States had great surpluses of wheat and corn which were exported. No one was trying to send these products into this country. American sugar growers were encouraged by a bounty of 2¢ per pound for their raw sugar and the American sugar refiners were favored by duty free raw sugar from abroad. The principle of reciprocity was written into the bill at the insistence of Secretary of State Blaine (see pp. 160-161).

There was more political maneuvering than usual in getting this tariff through Congress. The western states, including the new "omnibus states" (see p. 161) had to be promised support for silver legislation. To keep the South from combining with the West to defeat the bill, it was necessary for the Republican Party to promise to discontinue all efforts to enforce the 14th and 15th amendments in efforts to improve the civil rights of negroes. In 1890 the Republican House had passed the Federal Election Bill which would have had federal inspectors supervising, under certain conditions, elections in Southern states involving federal offices. With the assurance that the North would drop efforts to interfere with the South's own system of handling its race problem, the southern Democrats made no serious attempt to block the McKinley Tariff. Only five weeks after the bill was signed by President Harrison, the politics in making the tariff were matched by the politics in using it as an effective weapon against the Republicans in the 1890 Congressional election. In anticipation of the new tariff rates, a rise in prices occurred and continued during the election campaign. The Democrats made the most of the situation by blaming it all on the Republicans. The farmers felt the higher cost of living and discovered that the tariff did nothing for their wheat, corn, and potatoes. When the votes were counted the House contained 235 Democrats and only 88 Republicans. Even McKinley, who had served seven terms in the House, was defeated. It was a "landslide" for the Democrats. The Senate remained Republican, but by a smaller margin.

The Sherman Silver Act of 1890 provided that the government buy 4½ million ounces each month at the market price. This silver would be paid for in Treasury notes which would be legal tender and redeemable in gold or silver at the discretion of the government. The 4½ million ounces was about the total output of the silver mines in the United States. The Eastern Republicans disliked this law, but they voted for it in order to get the Western Congressmen to vote for the McKinley Tariff. The Westerners supported the McKinley Tariff only to get the support of the Easterners for the Sherman Silver Act. The situation was a good illustration of *log-rolling*. The farmers demanded the Bland-Allison Act and the Sherman Silver Act because they expected the increased amount of money to result in higher prices for farm products and an easier way to pay off mortgages. The silver mining industry favored these laws because it wanted a guaranteed market for silver. Yet neither of these groups achieved their aims. Farm prices continued downward, a fact which meant that, instead of getting cheaper, money was increasing in purchasing power. The silver mines were producing so much more silver that, in spite of the extensive government purchases, the surplus silver increased and the price fell. The value of the bullion in a silver dollar fell, but, as the Treasury redeemed all money in gold, the silver and the paper money were as good as gold. The farmers and the mining interests were still unhappy; their answer to the situation was free coinage of silver at the ratio of 16 to 1. The big struggle to apply this remedy was to come in the presidential campaign of 1896.

Civil War Pensions

Early in Harrison's administration it was evident that the G.A.R. (Grand Army of the Republic) had a friend in the White House. A past commander of the G.A.R., James Tanner, was appointed Commissioner of Pensions. When he took office he is reported to have said, "God help the surplus," a remark that apparently meant he intended to solve easily and quickly a problem that had bothered Cleveland for four years. The President gave support to this view about pensions and the surplus by saying that he was not going to "weigh the claims of old soldiers with an apothecary's scales." This remark was a slam at Cleveland who had vetoed the Dependent Pensions Bill. This bill would have given pensions to all Civil War veterans of at least 90 days service who were unable to earn a living other than by manual labor. Cleveland's stand on the pension issue was that all veterans who could show disability resulting from service in the Civil War deserved pensions. He approved a liberal interpretation of pension laws in favor of the veteran whenever there was some doubt about the disability or its connection with war service. He had signed many special pension bills and he had vetoed many. He was both generous with the veterans and decently considerate of taxpayers. The G.A.R. was naturally strongly Republican, and the return of their party to power was an opportunity not wasted. The Dependent Pensions Bill was revived and, with some modification, passed. The principle was established that pensions would be granted to disabled veterans regardless of the origin of their disability. Almost immediately the number of pensioners increased by over 300,000 and the annual expenditures by over $50,000,000.

Navy and Coast Defenses

We have seen that President Arthur began the construction of a modern navy. President Cleveland continued the good work by starting the building of about 30 steel ships. In 1890 Captain Alfred Mahan's monumental book, *Influence of Sea Power Upon History*, was acclaimed throughout the western world. Captain Mahan's writings made him unofficial spokesman for imperialism and aroused enthusiasm about the United States becoming a great naval power, perhaps one day the leading naval power of the world. The use of domestic steel for the new ships placed the business community solidly in favor of a large navy. The historical evidence compiled by Mahan in his nine-volume treatise was supported by the academic world of the universities. With a sense of pride the American citizens embraced the idea of a powerful United States navy. Congress appropriated the money. Late in Harrison's administration we had climbed to fifth place among the navies of the world and less than ten years later our navy held third place with only Great Britain and France ahead of us. In addition to the stepped-up expenditures for the new ships, large sums were spent for defenses along our coasts and for the improvement of rivers and harbors. The total appropriated by the first Congress under Harrison hit a new high at over a billion dollars. The Democrats raised the cry of extravagance, but the Republicans brushed it aside with the boast that the United States was a "billion dollar country."

* Populist Party Platform of 1892

Western farmers were not happy in the Republican Party; neither were the people in the silver-mining towns. Both were suffering from overproduction. Wheat was at the ruinous low price of 50 cents a bushel, and corn was being used by the farmers for fuel because it didn't pay to cart it to market. The silver mines had produced more than could be sold. The farmers of the South were, if anything, worse off with cotton too low in price to cover costs of production. The Southern farmers protested verbally with the other discontented groups, but they would still vote the Democratic ticket because they didn't dare split the white vote and thus provide the least little chance for the negro to become a political force. They felt that, regardless of economic distress, white supremacy must be preserved.

We have stated that the fundamental problem was overproduction; too much wheat, too much corn, too much silver, too much cotton, etc. But while there was "too much" of so many things, there was widespread poverty throughout the United States and the other advanced nations of the world. Man, presumedly the most intelligent of all the animal kingdom, seems to be the only one bothered by surpluses of the good things of life. The Populist Party (The People's Party) was formed to protest this suffering amidst plenty and to offer a corrective program. At Omaha, Nebraska, they nominated James B. Weaver for President and wrote a famous platform. It was a scorching blast at the status quo and a remarkable prophecy of things to come. Appropriately, they opened their nomination convention on July 4th, 1892.

From the Omaha Platform's Preamble

". . . we meet in the midst of a nation brought to the verge of moral, political, and material ruin. Corruption dominates the ballot-box, the Legislatures, the Congress, and touches even the ermine of the bench. . . . The newspapers are largely subsidized or muzzled, public opinion silenced, business prostrated, homes covered with mortgages, labor impoverished, and the land concentrating in the hands of capitalists. . . . The fruits of the toil of millions are boldly stolen to build up colossal fortunes for the few. . . . From the same prolific womb of governmental injustice we breed the two great classes—tramps and millionaires. . . . We have witnessed for more than a quarter of a century the struggles of the two great political parties for power and plunder, while grievous wrongs have been inflicted upon the suffering people. . . . They propose to sacrifice our homes, lives, and children on the alter of mammon; . . . the Civil War is over, and every passion and resentment which grew out of it must die with it, and we must be in fact, as we are in name, one united brotherhood of free men."

Demands of the Omaha Platform

1] Graduated Income Tax

2] Direct Election of Senators

3] Australian (Secret) Ballot

4] Extension of the Merit System in Civil Service

5] Restriction of Immigration

6] Initiative and Referendum

7] Eight Hour Day for Labor

8] Postal Savings Banks

9] Government Ownership of Railroads

10] Government Ownership of Telegraph and Telephone

11] Return to the Government of Lands granted to Railroads and Corporations in Excess of their actual Needs

12] Free Coinage of Silver at the Ratio of 16-1

One could hardly find a better working out of the cliché "The radical of today is the conservative of tomorrow." Two of these "radical" demands are now the 16th and 17th amendments of the Constitution. Most of the others have been substantially fulfilled or become accepted practice. The Populists did a superb job, far better than they knew, in setting up a substantial part of the agenda for Congress for a generation or two.

Grover Cleveland 1893-1897

Second Administration

DEMOCRAT

MAJOR ITEMS OF CLEVELAND'S SECOND ADMINISTRATION

Panic of 1893
Hawaiian Incident (1893)
Venezuelan Boundary Affair (1895)
Problem of the Gold Reserve

Wilson-Gorman Tariff (1894)
Pullman Strike (1894)
American Federation of Labor

Cleveland's Election (1892)

The Republicans nominated Harrison for a second term and the Democrats nominated Cleveland for the third consecutive time and a second term. Cleveland was still less than popular with the machine Democrats, but they knew he had the votes of the great bulk of the Party's membership. Tariff was again the main issue, with the Democratic platform restating Calhoun's position by asserting that "The federal government has no Constitutional power to impose and collect tariff duties, except for the purposes of revenue only." Cleveland took a firm stand for the gold standard and sound money, a position that won votes for him in the East and lost them in the West. The McKinley Tariff, which had been used so effectively as an issue in the midterm elections, was still hurting the Republican Party. In July the "massacre" (7 persons killed) at Homestead, Pa. occurred as Pinkerton's 300 private police shot it out with strikers of the Carnegie Steel Co. That a "private army" was hired by Henry Frick, general manager of Carnegie Steel, plus the fact that protection given steel by the McKinley Tariff failed to provide high wages, made the violence at Homestead an embarrassment to the Republicans. The presence of an articulate third party in the field, the Populists (see p. 164), which took Colorado, Idaho, Kansas, and Nevada with a total of 22 electoral votes, did not affect the outcome of the struggle between the two major parties.

	Popular Vote	*Electoral Vote*
Cleveland	5,554,414	277
Harrison	5,190,802	145
Weaver	1,027,329	22

The Democrats gained majorities in both the House and the Senate.

Panic of 1893

Cleveland's second term was four years of depression. In the spring of 1893 the National Cordage Company and the Philadelphia & Reading Railroad failed. Before the year was over, almost 500 banks and more than 15,000 businesses had failed. About 4,000,000 unemployed were roaming the streets looking for jobs that did not exist. Several factors seemed to contribute to this depression: the farmers had experienced no real prosperity since the early 1870's and their purchasing power had been low, strikes had cut the purchasing power of industrial and railroad workers, hard times in Europe stifled our export trade, the silver purchase acts had persuaded foreign holders of American securities to sell them while they could still get a good price, the McKinley Tariff had dried up the revenue usually received from imports, the "billion dollar" expenditures under Harrison had depleted the surplus and created a deficit, and the gold reserve to support our currency system had sunk some $20,000,000 below the legal minimum of $100,000,000. Cleveland did not create the depression, but he did get blamed for it. No President can weather a four-year depression and maintain the popularity, or even the confidence, of public opinion.

* Hawaiian Incident (1893)

Queen Liliuokalani came to the throne in 1891. At this time the McKinley Tariff with its bounty of 2 cents per pound for all the sugar grown in the United States had hit the Hawaiian sugar plantations with full force. The encouragement to American sugar growers was such a blow to Hawaii that the whole economy of the islands had been seriously threatened. The Queen decided to meet the situation by establishing a dictatorship and shifting Hawaiian economic dependence away from the United States. Her attempt to set aside the native Constitution met with a native revolt and the policy of orienting the Hawaiian economy away from the United States alienated the American citizens who had invested heavily in the island sugar plantations. The obvious move for the American sugar planters on the islands was to have Hawaii become a possession of the United States with free entry for her products to the mainland markets. The instability of native governments was another factor which favored annexation. John Stevens, our minister at Honolulu, was fully in sympathy with the American sugar planters on the islands and used his influence to aid the native revolt against Queen "Lil's" new policy. Marines from the U.S.S. *Boston* led the natives, deposed the Queen, and set up a provisional government with Sanford B. Dole as president. This government petitioned the United States to annex the Hawaiian Islands. President Harrison approved the request and submitted it to the Senate as a treaty. It was mid-February with only three weeks left in his term and before the Senate acted upon the treaty Cleveland had been inaugurated. Cleveland thought it strange that the government of Hawaii would be asking to be annexed to the United States, and upon investigation, he found that the revolution had been largely an American accomplishment. He withdrew the treaty, asked the Queen to pardon the revolutionists, and suggested that the provisional government step down in favor of Liliuokalani. But the Queen would not forgive; instead she made angry and unladylike comments about the United States while threatening to behead the revolutionists. With little difficulty the provisional government continued to rule the islands and wish for annexation. Cleveland's "retreat" from an angry native Queen gave rise to cries of disappointment in the United States and some silly charges of cowardice. But "Grover the Good" plodded along his decent, obstinate way getting more unpopular every day, but heading toward a rather high rating as one of our capable and worthy Presidents. When McKinley came along with the Spanish-American War, the urge to annex Hawaii was irresistible and no one in Washington wanted to resist it. On July 7, 1898, Hawaii was annexed by a joint resolution of Congress and in 1900 all the inhabitants of the Hawaiian Islands became citizens of the United States in the Territory of Hawaii.

* Venezuelan Boundary Affair (1895)

British Guiana and Venezuela had a boundary dispute of some 50 years standing. Twice Cleveland had suggested arbitration, once in 1887 and again in 1894. The dispute flared up again upon the discovery of gold deposits in the border areas. There was danger that either side might precipitate hostilities and thus involve the United States, for any loss of territory by Venezuela to Great Britain would involve the Monroe Doctrine. A European power would be colonizing at the expense of a republic in the western hemisphere. Secretary of State, Richard Olney, sent a message to the British Foreign Minister, Lord Salisbury, expressing the American view with great clarity and greater bluntness. Olney said that the United States "is practically sovereign on this continent" (What about Canada?) He went on to state that when the United States chose to enter into any situation in the western hemisphere, its word then became law. (What about the several republics there?) It contained the boast that the United States could take this position because it had the power to do so. "Its (The U.S.) infinite resources combined with its isolated position render it master of the situation and practically invulnerable against any and all other powers." The communication ended with an appeal for arbitration. After four months, Lord Salisbury replied with a refusal to arbitrate and an assertion that the Monroe Doctrine had no standing in international law and, in any case, did not apply to this situation. England sent troops to British Guiana. President Cleveland asked Congress to appropriate the necessary funds to send a commission to determine the proper boundary line which, if necessary, the United States would maintain against any attempt Great Britain might make to violate it. For a few weeks Cleveland was popular. Fortunately both sides calmed down. Neither really wanted war. The British navy was still five times as powerful as ours and trouble was brewing for England in South Africa. The abortive raid into the Transvaal by Dr. Jameson had been smothered by the Boers. A congratulatory telegram sent to the Boer leader, Kruger, by Kaiser Wilhelm II pointed up the growing hostility between England and Germany. England needed friends. The Venezuelan boundary dispute was arbitrated with the stipulation that any area actually occupied by either party for 50 years would belong to that party. The Monroe Doctrine had been respected, England got most of the land, and Venezuela need no longer fear encroachments by Britain. The settlement has been judged a fair one.

Problem of the Gold Reserve

As the price of silver fell, the value of the silver acquired by the Treasury under the terms of the Sherman Silver Purchase Act depreciated. Silver dollars and silver certificates were cheaper money than gold coins and gold certificates. It was true that all money could be redeemed in gold, but this was due to government policy which could be changed at short notice. The mere fact that one kind of money was more valuable than another resulted in people using the cheaper and saving the sounder money. Foreign traders would stipulate that their bills must be paid in gold. Before the Sherman Silver Purchase Act was passed about 85% of the customs duties had been paid in gold, but three years later over 90% had been paid in silver. This common sense tendency to get rid of cheap money and keep sound money had been formulated into Gresham's Law about 300 years earlier during the reign of Queen Elizabeth. Briefly stated, it says that cheap money drives good money out of circulation. Good money flows out of the country to pay foreign merchants and is hoarded by everyone who can manage to save. As long as the government exchanged gold for all legal tender, it was inevitable that gold would be drawn out of the Treasury while silver accumulated there. The minimum gold reserve required by law was $100,000,000, but it had fallen much below this limit and was inadequate to redeem the greenbacks and silver certificates then in circulation. Cleveland moved to correct this situation by calling a special session of Congress which repealed the Sherman Silver Purchase Act. This stopped the steady flow of new silver into the Treasury. The next problem was to get gold to come into the Treasury and stay there. Two issues of government bonds totaling $100,000,000 were sold for gold, but the purchasers then presented greenbacks or silver certificates to be redeemed in gold. There was a steady flow of gold through the Treasury, but no build-up of the gold reserve which had fallen to $41,000,000. At this point John Pierpont Morgan and a group of associates proposed to pay gold for bonds to the total of $62,000,000. Half of this gold was to come from abroad and the bankers pledged not to withdraw gold from the Treasury by redeeming legal tender paper. Cleveland accepted this plan. The gold reserve recovered, confidence in the currency system returned, the nation remained on the gold standard, and the credit of the United States had been preserved. But this transaction was political poison for a Democrat. "Wicked" Wall Street was the bailiwick of the tycoons of the financial world, a solid block of Republicans, and "J.P." was the king of Wall Street. The rank and file of the Democratic Party could neither understand nor forgive Cleveland for the Morgan "deal" which not only served the government but gave handsome profits to the bankers.

* Wilson-Gorman Tariff (1894)

During his second administration, Cleveland was as determined to achieve tariff reform as he had been when he fought unsuccessfully for the Mills Bill in his first term. Representative William Wilson of West Virginia introduced the bill Cleveland wanted. It put some raw materials on the free list (coal, copper, iron ore, sugar, wool), and some manufactured products had their rates cut to a moderate revenue level (china, cotton and woolen goods, glass, silk). The bill passed the House easily, but when Gorman of Maryland piloted it through the Senate, it was amended over 600 times. Democrats from Alabama, Louisiana, and West Virginia wanted protection for iron ore, sugar, and coal. When the Wilson-Gorman Tariff passed, it was protective with rates averaging about 40% as compared with the McKinley average of about 50%. Again Cleveland had been defeated on his tariff program. He angrily called the bill a piece of "party perfidy and dishonor," but allowed it to become law even though he didn't sign it. Had he vetoed the bill the higher McKinley Tariff would have remained in effect.

* Pullman Strike (1894)

This was a strike in the depth of a depression. The Pullman Company dismissed their employees and then hired about a third of them back with wage cuts of 20 to 25 per cent. A few of the Pullman employees were members of the American Railway Union which had just won a restoration of a wage cut from the Great Northern Railway System of James J. Hill. They appealed to Eugene V. Debs, president of the American Railway Union, for help. Debs had become disgusted with the railroad unions where conductors, engineers, firemen, switchmen, telegraph operators, etc. were in separate unions. They had fought each other during strikes as frequently as they had helped one another. So Debs organized the American Railway Union which invited all employees to join. It was an industrial rather than a craft union. The Pullman workers lived in a company town where the houses were owned by George M. Pullman. The town was neater and cleaner than most workingmen's neighborhoods; but rents, gas, and water rates were from 10 to 25 per cent higher than in nearby areas. Because a few employees formed a committee to discuss the situation with Mr. Pullman, he fired them. He had his own ideas about the proper relations between an employer and his employees. Debs suggested arbitration; Pullman said,

"We have nothing to arbitrate." He also observed that "The workers have nothing to do with the amount of wages they shall receive." More ill feeling was generated by the knowledge that the company had just paid its usual dividends totaling over $2\frac{1}{2}$ millions and had a surplus of some $25,000,000.

Debs ordered a boycott and within a week 100,000 workers refused to work on any train with a Pullman car. Debs warned them not to interfere with mail trains and not to try to prevent others from taking their jobs. He was confident that the railroads could not replace 100,000 skilled and semi-skilled employees, and that running the roads with incompetent help would prove intolerably dangerous and expensive. He was probably right. The strike was beaten by the United States Government through the use of injunctions issued by federal courts. An injunction is a negative court order directing someone not to do something he is about to do, or to stop doing what is already under way. The United States Attorney General was Richard Olney who for 33 years had been a corporation lawyer in Boston and had been on the Boards of Directors of several railroads. Both Olney and Debs saw that when thousands of skilled men quit work in any great industry, they could not be replaced in time to affect appreciably the situation. Such a strike became a contest to determine whether management could tolerate huge financial losses as long as workers could tolerate loss of pay and the risk of losing their jobs. In such a contest public opinion could become a tremendous asset for either side.

It was Olney who proposed the injunction as a method of dealing with the strike. A court order telling Debs not to interfere with the mails also could be defended as a proper procedure for stopping a violation of the Sherman Anti-trust Act; for was not the strike a conspiracy which restrained interstate commerce? Thus the Sherman Anti-trust Act was used to deny to labor the right to strike. The wording of the law certainly made such an interpretation plausible, but the purpose of the law had been to curb corporations. Workingmen, organized and unorganized, had looked upon the Sherman Act as their defense against exploitation by "Big Business." Olney asserted his position plainly and publicly. He held that any national railroad strike was automatically illegal. Here he put his finger on a point which has reached a critical stage today. Just what is to be done when a struggle between Big Labor and Big Business dangerously disrupts the national economy, or perhaps results in a deal satisfactory to both of them but detrimental to the public welfare? The Attorney General held that the causes of the strike were in no

way relevant to the legality of the strike. This was a reiteration of his first statement, with a strong implication that if one examined the causes of this particular strike, Mr. Pullman's acts and attitudes would compare most unfavorably with those of Debs. Mark Hanna, the Mr. Republican of his day, waxed profane when he expressed his opinion of George Pullman's refusal to "meet his men halfway." A third point made by Pullman was that local officials (state and city) could not be trusted with the enforcement of federal laws. This was a strange doctrine. The accepted view, then and now, is that federal troops enter a local situation only by invitation of the governor or mayor, or when it is clear beyond any doubt that the local authorities will not or can not maintain the peace. In the Pullman strike none of these conditions prevailed. Mayor Hopkins of Chicago and Governor Altgeld of Illinois bitterly protested the entrance of federal troops into their city and state. The strike was orderly and was being easily controlled by local authorities. There was no appreciable disorder until July 3rd when federal troops were ordered to Chicago; then extensive property damage occurred and twelve men were killed.

The injunction issued against Debs ordered him not to obstruct the mail, not to damage railroad property, and not to communicate with the strikers to direct their actions. Debs agreed with the first two prohibitions. But there was no way to escape the third. If he could not direct the strike, he could not maintain discipline and would then be arrested when violence occurred. If he did direct the strike and prevent violence, he would be arrested for directing the strike. Either way he was caught. Newspapers that opposed the strike were highly critical of this "government by injunction." After violence flared up, Debs issued the following instructions to the strikers and thus violated the injunction. "I appeal to you to be men, orderly and law-abiding. Our cause is just, . . . Let it be borne in mind that if the railroads can secure men to handle their trains, they have that right. Our men have the right to quit, but their right ends there. Other men have the right to take their places, . . . Keep away from railway yards, or rights of way, or those places where large crowds congregate. . . . Respect the law, conduct yourselves as becomes men and our cause shall be crowned with success." Debs was arrested. When tried for violating the Sherman Anti-trust Act, the jury voted 11 to 1 for acquittal. One of the jurors became too ill to continue serving so the judge dismissed them and no further action was taken on the conspiracy charge. Debs served a six months sentence. The Pullman strike was a severe blow to unions. The Knights of Labor had faded away and now the industrial union had been smashed.

Perhaps unfortunately, President Cleveland played a minor role in the Pullman strike situation. He left the problem with Olney and backed him to limit in whatever he did. When the furor over the injunction heaped criticism on the government, Cleveland supported his Attorney General with the statement that he would use every dollar in the Treasury and every soldier in the army if necessary to deliver a single postcard to Chicago. With the added wisdom given by distance and hindsight, the handling of the Pullman strike stands out as the one significant weak spot in Cleveland's strong and able handling of the presidency.

* The American Federation of Labor

In the 1870's Samuel Gompers organized a small craft, the cigar makers, into a union in New York City's lower East Side. He organized other unions in other crafts. In 1886 the A.F. of L. was born. The several groups forming the Federation were national organizations made up of local craft unions. The national organization advised and often aided their locals. The Federation advised the national organizations, aided in drives for membership, tried to prevent the formation of rival labor groups, and set the policy of keeping the union aims restricted to very practical and immediate goals such as collective bargaining, better pay, shorter hours, etc. The A.F. of L. avoided reform movements and political parties. Sam Gompers' program was a simple one aimed at better working conditions next year than existed this year. He had no economic or social philosophy and shied away from those who had. The A.F. of L. touched but a small fraction of the wage earners because it limited itself to organizing skilled workers. While Terence Powderly (see p. 154) and Gene Debs were going down to defeat, Gompers made progress throughout the 80's and 90's. By the outbreak of World War I the A.F. of L. had about two million members. With Sam Gompers as its president for 37 years, the A.F. of L. dominated the labor field for about forty years.

William McKinley

1897-1901

1843 - 1901

REPUBLICAN

☆

Vice-President THEODORE ROOSEVELT

Secretary of State JOHN HAY

McKINLEY'S PUBLIC SERVICE BEFORE HE BECAME PRESIDENT

Officer in the Union Army at Antietam and other Battles
Member of the House of Representatives from Ohio
Governor of Ohio

MAJOR ITEMS OF McKINLEY'S ADMINISTRATIONS

Spanish-American War (April 1898-
February 1899)
Governing Our New Possessions

Open Door Policy and the Boxer Rebellion
McKinley Assassinated by Czolgosz

* McKinley's Election in 1896 and 1900

The Republican convention met at St. Louis to adopt a platform advocating the gold standard, protective tariff, and the control of the Hawaiian Islands. They were confident of victory and boasted that any Republican could win. Marcus Hanna was an extremely wealthy merchant, industrialist, and financier who had great capacity for organization and a zest for power. It could almost be said that he was the Republican Party of Ohio. He dropped his business interests to groom McKinley for the presidency. His preconvention plans worked out perfectly with his candidate winning the nomination on the first ballot. Hanna, as National Republican Chairman, ran the successful campaign with a new technique for raising money. He "fried the fat" out of banks, insurance companies, railroads, and other corporations by persuading them to contribute generously for the party which gave them the kind of government they wanted—or perhaps to save them from the kind of government they didn't want.

The Democratic Party was in a sad state in 1896: it was blamed for the 1893 panic and the ensuing depression years; the Congressional elections of 1894 had put the Republicans in control of both House and Senate; and President Cleveland had managed to offend several blocs of voters. His scrutiny of pension bills had fastened the G.A.R. even more securely to the Republican Party; his vigorous support of the injunction against Debs in the Pullman strike had alienated labor; his insistence that the Sherman Silver Purchase Act be repealed had of-

fended cheap money advocates; his battles for a revenue tariff had divided his party; and his refusal to feed the party "machines" with "spoils" had deadened the enthusiasm of the regular Democrats who knew how to get out the vote on election day. At the Democratic convention in Chicago, Eastern leaders made speeches in support of the gold standard, and Tillman of South Carolina also presented a weak defense of free silver. Then the last of a too long list of speakers was a much younger man of 36, William Jennings Bryan. He paid brief and polite respects to the more distinguished Democrats who had preceded him. He then set the tone of his oration. "The humblest citizen in all the land, when clad in the armor of a righteous cause, is stronger than all the hosts of error. I come to speak to you in defense of a cause as holy as the cause of liberty— the cause of humanity." Almost every sentence brought applause and cheers. The speech had been carefully composed and thoroughly rehearsed. He concluded, ". . . we will answer their demand for a gold standard by saying to them: You shall not press down upon the brow of labor this crown of thorns, you shall not crucify mankind upon a cross of gold." Bryan had organized his supporters before the convention; he was thoroughly confident he would win the nomination. Perhaps his speech alone would have done it. On the 5th ballot he got the necessary two-thirds majority of the delegates and the "Boy Orator of the Platte" was the Democratic nominee. The gold standard Democrats withdrew from the convention.

The campaign was rather strange. McKinley gave polite little speeches from the front porch of his home in Canton, Ohio. Although the money raised by Mark Hanna was $3,500,000 it was estimated that the Republicans spent at least five times that amount hiring thousands of speakers and plastering the nation with posters. Many mills and factories in the northeast notified their employees on the Saturday night before the election that a Bryan victory would ruin the business and rob them of their jobs. The Democrats spent about $300,000 and had one speaker. Bryan covered about 20,000 miles in a special railway car and spoke as many as twenty times a day. It seems safe to say that no other person, before the time of radio, addressed so many people. Cleveland and the gold standard Democrats considered Bryan more a Populist than a Democrat (a "Popocrat") and either didn't vote or voted for McKinley. The early days of the campaign found the Republicans complacent and confident, but by late summer they were running scared. Twenty-two states went to Bryan and twenty-three to McKinley.

	Popular Vote	Electoral Vote
McKinley	7,035,638	271
Bryan	6,467,946	176

"Big Business" had won over the agrarian interests. The "Boy Orator of the Platte" had made a gallant fight in support of the common people, but he made that fight on an unsound economic doctrine of free silver at 16 to 1. Bryan seemed destined to devote his life to unfortunate causes, but his uprightness and his devotion to the "little man" attracted the affection of thousands and won him his title, "The Great Commoner."

McKinley Re-elected in 1900

The campaign of 1900 was an easy victory for the Republicans. Prosperity had returned early in McKinley's first term, and the Klondike gold rush, begun in 1896, had reached peak production in 1900, thus taking the life out of the demand for free coinage of silver. Theodore Roosevelt was a popular figure obviously climbing toward the top and equally obviously not an easy man for a party to control. Party loyalty induced him to accept the nomination as Vice-President, while the party bosses were anxious to put him safely out of the way on the Vice-Presidential "shelf" where his name would attract support to the ticket. The platform called for a continuation of the protective tariff, the gold standard, and an Isthmian canal under United States control across Panama. It also claimed credit for prosperity which, with their "full dinner pail" slogan, made the main issue of the campaign.

The Democrats nominated Bryan who again chose to hammer away at an issue that was bound to lose, anti-imperialism. The Spanish-American War had been an easy victory and, perhaps for that reason, a popular one. Bryan also continued to demand free silver at 16 to 1. Had the Democrats campaigned against the growing power of "Big Business" in government and the inadequacy of the laws to control abuses against the public welfare, they might have struck a sound and popular note; but anti-imperialism was hopeless and free silver was dead.

** Spanish-American War

The formal declaration of war was on April 25, 1898 and the ratification of the Treaty of Paris restored peace on February 6, 1899—a $9\frac{1}{2}$ months war. The fighting began at Manila Bay in the Philippines on May 1st and ended with the surrender of Santiago, Cuba on July 17th—an 11 weeks fight.

The United States had shown from time to time an interest in Cuba. President John Quincy Adams had written that it seemed in the nature of things to come that Cuba would one day belong to the United States. Buchanan, when Secretary of State under President Polk, had tried to purchase Cuba from Spain; and under President Pierce the Ostend Manifesto fiasco (see pp. 123-124) had embarrassed us. Spanish rule in Cuba was usually cruel and always inefficient. During most of the 1870's rebellion was rampant throughout the island, atrocities by Spanish authorities against the rebels were frequent, and an incident involving the death of several American citizens occurred. The incident was the capture by the Spanish of the ship *Virginius* which was running guns to the Cuban rebels. The 53 crew members, many of whom were Americans, were shot as pirates. Yet there was no great furor as our Secretary of State, Hamilton Fish, accepted a settlement of $80,000,000 for the families of the executed men. The late 1890's saw similar widespread rebellion with accompanying atrocities. But by this time the sugar crop of Cuba was more important to the United States, the American investments in Cuba were more extensive, and the United States navy was new and ranked second only to the navies of Great Britain and France. Our government and people found it easier to think in terms of world wide interests after the diplomacy of Secretary of State Blaine (see pp. 159-160) and the dispute with England over the Venezuelan-British Guiana boundary during Cleveland's second term (see p. 166). We were in a frame of mind to act the part of one of the great powers of the world and take part in colonialism, provided it could be done under the banner of rescuing an oppressed people or "sharing the white man's burden." But all of these factors combined would not have precipitated the war with Spain had it not been for the blatant jingoism and calculated fake atrocity stories and pictures by an irresponsible press. The Spanish-American War was an accomplishment of the *yellow press;* the most influential newspapers of this stripe were Hearst's *New York Journal* and Pulitzer's *New York World.* During the Cuban revolution, filibustering expeditions from New Orleans and other American ports were frequent, and the efforts of the government to stop them were less than vigorous.

President McKinley had said that there would be "no jingo nonsense" in his administration. Early in 1896 concentration camps established by General ("Butcher") Weyler imprisoned men, women, and children. Disease, semi-starvation, cruelty, and lack of sanitation gave the *Journal* and the *World* good copy for atrocity stories. A change in the Spanish ministry in November 1897 resulted in the recall of "Butcher" Weyler, a plan for local autonomy for Cuba, and the release of United States citizens from Cuban jails. But, like the "Olive Branch" offered by the British after the Battle of Saratoga, these concessions came too late to satisfy the rebels. The following month McKinley urged that Spain be given a reasonable opportunity to carry out her new policy. The "Old Guard" of the Republican Party and most of the business leaders approved McKinley's purpose to avoid war. The Cuban insurgents wanted to bring the United States into the war and the Spanish minister at Washington unwittingly played into their hands. A personal letter he wrote to a friend was stolen from the Havana post office. It described McKinley as a "would-be politician," a "bidder for the admiration of the crowd" and a weak official who took no strong stand, but always tried to "leave a door open behind himself" so that he might avoid responsibility. Hearst's *Journal* published the letter on February 9, 1898 and the Spanish Minister, Enrique Depuy De Lôme, resigned. On the evening of February 15th in Havana harbor an explosion killed 260 men on the battleship *Maine.*

McKinley asked the people to reserve judgment, but the newspapers had a field day. The *New York Journal* of February 17th displayed a front page picture (artist's drawing) showing the *Maine* with a submerged mine under it. Its biggest headline was, "DESTRUCTION OF THE WAR SHIP MAINE WAS THE WORK OF AN ENEMY." Other eye-catching headings were, "Assistant Secretary Roosevelt Convinced

the Explosion of the War Ship Was Not an Accident," "$50,000 REWARD! For the Detection of the Perpetrator of the *Maine* Outrage!," and "Journal Sends Divers to Report on the Condition of the Wreck." The *Journal* sold over a million copies that day and the *World* did almost as well by selling five million copies in a week. President McKinley's request for a suspension of judgment until some facts might be determined called forth a private comment from the Assistant Secretary of the Navy, Theodore Roosevelt, that the President had no more backbone than a chocolate éclair. Roosevelt was hungry for Cuba and a Panama Canal. There was no doubt about it: the *Journal,* the *World,* and Roosevelt struck the popular note. McKinley allowed himself to be swept away by the concocted hysteria of the moment.

On March 27, 1898 McKinley advised Spain that we had no territorial ambitions in Cuba; but we did desire that an armistice be arranged between the rebels and Spanish forces in Cuba, and that the concentration camp policy be discontinued. On April 10th McKinley received news that both of the conditions he had requested had been accepted by Spain. But before the President got this message he had reversed his anti-war policy and had decided to go along with the, to him, irresistible pressure of public opinion. He sent his war message to Congress on April 11th with the full knowledge that Congress would declare war. The agreement of the Queen Regent of Spain to both of his requests should have ended the war scare, but the only use McKinley made of it was to put at the end of his over 30 paragraph war message the following sentence.

"Yesterday, and since the preparation of the foregoing message, official information was received by me that the latest decree of the Queen Regent of Spain directs General Blanco, in order to prepare and facilitate peace, to proclaim a suspension of hostilities, the duration and details of which have not yet been communicated to me."

The response of Congress to this war message contained four points: (1) The United States recognizes the independence of Cuba; (2) Spain must withdraw its armed forces from Cuba; (3) The President of the United States is to use whatever armed force is necessary to carry out the first two resolutions; and (4) the United States does not intend to annex Cuba and will leave her government to her own people. This fourth point, known as the Teller Resolution, did not seem convincing to other nations at the time; but its substantial fulfillment after the war indicated that American imperialism never did have the robust abandonment of principles typical of true empire builders.

The Navy's Part in the War

Two months before Congress sent its declaration of war to Spain, Theodore Roosevelt, Assistant Secretary of the Navy, sent orders to Commodore Dewey in the Far East to be ready for an attack upon the Philippines. Dewey's four cruisers and two gunboats steamed into Manila Bay early in the morning of May 1st and opened fire on the Spanish squadron of 10 ships. After seven hours of bombardment the Spanish ships were sunk, silenced, or captured. The American casualties totaled 8 wounded and 1 man dead (from heat prostration); Spanish casualties were 381 killed and many more wounded. No damage was suffered by the American ships. Dewey did not have the men needed for an assault upon Manila until re-enforcements arrived late in July. In the meantime he occupied Manila Bay and set up harbor regulations which were annoyingly violated by a squadron of German warships under Admiral Von Diedrichs. If empire building was to take place, Germany wanted to share in it. Dewey threatened to take action against the German ships and received support from Admiral Chichester who commanded a British squadron in the area. The Germans yielded to the combined American and British pressure.

The Spanish fleet in the Caribbean took a position in Santiago harbor under the protection of land batteries. By June 1st both Commodore Schley and Rear Admiral Sampson had their squadrons blocking the harbor. The Spanish admiral, Cervera, had 4 cruisers and 3 destroyers while the United States blockading force had 5 battleships and 2 cruisers. Among the American ships was the *Oregon* which had steamed 14,000 miles from the north Pacific coast around South America to Cuba and was still in good fighting trim. Cervera attempted to escape on July 3rd and, in a running fight along the coast, the Spanish ships were totally destroyed. The American casualties were 1 killed and 1 wounded. There was no significant damage to our ships. Spanish losses were 474 killed and wounded and 1,750 taken prisoner.

The United States navy was modern, well built, and its man power was well trained. It was thoroughly prepared and effectively officered. Quite the opposite was true of the Spanish ships and men. Their equipment was in poor condition and the men were ineffective in its use.

The Army's Part in the War

President McKinley called for 200,000 volunteers. But there were neither uniforms nor modern rifles for them. Lack of lightweight khaki cloth resulted in men being sent to the tropics in heavy blue winter uniforms; contaminated meat ("embalmed beef") proved a more effective enemy than the Spanish; the volunteers were unbelievably undertrained; and the inexperience of the soldiers combined with poor organization resulted in dangerously unsanitary encampments. "All fouled up" is a good description of the army's logistics.

From the 20th-25th of June about 16,000 American troops landed at Daiquiri, less than 20 miles from Santiago, Cuba. Why they were allowed to land unmolested is still a mystery. Spain had about 200,000 troops in Cuba and there had been no element of surprise in the invasion. On July 1st a sharp battle was fought at El Caney, a few miles inland from Daiquiri, and on the following day another battle occurred at San Juan Hill. These encounters were severe. Casualties (killed and wounded) for the Americans reached 1,600. Santiago was now open to bombardment from high ground north and east of the city. Roosevelt had resigned as Assistant Secretary of the Navy to serve under General Leonard Wood with the rank of Lieutenant Colonel of the "Rough Riders," a cavalry unit made up of cowboys, Indians, hunters, and a sprinkling of Harvard and Yale graduates. This unit played a prominent part in the charge, on foot, up San Juan Hill, an engagement which gave a good boost to Roosevelt's public career. News of the naval victory over Admiral Cervera and of the victories at El Caney and San Juan Hill gave the United States a noisy, exuberent Fourth of July celebration. Two weeks later the city of Santiago, next to Havana in importance, surrendered, and on July 26th Spain asked for peace terms. It had been a short war full of victories for the United States and, as wars go, at minor costs. The *New York Journal* asked in gloating headline, "HOW DO YOU LIKE THE JOURNAL'S WAR?".

WAR COSTS

Killed in action	a few less than 400
Died from other causes	a few more than 5,000
Expense of conducting the war	about $250,000,000

* Treaty of Paris

(Accepted by Spain December 10, 1898) (Ratified by the Senate Feb. 6, 1899)

1] Spain gave up all claims to Cuba.

2] The United States got the Philippines for $20,000,000.

3] Spain ceded Puerto Rico and Guam to the United States.

It was not easy to get the Senate to ratify the treaty. The vote was 57 to 27, just one vote more than the required ⅔rds majority. The closeness of the vote reflected the anti-imperialist views held by many who disliked the acquisition by the United States of distant islands inhabited by people of an alien culture. Pushing Spain out of Cuba was popular, but acquiring Puerto Rico, the Philippines, and Guam was quite another matter. While most of the anti-imperialists were Democrats, the division cut across party lines. We had a few spokesmen for the "superior race" nonsense and many more who defended empire building on the basis that the United States needed Pacific Ocean outposts if we were to develop and protect our trading opportunities with the Far East. William Allen White, editor of the *Emporia Gazette* (Kansas) wrote, "It is the Anglo-Saxon's manifest destiny to go forth as a world conqueror. . . . This is what fate holds for the chosen people." Senator Albert Beveridge of Indiana told the Senate, "He (God) has made us master organizers of the world to establish system where chaos reigns. . . . He has made us adepts in government that we may administer government among savage and senile peoples. . . . He has marked the American people as His chosen nation to finally lead in the regeneration of the world." Senator Henry Cabot Lodge said, "Our trade with China has been growing rapidly. We ask no favors; we only ask that we shall be admitted to that great market upon the same terms with the rest of the world." The *Washington Post* thought empire building an incongruous path for our Republic to travel and its editor commented, "We are face to face with a strange destiny, the taste of Empire is in the mouth of the people even as the taste of blood in the jungle." While the debate raged in magazines and newspapers with a very articulate minority condemning the decision to govern alien and distant peoples, Mr. Dooley, a fictional Will Rogers of the 1890's created by Finley P. Dunne, remarked of the Philippines, " 'Tis not more thin two months since ye larned whether they were islands or canned goods, . . . they'se wan consolation; an' that is, if th' American people can govern thimsilves, they can govern anything that walks.' " The United States was not really comfortable with its foray into imperialism and almost immediately began plans to lead the subject people toward self-government—a long range program far more consistent with our own national origin and republican principles.

* Governing Our New Possessions

The Philippines

Before leaving Hong Kong for Manila Bay, Dewey had arranged to have Aguinaldo, a Filipino insurrectionist leader in exile at Singapore, go to the Philippines to lead the natives against the Spanish. Dewey promised to supply them with the necessary arms. The United States minister at Singapore and Dewey made some arrangements which Aguinaldo claimed was a promise to turn the Philippines over to the Filipinos under his leadership as soon as the Spanish had been driven out. Of course, neither Dewey nor the United States minister at Singapore had the authority to make any such arrangement. Just what agreements were made we don't know. The United States was expelling Spain from Cuba with the promise to turn the island over to native rule, so it is not surprising that Aguinaldo and the Filipinos sought and expected similar treatment. The anti-imperialists in and out of Congress were making several suggestions for the Philippines. The possibilities were: (1) turn the Philippines over to the natives and guarantee their independence from any attack by a foreign power. (2) take the Philippines, but have a definite plan to liberate them as soon as feasible, (3) occupy the island of Luzon and leave the rest of the archipelago to the natives, and (4) annex the Philippines. As soon as it was clear to Aguinaldo, whose men had helped Dewey take Manila, that the United States had replaced Spain as master of the islands he took to guerrilla warfare. From February 1899 to April 1902 a cruel war raged with too many atrocities on both sides. Over 4,000 American soldiers were killed and about 600,000 Filipinos lost their lives. The Manila area was pacified long before the rebellion was over. In April, 1900, William H. Taft was appointed with five commissioners to set up a civilian government at Manila. In July, 1902, Congress provided for a native assembly to act with Governor General Taft and his commission. By 1907 a native assembly had been elected and Taft's commission served as an upper house. In 1913 a policy was adopted whereby civil jobs were given to Filipinos whenever competent natives could be found to fill them. In 1916 the Jones Act allowed all male adults to vote if they could read and write in English, Spanish, or a native dialect. The Governor General's commission was replaced by a native upper house (Senate). The Governor General was still appointed by the

President of the United States and still had veto power over acts of the native legislature. In 1934 the Tydings-McDuffie Act provided that the native legislature draw up a constitution. President Franklin Roosevelt approved this constitution and in 1935 the first President of the Philippine Commonwealth, Manuel Quezon, was elected. A ten year trial-run of this native government was to culminate with complete independence. World War II brought a delay of one year, but on July 4, 1946 Manuel Roxas became the first President of the new Philippine Republic. The United States granted $600,000,000 to help restore damage from World War II and gave the Philippines an eight year guarantee of free trade with the United States to steady the economy.

Puerto Rico (Porto Rico)

In general Puerto Rico followed similar steps toward self government as had the Philippines. The Foraker Act of 1900 set up a Governor General and a council appointed by the President of the United States. A native assembly was elected and the council became the senate. In 1917 Puerto Rico became a territory and its people became citizens of the United States. In 1952 the natives drafted a constitution which President Truman approved. This gave the island the status of a free commonwealth voluntarily associated with the United States.

Cuba

True to the promise of the Teller Resolution (see pp. 172-173), Cuba was granted independence. In November, 1900, General Leonard Wood arranged a convention where a constitution for Cuba was drawn up. It was similar to that of the United States. In March, 1901, the United States Congress made certain additions which the Cubans accepted as an unamendable part of their constitution. These changes are known as the Platt Amendment.

1] Cuba shall make no treaty which endangers her independence.

2] Cuba shall borrow no money beyond her capacity to repay.

3] The United States may intervene in Cuba when necessary to preserve order.

4] Cuba will sell or lease coaling and naval stations to the United States.

In 1934 the terms of the Platt Amendment were abolished by treaty except for the naval base which the United States maintains at Guantanamo.

Insular Cases

During 1901 cases involving Puerto Rico and the Philippines came before the Supreme Court. Could a tariff be levied on goods coming from these possessions into the United States? According to the Constitution ". . . all duties, imposts and excises shall be uniform throughout the United States." Were Puerto Rico and the Philippines part of the United States? Would every child born in these islands after the United States took possession of them automatically be citizens because the Constitution states in the 14th amendment, "All persons born or naturalized in the United States, and subject to the jurisdiction thereof, are citizens of the United States . . ."? The Supreme Court said, probably having in mind some of the savage tribes in the Philippines, "It is obvious that in the annexation of outlying and distant possessions grave questions will arise from differences of race, habits, laws and customs of the people . . ." The question of what to do about the island possessions and the Constitution might be considered a political question to be decided by Congress rather than a legal one for the courts. On the specific point raised, the legality of a tariff on goods entering the United States from Puerto Rico, the Court ruled that "Porto Rico is a territory appurtenant and belonging to the United States, but not a part of the United States within the revenue clauses of the Constitution; . . ." Hence, Congress could levy tariffs on goods from Puerto Rico. Except for this decision on the revenue clauses the Supreme Court tossed the problem into the lap of Congress. The Insular Cases are confusing, but a workable summary seems to be that the Constitution applies, or does not apply, to possessions of the United States as Congress shall decide. With the Philippines independent, the Hawaiian Islands a state, and Puerto Rico a free commonwealth the question, "Does the Constitution follow the flag?" no longer seems important.

* Open Door Policy and the Boxer Rebellion

As early as 1844 Caleb Cushing had gained for the United States the right of extraterritoriality in China. Missionaries had been in China continuously since then, but after the era of the clipper ships, trade with China had lagged. Throughout the period American ships had traded in Chinese ports under the same terms as ships of other nations. But in the 1890's China was falling to pieces. Japan, after watching European powers grab Chinese ports and provinces, decided to follow suit. The Chino-Japanese War of 1894-95 proved that the modern-ized dwarf, Japan, was far more powerful than the tradition-ridden, disorganized giant, China. Japan took Formosa (Taiwan), the Pescadores Islands, the Liaotung peninsula, and Korea. But Russia, Germany, and France, under the pretext that they were defending China's territorial integrity, persuaded Japan to give back all but Formosa and the Pescadores. Their real motive was to keep Japan from getting what they themselves wanted. In 1898 Germany seized Kiao-chou at the base of the Shantung peninsula; France took the port of Kwang-chow-wan; England acquired Wei-hai-wei; and Russia bit off Manchuria and the Liaotung peninsula. As Russia took part of what Japan had been persuaded to give up, Japanese-Russian relations were particularly strained. With this scramble for spheres of influence, the advantage Great Britain had enjoyed in Far Eastern trade was being whittled away. With the acquisition of the Philippines, the United States had a quickened interest in China and looked with displeasure on its dismemberment. For the moment, British and American interests in Far Eastern trade made them share a common desire to check the setting up of spheres of influence.

When our Secretary of State, John Hay, wrote his famous Circular Letters, he knew that he would have the friendly cooperation of England. The first letter (September 1899) to the several nations with spheres of influence in China expressed the hope that the areas recently acquired by them were open to the trade of all nations on equal terms; that ports and railroads would be available to all; and that tariffs would be collected by the Chinese government. All of the nations except Russia replied with noncommittal generalities which seemed to say that each would be willing to comply with the ideas expressed by the Hay circular letter if all the other nations would do the same. In March 1900 Secretary Hay sent another letter to London, Paris, Berlin, St. Petersburg, Rome, and Tokyo informing them that their replies indicated a common willingness to permit equal trading rights for all nations within their respective spheres of influence. That being the case, the United States would "consider the assent given" . . . "as final and definitive." On paper, at least, it seemed that John Hay had won over the European nations and Japan to the acceptance of the Open Door Policy.

While the letter writing was going on, serious trouble developed in the Peking area. A Chinese nationalist organization, the Order of the Patriotic and Harmonious Fists, was intent upon driving the "foreign devils" out of their country. Missionaries and foreign traders were murdered and hundreds sought protection at the foreign legations in Peking. The Dowager Empress was secretly aiding the "Boxers." An international force with about 2,500 American troops from the Philippines arrived at Peking on August 14, 1900. The German ambassador had been murdered and a total of about 200 foreigners had been killed during the disorders. The attack on Peking lasted seven weeks while the hastily barricaded British legation served as the fortress for the beleaguered personnel of the legations, the missionaries, and foreign traders. The Empress and her court fled from the city before the arrival of the relief expedition. The Christian deliverers looted palaces and temples, killed many civilians, and committed other outrages. The nasty situation could have developed into tearing China apart and fighting over the spoils by the raiding nations. While the Boxers were besieging Peking, John Hay, sensing this danger, wrote another letter. In it he made it clear that the United States was interested in restoring order in Peking; "permanent safety and peace in China"; the preservation of China as an independent nation; and the safeguarding to "friendly powers . . . equal and impartial trade with all parts of the Chinese Empire." Japan and the European powers gave up any immediate designs they may have had for partitioning China. Letter writing, in itself, can not be the effective implement of foreign policy that it seemed to be in this case. There were several reasons why the nations may have wished to pursue the Open Door Policy advocated by Secretary Hay.

1] The scramble for additional spheres of influence carried with it a grave threat of war. England and Germany were in a state of "cold war"; while Russia and Japan were decidedly unfriendly. No one wished to "rock the boat" at this moment.

2] An Open Door situation could well mean better trading opportunities for all. It might allow the Boxer "foreign devils" attitude to become less violent, costly, and disruptive of trade.

3] Great Britain was in favor of the American idea, and whatever policy had the favor of London had influence in other capitals.

The timing of the John Hay letters was well nigh perfect. They gave prestige to the United States; expressed the desire of the American people to develop trade with the Far East on as favorable terms as any other nation; and reflected the opposition of Americans to the partitioning of China. The final settlement for the Boxer Rebellion was an indemnity against China of $333,000,000 of which the United States got $24,000,000. Because we thought it excessive, we returned half this amount which the Chinese government set aside to finance Chinese students in American colleges. American diplomacy during this period was especially wise and effective. The Open Door Policy and our moderating influence in the settlement of the Boxer Rebellion made the United States the least disliked white nation in Asia, while putting us in as favorable a position to develop Far Eastern trade as any other western nation.

McKinley Assassinated by Czolgosz

On September 6, 1901 President McKinley was shot by Leon Czolgosz, an American citizen. The tragedy occurred at the Pan-American Exposition in Buffalo, N.Y. The President was holding a reception at the Temple of Music, when a young man in the line of persons passing through to shake hands with McKinley extended his left hand to the President because his right hand was bandaged as if wounded. But the bandages concealed a revolver with which the assassin fired two shots. Czolgosz was immediately seized. He was an anarchist who thought he had a mission to kill "Czar McKinley." The President died eight days later. Czolgosz was electrocuted.

Marcus Hanna, then United States Senator from Ohio, rode on the funeral train from Buffalo to Washington. To a substantial degree, McKinley's public career had been built by Marcus Hanna. He felt both grief and anger, grief at the loss of a friend of many years and anger at the rise to power of Theodore Roosevelt. Noted as a man who said bluntly what he thought—which usually means a man who speaks spontaneously what he feels, without thinking—Hanna said, "I told William McKinley it was a mistake to nominate that wild man at Philadelphia . . . Now look, that damned cowboy is President of the United States!"

The day before his assassination McKinley had made a speech which has stood the test of time more successfully than his other public statements. It was a drastic modification of the views he held when, as a member of the House, he introduced the McKinley Tariff of 1890 and gained the reputation of being the high priest of protective tariffs. In part he said, "A system which provides a mutual exchange of commodities is manifestly essential to the continued and healthful growth of our export trade. We must not repose in fancied security that we can forever sell everything and buy little or nothing. If such a thing were possible, it would not be best for us or for those with whom we deal. . . . Reciprocity is the natural outgrowth of our wonderful industrial development. . . ." This reciprocity speech at Buffalo may have been the opening move by McKinley to modify the high protectionist policy which had so completely dominated the Republican Party. But it was to be many years before the good sense of McKinley's last public speech was to become the common policy of both major parties.

Theodore Roosevelt

1858 - 1919

REPUBLICAN

☆

Secretary of State JOHN HAY
ELIHU ROOT

THEODORE ROOSEVELT'S PUBLIC SERVICE BEFORE HE BECAME PRESIDENT

Assemblyman in the New York State Legislature
U.S. Civil Service Commissioner
New York City Police Commissioner
Assistant Secretary of the Navy
Organized and Led the Rough Riders in the Spanish-American War
Governor of New York
Vice-President During the Six Months of McKinley's Second Term

MAJOR ITEMS OF THEODORE ROOSEVELT'S ADMINISTRATIONS

Panama Canal
Trust Problem
Coal Strike (1902)
Conservation Program
Venezuelan Debt Controversy and the
  Drago Doctrine
Corollary to the Monroe Doctrine
Receivership of the Dominican Republic
Portsmouth Treaty (1905)

Agreements with Japan (Gentlemen's
  and Root-Takahira)
Algeciras Conference (1906)
Hague Conferences (1899 and 1907)
Hepburn Act (1906)
Pure Food and Drug Act and Meat
  Inspection Act and Muckrakers
Political Reforms of the Roosevelt Era

Theodore Roosevelt's Election in 1904

By 1904 the people had adopted "T.R." as their hero. In the popular mind he stood for what was fair and good. They liked his concern for the public during the coal strike; they liked his success in fighting the trusts; they liked his vigorous speeches extolling patriotism, displaying a warmth of feeling for people, and denouncing what was fradulent and false; they liked his family life; and they liked him. The "Old Guard" of the Republican Party felt "stuck" with him. They could call him a socialist and a demagogue and bemoan the "mistake" they had made in putting him on the ticket with McKinley in 1900; but to refuse him the nomination in 1904 would have been unthinkable, even had it been politically possible. The nominating convention at Chicago didn't bother to take a vote, they nominated Roosevelt by acclamation.

The Democrats passed by Bryan to nominate a very conservative candidate, Judge Alton B. Parker

of New York. There was nothing the Democratic Party stood for in 1904 that didn't seem more likely of accomplishment under Teddy Roosevelt than under Judge Parker. As Andrew Jackson had shown in 1828 and 1832, when a candidate has caught the affection of the people there is little the opposition party can do.

	Popular Vote	Electoral Vote
Theodore Roosevelt	7,628,834	336
Judge Alton Parker	5,084,401	140
Eugene V. Debs (Socialist)	402,460	0

Perhaps the Socialists did well enough to remind us that there was still a protest vote. Roosevelt acknowledged the tribute the people had paid him by announcing to the press that, as he had served all but six months of McKinley's second term, he would "under no circumstances be a candidate for or accept another nomination."

* Panama Canal

The 71-day trip of the U.S.S. *Oregon* from the northwest coast of the United States around South America to Cuba had dramatically called attention to the strategic value of an isthmian canal. Our acquisitions in the Pacific of the Philippines, Guam, and the Hawaiian Islands, and of Puerto Rico in the Atlantic gave the United States possessions stretching about half the distance around the globe. Great Britain and the United States had put the world on notice that the area through which such a canal was built, no matter who built it, would be policed by British and American forces, and the canal itself must be open to the use of ships of all nations on identical terms. (Clayton-Bulwer Treaty (1850), see p. 119.) Secretary of State Blaine had shown as early as 1899 more foresight than any other American statesman by urging closer Pan-American relationships. He had then suggested the abrogation of the Clayton-Bulwer Treaty as a first step in preparation for the day when an American canal would connect the Pacific and the Caribbean. French interests had purchased the right from Colombia to build a canal and had spent $260,000,000 on the project before they gave up in 1889. Malaria, yellow fever, engineering difficulties, mismanagement, and financial corruption had forced the French Panama Company headed by De Lesseps, builder of the Suez Canal, into bankruptcy. Some New York bankers had very quietly purchased the French Panama Company so that they might be in a position to sell the rights and deserted machinery to the United States if and when an American canal was built. To minimize the risk in this situation, the backers of the scheme contributed heavily to the 1900 Republican presidential campaign and received a degree of assurance by the plank in that year's platform favoring the acquisition of a canal across Panama (see p. 171). President Roosevelt, some of the army engineers, and many members of Congress favored cutting the canal through Panama; but there was considerable support for a sea level canal through Nicaragua. Congress approved expenditure of $40,000,000 for the purchase of the rights and machinery from the "French" Panama Company which had asked $100,000,000. The "French" Company accepted because there was the possibility that there might be a shift to the Nicaraguan route. But, above all, it was the Spanish-American War and an aggressive President that really got the project under way. In 1901 Secretary of State John Hay was able to reach an agreement with foreign minister Pauncefote of England. With the assurance by the United States that ships of all nations would be allowed to use the canal on equal terms, England readily gave up her right to share in the policing of the canal area. This Hay-Pauncefote Treaty cleared the way for negotiations with Colombia. Hay reached an agreement with Herran, the Colombian representative, which would have given the United States a 6 mile wide strip of land across Panama and a renewable 99 year lease. The United States would have paid $10,000,000 and an annual rental of $250,000. President Roosevelt and the Senate were pleased with these terms, but the Colombian Senate refused to approve because it considered the $10,000,000 too small a fee. Roosevelt was angry and the Colombian state of Panama was dismayed. Dr. Guerrero from Panama and Philippe Bunau-Varilla, who had been associated with the French attempt to build the canal, planned a revolution by Panama from Colombia. They did their plotting in New York City and Washington. President Roosevelt had no direct dealings with them, but on November 3, 1903, the day before the revolution, the U.S.S. *Nashville* arrived off the Caribbean coast of Panama to make sure that there would be "free and uninterrupted transit" across the Isthmus such as was our right to provide according to the New Grenada Treaty of 1846 (see p. 119). Other United States warships hovered off the Isthmus, and Colombia was unable to interfere with the revolution. A Colombian garrison already in Panama was bribed into submission, so no bloodshed occurred. Within a week Panama declared herself independent and within a few hours after the White House got the news, Secretary Hay extended official recognition to the new Republic. Philippe Bunau-Varilla turned up as the Minister of Panama and by November 18th the Hay-Bunau Varilla Treaty had been drawn up granting the United States a 10 mile wide strip across the Isthmus for $10,000,000 and a perpetual lease at $250,000 per year.

The medical work and splendid organization accomplished under the army doctor, Colonel Gorgas, changed a tropical jungle pest hole into a livable zone in which blasting through the mountains could proceed under the direction of army engineer, Colonel Goethals. It took about 10 years to dig the big ditch. The first ship went through August 15, 1914, but huge landslides soon closed it again. The canal was intermittently in service but not officially declared finished until 1921.

** Trust Problem

It has been pointed out that the Sherman Anti-trust Act of 1890 had failed to check the merging of businesses into huge aggregations of capital which the people commonly called "trusts" (see pp. 161-162). President Roosevelt considered that the ineffectiveness of the law denied a "square deal" to the people and to business in general. Unable to persuade Congress to pass new anti-trust legislation with teeth in it, he ordered his Attorney General to bring suit against the Northern Securities Company formed by Morgan, Hill, and Harriman. This company combined under one management the railroads of the northwest, an area roughly one-fourth of the United States. The Supreme Court by a 5 to 4 decision ordered the merger dissolved and thus gave the government its first substantial victory over a business combination.

The majority of the Court held that if a holding company could be formed to control the railroads in one section of the nation then, ". . . the entire railway systems of the country may be absorbed, merged and consolidated, thus placing the public at the absolute mercy of the holding corporation." The Court also said, ". . . it need not be shown that the combination, in fact, results or will result in a total suppression of trade or in a complete monopoly, but it is only essential to show that . . . it tends to restrain interstate commerce . . . and to deprive the public of the advantages that flow from free competition." The Court noted that the view had been advanced that the merger of the railroads might well have resulted in more efficient operation, better service, and lower rates to the public. This the Court found interesting but declared that even though such a view proved correct it had no bearing on the legal status of the merger under question. But such speculation does have meaning to the student, as it foreshadows the concept that railroads should be, in many respects, monopolies and thus shift their status from that of a purely private business to that of a public utility. But at the moment, the press accused Roosevelt of attacking big business in a cheap bid for popular approval. There was no doubt that "T.R." reveled in popular approval; but equally no doubt that he was sure that he was fighting for the people and justice against those he called "malefactors of great wealth" and "the mighty industrial overlords." He was intent upon bringing, as he put it, an end to the "immunity from government control" which big business had enjoyed in spite of the Interstate Commerce Act of 1887 and the Sherman Anti-trust Act of 1890. J. P. Morgan went to the White House to persuade the President to call off the suit against the Northern Securities Company; but Roosevelt seemed to view his appeal more as a challenge than a request and was more determined than ever to prove that Roosevelt and Uncle Sam were more powerful than Morgan, Hill, and Harriman. The trust busting program continued with successful suits against the Standard Oil Company of New Jersey, the American Tobacco Company, the beef trust, and the fertilizer trust. Anti-trust suits would usually begin only after malpractices had been suffered to exist for a long time; the government was bent upon punishment rather than prevention. The legal dissolution of a merger easily became an actual combination through informal agreements, the use of dummy directors, and a community of interest within an industry where one of the giants in the field would set the price and labor policies for all in the industry. Although about 40 anti-trust cases were prosecuted while Roosevelt was in office, the total effect was negligible and the problem still remained unsolved. In any economic field dominated by a few very large companies, cooperation among the leaders tends to prevail over free competition. In the Roosevelt Era the government was able only to irritate trusts, not control them.

One should not think of President Roosevelt as an opponent of "big business." His position was that large scale business operations were the strength of the American economy and accounted for the tremendous strides the United States was making in the world of manufacture and commerce. He appreciated the lower prices, the variety of products, and the constant introduction of new products which resulted from adequate capitalization and size of industrial units. His opposition was reserved for those business combinations which refused to operate within the law, or whose practices were so obviously against the public welfare that he would consider them morally wrong— incompatible with a square deal. Even the Supreme Court caught the flavor of "T.R's" square deal when it introduced the "rule of reason" into its anti-trust decisions. If the practices in restraint of trade seemed to the Court to be morally reprehensible, they would declare them "in restraint of trade" within the meaning of that phrase in the Sherman Anti-trust Act; but an action was allowed which, although it restrained interstate or foreign trade, seemed not to be morally questionable.

* Coal Strike (1902)

In May, 1902, about 140,000 miners went out on strike in the anthracite coal fields of northeastern Pennsylvania. For months the miners had protested working conditions, and the president of the United Mine Workers of America, John Mitchell, tried in vain to meet with the mine operators to talk over the situation. The grievances of the miners were many and real.

1] Their average annual wage was about $300.

2] The houses in the mining towns were owned by the company; they were usually miserable shacks.

3] The miners were sometimes paid per ton of coal dug, but the "ton" was measured at 3,000 lbs.

4] On certain jobs miners were paid by the number of cars they filled, but a "full" car was one topped nine inches above the edge.

5] Miners who needed dynamite, blasting powder, or other essential items for their jobs had to buy their own supplies from a company store at prices far above normal.

6] Some mines paid in token money good only at company stores where prices were high.

Bad as the above grievances may seem, the basic demand of the miners was the recognition of their union. They wanted the mine owners to talk to their president who would represent them. This is collective bargaining. Mr. George F. Baer was the spokesman for the mine operators. His state of mind was the greatest obstacle to a settlement. In the middle of the summer when Wilkes-Barre and Scranton were economically prostrate because of the prolonged strike, Baer wrote what he must have thought to be a reassuring letter. In it he said, "The rights and interests of the laboring man will be protected . . . not by labor agitators, but by the Christian men to whom God in His infinite wisdom has given control of the property interests of this country. . . ." By October a coal famine had set in and winter was very close. President Roosevelt called John Mitchell and George Baer to the White House. His view of the controversy was that a third party, the public, was the victim. Coal had risen from $5 per ton to $30 and house-holders were waiting in lines at coal yards to buy a few pounds at a time. Hard coal was the only fuel used in almost all the city homes of the northeast. To prevent widespread suffering, sickness, and death, the differences between miners and management must be settled quickly. With this purpose in mind the President brought the two leaders together. He made a strong plea for arbitration. Mitchell accepted, but Baer, who considered himself one of God's chosen custodians of coal mines, scolded Roosevelt for "negotiating with the fomenters of anarchy" and left the White House in a huff. He later expanded on his feelings by pointing out that the mine owners resented his being asked, even by the President, to meet with "a criminal" (John Mitchell). The "criminal" had

suggested that two prominent clergymen and another person selected by them might make a suitable committee of arbitration. Roosevelt was a wise, perhaps at times a wiley, politician. He knew how to compromise and he knew when not to fight. But once having entered a fight, "T.R." couldn't back down. In this coal strike he had just the kind of battle he liked. He was fighting to protect the public, and if he seemed to favor labor, it was only because labor in this instance was willing to arbitrate, while management was arrogantly unconcerned about the public. J. P. Morgan was the financial power behind the coal mines, so the President informed him that United States troops would seize and operate the mines unless arbitration began. Morgan told Baer to arbitrate and George did as he was told. The miners got a 10% raise and a few other improvements.

When Roosevelt threatened to seize the mines, he knew that there was nothing in the Constitution that gave him any such power. But he had a completely untenable theory about presidential powers; namely, that the president could do anything he thought necessary so long as there was nothing in the Constitution or laws that said he couldn't. Of course, quite the contrary is true. Our government is one of limited powers; no officer of the government can legally do anything unless the right to do so is in the Constitution or implied therein. In case of dispute over whether a power is implied, the issue may be settled in the courts. In his threat to commit an act beyond his proper powers, Roosevelt pin-pointed a major unsolved problem. Just what does the United States do when BIG labor and BIG business, both organized on a nationwide basis, engage in a fight which brings intolerable hardships and chaos to the nation? Only recently has it been true that several major industries are so organized by management and labor that the likelihood of a national crisis can be said to be probable rather than merely possible. One fact is clear, Uncle Sam will have to take essentially the same position that Roosevelt did. No factions of our society can carry their "private" fights to the extent of endangering the nation; the greatest power in our country must be the government. For the people of 1902 the important factor of the coal strike was that the federal government played a major role in bringing about a settlement of a strike, rather than joining the fight to assure victory to one side as it had done in the Pullman strike of 1894.

** Conservation Program

The first step indicating that the government realized that our natural resources were not inexhaustible was the Forest Reserve Act of 1891 which permitted the president to close timber areas to settlers and declare them national parks. Harrison, Cleveland, and McKinley had reserved a total of 45,000,000 acres, and Roosevelt added another 150,000,000. In addition he set aside 85,000,000 acres of mineral lands in Alaska. In June, 1902, the Newlands Act (Reclamation Act) provided that the money received from the sale of public lands in 16 western states would be used for the construction and maintenance of irrigation projects. The irrigated land was to be sold to settlers on a ten-year payment plan with the income therefrom used to create more irrigation projects. Semi-arid land blossomed into valuable fruit, sugar beet, and vegetable farms. The first great project was the Roosevelt Dam on the Salt River in Arizona. The reservoir created covered over 25 square miles and contained water enough to irrigate about 750,000 acres. Considered a big project at the time, it has been dwarfed by more recent dams on the Colorado and Columbia rivers and rivers in the T.V.A. area. In 1905 the supervision of public lands was put under the care of Gifford Pinchot, the first Chief Forester of the United States. Pinchot had studied forestry in Europe and had been an influence in stimulating Roosevelt's interest in conservation. He brought knowledge, enthusiasm, vision, integrity, and administrative ability into the federal program while his close friend and boss, the President, made speeches and held conferences which won popular support and set in motion conservation programs in the several states.

In May, 1908, Roosevelt held a conference at the White House on conservation. The delegates included governors of 34 states and 5 territories, representatives from 68 national societies devoted to the preservation of natural resources, members of the Supreme Court and the Cabinet, several Congressmen, and individuals who were prominent in conservation or allied fields. Pinchot and Roosevelt apparently succeeded in their efforts, for soon after this conference, forty states established conservation commissions. A National Conservation Committee with Pinchot as its chairman was set up to make the first inventory of the natural resources of the United States. Congress was under no obligation to appropriate money for a "National Conservation Committee" created by the President's White House conference. It didn't. When no funds were forthcoming Roosevelt received contributions from private sources, and many individuals performed the necessary clerical work and other services on a volunteer basis. "T.R." seemed to demonstrate that when he had the will, he found the

way. The total effect of the conservation program of the United States and the several states is by far Roosevelt's greatest achievement.

The conservation program and the coal strike illustrate the great use Roosevelt made of the *influence* of the office of president. He had no right to order the governors, judges, etc. to the White House Conference; but an invitation by the President is not refused. In the coal strike he could not order Mitchell and Baer to meet at the White House nor could he order J. P. Morgan to arrange for arbitration; but the invitations, requests, and suggestions of the President can wield a great deal of influence. Roosevelt was a master of this political skill, and his use of it served as an example for others to follow. He had built greater prestige into the office of the president.

Venezuelan Debt Controversy and the Drago Doctrine

Cipriano Castro, dictator of Venezuela, made no effort to meet debt payments due investors in England, Germany, Italy, and the United States. The European powers let it be known that they were considering the use of force even though they were aware of the Monroe Doctrine. As though in answer to the European powers, President Roosevelt included in his annual message of 1901 the statement that he did "not guarantee any State against punishment if it misconducts itself, provided that punishment does not take the form of acquisition of territory by any non-American power." Our government had been consulted by Germany and Great Britain before they established a blockade of Venezuelan ports in December, 1902. Italian ships soon joined in the blockade. This much was done with the consent of the United States and with a definite understanding that the European powers were not to seize any Venezuelan territory. But when the blockade resulted in the sinking of Venezuelan gunboats and the lobbing of shells into their ports, dictator Castro asked President Roosevelt to urge arbitration of the dispute. The European powers accepted Secretary of State Hay's proposal to submit the controversy to the Hague Tribunal. Apparently there was something to be said for Castro, as the final settlement cut the European claims from $40,000,000 to $8,000,000 and the United States claims from about $4,000,000 to $81,000. The episode was a clear recognition by European powers of the Monroe Doctrine; they had brought pressure by force against Venezuela only after consulting with the United States, and they had stopped the use of force when we asked for arbitration. It should have been obvious that Europe had decided not to challenge the Monroe Doctrine and that any future European investors in the bonds of unstable Latin-American Republics took their financial risks on their own shoulders; their governments would not attempt any forcible collection for them.

Dr. Luis M. Drago, foreign minister of Argentina, formulated a doctrine during the Venezuelan debt dispute of 1902 with the obvious purpose of making the blockading of harbors, engaging in naval battles, and bombarding coastal cities illegal methods of collecting money. His doctrine declared that any attempt by European powers to collect debts by force from American nations would be contrary to international law. This proposal was placed before the Hague Peace Conference of 1907 and adopted by the 46 nations there.

** Corollary to the Monroe Doctrine (1904)

President Roosevelt seemed to think the Drago Doctrine (see above) needed an answer from the United States. Unfortunately he gave one. In his annual message of December 1904 he said of the Latin-American nations, "Chronic wrongdoing, or an impotence which results in a general loosening of the ties of civilized society . . . may force the United States, however reluctantly, in flagrant cases of wrongdoing or impotence, to the exercise of an international police power. . . . We would interfere with them only in the last resort, and then only if it became evident that their inability or unwillingness to do justice at home and abroad . . . had invited foreign aggression. . . ." Thus the United States became the debt collector in Latin America for its European creditors. This Roosevelt Corollary led to our intervention in the Dominican Republic (Santo Domingo), Haiti, Nicaragua, and Cuba. The "Big Brother" of the original Monroe Doctrine became the "Big Bully" and the "Colossus of the North" of the Roosevelt Corollary. The words "made in U.S.A." became a distasteful symbol throughout most of Central and South America, and the United States entered upon an era of about twenty years of unnecessarily bad relations with our southern neighbors.

Receivership of the Dominican Republic

For about two years, 1903-05, European creditors were seeking through their respective governments to receive payment from the Dominican Republic, but political instability and financial chaos in the island nation presented a hopeless situation. When, in 1904, some American creditors were paid, the demands from European creditors grew louder. The Dominican Republic was under the shadow of President Roosevelt's Big Stick ("Speak softly and carry a big stick"). An agreement was reached between the President and the Dominican Republic whereby the United States could collect the customs duties at Dominican ports and administer the payment of its foreign debts. About 55% of the duties were turned over to creditors and 45% went to the running of the Dominican government. In two years the debts were paid and the finances of the island republic were in good shape. This was the first time the Roosevelt Corollary was put into operation. The United States Senate refused to ratify the agreement Roosevelt had made with the Dominican Republic until 1907 when the success of the receivership was apparent. The Senate had shown some doubt about the wisdom of carrying out the new corollary and the President had again demonstrated how to get things done his way.

Portsmouth Treaty (1905)

When the Russo-Japanese War broke out in 1904, Roosevelt was interested in an outcome that would best preserve the balance of power in the Far East. China was threatened by adjacent Russia and by the westernized island power, Japan. If either one of them got too strong, the Open Door Policy in China might well go down the drain. As we deemed Japan the weaker nation, the early Japanese victories pleased the United States; but her continued successes gave us second thought. Luckily Japan had quickly reached the end of her financial resources and Russia's unexpected defeats had touched off a revolution which put the Czar in a mood for a settlement of his foreign difficulties. President Roosevelt learned of the desire each belligerent had for peace, so he quickly invited them to send representatives to Portsmouth, New Hampshire for a conference.

It was Roosevelt's influence that persuaded Japan to give up her demands for a huge cash indemnity and induced Russia to give Japan the southern half of the island of Sakhalin. The results of the treaty as far as China and the Open Door Policy were concerned were negligible; Russia got out of Manchuria and Japan came in. As usually happens to peacemakers, each belligerent felt that the United States could have backed its claims more firmly. For bringing this war to an early conclusion President Roosevelt was awarded the Nobel Peace Prize in 1906.

* Agreements with Japan (Gentlemen's and Root-Takahira)

The Peace of Portsmouth seemed to usher in a period of ill feeling between Japan and the United

States. The easy victory of Japan over China in 1894-95 was surprise enough; the victory over Russia was a little frightening. When the Japanese learned that Roosevelt had opposed the cash indemnity demanded from Russia, there were anti-American demonstrations in Japanese cities. This state of mind was further inflamed when they learned that San Francisco made Japanese children attend segregated schools. Newspapers in both nations stirred racial hatreds. Hearst invented the "yellow peril" which led Americans to accept the idea that Japan was our natural enemy and might very well be about to take the Philippines. In 1907 the United States would have found it difficult to defend them. The San Francisco school situation and the marked increase in the number of Japanese immigrants entering California after 1900 did pose problems of international importance. Of course Roosevelt had no legal right to interfere with the San Francisco public school system, but he called the Mayor and other anti-Japanese leaders of California to Washington for a talk. The United States did have a treaty with Japan giving the Japanese in America the status of "the most favored nation." That is, they were legally entitled to the same rights accorded to any other aliens in the United States. The President pointed out that anti-Japanese measures taken by local governments could seriously embarrass the federal government. He might have pointed out that treaties are part of the "Supreme Law of the Land." The upshot of the Washington talks was the "Gentlemen's Agreement" of 1907 by which segregation in California schools was discontinued and the Japanese government agreed not to allow any more laborers to come to the United States.

It may have been the Japanese-American relations which inspired Roosevelt to send the "Great White Fleet" on a "good-will" mission around the world. When Congress heard of his idea of sending 16 battleships, 6 destroyers, and 6 other ships to visit many foreign ports, it objected because our shores would be left unprotected. It felt that poking our heavy artillery into foreign harbors constituted a questionable gesture of peace. Congress hesitated about appropriating the funds for this naval demonstration, but "T.R." said the fleet had coal enough to get from Hampden Roads to San Francisco, so he started them off on December 16th, 1907. A 14 months journey via the Straits of Magellan, San Francisco, Hawaii, Australia, the Philippines, China, Japan, the Indian Ocean, the Suez Canal, the Mediterranean, and the Atlantic brought the fleet home to Hampden Roads on Washington's birthday, 1909. The fleet was well received everywhere and the most enthusiastic welcome of all was at the port of Yokohama. It was a great tour without unpleasant incidents.

During the Great White Fleet's cruise around the world, Secretary of State, Elihu Root (John Hay had died) concluded the Root-Takahira executive agreement at Washington. The United States recognized Japan's dominance in Manchuria and Korea, and Japan recognized American sovereignty in the Philippines. Both nations reiterated their support of the Open Door Policy in China.

Algeciras Conference (1906)

By 1904 the Fashoda Affair (1898) and the Boer War (1899-1902) had led to British-French collaboration against Germany, the dominant partner in the Triple Alliance of Germany, Austria, and Italy. Russia was allied to France, but in 1904-05 she was suffering a humiliating defeat in the Russo-Japanese War and was in no position to play European power politics. The British-French combination, called the Entente Cordiale, and the Triple Alliance formed a hostile line-up which constituted a balance of power where neither side was expected to risk war with the other. England had extended her colonial control in Africa southward from the Sudan and northward from the Union of South Africa—with French approval. France had colonized Algeria and Tunisia in northern Africa and was in the process of annexing Morocco—with British approval. In 1905 Kaiser Wilhelm II visited the Sultan of Morocco publically to announce that Germany recognized the independence of Morocco. In diplomatic circles this was clearly understood to be a German demand that France stop her "peaceful penetration" tactics aimed at the absorption of Morocco. This was an opportune time for such a move by Germany, because Russia was helpless and no one knew whether the Entente Cordiale was a vague agreement of mutual friendship or a real alliance. London, Paris, and Berlin knew that a major war was a distinct probability. Wilhelm II called for a conference and asked President Roosevelt to arrange it. The conference met at Algeciras, Spain, where Roosevelt's influence and the good work of Henry White, our representative there, accomplished a settlement that avoided an immediate war. Moroccan independence was recognized, but in 1912 it became a French protectorate and in 1914 World War I began. Roosevelt had entered world politics in the Open Door Policy, the Boxer Rebellion, the Root-Takahira Agreement, and the Algeciras Conference. It was a new role for an American President and the Senate expressed its discomfort with a resolution that its ratification of the Algeciras agreement was not to be interpreted as a departure from "the traditional American foreign policy" which forbade our participation in purely European affairs.

* Hague Conferences (1899 and 1907)

Fervent, sincere, and sensible speeches deploring our armed-to-the-teeth "peace" and advocating disarmament do not express a recent wisdom born of modern means of destruction. In the mid-summer of 1898, Czar Nicholas II of Russia called for an international conference to seek ways and means of stopping the wasteful use of wealth in an "armed peace" which could lead only to cataclysmic horror. His immediate reason for calling a halt to the armament race was his plan to spend huge sums on a program of modernizing Russian agriculture and industry. But if his unfriendly neighbor, Germany, continued its rapid build-up of armaments, there was nothing Russia could do but follow suit. The conference was held at The Hague in Holland (Netherlands) in 1899 with 26 nations represented. Every move toward disarmament was blocked because several nations, especially Germany, still hoped their status might be improved some day by the use of armed force. Due largely to the efforts of the American delegation, an international court of arbitration, the Hague Tribunal, was established. There was no force behind the decision of the Hague Tribunal and no nation had to submit disputes to it. The court was used for minor differences that were no real threat to the peace. It was not so much a step in the right direction as merely a facing in the right direction.

In 1904 President Roosevelt suggested a second Hague Conference, but the Russo-Japanese war broke out and the meeting got under way at the call of Russia in 1907. The United States again stressed arbitration of international disputes and use of the Hague Tribunal. Great Britain and the United States had led the way among nations in resorting to arbitration, and Secretary of State Elihu Root by negotiating treaties of arbitration with 25 nations displayed our interest in peaceful settlements. As in 1899 the arbitration was not compulsory. Our Senate made the provision that no dispute to which the United States was a party could be submitted to arbitration without its approval. The Drago Doctrine (see pp. 182-183) was accepted by the conference. Both Hague conferences show the realization by nations of the necessity for abolishing war and also the inability of nations to submit to any plan which would limit their freedom of action. Will the fear of national extinction ever overcome the reluctance of nations to submit to exterior controls?

* The Hepburn Act (1906)

For 19 years the Interstate Commerce Act had been ineffective. The position as one of the Interstate Commerce Commissioners had become little more than a political plum, for any attempt really to regulate the railroads was doomed to failure. "T.R." was fed up with "the immunity from government control" which the railroads still enjoyed. To breathe some life into the Interstate Commerce Commission Roosevelt sponsored the Hepburn Bill which Congress passed in June 1906.

It's provisions were as follows:

1] The number of commissioners was increased from 5 to 7.

2] The Commission's authority was extended to cover sleeping cars, oil pipe lines, ferries, terminals, bridges, and express companies.

3] Reasonable maximum rates could be fixed for railroad services.

4] Rebates were forbidden.

5] With a few unimportant exceptions, free passes were prohibited.

6] Uniform accounting methods prescribed by the Commission must be used.

7] The orders of the Commission were to go into effect even though an appeal might be made to the courts.

The teeth of the act are to be found in the provision that made the railroads and others obey the orders of the Commission even though there was court action contesting them. Before the Hepburn Act the railroads frequently protested rate changes ordered by the Commission, no matter how reasonable, provided the old rates yielded more money than the cost of litigation. Some court cases had dragged on for years. The legal personnel available to the Interstate Commerce Commission were usually fewer in number and less experienced than the more impressive talent employed by the railroads.

An important weakness of the Hepburn Bill was its failure to fix any standard for evaluating the property of the railroads. "Just and reasonable" rates should allow a profit on investment. But how is one to determine the value of the railroads; that is, the dollar investment on which a reasonable profit should be made? Should the dollar value of railroad properties be the original cost, the present value, the replacement cost, or some formula taking account of all these factors? It was a complicated problem, but without a definite procedure it was most difficult to arrive at "just and reasonable" rates.

A lesson may be learned from the Hepburn Act. On first glance it seems unjust and arbitrary to give a government commission authority to enforce a ruling when it is protested and is about to go before the courts. Holding the commission's ruling in abeyance until the court reaches a decision would seem a proper protection against an overbearing government. Quite the contrary is true. If the courts find the commission in error, damages may be awarded to those affected. But if the commission does not have authority, its work will be so ineffective that the purpose of the law is defeated—as was the case for 19 years with the Interstate Commerce Commission.

* Pure Food and Drug Act and Meat Inspection Act and Muckrakers

Today, with our multitude of laws controlling the preparation and dispensing of food and drugs, one can hardly realize that not long ago the most effective control was the conscience and cleanliness of those who produced and handled it. President Roosevelt remembered that the canned meat was much more fatal to the troops in Cuba than Spanish bullets. When he read Upton Sinclair's book *The Jungle*, he couldn't believe it; and when word from investigators proved Sinclair's work to be substantially true, he demanded legislation. Federal interference in a field of regulation hitherto left to the states was opposed as socialistic. Several Congressmen felt that any federal laws would be a violation of the 5th amendment which gave the individual the *liberty* to buy whatever food or medicine he wished even though it was poison and he had no way of knowing it. There was widespread belief in "caveat emptor" (let the buyer beware) which held that any buyer stupid enough to be cheated by the seller would soon learn by experience; and, if he didn't, he deserved to suffer the consequences. In a relatively simple society "caveat emptor" made very little sense; in a complex society it became intolerable. Chemicals and dyes were used in food to preserve it and improve its appearance in almost complete disregard to what might happen to the consumer. Toxic dyes went into children's penny candy. The U.S. Department of Agriculture, the American Medical Association, and several *muckraking* magazine articles and books supported the President's efforts to get corrective

legislation, while the meat packers, patent medicine producers, and the Liquor Dealers' Association pooh-poohed the necessity for reform. *The Jungle* overwhelmed the opposition by arousing a public demand that literally drove the laws through Congress within a year. After the laws went into effect (1906) the United States had the best supervision of food, drugs, and meat of any nation. It was only a start, but it was a good start.

What had shocked Roosevelt in *The Jungle* had impressed a young Englishman, Winston Churchill, one day to be numbered among the greatest of England's Prime Ministers. He said, "This terrible book . . . pierces the thickest skull and most leathery heart." It told of cattle with tuberculosis and of pigs dying of cholera being slaughtered for food; it told of filth shoveled from the floors and of poisoned rats thrown into grinding machines to be processed into canned meat; and it cited an instance of a worker who fell in a vat where he was processed into lard. The heat and the chemicals had "processed" everything but a belt buckle, other insoluble bits of apparel, and some bones. All of these filthy and criminal practices were illegal under local laws, but bribing inspectors to overlook such conditions was common practice. The *muckrakers* uncovered corruption in many fields, but no matter where it came to the surface it had its roots in unholy alliances between government and business.

THE LEADING MUCKRAKERS

Lincoln Steffens	*Autobiography*
Lincoln Steffens	*The Shame of the Cities*
Upton Sinclair	*The Jungle*
Ida Tarbell	*History of the Standard Oil Co.*
Frank Norris	*Octopus*
Winston Churchill	*Coniston*
(American novelist)	

MAGAZINES

Cosmopolitan David Phillips *The Treason of the Senate*

McClure's carried *History of the Standard Oil Company* and *Shame of the Cities*

Collier's series of articles on patent medicines

Ladies' Home Journal series of articles on patent medicines

Everybody's Thomas Lawson *Frenzied Finance*

Political Reform of the Roosevelt Era

There is a school of thought that looks upon "T.R." as having shown more bluster than action in the field of reform. This may arise from the trust-busting that didn't really stop the trusts; from a Hepburn Bill that still left it difficult to establish "just and reasonable" rates; from settling a coal strike that did nothing to prevent a repetition of a similar emergency; and from meat, food, and medicine controls which have required many laws to strengthen them. But the job of reform is rarely accomplished in one grand attack with a single remedy; it is usually a long-time process that is never really finished. If the disappointment with Roosevelt as a reformer arises from the fact that there was so much to be done that was left undone, there is still a substantial defense to be made for him. Cleveland said Roosevelt was the ablest politician to occupy the White House. The art of the politician is to know when not to fight, when to compromise, and when to fight to a finish; to know when to let the loaf alone, when to accept half a loaf, and when to grab for the whole loaf. What Roosevelt accomplished he did in spite of his party, and he had to lead the party in a direction it was reluctant to take. He received the affection of the people who were stimulated to demand and achieve reforms on their own, so that political democracy was increased in state governments through the initiative, referendum, recall, and the direct primary. The spirit of the times reflected Roosevelt's vigorous concern for the welfare of the people and may justify calling the first decade of the 20th century The Roosevelt Era.

Initiative

A petition containing a draft of a proposed law must be signed by a designated per cent of the voters (5 to 8). This petition is then filed with the proper state official to be submitted to the state legislature which must act upon it. There are variations of this procedure. Some states permit the legislature to amend the draft submitted on the petition or to propose a rival bill. Where amendments or rival bills are proposed they must appear on the ballot at the next general election.

Referendum

The Protest Referendum—A petition signed by a designated per cent of the voters (5 to 8) asks that a law already passed by the legislature be submitted to the voters of the state so that they may have a chance to defeat it at the next general election. Sometimes the presentation of the petition suspends the law until after the election. This referendum gives the voters veto power.

The Ordinary Referendum—Many state constitutions require that certain laws can be passed only by being referred to the voters. This is often true of bond issues and amendments to state constitutions. Some states require constitutional amendments to be referred to the voters at two or three successive elections and to become law only when approved each time.

The total effect of the initiative and referendum has been to clutter up the ballots with too many propositions the voters are not interested in and don't understand. Their strength lies in the fact that a corrupt or lazy legislature can be goaded into action by the voters.

Recall

This is a device whereby the voters may start the machinery for the dismissal of an elected or appointed official. A petition requiring a designated per cent (25 or more) of the voters results in a special election to determine whether the official will retain his position. Some states arrange for another candidate to be on the ballot so that the one getting the greater number of votes fills the office. This device is seldom used.

Direct Primary

Anyone who wishes to run for office may circulate a petition and get the required number of signatures. The total number varies widely and usually there is a minimum needed in each county of the state. At the primary elections the registered party members elect the nominees from these candidates. While the use of some form of primary is widespread, it has disadvantages. It costs money to circulate petitions and run in a primary campaign. It forces the winner of the primary to conduct two election campaigns. Unless interest is running high in the primary election, the slate of candidates will be much the same as would be chosen by party leaders in a caucus. However, there are occasions where the primary may clean up or defeat an unsavory political organization.

All of these devices, initiative, referendum, recall, and direct primary, give the voters a more direct role in government. To a degree they substitute democracy for republicanism, direct participation for representation. They have made no marked change in American politics, but, as President Wilson said, they do give the voter "a shot gun behind the door."

William H. Taft

1909-1913

1857 - 1930

REPUBLICAN

☆

TAFT'S PUBLIC SERVICE BEFORE HE BECAME PRESIDENT

U.S. Solicitor General under Harrison
Judge of Federal Circuit Court
Head of Commission to Organize Government of Philippines
1st Governor General of the Philippines
Secretary of War under T. Roosevelt

MAJOR ITEMS OF TAFT'S ADMINISTRATION

*Tariff (Paine-Aldrich, 1909; Canada)
Conservation (Pinchot-Ballinger)
Mid-term Elections (1910)

Taft's Election in 1908

There was no contest at the Republican convention at Chicago. The Old Guard Republicans were happy to see Roosevelt leave the White House and glad to take advantage of his popularity by nominating his choice of successor. "T.R." campaigned for Taft on a platform pledging continuation of conservation policies, enforcement of antitrust laws, and a downward revision of the tariff. It is interesting to note that when Roosevelt was President he considered tariff reform too hot an issue to handle, but he was quite willing to put it in the lap of his less aggressive protegé. The Democrats nominated Bryan for the third time. Their platform was similar to that of the Republicans, but was more vigorous in its stand against monopolies and promised a sharper reduction in the tariff to revenue levels.

	Popular Vote	Electoral Vote
Taft	7,679,006	321
Bryan	6,409,106	162

The Republicans retained majorities in both Houses of Congress.

Tariff (Payne-Aldrich, 1909; Canada)

* Payne-Aldrich Tariff

Taft had pledged a tariff that would reduce rates appreciably without abandoning protection. This was a feasible plan because the Dingley Tariff of 1897 was extravagantly overprotective. The excess protection provided opportunity for high prices beyond anything justified as a defense against foreign competition. Representative Payne introduced a bill to carry out Taft's pledge. When it got to the Senate, Aldrich of Rhode Island managed to have some 600 rates increased and some 250 other changes made. Either through a wry sense of humor or a genuine attempt to deceive the public, Congress put several products of less than trifling commercial importance on the free list. The truth of the situation was brought out with genuine humor by Finley Dunne's newspaper comic character, Mr. Dooley. "The Republican party has been thrue to its promises. Look at th' free list if ye don't believe it. Practically ivrything necessary to existence comes in free. Here it is. Curling stones, teeth, sea moss, newspapers, nux vomica, Pulu, canary bird seed, divvy-divvy, spunk, hog bristles, marshmallows, silk worm eggs, stilts, skeletons, an' leeches. Th' new tariff bill puts these familyar commodyties within th' reach iv all."

Several progressive Republicans, among them La Follette and Norris, joined the Democrats in the Senate in angry opposition to the bill. But it passed, and Taft, instead of vetoing it, signed it. A few weeks later he made a speech in Minnesota praising the Payne-Aldrich tariff as the best the Republican Party had ever passed. This set the stage for a serious split in the party and a lively mid-term election.

Canada

Taft had started to negotiate for reciprocal tariffs with Canada. By late 1910 an agreement designed to increase trade to the benefit of both nations was ready to be presented to the Canadian Parliament and the American Congress. The reasonable expectation was that we would buy more Canadian foodstuffs and they would buy more American manufactured products. There was opposition from both nations, but it seemed that the plan would be adopted. Then the new Speaker of the House, Champ Clark (Democrat), put both feet in his mouth. In announcing his support for the reciprocal tariff agreement he chose a most undiplomatic way of expressing a desire for closer ties between the two nations. "I am for it because I hope to see the day when the American flag will float over every square foot of the British North American possessions clear to the North Pole." That was the end of President Taft's statesmanlike attempt at reciprocal tariffs with Canada.

* Conservation (Pinchot-Ballinger)

President Roosevelt frequently did what he thought was good for the country with little concern about his legal right to do it. Taft was much more aware of and sensitive to the constitutional limits of his office. Under Roosevelt, according to Taft, some water power sites had been set aside for public development without proper legal authority. These sites were opened to private enterprise. Coal deposits in Alaska, which Chief Forester Pinchot considered set aside as government reserves, were released for private use. Pinchot's superior, Secretary of the Interior Ballinger, defended this Alaskan deal which was investigated and approved by a committee of Congress. Pinchot was then dismissed. But the fat was in the fire. The members of Congress were not impressed with the findings of their own investigating committee; neither were the people, for Pinchot had the support of his old friend and colleague, Roosevelt. The Insurgent Republicans and the Democrats combined to oppose Taft. This attack on Taft over conservation really made no sense. He may well have been in the right in the instances cited above which started the rift. At any rate, his program of conservation as a whole was excellent. He retraced "T.R's" steps in setting aside natural resources of water power, forests, and minerals to plug legal gaps and thus make these reserves secure for the government. He persuaded Congress to set up a Bureau of Mines to watch over government mineral sites; his new chief forester added tremendous tracts of timber in the Appalachians to the national preserves, and set aside oil lands for government use and was thus the first president to give practical recognition to the importance of this natural resource. Yet, in spite of the facts, his contemporaries judged Taft to be either the betrayer of Roosevelt's conservation policies or, at best, a very weak supporter thereof.

Mid-term Elections (1910)

Taft's acceptance of the Payne-Aldrich tariff lost him much of the support of Republican voters who still looked upon Roosevelt as their political hero. It is sometimes said that Taft had to give in on the tariff issue, and pretend to like it, in order to keep the party together. But the political mistake was the introduction of tariff reform as a major promise in the Republican platform of 1908. No issue was required to lure voters when Taft, as the "crown prince" selected by Roosevelt, was assured of winning. The Pinchot-Ballinger tiff over conservation was interpreted by the public and the insurgent Republicans in Congress as proof that Taft had turned his back on Roosevelt's program. While this was grossly unfair to Taft (see above) it was a political factor of importance. Then there was the Speaker of the House, "Uncle Joe" Cannon of Illinois. He summed up his ignorance of conservation with brevity by declaring, "Not one cent for scenery." He had given Senator Aldrich every aid his powerful position as Speaker offered in getting the Aldrich version of the Payne-Aldrich tariff passed. Joseph Cannon had used the powers of the Speakership to the limit. He appointed the members to the several House committees, he was chairman of the Rules Committee and, as such, could get bills on or keep them off. He made himself a one-man bottleneck through which all legislation had to pass and over which he had control. Taft had avoided clashing with Cannon in an attempt to avert a party split. When, in the spring of 1910, a combination of insurgents and Democrats voted a change in the rules of the House which deprived the Speaker of membership on the Rules Committee, "Uncle Joe Cannon" could no longer control the flow of bills through the House. This defeat of the Old Guard by a coalition foreshadowed the Republican defeat at the polls in 1910.

In the summer of 1910 Roosevelt returned from his hunting trip in Africa and his visits with the heads of governments in Europe. He had taken a position against Taft on the tariff and conservation. He was heartily in sympathy with the views of the insurgents and reiterated his square deal slogan with appeals to the people such as "the power of the national government extends to the protection of the whole people against the special interests" and speaking of "the conflict between the men who possess more than they have earned and the men who earn more than they possess." While Roosevelt was re-establishing his political leadership, Taft was losing the confidence of the people. But at that very time (June, 1910) he was strengthening the Interstate Commerce Commission by supporting the passage of the Mann-Elkins Act which gave it the right to prevent new rates if challenged in the courts. The act also placed telephone, telegraph, cable, and wireless companies under the authority of the Interstate Commerce Commission. Taft also got Congress to set up Postal Savings banks as had been advocated in the Populist Platform of 1892. Certain post offices were designated as depositories for savings. But the insurgents and Roosevelt caught public attention while the deeds of Taft went unnoticed. For the first time in 16 years the Democrats gained control of the House and made large gains in the Senate. The nominal majority still held in the Senate by the Republicans lost control to the coalition of insurgents and Democrats. The Democrats also elected 26 governors, one of whom was Woodrow Wilson of New Jersey.

A mid-term defeat of such proportions was a defeat for the President. For the balance of his term Taft continued quietly at work. Before he left office he had initiated 90 anti-trust suits, 36 more than the record set by Roosevelt. Taft was to serve in two capacities better suited to his temperament and in which his specialized knowledge and keen intellect could achieve full effectiveness. During 1913-'21 he taught law at Yale University, and from 1921 until his death in 1930 he was Chief Justice of the U.S. Supreme Court.

Woodrow Wilson

1913-1921

1856 - 1924

DEMOCRAT

☆

WILSON'S PUBLIC SERVICE BEFORE HE BECAME PRESIDENT

Governor of New Jersey (1911-12)

MAJOR ITEMS OF WILSON'S ADMINISTRATIONS

16th, 17th, 18th, and 19th Amendments
Underwood Tariff (1913)
Federal Reserve System (Glass-Owen
   Act) (1913)
Federal Trade Commission (1914)
Clayton Anti-trust Act (1914)
U.S. in the Caribbean
   Nicaragua—Dominican Republic—
   Haiti—Virgin Islands
U.S. and Mexico
The Lusitania (May 1915)

Sussex Pledge Broken (February 1917)
Organizing for War
   Liberty Loans and War Revenue
   Acts—Railroads and Ships—Council
   of National Defense and War Indus-
   tries Board—Lever Food and Fuel
   Acts—Overman Act
"Fourteen Points" (January 1918)
American Expeditionary Force in France
Treaty of Versailles
The War Record

* Wilson's Election in 1912 and Re-election in 1916

The first story of the 1912 campaign is that of Roosevelt's unsuccessful attempt to get the Republican nomination away from Taft and his success at replacing La Follette as the leader of the Progressives. The Republican National Convention met at Chicago in mid-June. While Roosevelt had a large following among the Republican and independent voters, he did not have the support of the Republican organizations at any level, national, state, or city. Those who could supply the campaign funds could profit by the political spoils of victory, and could get the vote out on election day were backing Taft. Some opposed Roosevelt because he was running for a third term, although it was not a consecutive term and was only the second time he was running for election. His pledge of 1908 (see p. 178) not to seek re-election embarrassed him. The Republican insurgents under the leadership of Senator Robert M. La Follette of Wisconsin had organized a National Republican Progressive League in January 1911. They were threatening to take over the party much as the Populists had done in the Democratic Party in 1896. In the autumn of 1911 they had issued a statement that "the logical candidate for the Presidency of the United States" was La Follette. But as election day approached, the Progressive wing of the Republican Party realized that Roosevelt, if he would line up with the Progressives, could pull more votes than La Follette. Roosevelt, however, refused either to accept or reject their offer of leadership. In an unintelligible letter written in 1912 he stated, "I am not a candidate, and I never will be a candidate. But I have to tell the La Follette men and the Taft men that, while I do not wish the nomination, yet I do not think it would be right or proper for me to say that under no circumstances would I accept it if it came." Of course, this was political double-talk to be translated into "I want the nomination." Roosevelt was unwilling to commit himself to the Progressives until he had made an attempt to get the regular Republican nomination at the Chicago convention in June. But at the convention the machinery was controlled by the Taft forces. Where delegates had been chosen by state conventions the Taft forces won; where they had been chosen by primaries (13 states) Roosevelt got most of the delegates. Taft had the solid bloc of Southern delegates from states where there was only a handful of Republicans all of whom depended upon Washington for patronage. There were over 200 seats at the national convention claimed by both Taft and Roosevelt delegates. The committee on credentials was a Taft committee and settled most of these seats in favor of Taft delegates. On the first ballot Taft won the nomination with 561 votes to 107 for Roosevelt and 41 for LaFollette. That evening Roosevelt supporters met to denounce the "fraud" in nominating Taft and were addressed by Roosevelt who advised them to go home and organize a Progressive convention for later in the summer. He told them, "If you wish me to make the fight, I will make it, . . .". In August the Progressives had their convention in Chicago and nominated Roosevelt by acclamation. The man who had been a master politician in the White House had committed a major political blunder. Forming a separate political party could do nothing but split the Republican vote and hand the election to the Democrats. But at the convention all was enthusiasm, almost reaching religious fervor with the singing of "Onward Christian Soldiers." The popular leader declared himself "feeling like a bull moose" and ready for the fray. So the stage was set for the bull moose and the elephant to tear one another apart while the donkey ate the hay.

The second story of the 1912 campaign is that of how a college professor with only three years of political experience won the Democratic nomination and the presidency. Thomas Woodrow Wilson was a scholar. As an undergraduate at Princeton he had published an article on the irresponsibility of Congress. For his doctoral thesis at Johns Hopkins he wrote *Congressional Government*. He taught history at Bryn Mawr and Wesleyan, and political economy at Princeton where he became president in 1902. He was soon recognized as an outstanding educator, but he was having his troubles at Princeton. Wilson injected Princeton with his own high academic standards, perhaps too suddenly. His displeasure with the undergraduate social clubs and his insistence that the graduate school be more closely associated with the undergraduate college caused so much dissension that he resigned in 1910. By this time Wilson had become known as an orator of stature, and his books and magazine articles had made him the foremost American scholar in the field of government. George

Harvey, editor of *Harper's Weekly,* was seeking a replacement for Bryan as the spokesman for the Democratic Party and aspirant for the presidency. The first political move was to get Wilson the nomination for the governorship of New Jersey. The disreputable Democratic machine of New Jersey had long been out of power and could use to great advantage a figure-head to give it the appearance of respectability. When approached in 1910 about the possibility of running Wilson for governor, the bosses grabbed at the advantages he had to offer: personal dignity and respectability, high reputation in the academic world, authoritative knowledge of history and politics, and a superb ability in oratory. They had no idea, and less concern, about what kind of governor Wilson might make; but they knew he would be a wonderful candidate. He was. Two years before, the Republicans had a majority of 82,000 votes; Wilson polled a Democratic majority of 49,000. Within a little over a year the professor had the eyes of the nation focused on Trenton. He accomplished an unbelievable number of reforms: workmen's compensation law, direct primary, corrupt practices act, utility control act, and election reforms. He ignored the "machine" by explaining his program directly to the voters. In 1911 he visited the western states on an extensive speaking tour which enabled him to return to New Jersey as a truly national figure. The next contest would be at the Democratic National Convention at Baltimore in June 1912.

Bryan was still the most influential man in the Democratic Party. He was at the convention, not to get the nomination, but to see that the liberal faction of the party prevailed. Champ Clark of Missouri led in the early balloting. He was a middle of the road candidate favored by the professionals of the party. On the tenth ballot Clark had a majority, but not the necessary two-thirds, when the New York delegation shifted its votes from Judge Harmon of Ohio to Clark. This should have been the signal for getting on the band wagon and putting Champ Clark over. But Bryan made a dramatic plea to other states to follow the lead of Nebraska (which had voted for Clark) by changing their support from Clark to Woodrow Wilson, a true liberal. Bryan based his plea on the ground that any candidate who got the votes of the notorious Tammany Hall machine would not get the vote of his state, Nebraska. In ballot after ballot one or two states left Clark and went to Wilson until the New Jersey governor got the nomination on the 46th ballot.

There was nothing to choose between the Roosevelt Progressive program and the Wilson Democratic program, they were so very similar. The Democrats and many independents voted for Wilson and the Republicans split their votes between Taft and Roosevelt.

	Popular Vote	Electoral Vote
Wilson	6,286,214	435
Roosevelt	4,126,020	88
Taft	3,483,922	8
Debs	897,011	0

The Democrats gained control of both House and Senate.

The election of 1916 was close. The outcome was uncertain until the returns came in from California the Thursday after election day.

The Republicans nominated Charles Evans Hughes who resigned from the Supreme Court to run. The Progressive Party nominated Roosevelt but he refused and advised them to follow him back into the regular Republican fold. This caused the disintegration of the Progressive Party and repaired the rift in the Republican Party even though there were still Old Guard and Progressive members who would fight each other when they weren't fighting Democrats. As a united party Republicans far outnumbered Democrats, and unless there was a sharp difference on a major issue, the Republicans should win. In 1916 Hughes agreed with Wilson's policies. His campaign consisted of telling the voters that he would do essentially as Wilson had done, but that Republican administration would be more efficient and effective. Hughes was careful not to offend the "hyphenated" vote of the German-Americans and the Irish-Americans. Wilson had been vigorous in his protests against the submarine menace which had caused the loss of many civilians and had thus offended many German-Americans in the mid-west. His milder protests against Britain's violations of our rights on the high seas was interpreted by the Irish-Americans of the north east as a pro-English policy, and thus offended them.

The Democrats renominated Wilson whose greatest campaign asset was the slogan, "He kept us out of war." In the summer and fall of 1916 it did seem that Wilson's diplomacy had brought an end to the ruthless aspects of the submarine attacks. But there was neither promise nor implication by Wilson that changed circumstances might not result in war. When the states with the largest blocs of electoral votes, New York, Pennsylvania, and Illinois, had voted for Hughes, many papers conceded Wilson's defeat. But the next morning returns from western states began to change the picture until the final result depended on California, a state confidently reckoned to be Republican. On Thursday the tally was complete; California had gone for Wilson by the narrow margin of 3,773 votes. Hughes lost California because he and his campaign manager ignored Senator Hiram Johnson when they campaigned in his state. Johnson, a Progressive Republican, was extremely popular and the voters sensed the coolness between him and Hughes. Apparently thousands of them voted the Republican ticket except for the office of president. In the total popular vote Wilson got 590,000 more than Hughes, a very definite expression of confidence from the people. The Democratic Party did not fare as well as its leader. Their majorities in both House and Senate fell almost to the vanishing point, and they lost many governorships to the Republicans. The election was a personal, not a party, victory.

	Popular Vote	Electoral Vote
Wilson	9,129,606	277
Hughes	8,538,221	254

16th, 17th, 18th, and 19th Amendments (See p. 70.)

The 16th amendment was proposed in 1909 and ratified in February, 1913. (It is considered here, instead of under Taft, for the convenience of having these four amendments together.) It may be looked upon as a radical change in the Constitution. If Congress can tax incomes, it can use this tax to redistribute wealth. It can employ progressive taxation ("soak the rich" or "place the heaviest burden on the broadest back") to pay for all sorts of social services as Congress may decide and the courts permit. This amendment is more evidence supporting the judgment that Taft's alleged conservatism was an illusion fostered by his appearance and personality, but belied by his thinking and the accomplishments of his administration. In spite of their reputation to the contrary, the bulky, slow-moving, soft-spoken, deliberate, benign, and keen Mr. Taft was more "progressive" than the noisy, magnetic, dynamic, officious, and popular Mr. Theodore Roosevelt.

The 17th amendment was proposed in 1912 and ratified in May 1913. Both Taft and Wilson approved. It provided for direct election of Senators by the people, a reform long supported by popular opinion.

The 18th amendment was proposed in late 1917, ratified in 1919, and put into effect on January 16, 1920. It outlawed the "manufacture, sale, or transportation of intoxicating liquors." For decades the Anti-Saloon League and the Women's Christian

Temperance Union had been agitating for prohibition. Several factors combined to make 1917-20 a favorable time for the adoption of this amendment. Many people thought it a crime to use vast quantities of grain in the production of beer and liquor when food was needed for the allies and armed forces on the western front. A rather silly factor, but a real one at the time, was the association in the popular mind of breweries with German-Americans whose loyalty was under suspicion. (Some communities were foolish enough to stop teaching German in their schools.) The period of about two years when the amendment was before the states was the time when hundreds of thousands of American men were in Europe and elsewhere in the armed forces and were unable to exert political influence on the issue. On their return to a "dry" country they resented the loss of their "personal liberty" while they had been risking their lives and perhaps developing a taste for French beverages. The Volstead Act, passed over President Wilson's veto, defined "intoxicating" (as used in the amendment) as any beverage containing over ½ of 1% alcohol. From the beginning opposition to prohibition was too strong and widespread to permit enforcement. Corruption between federal agents and "bootleggers" reached serious proportions. Making "home-brew" became a fad throughout the land, and the "speakeasies" were a far more dangerous social hazard than the saloons they had replaced. In many "wet" areas the local police refused to cooperate with, and often worked against, federal agents. Supplying illicit alcoholic beverages was large scale business and the competition between suppliers expressed itself pretty much as pictured in the lurid T.V. versions of the "Roaring Twenties." No doubt the normal crime wave to be expected after a severe war was very much heightened by this unfortunate attempt to deal with a genuine social problem which still cries out for a solution. Had the words "is hereby prohibited" in the amendment been "is hereby subject to regulation by Congress," the 18th amendment might have proved the "noble experiment" President Hoover once called it.

The 19th amendment granted the vote to women. Susan B. Anthony started the campaign for women's suffrage in 1869. That same year the territory of Wyoming permitted women to vote. In the 1890's the states of Wyoming, Colorado, Idaho, and Utah granted women's suffrage, as had over a dozen states before World War I. The eastern states were the most reluctant to stop classifying women with others most commonly denied the ballot: the children, the illiterate, the insane, and the imprisoned. The way many thousands of women did "men's work" in war industries and drove trucks and busses helped their cause with many voters. Congress proposed the amendment in 1919 and it was ratified in August 1920 in time for the women to take part in the presidential election in November. Throughout the years women had promised benevolent results from their voting, but the only unquestioned fact is that the vote has more than doubled.

* Underwood-Simmons Tariff (1913)

On the day of his inauguration Wilson called a special session of Congress to meet April 7th to consider downward revision of the tariff. Cleveland had failed twice (Mills Bill & Wilson-Gorman Tariff) and Taft once (Payne-Aldrich Tariff) to achieve this result. For the first time since Jefferson, the President appeared in person to address both Houses in joint session. Wilson was well aware of his ability to speak effectively to an audience, just as he was aware of his inability to be persuasive in private conversations. His speech carried the conviction of authority; he knew what he was talking about. ". . . we have built up a set of privilege and exemption from competition behind which it was easy by any, even the crudest, forms of combination to organize monopoly; until at last nothing is normal, nothing is obliged to stand the tests of efficiency and economy." And "We must abolish everything that bears even the semblance of privilege or any kind of artificial advantage." The chairman of the Ways and Means Committee, Oscar Underwood of Alabama, got the bill through the House as Wilson wanted it. Rates were reduced on over 950 items, mostly necessities, while rates on luxuries were increased. Some 300 items were put on the free list. Altogether it was a reduction of from 25 to 30 per cent from the Payne-Aldrich level. As Wilson must have expected, the Senate took a different view. The chairman of the Finance Committee, Senator Simmons of North Carolina, started to arrange changes much as had Gorman and Aldrich in 1894 and 1909. Then Wilson spoke to the people through the press. "Washington has seldom seen so numerous, so industrious or so insidious a lobby. The newspapers are being filled with paid advertisements calculated to mislead the judgment of public men . . . and the public opinion of the country itself." And "It is of serious interest to the country that the people at large should have no lobby and be voiceless in these matters, while great bodies of astute men seek to create an artificial opinion and to overcome the interests of the public for their private profit."

After four months the Senators bowed to the pressure of withheld patronage by Wilson and the support given him by public opinion. The Underwood Tariff was the first substantial reduction in 56 years.

Part of the tariff was an income tax (made legal by the 16th amendment) with rates of 1% on single persons with incomes from $3,000 to $20,000 and on married couples with incomes from $4,000 to $20,000. The rate rose to 2% on incomes from $20,000 to $50,000 and was graduated until it reached the top limit of 6% on incomes above $500,000. In 1913 a foreman in an industrial plant or a highly skilled craftsman made about $1,300 to $1,800 a year.

For years the major parties had been arguing about tariffs. The Republicans had pictured tariff protection as a primary reason for the great industrial growth and prosperity of the United States, the protector of the "full dinner pail" of the workers. The Democrats had claimed that the protective tariff poured profits into the pockets of the rich squeezed from everybody by high prices. They saw the natural resources of the nation and the free trade area within the nation as more likely explanations of the economic strength of America. Now, for the first time since the United States had become industrialized, we had a tariff for revenue instead of protection. From practical experience we should get the answer as to where the greater wisdom lay, but such was not to be the case. Less than a year after the passage of the Underwood Tariff, war broke out in Europe (late July 1914). It started with Austria and Serbia, but within a few days Germany, Russia, France, and England were involved. With Europe shifting to a war economy imports to the United States dropped and the demand for American products rose. The tariff, no matter what its provisions, shriveled to a point of insignificance as a factor in international trade. Even for revenue purposes the tariff lost out to the much more productive income tax which soon took the lead as a source of government funds.

* Federal Reserve System (Glass-Owen Act) (1913)

In 1894 Henry Lloyd in his "Wealth Against Commonwealth" charged that a very small group of men controlled American industry, transportation, and credit. The muckrakers of the following decade uncovered evidence that there was truth in this charge. The Pujo Committee, set up by Congress, investigated. Its report in 1913 served as an excellent background for Wilson's financial and anti-trust legislation. The Pujo report listed 6 banks, headed by J. P Morgan & Co., which by their tremendous financial assets and interlocking directorates had control of banking resources of over $2,000,000,000; of 16 major transportation companies; of 9 industrial corporations; and of 7 public utilities. The Committee stated that its conclusions had been limited to facts that had been verified, so that the stated financial resources and the control through interlocking directorates was placed at minimum figures and thus represented the least possible, rather than the actual, amount of concentration of wealth and power. This situation was called the "Money Trust." *

As Wilson put it to Congress when he appeared before them to suggest a new banking system, ". . . the control of this system . . . must be public, not private . . . so that the banks may be the instruments, not the masters of business and of individual enterprise and initiative." Carter Glass of Virginia had been working on a plan for months in collaboration with several bankers and members

*   The 6 Banks
J.P. Morgan & Co.
1st National Bank of New York
National City Bank of New York
Lee, Higginson & Co.—Boston & New York
Kidder, Peabody & Co.—Boston & New York
Kuhn, Loeb & Co.

The 9 Industrial Corporations
Amalgamated Copper Co.
American Can Co.
J. L. Case Threshing Machine Co.
Cramp Ship & Engine Building Co.
General Electric Co.
International Harvester Co.
Lackawanna Steel Co.
Pullman Co.
United States Steel Co.

The 7 Public Utilities
American Telephone & Telegraph Co.
Chicago Elevated Railways
Consolidated Gas Co. of New York
Hudson & Manhattan Railroad
Interborough Rapid Transit of New York
Philadelphia Rapid Transit
Wesetrn Union Telegraph Co.

The 16 Transportation Companies
Adams Express
Anhracite coal carriers
Atchison, Topeka & Santa Fe RR.
Chesapeake & Ohio RR.
Chicago Great Western RR.
Chicago, Milwaukee, St. Paul RR.
Chicago & Northwestern RR.
Chicago, Rock Island & Pacific RR.
Great Northern RR.
International Mercantile Marine Co.
New York Central RR.
New York, New Haven & Hartford RR.
Northern Pacific RR.
Southern Railway
Southern Pacific Co.
Union Pacific RR.

of Congress. It became the Federal Reserve Act. The major provisions were as follows:

1] The nation was divided into 12 Federal Reserve Districts with a Federal Reserve Bank in each district.

1 Boston	7 Chicago
2 New York	8 St. Louis
3 Philadelphia	9 Minneapolis
4 Cleveland	10 Kansas City
5 Richmond	11 Dallas
6 Atlanta	12 San Francisco

2] All National Banks (under the National Banking Act of 1863) had to join the system and deposit 6% of their capital and surplus with the Federal Reserve Bank in their district. Other banks could join. These Member Banks thus supplied funds for the 12 Federal Reserve Banks. Only banks can do business with the Federal Reserve Banks; they are strictly banks for banks.

3] A Federal Reserve Board of 8 members appointed by the President supervises the system. The Secretary of the Treasury and the Comptroller of the Currency are on the Board (changed in 1935, see p. 221). One of the key powers of this Board is to regulate the rediscount rate charged the Member Banks for loans. This power exercises a major control over the credit available to business.

4] Money can be transferred from any Federal Reserve Bank to any other. The supply of money and credit can flow easily to any part of the nation as required by business conditions. The thousands of Member Banks can obtain funds for sound loans by applying to the Federal Reserve Bank of their district. Whether business conditions are sound is a decision made by the Federal Reserve Board and reflected in the rediscount rate.

5] Federal Reserve Notes, paper money, can be issued by the Federal Reserve Banks with commercial paper as security and the backing of a 40% gold reserve.

The way the system works may be clarified by following a loan. John Smith, a manufacturer, wishes to borrow $50,000 for materials and payroll. He has a contract to deliver his product, but he needs cash to meet the costs of making it. The local bank knows he can fulfill the contract he has with his customer. The local bank is a Member Bank of the Federal Reserve System. Smith gets the $50,000 loan discounted at 5%. Discounted means that the banker takes the 5% interest when the loan is made. Smith gives the Member Bank some legal document (security) representing value enough to cover the loan so that, no matter what happens to Smith, the bank can get its money back. This legal document is called commercial paper. With thousands of businessmen getting similar loans, the Member Bank gets low on cash and overstocked with commercial paper. To get more funds to lend to businessmen, the Member Bank borrows from the Federal Reserve Bank in its district and uses commercial paper for security. The loans to Member Banks from its Federal Reserve Bank may be discounted (rediscounted) at about 1½% or 2%. This is the second time the commercial paper has been discounted and is therefore called the rediscount rate. Now the Federal Reserve Bank has the commercial paper and the Member Bank has more cash to lend to local businessmen. So far, money has been moving from the Member Bank to businessmen and from the Federal Reserve Bank to the Member Bank. When the loans are repaid the process is reversed. Of course many loans are being made while many others are being repaid so that there is a continuous flow in both directions of both money and commercial paper.

The rediscount rate is an important feature. If the Federal Reserve Board judges business conditions in a given district to be verging on the speculative side, to be a bit too active to be sound under the conditions that exist there, it will increase the rediscount rate. When that happens, the Member Banks in that district will raise the discount (interest rate) to the local businessman when he applies for a loan. Money is getting "tight" or more expensive to borrow. The businessman will take the increased rediscount rate as a danger signal; as a sign to be cautious. The resulting slow-up in business was exactly the result the Federal Reserve Board desired in order to promote safety and business stability. If business is slow in an area which the Federal Reserve Board judges should be enjoying a more active business climate it may lower the rediscount rate. This will result in lower interest charges by the Member Banks to businessmen who will interpret the lower rates as a signal to go ahead with plans they may have had for plant expansion, new machinery, bigger inventory, or new ventures. The scheme is elastic; it can be adjusted at any time in one or any number of Federal Reserve Districts to suit business conditions as evaluated by the Federal Reserve Board, a group of banking experts with financial knowledge and know-how.

* Federal Trade Commission (1914)

When Wilson gave the title "New Freedom" to his program he was talking about freedom for consumers and workers from unfair practices commonly, but by no means exclusively, associated with monopoly power such as the Pujo report indicated. In his address to Congress in January 1914, he made several specific recommendations which were, in large part, carried out by the establishment of the Federal Trade Commission and the passage of the Clayton Anti-trust Act.

The Federal Trade Commission consisted of 5 members appointed by the President. Both parties were to be represented on the Commission whose members served a 7 year term. Except for banking and transportation, they had jurisdiction over large corporations. Their powers included the right to demand annual and special reports to assist them in fact finding; to publish their findings if such publicity served the public interest; and to issue cease and desist orders which were subject to review by the courts. The unfair practices most frequently encountered were deceptive and false labeling, adulteration of products, conspiracies to maintain prices, and false claims to patents. The Commission operated as an effective traffic cop, one who stays in plain sight in order to discourage violations and makes himself generally helpful to motorists, but who can hand out a ticket or escort an offender to jail. It was set up to warn and advise corporations in order to prevent violations of law. Corporations sometimes found themselves in genuine doubt about the legality of contemplated business arrangements and practices, for regulatory laws are numerous and often complex. A corporation could seek advice from the Commission and, if the corporation's attitude displayed an intent to obey the law, would be allowed to adjust its practices according to the Commission's suggestions, thus avoiding penalties. The Commission proved very useful in advising the government of situations that invited prosecution under the anti-trust laws and supplying facts to support anti-trust suits.

** Clayton Anti-trust Act (1914)

This law was made to correct weaknesses in the Sherman Anti-trust Act, add new provisions, and remove labor unions from liability under anti-trust laws. To prevent monopoly by preserving competition it forbade

1] Interlocking directorates which would lessen competition among large corporations.

2] Ownership of stock by one corporation in a competing corporation.

3] Tying contracts which restricted the retailer to handling only the product of one supplier. (For example, an agreement by which a grocer must sell only one brand of soft drinks.)

4] Price cutting below cost in an effort to eliminate a competitor.

The provisions especially favorable to labor provided that

1] Anti-trust laws do not apply to labor unions, farm organizations, or other non-profit mutual help associations.

2] Injunctions shall not be issued in labor disputes unless there is a threat of irreparable damage to property. (This grew out of the injunction against Debs in the Pullman strike of 1894.)

3] Boycotts, peaceful strikes, and peaceful picketing are legal.

4] "The labor of a human being is not a commodity or article of commerce."

These labor provisions were hailed by Samuel Gompers, president of the A.F. of L., as the Magna Carta of labor; but his enthusiasm was premature. Interpretation by the courts robbed the labor provisions of the vitality Wilson, and probably Congress, intended. From the Sherman Anti-trust Act of 1890 until after the financial crash of 1929, court decisions leaned heavily in favor of the views of business leaders, just as for the past quarter century or more they have leaned heavily in favor of individual civil rights. It is well to recognize that a worthwhile judgment about a law must consider three factors: its provisions, its enforcement, and its interpretation.

U.S. in the Caribbean

The Roosevelt corollary initiated a relationship between the United States and Latin America termed "Dollar Diplomacy." This means that the diplomacy of our government toward the republics to the south had as its main consideration the protection of investments made by American citizens in those countries. There was considerable truth in this view, but it was not the whole truth. Wherever there were large scale American businesses in Latin America, such as the United Fruit Co. and oil companies, they dominated the economy of the area and sometimes the government of the republic. Corrupt deals between business and government were probably easy to arrange, perhaps difficult to avoid. Contributions to a dictator in return for freedom to maintain a near slave-labor policy would be a practical two-way bargain. The American business would keep costs down and profits up, while the dictator could rely upon U.S. Marines to put down any revolt against his rule. The U.S. Marines would not be employed to support the dictator, but to protect American lives and property. This was a legal distinction only. To the revolutionists the obvious fact was that American business exploited native labor with the connivance of the hated dictator and that this situation was maintained by the power of the United States. Had American businessmen been saintly in their dealings with Latin American governments and generous in their treatment of native labor, the explosiveness of Latin American politics would have resulted in repeated revolutions and destruction of property. There simply was no way to avoid serious trouble between these unstable governments and foreign businesses. A good case can certainly be made in support of the view that American investments have been much to the advantage of the republics. But more important, no matter how unfortunate the presence of U.S. Marines may have been in particular instances, the fact of historical significance is that at no time was the United States following a policy of "peaceful penetration" as a prelude to empire building. Our armed forces may have been too frequently uninvited and unwelcomed guests, but there was never any doubt that they would go home. During the time of dollar diplomacy, England, France, Germany, Japan, and Russia were grabbing pieces of Asia and Africa. United States power, misdirected into dollar diplomacy, was the same power that stood behind the Monroe Doctrine and put Latin America off bounds for the colony seekers. Measured by an artificial ideal of how nations should behave, dollar diplomacy has a shabby appearance; measured by a realistic standard of how nations were then behaving, dollar diplomacy was a minor misdemeanor under conditions that would have tempted other great powers into unabashed colonialism.

Nicaragua

In 1911 President Taft approved a loan by New York bankers of $1,500,000 to Nicaragua. To make sure the terms of repayment were fulfilled, Americans operated the National Bank of Nicaragua and U.S. marines were stationed there until 1933.

In 1916 under Wilson the Senate ratified the Bryan-Chamarro Treaty by which the United States paid $3,000,000 for a right of way for a canal through southern Nicaragua, the right to build a naval base on Fonseca Bay, and the islands of Great and Little Corn off Nicaragua's east coast. This purchase of a canal route and defense points at the Pacific and Atlantic ends of it was prompted by the fear that some other nation might do the

same. As a result of the treaty, Nicaragua has been called a dependency or a protectorate of the United States.

In 1926 General Sandino led a liberal insurrection against the just elected President, Chamarro. President Coolidge refused to recognize Chamarro, neither did he approve of Sandino who was pictured in many American newspapers as a bandit leader. U.S. troops intervened by supporting a conservative candidate, Adolfo Diaz, who became President. After he had served out his term an election was supervised by the United States. As a result a liberal candidate became President in 1928. Five years later the last of the marines were withdrawn from Nicaragua by President Hoover.

Dominican Republic

Under T. Roosevelt the finances of the Dominican Republic had been put in good order in 1907 (see p. 183), but from 1912-15 revolution and general irresponsibility brought the Dominican finances to a chaotic state. President Wilson sent in troops which established a military government in November 1916. By 1922 the finances were in good order. The next two years settled the political disorders as authority was gradually transferred to the Dominicans. With the election of a president in July 1924 the U.S. forces were withdrawn.

Haiti

Haiti had two revolutions within six months early in 1915. Because she was unable to meet her financial obligations, President Wilson sent in U.S. troops and took over the island which we governed until 1934. During this time the United States held Haiti in receivership; that is, the people of Haiti elected their own officials whose decisions, especially in the field of finances, were subject to our approval. An occupation of this duration may have seemed permanent to the people of Haiti, but there was no doubt on the part of the governments of Haiti and the United States that the arrangement was temporary.

Virgin Islands

In 1917 both Denmark and the United States feared Germany might take the Virgin Islands, an eastern outpost of the Caribbean Sea. President Wilson arranged the purchase of the islands for $25,000,000. Prohibition wrecked their economy to such an extent that President Hoover called them "an effective poorhouse." In 1927 the natives were made citizens of the United States, in 1936 the islands were organized as a territory, and in 1938 universal suffrage was adopted. The repeal of prohibition in 1933 improved the economic status of the islands which, nevertheless, remained a serious problem.

* U.S. and Mexico

By 1910 Porfirio Diaz had been dictator of Mexico for over 30 years. During his regime foreign investments, mostly American, totaled about $2 billion with the biggest single investment in oil. Diaz had maintained order and granted liberal concessions to foreign companies. In 1911 Diaz was forced by the liberal revolutionary leader, Francisco Madero, to resign, but not until there had been considerable destruction of property and some Americans had lost their lives. President Taft recognized the Madero government and made no move toward military occupation. In February, 1913, Madero was assassinated by an agent of General Huerta. American business interests strongly urged the recognition of Huerta, but Taft refused. Within two weeks President Wilson was inaugurated. He expressed disapproval of dictators who attained their position by assassination, declared that he would not pursue a policy of dollar diplomacy, refused to recognize Huerta as president, and announced a policy of "watchful waiting." Wilson soon told Huerta that the United States would use its influence to force him from power. An embargo was put on arms shipments to Huerta, but their sale to his enemies was encouraged. In addition a naval blockade off Veracruz was established to prevent military supplies getting to Huerta from other countries.

On April 9, 1914 unarmed marines from the U.S.S. *Dolphin* went ashore for supplies at Tampico. They inadvertently entered a restricted zone and were arrested. A superior Mexican officer quickly released them with apologies. Admiral Mayo demanded a formal apology and a 21 gun salute to the American flag. Huerta pointed out that formal apologies and 21 gun salutes could hardly be official until the American President recognized the Mexican President. This was interpreted as a refusal by Huerta, and Wilson ordered the occupation of Veracruz, Mexico's greatest port. The real reason for the seizure of the port was the shipment from Germany to Veracruz of arms to Huerta. The Tampico episode was merely a convenient excuse. On April 21, 1914, U.S. ships bombarded Veracruz, and the marines occupied the city. Wilson was determined on two points: not to permit Huerta to retain power and not to allow this incident to develop into war. When Argentina, Brazil, and Chile suggested arbitration, Wilson quickly agreed. These three nations met with the United States and Mexico at the A.B.C. Conference at Niagara Falls, Canada during late May and all of June 1914. The result was that Huerta went into exile (to Long Island, N.Y.); Carranza, favored by Wilson, was recognized as president of Mexico, and late in 1914 the marines left Veracruz.

The Zimmermann note was an interesting bit of news that broke on March 1, 1917. The British navy had intercepted and decoded a message sent by the German foreign minister to the German ambassador at Mexico City. It contained instructions to be carried out by the ambassador if and when the United States entered the war against Germany. Mexico was to be promised her "lost territory in New Mexico, Texas, and Arizona" in return for entering the war as an ally of Germany.

* The Lusitania (May 1915)

A few days before the *Lusitania* left New York on her last voyage, a notice signed by the Imperial German Embassy was printed in the New York *Times* and some other papers. It stated that ships flying the British flag and traveling in the war zone adjacent to the British Isles were liable to destruction. A direct communication from the German Embassy to the American people was a gross violation of diplomatic procedure. As the largest luxury liner afloat, the *Lusitania,* was about to sail, many took the notice as a warning for that particular trip. Some cancelled their reservations; others bought them up on the chance that something exciting might happen. The queen of the seas with several watertight compartments was alleged to be unsinkable. But on May 7th at 2 P.M. off the Irish coast Submarine Captain Schwieger wrote in his log, "Right ahead appeared four funnels and two masts of a steamer. Clean bow-shot from 700-meter range. Shot hits starboard side right behind bridge. An unusually heavy detonation follows . . . In the front appears the name *Lusitania* in gold letters." (Total aboard—1,924; total lost—1,198; Americans killed—128.) Part of the *Lusitania's* cargo, over 4,000 cases of rifle cartridges, was contraband. International law made such a ship a legal target for enemy action, but it also provided that a warning shot be fired across her bow to stop her and, if she then stopped, there must be reasonable provision made for the safety of the passengers and crew. The Germans were faced with a choice of not using submarines against merchant ships or violating international law. The choice they made was inevitable just as it was in World War II when swarms of bombers blasted whole cities off the map, and when finally two bombs were dropped on two Japanese cities. In 1915 people seriously discussed the rules of war; now we know better.

Reactions differed sharply throughout America. "Deliberate murder," "savages drunk with power" expressed one view; "Real patriots keep cool" was another; and President Wilson, determined to stay neutral, said there was such a thing as "being too proud to fight." Congress talked of passing laws forbidding American citizens to travel on ships of belligerents. Wilson favored protests and insistence on our rights as a neutral. But Secretary of State Bryan resigned because he thought such a course would lead to war. Theodore Roosevelt wanted war right away, or at least a break in relations with Germany. In such times of crisis the president is a lonely man. He must sometimes make decisions based upon information that can not be made public. For example, in this instance Wilson could have known that German espionage was well established and poised for action throughout the United States, while we had not yet built a defense against it. If so, a premature declaration of war for any reason would result in industrial plants, railroads, bridges, etc. sabotaged or destroyed—a national disaster. Such a situation could not be publicly acknowledged. Perhaps there is some virtue in the thought that simply because a person is president, in time of crisis he deserves an extra bit of confidence from the people.

* Sussex Pledge Broken (Feb. 1917)

On August 19, 1915 two American lives were lost when the British passenger ship *Arabic* was torpedoed. The German Ambassador at Washington, Von Bernstorff, assured our government on September 1st that "Liners will not be sunk by our submarines without warning and without safety of the lives of non-combatants, provided that the liners do not try to escape or offer resistance." A month later the German government offered an indemnity for the loss of American lives on the *Arabic*. Wilson's insistence on our rights as a neutral seemed to be bringing results, although this pledge referred only to passenger ships.

On March 24, 1916 the French passenger liner *Sussex* was sunk in the English channel with the loss of several lives and injury to some Americans. President Wilson sent an ultimatum to Germany on April 18th demanding an immediate end to Germany's "present method of submarine warfare" under penalty of an immediate severance of relations, a diplomatic action preceding a declaration of war. On May 4th Germany pledged that she would abide by Wilson's demands on condition that the United States would compel the Allies to respect international law in their naval warfare. Wilson accepted the pledge and rejected the condition. From the spring of 1916 to February, 1917, there was a lull in submarine activity. We believed it to be the result of the "Sussex Pledge" and, as it coincided with the presidential campaign of 1916, the slogan "He kept us out of war" helped Wilson tremendously. Later we learned that submarines were being called back to German shipyards for improvements and that Germany was considering diplomatic moves toward a negotiated peace. In short, the Germans had their own reasons for calling off the submarine activity.

On January 31, 1917 Ambassador Von Bernstorff informed Secretary of State Lansing that on the following day the German government would begin a new submarine campaign. The United States was to be allowed one ship a week to the British Isles and three a week to Mediterranean ports. They were to travel in designated shipping lanes, have their funnels and hull painted with broad red and white stripes, and fly a red and white checkered flag at each funnel and mast. This was both an insult and a breaking of the Sussex pledge. On February 3rd an American ship was torpedoed and that same day President Wilson announced that the relations between Germany and the United States were severed. He made it clear that additional "actual overt acts" would result in war. On March 16 three American vessels were sunk by submarines. On April 2nd Wilson asked Congress for a declaration of war which the Senate approved by a vote of 82 to 6 on April 4th, and the House approved by 373 to 50 on April 6th. The United States was at war.

* Organizing for War

Liberty Loans and War Revenue Acts

The government's policy was to raise about 2/3rds of the war's cost by borrowing (selling bonds) and the other 1/3rd by taxes. During the war there were four Liberty Loans (bond issues) and after the war in 1919, a Victory Loan. Instead of borrowing in large sums from banks, as was the case in the Civil War, the government borrowed as little as $50 from individuals. One could buy war stamps at any post office for 25¢ and stick them in a booklet provided for the purpose; when the book was full it could be turned in for a $50 liberty bond. These five bond issues raised over $21 billion.

The most important special war tax was the increased levies on incomes with a graduated rate beginning at 4% and reaching a maximum at 65%. Corporations were taxed from 20% to 60% on excess profits, excess meaning profits above the level the corporation earned before the war in 1911-13. Railroad tickets, telephone and telegraph messages, theater tickets, liquor, gasoline, and whatever else Congress could think of bore a special war tax. Income from taxes totaled about $11¼ billion.

Railroads and Ships

In the summer of 1916 the railroad workers' unions were demanding more pay and shorter hours. The war in Europe had caused a boom in business which was reflected in higher wages, higher prices, and a manpower shortage in many occupations. As a public utility with rates subject to regulation by the Interstate Commerce Commission, a railroad's income did not respond to market conditions as easily and quickly as that of private business. The wages of railroad employees also failed to keep pace with those of other workers. A strike was set for September 8th. President Wilson pointed out that the nation was mobilizing its strength under the threat of war; under no conditions could a stoppage of the railroads be permitted. At the last minute Congress passed the Adamson Act which gave railroad workers an 8 hour day with the same pay they had received for a 10 hour day, plus time and a half for overtime. It also gave the President power to take over the railroads if, for military reasons, he thought it necessary.

Soon after we entered the war, several railroad presidents organized an association to promote efficiency and to do their full share in the war effort. Even though rates had been adjusted to meet the added costs of the Adamson Act, the price-wage spiral kept climbing to create special problems for railroads. With industry booming there was a shortage of freight cars, which meant that railroads sent them where the demand of high-paying freight was greatest. Within a few months railroads were busy shuttling valuable freight (good pay-loads) up and down the eastern seaboard. But the war effort required the movement of vast stores of grain from west of the Mississippi to ships waiting empty in Atlantic ports; it needed miles and miles of cars hauling soft coal to war plants. As there was not enough equipment to do both jobs well, the most profitable task got the most attention. Empty ships, hills of grain exposed to the weather, railroads busy hauling freight of secondary importance, and a food shortage threatened on the western front was a combination that led on December 12, 1917 to the seizure of the railroads by President Wilson. William G. McAdoo became Railroad Administrator and soon had the traffic difficulties straightened out. He enforced a system of priorities, discouraged un-necessary passenger traffic, placed embargoes on non-essential freight, and coordinated all roads into serving the war effort. The cost was tremendous and the railroad equipment was not well maintained; but the real job, getting what Uncle Sam needed to the place he needed it at the time he had to have it, was superbly done.

The Esch-Cummins Act of 1920 (Transportation Act of 1920) returned the railroads to private operation. In running all the roads as one coordinated system, the government had become convinced of the efficiency and economy consolidation promoted. What Morgan, Hill, and Harriman had tried to do in forming the Northern Securities Co. was the economic way to organize the roads (see p. 180). The main features of the act were as follows:

1] The Interstate Commerce Commission can evaluate railroad property and fix rates that will yield a fair return.

2] The Commission was to work out a plan for consolidating the railroads into fewer systems in order to improve service.

3] A railroad Labor Board was set up to settle disputes between labor and management.

The end of World War I just about marks the beginning of the decline of railroads. Automobiles, trucks, busses, and finally planes became stronger competitors year by year. The depression '30's hit railroads hard and they have been sick ever since. But they are still indispensable to the national economy and promise to remain so for the indefinite future.

In September, 1916, Congress set up a shipping board of five members empowered to build, lease, requisition, and purchase ships; that is, to get ships any way they could. This was done effectively through the Emergency Fleet Corporation created 10 days after we declared war. Enemy merchantmen in American ports were seized, neutral ships were bought, private ships were requisitioned, ship yards, some newly built, performed miracles of construction in wooden, steel, prefabricated, and even concrete ships. By such means the Emergency Fleet Corporation supplied 10 million tons of shipping which meant that we were increasing our tonnage about twice as fast as the submarines were sinking it. It was a marvelous job of meeting the demands of the war and, as with the railroads, it was done at a very high cost.

Council of National Defense and War Industries Board

In the late summer of 1916, Secretary of War Newton D. Baker was appointed head of the Council of National Defense formed of six other cabinet members. Seven prominent civilians served as advisors to the Council. It took an inventory of our resources, raw, human, professional, industrial, educational, and managerial. It assessed farms, factories, and transportation facilities. Because this Council did the preliminary planning to put the nation on a war footing, it was possible to set up the War Industries Board early in the war.

In late July, 1916, the War Industries Board was created to supervise all war industries. Bernard Baruch was its chairman for most of the war. He had authority to convert factories to war work, to allocate fuel and materials, to fix prices and purchase supplies. He was truly a czar of industry. One writer described the size of his job by saying that he united 28,000 factories into one production "trust." Another emphasized the difficulty of his job by listing a few of the problems he faced. "Should locomotives go to Pershing to help him get ammunition to the front, or should they go to Chile to haul nitrates, without which there would be no ammunition? Should steel go to destroyers whose mission was to sink the submarines, or to merchant ships, which the submarines had thinned to the point of breaking down the food supplies to the Allies? Should nitrates go to munitions, without which the guns were useless, or to fertilizers, without which the artillerymen would be foodless? Should cranes go to the American wharves for loading ships for France, or to French wharves for unloading the same ships?" Our industrial production during the war was so great that it amazed ourselves, our Allies, and our enemies.

Lever Food and Fuel Act

Herbert Hoover headed the Food Administration. He had already won a world-wide reputation by his work in Belgian War Relief. As Food Administrator he could fix prices on staple foods and do whatever seemed effective to "stimulate and conserve the production and control the distribution of foods." The law prevented the use of grain for the manufacture of alcoholic beverages. A very effective program worked well because the public cooperated wholeheartedly; it included wheatless Mondays, meatless Tuesdays, and porkless Thursdays. The farmers expanded acreage and stepped up production until they were feeding America, much of war-torn Europe, and the allied armed forces. The farmers' great contribution to the war effort was to turn into the "farm problem" soon after the armistice.

Harry Garfield was Fuel Administrator. His powers and responsibilities paralleled those of Hoover for food. Monday was fuelless day when householders kept the temperature no higher than 65 degrees. Sunday was gasless day when anyone driving a private car other than in a funeral procession felt embarrassed. Non-essential factories often were shut down so that their fuel supply could be transferred to a war plant. Electric advertising signs remained unlighted and daylight saving was instituted.

Overman Act

In May, 1918, President Wilson was given unprecedented powers by the Overman Act which was to be in effect only during the war. It allowed him to create or abolish executive bureaus, agencies, and offices; to shift personnel from one to another; to reallocate funds from one to another; in short, to do as he thought best for the conduct of the war. Congress had granted his requests when based on war necessity, and it seemed as if it had decided to let the President go ahead as he saw fit, instead of rubber-stamping his requests one by one.

** "14 Points (Jan. 1918)

On January 8th the President addressed Congress to state the war aims and peace terms of the United States. He called it the "only possible" program that could maintain world peace. Some points dealt with territorial adjustments of immediate concern, and others stated principles which Wilson thought should guide and permeate international relationships. We are concerned with the latter only.

1] Open covenants (treaties) openly arrived at.

When nations know that there may be secret agreements, they can never be sure that the treaties they have made are not undermined. Secret treaties weaken all treaties and create mutual distrust among nations. "Openly arrived at" does not prevent confidential discussions, but it does mean that any agreements made by such secret diplomacy must be publicized.

2] Absolute freedom of the seas in peace and war.

There is rarely any trouble about freedom of the seas in time of peace. During a major war freedom of the seas has never been maintained. Wilson looked to the "association of nations" of his 14th point to enforce freedom of the seas in time of war.

3] Removal of barriers to international trade.

This referred to tariffs, quota systems, and any artificial hindrances to commerce.

4] Reduction of armaments to the point where

each nation has only a police force to keep domestic order.

5] Self determination of peoples.

Throughout the world any area which has the extent and resources to be a nation should be governed according to the free choice of its people.

6] A general association of nations must be formed.

Wilson stated this to be the most important of the 14 points. It could be a continuing force working to achieve a better world. To permit the continuance of international anarchy was to invite international suicide.

These six ideas are worth mulling over. How were they received in 1918? How much did they affect the Treaty of Versailles? What has been done about them? Are any of them now considered unwise or outmoded? Do any of them have historic roots?

The American Expeditionary Force in France

The month the United States entered the war was the peak of the submarine offensive. That April over 880,000 tons of shipping went to the bottom. The average monthly loss was 200,000 tons. The last six months of 1917 found the allies at their lowest point. They were maintaining a desperate defense with no capacity to mount an attack. The arrival of the first American troops in France on June 26th was a boost to allied morale, but little else. These troops took positions in the fighting front in late October. But there was bad news. In October the Italian army in the Caporetto campaign began to crumble; by December it had collapsed and left northeastern Italy to the Germans. The November revolution in Russia released huge German forces for use in France. American troops arrived at an accelerating rate to reach a total in one month, April 1918, of over 313,000. Before the war ended, American troops in France totaled 2,084,000. General John J. Pershing was in command of this A.E.F.

Chronology of Major Actions Involving Substantial American Forces

June 3-4 1918 Chateau-Thierry (Defensive)

June 6-July 1 Belleau Wood—27,500 U.S. troops with the French. Successful counter attack.

July 18-Aug. 6 2nd Battle of the Marne (Defensive) 85,000 U.S. troops. The German offensive begun in March was stopped here.

Aug. 8-Nov. 11 The Somme (Offensive) 54,000 U.S. troops with the British.

Aug. 19-Nov. 11 Ypres (Offensive) 108,000 U.S. troops with the British.

Sept. 12-16 St. Mihiel (Offensive) 550,000 U.S. troops wiped out a dangerous salient south of Verdun.

Sept. 26-Nov. 11 Meuse-Argonne (Offensive) 1,200,-000 U.S. troops.

The Armistice terms were signed at 5 A.M. and hostilities stopped at 11 A.M. Joy and thanksgiving throughout the United States were unbounded. Everyone seemed to be out in the streets laughing and half-crying. Utter strangers greeted one another as life-long friends. The usual barriers were down —the well dressed and the shabby; the educated and the uneducated; the upper crust and the under privileged; the "real" Americans and the first or second generation Americans; the genteel and the crude; the white, the brown, and the black for one glorious day recognized each other for what they really were, human beings. They shared one overwhelming emotion, "Thank God the war is over."

WAR COST

Dead   112,432 Americans (over ½ from disease, chiefly influenza)

Money Spent $21,850,000,000

Money loaned to Allies $10,350,000,000

* Treaty of Versailles

On October 24, 1918, President Wilson addressed the people through a press release devoted entirely to the Congressional elections less than two weeks away. He asked for the election of Democratic majorities in both Houses of Congress, not because "any political party is paramount in matters of patriotism," but because the times demand a "unified leadership, and that a Republican Congress would divide the leadership. . . . The return of a Republican majority to either House of Congress would, moreover, be interpreted on the other side of the water as a repudiation of my leadership. . . . It is well understood there as well as here that Republican leaders desire not so much to support the President as to control him." This was a most unfortunate and impolitic message. Unfortunate because the opportunity for successful compromise with the Republicans on plans for the peace should have been obvious to the President. There was no need to picture a successful treaty as something only Democrats could achieve. Whatever the outcome of the Congressional elections, bypartisan participation in the task of building the peace held the greatest promise. Impolitic because Wilson must have known that his message to the people might be resented by them as an attempt to wield undue influence in state affairs. His appeal for a Democratic Congress backfired. The Republicans won the House by 50 seats and the Senate by 2. According to his own words the President had been "repudiated" in the eyes of the governments of the Allies. Two weeks after the election he announced that he was going to Paris for the Peace Conference. A substantial objection to his trip was that, among the four advisors he had selected to go with him, only one was a Republican and none were Senators. If he came back with a treaty it would be the Senate that would either ratify it, or refuse to!

Wilson negotiated with Clemenceau of France, Lloyd George of Great Britain, and Orlando of Italy. These men, the Big Four, made most of the decisions. In order to get the League of Nations written into the treaty, Wilson gave in on some terms neither he nor the United States approved. He made the point that some inequities and mistakes, as we saw them, could be corrected later through the League of Nations as time proved them to be unwise. Wilson was a tough bargainer. He prevented France from annexing the Saar, kept Italy from getting Fiume, kept the Poles from getting East Prussia, stopped France from annexing the German Rhineland, and agreed to give Shantung to Japan only with a pledge that it would soon be given to China—as it was in 1921. There was nothing wrong with Wilson as a strong representative of the United States at the peace table; the trouble was that he did not have at least two Republican Senators with him.

The bulk of the Versailles Treaty was the Covenant of the League of Nations. Other terms included the forced admission of guilt by Germany for the war, the return of Alsace-Lorraine to France, the Saar Basin (rich in iron and coal) was put under the League of Nations for 15 years, after which the people could vote to go with either France or Germany; Danzig was made a Free City (To give Poland a seaport); the German Rhineland was demilitarized; and German colonies were mandated under the League of Nations. The ratification of this treaty, with the Covenant of the League of Na-

tions as the heart of it, became the great debate of the campaign of 1920.

* The War Record

A brief look back over World War I shows a job remarkably well done. The President, Congress, industry, agriculture, shipping, labor, the armed forces, and the people became an effective team. General Pershing proved to be a more than capable head of the A.E.F. About $4\frac{1}{2}$ million men were in the armed forces. Liberty Bonds and the Selective Service Act raised money and men wisely, effectively, and fairly. This was quite a contrast to the Civil War when about the only factors that were right were the strength and wisdom of Lincoln and the determination of the Union soldiers to outlast the Confederates. There was one blot on the picture, the almost hysterical behavior of too many people encouraged by Attorney General Palmer, the Espionage Act, and the Sedition Act. Not too thoughtful old ladies of both sexes equated a German accent with sabotage. Some schools dropped German and some libraries removed German books from the shelves, and some colleges revoked honorary degrees they had given to distinguished Germans. All this suggests that knowledge without understanding is still ignorance. After the war was over, the continuance in power of the Bolsheviks in Russia and the world-wide propaganda of the Third International created intolerance throughout the United States toward all sorts of non-conformists. New York expelled five Socialists elected to the state Assembly. They had won their seats legally in a regular campaign. The only reason given was that, in the opinion of the other members of the Assembly, Socialism was "absolutely inimical to the best interests of the state of New York and of the United States." Charles E. Hughes, ex-Republican Governor of the state and to become Chief Justice of the Supreme Court, and Governor Alfred E. Smith vigorously protested this action, but to no avail. Getting down to bed rock, ballots are a civilized substitute for bullets as a means of settling differences of opinion. If the ballot is made completely useless, men are likely to have recourse to bullets.

Warren G. Harding

1921-1923

1865 - 1923

REPUBLICAN

☆

Vice-President CALVIN COOLIDGE

Secretary of State CHARLES E. HUGHES

HARDING'S PUBLIC SERVICE BEFORE HE BECAME PRESIDENT

> Senator in the Ohio Legislature
> United States Senator from Ohio (1915-21)

MAJOR ITEMS OF HARDING'S ADMINISTRATION

> Washington Conference (1921-22)
> Fordney-McCumber Tariff (1922)

Election of Harding (1920)

Ohio's Senator Harding was nominated at the Republican Convention with Governor Coolidge of Massachusetts as his running mate. After their victory at the mid-term elections, the Republicans felt that any good Republican could beat any Democrat. This made political sense because, with Republicans still the larger party, the Democrats could win only when the Republicans split (mugwumps vs stalwarts—Old Guard vs insurgents—Taft regulars vs Roosevelt progressives). Harding was a dark horse selection made after more prominent candidates had fought to a deadlock through 9 ballots. The Old Guard picked him. His qualifications included a pleasing personality, party regularity, handsome appearance, and no enemies. Harding's speeches reflected faithfully the confusion written into the Republican platform which at the same time opposed the League of Nations and favored an "agreement among nations to preserve the peace of the world." He seemed sometimes to be flatly against the League and at others to favor it with a few modifications. This strategy resulted from differences within the party. Those who were strongly opposed to the League would certainly support Harding; but, on the other hand, such Republican leaders of caliber as Elihu Root, Charles E. Hughes, and Herbert Hoover said that a vote for Harding was the best way to get the United States into the League with some reservations to safeguard American interests.

James M. Cox, also from Ohio, was nominated at the Democratic Convention with Franklin Roosevelt as his running mate. The platform advocated ratification of the Versailles Treaty which contained the Covenant of the League of Nations. On the question of accepting the League with reservations, the platform stated that there were no objections to "any reservations making clearer or more specific the obligations of the United States to the League associates." The Democrats were intent upon making the League of Nations the one issue of the campaign; but the Republican tactic of facing in all directions prevented it. The real debate on the League was over. It had begun in September 1919 when Wilson decided to take his cause to the people. He had started on a western tour speaking to large enthusiastic audiences. He had been followed a few days later by Republican Senator Lodge who spoke against the League. On September 26th Wilson had started back east from Colorado when he collapsed and was incapacitated for the rest of his term. With the loss of his eloquence and crusading zeal the vitality had gone out of the debate.

Harding advocated a "return to normalcy." *Normalcy* wasn't then in the dictionary, but it caught the public fancy. It certainly suggested a return to the days when we were not entangled in foreign problems, pestered by demands for reforms, and annoyed by government regulations. During the war the people had responded to the idealism of Wilson, they had accepted government controls, they had sacrificed individual freedoms for a cause bigger than themselves—and now they were weary. Let's "return to normalcy" were welcome words, even though they were nonsense. There never have been any "good old days" to which to return, and war creates problems as our generation should well know. Ignoring difficulties does not make them dissolve; but turning away from difficulties was, understandably, the temper of the people in 1920. When the ballots were counted, the overwhelming Republican victory was "explained" in terms of a protest against government regulation, high taxes, the H.C. of L. (high cost of living), weariness from the war, and perhaps the League of Nations.

	Popular Vote	Electoral Vote
Harding	16,152,200	404
Cox	9,147,353	127
Debs	919,799	0

This was the first presidential election in which women voted.

Debs had been convicted of sedition and ran his campaign from the federal penitentiary in Atlanta.

* Washington Conference (November 12, 1921-February 6, 1922)

This conference was called to ease tensions that existed over the situation in the Far East and to reduce naval armaments. The nations represented were Belgium, China, France, Great Britain, Italy, Japan, Netherlands, Portugal, and the United States. Secretary of State Hughes was chairman of the conference.

The trouble in the Far East had started in 1915 when the Japanese made "21 Demands" upon China, some of them violating the Open Door (see pp. 175-176) and the Root-Takahira agreement (see pp. 183-184). Our protests carried little weight because we were in no position to use force in that area. Japanese-American relations were strained at the time by the action of California in passing laws prohibiting ownership of land by Japanese. In spite of protests by President Wilson, California persisted in this discriminatory policy which violated the "most favored nation" agreement we had made, an agreement which obligated the United States to give all Japanese in America equal privileges with others. During World War I the Japanese took the German islands in the Pacific and the German sphere of influence in China, the Shantung peninsula with its port of Kiao-chow. When Russia was weakened by revolution, Japan moved into Manchuria.

The Conference resulted in a series of treaties.

1] The Five Power Pact (United States, Great Britain, Japan, France, and Italy) provided for the limitation of naval armaments. The ratio of capital ships (over 10,000 tons displacement) was to be United States—5; Great Britain—5; Japan—3; France—1¾; and Italy—1¾. For a period of 10 years no new capital ships were to be built. The United States and Great Britain already had more than their quota of capital ships so both destroyed some and cancelled their plans for others. The United States, Great Britain and Japan agreed to maintain the "status quo" of their "fortifications and naval bases" in the Far East. Japan returned Shantung with its port of Kiao-chow to China. The fact that smaller cruisers, submarines, destroyers, etc. were not limited made the treaty meaningless as far as maintaining any ratio of strength of one navy to another. But the treaty reduced naval appropriations for a while and gave hope (which turned out to be false) for the future.

2] A Four Power Pact (United States, Great Britain, France, and Japan) agreed to respect each others rights in the Pacific Ocean region and to settle by peaceful means disagreements that might arise. This replaced an Anglo-Japanese Alliance of 1905 which had worried Australia, New Zealand, Canada, and the United States.

3] A Nine Power Pact (including all nations at the conference) provided that China's political and territorial sovereignty would be respected. It was also agreed that submarines should be used only in accordance with the recognized rules of war. The use of asphyxiating gases in warfare was outlawed.

* Fordney-McCumber Tariff (1922)

The Republicans were anxious to get back to the protective tariff policies of McKinley, Dingley, and Aldrich. Europe's industrial plant had not recovered appreciably from the war, and her only path toward economic improvement was the gradual increase of manufacturing for export trade. Not until their peoples became prosperous enough to pay taxes could the governments get money to pay war debts. Fearing Europe's efforts to sell in the American market, Congress passed the Fordney-McCumber tariff. It was the highest yet. Apparently Congress was not attracted to Wilson's idea that lowering trade barriers was essential to international peace. There were no immediate ill effects from the tariff. The twenties were to be known as the "gilded twenties" because we experienced a frothy prosperity as we headed for the 1929 crash. The real harm in the Fordney-McCumber tariff was the example it set. Other nations were bound to retaliate. We started the same merry-go-round that the thirteen states rode to destruction under the Articles of Confederation; only this time, a large part of the world was involved. As tariff walls went up, many American manufacturers established plants in foreign countries. Some leading industrialists and bankers retreated from their support of protection as they awoke to the fact that foreign trade has to be a two-way street. This economic truth did not penetrate quickly or easily. It was after the depression '30's that more and more nations turned to reciprocal trade agreements as a method of chipping away at the tariff walls that never should have been built.

Calvin Coolidge

1923-1929

1872 - 1933

REPUBLICAN

☆

Secretary of State FRANK B. KELLOGG

COOLIDGE'S PUBLIC SERVICE BEFORE HE BECAME PRESIDENT

Mayor of Northampton, Mass.
Lieutenant Governor of Massachusetts
Governor of Massachusetts
Vice-President of the United States

MAJOR ITEMS OF COOLIDGE'S ADMINISTRATION

Oil in the Cabinet
Oil in Mexico
Kellogg-Briand Peace Pact (Pact of Paris) (1928)

Election of Coolidge (1924)

While returning from a trip to Alaska, President Harding died at San Francisco on August 2nd 1923. He had found the responsibilities of the office of President too great for his capacities. Under the most favorable circumstances Harding would probably have been miserable under the strain, and conditions were far from favorable. He had brought too many "friends" with him from Ohio, some of whom had helped him up the political ladder. In the Ohio legislature and in the United States Senate, Harding had enjoyed fronting for the political bosses behind him and he clearly understood that political debts were to be paid. He had not been President long, before he realized that several important appointments made on the basis of political spoils had gone sour. Harding lacked the moral courage to attack corruption when those involved were his friends. His suspicions, if not actual knowledge, of criminal malfeasance by high officials may well have been an important factor in the illness which sent him on the trip to Alaska in an attempt to rest. Had he returned to Washington it would have been to face a major scandal.

Vice-President Coolidge was visiting his father in the little Vermont village of Plymouth Notch when the news of Harding's death aroused the household from their beds. By the light of a kerosene lamp, Coolidge took the oath of office as President of the United States. His father, Justice of the Peace John Coolidge, administered the oath.

Coolidge was quite unlike Harding; he was neither handsome nor congenial; no one could lead him where he didn't want to go; he was thrifty and honest; a modest bit of granite out of the cold Vermont hills. The end of Harding's term was a sordid story of scandal. Nothing could have been better for the Republicans than the presence of Calvin Coolidge in the White House.

The Republican Convention met at Cleveland and nominated Coolidge by an almost unanimous vote. The platform called for a continuation of the Fordney-McCumber tariff, membership in the World Court, international coöperation to prevent war, and limitation of armaments. Our attitude toward the League of Nations was still one of confusion. We wouldn't join it, but we favored its purposes and frequently worked with it.

The Democrats tore their party apart at the Convention in New York. William G. McAdoo of Tennessee and Alfred E. Smith of New York battled for 101 ballots. Each controlled over ⅓ of the votes and, under the ⅔ rule of Democratic nominating conventions, could prevent the other from winning. Finally both candidates withdrew and on the 103rd ballot John W. Davis, a conservative, was nominated. There was no such thing as a better conservative than Calvin Coolidge so, in a listless election, the Republicans won almost without a contest.

	Popular Vote	Electoral Vote
Coolidge	15,725,016	382
Davis	8,385,586	136

* Oil in the Cabinet

Before Harding had gone on his Alaska trip, there were rumors of graft in the President's official family. About two months after his death, a Senate committee under Thomas Walsh of Montana was formed to investigate oil leases made to private companies from government reserves in Wyoming (Teapot Dome) and California (Elk Hills). These reserves of oil had been set aside under Taft and Wilson for the use of the navy. In its essentials, the story uncovered was as follows. Soon after his inauguration, President Harding transfered the Teapot Dome and Elk Hills oil reserves from the Navy Department (Secretary Denby) to the Interior Department (Secretary Fall). Denby approved of this transfer. Fall then entered into a secret, illegal, and corrupt deal with two oil men, Harry Sinclair and Edward Doheny. Without competitive bidding and at a bargain price, Teapot Dome was leased to Sinclair who had made a large contribution to the Republican campaign in 1920; and the Elk Hills reserve was leased to Doheny, a close friend of Fall. In March, 1923, Fall resigned from the cabinet much richer than before he entered it.

The investigating committee discovered that Fall had received a "loan" of $100,000 from Doheny on which he was charged no interest, for which he put up no security, and for which no arrangements had been made for repayment. Fall also received a "loan" of about $300,000 from Sinclair. His private financial situation had suddenly changed from near bankruptcy to high prosperity. Fall went to jail for accepting a bribe from Doheny, but stangely enough, in a separate trial a jury found Doheny not guilty of giving Fall the bribe. Doheny and Sinclair were tried on charges of "conspiracy to defraud the government" and were acquitted; but the Supreme Court declared the leases cancelled because they were a "conspiracy" involving "fraud" and "corruption." Secretary of the Navy Denby resigned during the Senate investigations.

Attorney General Daugherty should have been aware of the oil deal before the Senate started to investigate. He was one of Harding's appointees known as the Ohio gang. The apparent ignorance of the Justice Department of what was going on suggested, at the very best, incompetence. Investigation brought out gross irregularities. Daugherty had been bribed by prohibition law violaters and he had known of graft in the Veterans' Bureau, but had done nothing about it. He was tried for conspiracy and acquitted. President Coolidge forced him to resign.

Colonel Forbes, head of the Veterans' Bureau went to jail for conspiring to sell narcotics, liquor, and other government property. Colonel Thomas Miller, Custodian of Alien Property, sold German chemical patents for such small sums that bribery seemed the only explanation. He went to prison for "conspiring to defraud the government."

** Oil in Mexico

Under Coolidge a long and difficult controversy with Mexico was finally put on the right road to a settlement. The trouble started with the new Mexican constitution of 1917. Article 27 stated that all mineral wealth (including oil) in Mexico belonged to the government and concessions to develop mineral resources could be granted only to Mexican nationals. This was not a necessary source of friction unless Article 27 was made retroactive. The United States was ready to accept the view that Mexico could do what it wished with its natural resources provided property rights already acquired by Americans were not disturbed. Americans had about $300,000,000 in such investments by 1919. Under Wilson's protégé, Carranza, we had no trouble. In 1919 Obregon became President and would give no assurance one way or the other, an attitude we took to be unfriendly. We increased our border patrol to proportions suggesting intervention, but tension was relieved when the Mexican Supreme Court declared that Article 27 did not apply to properties acquired before the adoption of the constitution of 1917. In 1925 President Calles embarked on a revolutionary reform program to redistribute land, to break the power of the Roman Catholic Church, and to confiscate foreign holdings of mineral wealth under Article 27. Secretary of State Kellogg advised Coolidge to consider intervention, but the Senate disapproved and public opinion was not in favor of a war over American oil properties in Mexico. President Coolidge sent his friend of Amherst College days, Dwight W. Morrow, as ambassador to Mexico. Painstakingly and patiently Morrow persuaded President Calles that the United States basically approved of his revolutionary aims and that it was only the confiscation of lawful property to which we objected. We agreed with Mexico that it would be good to have Mexico own her own natural resources, but the transfer of ownership must be accomplished by purchase at a fair price, not by confiscation. Morrow made himself a very welcome ambassador in Mexico City and set the pattern for the eventual solution of American investments in Mexican land and minerals. There were difficulties along the way. Mexico passed minimum wage laws in 1938 which applied to oil companies and set a date for them to go into effect. The American oil companies claimed they would go bankrupt if they paid the new wages. The deadline passed, the Mexican government declared the oil properties seized, the oil companies then agreed to pay the new wage, but the government refused to allow it. This would have accomplished confiscation through the ruse of a minimum wage law. The United States threatened to stop the purchase of silver from Mexico, a move that would be a serious economic blow. This episode was handled by Secretary of State Cordell Hull under F. D. Roosevelt. Through such situations the United States did not threaten intervention, but persisted along the lines drawn out by Morrow. By 1942 a settlement set a fair price and a schedule of payment. With the foreigners gone, the Mexicans made a dismal failure of operating the wells and refineries; which, instead of yielding handsome profits went into the red. Mexico called for help, which meant the hiring of American and other foreign personnel to come to Mexico to teach Mexicans how to operate the oil business. This took a few years and worked out well. This record of peaceful withdrawal from Mexico, of preventing confiscation, and helping Mexico to gain control of her own natural resources was an accomplishment of which to be proud. We got started in the right direction under Coolidge and the program was carried to completion under Hoover and F. D. Roosevelt.

* Kellogg-Briand Treaty (Pact of Paris) (1928)

Ten years after the end of World War I, Secretary of State Frank Kellogg decided to give the anniversary suitable recognition. Briand, the French foreign minister, had suggested a bilateral agreement to outlaw war. Kellogg suggested a multilateral agreement. Eventually 62 nations signed it.

The "outlawry of war" was a pledge to reject war as an instrument of international policy. Up until this time, war had been a legally respectable, though drastic, procedure by which nations sought to accomplish their purposes. The Kellogg-Briand Treaty made war a criminal act on the part of any nation signing the agreement.

There was no force to back it up except the moral influence of world opinion, and war was restricted to mean only offensive war. What nation started a particular war or was to blame for it, is a question about which another war may be started. In spite of these two weaknesses, the treaty brought some hope to the people at the time and, if war is ever outlawed, the Kellogg-Briand Treaty will be considered a mile post along that road.

Herbert Hoover

1874 - 1964

REPUBLICAN

☆

Secretary of State HENRY L. STIMSON

HOOVER'S PUBLIC SERVICE BEFORE HE BECAME PRESIDENT

Headed War Relief in Belgium
Food Administrator in World War I
Secretary of Commerce under Harding and Coolidge

MAJOR ITEMS OF HOOVER'S ADMINISTRATION

National Origins Immigration Act (1929)
Panic and Depression
Hawley-Smoot Tariff (1930)

* Hoover's Election (1928)

President Coolidge could have had the nomination, but he had said several months before the convention, "I do not choose to run." New Englanders knew that when one of them did "not choose" to do something it meant he was *not* going to do it. At the convention in Kansas City, Mo. the Republicans nominated Herbert Hoover. He had shown great capacity as an administrator in Belgian Relief and as Food Administrator; he had become a very wealthy man as a mining engineer and consultant, a business career that had taken him to China, Africa, Latin America, and Russia. He was looked upon by the people as a humanitarian and a businessman, one who combined a sympathetic understanding of great human needs with the practical ability to administer a program with businesslike efficiency. He seemed the ideal man to give more business in government and less government in business. The platform favored the continuance of prohibition and protective tariff. In his "rugged individualism" speech at the close of the campaign (Oct. 22nd), Hoover expressed his philosophy of government. The following quotations are worth consideration.

"To a large degree we regimented our whole people temporarily into a socialistic state. However justified in time of war if continued in peace-time it would destroy not only our American system but with it our progress and freedom as well."

"If anyone will study the causes of retarded recuperation in Europe, he will find much of it due to stifling of private initiative on the one hand, and overloading of the government with business on the other."

"Every step of bureaucratizing of the business of our country poisons the very roots of liberalism—that is, political equality, free speech, free assembly, free press, and equality of opportunity."

". . . economic freedom cannot be sacrificed if political freedom is to be preserved."

"Nor do I wish to be misinterpreted as believing that the United States is free-for-all and devil-take-the-hindmost. . . . On the contrary, it demands economic justice as well as political and social justice. It is no system of laissez faire."

"By adherence to the principles of decentralized self-government, ordered liberty, equal opportunity, and freedom to the individual, our American experiment in human welfare has yielded a degree of well-being unparalleled in all the world."

"We are nearer today to the ideal of the abolition of poverty and fear from the lives of men and women than ever before in any land."

At the Nominating Convention at Houston, Texas, the Democrats nominated Alfred E. Smith, four-time governor of New York. His name was presented to the convention by Franklin Roosevelt who called him the "Happy Warrior," a description so apt that it stuck. The platform advocated the enforcement of prohibition, regulation of water resources, independence of the Philippines, and better enforcement of the anti-injunction provision of the Clayton Anti-trust Act. In the campaign, Smith advocated repeal of prohibition. Al Smith was very popular in the cities of the northeast, but his reception in the west and south was less than friendly. He had grown up in Manhattan almost in the shadow of Brooklyn Bridge, worked in the Fulton Fish Market, and got his political training in Tammany Hall. That he favored repeal of prohibition and was the first Roman Catholic to run for the presidency led many in the west and south to consider him not the type of person for the White House. Governor Smith lost votes as a result of the same kind of prejudice that had turned the seaboard aristocracy of the South away from Jackson. There was a marked religious prejudice in both directions, many voting for him because he was a Catholic and many against him for the same reason. There was much ridiculous, and some vicious, anti-Catholic propaganda to mar the campaign.

	Popular Vote	Electoral Vote
Hoover	21,392,190	444
Smith	15,016,443	87

** National Origins Immigration Act (1929)

This act established a policy of immigration control that is still in effect. But to treat immigration as a unit and to understand the background of our present policy it may help to go back to the first real immigration law, the Chinese Exclusion Act of 1882. The United States had a treaty with China which allowed us to "regulate, limit or suspend" but not to prohibit Chinese immigration. This treaty displays a basic fact Americans may easily overlook; the sensitivity of any people to laws that seem to stamp them as inferior. Obviously the Chinese government was disinterested in how many Chinese were allowed to come to the United States, it simply wanted to avoid exclusion. The Knights of Labor and the people of California demanded the 1882 Exclusion Act which "suspended" Chinese immigration for 10 years; but as the act was renewed each time, it violated the intent, if not the letter, of our agreement with China. From 1900 to 1907 difficulties in California with the Japanese (see pp. 183-184) resulted in the "Gentlemen's Agreement." California then limited the right of Japanese to own or lease farms, thus again violating the intent of the "Gentlemen's Agreement." When American courts upheld the right of California to pass such discriminatory land laws, the

Japanese set aside a day as "Humiliation Day" so that "Hate Americans" mass meetings could be held. People in the United States were probably quite unconscious of the ill will being created. The long sustained assumption of superiority based on color (or lack of it) is an historical fact which may be too long remembered by people of color.

The census of 1890 showed a new trend in immigration. In the preceding decade a great increase of people from eastern and southern Europe occurred. By 1910 our large cities had foreign districts within them. Italians, Poles, Russians, Russian Jews (fled from persecution), Serbs, Rumanians, and Chinese lived in slum or semi-slum areas in compact groups of their own nationality. In 1914 almost 75% of all immigrants came from eastern and southern Europe. This called for a drastic revision of our "everybody welcome," "land of opportunity," "melting pot" attitude which had been our proud tradition. Unfortunately the thinking applied to the problem was dangerously superficial. We made laws designed to keep certain nationalities out and let others in, thus assuming certain nationalities to be inferior and others superior. Those labeled inferior by our laws resented it. Inferiority and superiority are individual differences, not racial or national; thus a wise immigration policy will be based on individual differences. For example: we might decide to allow a certain number of doctors, scientists, building trades workers, unskilled laborers, nurses, clerks, farmers, electrical workers, etc., based on the estimated needs of our economy each 3 to 5 year period. There need be no national quotas, no religious or color bars, and everyone who enters America as an immigrant would do so with the knowledge that our law makers think he is needed here. But the laws Congress passed were not like this.

In 1921 the first quota law allowed 3% based on the census of 1910. For example: if the census showed 10,000 persons in the U.S. who had been born in X nation, this law would give that nation a quota of 300. In 1924 a new law provided for 2% based on the census of 1890. The earlier the census date, the smaller the proportion of eastern and southern Europeans to the total population. This is so because they didn't begin to come here until 1880 and didn't reach their highest yearly peak until 1914. The 1924 law not only cut the number by 1%, but also held back the eastern and southern Europeans while making comparatively little difference to quotas for western and northern Europe. On July 1, 1929 the National Origins formula became law. This was the most drastic in its discrimination on the basis of nationality.

THE FORMULA

$$\frac{X}{150,000} = \frac{\text{Number of persons who trace their origin to X nation according to the census of 1920}}{120,000,000 \text{ (approximate population in 1920)}}$$

Asians were excluded.

Quotas did not apply to Latin America and Canada or to a few individuals such as college students, professors, and ministers.

If a quota was less than 100, that nation could send in 100 provided the total of 150,000 had not been reached.

Immigration policy was one subject on which Hoover and Smith agreed in the campaign of 1928. Both opposed the national origin formula which was before Congress. They considered it unfair and arbitrary. Unfair for reasons already stated and arbitrary because one's national origin is frequently elusive and a great many people don't know their national origin. Origin goes a long way back. What is your origin? Having paternal and maternal ancestors leads to real confusion; for instance; on the maternal side it may go French-Dutch-English-Italian-Swiss and on the paternal side German-Austrian-Serbian-Russian-Russian. In what national group will the Census Bureau classify this person? Whatever the decision, it will have to be arbitrary because there is no sensible way to do it. In case of doubt, and that is a great many cases, the decisions will be made to support our policy of holding down immigration from eastern and southern Europe.

In 1952 the McCarran-Walter Act modified the 1929 law by including Asians in the formula. Some provisions were also added to keep out "subversives" and to expel immigrants belonging to "Communist or Communist-front" organizations.

Our immigration laws, though unnecessarily offensive to others and embarrassing to us, work satisfactorily in controlling the number of people coming to the United States. We have no immigration problem in this respect.

** Panic and Depression

Some of the Causes

For a week before October 29, 1929, stock prices slumped, but on that date the bottom fell out of the market. From October 21 to November 13 total prices of securities declined about $30 billion and by June about $75 billion. Why? Several factors contributed, but the one most often given is overspeculation in securities (shares of stock of all kinds of enterprises). During the "gilded prosperity" of the '20's the middle income group, which had

rarely bought stock before, entered the market. Their very numbers, in combination with their lack of any sound basis for financial judgment, created a very speculative situation. Tens of thousands of these new purchasers of stocks began scanning the financial pages instead of the sports pages of the newspaper. A gambling mania hit the people. They would buy stock on 10% margin which meant that they could purchase securities priced at $500 by putting down $50 plus a small brokerage fee. The broker would put up the balance. If he sold the stock a few days later at a higher price the speculator made a profit and probably judged himself to be a financier; if the stock fell in price the broker would sell before the loss exceeded the $50 deposit, or he would demand payment of more margin by the speculator if he cared to hang on to the stock in the expectation that it would come back. The broker was the middleman bringing the buyer and seller together; he sold this service for a fee and was not a party to the speculation. If the speculator either couldn't or wouldn't supply the extra margin on a declining stock, the broker sold and the speculator lost whatever he had paid. With a few years of almost steadily rising stock prices this seemed good fun, but the price of securities had risen far beyond the value behind them. If a share of stock in 1922 representing $100 actually invested in a corporation were sold many times at a higher price each time, it might reach a market price in 1929 of $500; but only its price would have risen, not its value. Anyone owning several shares of such a stock in 1922 who sold them in 1929 would be quite happy about it. How long can this sort of "bull market" (rising prices) last and how high can it go? "What goes up must come down" applies to such a stock market situation as prevailed throughout the '20's. But going up the road is a pleasant rise with a few little dips only deep enough to produce an exciting little queasy feeling in the stomach and then up again to new heights. There will come a change, there'll be a sharper dip and a longer one that will be more than exciting, it will be temporarily frightening; but probably will be followed by another rise in the road, maybe one, maybe two sharp drops and recoveries; then off the cliff—crash! It's a panic, it's Oct. 29, 1929. Overspeculation is part of the story of every financial panic, but it is only part of the story.

During the 1920's a substantial part of the goods we sold to Europe was purchased with money loaned by American investors. No business can prosper by lending money to its customers so that they can buy its products. While not quite as simple as this, it was essentially the explanation of the apparently healthy export trade the United States enjoyed. When the loans were not repaid and no more were made, business stopped. From 1929 to 1931 foreign trade fell over 55%.

War diverts manpower and resources to the production of goods to be destroyed (tanks, planes, ships, ordnance, bombs, etc.) in a manner aimed at the destruction of as much enemy property as possible. Four years of this economic insanity made nations and people poor. A war impoverished Europe was a strong force pulling the American economy down; poverty anywhere is a threat to prosperity elsewhere. By the late '20's there was some suspicion that war debts might not be paid; by June 1931 President Hoover declared a moratorium on a $1/4 billion war debt installment then due. Moratorium followed moratorium until it was recognized that the debts wouldn't be paid. Finland was the only nation which paid its war debt in full to the United States, and almost surely the only nation that could do so. Finland's debt was not large for her to bear and her major export, wood pulp, was a product American paper mills were glad to buy. This was good business for the Finns, a source of tax revenue for the Finnish government, and the means by which the debt was paid.

The farmers of America had been in a depression since about 1920. Rural America was still a large enough segment of the population to affect the economy as a whole. When farm families slow down on their purchases over a period of years, the farm machinery companies and the merchants in the smaller towns feel the pinch and eventually the factories which supply the rural retailers become idle.

Wages rose slowly, about 12%, during the '20's before the crash. Those whose chief income was in the form of dividends, profits, and rents fared much better. This is another way of saying that a maldistribution of wealth developed until it became marked enough to affect adversely the economy. It was estimated that 1/20 of the people had 1/3 of the purchasing power. Our foreign trade had fallen away and most of our own people were unable to buy the products of our own factories. When too many have too little and too few have too much, business stagnates.

Installment buying went to great extremes during the '20's. Although the installment system has its proper place, it can be a serious deterent to business. For example, if a family buys several items (house, car, furniture, vacuum cleaner, refrigerator) on the installment plan, the purchasing power of that family is curtailed. In addition to the cost of the items, the accounting and carrying services involved must be paid for; they may be called interest on the unpaid balance, service charge, or they may be hidden in a higher original price. If the family over-extends itself and is unable to meet all these payments, it will have some purchases reclaimed by the merchant and thus lose the money already paid and the item. If the family is hard-pressed to meet all payments, it will curtail expenditures for food, medical care, fuel, and other essentials which are more important to the family welfare than the installment purchases. Without proper judgment and self-control, installment buying can get out of hand and result in a family's getting less for its expenditures while using its money for the wrong things. Multiply this unsound family financing by a few million and the result is an unsound economy. There is virtue in the savings banks' advice to save money for purchases and let it earn while you save.

A Few Immediate Results

1] About 15,000,000 unemployed.

2] About 1/3 of the railroad mileage bankrupt.

3] About $132 billion loss in national income from 1930 to 1938.

4] Over 5,500 banks closed between the market crash in 1929 and the bank "holidays" proclaimed by several governors and the president in 1933.

5] Pitiful shacks made from whatever materials the city dumps supplied grew into sizeable communities ("Hoovervilles") at the dump sites. Empty box cars constituted some of the better homes of the destitute. Jobless veterans were permitted to sell apples at 5 cents apiece on busy city corners; it was thinly disguised begging referred to as "ragged individualism."

6] About 1/4 of the farms were lost through nonpayment of taxes or mortgages. There were several instances in the west of armed farmers appearing at auctions and preventing foreclosures. This was really revolution, but the mood of the community and the circumstances made the law one thing and the prevailing idea of justice another.

7] The "Bonus Marchers" converged on Washington from as far away as Portland, Oregon. Most of them had a $1,000 bonus payable in 20 years. Over President Hoover's veto Congress passed a law in February 1931 to pay them half their bonus immediately. In July, 1932, 10,000 veterans were at the capitol building demanding the other half. They encamped at several places in Washington, the largest being at Anacosta Flats. These unemployed veterans, some with their families, made a sorry spectacle in the capital city. Many left after the Senate refused to pass the second bonus bill, but those who stayed in the tumble-down encampments because they had no jobs and no reason to go anywhere else were finally driven off by tanks, tear gas, and some gun fire. Two soldiers, later to become famous, were officers in charge of this very distasteful job, Douglas MacArthur and Dwight Eisenhower.

8] Cities and towns all over the United States and the private charitable organizations did what they could for relief; but the bread lines were long and the need for shelter too great.

9] The unemployed were a cross section of our population; from unskilled laborers to highly paid executives, from the illiterate to the highly competent professionals.

Some Things Hoover Did

1] Businessmen were urged to maintain their payrolls at normal levels.

2] To keep prices up, the Federal Farm Board attempted, with little success, to stabilize prices in cotton, grain, wool, and some other commodities by purchasing them on the open market.

3] The Federal government supplied leadership at state and local levels in organizing voluntary relief agencies.

4] In December, 1930, a small program of public works called for expenditures up to $150,000,000.

5] In February 1932 the Reconstruction Finance Corporation was formed. It was empowered to lend up to $2 billion to railroads, insurance companies, banks, farm mortgage associations, and building and loan associations. This was a "pump priming" measure. If such a corporation was threatened with bankruptcy, the R.F.C. could decide whether a loan might save it; if a loan restored the business to a sound economic footing, the benefits would spread to the share holders, the employees, and thousands of persons doing business with the corporation. In such a case the loan would be repaid. In some cases the corporations failed and the loans were lost.

6] In July, 1932, when unemployment had climbed to about 10,000,000, the Relief and Construction Act was passed making available $3 billion for public works of a "self-liquidating" type (something that, once completed, would bring in revenue to pay for itself). States and cities could become part of this program. About $300 million was set aside for loans to states which were unable to finance their relief burdens.

President Hoover suffered two injustices. One was that he was blamed for the depression, a public reaction as silly as it was certain. Presidents always have been,* and perhaps always will be, credited with prosperity (Coolidge) and blamed for depressions. Anyone in politics is expected to accept this as a fact of political life. The other injustice was the charge that he did nothing to relieve the depression. As we have noted he did do several things; but they were woefully small in scope until early 1932 (the R.F.C.) and then it seemed to the people that the government would make but the feeblest moves for relief of individuals but had billions to help bail out distressed corporations. The President's approach to the problem of the depression was a thoughtful one quite consistent with the ideas he had many times expressed. Handing out relief for multitudes of individuals that they might eat would never end, as they soon got hungry again. That sort of relief, imperative as it was, should, he thought, be done by private charity and at the local levels of government. The R.F.C., however, was a constructive relief that sought to put corporations in a position to prosper and thus maintain productive employment; it was reviving economic life to a self-sustaining status. If the government can set the economic stage so that business can operate profitably, people with money to invest will do so and the nation will prosper. Hoover was not alone in holding these convictions. Soon the "New Deal" philosophy was to emerge with a different answer to the question, what makes our private enterprise economy tick? Anyone with a genuine spark of interest in political economy (the interaction of politics and economics) should seek an understanding of right wing Republican and the left wing Democratic thinking; they are the two major patterns of thought within what is generally called the "private enterprise" or "capitalist" or "American" system.

It should be remembered that the depression of the '30's was the first one that required planning by governments, city, state, and federal. Our procedure in all previous depressions was the same as that of any normally healthy person with an ordinary cold: just wait it out in mild misery and it will pass over. In the past, "waiting it out" had been miserable for many, but tolerable for the nation. This explains Hoover's early, and too long continued, assertions that the country was "fundamentally sound," that "all we need is confidence," and that "prosperity is just around the corner." This was no cheap attempt to fool the people and stall for time; it was a conviction based upon his economic philosophy and apparently backed by America's experience.

In addition to the general helplessness of business leadership displayed in the national crisis, there was corruption, much of it uncovered in the '30's by the Pecora Committee. The Samuel Insull public utility empire proved a gigantic swindle; Insull fled to Greece to avoid arrest but was finally apprehended. The partners of the House of Morgan had failed to pay income taxes for two years. Investment banks had deliberately unloaded worthless securities on thousands of unsuspecting customers. Before the middle '30's the temper of the country had shifted violently from its attitude of almost awesome respect for the capacity of business leadership to one of deep distrust. Big business was in the national "dog-house."

* Hawley-Smoot Tariff (1930)

Hoover had asked for a slight revision of the tariff; what he got was a very considerable revision which pushed protection to a new high and brought protests from importers, some bankers, and a few industrialists. Joseph Grundy, President of the Manufacturers Association of Pennsylvania, had been appointed to fill a vacancy in the United States Senate. In his double capacity as tariff lobbyist and Senator he played so prominent a part in boosting the rates that the bill was called the "Grundy Tariff." Congress considered the bill for over a year during which it became a matter of sharp controversy. A petition signed by about 1,000 economists urged President Hoover to veto it. As it turned out, the Senate passed it by a margin of only two votes and a veto would have killed it. Had Hoover vetoed the law, he would have alienated the most powerful faction of his party and pleased only a handful of Republicans and most of the Democrats. He found himself in the same political position that Taft had experienced with the Payne-Aldrich tariff. Beginning with the Fordney-McCumber tariff of 1922, the Tariff Commission had been empowered to recommend a change in any rate within 50% of that set by the law, and Hoover hoped that, away from the noise and heat of Congressional dispute, the Tariff Commission could achieve modifications under conditions more suitable to considered judgment. No such modifications took place. Foreign reaction to the Hawley-Smoot tariff was marked and fast; 25 nations put up tariff barriers against American goods, and our foreign trade, both exports and imports, fell off over 50% within 18 months. Of course the depression must have been an important factor, but some of the decline in trade can be put at the door of the Hawley-Smoot tariff. More American manufacturers built factories in European countries.

Franklin D. Roosevelt

1933-1945

1882 - 1945

DEMOCRAT

☆

FRANKLIN ROOSEVELT'S PUBLIC SERVICE BEFORE HE BECAME PRESIDENT

State Senator in New York
Assistant Secretary of the Navy
Governor of New York (1928-32)

MAJOR ITEMS OF FRANKLIN ROOSEVELT'S ADMINISTRATION

20th and 21st Amendments
  ("Lame Duck" and Repeal of
  Prohibition)
New Deal
  Its Point of View—Major Financial
  Measures—Unemployment—

Housing—Agriculture—Labor—Business and
Industry—Youth—Social Security—Tennessee
Valley Authority—Supreme Court Fight
Approaching World War II
Fighting World War II
Building the Peace

Franklin Roosevelt's Election in 1932, 1936, 1940, and 1944

Any Democrat was bound to win in 1932. After more than three years of constantly deepening depression, President Hoover and the Republican Party had lost the support of the people. Some of the most prominent Republican leaders deserted Hoover; Nicholas Butler, President of Columbia University, and Senator Borah of Idaho by their silence during the campaign, and Senators Hiram Johnson (California) and George Norris (Nebraska) by campaigning for Roosevelt. Hoover was nominated at the Chicago Convention on the first ballot; no one else made any effort to get the nomination.

The Democratic Convention met in the same hall a few days later and nominated the governor of New York State on the 4th ballot. Al Smith made a try for the nomination, but the party feared a revival of the religious issue. Besides, Roosevelt had shown great vote-getting ability in New York by winning the governorship in 1928 and 1930; the first time while Smith was losing the state in the presidential race, and the second time by the largest vote ever given to any candidate by the Empire State. On the 3rd ballot Roosevelt had 682 votes to 190 for Smith and on the next ballot Jack Garner of Texas (Speaker of the House) threw his support to give the nomination to Roosevelt in

return for the vice-presidential spot on the ticket with him.

During the campaign, Roosevelt not only used radio effectively, he made a tour of the country. He wished to demonstrate his physical vigor in spite of the paralysis in his legs (polio), to take full advantage of personal appearances which he had found such an effective vote-getter, and to have the fun of the campaigning he liked so well. He pictured the depression as an emergency every bit as real as war and a situation demanding "action." He promised a "new deal" especially in behalf of "the forgotten man at the bottom of the economic pyramid." He asserted it to be the proper concern of the federal government to see that no American citizen starved. President Hoover in uninspiring speeches blamed the depression on world conditions and claimed his administration had prevented the situation from becoming worse. The Republican platform pledged continued protective tariffs, revision of prohibition, decrease in public spending, and a balanced budget. The Democratic platform pledged a revenue tariff, a balanced budget, decreased public spending, repeal of prohibition, aid to farmers to bring farm prices above costs, banking and stock exchange reforms to prevent fraud, and regulation of holding companies to prevent a repetition of the Insull public utilities abuses.

	Popular Vote	Electoral Vote
F. D. Roosevelt	22,809,638	472
Hoover	15,758,901	59

Hoover won Maine, Vermont, New Hampshire, Connecticut, Pennsylvania, and Delaware.

The Democrats swept the Congress—60 to 35 in the Senate and 310 to 117 in the House.

Election of 1936

This campaign presented the voters with a chance to pass judgment on the New Deal. Four years crammed with legislation offered plenty of opportunity for differences of opinion. Recovery, though far from complete, had restored the will and the strength to the opposition to unite their forces. Those Republicans who had kept silent in 1932, or joined the Democrats, were back in their party again.

The Republicans nominated Governor Alfred (Alf) Landon of Kansas who had been among the very few Republicans strong enough to win during the Democratic landslide of 1932. He attracted further attention by maintaining a balanced budget in his state. Two former Democratic presidential candidates, Al Smith and John W. Davis, broke with the New Deal and came out for Landon. The Republicans waged a spirited attack on the ideology of the New Deal, but did not urge the repeal of any major New Deal legislation; they even criticized Social Security for not including professional people, farmers, and domestic help. The following quotations from the Republican platform express its tone.

"America is in peril. . . . We dedicate ourselves to the preservation of their (the peoples') political liberty, their individual opportunity and their character as free citizens, which today for the first time are threatened by Government itself."

"The powers of Congress have been usurped by the President."

"The integrity and authority of the Supreme Court have been flouted."

"The rights and liberties of American citizens have been violated."

"Regulated monopoly has displaced free enterprise."

"It (New Deal) has destroyed the morale of many of our people and made them dependent upon Government."

"We invite all Americans, irrespective of party, to join us in defense of American institutions."

The Democrats nominated Roosevelt and Garner by acclamation. Their platform was a recital of their record and a promise to continue along the same lines. It labeled the Republicans a do-nothing party. They changed their long-standing 2/3rds rule for nominating candidates for President and Vice-President to a simple majority.

Because the campaign was waged on a clash of ideas rather than the approval or rejection of separate laws or measures, feeling ran high and the campaign was bitterly fought even though the result was extremely one-sided. "F.D.R.'s" acceptance speech illustrated this when he said, "The royalists of the economic order have conceded that political freedom was the business of the Government, but they have maintained that economic slavery was nobody's business. . . . These economic royalists complain that we seek to overthrow the institutions of America. What they really complain of is that we seek to take away their power."

	Popular Vote	Electoral Vote
F. Roosevelt	27,751,612	523
Landon	16,681,913	8

Landon got Maine and Vermont. The Democrats won control of the Senate by 76 to 16 and of the House by 331 to 89.

Election of 1940

In 1940 the attention of America was focused on the war in Europe. In a speech at the University of Virginia President Roosevelt said, "The people and Government of the United States have seen with the utmost regret and grave disquiet the decision of the Italian Government to engage in the hostilities now raging in Europe. . . . On this 10th day of June, the hand that held the dagger has struck it into the back of its neighbor." In September Congress passed the first peacetime draft in our history and a few days later Great Britain gave us a lease on several air bases in exchange for 50 destroyers. There was a nation-wide committee, "Defend America by Aiding the Allies," and another to keep us isolated, "America First." The pro-Ally and the pro-isolation groups cut across party lines.

The Republicans met at Philadelphia where Taft (Ohio), Vandenberg (Michigan), and the New York Attorney General, Dewey, were considered the leading candidates. But a group of non-professional Republicans had organized to present the name of Wendell Willkie before the Convention. Willkie had fought the establishment of T.V.A. and had been a leading critic of the New Deal (its performance rather than its program). His charm, youthful vigor, and lively good sense enabled the amateur politicians to put him over on the 6th ballot. "Win with Willkie" became the Republican cry.

The Democrats met at Chicago faced with a third term problem. The two-terms-only tradition had never been broken and on the second day of the Convention a message from the President stated that he had no desire to be a candidate for a 3rd term. Roosevelt was careful not to make any move, directly or indirectly, beyond this one message. On the 4th day the Convention broke the 3rd term tradition by nominating Roosevelt who replied by radio that "in the face of the danger which confronts our times" he felt that he could not refuse. There seems little doubt that F.D.R. was anxious to stay in power to see the European situation to a conclusion.

In the campaign there was not much of an issue except the third term. Willkie approved most of the New Deal but deplored what he termed its inefficiencies and wastefulness. He had supported the Defend America by Aiding the Allies committee, so there was no important issue in foreign policy. The Democrats warned against "changing horses in midstream."

	Popular Vote	Electoral Vote
F. Roosevelt	27,244,160	449
Willkie	22,305,198	82

Election of 1944

Before the Republican Convention met at Chicago, Wendell Willkie withdrew from the race for the nomination, thus leaving the path clear for Governor Thomas E. Dewey of New York who had become nationally famous as the courageous and clever Attorney General of New York State in the successful prosecution of some of gangland's most notorious criminals. The Democrats nominated Roosevelt who selected Harry Truman of Missouri as his running mate. Dewey had a sharp mind practiced in the art of attack. His supporters could find much to respect in his ability but little warmth to draw their affection. In the campaign Dewey advised the replacement of "tired old men" by a new and vigorous administration. "It's time for a change" was the gist of his campaign message. On the domestic front he attacked the operation of the New Deal more than its content, while in the field of foreign affairs, he could hardly attack a war policy that was clearly approaching victory. Both parties favored an international organization to preserve the peace. For the first time, organized labor set up a Political Action Committee (P.A.C.) to campaign for individual candidates whose records or promises they approved.

	Popular Vote	Electoral Vote
F. D. Roosevelt	25,602,505	432
Thomas Dewey	12,006,278	99

20th and 21st Amendments
(See p. 70.)
** New Deal

Its Point of View

When Franklin Roosevelt took office on March 4, 1933, businessmen, bankers, organized labor, the general public, and Congress were ready to accept positive, confident leadership. "F.D.R." supplied that leadership. Under his direction the government began to plan, to pass laws, to spend money, and to assume the burden of lifting the nation out of the depression. There were many laws, some wise, some unwise—with considerable difference of opinion as to which was which. Altogether the vast program of legislation constituted the New Deal.

There is no political and/or economic dogma or philosophy that is an official statement of New Deal thinking. But from the numerous speeches by leading figures of the liberal wing in the Democratic Party, from F.D.R. to John F. Kennedy, some very definite trends of thought are evident. Emphasis is placed upon the purchasing power of the middle and lower income groups as the foundation of economic prosperity. Two reasons are advanced to support this view: the total purchasing power of the middle and lower income groups is a very large part of the gross national income; and these income groups spend their money about as fast as they get it, thus stimulating the economy by rapid turnover as well as by its volume. ($1 spent five times does as much business as $5 spent once.) When these people have money in their pockets, they'll keep the economy humming. To maintain this effective purchasing power, wages should be as high as possible. To further stimulate purchases, prices should be low. Profits must be high enough to attract investment capital (risk capital) but need not be, and ordinarily should not be, higher. Presumably this would be somewhat above savings bank interest or the return on gilt edge bonds. Keen competition among efficient producers operating under conditions of mass production creates a favorable setting for a prosperous economy. Simplifying this into a sort of formula, one might say that mass production + high wages + low prices + moderate profits = a sound and vigorous economy. If high wages and low prices seem contradictory, it can be shown that mass production often achieves this combination. If one asks why anyone would be willing to invest money for no greater expectation than a moderate profit, there are two answers: a moderate profit per unit produced can be a handsome income as is often the case when the number of units get into very high numbers in mass production; and there is nothing to worry about because "moderate" profit, by definition, means just enough to attract the required investment capital. New Dealers are fond of pointing to the achievement of Henry Ford of Model T fame, the man who literally put America on wheels, as an industrialist who actually made his millions under the New Deal "formula." He had mass production, he paid wages about twice as high as the rest of the automobile industry, he priced his car considerably lower than the others, and he made a small profit on each car. But he sold so many cars that he made more money than anyone else in the automobile business at the time. Henry Ford never considered himself to be a political economist; he was a manufacturer developing his business with astounding success by the application of what to him probably appeared to be just plain common sense. If this sort of thinking seems to place too much stress on mass production, the New Dealer might point out that mass production not only accounts for a large part of all manufactured goods, but that new techniques are continually standardizing more and more products so that they, too, become part of mass production procedures. In short, mass production already dominates American production and it will do so to a greater degree as time goes on.

A point to notice is that the New Deal thinking is inclined to ignore, or at least minimize, the economic importance to the nation of the upper income group. Individuals therein have great purchasing power, but their total purchasing power as a group is not great compared to that of the whole population. The New Deal rejects the "trickle down" theory of prosperity where the expectation of high profits attracts ample investment capital which runs industry and commerce so that workers get jobs and take home fat pay envelopes. This "trickle down" theory is sometimes disparagingly referred to as the poor man living off the crumbs that fall from the rich man's table. What is the "key" to a steadily prosperous economy, ample investment capital or ample purchasing power? Which is more likely to produce the other? Certainly, in a complex economy such as ours, both must be present if we are to prosper. But which is the hen and which is the egg? The New Deal says that purchasing power of the middle and lower in-

come groups is the hen that lays the golden eggs.

The New Deal also has ideas about depressions and how to avoid them. Briefly, and probably too simply stated, they look to private enterprise as the mainstay of our economy. Depressions are manmade and result from faults in our economy, especially in distribution rather than in production. When private enterprise falters, the government should stand ready with plans to prevent depression; and when private enterprise regains vitality, the government should withdraw. A steady economy might be attained by

a. High taxes in prosperous times.
b. Public works at a minimum in prosperous times.
c. Low taxes in hard times.
d. Increased public works in hard times.

Theoretically this would avoid or lessen the violence of swings from boom to bust. Private enterprise carries the major load most of the time, and the government stands by to supplement it when depression threatens. This concept of government standing on the side lines always ready to help and always anxious not to help until necessary is sometimes called the two-front economy. Of course the rough and tumble of every day politics has not permitted any neat and orderly experiment in working out such a program. For instance, in prosperous times what are the chances of a member of Congress getting elected by advocating high taxes which are not immediately needed, but are to be set aside for a future public works program when the next depression threatens? Would such sums, if collected and set aside, be used properly or would they invite extravagance and graft? Most public works (roads-hospitals-schools-parks-etc.) are rarely emergency projects; they can be built now or a few years from now. It would seem possible that a well planned program of public works could be put into effect at times best calculated to maintain a steady economy. But this foresight takes intelligent planning and integrity. Perhaps this is enough to show how inseparable politics and economics are, and how demanding a complex economy may be upon the capacity of a people for self-government.

Major Financial Measures

1] Emergency Banking Relief Act (1933).

The day after his inauguration the President called Congress into a special session to begin on March 9th and declared a 4-day bank holiday which stopped all activities of the Federal Reserve System and other banks, loan associations, and credit unions. Most such financial institutions had been closed a day or two earlier through the action of the several governors. The first day of its special session Congress passed the Emergency Banking Relief Act which confirmed the bank holiday and provided for the reopening of the banks as soon as examiners had found them sound. A rapid inspection resulted in an end to the bank panic as over 5,000 banks opened within three days. March 9th was the beginning of The Hundred Days when the "action and more action" Roosevelt had advocated resulted in an unprecedented number of laws —the 1st New Deal. Legislation passed under Roosevelt after this first 100-day session is sometimes called the 2nd New Deal.

2] Federal Securities Act (1933 and 1934).

This law made sweeping reforms in the selling of securities. Securities offered for sale had to be accompanied with full and true information concerning the properties represented. Misleading information or the absence of pertinent information could result in prosecution. The Federal Trade Commission supervised the stock market for about a year and then a separate body, the Securities and Exchange Commission, took over the police job in 1934. While there was quite a bit of grumbling when the supervision began, it has since been welcomed by the New York Stock Exchange and brokers generally.

3] Gold Standard Abandoned '33 and Gold Dollar Devalued '34.

In April 1933 all gold and gold certificates were called in and all debts were made payable in legal tender. Any contract calling for payment only in gold was made void as well as the promise of the United States on gold certificates to pay gold on demand to the bearer. The Supreme Court ruled that this breaking of its contract, however reprehensible, was legal because Congress had the right to regulate the currency. In its own words, "Contracts, however express, cannot fetter the Constitutional authority of Congress."

In June, 1933, President Roosevelt, in order to "make possible the payment of debts at more nearly the price level at which they were incurred," lowered the gold content of the dollar to 59.06% of its former content. Other reasons for going off the gold standard and lowering the gold content of the dollar were to raise commodity prices and increase the funds in the treasury.

4] Banking Acts of 1933 (Steagall Act) and of 1935. The more important terms of these two acts were

a. The Federal Reserve Board was given tighter control of the investment practices of Member Banks.

b. The Federal Deposit Insurance Corporation was set up to insure all deposits in Federal Reserve Member Banks up to $5,000. (since raised to $10,000.)

c. Investment banking was separated from commercial banking so that a commercial bank with an investment department would no longer be under any temptation to unload its own bad investments on its customers.

d. Savings banks and industrial banks were permitted to join the Federal Reserve System.

e. The Federal Reserve Board was changed to the Board of Governors. There were 7 members, but the treasurer and comptroller of the currency no longer serve.

Unemployment

Works Projects Administration (W.P.A.) 1935. This huge undertaking was directed by Harry Hopkins. There were subdivisions such as the C.C.C. and the N.Y.A. which we will take up separately as plans to help young men just out of school or still in college. Another subdivision was the Public Works Administration (P.W.A.) under Harold Ickes, Secretary of the Interior.

The W.P.A. was intended to put wages into the possession of as many unemployed as possible. The pay was the going hourly rate for whatever job was being done, but the work week was shortened about 25% to 30% to spread the work and to make full time employment in a private job more attractive if available. By early spring in 1936 about 3½ million persons were on W.P.A. The type of work done was deliberately picked to put most of the money, about 85%, into wages rather than into materials and machinery. Laborers, writers, musicians, actors, and clerks were given work in their own fields. Harry Hopkins' idea behind this organization was that work was better than a dole, and work in one's own specialty was a good morale builder. Writers went to work compiling state histories, musicians formed orchestras and gave concerts, actors formed companies and put on dramas and other entertainment. Critics of the program thought much of the employment useless work and called it "boondoggling."

The P.W.A. under Secretary of the Interior Harold Ickes went in for construction jobs such as schools, hospitals, post offices, roads, and even the Grand Coulee Dam on the Colorado River. Of course, unemployment was aided just as effectively by these jobs as by the W.P.A., perhaps more so, as the suppliers of building materials had to hire men to make bricks, cement, steel, and build the machines used on the jobs. The distinction between the type of jobs under W.P.A. and under P.W.A. was not as clear as this account suggests. W.P.A. also built roads and public buildings. The total employed was about 8½ million persons at a cost of about $11 billion.

Housing

1] Home Owners Loan Act 1934.

By refinancing mortgages at lower rates of interest over longer periods of time this act was aimed at preventing the foreclosure of home mortgages. Loans were offered on easy terms for remodeling or repairs, and a great deal of publicity urged home owners to take advantage of this opportunity to improve their property and stimulate employment.

2] National Housing Act 1934 (F.H.A.).

This law set up the Federal Housing Authority (F.H.A.) which encouraged banks, building and loan associations, etc. to make loans for building homes, small business establishments, and farm buildings. If the F.H.A. approved the plans, it would insure the loan. This resulted in many loans that otherwise would not have been made.

3] National Housing Act 1937 (U.S.H.A.).

This act set up the United States Housing Authority to encourage slum clearance. It made 60-year loans at low interest to local governments which would put up 10% of the cost of the slum clearance project. Rents in these apartment-house blocks were fixed and available only to low income families.

Agriculture

Agricultural Adjustment Act 1933 (A.A.A.) and in 1938.

Whatever the faults of this legislation it struck at the heart of the farm problem, over-production. Some may point out that *under-consumption* might be a more realistic appraisal of the vast stores of agricultural products, for it was true that, while there was too much cotton and wool, there were many in desperate need of clothing; while there was too much corn, wheat, meat, butter, milk, etc. there were many families suffering from malnutrition. But when any product is in such great supply that it cannot be sold at a price above the cost of production, it is said to be surplus production no matter how much people who can't buy it may want or need it. The A.A.A. paid the farmers not to raise crops and livestock, it paid them to destroy acreage under production and to kill pigs and lambs before they became hams and lamb chops. The money to pay the farmers for cutting back production about 30% was raised by a tax on companies that bought the farm products and processed them into food or clothing. It was called a processing tax. In 1932, farm income was about $5½ billion and in 1935 it was $8½ billion. Not all of this increased farm income was due to the A.A.A.; nature took a cruel hand in the situation in 1933 to 1935 when severe drought and heavy winds created dust storms that lifted top soil in such huge amounts off western farms that the air along the eastern seaboard was hazy. This removal of farms and farmers, along with the A.A.A., cut production. The plight of thousands of farm families suffering from depression and drought is vividly and realistically told by John Steinbeck in the *Grapes of Wrath*.

By a 6-3 decision (*U.S.* v. *Butler*) in 1936 the Supreme Court declared the A.A.A. unconstitutional. The majority ruled that it was illegal to levy a tax on one group (the processors) in order to pay it to another (the farmers). They ruled that farming was not interstate commerce and hence not subject to federal regulation. In 1938, another A.A.A. was passed without the processing tax. It was financed out of the general tax funds and thus met one of the objections of the court. In 1939 (*Mulford* v. *Smith*) and again in 1942 (*Wickard* v. *Filburn*) the Supreme Court completely reversed the 1936 decision that farming was not interstate commerce. It accepted the fact that the crops commonly became part of interstate trade as justifying Congress in the regulation of these crops. In both the 1933 and the 1938 Agricultural Adjustment Acts, the farmers were free to join the program or to operate independently. But if they accepted payment for their restriction of output, they had to fulfil the provisions of the plan.

Labor

Wagner-Connery Act 1935.

This law was the beginning of what was to be referred to as Big Labor. For many years labor had had the right to organize and to strike, but employers had had the right to fire employees because they joined unions or went on strike. As it is almost always easier for an employer to find another employee than it is for an employee to find another job, the right to belong to a union and to strike tended to be rather anemic compared to the right of the employer to fire. The result was that the pressures employers could bring to bear on employees were far more real than any bargaining power held by the employees. Under these conditions organized labor embraced about 10% of the workers and was concentrated among those who were highly skilled. By and large those workers who most needed the strength organization might give were the ones who remained unorganized. Senator Wagner of New York introduced a completely one-sided bill filled with pro-labor provisions. When his bill was vehemently attacked on this basis, Senator Wagner's response was that it was his intention to present just such a bill in order to balance the bargaining positions of employer and employee.

A National Labor Relations Board (N.L.R.B.) was set up to make truly effective labor's right to organize. At the request of the workers the N.L.R.B. would conduct an election to determine whether the employees wanted a union. If two groups of employees disagreed on which should be the official union in a plant, the N.L.R.B. would settle the question by a supervised election. It would hear complaints by employees of unfair labor practices on the part of the employer. Some of the practices the Wagner Act declared unfair were attempts by the employer to dominate a union; attempts by word of mouth, pamphlets, posters, notices, etc. to discourage union membership; to fire anyone for union activity; to adopt a hiring policy intended to discourage union activity; and to refuse to bargain with accredited representatives of the unions. The N.L.R.B. sometimes arbitrated disputes. The Wagner Act removed most of the fear of employees concerning union activity and, of course, stimulated the unions to step up their organizing efforts. The clauses in the law denying the employer the right to express opposition to unions to his employees was considered by some as a violation of the employers' right to freedom of speech. Others considered any attempt by management to persuade employees against unions was intimidation. In 1937 the Supreme Court, Chief Justice Hughes giving the decision, declared the Wagner Act constitutional. Organized labor at its height has reached about 40% of all employees, but its membership is concentrated in relatively few large industries. In these industries the power of labor organized on a national scale is comparable to the power of industry similarly organized; which is the stronger is a matter upon which there is little agreement. If Big Labor and Big Industry cooperate with one another to continually raise prices and wages, the consumers (everybody) pay the bill and inflation threatens the economy. If they fight to a deadlock and a strike ensues, the total economy may be seriously disrupted and, if carried far enough, the government must intercede. If the federal government is given power to prevent or control such labor *vs.* management fights, then government itself exercises a degree of power many believe to be dangerous. There is a real problem here.

Business and Industry

National Industrial Recovery Act 1933 (N.I.R.A. & N.R.A.).

General Hugh S. Johnson was in charge of the administration of the National Industrial Recovery Act. Its purpose was to restore prosperity by organizing thousands of businesses under fair trade codes drawn up by trade associations and industries. Just as the War Industries Board under Bernard Baruch had organized industry for war, Hugh Johnson was to organize the business enterprises of America for prosperity. Congress had some doubt about its constitutional rights in this respect. This doubt expressed itself in the wording of the National Recovery Act which stated that its purpose was to remove obstructions to the free flow of interstate commerce. If prosperity could be achieved through the regulation of interstate commerce, a power specifically granted to Congress by the Constitution, the N.R.A. might pass the scrutiny of the Supreme Court. During the summer of 1933 the President had been authorized by Congress to issue a blanket code for all business to follow until the individual codes had been worked out. This blanket code set a 40 hour week for clerical workers, a 36 hour week for industrial workers, a minimum wage of 40 cents an hour, and a guaranteed right that labor could organize and exercise the right of collective bargaining. The codes were to avoid monopolistic practices and were to be free from the restrictions of the anti-trust laws. Most of the several hundred codes were prepared by prominent businessmen drawn from the leading companies in their particular field; naturally the finished codes reflected their business practices. When the codes were ready, all businessmen were urged to operate under them in a huge national effort to pull out of the depression. Great emphasis was placed on holding prices down, at least until signs of substantial recovery, and keeping employment up. Parades were held in thousands of cities and towns to create enthusiasm for the N.R.A. Never were parades so long; every business from a great factory to a small family business put crepe paper bedecked wagons and trucks in the line. The blue eagle, adopted as the symbol of the N.R.A., appeared everywhere. Publicity for the N.R.A. had been expert and thorough. The depression was so severe that people were in a mood to follow any plan for recovery so long as they were told what to do; and the business community was no different in this respect from the general public. The program was voluntary, no company had to agree to operate under its N.R.A. code. Those businessmen who accepted the N.R.A. had the blue eagle to post in their windows. Doing business without a blue eagle on display was well nigh impossible, for almost everyone interpreted the absence of the N.R.A. symbol as a defiant unwillingness to join with others in an effort to lick the depression. The pressure of public opinion was probably more compelling than any legal provision could have been. The task the N.R.A. attempted was too large and too complex; it was bound to fall of its own weight, to become entangled in its own regulations. The codes actually encouraged monopoly by setting regulations impossible for small companies to follow and by being immune from anti-trust laws. About 23,000,000 people worked under the blue eagle and unemployment was reduced by about 4,000,000. The initial good morale and high purpose with which this "planned economy" started soon dissolved, and violations of codes became common. Regional, state, and local boards established to aid in the implementation of the codes and to correct abuses thereof through court action, if necessary, were bogged down in work and confusion. Before this gigantic scheme collapsed from its own unwieldiness, the Supreme Court declared it unconstitutional in 1935 (*Schechter Poultry Corp.* v. *U.S.*). The reasons given were that many codes were an illegal delegation of legislative authority; that the federal government had invaded fields reserved to the states; and that the N.R.A. stretched the commerce clause of the Constitution beyond all reason.

Youth

1] Civilian Conservation Corps (C.C.C.) 1933.

This program tackled the problem of the unemployed young men 18 to 25 years old. C.C.C. camps were set up all over the United States, most of them in the forests convenient to conservation work. At its peak the program had about 500,000 enrolled, and the total served throughout its existence (1933-41) was almost 3,000,000. The Agriculture, Interior, Labor, and War Departments cooperated in the program. The organization was semi-military with army officers and forest rangers in charge of the men. The typical routine provided opportunities to learn to handle tools and lathes, plenty of outdoor work, time for recreation and instruction, and plenty to eat. The pay was $30 a month with $22 dollars of it being sent home to dependents or family. Many of the boys in the C.C.C. came from families on relief. They planted billions of trees,

built thousands of miles of firelanes and fire-breaks in the forests, built public parks and camp sites, drained swamps to fight malaria, worked on flood control projects, helped control forest pests and diseases, restocked streams with fish, and did anything and everything to preserve and improve "the great outdoors." This useful work under well-nigh ideal conditions for the building of the body and renewing of the spirit sent many C.C.C. boys back into private employment with new skills, a vigor born of good living, and a confidence that society recognized their age group as a great national asset. Without the C.C.C. these youths would have been a burden to their families and a serious threat to law and order; with the C.C.C. they became a help to their families, to themselves, and to the country.

2] National Youth Administration (N.Y.A.) 1935.

This program helped those who were between the ages of 16 to 25 who, because they desired to continue with their education, had not definitely entered the labor market to be included among the unemployed. They needed part time jobs and an opportunity to continue in secondary school or college. The range of the educational program went from the manual arts to college work on the graduate level. More than 700,000 enrolled in this program, most of them from families on relief. These young people attended schools in their own communities, some especially set up for the purpose, and lived at home. The program necessarily centered in the cities and the part time jobs and educational opportunities were decidedly makeshift arrangements compared with the educational programs that had been disrupted by the depression. The morale in this program was always poor, probably because the young people were continually in the presence of depression hardships of their families and the obvious tragedy of widespread unemployment in urban communities. They had too much time to "feel sorry for themselves" and were too available for, and susceptible to, the propaganda of communist agitators and other extremists of the right and left. The C.C.C. youths had been lifted right away from the depression scene while the N.Y.A. lived surrounded and saturated by it. The discontent and radicalism prevalent in the N.Y.A. caused public opinion to turn against it. Just as the C.C.C. was the most popular of the New Deal programs, so the N.Y.A. was the most unpopular.

Tennessee Valley Authority (T.V.A.) (1933)

During World War I at Muscle Shoals, Alabama, on the Tennessee River, a $145,000,000 hydro-electric plant and two munitions factories had been built. Senator George Norris of Nebraska, an "insurgent" and "progressive" Republican, had twice succeeded in getting a bill through Congress providing for government operation of the Muscle Shoals facilities for peacetime purposes. But each time the bill had been vetoed, first by Coolidge and then by Hoover. But when Franklin Roosevelt got under way with the New Deal, the Tennessee Valley Authority was established. The munitions factories became chemical plants for the manufacture of fertilizer and the hydro-electric plant generated power for distribution throughout parts of seven states (Virginia, North Carolina, Georgia, Tennessee, Kentucky, Alabama, Mississippi). The T.V.A. is a multipurpose project of tremendous scope which changed the economy of a large section of the United States. It is government owned and operated and is therefore a major experiment in Socialism, the basic reason for the previous presidential vetoes. The several purposes of T.V.A. include flood control, reforestation, improved use of land, irrigation, navigation, preservation of wild life, recreation, production of fertilizer, and the development of electric power. While the Socialistic nature of the program was a reason for opposition, the most spirited fight against it developed because T.V.A. would compete with private utility companies in the production and distribution of electric power. Most of T.V.A.'s other activities were valuable parts of conservation, and were not in competition with private enterprise. T.V.A. power has been sold at much lower rates than those charged by private utilities and has given the government what some call a "yardstick" by which to judge the fairness of private utility rates. Opponents point out that T.V.A. pays no taxes, but proponents point out that it does pay the communities in which it operates sums "in lieu of taxes" which are greater than the taxes would be. Cost accounting is a complex matter in this case. The 34 dams on the Tennessee and Cumberland Rivers and their tributaries not only play a part in the production of electric power, but also are part of flood control, irrigation, and navigation. How does one allocate a precise share of the costs to each service? Then again, the engineers and other personnel working for T.V.A. may perform services valuable to several of its purposes. How does one allocate a precise part of the payroll to each? If one doesn't like T.V.A., it is easy to cast doubt on its dependability as a "yardstick"; but if one likes it, it is easy to assume that normal accounting procedures are used and that comparative figures are as valid for T.V.A. as for many other complex cost accounting situations which go unquestioned. One thing is certain: T.V.A. is very popular in the region it serves. Chambers of Commerce, mayors, governors, farmers, newspapers, and householders like it. Many once isolated and backward areas now have roads, telephones, libraries, electric lights, electric appliances, and have become fairly good customers. The standard of living in T.V.A. land has risen appreciably. But if one still doesn't like T.V.A., it may be that the rest of the United States is unjustly bearing the tax load for the special benefit of one section of the nation. During World War II the Muscle Shoals plants produced munitions, and T.V.A. power was a key factor in producing aluminum and the atomic bomb at Oak Ridge, Tenn.

Social Security Act (1935)

During the first century under our Constitution the local solution to the problem of indigent old age was never satisfactory. The most fulsome praise one can give to "over the hill to the county poor house" is that it was better than nothing. The problem of care for the indigent handicapped had also been ignored or inadequately handled. During our second century the growing urbanization and the increasing span of life has made the problem more acute. The Social Security Act is the official acknowledgement that families and local governments had failed miserably over a long period of time, and that these social problems are best met through a gigantic plan of compulsory insurance.

The major feature of the law is the Old Age and Survivors Insurance which allows up to $127 a month to those who come under Social Security. To finance the plan, a 3% payroll tax is paid by the employer and employee in equal amounts. Individuals become eligible for the payments upon retirement if they have reached the age of 65. The other provisions of the law encourage states to meet social problems by offering to the states substantial financial help for such purposes as the following.

Unemployment insurance
Old-age pensions
Aid to the blind, the crippled, and the destitute
Aid to delinquent children
Maternity and infant care
Public health work
Vocational rehabilitation

The law has been amended to be made more liberal in its payments, broader in its coverage, and higher in its taxes. Changes were made in 1950, 1952, 1954, 1956, 1958, 1959, and 1961. Current terms of the Social Security Act are easily available at local offices in any community.

* Supreme Court Fight (1937)

Early in February, President Roosevelt sent Congress a plan for reorganizing the Supreme Court and making several changes in Federal court procedures. He had just won re-election by a margin of over 10,000,000 votes and carried all but two states, a political victory which seemed to him to mean that the people wanted the New Deal continued. The Supreme Court, when it struck down the N.R.A. and the A.A.A., as well as some less important New Deal laws, was the only effective opposition to his program. He decided to strike back. Six of the judges on the Court were over 70, and Roosevelt had said that they were still living in the horse and buggy days. A popular book with the impolite title *The Nine Old Men,* in classifying the justices as liberal or conservative, described Chief Justice Charles E. Hughes as the "man on the flying trapeze" because he sometimes agreed with the liberal associate justices and sometimes with the conservatives. Seven of the justices had been appointed by Republican Presidents, and four of them formed a conservative bloc that seemed to be an immovable barrier to New Deal legislation.

The Roosevelt plan called for an additional judge for every justice still on the Court at age 70, until the number of judges reached 15. If none of the six justices over 70 then on the Court would retire with full pay, the President would be allowed to appoint six additional judges. The plan was simplicity itself and completely within the constitutional power of Congress to enact into law. The debate over the bill lasted about six months, and it soon became clear that this was one political fight F.D.R. would lose. His own party in Congress failed to go along with him, and public opinion seemed to consider the move too drastic. Early in the fight, in March, Justice VanDevanter, an "immovable conservative," announced his intention to resign. From late March through May the Supreme Court declared constitutional the Social Security Act and the Wagner-Connery Labor Act as well as a few lesser New Deal laws. With the prospects good for further retirements and the more friendly view of the Court toward the New Deal, there seemed no necessity for reorganization. On July 22nd the Senate killed the Court Reorganization Bill. During the next four years, Roosevelt appointed 7 judges, and the Supreme Court was then called "the Roosevelt Court." Talk of "packing" the Supreme Court makes very little sense. Any president will appoint as justices men whose general point of view he believes to be in accord with his own. But this by no means assures the President that, in any particular case, the decisions reached by his appointees will conform with his own opinion. Justices who, when appointed, have been thought to be "conservatives" have turned out to "liberals" on the Court, and vice-versa.

* Approaching World War II

Europe Blunders Toward War

With the close of World War I, even though we were reluctant to accept the fact, the United States had replaced Great Britain as the leading power of the world. We could stand aloof for a time or we could accept the responsibilities of world leadership. But, in either case, events anywhere in the world had significance for us. In the 1930's this was particularly true of events in Europe. After World War I, American history is World history from a United States' approach. This makes a chronology of events in the '30's in Europe an integral part of our story.

1933—Hitler became Chancellor of Germany.

1934—Hitler took Germany out of the League of Nations.

1935—Hitler renounced the Versailles Treaty by rearming Germany in direct violation of its terms. Nothing was done to stop him.

1935—Mussolini attacked Ethiopia. A League of Nations embargo on oil and steel, with which the United States was willing to cooperate, would have brought the Italian war machine to an early halt. England could have closed the Suez Canal to Italian shipping. Nothing was done.

1936—Hitler sent German troops into the demilitarized Rhineland in direct violation of the Versailles Treaty. The French army was overwhelmingly superior to the German forces, but the French government seemed incapable of making positive decisions. England, also a party to the treaty, could have nudged France into action. This move of Hitler's was pure bluff and worked perfectly.

1936—Germany, Italy, and Japan formed the "Axis," an alliance of aggressive dictatorships.

1936-1939—A vicious civil war in Spain ended in the defeat of a republican government and the re-establishment of a dictatorship under General Franco. Germany and Italy, adjacent to Spain, supported the rightist dictatorship, while distant U.S.S.R. gave air support to the leftist "United Front" Loyalists. It was a good workout for Germany and Italy in preparation for the main bout soon to come. The western democracies maintained a neutrality which played into the hands of Hitler and Mussolini.

1938—Hitler took Austria.

1938—Hitler took the Sudeten district of Czechoslovakia. This was arranged at Munich with the consent of England and France in violation of their pledge to Czechoslovakia. It is this Munich betrayal that made "appeasement" an indecent word in the jargon of diplomacy. Prime Minister Neville Chamberlain hailed the sell-out as a guarantee of "peace in our time." In less than a year, World War II had begun.

1939—Hitler took the rest of Czechoslovakia.

1939—Mussolini took Albania.

1939—Russia and Germany made a pact which startled the world. Many in western Europe and the United States had hoped that the two dictatorships would clash and annihilate one another; but instead they made an agreement that neither would attack the other, and that if a third party attacked one of them, the other would remain neutral.

1939—On September 1st the "blitzkrieg" began as Warsaw became the first city to be wiped off the map by massive air attack. This act by Hitler brought a declaration of war from England and France. World War II was on. By September 28th Poland had disappeared, split between Germany and Russia.

1939 (Oct.) to 1940 (Mar.)—Russia invaded Finland to take a slice of it and then annexed the small Baltic nations, Estonia, Latvia, and Lithuania.

The United States Approaches War

1932—The Stimson Doctrine made a formal protest against Japan's aggression in Manchuria. The doctrine stated that the United States would not recognize any change in sovereignty brought about by external aggression; in short, we would not recognize Manchukuo. The situation which brought forth this doctrine was as follows. In the fall of 1931 Japan invaded Manchuria and about a year later recognized a new nation, Manchukuo. Our Secretary of State, Henry Stimson, claimed Manchukuo represented nothing other than a thinly disguised conquest of South Manchuria by Japan at China's expense. It was our contention that Japan had violated the Nine Power Pact of the Washington Conference of 1921, the Kellogg-Briand Treaty of 1928, and the Covenant of the League of Nations. The League sent a commission under Lord Lytton to Manchuria to get the facts. The Lytton report confirmed the United States' claims. Having been caught in a deliberate lie by an official investigation, Japan withdrew from the League of Nations in February, 1933.

1935—*Neutrality Act* This was a reaction to Italy's attack upon Ethiopia. It provided that, after the President formally recognized that a war was in progress, American citizens could not sell arms to belligerents. Such embargoes were to last six months and were renewable. The law also stated that American citizens traveling on ships of belligerents did so at their own risk.

1936—*Neutrality Act* This law merely renewed the Act of 1935 and forbade loans or credits to belligerents.

1937—*Neutrality Acts* The Spanish conflict broke out in July, 1936, but the previous neutrality laws did not apply to civil wars. So in January 1937 Congress placed an embargo on munitions to either side. This was a strange action. The normal procedure would have been to continue trade as usual with the government of Spain, in this case the Loyalists, and ignore the rebels unless and until they won the war. This embargo kept munitions from the Loyalists while the rebels got massive help from Germany and Italy. Our action was not only irregular, but against our own interests. In May, another Neutrality Act gave the President discretion in the use of embargoes and forbade travel by United States citizens on ships of belligerents. This act was aimed at the renewed Sino-Japanese conflict. The President forbade any U.S. government vessels to carry munitions to belligerents, but allowed any private ships to do so at their own risk. As Japan had control of the waters in the Far East, this worked out to her benefit. Again a neutrality act was working for the wrong side.

1937—*The "Quarantine" Speech* In October, President Roosevelt said that, more often than not, our neutrality laws had aided the aggressors (the rebels in Spain and the Japanese in Asia). He urged a "world-wide quarantine" against aggressors and by these remarks clearly took a partisan position which created quite a bit of criticism. However, he proved to be just a step or two ahead of public opinion which soon caught up with him.

1937—*Panay Incident (Dec. 12th)* Japanese planes bombed the U.S. gunboat *Panay* in the Yangtze River. The attack, which killed two Americans and wounded several, was deliberate on the part of the Japanese pilots although their government called it an accident and agreed to our demands for an apology and reparations. As Asia seemed very remote, public opinion in the United States was strongly opposed to war with Japan. Representative Ludlow of Indiana sponsored an amendment that would have required a nationwide referendum before Congress could declare war unless we were invaded. It seemed sure to pass Congress until President Roosevelt sent a message in January 1938 to be read before the House by Speaker Bankhead. It said, "Such an amendment to the Constitution as that proposed would cripple any President in his conduct of our foreign relations, and it would encourage other nations to believe that they could violate American rights with impunity." This message turned the tide, and the House defeated the Ludlow amendment 209 to 188.

1938—Japan denounced the Five Power Pact of the Washington Conference of 1921 because she was no longer willing to accept a ratio of capital ships inferior to that of Great Britain and the United States. The reaction of our Congress was the appropriation of over $1 billion to start building a two-ocean navy.

1939—*Neutrality Act* This was a "cash and carry" plan. All arms embargoes were lifted so that any ships could come to our ports, pay cash, and carry away anything they could buy. Here, finally, was a "neutrality" law which served our purposes. The British and French had control of the surface of the seas and their merchant marine could have almost a monopoly of this "cash and carry" trade. This was our first step toward becoming the "arsenal of democracy."

1940 (Jan.)—President Roosevelt called for 50,000 planes a year and $18 billion for national defense—and got them both. Four months later he got another $1.3 billion.

1940 (Apr.-June)—Hitler took Norway and the name Quisling became a synonym for traitor.

1940 (May-June)—Hitler took the Netherlands and Belgium.

1940 (May 28-June 4)—British and French troops totaling about 340,000 were rescued from the beaches at Dunkirk.

1940 (June)—Prime Minister Churchill appealed for war supplies, "Give us the tools and we'll do the job." The United States responded so wholeheartedly that we were soon extending "all aid short of war."

1940 (June)—President Roosevelt appointed two Republicans to cabinet posts; Henry L. Stimson as Secretary of War and Frank Knox as Secretary of the Navy.

1940 (July)—France fell.

1940 (Aug.-Oct.)—*Battle of Britain* The R.A.F. (Royal Air Force) beat off the "Luftwaffe" and prevented an invasion of the British Isles.

1940 (Sept.)—The United States transferred to England 50 "overage" destroyers in return for air bases on Newfoundland, Bermuda, Jamaica, Trinidad, and several smaller islands in the Caribbean area.

1940 (Sept.)—*Selective Service Act* This was the first peace time draft in our history. All men between the ages of 21 and 35 were registered.

1941 (March)—*Lend-Lease* Britain had spent all her money and exhausted all her credits, so Congress passed the Lend-Lease Act to permit the President to "sell, transfer, exchange, lease, or otherwise dispose of" war equipment to any nation for use in the interests of the United States. The official title of the law was "An Act to Promote the Defense of the United States."

1941 (April)—The United States agreed to defend Greenland for Denmark in return for the use of the island during the war.

1941 (June 22)—Hitler astounded the world, and probably defeated himself, by attacking the U.S.S.R. The reason for this break with Russia was the refusal of the Soviet Union to give up her ambition to control the Dardanelles. Both F.D.R. and Churchill immediately welcomed the U.S.S.R. as a partner in war and hoped she could keep Hitler occupied on the eastern front for as long as six months. She did. Lend-Lease was extended to Russia.

1941 (July)—Iceland agreed to U.S. occupation for the duration of the war.

1941 (Aug.)—*The Atlantic Charter* A few days' conference between Roosevelt and Churchill on British and American warships off Newfoundland brought forth a declaration of war aims. Some of them were:

1] No territorial gains are sought by the U.S. or Britain.

2] Readjustment of territories must be in accord with the wishes of the inhabitants.

3] People have the right to choose their own form of government.

4] Trade barriers should be lowered.

5] There must be disarmament, first of the aggressors and then of all other nations.

6] There must be freedom from fear and want. (With speech and religion these are the "four freedoms.")

7] Freedom of the seas must be established for all.

8] An association of nations must be formed.

1941 (Sept.-Oct.)—*"Shoot on sight"* German submarines had attacked U.S. naval vessels. The *Greer* and the *Kearny* were attacked, but not sunk; the *Reuben James* was sunk with about 100 lives lost. Roosevelt gave orders for U.S. naval craft to "shoot on sight" any submarines in the North Atlantic.

1941 (Dec. 7)—*Pearl Harbor* At 7:55 A.M., Hawaiian time (1:20 P.M., Washington time) the surprise attack sunk or damaged 19 naval vessels, destroyed 150 planes, killed 2,335 soldiers and sailors, and 68 civilians.

1941 (Dec. 8)—Congress declared war by a unanimous vote in the Senate and only one dissenting vote (a pacifist) in the House.

1941 (Dec. 11)—Germany and Italy declared war on the United States.

Fighting World War II

In the Pacific

1941 (Dec.)—Japan took the islands of Guam and Wake.

1942 (April 18)—Major General "Jimmy" Doolittle's squadron of B-25's carried the war to Japan by bombing Tokyo.

1942 (May 6)—General MacArthur was forced to evacuate Corregidor and surrender the Philippines. Upon leaving, after a severe and heroic struggle, MacArthur said, "I shall return."

1942 (May 7-8)—In the Coral Sea off the northeast coast of Australia a carrier based air battle took place. None of the ships got near enough to engage each other, but the planes sank one carrier on each side and, in addition, U.S. planes damaged other Japanese naval vessels.

1942 (June 3-6)—An air-naval battle off Midway Island was the first major U.S. victory over Japan. Japan's attempt to take Midway was repulsed with losses to the enemy of 4 carriers and about 275 planes.

1942 (Aug. 7, '42 to Feb. 9, '43)—United States started its island hopping offensive toward Japan with a landing at Guadalcanal in the Solomon Islands.

The character of the fighting, as the United States' landing forces took key islands in each island group, took on the same patterns. The Japs fought from caves and dug-outs until annihilated; they often preferred death to surrender and had to be burned out or burned to death by flame throwers. It was foot by foot fighting of the toughest kind. On some islands an attack was a matter of inching along, literally crawling through jungle-like growth seeking an enemy cleverly camouflaged in trees and grass. The price in men paid for these islands was great.

1943 (Nov.)—Landings on Tarawa and Makin gave the United States control of the Gilbert Islands.

1944 (Feb.)—Landings on Kwajalein and Eniwetok gave the United States control of the Marshall Islands.

1944 (July)—Landings on Saipan and Guam gave the United States control of the Mariana Islands.

1944 (Oct.)—The battle in Leyte Gulf in the southern Philippines broke the back of the Japanese fleet. Their losses included 2 battleships, 4 carriers, 9 cruisers, and 9 destroyers. Japan lacked the reserve strength to replace or to sustain such losses.

1944 (Dec.)—MacArthur's "I shall return" promise was fulfilled when he led a landing force onto the island of Mindoro.

1945 (Feb.)—Tokyo suffered its first heavy bombing raid by 90 B-29's.

1945 (Feb.)—The island of Iwo Jima was taken at the cost of 4,000 marines killed and over 15,000 wounded. The American flag was placed on top of Mt. Suribachi on February 23rd.

1945 (March-June)—The island of Okinawa was taken at the cost of over 11,000 killed and about 34,000 wounded. The United States had fought its way to within 360 miles of Japan.

1945 (Aug. 6)—The first atomic bomb dropped on Hiroshima. The death toll was about 160,000.

1945 (Aug. 9)—The second atomic bomb was dropped on Nagasaki.

1945 (Aug. 15)—*V.J. Day.*

In Africa and Europe

1942 (Nov.)—General Dwight D. Eisenhower, in cooperation with the British, made landings in Africa and took Casablanca, Oran, and Algiers.

1943 (Feb.-May)—On February 14th General Eisenhower took command of the allied forces in North Africa. Aided by General George S. Patton and British General Montgomery, he forced the surrender on May 13th of 250,000 troops and brought the African campaign to a close.

1943 (Sept.)—General Mark Clark led an American invasion of Italy at Salerno, south of Naples.

1944 (Jan.)—General Eisenhower was made Supreme Commander of the Allied Expeditionary Forces. His headquarters (SHAEF) were in London.

1944 (June 6)—*"D-Day"* Invasion by allied forces of western Europe was the start of "Operation Overlord," the greatest naval-military assault of all time. The men in England had been trained for this venture for months and were well over 2,000,000 in numbers. The first few hours of Operation Overlord included heavy air bombardment all along the French and Belgian coasts; 4,000 troop ships crossing the channel; 176,000 troops; air cover by 11,000 planes; glider planes with parachute troops being dropped behind enemy lines; and about 600 fighting ships escorting the troops and bombarding the enemy batteries which defended the landing areas. This mammoth operation was under the command of General Eisenhower. By July a million troops had crossed into France and by September the number had reached more than two million.

1944 (Sept. 12)—United States troops entered Germany.

1944 (Dec. 16-26)—The Battle of the Bulge was Germany's last counter offensive. It took place near the French-Belgian border in the Ardennes sector along the Meuse River and cost the Americans 8,000 killed and 21,000 wounded.

1945 (May 1)—Hitler's death was reported. Berlin was occupied on May 2nd.

1945 (May 8)—*V.E. Day*   Unconditional surrender.

STATISTICS (*to the nearest 1,000*)

Total U.S. forces	12,466,000
Dead	322,000
Wounded	676,000
Captured	124,000
Captives returned	111,000

Due to improved medical care, penicillin and sulfa drugs, blood plasma, and air transport to hospital centers, the losses from sickness and wounds were minimal.

** Building the Peace

Apparently the experience of World War I taught the necessity of preparing for peace while still fighting the war. Partners in war are in the mood for reasonable cooperation when the horrors of war are staring them in the face daily and their people are resolved against any re-occurrence. Partners in war so soon fall out with one another after the battles are over that it was a wise move to build the foundations for peace as early as possible. Unlike the climate of opinion during World War I, there was no inclination in the 1940's to do only one job at a time, finish the war and then build the peace; sentiment among governments and peoples alike favored planning for peace while winning the war. At many conferences called primarily

to plan the next moves and objectives of the war there was also serious attention given to preparing the peace. The following list gives a skeletal account in chronological order of peace moves leading to the formation of the United Nations.

1943 (Sept.)—Representative James W. Fulbright introduced a resolution favoring United States' participation in an international organization with power enough to establish and maintain "a just and lasting peace." This was a very unusual move as the House has little influence on foreign policy and is not expected to voice an opinion or to suggest a policy. But as the branch of our government closest to the people, it was undoubtedly reflecting popular opinion and feeling. The House resolution passed by a vote of 360 to 29.

1943 (Oct.)—The Moscow Conference was the first meeting during the war of the United States, Great Britain, and the U.S.S.R. The heads of foreign affairs, Cordell Hull, Anthony Eden, and Vyacheslav Molotov recognized the "necessity of establishing at the earliest practicable date a general international organization based on the principle of the sovereign equality of all peace-loving states, and open to membership by all states, large and small, for the maintenance of international peace and security."

1943 (Oct.)—Senator Tom Connally, chairman of the Foreign Relations Committee, introduced a resolution which quoted the above Moscow declaration. It was adopted in the Senate by 85 to 5. This was significant as an assurance to other nations that the United States would ratify a treaty making us a member of whatever peace machinery was set up. It was a promise that the United States was not about to present the world with another international organization and then back away from it at the last minute.

1943 (Nov.)—Roosevelt, Churchill, and Stalin met at Teheran, the capital of Iran, marking the first meeting of the heads of state for the Big Three. Some tentative plans were made to start the international organization for peace that the Moscow conference had recently declared to be necessary.

1944 (July)—The Bretton Woods Conference met in the White Mountains of New Hampshire with the representatives of 44 nations present. An International Monetary Fund was established to help stabilize the currencies of Western Europe and hence promote trade. An International Bank for Reconstruction and Development was created to aid devastated nations.

The United States contributed about 25% of the $8.8 billion for the Monetary Fund and about 35% of the $9.1 billion for the Bank. The U.S.S.R. had been invited, but did not attend.

1944 (Aug.-Oct.)—The Dumbarton Oaks Conference was held in Washington, D.C. The United States, Great Britain, the U.S.S.R., and China drew up a charter which was to serve as a starting point from which to work at the San Francisco Conference to be held later. Concerning their rights on the Security Council of the proposed United Nations, the big powers were unable to reach definite conclusions, except that they would each insist on a veto. The U.S.S.R. was inclined to have the veto enable a member to keep any issue from coming before the Council for discussion. The Russian position here closely paralleled the position taken by the United States under the Root Formula for our entrance to the World Court.

1945 (Feb.)—The Yalta meeting in the Crimea found Roosevelt, Churchill, and Stalin considering plans to attempt a quick end to the war they were obviously winning. Russia promised to set up a front against Japan, a pledge which Roosevelt thought, by having Russia share the burden of attack, would save a great many American lives. The three powers agreed to see that the liberated states had representative governments chosen by free elections. The date was set for the San Francisco Conference on April 25, 1945.

The Yalta Conference has long been a controversial issue in America. The Russians did set up a front in Manchuria and occupy northern Korea as agreed at Yalta, but the atomic bomb made the presence of Russian forces unnecessary for victory, and much too handy for Soviet pressure in Korea. Stalin broke his promise to promote, or at least allow, free elections and representative government in the nations adjacent to her. How much of this should have been foreseen and how much is now "Monday-morning quarterbacking" is everyone's privilege to judge. Certain it is that had Stalin refused at Yalta to promise free elections and representative governments, there was nothing Roosevelt or Churchill could have done. No move would have been made that would have lessened the Russian war effort. At the time, Roosevelt was especially pleased with the Yalta meeting because he had a definite pledge of help against Japan and a definite assurance that Russia would attend the San Francisco meeting to help form the United Nations.

1945 (April-June)—The San Francisco Conference which drew up the United Nations charter was attended by delegates from 50 nations. Early in the Conference the U.S.S.R. insisted that the veto power must include the right to prevent discussion of any issue that came before the Security Council. Secretary of State Edward Stettinius threatened United States' withdrawal from the Conference unless Russia modified her position. Our representative in Moscow, Harry Hopkins, was instructed by President Truman (President Roosevelt had died on April 12th.) to make Stalin aware of the seriousness of the issue and urge a shift in the Russian position. Stalin sent word that Russia would not insist on the veto power extending to the right to prevent an issue coming before the Council for discussion. The other nations vigorously opposed the veto power given to the United States, Great Britain, the U.S.S.R., France, and China, but it became evident that without such a favored position the five nations would not join the United Nations. Other than this one defeat, the smaller nations wrote a great many changes into the Dumbarton Oaks version of the charter, so that it was truly representative of the 50 nations at the Conference. The main organs of the United Nations were: a Council of 11 members with five of them permanent and having veto power, while the other six members served two-year terms; a General Assembly where every member nation had one vote; an Economic and Social Council of 18 members chosen by the General Assembly to deal with a great variety of problems other than military; an International Court of Justice composed of 15 judges selected by the Assembly and the Security Council; a Trusteeship Council consisting of members from all nations administering trust areas and an equal number of nations without such trusteeships; and a Secretariat, presided over by the chief officer of the U.N., the Secretary General, to do the administrative work of the U.N.

1945 (July 28)—By a vote of 89 to 2 the United States Senate ratified the treaty, making us members of the United Nations. It is interesting to note that this action was taken before V.J. Day, even before the disasters that struck Hiroshima and Nagasaki.

Harry S. Truman   1945-1953

1884

DEMOCRAT

☆

After having served less than three months of his fourth term, President Franklin D. Roosevelt died on April 12th of a cerebral hemorrhage. Vice-President Harry Truman assumed office faced with a war to be finished and the difficult problems of a postwar period.

Truman's Election in 1948

This was an election the Democrats expected to lose, that is, almost all the Democrats except Harry Truman. The Nominating Convention at Philadelphia was a dispirited affair. The Democrats had approached General Eisenhower to see if he would accept the nomination, but he had already refused a similar offer from the Republicans on the ground that a civilian would more suitably occupy the office. It was a bit awkward for Truman when, after having been President for almost four years, his party nominated him only after trying to get someone else to run. Justice William O. Douglas didn't help matters when he refused to step down from the Supreme Court to run as the candidate for Vice-President. The 70-year-old Senator Barkley of Kentucky was persuaded to help the Party by accepting the second spot on the ticket. Truman had offended the deep South by a strong stand in favor of civil rights, and it was hoped that the Kentucky Senator would hold the South in the Democratic column. Nevertheless, several delegates from Southern states (Louisiana, Mississippi, Alabama, Florida, Georgia, South Carolina) walked out of the Convention and formed the States' Rights Party (Dixiecrats) with Governor Thurmond of South Carolina as their candidate. The Democratic Party was still further weakened when Henry Wallace, Secretary of Agriculture, organized and headed a Progressive Party which promised to expand the New Deal more vigorously and to accomplish good relations with the U.S.S.R. Both Thurmond and Wallace cut into the regular Democratic vote. With this drab outlook most Democratic leaders sat out this election; but President Truman made an aggressive campaign. His speeches during his "whistle-stop" tours were brief, caustic, and sincere. He carried the conviction that he knew what he was talking about and he pulled no punches. He lambasted the "do-nothing" 80th Congress (Republican-elected in 1946) whose only accomplishment was the "slave-labor" Taft-Hartley Act passed over his veto. He delighted many of his listeners who encouraged him with, "Give 'em hell, Harry."

After General Eisenhower had refused the nomination, the Republicans met at Philadelphia and, for the second time, nominated Governor Dewey of New York. Dewey expected to win, and his expectations were shared by the highly impartial betting fraternity which gave odds as high as 15 to 1. Dewey's speeches were longer and fewer than Truman's. His language was more polished, his manner suave, and his attitude toward his opponent condescending. He kept to generalities as if unwilling to make commitments that might later come home to roost. His campaign showed him to be able, clever, confident, and noncommittal.

	Popular Vote	Electoral Vote
Truman	24,105,812	303
Dewey	21,970,065	189
Thurmond	1,169,063	39
Wallace	1,157,172	0

The Democrats regained control of both Houses of Congress and won 20 of the 33 gubernatorial contests. President Truman had won a campaign while his own party practically sat on the sidelines and watched; he had fought his way to the undisputed leadership of the Party.

* Taft-Hartley Act (1947)

This act reflected the views of the Congress elected in 1946 which had Republican majorities in both Houses for the first time since Hoover's administration. Congress felt the Wagner-Connery Labor Act had tipped the advantage heavily in favor of labor and so it passed the Taft-Hartley Act to restore the balance. It passed over President Truman's veto.

Major Provisions

1] Unions, as well as employers, were subject to being sued for breach of contract.

2] The closed shop was declared illegal. (A closed shop is one which requires a worker to belong to the union at the time he is hired.)

3] Unions must submit financial reports to public authorities.

4] The "check-off" system of paying union dues was made illegal. (The check-off was a deduction from the worker's pay to be given to the union and thus made the employer collect dues for the union.)

5] Union officers had to take an oath that they were not members of the Communist party.

6] The National Labor Relations Board could issue an injunction to delay a strike for 80 days if the strike threatened "irreparable damage" to the public interest.

7] Secondary boycotts and jurisdictional disputes were outlawed. (A jurisdictional dispute is one between two unions over which has the right (jurisdiction) to perform a certain job. Should the carpenters' union install metal window frames in a hotel building or should the steel workers' union do the job? The employer should not be the victim of a dispute between two unions.)

Organized labor bitterly attacked the Taft-Hartley Act, calling it a "slave-labor" law, but time has proved that it has not hurt labor's position. The communist oath provision is probably useless and perhaps unfair; useless because any real Communist who managed to become an officer in a labor union would gladly take the anti-Communist oath, and unfair because only the representatives of labor are required to take the oath, not the spokesmen for the employers. The 80-day injunction can easily be made ineffective by setting the date for a strike 80 days before the most strategic time to call it.

* Presidential Succession Act

At President Truman's request Congress passed a Presidential Succession Act which provided for the Vice-President to be followed in order by the Speaker of the House, the President pro-tempore of the Senate, the Secretary of State, and down the Cabinet according to rank. This replaced the order in effect since 1886 which had gone right from Vice-President to the Cabinet officials. So far, the matter of succession beyond the Vice-President has fortunately been purely academic; but Truman felt that the law should be changed to make it almost certain that only an elected official, such as the Speaker of the House or the temporary chairman of the Senate, should become President. One may question the significance of the election of a member of Congress as a measure of the popular choice by the nation as a whole; a congressional district, or even a state, is an insignificant sampling of the entire country. As either the House or the Senate, and sometimes both at once, may be controlled by the opposition party, a shift in the office of the President from one party to the other without an election is much more likely now than before. A more immediate problem concerning the Presidency is the lack of any provision for determining just when a President is incapacitated by illness, or some other cause, from carrying on the responsibilities of his office; or just when his recovery justifies his resumption of responsibility. There had been considerable talk, but no action, about this question of disability.

Trials of War Criminals

An International Military Tribunal was established under the direction of Supreme Court Justice Robert Jackson who also served as chief counsel for the prosecution. The crimes were classified as against "peace," "humanity," and "international law." A crime against peace meant the violation of the Kellogg-Briand Treaty of 1928 in which nations pledged not to engage in aggressive war. It may be a step forward if men in responsible political positions can be tried and punished for having started a war; but such trials can take place only when the aggressors happen to lose. As to fighting a modern war with due regard to "humanity" and "international law," the idea appears to many to be intrinsically ridiculous. One lesson of fairly recent history is that any new weapon that is effective will be used, humanity or international law to the contrary notwithstanding. The submarine, the massive bombing raids, and the atomic bomb are cases in point. The atomic bombs of 1945 are now crude old-fashioned toys compared with those already stockpiled in the U.S. and the U.S.S.R.; and the delivery service for the up-to-date models is said to be rather sudden to any point on the world's surface. Scores of such missiles are presumedly all set for dispatch to hit long-since-determined targets. If, or should one say *when,* germ warfare and poison gas become controllable so that they will not boomerang, they will receive official sanction and be added to the arsenals of all truly advanced nations: Trying to regulate and classify the many ways of destroying each other, either en masse or bit by bit as a crime, or not a crime, against humanity has an air of unreality about it. The crime, of course, is war itself; not the way in which it is waged. If the execution of a score or so of top brass and government officials of Germany and Japan have served to make another war less likely, the trials have been of use; otherwise many will consider them to have been pointless and a bad precedent.

** Truman Doctrine (1947)

Late in 1946 about 13,000 communist-led guerrillas entered northern Greece from Albania, Yugoslavia, and Bulgaria. Greece complained to the Security Council of the United Nations which sent a commission to investigate. The U.N. commissioners were allowed to move freely throughout Greece but were not allowed in Albania, Yugoslavia, or Bulgaria. The U.S.S.R. and her satellites claimed that there was a genuine revolt of the Greek people against the government, but the fact was that the guerrillas were Communist invaders. The situation in Greece reached a climax at this time because UNRRA (United Nations Relief & Rehabilitation) was closing up shop on March 31, 1947 and, in addition, British troops which had helped to discourage Communist aggression were being pulled out of Greece because England was on the edge of financial collapse and couldn't afford to maintain them any longer. In short, with Communist nations, directed by the U.S.S.R., closing in to take her over, Greece was helpless.

At the same time, Turkey was being pressured by Russia. In 1945 Russia refused to renew a 20-year-old friendship pact which placed control of the Dardanelles under a commission of 9 nations. Russia was insisting that the nine-nation control be changed to a two-nation control, Russia and Turkey. At the same time the Russian press was strongly anti-Turkish, referring to the Turks as fascists and reactionaries while reviving old claims Russia had on Turkish territory. Turkey reacted to this ominous pressure in two ways: she stopped her internal bickerings and generated an intense hostility against Russia, and she appropriated so large a share of her budget to armaments that her economy was in danger of collapse. The Turks much preferred fighting and going broke to remaining solvent and being gobbled up.

This was the setting for the Truman Doctrine. The perfect solution would have been action by the United Nations to arrange economic assistance to Greece and guarantee both Greece and Turkey against aggression. Obviously the U.N. could do no more than investigate, no more than clearly tell the world just what the situation was. This, in itself, is often a service of great value, but in this case it would not suffice. President Truman said he would base the policy of this country on "the frank recognition that totalitarian regimes imposed on free peoples, by direct or indirect aggression, undermine the foundations of international peace and hence the security of the United States." On March 12, 1947, he began aid to both Greece and Turkey. For Greece there were relief supplies as well as military equipment and military personnel to help organize anti-guerrilla forces. For Turkey the aid was almost completely military and much of it was good equipment a bit outmoded for our army and air force, but far superior to anything Turkey had. This unilateral action stopped the penetration of the U.S.S.R. toward the Mediterranean. Three years after the Truman Doctrine, the guerrillas were no longer in Greece, railroads were operating, and roads were passable. Farm production had climbed higher than pre-war levels, about 40,000 new houses had been built, and cases of malaria had dropped from over 1,000,000 annually to 50,000. Turkey built an effective mechanized army and an air force of far greater striking power than before. For the first time in 27 years, Turkey held an election with more than one party running for office.

The Truman Doctrine was often said to be a policy of opposing Communism all over the world. A more accurate statement would be that it advocated opposing *aggressive* Communism all over the world. A completely realistic interpretation of the Truman Doctrine is that the United States will oppose aggressive Communism all over the world only when circumstances favor the success of our intervention. For example, to have intervened when Communist China invaded Tibet would have been foolish.

** The Marshall Plan (1947)

About three months after the President announced the Truman Doctrine, Secretary of State General George C. Marshall announced a gigantic plan for European Recovery (E.R.P.), usually called the Marshall Plan. As Marshall said in his speech at Harvard University on June 5, 1947, it was aimed against "hunger, poverty, desperation, and chaos"; it was an economic program of reconstruction which European nations were invited to join. They were asked to form plans for putting their transportation systems, their industrial plants, their agriculture, etc. into good working condition. The United States was offering to underwrite a receivership for war-devastated Europe. Twenty-two nations met at Paris in late June to consider the Marshall Plan and, although foreign minister Molotov of the U.S.S.R. called it an "imperialist plot" to enslave Europe, 16 nations continued the conference until a four-year plan had been formulated that would cost from $16 to $24 billion dollars. The debate in this country, in and out of Congress, went on for months. Some said the United States had better give up playing Santa Claus and they called the E.R.P. "operation rat-hole." Others believed that an economically prostrate Europe was fertile soil for Communist ideology and that Russia would roll over western Europe. Then Russia would have the technical know-how of the people of western Europe and its equipment, both to be organized for world conquest. The United States could wait for that kind of war and fight it alone, or it could revive Europe to become our allies against the Communist bid for world domination.

Russia helped measurably to decide the issue by her attack upon Czechoslovakia in March, 1948. Czechoslovakia's loss of freedom through Communist infiltration and a Moscow-directed coup was answered in the United States Congress by an overwhelming vote for the Marshall Plan which became law on April 3, 1948. Congress appropriated $6.8 billion for the first 15 months and contemplated further expenditures over four years totaling $17 billion. Some of Russia's satellites had shown an inclination to come into the E.R.P. but were quickly ordered by Moscow to stay away. As a very feeble counter-balance to the Marshall Plan, Russia formed the Council of Mutual Economic Assistance (U.S.S.R., Poland, Czechoslovakia, Bulgaria, Hungary, and Rumania).

* Germany and Berlin

While the San Francisco Conference was in progress shaping the hope of the world for peace, the diplomatic maneuverings of the Soviet Union in central Europe were pointing ominously in the opposite direction. In order to bring the war to a close, it was necessary to arrange treaties with several nations. From the outset, Russia used tactics of delay; arrangements that should have required several days or a week or two, took over a year. For instance, it was not until February 1947 that treaties were concluded with Bulgaria, Finland, Hungary, Italy, and Rumania. The masterpiece of Russian stalling was the settlement about Germany. Over two months before V.E. Day a temporary plan for the occupation of Germany had been agreed upon. Some of eastern Germany was added to Poland and some to Russia. Then Germany was divided into an eastern zone occupied by Russia, and a somewhat larger western zone divided among Britain, France, and the United States. Berlin was 100 miles within the Russian zone and was itself divided into East Berlin as the Russian area and West Berlin for the British, French, and American sectors (see map). At first the British, French, and American authorities were so affected by the horrors discovered in prison camps that their first reaction was to reduce Germany to a simple agricultural community which would have no capacity for future war. A few months went by with nothing done to establish either a government or an economy, and poverty and misery among the German people deepened with each day. German money was worthless, so the people bartered their possessions for food. As poverty and hopelessness are natural preludes to Communism, this situation served Stalin's purpose. By late 1946 the western allies revised their ideas about keeping Germany a weak agri-

Germany and Berlin—Divided

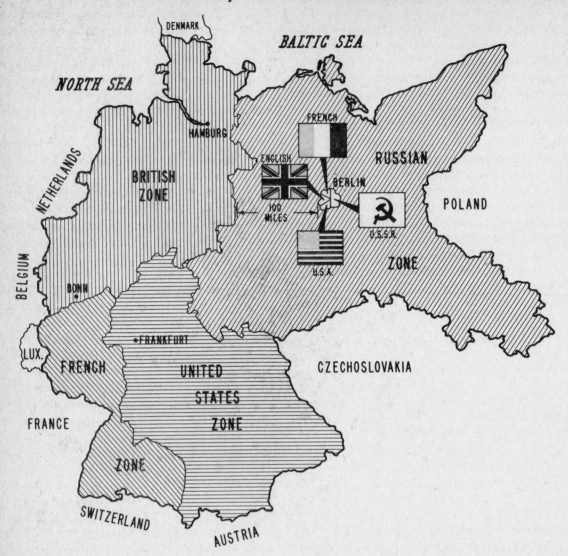

cultural nation. Russia's delaying tactics had convinced them that Stalin would accept no agreement unless it made Germany a Communist nation under Soviet control. The allied answer was the unification of the British, French, and American zones into West Germany which they proceeded to build into a vigorous commercial and industrial economy. Under allied direction a constitution was drawn up for a federal government with a bicameral legislature. A President had duties that were more ceremonial than important and a Chancellor was the real chief executive. These political and economic buildups made substantial progress in 1947 and brought from Russia the charge that the western allies had violated the Potsdam Agreement. The allies suggested the extension of the Bonn government to include East Germany as it was a people's government established through free elections; but the U.S.S.R. set up a militarized puppet state in

East Germany which they called "The People's Republic."

In an attempt to force the western allies out of Berlin the Russians created a crisis in June, 1948. For some almost unbelievable reason or oversight, the western powers had allowed themselves to be buried 100 miles within the Russian sector of Germany with no path under their control for getting in or out of Berlin. Russia placed barriers on highways, waterways, and railways and allowed no traffic between Berlin and West Germany. Russia was saying, in effect, "Get out of Berlin or stay and watch the people in the British, French, and American sectors of the city starve." The Americans, with some British help, organized the "Air Lift" to perform "Operation Vittles." The apparently impossible was achieved. From June 24, 1948 through May 17, 1949 a population of 2¼ million was supplied by planes with food, fuel, and other necessities. This remarkable display of organizational skill and air power brought a settlement and resumption of normal transportation facilities. The Air Lift convinced the West Germans that the allies would stand with them against Soviet pressure and has probably convinced the Russians that the Berlin issue cannot be settled by force short of a major war.

** North Atlantic Treaty Organization (NATO) (1949)

On March 17, 1949 Great Britain, France, Belgium, the Netherlands, and Luxembourg signed a fifty-year agreement at Brussels "to secure the principles of democracy, personal freedom, and political liberty." That very same day President Truman proclaimed the Brussels Pact a noble and notable step which deserved the full support of the United States. On April 4, 1949, at Washington, twelve nations signed the North Atlantic Treaty Organization (NATO). On July 21st the Senate ratified the treaty which stated in part that "the parties agree that an armed attack on one or more of them in Europe or North America shall be considered an attack against them all . . . and agree that if such an attack occurs, each of them will assist the party or parties so attacked by taking such action as it deems necessary, including the use of armed force, to restore and maintain the security of the North Atlantic area." This purely military defensive alliance went ahead and early in 1951 General Dwight D. Eisenhower took command of NATO with headquarters in France. Turkey, Greece, and West Germany joined to make a total membership of 15 nations. (Belgium, Britain, Canada, Denmark, France, Greece, Iceland, Italy, Luxembourg, the Netherlands (Holland), Norway, Portugal, Turkey, West Germany, and the United States.)

The Truman Doctrine turned back a serious threat of Soviet expansion to the Mediterranean, The Marshall Plan (ERP) started recovery in western Europe, and NATO started a military defense against Soviet expansion westward into Europe. The fact that the United States possessed the atomic bomb may have been an important factor in checking Russia enough to permit these policies to become effective.

** Korea (1950-'53)

At both Cairo in 1943 and Potsdam in 1945 it was agreed by the major powers that Korea would "in due course" be free and independent. Russia re-affirmed this pledge when she declared war on Japan, August 8, 1945. When Japan accepted surrender terms the United States proposed that the Japanese in Korea north of the 38th parallel surrender to Russian troops, and those south of the parallel surrender to U.S. forces. While it was not the intention of the United States that the division of Korea would be permanent, it soon became clear that the Soviet Union had assumed otherwise. In December, 1945, foreign ministers of Great Britain, Russia, and the United States agreed at Moscow that a Joint Commission of Russians and Americans would consult with Koreans to set up a democratic government for Korea. For almost two years Russia blocked every move toward the accomplishment of this purpose, and in November of 1947 a United Nations Temporary Commission was formed to supervise the drafting of a constitution for a National Korean Government. Russia claimed that the U.N. had no jurisdiction and refused to allow their Commission to enter North Korea. Nothing was acceptable to Russia except a Communist Korea under Moscow domination. So the U.N. formed a representative government chosen by free elections and thus the Republic of Korea (South Korea only) was officially established on August 15, 1948. By January 1, 1949 thirty-two nations had recognized the Republic of Korea, but the Russian veto kept her from becoming a member of the U.N. Russia set up the People's Republic of Korea, a militarized Communist dictatorship, north of the 38th parallel. In response to a request by the U.N. for the withdrawal of foreign troops from Korea, United States forces left by July 1949 and Russia claimed that her troops had also left; but, unlike the United States, she refused to allow any inspection by the U.N. to verify the alleged fact.

At dawn on Sunday, June 25, 1950, the North Koreans crossed the 38th parallel in force. On Saturday night at 9:40 (because of the time difference) the United States got news of this aggression. At the request of the U.S., the Security Council met at Lake Success, N.Y., at 2 P.M. Sunday, and by a vote of 9 to 0 adopted a resolution calling for withdrawal of North Korean forces to the 38th parallel and cessation of hostilities. It also called upon "all Members to render every assistance to the United Nations in the execution of this resolution and to refrain from giving assistance to North Korean authorities." A few hours later, President Truman ordered United States' forces to Korea. Public announcement that the U.S. was backing the U.N. resolution with "air and sea forces to give the Korean Government troops cover and support" was made on June 27th. This fast action by the U.N. was made possible by the absence of the Soviet delegate on the Security Council. On January 13, 1950 he had walked out of the Security Council because

"Red" China was not recognized as the official China, given membership in the United Nations, and made a permanent member of the Council. Russia was without a member on the Council until August 1, 1950 when it became the Soviet's turn to preside over it. Absenting herself at this critical time was a sizeable blunder by the Soviet Union, and a very fortunate one for the United Nations and the United States. Russia's absence made it possible for the Security Council to vote, as it did on July 7, 1950, to ask the U.S. to designate the commander of U.N. forces under the U.N. flag and the flags of such nations as took part in the Korean operation. The next day, President Truman appointed General MacArthur as commanding general of United Nations forces.

There seems no doubt that Mao Tse-tung, the leader of Communist China, and Stalin had expected no action, only protests, when North Korean forces crossed the 38th parallel. Although the Security Council acted a few hours before President Truman and therefore established the legal fact that the United Nations was opposing aggression in Korea; the actual fact was that the determination of the United States to use its power in support of South Korea probably accounted for the Security Council's resolution and certainly made possible its implementation. Somewhat over half of the manpower opposing the North Korean Communists were South Koreans; the bulk of the remainder were Americans with a scattering of help in men and equipment from about a dozen other U.N. members. During the first six weeks of the fighting, the U.S. Navy and Air Force bombed enemy supply lines and positions while troop re-enforcements arrived to bolster the South Koreans who had been pushed almost off the southern tip of the peninsula. But by mid-September the buildup of U.N. troops and superior air and sea support turned the North Koreans back up the peninsula so that, by the last week of September, the fighting was at the 38th parallel. A month later, General MacArthur had taken the North Korean capital, Pyongyang, and gone on to within five miles of the Yalu River which separated North Korea from Manchuria. President Truman and General MacArthur had met on Wake Island on October 14th to discuss the advisability of pressing the attack north of the 38th parallel. On October 11th Mao Tse-tung had said that his government "cannot stand idly by" while U.N. forces penetrated North Korea; but it was MacArthur's judgment that the Chinese would not interfere and that the best way to settle the Korean problem, once and for all, was to launch an "end-the-war" offensive and have it over with before

Christmas. President Truman accepted this judgment. On November 26th a veritable horde of Red Chinese troops came down from the Yalu River and forced a bitterly contested and very costly retreat down the peninsula and back across the 38th parallel.

General MacArthur called this a new war that called for a new policy. His new policy included bombing enemy supply lines and depots in Manchuria, bombing major Chinese cities, blockading Chinese ports, and mounting an invasion of the Chinese mainland with the Nationalist Chinese army under General Chiang Kai-shek. President Truman flatly rejected this plan, and General Omar Bradley, Chief of Staff, opposed MacArthur's policy because it would get the United States into "the wrong war, at the wrong time, in the wrong place, with the wrong enemy." MacArthur made public statements in support of his ideas and in opposition to those of the President; he wrote a letter to Joseph Martin, Republican minority leader of the House, which emphasized his differences with the President and contained the phrase, "there is no substitute for victory." This flare-up between a popular general and the President recalls the McClellan-Lincoln disagreements. As McClellan had many supporters against Lincoln, so too MacArthur had his adherents. He was clearly guilty of insubordination and had tried to *make* policy instead of just carry it out. There was nothing for President Truman to do except fire him. MacArthur came home and made speeches to enthusiastic audiences, and there the parallel with McClellan ended, because he did not, as McClellan did, run for President. Western Europe was solidly in agreement with Truman, and it is safe to say that the possibility of becoming bogged down in a war in the tremendous expanse of remote Asia was unattractive to the great majority of Americans. If World War III had to be fought, Europe, where we had some allies, seemed the better battleground for the United States; and Russia seemed the more important enemy.

As the U.N. forces were pushed south below Seoul, the capital of South Korea, they faced a winter to remember (January through March, 1951). Intense cold, blizzards, mountains, swamps, atrocities in the fighting, atrocities in the prison camps, and the fanatical tenacity of the enemy made this fighting as tough as war has witnessed. In late March, General MacArthur threatened to launch an air and naval attack on Red China. As such an action would be a gross violation of the policy of President Truman, MacArthur was removed from command and replaced by General

Matthew Ridgeway. In April the U.N. forces started a spring offensive which, by June, took them back to the 38th parallel, and just a bit beyond it. Here the fighting stopped after it had lasted almost exactly a year. The aggressors had been thrown back, but their miscalculation that no one would come to the aid of South Korea had been a costly one. North Koreans and Red Chinese suffered 1½ million casualties, the South Koreans about 400,000, and the Americans 33,000 dead and 103,000 wounded.

Traitors

The Cold War, which was on in earnest when the Truman Doctrine counteracted the Russian push toward the Mediterranean, brought with it a fear of Communist infiltration into labor unions, government, education, scientific research, and even the clergy. That such dangers existed was obvious, but to what extent the Moscow-directed Communists had infiltrated such areas was difficult, if not impossible, to know. The Republicans over-emphasized the success of the Communists in penetrating sensitive areas, and the Democrats underestimated it. This was to be expected as normal political reactions of the OUTS and the INS. Attempts to screen government employees through Loyalty Boards produced very questionable results, in part because the members of such Boards usually had neither the training to make valid judgments in the field of civil rights nor any special qualifications in the art of detecting espionage. Even the courts had their troubles with the Smith Act of 1940 (Alien Registration Act), which tried to control Communists by

making it a crime to advocate the overthrow of the United States by force and violence. Loyalty oaths became popular as a prerequisite for holding certain positions; but the person who would be most willing to take a loyalty oath would be the genuine Communist spy. Congressional hearings often denied witnesses civil rights that would be accorded them in a court trial. Senator McCarthy was eventually censured by his colleagues for his extreme disregard for facts and the rights of individuals who might be seriously hurt by his investigation tactics. But, on the whole, both the government and the people exercised better judgment in the anti-Red crusade of the 1950's than they had during the more hysterical Red-hunts of the 1920's.

There were spies in America. Alger Hiss, Judith Coplon, Harry Gold, Ethel and Julius Rosenberg, and Morton Sobell were all convicted and some were executed. The scientist, Klaus Fuchs, who fled from England to Russia, had worked among our scientists at the Los Alamos atomic research laboratories. We still have the Cold War and we almost certainly are victims of spies; we should hope that we have our share of successful agents working in key spots the world over. Screening of personnel by Loyalty Boards, demanding loyalty oaths, and making the security of the nation and the loyalty of individuals a political football have been ineffective ways of dealing with a complex problem. Detecting subversion may best be left to trained organizations such as the F.B.I. and the C.I.A. whose methods and effectiveness are always subject to Congressional inquiry and Executive control.

Dwight D. Eisenhower

1953-1961

1890-

REPUBLICAN

☆

EISENHOWER'S PUBLIC SERVICE BEFORE HE BECAME PRESIDENT

Assistant Military Advisor to the Philippines (1935-39)
Chief of War Plans Division in Office of Chief of Staff
Chief of Operations Division in Office of Chief of Staff
Commander of Invasion of North Africa (1942)
Commander of Invasion of Europe-SHAEF (1944)
Chief of Staff (1945)
Supreme Commander of Allied Powers in Europe-SHAPE (1951)

MAJOR ITEMS OF EISENHOWER'S ADMINISTRATIONS

Amendment XXII (See p. 70)
Brown v. Board of Education of
  Topeka, Kansas
French Indo-China
Southeast Asia Treaty Organization
  (SEATO)
Taiwan-Quemoy-Matsu

Suez Crisis (1956)
Eisenhower Doctrine
The Race for Space
St. Lawrence Seaway
Alaska and Hawaii Become States (1959)
"Summit" Conference and the U2

Eisenhower's Election in 1952 and Re-election in 1956

The Republican National Convention at Chicago witnessed a divided party with Senator Taft ("Mr. Republican") leading the conservative (right wing) faction in opposition to liberal Republicans. Taft claimed that the 20 years of Democratic supremacy resulted from the similarity of the two parties; that a Republican watered-down liberalism *vs.* a Democratic liberalism aroused no enthusiasm among voters opposed to F.D.R's New Deal and Truman's Fair Deal. But the liberal Republicans feared that a return to Hoover's "rugged individualism" would be an invitation to oblivion. Governors Dewey of New York and Adams of New Hampshire had talked with General Eisenhower in 1951 while he was commander of NATO. By this time Eisenhower was sure that he was a Republican (he had been offered the nomination by both parties in 1948), but he said his duties with NATO would not permit him to campaign for the nomination. This was an acceptance, and his name was entered in several state primaries. Taft campaigned vigor-

ously for the nomination and his success in some states brought Eisenhower away from NATO into active primary campaigning. At the Convention most of the disputed seats claimed by both Taft and Eisenhower delegates were finally awarded to Eisenhower who then was nominated on the first ballot. Senator Richard Nixon of California shared the ticket with him.

The Democrats met in Chicago with no candidate having a distinct advantage. Four months earlier, President Truman had made it clear that he would not run again. Governor Adlai Stevenson of Illinois was nominated on the third ballot.

Stevenson supported the New Deal-Fair Deal foreign and domestic policies and advocated the repeal of the Taft-Hartley Labor Law. He was a good campaigner with an unusual capacity for witicisms to lighten and enlighten the discussion of heavy and complex issues. Perhaps he was too much the professor-type speaker delivering a lecture before university students; his appeal was set on a high plane of idealism and understanding, much as had been typical of Woodrow Wilson. General Eisenhower was a great military hero; and he was more than that. With his proven capacity for toughness and heavy responsibility he had a mildness of manner, an openness of countenance, and a friendliness that inspired great trust. His career had demonstrated strength and ability, his personality inspired affection. "I like Ike" was more than a slogan, it was the truth. In his campaign he offered nothing new or different. He was not going to attempt to undo any New Deal-Fair Deal achievements. His foreign policy was to take no new direction; it was to be more effectively carried out. He promised to go to Korea and get the long drawn out arguments over the exchange of prisoners settled quickly. He promised a house cleaning in Washington which, the people were convinced, needed some attention. The Truman administration had become a bit shabby around the edges. There were men claiming to have special "pull" in the right places who would, for a 10% commission, assure businessmen success in getting government contracts. Several officials received such "gifts" as refrigerators and fur coats for their wives from grateful recipients of contracts or other favors. It was all petty graft compared to the Grant and Harding administrations, but it put a good deal of sense in the slogans "it's time for a change" and "throw the rascals out."

	Popular Vote	Electoral Vote
Eisenhower	33,936,252	442
Stevenson	27,314,922	89

Stevenson carried only 9 states, but the Republican Party did not fare well. It won a majority of only 8 in the House and broke even in the Senate. The election was a tremendous Eisenhower victory; the man, not the Party, had won.

The re-election of Eisenhower in 1956 was a foregone conclusion. He had made a remarkable recovery from a heart attack and had resumed his usual work schedule early in 1956, so that his announcement in February that he would run again was welcomed and came as no surprise. At the Republican Nominating Convention in San Francisco, "Ike" was nominated by acclamation. Vice-President Nixon was again to be his running mate.

The Democrats met at Chicago and nominated Adlai Stevenson on the first ballot. The campaign was not very interesting as the issues and the candidates were the same as in 1952 with the similarities between the parties being more real than the differences. Stevenson kept the support of the intellectual idealists, "eggheads," Eisenhower called them; and the term was difficult to resent because,

although not intended as a compliment, it surely meant a person possessing superior intelligence and knowledge even though lacking the "common touch." Even the "eggheads" who voted for Stevenson probably liked Ike as a man; but the vast majority of voters not only liked Ike, they voted for him.

	Popular Vote	Electoral Vote
Eisenhower	35,585,316	457
Stevenson	26,031,322	74

While Eisenhower was winning all but 7 states and a plurality of about 9½ million votes, the Republican Party lost ground in the House and made no gain in the Senate. Again it was a personal victory.

In September, 1955, President Eisenhower had a heart attack; in June, 1957, he underwent a major operation, and in November, 1957, he suffered a slight stroke; but Congress has not yet passed any legislation to deal with the circumstance of a President who is unable to carry the responsibilities of the office. Fortunately, except for very brief periods of time, President Eisenhower's illnesses did not incapacitate him.

** Brown v. Board of Education of Topeka, Kansas

The 14th Amendment was adopted in 1868 (see pp. 69-70) and was part of the terms imposed upon the South by a victorious North after the Civil War. The ex-Confederate States, all except Tennessee, at first refused to accept this Amendment and were therefore referred to as "the sinful ten." The Amendment begins with a definition of a citizen which included the recently freed negro and then goes on to guarantee to all citizens equal rights and equal treatment under the law. In its historic setting there can be no doubt that the purpose of the Amendment and the intent of its framers were to force the ex-Confederate States to refrain from any discrimination by law against the black race. During the Reconstruction years when the scalawag and carpetbag governments were kept in power by the presence of federal troops, negroes did vote and hold office as every effort was made to enforce the letter of the 14th and 15th Amendments. After the election of Hayes in 1876, with the withdrawal of federal troops from the South, the complete supremacy of the whites was quickly re-established. Thus the issue rested for several decades with nothing more than an occasional futile attempt by negroes to get redress through court action. The Plessy v. Ferguson case of 1896 stated the legal reasoning that prevailed since the end of the Reconstruction Era until *Brown* v. *Topeka Board of Education* in 1954.

In *Plessy* v. *Ferguson* the case involved a ⅛th negro, Plessy, who had been fined $25 for riding in the white section of a railroad coach. Some of the key statements of the court follow.

> "Laws permitting, and even requiring, their (negroes & whites) separation in places where they are liable to be brought into contact do not necessarily imply the inferiority of either race to the other, and have been generally, if not universally, recognized as within the competency of the state legislatures in the exercise of their police power. The most common instance of this is connected with the establishment of separate schools for white and colored children, which has been held to be a valid exercise of the legislative power even by courts of states where the political rights of the colored race have been longest and most earnestly enforced."

> "We consider the underlying fallacy of the plaintiff's argument to consist in the assumption that the enforced separation of the two races stamps the colored race with a badge of inferiority. If this be so, it is not by reason of anything found in the act, but solely because the colored race chooses to put that construction upon it." This is the "separate but equal" argument that was the law until 1954.

In *Plessy* v. *Ferguson* Justice Harlan gave an interesting dissenting opinion.

> "But in the view of the Constitution, in the eye of the law, there is in this country no superior, dominant, ruling class of citizens. There is no caste here. Our Constitution is colorblind and neither knows nor tolerates classes among citizens. In respect of civil rights, all citizens are equal before the law. The humblest is the peer of the most powerful. The law regards man as man and takes no account of his surroundings or of his color when his civil rights as guaranteed by the supreme law of the land are involved."

This dissenting opinion became the prevailing opinon 58 years later.

Brown v. *Topeka Board of Education* involved suits by citizens from Kansas, South Carolina, Virginia, and Delaware. They all protested segregated schools and were essentially the same, so the Court considered them as part of this case. Negro parents claimed that the refusal to permit their children to attend schools with white children deprived them

of the equal protection of the laws under the 14th Amendment. Chief Justice Warren in delivering the unanimous decision of the Court made the following statements.

> "In approaching this problem, we cannot turn the clock back to 1868 when the Amendment was adopted, or even to 1896 when *Plessy* v. *Ferguson* was written. We must consider public education in the light of its full development and its present place in American life throughout the Nation. Only in this way can it be determined if segregation in public schools deprives these plaintiffs of the equal protection of the laws."

> "In these days, it is doubtful that any child may reasonably be expected to succeed in life if he is denied the opportunity of an education. Such an opportunity, where the state has undertaken to provide it, is a right which must be made available to all on equal terms."

> "Does segregation of children in public schools solely on the basis of race, even though the physical facilities and other "tangible" factors may be equal, deprive the children of the minority group of equal educational opportunities? We believe that it does."

> "Separate educational facilities are inherently unequal. Therefore, we hold that the plaintiffs and others similarly situated for whom the actions have been brought are, by reason of the segregation complained of, deprived of the equal protection of the laws guaranteed by the Fourteenth Amendment. This disposition makes unnecessary any discussion whether such segregation also violates the Due Process Clause of the Fourteenth Amendment."

> ". . . the courts will require that the defendants (school boards) make a *prompt and reasonable* start toward full compliance with our ruling. Once such a start has been made, the courts may find that additional time is necessary to carry out the ruling in an effective manner. The burden rests upon the defendants to establish that such time is necessary in the public interest and is consistent with *good faith compliance at the earliest practicable date.*" (Italics added.)

A separate case, *Bolling* v. *Sharpe,* in 1954 applied to the District of Columbia and the Court gave the same ruling, but based it on the due process of law guaranteed by the 5th Amendment.

It may be worth speculating on the probable reasons that brought such a sharp reversal, and by a unanimous decision, in 1954 as compared with 1896. Some possibilities are: two World Wars found the negro citizens quite as patriotic as the whites and many white soldiers may have been made more deeply conscious of the intrinsic injustice of racial discrimination; many more negroes are now educated and prosperous and, when this is so, it becomes more evident that aversion by whites to association with negroes is not altogether a matter of color, but a matter of cultural and economic differences; many large northern cities have a negro population with enough votes to hold the balance of power in the city, or even state, elections and therefore white city councilmen and state legislators support negroes' efforts for greater recognition; the presence of the United Nations in New York City brings the United States under the scrutiny of non-whites from the world over, and it is increasingly embarrassing to try to explain the difference between our belief about "all men are created equal" and our mode of living; race discrimination has become a severe handicap for the United States in its struggle against Communism and the influence of the U.S.S.R.; and perhaps the basic hypocrisy in the "separate-but-equal" theory has become too much for the nation to tolerate any longer. All of these factors have been creating a shifting climate of opinion for many years, and justices of the Supreme Court are also creatures of their changing environment.

It is a mistake to think that the shift away from segregation is an exclusively Southern problem; it is a national problem that will arouse deep antagonisms in every state of the Union, with the possible exception of Hawaii. We are witnessing the beginning of the end of second-class citizenship for negroes.

French Indo-China

The break-up of the French colonial empire in Indo-China was a matter of considerable difficulty for the United States. France showed no talent for letting go of colonies she had every reason to know she soon must lose. Her strong inclination was to maintain her colonies to the bitter end, and she resented as unfriendly any different attitude by other nations. We valued France as a European ally, but looked with grave misgivings on her colonial policy. In 1953 Communist guerrillas, called Viet-Minh, had occupied the northern part of Vietnam in Indo-China. Laos, the adjacent state in Indo-China was in imminent danger and, if that collapsed, the whole of Southeast Asia could fall to the Communists who were backed by Red China. The United States had no desire to bolster up the French colonial Indo-China, but we had every interest in preventing the spread of Communist influence throughout Southeast Asia. The United States had paid about 75% of the expense of the French fighting in Indo-China, but President Eisenhower would not commit troops in the struggle. When the Viet-Minh captured the French fortress of Dienbienphu on May 7, 1954, the French had been thrown out of Indo-China. At a conference in Geneva in July a settlement was made. This was the first meeting where the United States met with delegates from Red China which was among the 19 nations present. Vietnam was split at the 17th parallel much as Korea had been divided at the 38th. North of the 17th parallel was to be a Communist state and south of it was to be independent. Laos and Cambodia were to be independent. South Vietnam, Laos, and Cambodia were feeble states with unstable governments unable to stand by themselves. Laos and Cambodia are members of the United Nations, while South Vietnam, like South Korea, is half a nation hoping someday to be reunited without becoming the victim of its Communist half. The end of French colonialism in Southeast Asia was, in itself, a good development; but that it was brought about by Communist pressure while the United States was backing France was unfortunate. To resist further Communist successes, President Eisenhower and Secretary of State Dulles organized the Southeast Asia Treaty Organization (SEATO).

* Southeast Asia Treaty Organization (SEATO)

In November, 1954, SEATO was formed. Eight nations combined under a pledge to meet any threat of armed aggression by united action. They will "meet in order to agree on the measures which should be taken for common defense." They have established headquarters at Bangkok, the capital of Thailand, where a secretariat functions. There is a small armed force at SEATO's command, but its effectiveness as a military power rests in the willingness of the United States to lead, and the others to follow, whenever a crisis arises. In view of our action in Korea this may be a substantial deterrent to aggression; but it has none of the immediate striking force of NATO. The members of SEATO are the United States, Great Britain, France, Australia, New Zealand, Thailand, Pakistan, and the Philippines.

Taiwan-Quemoy-Matsu

In February, 1953, President Eisenhower lifted the blockade of Taiwan (Formosa) which had prevented any move by Chiang Kai-shek against the mainland of China. This released Taiwan naval forces for hit and run bombardments of Amoy or other points on the Red China coast opposite Taiwan. The Chinese declared their intention of taking Taiwan, and President Eisenhower said that it could be done only after the 7th fleet had been driven off the sea or sunk. Red China threatened to take Quemoy and Matsu islands which, although very close to the shore of Red China, were occupied by Nationalist China. In September, 1954, Eisenhower rejected proposals that direct action be taken against Red China and based this decision on much the same grounds Truman had given during the Korean conflict (see pp. 237-238). In December, 1954, the President assured Nationalist China that the United States would come to their aid if they were attacked, but this promise did not include the small islands of Quemoy and Matsu. As to those two islands so near the Red China shore, the President asked Congress to leave to his judgment what to do in case an attack was made against them. If he considered such an attack part of a move against Taiwan he would repel it; but if he did not so interpret the attack he might not take action. The Pescadores Islands, much nearer to Taiwan than to Red China, would be protected by the 7th fleet. This statement of policy was made early in 1955, and the uneasy peace was maintained quietly until 1958 when Red China began bombardments of Quemoy and Matsu islands. The 7th fleet convoyed Nationalist Chinese supply ships to these islands and carefully avoided entering waters within three miles of Red China's coast. Both Red China and the United States were being careful not to provoke the other into large scale attack. It was an uneasy situation.

* Suez Crisis (1956)

The Suez crisis resulted when Colonel Gamal Abdel Nasser, dictator of Egypt, used the power-politics maneuvers of the Soviet Union and the United States to advance his position as leader of the Arab states of the Middle East. In 1954, Secretary of State Dulles arranged the Bagdad Pact composed of Iran, Iraq, Pakistan, and Turkey to serve as a protection against the spread of Communism in the Middle East; much as NATO and SEATO were intended to do for Europe and Southeast Asia. While the United States was not a member of the Bagdad Pact, it was obviously an American creation and, if need be, would presumably have United States' support. Nasser saw the Pact as a device to split the Arab-Moslem states of the Middle East by making some of them pro-western and leaving some neutral (Syria, Jordan, Saudi Arabia).

It was Nasser's ambition to unite all of them to accomplish the annihilation of Israel which had fought its way to independence in 1949. With Egypt enraged by the Bagdad Pact, Russia immediately arranged to supply her with arms, but, instead of doing it directly, did it through her satellite, Czechoslovakia. Thus Russia had "leap-frogged" over the Bagdad Pact barrier. While getting arms from the Communist bloc, Nasser asked both the U.S.S.R and the United States to finance the building of the Aswan dam on the upper Nile, a project that could tremendously improve irrigation and produce vast hydroelectric power. The plans called for construction of the largest dam in the world, and its completion could transform Egypt's miserable, poverty-stricken economy to one of vigor and promise. In December, 1955, the United States and Great Britain, in cooperation with the International Bank of the United Nations, agreed to finance the Aswan dam. The details of the financing were worked out and accepted on July 17, 1956, and two days later the United States withdrew its offer, as did Great Britain and the International Bank. The enthusiasm of the United States for the project had been cooling during the 18 months since the offer was first made. Egypt had leaned more and more toward Russia as she built her armaments via trade with Czechoslovakia. It was obvious that Nasser's chief interest was in becoming head of an Arab league in order to re-open the war against Israel.

Back in 1869 the French had finished construction of the Suez Canal and shared its ownership with the khedive of Egypt who later, in 1875, sold his canal shares to England. This link in Britain's "life-line" to the Far East was so important to the empire that British troops occupied the canal area from 1882 until June of 1956 when they were finally withdrawn after continued pressure from Nasser to get foreign troops off Egyptian soil. All the time France and England managed the canal there was an international agreement to allow ships of all nations the use of the canal on equal terms; but no sooner had British troops left, than Nasser announced he was going to "nationalize" it; that is, take it over and run it as Egyptian property. Nasser rejected all attempts by the United States, France, and England to persuade him to permit international supervision of the canal's operation or, at least, to observe previous international rules concerning its use. Nasser closed the canal to Israeli shipping, justifying his action on the ground that they were still legally at war. From 1949 to 1956 the Egyptian fedayeen (commandoes) and Israeli troops had raided each other's border settlements from time to time. The take-over of the canal by Nasser was a severe blow to Britain and France as well as a crippling action against Israeli commerce. On October 25, 1956, Israeli forces drove into the Sinai Peninsula and fought their way to the Suez canal by October 29th. On October 31st French and British forces arrived by air to cooperate with Israel in the seizure and control of the area. Nasser had blocked the canal by sinking ships at strategic points. The day France and England made their attack, President Eisenhower expressed strong disapproval of the use of force as an instrument of international policy, a statement which reiterated the Kellogg-Briand Treaty. Russia threatened to intervene. The United Nations General Assembly met in continuous session, day and night, during the first days of November. Under pressure of the Russian threat, the world opinion expressed through the U.N., and United States' disapproval, France and England announced a cease fire agreement for November 6th. An unusual aspect of this dangerous approach to World War III was the debate and voting in the U.N. Assembly, where delegates of the U.S. and the U.S.S.R. united to condemn aggression by France, England, and Israel. U.N. forces took over supervision of the canal area and cleared the canal for traffic by the middle of April. President Eisenhower found persuading Israel to withdraw a difficult task; but they did leave upon the assurance that the United States would use its influence to have the canal open for Israeli shipping. As it turned out, our influence proved unavailing and the canal remained closed to Israel. It is still true that a determination to liquidate Israel is the one point of agreement among the Arab states. The Suez crisis greatly strengthened Nasser's prestige in the Middle East and, temporarily at least, put a severe strain on Anglo-American relations. The United States gained stature in the eyes of the many new and small nations of the world for opposing aggression, even when committed by our friends.

* Eisenhower Doctrine (1957)

The Suez crisis had lessened British and French prestige in the Middle East and put a rift in Anglo-American relationships. As the western allies' position was made weaker, so the Communist's was enhanced. President Eisenhower recovered some ground by proclaiming the Eisenhower Doctrine. After requesting and receiving the approval of Congress, he offered economic and financial aid to any Middle East nation asking for it (a tiny $200 million Marshall Plan) plus the support of American armed force to resist aggression, or threatened aggression, by any communist nation. A communist take-over was much more likely to be accomplished by 5th column infiltration, culminating in a coup d'état directed from Moscow and executed by native communists, than by aggressive action by Russia or one of her satellites. The Eisenhower Doctrine would not stop this boring-from-within type of aggression. During much of 1957 and 58 the 6th Fleet was in the Mediterranean ready to give quick assistance on call. When, in May, 1958, Syria and Egypt stirred up a rebellion in pro-Western Lebanon, President Chamoun called to the United Nations for help. While the U.N. discussed the situation, President Eisenhower sent in 14,000 marines who restored order in Lebanon, re-established Lebanese authority, and got an agreement from the offending Arab states to leave Lebanon alone.

For the economic and financial aid offered by Eisenhower, the consent of Congress was essential; but for the intervention with United States forces to stop aggression, the President had full authority, by virtue of his office, to act without consulting Congress. In the Far East crisis over Taiwan, Quemoy, and Matsu, the President had full authority to use his judgment concerning their defense, yet he did ask Congress to approve beforehand whatever decision he might make. This tendency to request authority, which he already possessed, was criticised as weakening the power of the presidency; but it probably merely reflected Eisenhower's consciousness of his completely military background coupled with his feeling that American tradition held the presidency to be an essentially civilian position. At any rate, it is interesting, if not important, that the complete soldier in the President's office subdued his authority as commander-in-chief of our armed forces; while the almost completely civilian President, Truman, ordered our massive armed intervention in Korea within a few hours of the crisis and told Congress about it later. Faced with many years of "brush-fire" outbreaks and the ever present possibility of nuclear war, it is a practical certainty that Congress will have no opportunity to discuss the commitment of American forces to action. That heavy responsibility lies more completely on the shoulders of the President than ever before.

The Race for Space

Nobody knows who's ahead and there is some doubt as to the worthwhileness of the race. Some facts are known: the United States and the U.S.S.R. are far in the lead; in 5-10-20 years other nations will have considerable space capability; offensive power is far ahead of defensive; it's a very expen-

Early Stages of
The Orbit Race in Space

UNITED STATES	THE U.S.S.R.
1958 Jan. Explorer I Discovered Van Allen radiation belt	**1957** Oct. Sputnik I 1st orbit
1958 May Vanguard I	**1957** Nov. Sputnik II 1 orbit with dog
1958 March Explorer III	
1958 July Explorer IV	**1958** May Sputnik III 2,925 lbs.
1959 Feb. Vanguard II	**1959** Jan. Lutnik I Solar orbit
1959 March Pioneer IV Solar orbit	**1959** Sept. Lutnik II Hit the moon
1959 August Explorer VI First to televise earth's cloud cover	**1959** Lutnik III Photographed far side of the moon
1960 Pioneer V Set distance communication record— 22,500,000 miles	**1961** Vostok I 1 orbit with Gagarin
1961 Nov. Atlas Missile 2 orbits with chimpanzee	**1961** August Vostok II 17 orbits with Titov
1962 Feb. Friendship 7 3 orbits with John Glenn	**1962** August Vostok III 64 orbits with Nikolayev
1962 May Aurora 7 3 orbits with Scott Carpenter	**1962** August Vostok IV 48 orbits with Popovich
1962 Oct. Sigma 7 6 orbits with Walter Schirra	**1963** June Vostok V 82 orbits with Valery Bykovsky (5 days) Vostok VI
1963 May Faith 7 22 orbits with Major Gordon Cooper, Jr. (1½ days)	49 orbits with Valentina Tereshkova (3 days) First woman astronaut Part of the time these two space vehicles orbited together within three miles of one another.

sive race; and the immediate goal is to land a man on the moon. Of course, any advance in lifting heavier satellites into orbit means greater ability to launch heavier weapons more accurately directed. If it is not already a fact that the U.S. and the U.S.S.R. can hit any place any time with scores of nuclear bombs, it soon will be. Everyone is agreed that the only sensible program is disarmament, and there seems no prospect that disarmament will be accomplished. The effort to get to the moon may result in scientific developments with important applications to earthly affairs; by-products have a way of becoming far more important than the immediate goal. The climate of opinion in the early 1960's was unmistakably in full support of the Eisenhower and Kennedy program

of winning the race in space, cost what it may. A few scientists and a few just plain citizens believe the capacity for offensive war has already guaranteed success in the total destruction of the enemy, to be surely followed by the enemy's total destruction of us, or vice versa; and that further crash programs in space research directed primarily toward military purposes is good evidence that there is no necessary relationship between man's cleverness and his sanity.

By the end of 1966 about 100 man-made satellites were orbiting the earth. Four of them are expected to continue in orbit for 100 years, one for 250 years, five for 500 years, one for 700 years, seven for 1,000 years, one for 2,000 years, one for 5,000 years, and four for 1,000,000 years.

* St. Lawrence Seaway

Making a deep water passage through the St. Lawrence to the Great Lakes had been a dream for years. The Senate had rejected a treaty with Canada in 1934 and thus delayed the start of the project. But in June, 1959, President Eisenhower and Queen Elizabeth officially opened the St. Lawrence Seaway for traffic. Canada and the United States shared the cost and the regulation. New York State and Canada made agreements for the development of hydroelectric power; a situation that raises the constitutional question of the right of a state to make agreements with a foreign power. The Constitution put treaty-making exclusively in the hands of the Federal government, but it is permissible for a state to make agreements with a foreign nation if Congress approves and if the terms of the agreement do not encroach upon Federal powers.

Some St. Lawrence Seaway Facts

1] From the Atlantic coast to Duluth, on Lake Superior, is 2,342 miles.

2] From Montreal through the Welland Canal, which by-passes Niagara Falls, is 369 miles.

3] There are 15 locks; 7 in the new section (St. Lawrence Seaway) and 8 in the old section (Welland Canal).

4] Ships are raised, or lowered, a total of 552 feet.

5] All locks are emptied and filled by gravity. Raising or lowering a ship in a lock can be done in about 10 minutes.

6] Ships 750 feet long, 72 foot beam, and 27 foot draft can be accommodated.

7] Seaway tonnage increased 75% the first year of its operation.

Alaska and Hawaii Become States (1959)

Alaska was admitted on January 3rd and Hawaii on August 21st. Some members of Congress were hesitant about admitting Hawaii because it was expected to stand firmly for civil rights and against any discrimination based on race. The assumption was made that it would become a Democratic state, so the Republican Congressmen and the Southern Democrats formed what opposition there was against its admission. There was no appreciable opposition to admitting Alaska except that those Congressmen strongly in favor of Hawaii would hold back on Alaska until they had assurance that Hawaii would be admitted. This political maneuvering delayed admission for a few years, but in 1959 they came together, the 49th and 50th states.

"Summit" Conference and the U2

President Eisenhower, in order to discuss nuclear testing and disarmament, wished to arrange with Khrushchev for a meeting of the heads of states sometime in the spring of 1960. When Khrushchev came to Washington in September, 1959, he and the President retired to Camp David where they could be undisturbed. The two men got along so well that, if the "spirit of Camp David" continued, the summit conference they arranged could be a success. In his State of the Union message of January 7, 1960, the President foresaw "a somewhat less strained period in the relations between the Soviet Union and the rest of the world." Two weeks later, Secretary of State Herter said that in any conference where disarmament was discussed, it was "inevitable" that Communist China be represented. While willingness to meet with Red China did not amount to official recognition, it did suggest a softening toward her by the United States. It was Eisenhower's hope that he might do something substantial toward furthering the cause of peace.

With all arrangements completed and the conference only days away, the U2 incident occurred. On May 1, 1960, a U2 high altitude plane was shot down over central Russia (near Sverdlovsk). At first the United States said that it must be a meteorological plane which had drifted off course, but central Russia was a long way to drift. This story wouldn't hold, as the Russians had the plane's equipment practically intact and the pilot, Francis Powers, was alive. It was admitted that the U2 was an espionage plane on a routine picture-taking mission. Khrushchev squeezed every bit of publicity out of the incident. On May 9th Secretary of State Herter said that the U2 espionage flights would continue; but on May 16th, the opening day of the Summit Conference, President Eisenhower said that he had ordered such flights stopped. Khrushchev demanded an apology and a statement condemning the violation of Russian territory; Eisenhower refused both demands. The Conference broke up before it got under way. There is no doubt that Khrushchev knew of the U2 flights which had been going on for about 4 years. His bluster and apparent anger may well have been a device for breaking up a conference that he no longer wished. He had learned he could get no concessions on Berlin and he had no desire to make concessions on nuclear testing or armaments. Red China was criticizing the

Soviet Union's leadership of the Communist nations with charges that Russia was too soft toward the West and too fearful of war. The U2 incident gave Khrushchev an opportunity to placate China, to put on an act of righteous indignation, and to avoid a conference that he no longer wanted.

John F. Kennedy

1917 - 1963

DEMOCRAT

☆

Vice-President LYNDON B. JOHNSON

KENNEDY'S PUBLIC SERVICE BEFORE HE BECAME PRESIDENT

Distinguished Record in Pacific Theater of World War II
Member of the House of Representatives from Massachusetts
Member of the Senate from Massachusetts

MAJOR ITEMS OF KENNEDY'S ADMINISTRATION

Alliance for Progress
The Peace Corps
Cuba

Nuclear Test-ban Treaty
Kennedy Assassinated at Dallas, Texas
(Nov. 22, 1963)

Kennedy's Election in 1960

President Eisenhower was ineligible for another term (Amendment 22), but he left no doubt that he favored his Vice-President, Richard Nixon, as his successor. Nixon won the nomination at the Chicago Convention on the first ballot. Henry Cabot Lodge of Massachusetts was his running mate.

Adlai Stevenson, who had lost two campaigns, showed no enthusiasm for a third attempt even though, with "Ike" out of the race, the Democratic hopes were high. Senator John F. Kennedy entered 7 state primaries and won them all as he made himself known in widely scattered parts of the United States. He was nominated at the Los Angeles Convention on the first ballot. Senator Lyndon Johnson of Texas was his running mate.

The platforms of both parties had strong civil rights planks and favored federal aid in financing a national health program (two different programs). There was no substantial difference in foreign affairs.

	Popular Vote	*Electoral Vote*
Kennedy	34,226,925	303
Nixon	34,108,662	219

Kennedy's margin of victory was less than 1/5 of 1% of the popular vote. As minor candidates polled over 600,000 votes, he received less than half the total vote. He was the youngest president to be elected (43 years old) although Theodore Roosevelt was only 42 when McKinley was shot. Kennedy was the first Roman Catholic to be elected, and the religious bigotry so prominent in the 1928 Al Smith campaign was almost non-existent in 1960.

Alliance for Progress

The Cuban Crisis of April, 1961 (see p. 250, pushed Latin American nations more firmly into a pro-Western position. The Alliance for Progress program needed every assistance, because attainment of its goal seems both impossibly difficult and absolutely necessary. The goal is the creation in Latin American republics of a middle class able to buy decent housing, food, and clothing; a middle class with opportunity for education; and a middle class capable of representative government through the use of ballots (not bullets). Every republic needs tax reform, land reform, and political stability. The Alliance for Progress supplies funds for building economic strength, much as did the Marshall Plan in Europe, but in Latin America the problem is not one of recovery, it is one of creating *for the first time* something better than extreme poverty with its many attendant evils (ignorance, disease, despair, suspicion, hate, fear). The Kennedy program tried to grant financial aid only for approved purposes when some specific reform was undertaken. Any tax or land reform is basically a redistribution of existing wealth as well as an attempt to create additional wealth. Latin American republics are under the control of a few very wealthy families. This has been a pattern of life since Spain and Portugal colonized Central and South America; it is a pattern that will not be tolerated much longer. The Communists would like the economic situation to blow up in revolution. Trained Communist personnel can guide revolution into a Communist totalitarian state. The Western world wants improvement without violence, a program that contemplates two or three generations to achieve its goals. The first year under the Alliance for Progress had satisfied no one. The United States felt that the reforms achieved had been too few and too feeble; the Latin American republics felt the amount of aid had been too small. The aid extended during the first year was $1 billion, 29½ million.

* Peace Corps

In March, 1961, Congress approved President Kennedy's Peace Corps and soon appropriated $30 million for the first year. This put American citizens to work side by side with those they helped. The first year about 3,000 volunteers were serving abroad and another 1,000 were in training in the United States. The program expects to build up a corps of about 10,000 serving in 50 or more nations, most of which will be in Africa, Asia, and Latin America. Peace Corps members learn the native language and make a point of living in native communities in the same style as the natives. The volunteers get $75 a month which is deposited to their credit in a bank in the United States to be available at the end of their service. Peace Corps workers are sent only upon the request of the nation wanting them. The expected term of service for a Corps member is 2 years and the age limit is from 18 up. A very few members are over 60, but the great majority are in their twenties or early thirties and many have been to college. The United States allows Corps members expenses for travel and a living standard suitable for the area in which they are stationed. America is exporting some of its finest young people who may be engaged in a practical, inexpensive, person-to-person program that will plant trust, good will, and a capacity for self-help in Asia, Africa, and Latin America.

** Cuba

Rumors of impending invasion of Cuba were common in 1960 and early 1961. Less than two months after his inauguration, President Kennedy felt called upon to say "there will not, under any conditions, be an invasion in Cuba by the United States' armed forces." In its literal sense this pledge was kept. But Cuban refugees were training in Guatemala and receiving aid from the United States. On April 17, 1961, an invading force landed at the Bay of Pigs on the south shore of Cuba. Without

air cover their supply ships were sunk by Castro's 9-plane airforce and they were soon stranded in a swampy area with insufficient ammunition. After 400 had been killed and about 1,200 taken prisoners, the abortive attack was smothered in two days. Fidel Castro made his May Day (May 1st) speech in which he blamed the United States for the invasion attempt and declared that there would be no more elections. He left no doubt that he had taken Cuba into the Communist camp and looked to the Soviet Union and Red China for aid and leadership. Over a two-year period, Fidel Castro released most of the invasion prisoners and several American citizens who were political prisoners. Private sources, with some government help, arranged their release by paying ransom in money and goods.

Apparently Cuba did not turn to Russia in vain, for, on October 22, 1962, President Kennedy announced that the U.S.S.R. had placed medium and intermediate-range ballistic missiles and some jet bombers in Cuba. We had pictures to prove it and to help Adlai Stevenson, our U.N. chief delegate, to convince the world of Cuba's build-up in offensive weapons supplied by Russia. President Kennedy demanded the removal of the offensive weapons and the jet bombers. He established an air-sea blockade of Cuba until the removal took place. Within 5 days Khrushchev promised removal of the missiles and planes on condition that the U.S. would pledge not to invade Cuba. The President promised not to invade Cuba if the missiles and planes were removed and we were permitted to verify their removal by an on-site inspection. The missiles and planes were removed, but as there had been no on-site inspection, President Kennedy pointed out that our pledge not to invade Cuba was not in effect. A few thousand Russian "technicians" left Cuba during 1962-63 and some may have entered. Just how many Russians there were in Cuba by the summer of 1963 was a matter of uncertainty and controversy. The first few days of the air-sea blockade of Cuba, when the U.S. and the U.S.S.R. stood toe to toe on the brink of war, was also the climax of the mid-term Congressional elections. The usual pattern of mid-term elections is a moderate loss for the party in power, but this time the Democrats made a slight gain in the Senate (4 seats) and a loss of only 2 seats in the House; all of which could be interpreted as popular support for the President's Cuban action.

* Nuclear Test-ban Treaty (1963) (Ratified by the Senate 80 to 19)

This treaty prohibits nuclear testing in the atmosphere, in space, and under water. Underground tests are not banned as there is no way to detect them without an inspection system. The U.S. and the U.S.S.R. are still unable to agree on a method of inspection. Fortunately, dangerous contamination from underground testing is at a minimum.

France and Communist China are the only nuclear powers not signing the treaty. Over 100 nations signed the treaty very soon after the U.S. and the U.S.S.R. had reached an agreement. Whether the treaty reflects fear of contamination if nuclear testing continues, a break in the "cold war," or both is anyone's guess.

Kennedy Assassinated at Dallas, Texas (Nov. 22, 1963)

President Kennedy and Mrs. Kennedy were seated in the rear seat of an automobile with the top down. Texas Governor Connally and Mrs. Connally were seated directly in front of them. The presidential motorcade, formed at the city airport, was nearing downtown Dallas. Happily enthusiastic crowds lined the street. At 12:30 P.M. two shots were fired; both hit the President wounding him in the head and neck and causing death within half an hour. The second shot also seriously wounded Governor Connally who recovered several weeks later. The bullets were fired from an upper window in the Texas Book Depository Building used for storage space by the Dallas school department.

About an hour and a half after the assassination a suspect, Lee Harvey Oswald, was arrested. But within that 90 minutes Oswald had shot and killed a policeman who got out of his squad car to approach him for questioning. Throughout the 30 hours Oswald was under close examination by the police, he stuck to his story that he was innocent of the assassination of President Kennedy. On November 24th the Dallas police were escorting Oswald from the city to the county jail. While still in a basement corridor of the city jail the police were proceeding with their prisoner through a jumble of people, most of whom were reporters and television men. One bystander, Jack Rubenstein (Jack Ruby), stepped forward directly in front of Oswald and fired at point-blank range. Oswald died forty minutes later with no opportunity for further questioning. The murder of the President was a world tragedy; the televised murder of Oswald was a national disgrace. Technically, at least, we should refer to Oswald as the alleged assassin, a man legally innocent because he had not received a trial and been convicted. The F.B.I. moved into Dallas to re-examine the sequence of events. A commission appointed by President Lyndon Johnson made a separate investigation. Their reports may "prove" an airtight case in minute detail against Oswald, but the horrible ineradicable fact must ever remain—Oswald did not receive a trial.

The nation was truly grief-stricken. Television had brought the young and vital presidential family close to the American people. The first lady, Jacqueline Kennedy, had shown herself to be a woman of quiet, intense patriotism built on religious faith, belief in people, and a high intelligence made doubly attractive by a natural modesty and a touch of shyness. Her guided television tour of the White House had given the American people an appreciation of its value as an historic shrine and an awareness of the dignity, graciousness, and competence of Jacqueline Kennedy in the role of first lady. The two children, Caroline almost six and John almost three, had entered most American homes through television to capture, as children do the world over, the affection of the people. John Fitzgerald Kennedy reached the presidency while still a young man of forty-three. He was obviously an intellectual with ideals, but his feet were on the ground and he had long since learned the ways, wiles, and the art of politics. His Pulitzer Prize winning essays, *Profiles of Courage*, clearly show the kind of living he most admired. Each of the profiles was of a politician who had the courage to deliberately follow a course of action he knew would result in political suicide; but each man could do nothing else because his urge to serve the nation and be true to himself had to be realized regardless of any personal consequences.

The public reaction to the tragedy of Kennedy's assassination was based on more solid ground than already mentioned. President De Gaulle of France, one of scores of heads of nations who attended the funeral, said that the "little" people of France had sent him. An oft-repeated thought was that the late President had felt that he was working for the "ordinary" people all over the world. President Kennedy would no doubt have appreciated this recognition of his deepest concern, but almost surely would have had a good natured intellectually effective barb to spear those well-meant, but nevertheless inept, words "little" and "ordinary." Jefferson, Jackson, and Lincoln couldn't think of people as little and ordinary; it is part of the American creed of democracy not to do so. Populations sense when a leader has that kind of faith in people. Many shared with President Kennedy his principles and goals while holding quite different convictions as to policies and procedures. In the shock and grief at the assassination these differences were set aside as the nation realized how much it had come to love and respect the youngest man it had ever elected to the presidency.

Shortly after 2:30 P.M. Lyndon B. Johnson took the oath of office as President of the United States. The ceremony took place in the cabin of the plane at Dallas which was about to take off for Washington with the body of the slain President.

Lyndon B. Johnson

1963-

1908 -

DEMOCRAT

☆

JOHNSON'S PUBLIC SERVICE BEFORE HE BECAME PRESIDENT

Member of the House of Representatives from Texas (1937-49)
Member of the Senate from Texas (1949-61)
Minority Leader (1953-55)   Majority Leader (1955-61)
Vice-President (1961-63)

MAJOR ITEMS DURING THE ADMINISTRATION OF JOHNSON

The "Cold War"	Wesberry v. Sanders (1964) and
Cuban Policy	Baker v. Carr (1962)
Income Tax Cut	Civil Rights Act (1964)
	Antipoverty Act (1964)

The "Cold War"

The transition from President Kennedy to President Johnson was accomplished with a smoothness and lack of confusion which gave great emphasis to the stability of the federal government. Both the personnel and the policies in the field of foreign affairs established under Kennedy were satisfactory to President Johnson who, as Vice-President, had been well informed about and active in the making of foreign policy. The Nuclear Test-ban Treaty did point toward co-existence rather than increased tension between the "East" and the "West." However, there was nothing really both definite and important to substantiate the feeling that U.S. and U.S.S.R. relations were improving. There was, however, ample proof that the rivalry within the communist camp between Russia and Red China was rapidly getting noisier and hotter. Khrushchev's propaganda line for home consumption stressed the complete destructiveness of nuclear war. He posed as a leader who wished to take his people into a pleasanter world of greater prosperity. He talked of co-existence and pictured the conflict between communism and capitalist imperialism as one to be fought on the battlefield of political economy where success will go to that system which produces the better standard of living for its people. This is precisely the type of conflict the United States and the "West" would welcome. Mao Tse Tung's propaganda line declared the U.S.S.R. was betraying Karl Marx, Lenin, and Stalin with its humiliatingly weak leadership. He minimized the horrors of nuclear war and seemed to view a forceful conquest of the non-communist world as the inevitable path history must take. Thus, early in Johnson's presidency the U.S.S.R. and Red China were so busy competing for the leadership of the communist world that their attention was diverted from harassment of the "West." Relaxed tension on such a basis is obviously subject to change without notice.

* Cuban Policy

Cuba shut off the fresh water supply to the United States naval base at Guantanamo. President Johnson's response was to supply fresh water by tankers while setting up a huge converter at the base to transform salt water to fresh in ample quantities. This not only made Guantanamo independent of Cuba for its fresh water, but deprived Cuba of revenue she had been getting and also eliminated many jobs held by Cubans in connection with the water supply.

President Johnson announced that American U2 planes will continue to fly inspection missions over Cuba. Castro has said he will shoot them down and Khrushchev has stated his approval of Castro's position. Johnson has made it clear that attacks on U2's will be met with severe action. There is still a Cuban crisis.

The President's policy toward Cuba seeks to avoid war while refusing to negotiate. He hopes to restrict trade with Cuba enough to force Castro from power. Cuba's major threat to the United States is that it can serve as a base for communist infiltration into other Latin American republics. Some of our N.A.T.O. allies do not cooperate with our trade policy toward Cuba. Their selling to Cuba seems to them much the same as the United States' selling wheat to Russia. England suggests that increasing trade with the communist world is a natural avenue along which a favorable climate for amicable relations may develop. But President Johnson points out that Cuba's economy can be seriously affected by trade restrictions because it is a small nation with limited natural resources. Russia, on the other hand, has vast resources with a many-sided economy so that any trade restrictions possible to enact would have slight impact upon her total economy.

Income Tax Cut (1964)

Late in February the income tax was reduced to some extent all across the board. Most people were affected by the cuts in the income brackets up to $8,000 per year. Based on a family of four an income of $5,000 was taxed $290 instead of $420; an income of $8,000 was taxed $772 instead of $972. If the increased money available for private expenditure and investment results in fuller employment without a general rise in prices (inflation), the President has predicted that a further tax cut may be in the making. Along with the tax cut, and part of the same financial policy, cuts have been made in government spending. Several armed forces installations have been shut down. While stating that army, navy, and air force must not be used as W.P.A. projects, the President will not curtail defense expenditures where needed nor continue them where no longer needed.

** Wesberry v. Sanders (1964) and Baker v. Carr (1962)

The *Wesberry* v. *Sanders* case originated in Georgia as a test case to find out whether grossly unequal congressional districts within a state were constitutional. Such districts give one voter a very different amount of influence as a voter than another in a different district. The decision of the Supreme Court was that all congressional districts within any state must "as nearly as practicable" have the same number of voters. As population shifts have taken place over the years many states have neglected to readjust their congressional districts. The result has been that urban areas are often very much under represented and rural areas very much over represented. Each congressional district has one member in the House of Represent-

atives no matter how many people live in the district. This "rotten borough" situation is not sectional, it exists throughout the United States. The total population according to the 1960 census was 191,000,000. As there are 435 seats in the House of Representatives each congressional district should have about 439,000 people. Yet there are numerous situations such as the following: in Texas one district has about 950,000 people while another has about 200,000, in Connecticut one district has about 700,000 while another has 300,000, and in Georgia one district has about 800,000 and another 300,000. To make the adjustments this court decision requires will take time. It may take further court decision to get answers to such questions as —how much time may a state have for redistricting? —and—how nearly equal must the congressional districts be?

In a previous case, *Baker* v. *Carr* (1962) the Court had ruled that election districts within each state from which members of the lower house of the state legislature are sent must be of approximately equal population. There are many more such election districts in each state than there are congressional districts. Compliance with this decision will require changes in 40 states or more.

Both of these decisions were based on the clause of the 14th Amendment stating, ". . . nor shall any State deprive any person within its jurisdiction the equal protection of the laws." Any person's vote for a representative in the federal Congress or in a state legislature should have approximately as much weight as the vote of any other resident of the state. It is interesting to speculate about the effect the new apportionments may have upon the political complexion of the federal Congress and the several state legislatures. How about your state?

** Civil Rights Act (1964)

After a three months filibuster by southern Senators was ended by cloture, the Civil Rights Act was passed. After a delay of almost 100 years this act created federal law in support of the original purpose of the 14th amendment, equal treatment under the laws for blacks and whites. Its most important provisions are the following.

1] Uniform standards must prevail for establishing the right to vote. Schooling through the sixth grade constitutes legal proof of literacy. Literacy tests must be in writing and copies of the applicants' answers must be supplied on request. The attorney general may institute legal proceedings if he finds a pattern of discrimination in any voting district. Voting cases will be tried by a court of one or three judges without a jury and must be given priority over other cases.

2] A public accommodations' provision makes establishments offering food, lodging, gasoline or entertainment available to all persons without discrimination based on race, color, religion or national origin. Private clubs and proprietor occupied houses with five rooms or less for rent are exempt. Any complainant may have the service of an attorney without cost. The attorney general may initiate legal action in any area where he finds a pattern of resistance to the law.

3] When the attorney general receives a complaint in writing which charges segregation in public schools, parks, playgrounds, swimming pools, libraries, or similar public facilities, he may bring suit on behalf of the complainant. Orders by a court or federal official to transport children to achieve racial balance in schools are barred.

4] Projects involving federal funds will have such funds cut off if there is discrimination based on race, color or national origin.

5] An employment agency, a union or an employer may not discriminate in the hiring, firing or promotion of persons on the basis of race, color or national origin. Racial quotas shall not be used nor will merit or seniority systems be disturbed.

6] The attorney general may intervene in any civil rights case under the 14th amendment if he considers it of general public significance.

7] If a case of criminal contempt arises in a voting rights trial, there will be a jury if the penalty exceeds 45 days in jail or a $300 fine. In all other criminal contempt cases arising under the Civil Rights Act, the defendant shall be entitled to a jury trial.

It is to be noted that throughout the Civil Rights Act the repeated reference to the attorney general clearly recognizes that resistance to the enforcement of its several provisions is likely and that the federal government is determined to enforce them. This emphasizes that this legislation requires deep and difficult social, political and economic readjustments. The passage of the act does not immediately raise the negro from his status of second class citizen, but it does assure him that Uncle Sam is earnestly and energetically supporting him in his struggle toward genuine equality under law. We may expect years of struggle before the Civil Rights Act is fact as well as law and has become accepted not only as proper but as a normal part of the American Way of Life.

Antipoverty Act (1964)

This was the first major law that was wholly a Johnson measure, one not initiated·by President Kennedy. President Johnson called it the opening gun in his total war on poverty. The act aims to help people to climb out of poverty and stay out, not merely to alleviate poverty. The $947.5 million appropriation provided for:

job training centers
conservation camps
basic education
aid to needy college students
loans to low income farmers
loans to low income businessmen
a domestic peace corps

The bill passed in August, 1964, during the early days of the presidential campaign. It received overwhelming support from Democratic members of Congress and scattered support from a few Republicans in both Houses. Senator Barry Goldwater, the Republican candidate for President, voted against the bill and labeled it an election-year bid for votes. No doubt the timing of the bill was a political stratagem, but the problem of poverty was real. The struggle, most marked in the South, to adjust to the new Civil Rights Act, the poverty riots in negro sections of large cities in the North, and the growing economic dislocations resulting from automation combined to persuade many that poverty pockets throughout the United States required legislative action by the federal government.

Test I

TO MAKE EFFECTIVE USE OF THESE TESTS
CONSIDER THE FOLLOWING FACTS

1] The forms used for the questions are often similar to College Entrance Examination Board Scholastic Aptitude Tests (S.A.T's and P.S.A.T's). There is a danger in becoming accustomed to any form of questioning. It encourages careless reading of the questions so that deviations from the familiar pattern go undetected. Always read every question with deliberate care. If you must hurry, make up your mind quickly about the answer but be sure you have the question accurately in mind.

2] Most questions are answered by a number or a letter. This means the questions contain the answers and therefore there is a substantial probability the correct answer may be selected by chance. Realize that "I guessed right" is equivalent to "I didn't know".

Multiple choice groups designated as three questions (13-15, 27-29, 75-77, 91-93, etc.) are considered sufficiently difficult to justify a weight of 3%. Some matching questions are considered relatively easy and, as in Questions 1-12 in Test I, two correct matches are required for each question. In this pattern each test can be quickly rated on the basis of 100 questions and 100%.

3] Selecting the true, or false, statements from a group of five to eight of them is usually given a score of 3%. Care has been taken to use statements that appear plausible to any student who is not well informed.

4] Consideration of why the wrong answers are wrong is a valuable learning technique. Approach the tests as teaching, as well as measuring, devices.

5] Several answers must be judgment rather than factual responses. Differences of opinion as to the best choice for an answer will occur. In such cases try to see why the choice you make may be considered a weaker one than the response designated as the answer. Whatever your conclusion, the careful consideration of the topic is much more significant than your score on the test.

6] Several questions demand knowledge in depth about a particular topic or circumstance. Such questions can serve as an effective starting point for a full discussion of fact and evaluations. *Using* questions can be much more beneficial than merely going over them to compile a score.

1.-12.

The items in both columns are associated with the period of exploration. Match each of the numbered items in Column II *with an item in* Column I. *In some cases more than one item in* Column II *matches the same item in* Column I.

COLUMN I	COLUMN II
A. Dias	1. (a) Discovered the Grand Canyon
	(b) King of the Aztecs
B. Columbus	2. (a) First white man to see the Pacific Ocean
C. Cortez	(b) Landed at Bahamas, probably at Watling Island
D. Coronado	
E. John Cabot	3. (a) First to reach India from Europe by water
F. Gutenberg	(b) "Father of New France"
G. Aristotle	4. (a) Sailed in the "Half Moon"
	(b) Had a "school of navigation" in Portugal
H. Da Gama	
I. Ponce de Leon	5. (a) Sailed along northeast coast from Newfoundland to Chesapeake Bay for England
J. Montezuma	(b) Printed first Bible
K. Cartier	6. (a) Seventeen years in China

256

COLUMN I

L. H. Hudson

M. Marco Polo

N. Eratosthenes

O. Vespucci

P. Balboa

Q. Magellan

R. Champlain

S. Prince Henry

COLUMN II

(b) First to estimate the circumference of the world

7. (a) First to think the world was a sphere

(b) Rounded Cape of Good Hope but did not proceed to India

8. (a) Sailed along coasts of South America and proved it a continent

(b) Explored Florida—"Fountain of Youth"

9. (a) Discovered Mexico and gold

(b) First to circumnavigate the world

10. (a) Explored St. Lawrence River and Gulf

(b) Lived about 350 B.C.

Each of the following five dates gives the year or years when one of the events in Column II *was accomplished by a man named in* Column I. *Match the date with the correct name in* Column I.

11. (a) 1454
    (b) 1498
12. (a) 1519-22
    (b) 1609

13.-15. In order to pass Congress a bill must conform to which of the following conditions?

(a) Receive a majority of the votes in Congress

(b) Receive a 2/3rds majority of the votes in Congress

(c) Receive a majority of the votes in each House of Congress

(d) Receive a 2/3rds majority of the votes in each House of Congress

(e) Pass both Houses of Congress in identical form

(f) Pass as amended in the last House to consider it

(1) d, e **(2)** c, e **(3)** d, f **(4)** c, f **(5)** a, e **(6)** a, f **(7)** b, e **(8)** b, f

16. Where does the sole power to impeach the President lie?

17.-21. Give the number of the Amendments in the U.S. Constitution for each of the following.

17. Prohibition

18. Provides for the reduction of a state's representation in the House if the state denies suffrage to its male adult citizens

19. Provides the method of electing the President

20. Gives the District of Columbia electoral votes for President

21. Abolishes slavery

22. In the Bill of Rights of our Constitution the following words occur. All of them except one take into account the permanent nature of the Constitution. Which is the exception?

(a) cruel (b) unusual (c) twenty dollars (d) excessive (e) speedy

23.-32.

Each of the following statements presents a typically Federalist viewpoint or a typically Republican (Democratic Republican) viewpoint. Indicate the Federalist statements with an F, *the Republican statements with an* R. *All statements deal with the period 1789 to 1800.*

23. If "necessary" in the Implied Powers Clause can be interpreted to mean anything less than absolutely necessary, there is then no point at which a line can be drawn and thus "necessary" may mean anything Congress wants it to mean. Congress can become powerful beyond all intention.

24. A bank of the United States would obviously help in carrying into execution such powers of Congress as the collection of taxes, the borrowing of money, and the payment of the public debt.

25. We have no obligation to help the French. The situation is so changed by the French Revolution that the Treaty of Alliance made in 1778 no longer holds.

26. Sending thousands of troops into western Pennsylvania to collect small change from almost penniless corn farmers is ridiculous!

27. It is true that the Bank of the United States is proving a good investment for its stockholders but, more important, it is having a steadying influence on other banks.

28. Treaty or no treaty, the important fact is that this new government is too uncertain and too weak to follow any policy other than that of neutrality.

29. The treaty is an insult. Jay should be tarred and feathered.

30. It is too late to pay the domestic debt. The original bondholders have sold out to speculators. There's no sense in putting more money in the pockets of wealthy speculators.

31. The credit of the federal government and of the several states must be made secure by the payment in full of all public debts. How such a sound policy helps or hurts individuals is a matter of no lasting importance.

32. It is clear that government policies favor the

interests of commerce while the only attention paid to farmers is to make sure they pay taxes.

33.-42.

The words or phrases in parentheses with each of the following items have a relationship with the item as indicated by A, B, or C. Designate which letter best applies in each case.

A—to bring into effect, to support, or to make more effective

B—to bring to an end, to oppose, or to make less effective

C—neither A nor B apply

33. Judicial review of federal laws (John Marshall)

34. American invasion of Canada (Andrew Jackson)

35. Clay's chance to be elected by the House of Representatives in the campaign of 1824 (12th Amendment)

36. The success of the Democrats in the election of 1844 (Liberty Party)

37. Seward's "higher law" point of view. (Personal Liberty Laws)

38. The Tweed Ring (Harper's Weekly & the New York Times)

39. Effectiveness of the Sherman Anti-trust Act (U.S. v. E. C. Knight & Co.)

40. Spheres of influence in China (Secretary of State John Hay)

41. Segregation of oriental children in the San Francisco schools (Root-Takahira Agreement)

42. The slogan, "He kept us out of war" (Sussex Pledge)

43.-45. Which three of the following statements would have received the approval of John Quincy Adams?

(a) Clay's American System is a sound program for the nation.

(b) Continued debate of the slavery issue wastes the time and consumes the energy of Congress without bringing compensating benefits. Such discussion should be declared out of order.

(c) In making appointments a president will be wise to consider not only the welfare of the nation, but also the reaction of the public to the appointments and their subsequent effect upon the President himself.

(d) Any person who has served as President of the United States should protect the dignity and prestige of that office by refusing to serve in public office thereafter, even though it be that of chief justice of the Supreme Court.

(e) Gag resolutions violate the Constitution and the rights of the people.

(f) Because England and America both object to the Holy Alliance raiding the ex-Spanish colonies in Latin America is no reason why the United States should unite with England in a policy to prevent such aggression.

46.-65.

Match the items in Column II *with the names in* Column I. *The items are slogans and quotations (or close paraphrases thereof) associated with the names. Some of the men named are associated with more than one of the slogans or quotations.*

COLUMN I	COLUMN II
A. Calvin Coolidge	**46.** *Watchful waiting*
	47. *We must be the great arsenal of democracy.*
B. Wm. L. Garrison	**48.** *Return to normalcy*
	49. *I will not equivocate—I will not excuse—I will not retreat a single inch.*
C. Warren G. Harding	**50.** *I thought what was good for General Motors was good for the country, and vice versa.*
D. Andrew Jackson	**51.** *The Republicans tell me that they stand for unity. As Al Smith would have said, "That's a lot of hooey". And if that rhymes with anything, it's not my fault.*
E. Abraham Lincoln	
F. Douglas MacArthur	**52.** *I do not choose to run.*
	53. *The only thing we have to fear is fear itself.*
G. James K. Polk	**54.** *Labor is prior to, and independent of capital. Capital is only the fruit of labor, and could never exist if labor had not first existed.*
H. Franklin Roosevelt	**55.** *Don't swap horses in the middle of a stream.*
I. Theodore Roosevelt	

COLUMN I   COLUMN II

J. Harry Truman   56. *I regret that I was unable to shoot Henry Clay or to hang John Calhoun.*

57. *I now close my military career and just fade away.*

K. Cornelius Vanderbilt   58. *There is no right to strike against the public safety by anyone, anywhere, any time.*

59. *We should have open covenants openly arrived at.*

L. Earl Warren   60. *I am as strong as a bull moose.*
                             61. *The public be damned.*

M. Daniel Webster   62. *Liberty and Union, now and forever, one and inseparable.*

63. *In public education the "separate but equal" doctrine has no place.*

N. Charles E. Wilson   64. *Fifty-four forty or fight*
                             65. *Speak softly and carry a big stick; you will go far.*

O. Woodrow Wilson

66. Name the Secretary of State at the time Alaska was purchased by the United States.

67.-71.
Arrange the following items in chronological order.

A. First law excluding Chinese laborers
B. Peak of Irish immigration resulting from famine
C. McCarren Walter Act
D. Gentlemen's Agreement
E. National Origins Formula

72.-77.
Arrange the following in chronological order.

A. Hepburn Act
B. Wagner-Connery Act
C. Interstate Commerce Act
D. Clayton Anti-trust Act
E. Taft-Hartley Act
F. Sherman Anti-trust Act

78. *Which of the following is the best expression of the meaning of dollar diplomacy?*

(a) Foreign affairs carried out with a sharp eye to curtailing expense
(b) Foreign affairs carried out without regard to expense
(c) Use of money for bribing foreign agents or for other methods which usually would be considered unethical—except in diplomacy
(d) Conducting foreign policy with protection of American investments abroad as its main objective
(e) A term used to emphasize the inadequate pay received by those who make a career of serving the U.S. as consuls, ministers and ambassadors

79.-88.
Items in Column I *and* Column II *are associated with events shortly before World War I. Match each item in* Column I *with an item in* Column II.

COLUMN I   COLUMN II

A. Zimmerman   79. "He kept us out of war"
B. T. Roosevelt   80. German instructions to U.S. ships to use only certain shipping lanes and to paint our ships as they suggested
C. Charles E. Hughes
D. Wm. J. Bryan   81. Resigned because Wilson's protests to Germany were severe and likely to cause war
E. Von Bernstorff
F. Woodrow Wilson   82. Sent a note to Mexico which the British decoded and sent to the U.S.
G. Walter H. Page
H. Robert Lansing   83. A French ship sunk in the English channel with injury to some Americans
I. Eugene Debs
J. Von Papen   84. German ambassador at Washington
K. Boy-Ed   85. May 7, 1915
L. Lusitania   86. There is such a thing as "being too proud to fight."
M. Sussex
N. Titanic   87. The U.S. should declare war or at least break off diplomatic relations with Germany.
O. Seemed justified by Germany's Sussex Pledge
P. Sussex Pledge broken   88. Our ambassador to England at the outbreak of the war.

89.-91. After his re-election in 1936, Franklin Roosevelt attacked the Supreme Court which had declared the A.A.A. and the N.I.R.A. unconstitutional. Which of the following statements about this executive-judicial conflict are true?

(a) Congress, which has passed the laws struck down by the Court, naturally sided with the President.

(b) The President's plan to enlarge the Supreme Court was of questionable constitutionality.

(c) The extreme complexity of the President's plan was one of the factors that led to its defeat.

(d) From the beginning, Roosevelt got little support for his plan.

(e) While Roosevelt was urging his plan upon Congress and the nation, the Supreme Court declared some important New Deal laws to be constitutional.

(f) Congress refused to pass any law changing the number of justices on the Supreme Court.

(g) While Roosevelt was President he had the opportunity to make so many appointments to the Supreme Court that it was called, by those who didn't like it, a "Roosevelt Court."

(1) d, e, f, g (2) a, c, g (3) b, d, f (4) b, d, e, g (5) a, c, g

92.-94. Which of the following statements are true concerning the Truman Doctrine and the circumstances to which it was directed?

(a) The Truman Doctrine was a unilateral action by the United States.

(b) While taking no part in carrying out the Truman Doctrine, the U.N. Council approved the action taken by the U.S.

(c) Greece and Spain were the principal beneficiaries of the Truman Doctrine.

(d) Greece had appealed to the U.N. for help.

(e) The Soviet Union was pushing toward an outlet and control on the Mediterranean Sea just as had Czarist Russia throughout modern times.

(f) Under the Truman Doctrine substantial military aid was sent to Turkey.

(g) The Truman Doctrine was brought into play when Red China attacked Tibet.

(1) a, d, e, f (2) a, b, d (3) c, d, g (4) b, c, e, g (5) a, f, g

95.-97. Which of the following statements are

true of the 14th Amendment of the U.S. Constitution?

(a) It's purpose was to force the ex-Confederate states to grant the ex-slaves equal treatment under the law with whites.

(b) ". . . *nor shall any state deprive any person of life, liberty, or property, without due process of law, nor deny to any person within its jurisdiction the equal protection of the laws*" is a quotation from the 14th Amendment.

(c) ". . . *nor shall any State deprive any citizen of the right to vote on account of race, color, or previous condition of servitude*" is a quotation from the 14th Amendment.

(d) As long as the Reconstruction Period lasted in each of the ex-Confederate states the civil rights provisions of the 14th Amendment were substantially enforced.

(e) After the Reconstruction Period and until 1954 the *"separate but equal"* criterion prevailed.

(f) The provision of the 14th Amendment which places a penalty upon any state for depriving adult male citizens from voting has never been enforced.

(1) a, b, d, f (2) b, c, e (3) all but f (4) b, d, e (5) all but c

98.-100. Which of the following statements concerning President Kennedy's administration are true?

(a) The Alliance for Progress is directed toward Latin America.

(b) Latin American governments are usually anxious to institute political and economic reforms in return for aid under the Alliance for Progress.

(c) Selling surplus food products to the U.S.S.R. and other communist nations gained considerable support from both major political parties.

(d) The Peace Corps program is a comparatively inexpensive foreign aid program.

(e) United States on-sight inspection confirmed the removal of offensive missiles from Cuba.

(f) President Kennedy accepted from Congress a much weaker civil rights bill than he had recommended.

(1) a, b, f (2) a, c, d (3) b, d, e (4) a only (5) all except e

Test II

1.-3. The Demarcation Line of 1493 was agreed upon by Spain and Portugal as the dividing line of their claims in the New World. Pope Alexander VI was consulted in the fixing of this line. Which of the following statements are true?

(a) The pope had very limited knowledge of the geography of the New World.
(b) The New World west of the Demarcation Line was given to Spain.
(c) Portugal received only a portion of what is now Brazil.
(d) The division made by the Demarcation Line had little effect on the eventual disposition of the New World among the exploring nations.
(e) Spain and Portugal were more vigorous and earlier in exploring the New World than were either England or France.
(f) Bartholomew Diaz, Vasco da Gama, and Hernando de Soto explored for Portugal.
(g) Balboa, Cortez, and Sebastian Cabot explored for Spain.

(1) all but d (2) all but a (3) b, c, e, g (4) a, d, e, f (5) a, b, c, d, e (6) a, d, e, g

4.-13. The preamble of the Constitution reads, *"We the people of the United States, in order to . . . , do ordain and establish this Constitution for the United States of America."*

Did "We the *people*" or did the *states* establish the Constitution?

Classify each of the following statements as P, S, *or* X.

    P—when the statement supports the idea that the people did establish the Constitution
    S—when the statement supports the idea that the states did establish the Constitution
    X—when the statement supports neither idea.

4. Delegates to the Constitutional Convention were chosen by governors and by state legislatures. No popular elections were held to select the delegates.

5. In no way did the 55 delegates at the Convention represent a cross section of the population of the several states.

6. The Convention may be considered illegal or extralegal in that it was called to amend the Articles of Confederation and then proceeded to do something else, namely, form a new constitution.

7. Conventions were held in each state to ratify or to reject the proposed Constitution. Some delegates were sent from their districts to oppose ratification and others were sent to their state convention to support ratification.

8. The great compromises resolved in the Constitution involved conflicting views between big and little states, commercial and agricultural states, and free and slave states.

9. Before each state voted to accept or to reject the Constitution, its voters had ample time for campaigning on the issue.

10. It may well be true that in no election anywhere before had so large a portion of the adult males been allowed to vote and been exposed to such full publicity of the issues involved as was the case when the Constitution was submitted for ratification.

11. "We the people" was purely literary form for convenience. The first draft had named the states in the preamble. But this was revised because the addition of new states would have then required changing the preamble.

12. The United States Constitution has been in continuous operation longer than any other written constitution.

13. In order to assure ratification it was necessary to promise that a bill of rights would be added to the Constitution very soon after its adoption.

14. Where does the sole power lie to try a President who has been impeached?

15.-18. Give the number of the Amendment in the U.S. Constitution for each of the following.

15. Forbids states to deny any person equal protection of the laws.

16. Limits the President's term in office

17. Forbids payment of the war debt of the rebellious states

18. Makes a Lame Duck session of Congress most unlikely

19. Name the act which was passed as a "frame-up" to lead to the impeachment of President Johnson in 1868.

20.-22. The Supreme Law of the Land Clause of the Constitution establishes *three* legal authorities which constitute the supreme law of the land. List these three authorities.

23.-25. Which of the following circumstances illustrate *log-rolling* in a political sense?

(a) The McKinley Tariff and the Sherman Silver Act

(b) The 1894 Income Tax and the Payne-Aldrich Tariff

(c) The National Origins Immigration Law of 1929 and the McCarran-Walter Act

(d) Assumption Act and the location of the capital on the Potomac River

(e) Wagner-Connery Act and the Taft-Hartley Act

(1) a, b, d   (2) b, c, e   (3) c, d, e   (4) b, c   (5) a, d

26.-35.
The words or phrases in parentheses with each of the following items have a relationship with the item as indicated by A, B, or C. Designate which letter best applies in each case.

   A—to bring into effect, to support, or to make more effective

   B—to bring to an end, to oppose, or to make less effective

   C—neither A nor B apply

26. The desirability of the acquisition by the U.S. of the Louisiana Territory (France took Louisiana Territory from Spain)

27. Manufacturing in America (Tariff of 1816)

28. Era of Hard Feelings (Election of 1820)

29. War between Mexico and Texas (Battle of San Jacinto)

30. The Democratic Party split between Douglas and Breckenridge (Lecompton Constitution)

31. Acceptance of the decision of the Electoral Commission in 1876 (Democratic states of the South)

32. Effectiveness of the Sherman Anti-trust Act (Northern Securities Case)

33. The build-up of the demand for war against Spain in 1898 (Business interest and the conservative wing of the G.O.P.)

34. A crisis which might have set off a major war (Algeciras Conference)

35. The likelihood that the U.S. would accept the Versailles Treaty with the League of Nations in it (Wendell Willkie's slogan, "One World")

36.-49.
Match the items in Column II with dates taken from Column I. All of the items have some association with slavery.

COLUMN I		COLUMN II
1607	1845	36. Admission of California as a state
1609	1848	37. John Brown's raid at Harper's Ferry
1619	1850	38. First law of Congress outlawing the importation of slaves
1620	1854	39. Lincoln's Cooper Union speech
1765	1857	40. First slaves brought to Virginia
1775	1858	41. First issue of Garrison's *Liberator*
1783	1859	42. Slavery recognized as legal in the Constitution
1788	1860	43. Missouri Compromise
1803	1861	44. Lincoln-Douglas debates
1808	1863	45. Admission of Texas as a state
1812	1865	46. Emancipation Proclamation went into effect
1820		47. Kansas-Nebraska Bill
1824		48. Firing on Ft. Sumter
1831		49. Dred Scott Decision

50.-53. The following four questions deal with the Compromise of 1850.

50. What parallel was part of the Compromise?

51. What two states were part of the Compromise?

52. Name the territory north of the parallel referred to in question #50.

53. Name the territory south of the parallel referred to in question #50.

54. The election of what president put an end to the "Virginia Dynasty"?

55.-60.
Arrange the following items in chronological order.

A. Share cropping began

B. Tobacco became a commercially important crop
C. Agricultural Adjustment Act
D. McCormick Reaper invented
E. Cotton became a commercially important crop
F. Cotton picking machine

61.-72. *Resolved that big business corporations such as exist in automobiles, chemicals, electronics, steel, oil, etc. constitute an asset to a dominantly private-enterprise economy.*

The statements below, all arguments which may or may not have merit, are to be marked S, O, or X.

   s—if they support the above resolution
   o—if they oppose the above resolution
   x—if they do neither

61. They can maintain research laboratories too costly for smaller corporations to operate.

62. They carry specialization in operations to a greater degree than smaller units and employ specialists whose salaries are too costly for small or medium sized corporations to pay.

63. Their size frequently goes beyond the point of greatest efficiency and serves no purpose other than to give them monopolistic advantages.

64. Prices of their products react quickly to economic factors which tend to raise prices, but react sluggishly, if at all, to economic factors which tend to lower prices.

65. When a few large corporations sell a large portion of any product they become price leaders in that field and set prices which scores of small producers dare not under-cut.

66. Some of the very large corporations have grown from a small business as a result of years of continuing success.

67. Many of the very large corporations have been formed by mergers with other corporations in the same field.

68. When huge corporations with plants scattered all over the United States bargain with the A.F. of L.-C.I.O. they can conspire against the general public and raise both wages and prices.

69. Big business organizations battling big labor unions will bring big government into existence and thus threaten the private enterprise economy.

70. For the most part it is the larger corporations that have the necessary specialists, capital equipment, and managerial know-how to maintain national defense in this nuclear age.

71. There is frequently close cooperation between scientific research in our universities and in private corporations.

72. More private industry is organized on a large scale in the United States than in any other nation.

73.-75. Which of the following statements are true concerning the railroad situation during World War I?

(a) The government took over the railroads before the war was over.

(b) Under private management grain was not moved to ships nor coal to factories fast enough.

(c) Wilson called a conference of railroad presidents who then coordinated the efforts of many railroad systems to improve service.

(d) The Adamson Act and the Esch-Cummins Act both dealt with railroads.

(e) The total war record of American railroads was excellent in terms of getting freight moved to the places where it was most needed.

(1) All of them   (2) b, c, d, e   (3) a, e   (4) a, c, d, e   (5) a, c, e   (6) b, c, d

76. One of Wilson's *Fourteen Points* was reduction of armaments. Which of the following is closest to his stated goal in this respect?

(a) All nations should reduce their armaments by 25% three times at five year intervals. Then they should hold a conference to decide how further to reduce them.

(b) The defeated nations should disarm immediately. The allies should maintain their armaments until the stability of the postwar period was assured.

(c) Armaments should be reduced to the point where nations had only sufficient forces to maintain police protection against smuggling, piracy, etc. and to maintain domestic tranquility within their borders.

(d) The United States should make the first substantial move toward disarmament as an encouragement for other nations to follow suit.

(e) The United States and Great Britain should pledge sharp reductions in their naval power as an inducement to other nations to move in the same direction.

77. Which one of the following statements comes closest to Franklin Roosevelt's meaning of the "New Deal"?

(a) These times call for policies that will bring a decent standard of living to the forgotten man at the bottom of the economic pyramid.

(b) It is time for a change, a change that will call forth abundant capital to turn the wheels of industry and activate the channels of trade.

(c) Our policy calls for a full dinner pail for every worker. It can be best accomplished by a moderate protective tariff.

(d) The farmer has too long been aided by federal laws. We need a new deal that favors no segment of our people but assures opportunity for all.

78.-80. Which of the following statements about the Wagner-Connery Act are true?

(a) The act encouraged the growth of unions so that, for the first time in our history, "Big Labor" came into being.

(b) The terms of the act were pro labor and the law made no pretense of treating both labor and management equally.

(c) It was one of the major laws of the New Deal.

(d) Some labor leaders objected to certain provisions of the act and called it a "slave labor law."

(e) The Supreme Court ruled that the law was constitutional.

(f) The law forbade employers to urge their workers not to join a union.

(1) All except f   (2) All except e   (3) All except d
(4) a, c, e, f   (5) b, c, d, e   (6) a, c, d, e

81.-92.

Match the items in Column I *with those in* Column II. *All items are associated with World War II.*

COLUMN I	COLUMN II
A. Jimmy Doolittle	81. Mt. Suribachi
B. General Eisenhower	
C. General Mark Clark	82. Philippines
D. General MacArthur	83. Dropped first bombs on Japan
E. Prime Minister Chamberlain	84. Allied Invasion of western Europe
F. Prime Minister Churchill	85. Head of SHAEF
G. General Montgomery	86. Atom bombs
H. Kwajalein & Eniwetok	87. "I shall return"
I. Tarawa & Makin	88. Marshall Islands
J. Iwo Jima	89. Beginning of U.S. offensive in island hopping to Japan
K. Hiroshima & Nagasaki	
L. Corregidor	90. "Peace in our time"
M. Guadalcanal	
N. Operation Overlord	91. Led Salerno invasion of Italy
O. Battle of the Bulge	
P. Dunkirk	92. Last German counter offensive

93.-95. Which of the following statements are true concerning the Marshall Plan?

(a) The plan was primarily a military alliance to assure peace in Europe.

(b) It was known as the European Recovery Plan (E.R.P.).

(c) The fall of Czechoslovakia from an independent republic to a satellite of the U.S.S.R. helped convince Congress to appropriate the billions of dollars the plan required.

(d) General George C. Marshall, then our Secretary of State, so effectively organized the plan that it grew into a strong NATO alliance.

(e) The Soviet Union's hostile reaction to the Marshall Plan made it very definite that the "cold war" was on in earnest.

(f) As first presented by the United States, the communist bloc of nations in eastern Europe could have joined in the Marshall Plan.

(1) c, e (2) b, c, d (3) a, b, d (4) b, c, e, f (5) a, d, f

96.-100. *All of the following events occurred within four years. They are high points in the United States-Soviet Union relations. Arrange them in chronological order.*

A. Beginning of the Berlin Airlift
B. Truman Doctrine
C. Formation of NATO
D. Formation of the Marshall Plan
E. Potsdam Conference

Test III

___

1.-3. While settling the New World the French got along very well with the Indians. The Spanish treated them very cruelly. The English were usually on bad terms with the Indians but tended to have as little to do with them as circumstances permitted. Which of the following statements are acceptable as explanations of these different relationships with the Indians?

(a) The Spanish lived under a cruel monarchy in Spain and accepted that type of authority as the natural way to govern any people.

(b) The Spanish temperament as indicated by their culture and customs nurtured cruelty.

(c) Conquering the natives and enslaving them was a practical program for stealing their treasure and mining for more. Mexico and Peru were examples of such successes by the Spanish.

(d) The French government was absolute, but paternalistic. The French settlers in America tended to look upon Indians as children to be treated in a fatherly manner.

(e) The French were more advanced in nationalism and culture than any other people on the continent of Europe and this was reflected in their treatment of the natives in their colonies.

(f) Collecting furs along the St. Lawrence, Great Lakes, and Mississippi River made good relations with the Indians an economic necessity.

(g) The English had already developed representative government which recognized the dignity and importance of those who were ruled as well as those in authority.

(h) Settling towns and farms along the Atlantic seaboard antagonized the Indians as they were pushed off the land. But, for the most part, the English and Indians lived separately so that their ill-will toward each other was expressed by infrequent raids and attacks.

(1) a, e, c, f, h   **(2)** c, f, h   **(3)** a, d, g   **(4)** b, e, g   **(5)** all of them   **(6)** none of them

4.-15. *According to the United States Constitution by what majority may each of the following be accomplished? If by a simple majority indicate it by the letter* S; *if by some other majority indicate the fact by writing the correct fraction.*

4. To pass a tariff bill

5. To declare war

6. To ratify a treaty

7. To expel a member of the House of Representatives

8. To expel a member of the Senate

9. To propose an amendment to the Constitution

10. Number of states required to ratify an amendment

11. Approval of an appointment of a Secretary of State

12. Approval of an appointment of a Chief Justice of the Supreme Court

13. To pass an immigration law

14. For the Electoral College to elect a President

15. For the Senate to find a President guilty at an impeachment trial

16. What is the number of the Amendment of our Constitution which forbids involuntary servitude except for punishment of a crime?

17. What percentage of the seats in the House of Representatives is up for election at each national election?

18. What is the least percentage of Senate seats up for election at each national election?

19. It is the Constitutional duty of what government official to preside over the Senate?

20. Who makes the rules that govern the procedures of the House of Representatives?

21. Quote or paraphrase the 9th Amendment of the U.S. Constitution.

_____

_____

_____

22.-23. In his Farewell Address President Washington gave two bits of advice he thought the nation should follow. In substance, they are among the following statements. Identify them by letter.

(a) Avoid making treaties with other nations.

(b) Maintain at least two independent and strong political parties.

(c) Avoid permanent entangling alliances.

(d) It is better to err on the side of freedom for individuals than on the side of excessive power for the government.

(e) Make sure that attachment to a political party does not become a stronger influence than attachment to the nation.

(f) Office holders must ever strive to so conduct public affairs that the word, politician, will become a noble word.

24.-33.

The words or phrases in parentheses with each of the following items have a relationship with the item as indicated by A, B, or C. Designate which letter best applies in each case.

> A—to bring into effect, to support, or to make more effective
>
> B—to bring to an end, to oppose, or to make less effective
>
> C—neither A nor B apply

24. The strength of Jefferson's Democratic Republican Party (X.Y.Z. Affair)

25. Maryland's attempt to tax the Baltimore branch of the Bank of the United States (Gibbons v. Ogden)

26. Calhoun's "Exposition & Protest" (Kentucky Resolutions)

27. Slavery controversy (Mexican War)

28. Douglas' election to the U.S. Senate in 1858 (John Brown's raid on Harper's Ferry)

29. Bland-Allison Act (Increased production of the silver mines)

30. Democratic success in the 1890 election (McKinley Tariff)

31. A strong demand for war against Spain in 1898 (The New York Journal and the New York World)

32. The Hague Conference of 1899 (Dollar Diplomacy)

33. Coolidge's rise to the presidency (Boston Police strike)

34.-45.

The following statements are associated with foreign policy under Jefferson and Madison. Classify each statement as S, O, or X.

> S—if it supports the policy of this period
>
> O—if it opposes the policy of this period
>
> X—if it does neither

34. The Embargo Act of 1807 kept American ships off the high seas and prevented impressment of our sailors by England.

35. England and France needed our goods more than we needed their trade. They were at war and needed all the imports they could get.

36. The Embargo Act ruined the New England shipping companies.

37. Scores of small manufacturing establishments started up in the northeast between 1800 and 1815.

38. The Embargo Act and the Non-Intercourse Act were embarrassingly close to a peace-at-any-price policy.

39. Circumstances can make avoidance of war a wiser policy than insistence upon national rights.

40. The Macon Act lifted all restrictions on U.S. shipping.

41. Had local officials aided the federal government in preventing smuggling, our rights as neutrals would soon have been observed by England and France.

42. The Macon Act eventually got the U.S. in such an awkward position that we declared war more through embarrassment than any other reason.

43. In such major wars as the Napoleonic War the rights of neutrals have always been violated. It happened again in World Wars I and II. When a big fight is on, neutrals get hurt.

44. The United States was allied with a despot, Napoleon, against a democratic monarchy, England.

45. Francis Scott Key was inspired to write our national anthem as he witnessed the bombardment of Ft. McHenry.

46.-48. Which of the following statements about the Hartford Convention are true?

(a) Only New England was represented at the Convention.

(b) Every delegate there was a Federalist.

(c) The meeting was either illegal or extralegal.

(d) Such a protest meeting held during the war was traitorous.

(e) Not one of their proposed amendments was adopted.

(f) The fact that the vote for the declaration of war in the Senate passed by only 19 to 13 strongly suggests that many Americans shared the views of the Hartford Convention.

(g) The Convention killed the Federalist Party as an influence on a national scale.

(1) All of them (2) All but a & b (3) All but c & g (4) All but e & f (5) a, c, e, g (6) a, b, e, f, g

49. The Battle of New Orleans did not affect the outcome of the War of 1812, but it did make a president. What president?

50.-56.

All of the following items are boundary lines. Arrange them in chronological order.

A. Final adjustment of the northeastern border between Maine and Canada

B. The Mississippi River set as our western border

C. Establishment of our present southwest border between the Rio Grande River and the Pacific Ocean

D. Establishment of the border between Spanish Florida and the United States

E. Establishment of the northern border from the Lake of the Woods to the Rocky Mountains

F. Establishment of the "step line" along much of the western border of the Louisiana Purchase

G. Establishment of the northern border from the Rockies to the west coast

57.-66.

The following treaties and events had some bearing on the United States' interest in acquiring the

Panama Canal. Arrange them in chronological order.

A. Hay-Bauna Varilla Treaty
B. Guadalupe-Hidalgo Treaty
C. Treaty with New Granada
D. Hay-Herran Treaty
E. Acquisition of Puerto Rico & the Philippines
F. California gold rush
G. Trip of the *Oregon*
H. Hay-Pauncefote Treaty
I. French attempt to build an isthmian canal
J. Clayton-Bulwer Treaty

67. Which *one* of the following statements about the coal strike of 1902 is *not* true?

(a) The strike was in the anthracite coal fields of eastern Pennsylvania.
(b) J. P. Morgan played a part in bringing about a settlement.
(c) President T. Roosevelt intervened on the part of the public.
(d) Refusal of the mine operators to recognize the union as a bargaining agent was a major issue in the strike.
(e) The intervention by the President in the strike was strongly resented by the union, but accepted willingly by the mine operators.

68.-69.
Both Group A *and* Group B *contain one item which does not belong with the other items in its group because it lacks a factor common to the other five items. Select, by number, the odd item in each group.*

GROUP A	GROUP B
1. Interstate Commerce Act	1. Pullman strike
2. Esch-Cummins Act	2. Injunction
3. Wabash v. Illinois	3. Molly Maguires
4. Adamson Act	4. Force Bill
5. Hepburn Act	5. I.W.W.
6. Pendleton Act	6. Haymarket Square

70. One of Wilson's *Fourteen Points* called for freedom of the seas in peace and war. Which *one* of the following statements is false?

(a) Freedom of the seas is rarely any problem in time of peace.
(b) The United States was not permitted freedom of the seas during the Napoleonic War.
(c) The United States was not permitted freedom of the seas from 1914 to its entrance into World War I.
(d) With freedom of the seas in time of war all neutral nations would be allowed to trade with each other without molestation or hindrance.
(e) With freedom of the seas in war time the operation of a blockade against neutral shipping would be prohibited.

(f) Under conditions expected to prevail if there is a World War III, the concept of freedom of the seas will have little, if any, meaning.

71.-85.
Mark each of the following statements as A, B, *or* C.

A—if they support or go along with the thinking of the New Deal "liberal" wing of the Democratic Party.
B—if they support or go along with the thinking of the "conservative" wing of the Republican Party.
C—if they cut across party lines and can't be identified as "liberal" or "conservative" or as politically "left" or "right."

71. The key to economic health lies in the purchasing power of the lower and middle income groups.
72. The federal government is not pressing hard enough on the civil rights issue in connection with the race problem.
73. Minimum wage laws keep people from being employed and thus force them on the public relief rolls.
74. Cutting the gold content of the dollar by about 40% was a legitimate method of counteracting deflation in the 1930's.
75. A minimum wage set by law should be an hourly wage high enough to keep people off the public relief rolls.
76. The possibility of very high profits is a desirable factor to stimulate business enterprise into new ventures.
77. Present methods of meeting medical costs are inadequate and some legislation is called for to remedy the situation.
78. The federal government is pressing too hard on the civil rights issue in connection with the race problem.
79. Parity payments on agricultural products should be about 75% or less and every effort should be made to get rid of parity payments altogether.
80. Taxation results in the government spending the money it collects and has no influence in reducing or checking inflation.
81. Parity payments on agricultural products should be in the range of about 80% to 100%.
82. An ample supply of risk capital and a political climate that encourages investment is the best stimulus for a healthy economy.
83. High taxes in prosperous times tends to control inflation by leaving in the people's hands less money to spend.
84. Cutting the gold content of the dollar was an actual steal by the government even though its legality was upheld by a split decision of the Supreme Court.
85. The race to the moon is not a wise expenditure of the vast sums required.

86.-100.
All of the following were newsworthy during the   *presidency of Dwight Eisenhower. Match the items*
in Column II with those in Column I.

COLUMN I   COLUMN II

A. Dienbienphu   86. Changed to CENTO
B. Viet Minh   87. Member of SEATO
C. 38th parallel   88. Part of Red Sea coast
D. Bangkok   89. Vietnam
E. Philippines   90. U.S. met with delegates of Red China
F. Taiwan   91. French collapse in Indo China
G. Quemoy & Matsu   92. Headquarters of SEATO
H. Pescadores Islands   93. Islands near Taiwan
I. Laos   94. Islands bombarded by Red China
J. Bagdad Pact   95. Communist forces in Vietnam
K. Aswan   96. Formosa
L. Gaza Strip   97. Objective of Arab nations
M. Sinai Peninsula   98. On the Israeli border
N. Liquidation of Israel   99. Dam in Egypt
O. 17th parallel   100. Breakup of "Summit" Conference
P. Geneva Conference 1954
Q. U 2

Test IV

1.-3. Which of the following items are associated with the colony of Virginia?

(a) A terrible starving time **(b)** John Rolfe **(c)** Governor Berkeley **(d)** William Brewster **(e)** Religious Toleration Act of 1649 **(f)** Pocahontas **(g)** John Davenport

(1) a, b, c, f   **(2)** a, c, f, g   **(3)** c, e, g   **(4)** b, e, f   **(5)** a, b, e, g   **(6)** a, c, d, e

4.-13.

The words or phrases in parentheses with each of the following items have a relationship with the item as indicated by A, B, or C. Designate which letter best applies in each case.

A—to bring into effect, to support, or to make more effective

B—to bring to an end, to oppose, or to make less effective

C—neither A nor B apply

4. Proclamation Line of 1763 (Chief Pontiac's War)

5. Policy of Salutary Neglect (Gresham's Law)

6. Mercantilism (Laws forbidding trades and crafts in the colonies)

7. New England rum distilleries (Theocratic government in Mass. Bay Colony)

8. Favorable balance of trade for England (Trade & Navigation Acts)

9. Dependence of the American colonies on England (Expulsion of the French from America)

10. American colonial boycott against England (Sons of Liberty)

11. Indecision concerning revolution (Paine's *Common Sense*)

12. First Continental Congress (Battles of Lexington and Concord)

13. Government regulations over trade and business (Laissez faire)

14.-16. Article I Section 8 of the Constitution gives to Congress the power to lay and collect taxes for certain purposes. Which of the following list of purposes are contained in this clause of the Constitution?

(a) to aid the several states in financing public education

(b) to provide for the common defense

(c) to more equitably distribute wealth

(d) to pay the public debt

(e) to provide for the general welfare

(f) to stabilize the economy

(g) to encourage a rising standard of living

(1) a, b, d, e   **(2)** b, c, d, f   **(3)** b, c, d   **(4)** b, d, e   **(5)** b, d, g   **(6)** b, e, g

17.-21. The following questions are to be answered by giving the correct number of years.

17. State the minimum age for a member of the House of Representatives.

18. State the minimum age for a member of the Senate.

19. State the minimum age for a President.

20. What is the term for a member of the House?

21. What is the term for a member of the Senate?

22.-25. Give the number of the Amendment in the Constitution which provides for each of the following.

22. Income tax

23. Defines a citizen

24. Forbids states to deny life, liberty or property without due process of law

25. Modifies the original jurisdiction of the federal courts

26.-27. A writ of habeas corpus will, under most conditions, protect the individual in which *two* of the following ways?

(a) Assure him of the services of a competent lawyer

(b) Afford the opportunity to get out on bail within a brief period after arrest

(c) Guarantee a prisoner the right to have his accusers cross-examined

(d) Make it very unlikely that a person will be deliberately arrested on false charges

(e) Make it illegal to try a person a second time for an act for which he has been tried and found innocent

(f) Prevent martial law from applying to civilians during war or insurrection

28.-30. When the Electoral College fails to elect the Vice-President, which of the following statements are part of the Constitutional provisions dealing with such a situation?

(a) The election goes to the House of Representatives.

(b) The election goes to the Senate.

(c) Each state has one vote.

(d) Each state has two votes.
(e) Each state has as many votes as it has members in Congress.
(f) Each state has as many votes as it has members in the House.
(g) The Vice-President must be chosen from the top five candidates.
(h) The Vice-President must be chosen from the top three candidates.
(i) The Vice-President must be chosen from the top two candidates.

(1) b, d, h (2) b, d, i (3) b, c, h (4) a, e, g
(5) a, c, g (6) a, c, h

31.-35.
List, in any order, the five freedoms contained in the first Amendment of the Constitution.

36.-45.
The words or phrases in parentheses with each of the following items have a relationship with the item as indicated by A, B, or C. Designate which letter best applies in each case.

A—to bring into effect, to support, or to make more effective
B—to bring to an end, to oppose, or to make less effective
c—neither A nor B apply

36. The strength of Jefferson's Republican Party (The Alien, Naturalization, and Sedition Acts; the *Midnight Judges,* and the Kentucky & Virginia Resolutions)
37. The doctrine of states' rights (*Strict Construction* of the Constitution)
38. The *Compact Theory* of the Union (Daniel Webster)
39. Slavery in the District of Columbia (Carry Nation)
40. The likelihood of Douglas being elected president (Lincoln-Douglas debates)
41. Pendleton Act (C. Julius Guiteau)
42. Farm support for the Populist Party (Panic of 1873)
43. Pacification of the Philippines (Aguinaldo)
44. The philosophy of caveat emptor (Department of Agriculture of the U.S. and the American Medical Association)
45. Hawley-Smoot Tariff (Petition signed by about 1000 economists)

46.-55.
The following items are associated with the War of 1812. Match the items in Column II *with those in* Column I.

COLUMN I
A. Oliver Perry
B. Jackson
C. Monroe
D. William Hull
E. Thomas Macdonough
F. Madison
G. *Constitution*
H. *Shannon*
I. *Little Belt*
J. *President*
K. Ft. McHenry
L. Lundy's Lane

COLUMN II
46. *Guerriere*
47. *Chesapeake*
48. Put-in-Bay
49. Bombardment of Baltimore
50. President during the war
51. Battle in Canada—both sides claimed victory
52. New Orleans
53. Surrendered Detroit
54. Drove British off Lake Champlain
55. Secretary of State & Secretary of War

56.-65. *Resolved that the Civil War was an irrepressible conflict.*
Classify each of the following statements as A, N, or X.

A—if it supports the affirmative of the above resolution
N—if it supports the negative of the above resolution
x—if it does neither

56. If not on the issue of slavery, then on some other issue the battle over states' rights had to be fought.

57. Back in 1830 Calhoun said the tariff issue was a surface issue and that the basic quarrel resulted from the "peculiar domestic institutions of the Southern States."
58. The northern defiance of the federal fugitive slave law of 1850 by operating the *Underground Railway* and passing Personal Liberty Laws created an intolerable situation.
59. Due to the conditions of weather and soil prevailing in the Mexican Cession and in the Kansas-Nebraska Territory the furor over slavery made no sense.
60. The Congress of Vienna had condemned slavery as early as 1815.

61. England had made slavery illegal throughout her empire and even the czar of Russia was on the verge of abolishing serfdom.

62. Many southerners were finding out that slave labor was more expensive and more trouble than hired labor. Helper's *Impending Crisis* pictured slavery as a weakness, not a strength of the southern economy.

63. Comparatively few southerners owned slaves. Confederate soldiers would have stayed home gladly if only the federal laws were obeyed and the northerners minded their own business. "Let us alone," not "Slavery forever," was their cry.

64. There was no need to stir up the Kansas-Nebraska struggle in the middle 1850's. Calm and prosperity marked the early years of the 1850's. The unnecessary Kansas-Nebraska Act of 1854 then set off a chain of violent actions and reactions which led to secession.

65. In 1856 many settlers in Kansas were there not to build homes and work farms, but to win a political battle. Men from Missouri rode over the border to become temporary Kansans and the New England Emigrant Aid Company financed northerners to go west armed with "Beecher Bibles."

66.-68. Which of the following statements about the Bland-Allison Act are true?

(a) It was generally favored by farmers of the west.
(b) The Greenback Party opposed it.
(c) Some termed its passage the "Crime of '73."
(d) The bill was vetoed by the President.
(e) The bill provided for unlimited (or free) coinage of silver at 16 to 1.
(f) The discovery of the Comstock Lode substantially reduced the political controversy over silver.

(1) a, b, e   **(2)** a, f   **(3)** b, c, d   **(4)** a, c, e, f   **(5)** a, d

69.-79. *Resolved that the protective tariff policy which prevailed almost all the time from the Civil War to the depth of the great depression in 1933 was beneficial to our economy.*

Classify each of the following statements as S, O, or X.

s—if it supports the above resolution
o—if it opposes the above resolution
x—if it does neither

69. Protected industries keep a full dinner pail for the workers.

70. Products of foreign pauper labor are kept out of the U.S.

71. Protective rates levied by the U.S. invite corresponding rates against our products.

72. Protective tariffs tend to provoke international friction.

73. Development of natural resources and a growing population are the true explanation of our rising standard of living.

74. Protection encourages inefficiency in production and in marketing.

75. Our growth as an industrial and commercial nation was phenomenal during this period.

76. The farmers received almost no protection through tariff.

77. The tariff, as a single factor in the economy, had no more than a trifling effect upon the ups and downs of our economy.

78. Without protection by tariffs for our manufacturers, England could have smothered our industries with her greater financial assets and her industrial "know-how" during the early and middle 1800's.

79. Promise of high profits, almost guaranteed by high tariffs, kept a flow of risk capital available for expansion and experimentation.

80.-83.
Column I *is a list of Supreme Court cases.* Column II *is a list of statements about these cases. Match the statement with the proper case.*

COLUMN I	COLUMN II
A. Marbury v. Madison	**80.** This case involved a Justice of the Peace.
B. U.S. v. E. C. Knight	**81.** This case was soon followed by a President saying, John Marshall has made his decision, now let him enforce it.
C. Schechter v. U.S.	**82.** This case was a great set-back to early New Deal legislation.
D. Cherokee v. Georgia	**83.** This case made the Sherman Anti-trust Law appear very ineffective.

84.-89.
Match the numbered items in Column II with the lettered items in Column I. All items are associated with the career of Theodore Roosevelt.

COLUMN I

A. College boys and cow-
   boys
B. Dominican Republic
C. Arizona
D. Argentina
E. Panama
F. Nobel Peace Prize
G. Algeciras
H. Interstate Commerce
   Act
I. Pure Food & Drug Acts
J. Venezuela
K. California
L. "Trust Buster"

COLUMN II

84. (a) Revolution
    (b) Northern Securities Co.
85. (a) Roosevelt Dam
    (b) Roosevelt Corollary
86. (a) Muckrakers
    (b) Debt Controversy
87. (a) Drago
    (b) Gentlemen's Agreement
88. (a) Rough Riders
    (b) Portsmouth Treaty
89. (a) Moroccan Crisis
    (b) Hepburn Act

90. Which of the following groups of nations came into being before World War II as a result of World War I?

GROUP A	GROUP B	GROUP C	GROUP D
Estonia	Hungary	Lithuania	Congo
Ethiopia	Yugoslavia	Czechoslovakia	Egypt
Poland	Israel	Finland	Latvia

91.-93. Which statements are true? They are all associated with Hoover's term as president.

(a) The National Origins Immigration Formula went into effect during his term.
(b) As he assumed the presidency he felt that our American Way of Life was showing the way to banish poverty.
(c) He had defeated the Democratic candidate, John W. Davis, by a wide margin.
(d) Within the first year after the 1929 crash he ordered banks closed in order to check further collapse of even sound banks.
(e) "Hoovervilles," towns where extraordinary relief efforts were being put into effect, sprang up in several states.

(f) President Hoover said, as the depression deepened, that it was a postwar economic reaction made more severe by the widespread poverty in Europe.

(1) b, c, f   (2) a, c, d   (3) c, d, e, f   (4) a, b, f
(5) a, b, c, e   (6) b, d, e

94.-98. *The following events happened in the 1930's. Arrange them in chronological order.*

A. Hitler annexed Austria.
B. Italy attacked Ethiopia.
C. Japan attacked Manchuria and set up a puppet state.
D. Hitler violated the demilitarized Rhineland.
E. England and France deserted Czechoslovakia at Munich.

99.-100. When General Bradley said that General MacArthur's policy in Korea would have the United States in the *"wrong war, at the wrong time, in the wrong place, with the wrong enemy"* what did Bradley consider to be the right place and the right enemy?

Test V

1.-3. Which of the following items are associated with the Massachusetts Bay Colony?

(a) Ann Hutchinson **(b)** Theocratic government **(c)** John Winthrop **(d)** Edmund Andros **(e)** Calvert **(f)** Haven for Catholics **(g)** Oglethorpe

(1) a, c, d, f **(2)** a, b, e, g **(3)** c, d, e, f **(4)** b, c, d, g **(5)** a, b, c, d **(6)** a, d, f, g

4.-6. The following statements are points in Grenville's program of 1764-'65. After each statement write a sentence of not over 25 words giving Grenville's reason for the regulation.

4. A vice-admiralty court was established at Halifax where tax cases arising in America could be taken for trial without a jury.

5. Colonial shippers were required to post a much heavier bond than before.

6. Local deputies were no longer allowed to collect taxes. The tax collector had to come to America from England and perform his duties in person.

7.-8. What building is known as the "cradle of liberty"? In what city is the "cradle of liberty" located?

9.-16.
Match the items in Column II *with the quotations in* Column I.

COLUMN I

A. *"I shall return."*
B. *"I have not yet begun to fight."*
C. *"Millions for defense, not one cent for tribute."*
D. *"Don't give up the ship."*
E. *"I only regret that I have but one life to lose for my country."*
F. *"We have met the enemy and they are ours."*
G. *"We must all hang together, or assuredly we shall all hang separately."*
H. *"I know not what course others may take, but as for me, give me liberty or give me death."*

COLUMN II

9. A spy
10. *Bonhomme Richard*
11. Virginia Convention
12. Lake Erie
13. Evacuation of Corregidor
14. *Chesapeake*
15. Declaration of Independence
16. X.Y.Z. affair

17.-20. Give the number of the Amendment of the United States Constitution which provides for each of the following.

17. Forbids denial of suffrage on account of race or color.

18. Repealed prohibition.

19. Forbids states to deny any person equal protection of the laws.

20. Forbids denial of suffrage on account of sex.

21.-23. Which of the following are special privileges or restrictions of members of Congress contained in the Constitution?

(a) In some instances they are not subject to arrest when other citizens would be.

(b) Attendance at half the meetings of Congress each session is compulsory unless due to physical disability.

(c) While a member of Congress they can't hold another federal office.

(d) Salaries of Congressmen are not subject to the federal income tax.

(e) Congressmen may not use funds for secretarial work for the employment of close relatives. (Nepotism)

(f) Any pay raise Congress passes for its members does not apply to any member until his election *after* the new salary became law.

(g) Congressmen are not subject to the same restraints or penalties for the abuse of freedom of speech as are other citizens.

(1) a, c, e, f, g **(2)** all of them **(3)** a, c, f, g **(4)** b, e, g **(5)** a, d, e **(6)** a, c, d, e, f

24.-26. The following statements are about the Kentucky Resolutions written by Jefferson. Which are true?

(a) They declared the Sedition Act unconstitutional.

273

(b) While an important political pronouncement, these resolutions were not the formal act of any government.

(c) The immediate purpose of the resolutions, and probably their only purpose, was to win the election of 1800 for the Republicans.

(d) James Madison wrote the Virginia Resolutions which pointed in the same direction as the Kentucky Resolutions but were more moderate in tone.

(e) Jefferson's reasoning in these resolutions would apply to secession as logically as to nullification, but Jefferson did not claim the right of a state to secede.

(f) At the turn of the century, 1798-1802, no other states accepted the reasoning of the Kentucky and Virginia Resolutions.

(1) All but f   (2) a, d, e   (3) a, e, f   (4) b, c, d, e
(5) All but b

27.-29. Which of the following statements about the Marbury v. Madison Case are true?

(a) The case involved the appellate jurisdiction of the Supreme Court.

(b) The case involved the Judiciary Act of 1789.

(c) Chief Justice Marshall issued a mandamus ordering Secretary of State Madison to deliver the commission of Justice of the Peace to Mr. Marbury.

(d) The Court upheld a law of Congress that was challenged by Jefferson.

(e) The Court declared an act of Congress unconstitutional.

(f) Chief Justice Marshall and President Jefferson held opposing political views.

(1) b, e, f   (2) a, c, f   (3) a, d, b, f   (4) b, c, d
(5) a, b, c, e   (6) a, b, d

30.-39.

The words or phrases in parentheses with each of the following items have a relationship with the item as indicated by A, B, or C. Designate which letter best applies in each case.

A—to bring into effect, to support, or to make more effective

B—to bring to an end, to oppose, or to make less effective

C—neither A nor B apply

30. Napoleon's plans for an empire in the western hemisphere (Toussaint L'Ouverture)

31. The action of the New Hampshire legislature which changed Dartmouth College, a private institution, into Darmouth University, a state institution (Dartmouth College Case)

32. The Second Bank of the United States (Martin Van Buren)

33. Abolitionist sentiment (Seward's "higher law")

34. G.O.P. control in the South 1867-'75 (Waving the *bloody shirt*)

35. The strength of organized labor (Haymarket Riot)

36. Prosperity in Hawaii (2¢ bounty for American sugar passed with the McKinley tariff)

37. Dewey's occupation of the city of Manila (Admiral Cervera)

38. The split between Taft and T. Roosevelt (Pinchot-Ballinger)

39. Blaine's leadership in the Republican Party ("Stalwarts")

40.-42. Which of the following statements associated with the Lincoln-Douglas debates are true?

(a) The Freeport Doctrine, advanced by Lincoln, grew out of these debates.

(b) Lincoln pointed out the incompatibility of the Dred Scott Decision and the Kansas-Nebraska Bill.

(c) Douglas had to win re-election to the U.S. Senate in 1858 in order to be in line for the Democratic presidential nomination in 1860.

(d) Douglas went against the Supreme Court and stuck to the popular sovereignty principle of his Kansas-Nebraska Bill.

(e) Douglas defeated Lincoln for the senatorship.

(f) The Freeport Doctrine was heartily disliked by southern Democrats.

(1) All of them   (2) a, b, f   (3) b, c, d   (4) a, c, d, e   (5) c, d, e   (6) b, c, e, f

43.-45. Which of the following statements are true about the provisions and effects of the Homestead Act of 1862?

(a) The purpose of the act was to encourage more rapid settlement of the West.

(b) There was nothing in the act to prevent land companies and banks purchasing tracts of land for resale to settlers.

(c) An adult could acquire 160 acres by living on it and working it for five years with no money payment required other than a modest registration fee.

(d) Land could be purchased at $1.25 per acre with a six months' residence provision.

(e) The residence provisions of the law were carefully administered to assure that only true homesteaders acquired land under this act.

(f) Homesteading was one way to avoid the Civil War draft back home and also to escape the embarrassment of not enlisting.

(1) a, b, c, d   (2) b, c, d, f   (3) a, c, d, f   (4) a, e
(5) a, c, d, e   (6) All but b

46.-55.

Match the items in Column II *with the names of the presidents in* Column I.

COLUMN I	COLUMN II
A. John Adams	46. Tie vote in the Electoral College
B. Buchanan	47. Had the greatest electoral and popular vote, but an opponent won
C. Cleveland	48. Won the electoral vote but not the popular vote
D. Harding	49. His Vice-President belonged to the opposing party
E. B. Harrison	50. Served two non-consecutive terms
F. Hayes	51. Broke the no-third-term tradition
G. Jackson	52. Died a month after his inauguration
H. Jefferson	53. His election marked the end of the *Crime of Reconstruction*
I. Polk	54. The first "Crown Prince" of the U.S.
J. F. Roosevelt	55. The first "Dark Horse"
K. W. Harrison	
L. Van Buren	

56.-63.
Match the items in Column II *with those in* Column I. *All of the answers are associated directly or indirectly with James G. Blaine.*

COLUMN I	COLUMN II
A. Mugwumps	56. Railroad scandal
B. Somoan Islands	57. Blaine's faction of the G.O.P.
C. Reciprocity	58. Written into the McKinley tariff
D. Hawaiian Islands	59. Blaine's most forward-looking public program
E. Mulligan Letters	60. Pago Pago
F. Bering Sea	61. "mare clausum"
G. Mafia ("black hand")	62. New Orleans
H. Lake Michigan	63. Valparaiso, Chile
I. Grant	
J. Stalwarts	
K. Income tax	
L. Pan-Americanism	
M. Amercian marines killed	

64.-74.
All of the items listed below are associated with reform movements or the struggle between employ-ees and management. Each item can be placed in one of the time periods designated as I, II, III, & IV.

COLUMN I	PERIODS OF TIME
64. (a) Knights of Labor	
(b) Frances Wright	
65. (a) Establishment of the U.S. Department of Labor	
(b) Adamson Act	
66. (a) New Harmony established by Robert Owen	I. Before 1861
(b) Rochdale Cooperatives started	
67. (a) Sit-down strike at General Motors	
(b) A. F. of L. formed	
68. (a) State "Right to Work" laws	
(b) John Mitchell and the Anthracite Coal Strike	
69. (a) Danbury Hatters' Strike	II. 1862—1900
(b) Taft-Hartley Law	
70. (a) Homestead, Pa. Massacre	
(b) Brook Farm	
71. (a) "Molly Maguires"	
(b) Esch-Cummins Act	
72. (a) Wagner-Connery Act	III. 1901—1929
(b) Formation of the I.W.W.	

73. (a) Formation of the Political Action Committee of the C.I.O.
    (b) Haymarket Square Riot
74. (a) Formation of the National Association of Manufacturers
    (b) Pullman Strike

IV. After 1929

75.-94.
Match the items in Column II *with those in Column I.* *All items are associated with the period following World War I.*

COLUMN I	COLUMN II
A. Unconstitutional	75. Harding
B. Rural electrification	76. Alfred E. Smith
C. Lame Duck	77. Hoover
D. Parity	78. Coolidge
E. Presidential candidate defeated in 1940	79. T. V. A.
F. Labor-management relations	80. Taft-Hartley Act
G. Inflation	81. Rejection of the League of Nations
H. Ramsay MacDonald	82. Make Germany pay for the war
I. *Pump priming*	83. Gold content of the dollar cut about 40%
J. Boston Police Strike	84. Allied War Debts
K. Reparations	85. Reconstruction Finance Corporation
L. Economic sanctions	86. Price fixing
M. The choice is between American rugged individualism and European state socialism	87. No trade in strategic goods to aggressors
N. Isolation	88. Esch-Cummins Act
O. Happy Warrior	89. Amendment #20
P. Moratorium	90. Bonus marchers
Q. Railroads were returned to their owners	91. A.A.A.
R. Back to normalcy	92. Samuel Insull
S. Attorney-General Palmer	93. War outlawed
T. Public utilities empire	94. Immigration
U. McCarren-Walter	
V. Anacosta Flats	
W. Kellogg-Briand	

95.-100.
Each of the following items is to be classified as A, B, or C.

  A—prohibited by the Taft-Hartley Act
  B—provided by the Taft-Hartley Act
  C—not included by the Taft-Hartley Act

95. (a) Unions are made subject to suit for breach of contract.
    (b) Employers are made subject to suit for breach of contract.
96. (a) Union officials must take an oath that they are not members of the Communist Party.
    (b) Management officials bargaining with unions must take an oath that they are not members of the Communist Party.
97. (a) Closed shop
    (b) Union shop
98. (a) "Compulsory check-off"
    (b) Injunction to postpone a strike for 80 days
99. (a) Contributions by unions to political parties
    (b) Contributions by corporations to political parties
100. (a) Secondary boycotts
    (b) Unions liable for damages resulting from jurisdictional strikes

Test VI

1.-12.

Match the items in Column II *with the items in* Column I.

COLUMN I

A. Leyden
B. 1636
C. 1732
D. John Davenport
E. Virginia
F. James II
G. Connecticut
H. "Hundreds"
I. 1688
J. Salem
K. Pennsylvania
L. Culture of Tobacco
M. Quakers
N. Roger Williams
O. Pilgrims
P. Henry VIII
Q. Nathaniel Bacon
R. Delaware
S. Charles 1
T. Hartford
U. Winthrop
V. Duke of York
W. Ann Hutchinson
X. 1588

COLUMN II

1. (a) Left Mass. Bay Colony for R.I. to join settlement on Narragansett Bay
   (b) A type of desk still commonly in use
2. (a) Colony where House of Burgesses was established
   (b) Last of the Stuarts
3. (a) City of the "charter oak"
   (b) Separatists
4. (a) Date Georgia was founded
   (b) Settled in Pennsylvania
5. (a) Date Harvard was founded
   (b) Temporary home of the Pilgrims
6. (a) Founder of New Haven
   (b) Fundamental Orders
7. (a) Tudor
   (b) John Rolfe
8. (a) Opposed Gov. Berkeley
   (b) Beheaded
9. (a) Settled by Swedes
   (b) Took New Amsterdam
10. (a) "The Holy Experiment"
    (b) Witches burned
11. (a) Spanish Armada
    (b) Date of Bloodless Revolution in England
12. (a) Sent delegates to the House of Burgesses
    (b) Complete religious freedom

13. As applied to the American colonial scene which one of the following statements best explains the term *salutary neglect?*

(a) Colonials neglected to pay taxes as required by law.

(b) England neglected to support the war against the French and Indians until Pitt took over.

(c) France neglected to put forth strenuous efforts to back up her settlers in America.

(d) American settlers neglected to enter wholeheartedly into the French and Indian War.

(e) England did not enforce, either strictly or regularly, the trade and navigation acts.

14.-20. The following questions can be answered very briefly, usually in one or two words.

14. In what year did the 2nd Continental Congress convene?

15. Name the last state to ratify the Articles of Confederation and thus bring them into effect.

16. In 1787 what was the name of the area now occupied by Ohio, Indiana, Illinois, Michigan, Wisconsin and part of Minnesota?

17. What Revolutionary War captain led a revolt of debtors in central and western Massachusetts?

18. Name the British general who surrendered at Saratoga.

19. Name the British general who surrendered at Yorktown.

20. Which was the "Critical Period"? **(a)** 1763-1775 **(b)** 1775-1783 **(c)** 1781-1789 **(d)** 1789-1800 **(e)** 1800-1815

21.-23. Articles I, II, and III of the Constitution of the United States deal with the three major departments of government. Name the department for each Article.

24. What type of bill must originate in the House of Representatives?

25. Where does the authority lie to ratify a treaty?

26. Which weakness of the Articles of Confederation was most closely associated with the Mt. Vernon and Annapolis Conventions?

(a) No courts to handle interstate disputes.
(b) No authority to regulate interstate commerce.
(c) No power to collect the taxes it levied.
(d) No power to recruit an adequate armed force.
(e) No power to change its constitution except by unanimous approval of all 13 states.

27.-29. Which is the best definition of an ex post facto law? An ex post facto law is one which

(a) punishes a crime which was legal when committed.
(b) makes an act illegal which, before the law was passed, was legal.
(c) makes punishable an act which was legal when committed.
(d) is so unjust as to be intolerable.
(e) neither the states nor the federal government may pass.
(f) was an important factor in our dispute over oil with Mexico in the early 1900's.

30.-31. All but *two* of the following items were controversial as between the Federalists and the Democratic Republicans during President Washington's administrations. Which two?

(a) Whisky Rebellion (b) Bank of the United States (c) Handling of federal domestic debt (d) Handling state debts by the Assumption Bill (e) Handling the foreign debt (f) Genet and the Treaty of Alliance of 1778 (g) Jay Treaty (h) Pinckney Treaty

32.-41.
The words or phrases in parentheses with each of the following items have a relationship with the item as indicated by A, B, or C. Designate which letter best applies in each case.

   A—to bring into effect, to support, or to make more effective
   B—to bring to an end, to oppose, or to make less effective
   C—neither A nor B apply

32. American shipping companies (Embargo & Non-Intercourse Act)

33. Fulton's and Livingston's franchise from New York State granting them a monopoly of steamboat trade on the Hudson (McCulloch v. Maryland)

34. "King Caucus" (Referendum)

35. Mutual suspicions and hostility of the United States and Great Britain toward each other over Central America (Clayton-Bulwer Treaty)

36. The continuance of slavery (Emancipation Proclamation)

37. The right of a state to fix maximum rates for the use of grain storage elevators (Munn v. Illinois)

38. Cleveland's popularity with his own party (Gold Standard Act of 1900)

39. The right of Cuba to govern itself (Platt Amendment)

40. The Volstead Act (President Wilson)

41. Segregation in public schools (Plessy v. Ferguson)

42.-53.
The following statements are associated with the period from 1816 to 1824 inclusive. Label each statement C, Ch, CCh, or X.

   C—if it represents the position of Clay
   CH—if it represents the position of Calhoun
   CCH—if it represents the position of both Clay and Calhoun
   X—if it does not fit any of the above classifications

42. The tariff of 1816 is a wise move to protect American infant industry.

43. British ships were off shore at the end of the War of 1812 with cargoes of manufactured goods ready to be dumped on the American market.

44. In this moment of a second victory over England we cease to be Kentuckians, South Carolinians, New Englanders, Southerners, or Westerners; we are all Americans.

45. The South has ample water power and an inexpensive labor force in its slaves. Textile mills will move to where the cotton is grown.

46. Import duties collected under the tariff of 1824 should be used to build roads to connect the West and South with the Northeast.

47. Ships made north-south transportation reasonably adequate, but lack of roads made east-west commerce almost impossible.

48. Roads built at federal expense are paid for by all the people, but benefit only those who live near them.

49. Roads connecting the seaboard with the Mississippi River will strengthen the nation and the benefits of increased commerce will spread throughout the United States.

50. Before the Cumberland Road got to St. Louis, railroads were a more practical connecting link and enthusiasm for turnpikes dwindled.

51. Federal financing of improvements located in states opens the door to federal control of matters properly belonging to the states. This policy could be the beginning of the end of state sovereignty.

52. The Bank of the United States is an important factor in the encouragement and support of a prosperous economy.

53. The banks chartered by the several states are adequate to the business needs of the nation.

54.-55. The historical term, "the sinful ten," has the closest association with which *two* of the following?

(a) The formation of the Confederate States of America in 1860-'61.
(b) The 10 deadly sins
(c) The 10 men (bankers, railroad presidents, industrialists), called by T. Roosevelt the "malefactors of great wealth."
(d) Senator Henry Cabot Lodge and his 9 colleagues who led the fight against President Wilson on the issue of the League of Nations.
(e) Thaddeus Stevens and Charles Sumner
(f) Fourteenth Amendment

56.-62. Each of the following statements fits a tariff bill passed in a year included among the dates listed below. Match the dates with the statements.

1816 1824 1828 1833 1890 1913 1930

56. It marked the culmination of a bitter controversy over tariffs and introduced a temporary, but prolonged, lull in this strife.

57. It was one side of a logrolling deal when several western states had recently entered the Union.

58. It protected scores, perhaps hundreds, of infant manufacturing establishments in the United States.

59. It made no sense in anyone's eyes as an economic measure, but it was loaded with politics.

60. About 1000 economists made a formal protest against this tariff bill, but Congress passed it.

61. This bill clearly illustrated for the first time the sharp sectional cleavage on the tariff issue between the South and the Northeast.

62. It marked a substantial downward revision in rates, but its effects were smothered by developments in Europe.

63.-68.

Match the items in Column II *with those in* Column I.

COLUMN I	COLUMN II
A. Gorgas	**63.** (a) Represented England in a treaty with the U.S. in 1850
	(b) Suppressed malaria and yellow fever in the Canal Zone
B. Bunau-Varilla	
C. Goethals	**64.** (a) Had an alternate route for a canal
	(b) Granted the U.S. the right of free passage across the Isthmus of Panama in 1846
D. DeLesseps	
E. Nicaragua	**65.** (a) Represented England in a treaty with the U.S. in 1901
	(b) Represented the U.S. in a treaty with England in 1850
F. Panama	
G. Colombia	**66.** (a) Engineer in charge of building the Panama Canal for the U.S.
	(b) Engineer in charge of building the Suez Canal
H. New Granada	
I. Hay	**67.** (a) Represented the U.S. in a treaty with England in 1901
	(b) Represented Panama in making the treaty by which the U.S. acquired the Canal Zone
J. Bulwer	
	68. (a) Won a bloodless revolution with an assist by the U.S.
K. Pauncefote	(b) Rejected T. Roosevelt's offer for a renewable 99 year lease of a strip of land across Panama
L. Clayton	

69.-76.

Classify each of the following statements about T.V.A. as S, A, or X.

s—if the statement supports T.V.A.
a—if the statement attacks T.V.A.
x—if the statement does neither

69. Senator George Norris, a "progressive" Republican might well be considered the man who put T.V.A. across.

70. Huge munitions plants were converted into chemical fertilizer factories.

71. Coolidge and Hoover both vetoed T.V.A. because it was a socialistic plan incompatible with our way of life.

72. As a producer of electric power the T.V.A. furnishes a phony yardstick.

73. Though tax free, T.V.A. pays more "in lieu of taxes" than private utilities would pay in taxes.

74. While the controversy over T.V.A. centers around its production of hydroelectric power, T.V.A. is also engaged in large scale irrigation, soil conservation, flood control, manufacture of fertilizers, and improved use of land.

75. Chambers of Commerce, mayors, governors, and newspapers of the seven-state T.V.A. area are enthusiastic in their support of T.V.A.

76. Whatever benefits T.V.A. may have brought to its area have been paid for by the people who, for the most part, live outside the T.V.A. area.

77.-78. One item in each of the two groups below is out of place. It lacks a factor common to all of the other items in its group. Select the odd items.

77. GROUP A	**78.** GROUP B
1. George Westinghouse	1. Thomas Dewey
2. Eli Whitney	2. Frank B. Kellogg
3. Benjamin Franklin	3. Henry Stimson
4. Cyrus McCormick	4. John Hay
5. George Norris	5. Charles E. Hughes
6. Robert Fulton	6. Dean Acheson

79.-81. Which of the following statements about our difficulties with Mexico over oil in 1920-1945 are true?

(a) The United States followed a policy of dollar diplomacy.

(b) As President Wilson had done in opposing Huerta, we continued to exert influence in Mexican politics to assure the election of friendly Mexican presidents.

(c) Eventually the U.S. tolerated the confiscation of American oil properties in Mexico valued at hundreds of millions of dollars.

(d) Ambassador Dwight Morrow established workable relations with Mexico by convincing them that our government would insist on a fair payment for all American oil properties, but would not hinder the transfer of such properties to the Mexican government.

(e) Mexican moves toward confiscation were met by American economic pressure exerted through decreasing our purchases of Mexican silver.

(f) After many years and several incidents foreign oil companies were squeezed out of Mexico, but were paid for their properties.

(1) a, e, f   **(2)** b, c   **(3)** d, f   **(4)** a, b, c,   **(5)** a, c, e **(6)** d, e, f

82.-87.
Arrange in chronological order.

A. Hay-Pauncefote Treaty
B. Hay-Bunavu-Varilla Treaty
C. Kellogg-Briand Treaty
D. Treaty of Ghent
E. Pinckney Treaty
F. Webster-Ashburton Treaty

88.-90. Which of the following statements are true?

(a) The day after his inauguration, President F. Roosevelt declared a bank holiday. Many banks and loan associations had already been closed by order of governors in some states.

(b) The Federal Securities Act of 1933 and the Securities & Exchange Commission were devices to stimulate trading in shares of stock with better prospects of quick profits.

(c) In the early 1930's all gold coin and gold certificates were called in and all debts were made payable in legal tender.

(d) As a result of the financial measures of the New Deal, gold ceased to be an important factor in our currency system.

(e) The New Deal financial legislation separated investment banking from commercial banking.

(f) The C.C.C., the N.Y.A. and the I.L.O. were New Deal organizations established by the federal government in an effort to speed recovery.

(1) b, c, f   **(2)** b, c, d, f   **(3)** c, d, e, f   **(4)** a, d, e **(5)** a, c, e

91.-100.
Put A, B, C, or D after each of the following President's names.

A—if he served less than one full term
B—if he served just one term
C—if he served more than one term but less than two full terms
D—if he served two full terms

91. John Adams
92. John Quincy Adams
93. James Madison
94. James Polk
95. Millard Fillmore
96. Andrew Johnson
97. Grover Cleveland
98. Calvin Coolidge
99. Herbert Hoover
100. Harry Truman

Test VII

1.-3. Which of the following statements about mercantilism are true?

(a) Colbert in France and Adam Smith in England advocated this economic theory.
(b) Colonial trade was to be regulated in a manner which would create a favorable balance of trade for the mother country.
(c) While England was following the mercantile theory of trade she was also treating the American colonies with salutary neglect in regard to the trade and navigation acts.
(d) Laissez faire was a basic concept of mercantilism.
(e) Laws requiring ships engaged in imperial trade be owned by British subjects and have a captain and most of the crew who were British was resented in the seaport towns of New England.
(f) An assumption inherent in mercantilism was that in business deals one party got the better of the other.
(g) Under mercantilism the natural resources of colonial America were seriously depleted in order to supply craftsmen and factories in England.

(1) a, c, e (2) b, d, f, g (3) c, e, f, g (4) a, d, e
(5) b, c, f

4.-13.

Resolved that the fixing of the Proclamation Line of 1763 was justified.
Classify each statement as S, O, or X.

　s—if it supports the resolution
　o—if it opposes the resolution
　x—if it does neither

4. The line followed the Alleghenies.
5. The destruction of several English forts in the Ohio region by Indians under Chief Pontiac could have been only the beginning of a serious military problem.
6. The area east of the Alleghenies to the Atlantic coast left plenty of land for the settlers of the 1700's.
7. Settlers who had already gone west of the mountains could not be expected to give up their land claims and their livelihood.
8. Transportation from west of the Alleghenies to the seaboard was so difficult as to be practically non-existent.
9. Keeping Indians in a designated area by military force was impractical and necessitated an agreement they would willingly accept.

10. Restricting the colonists to land east of the Alleghenies gave them less freedom of movement than they had enjoyed before the French were driven out of America.
11. King George could issue a proclamation setting a boundary, but he had no possible way of enforcing it.
12. The French and Indian War had benefited the American colonies more than any other part of the British Empire and it had been a costly war.
13. Most of the Indians had aided the French during the war.

14.-15. What building in what city housed the Constitutional Convention of 1787?

16.-20. The following questions can be answered by giving the number of years.
16. What is the citizenship qualification for a Representative?
17. What is the citizenship qualification for a Senator?
18. What is the residence qualification for the President?
19. What is the maximum number of years a President may serve?
20. What is the minimum number of years to which a President's term in office may be restricted by Constitutional provision?

21. Which *one* of the following is *not* in the Preamble of the Constitution?

(a) to form a more perfect union
(b) to insure domestic tranquility
(c) to establish justice
(d) to protect life, liberty and property
(e) to promote the general welfare
(f) to secure the blessings of liberty
(g) to provide for the common defense

22.-24. Which of the following is a correct paraphrase of the Implied Powers (or Elastic Clause) of the Constitution?

Congress shall have power to make all laws necessary and proper

(a) to promote the general welfare of the United States.
(b) to provide for the common defense, pay the public debt, and promote the general welfare.
(c) to carry out the provisions of this Constitution.
(d) to carry out the list of powers of which the Implied Powers Clause is the last.

(e) to do whatever a majority of the members of the House of Representatives and the Senate agree to do, subject only to the suspensive veto of the President.

(f) to maintain the union.

25.-29.

The following statements are about the Alien, Sedition, and Naturalization Acts of John Adams' administration. Mark each statement with an F, R, or X.

F—if the statement expresses a Federalist point of view

R—if the statement expresses a Republican point of view

X—if it does neither

25. There is a real danger that the revolutionary spirit of the French Reign of Terror may spread to America.

26. The X.Y.Z. Affair coupled with the undeclared war with France in the Caribbean makes tolerance of false, scandalous, and malicious statements about our government or its officials a threat to national safety.

27. The political strife over these acts illustrates the excesses in party factionalism so strongly deplored by President Washington.

28. The Sedition Act brought forth the Kentucky and Virginia Resolutions.

29. Newspaper editors, not Jacobins or aliens, were the intended victims of the Sedition Act.

30.-39.

The words or phrases in parentheses with each of the following items have a relationship with the item as indicated by A, B, or C. Designate which letter best applies in each case.

A—to bring into effect, to support, or to make more effective

B—to bring to an end, to oppose, or to make less effective

C—neither A nor B apply

30. The Embargo Act (The *Chesapeake* incident)

31. The Spanish Step Line (Treaty of 1819)

32. Organized Labor (Panic of 1837)

33. Westward movement of settlers (Kansas-Nebraska Bill)

34. Impeachment of President Johnson (Electoral Commission)

35. The effectiveness of the Granger Laws. (Wabash v. Illinois)

36. The Pullman strike ("Molly Maguires")

37. Theodore Roosevelt's becoming president (Leon Czolgosz)

38. The 18th Amendment (Volstead Act)

39. Republican strength in the 1890 election (Klondike Gold Rush)

40.-49. *Match the items in* Column II *with those in* Column I.

COLUMN I	COLUMN II
A. William J. Bryan	40. First governor general of the Philippines
B. Grover Cleveland	41. "Tippecanoe & Tyler too"
C. Calvin Coolidge	42. He would use every dollar in the treasury and every soldier in the army if necessary to send one postcard to Chicago.
D. Thomas Edison	
E. Albert Einstein	
F. Henry Ford	
G. Warren G. Harding	43. One World
H. Wm. H. Harrison	44. The Great Commoner
I. Richard Nixon	45. T.V.A.
J. George Norris	46. "I do not choose to run."
K. Wm. H. Taft	47. ". . . uranium may be turned into a new . . . source of energy. . . ."
L. Wendell Willkie	48. *Oscar II,* the "Peace Ship"
	49. Return to normalcy

50.-52. Pick out the *two* statements which make the most sense.

A. The Specie Circular caused the Panic of 1837.

B. The Specie Circular precipitated the Panic of 1837.

C. The Panic of 1837 was merely the low spot of an economic cycle which regularly recurs according to natural economic law.

D. Overspeculation in land, unsound financial policies of many wild-cat banks, irresponsible financing of state governments, and other discernible factors combined to cause the Panic in 1837.

E. Jackson's defiance of the federal courts, his illegal refusal to deposit government funds in the Second Bank of the United States, his open dislike of the wealthy and aristocratic frightened the business community into inactivity and hence depression.

53.-54. Name the slave states that did not join the Confederate States of America.

55. Name the president whose election depended upon the decision of the Electoral Commission.

56.-65.
Match the items in Column II *with those in* Column

I. *All items are associated with the Spanish-American War.*

COLUMN II

COLUMN I

A. Asst. Sec. of the Navy
B. Aguinaldo
C. $20,000,000
D. San Juan Hill
E. Admiral Dewey
F. New York Journal
G. General Weyler
H. Enrique Depuy De Lôme
I. The *Oregon*
J. The *Maine*
K. Teller Resolution
L. Platt Amendment
M. Admiral Chichester
N. Admiral Von Diedrichs
O. Admiral Cervera
P. Admiral Sampson
Q. Finley P. Dunne
R. William H. Taft
S. Foraker Act
T. Hawaiian Islands
U. Puerto Rico & Guam
V. Japan
W. Col. Leonard Wood

56. (a) jingoism
    (b) Mr. Dooley
57. (a) Became T. Roosevelt's Secretary of War
    (b) T. Roosevelt
58. (a) Concentration camps
    (b) U.S. promise not to annex Cuba
59. (a) Philippines
    (b) Puerto Rico
60. (a) Ceded in Treaty of Paris 1898
    (b) Took Manila
61. (a) "Rough Riders"
    (b) Havana harbor
62. (a) Demonstrated need for interoceanic canal
    (b) Sought to share in the spoils of war
63. (a) Blockaded Spanish ships in Santiago harbor
    (b) A diplomat who wrote an undiplomatic letter
64. (a) Cost the U.S. more casualties than the Spanish-American War
    (b) Secured a naval base for U.S. on Cuba
65. (a) Lost the naval battle along Cuba's southeastern coast
    (b) Cooperated with Admiral Dewey in repulsing foreign interference

66.-69.
Column I *is a list of Supreme Court cases.* Column

II *is a list of statements about these cases. Match each statement with the proper case.*

COLUMN I

A. Dred Scott Case
B. Ex Parte Milligan
C. Plessey v. Ferguson
D. Adkins v. Children's Hospital

COLUMN II

66. This case involved civil versus military jurisdiction.
67. This case involved minimum wage laws.
68. This case nullified a law that had stood for 37 years.
69. This case upheld segregation in public transportation.

70.-84.
Classify each of the following statements about automation as belonging in category A, B, C, *or* D.

   A—A sound opinion, almost certainly true
   B—An opinion on which well informed people will differ
   C—An opinion which will be generally rejected by well informed people, but accepted by a minority of them.
   D—A rather ridiculous opinion held almost exclusively by the ill-informed.

70. It is difficult to determine just how much unemployment is due to automation, particularly when considering those entering the labor market for the first time.

71. Concern over automation is unjustified. We did all right changing from livery stables to garages. Let economic forces adjust themselves.

72. With unskilled and semi-skilled jobs decreasing in proportion to those demanding above average abilities, automation is building an employment situation where eventually over half the adult population will be incapable of gainful employment.

73. Whatever problems automation presents, the answers lie in going ahead with automation while doing our best to handle the problems it creates.

74. An employer who cuts his labor force by automation should be required to retrain the displaced workers and pay them their accustomed wages.

75. The transitions required by automation create the economic hardship, just as did the transition into the industrial revolution; but its long-run effects will be highly beneficial as were those of the industrial revolution.

76. Collective bargaining unhindered by any new legislation can be depended upon to carry the economy through the growing pains of automation.

77. Automation should be delayed, perhaps completely held back, so long as unemployment remains a problem.

78. Considerable "featherbedding" is justifiable while going through adjustments caused by automation.

79. For those who know they can't go to college it is better to get into the labor market as soon as possible.

80. Profits derived from automation should be heavily taxed and the money used to alleviate economic distress caused thereby.

81. Unemployed workers do not purchase much. Automation can kill the market for its own products. As Walter Reuther said on looking at an automated automobile plant where one man could do the work of fifty men, "Are those machines going to buy cars?"

82. Automation creates highly skilled jobs for which there are too few capable workers.

83. Retraining programs are expensive and promise only moderate success. Too few workers can be retrained and many who do complete the training will find no market for their new skills.

84. Retraining programs, both by industry and government, constitute one constructive measure dealing with unemployment caused by automation.

85.-86. One item in each group is out of place. It lacks a factor common to all of the other items in its group. Select the odd items.

85. GROUP A	**86.** GROUP B
1. Zachary Taylor	1. Teapot Dome
2. John Tyler	2. Carpetbaggers
3. John C. Calhoun	3. Tweed Ring
4. Millard Fillmore	4. Whisky Ring
5. Franklin Pierce	5. Credit Moblier
6. William Harrison	6. Mugwumps

87.-91.
Arrange in chronological order. All items are associated with World War I.

A. Wilson re-elected
B. Bolshevik Revolution
C. England declared war on Germany
D. Germany declared war on France
E. United States entered the war

92. The wording of the Agricultural Adjustment Act (A.A.A.) made it clear that Congress depended upon which of the following Constitutional powers as a support of its right to pass such a law.

(a) The General Welfare Clause in the preamble
(b) The General Welfare Clause in the taxing power
(c) The Elastic Clause (Implied Powers Clause)
(d) The Supreme Law of the Land Clause
(e) The Interstate Commerce Clause

93.-98.
Arrange in chronological order of their being written.

A. Uncle Tom's Cabin
B. Common Sense
C. The Star-Spangled Banner
D. Grapes of Wrath
E. The Liberator
F. The Jungle

99. Which one of the following statements best expresses Theodore Roosevelt's views on presidential powers?

(a) The president may do whatever he thinks is right and for the national welfare so long as there is no prohibition in the Constitution or laws to prevent such action.
(b) The president must restrict his official actions to carrying out powers specifically granted to him in the Constitution.
(c) The president may do anything the Constitution specifically permits or anything else reasonably implied by Constitutional provisions.
(d) In time of war or other national emergency the president may do as he thinks best, without regard to the Constitution.
(e) Whenever a President is in doubt about the extent of his legal powers he may confer with the Supreme Court for authoritative advice.

100. Name the political party famous for its 1892 Omaha Platform.

Test VIII

1.-3. Which of the following statements about the trade and navigation acts of the colonial period are true?

(a) The rival colonial powers had similar trade and navigation laws to control the trade of their respective colonies.

(b) Because England was more energetic and thorough in the enforcement of her trade and navigation laws she gained a solid advantage over France and Spain in the struggle for empire.

(c) Had the sugar and molasses acts passed by the British Parliament been enforced they would have had a substantial adverse effect on the New England rum trade.

(d) The triangular trade routes established by American colonials were in defiance of the trade and navigation acts.

(e) The regulations governing the tobacco trade practically assured the British Isles as a market for Virginia and Maryland tobacco.

(f) The beaver trade centered in the Hudson valley resulted in scores of small establishments in Connecticut and New York coastal towns which were well known for the manufacture of fine beaver hats and cloaks.

(g) No real trouble between England and the American colonies developed over trade and navigation acts until after the French and Indian War.

(1) b, c, d   **(2)** c, d, e, f   **(3)** a, c, e, g   **(4)** a, b, f, g
(5) a, b, d

4.-11.

Match the items in Column II *with those in* Column I. *Most of the items are closely associated with the French and Indian War.*

COLUMN I

A. Iroquois
B. Albany Plan of Union
C. Plains of Abraham
D. Pitt the Younger
E. Treaty of Utrecht 1713
F. England got Newfoundland and Nova Scotia from France
G. Dinwiddie
H. General Braddock
I. General Wolfe
J. Treaty of San Ildefonso 1762
K. Marked the end of the American colonies' need for England's protection
L. Ft. Necessity
M. Ft. William Henry
N. General Amherst
O. Treaty of Ghent
P. Great Meadows
Q. Treaty of Paris 1763
R. Pitt the Elder
S. Ft. Duquesne

COLUMN II

4. (a) Treaty of Paris 1763
(b) Prime Minister who directed England to victory in the 7 Years War

5. (a) British garrison wiped out by French and Indians under General Montcalm
(b) Captured Quebec

6. (a) French victory over George Washington
(b) Treaty by which France ceded lands in America to Spain

7. (a) Enemies of the French
(b) Governor of Virginia in the middle 1750's

8. (a) Benjamin Franklin
(b) France gave up all lands she had on the continent of North America

9. (a) Spain ceded Gibraltar to England
(b) Captured Montreal

10. (a) Fort built by George Washington
(b) Defeated by French near Ft. Duquesne

11. (a) Name changed to Fort Pitt
(b) Battle of Quebec

12.-18. *The "three great compromises" written into the Constitution contained the provisions stated in the following statements. Classify each statement as A, B, or C.*

A—If it is part of the compromise between states with large and those with small populations.

B—If it is part of the compromise between states where commercial interests prevailed and those where agricultural interests prevailed.

c—If it is part of the compromise arising from the fact that some states had slavery and others did not.

12. The migration or importation of such persons as any state shall think proper to admit, shall not be prohibited by Congress before 1808.

13. No export taxes can be levied.

14. Representation in the House will be based on total population in each state counting all free persons, exclusive of Indians not taxed, and three-fifths of such other persons as may reside in a state.

15. Each state shall have the same number of Senators and this provision can't be altered without the consent of every state.

16. Tariff bills may pass Congress, as do other bills, by a simple majority vote in each house.

17. Direct taxation by the federal government must be apportioned among the several states according to the population of each state counting all free persons, excluding Indians not taxed, and three-fifths of such other persons as may reside in a state.

18. Representation in the House of Representatives will be in accordance with the population of each state.

19. How are the *number* of judges on the Supreme Court determined?

(a) by Congress   (b) by the Senate   (c) by the Constitution   (d) by a convention which at least ¾ of the states must attend   (e) by a convention which at least ⅔ of the states must attend

20. How is a new state admitted into the Union?

(a) by Congress   (b) by the President   (c) by the Senate   (d) by the Supreme Court if it approves of its constitution   (e) by the Congress with the approval of the Supreme Court

21. The Constitution provides that each state must have what form of government?

22. The Constitution forbids what type of test as a qualification for holding a federal office?

23.-32.
The words or phrases in parentheses with each of the following items have a relationship with the item as indicated by A, B, or C. Designate which letter best applies in each case.

A—to bring into effect, to support, or to make more effective

B—to bring to an end, to oppose, or to make less effective

C—neither A nor B apply

23. The Embargo Act (Smuggling)

24. United States' claim to Texas (Monroe Doctrine)

25. The spoils system (Andrew Jackson)

26. Realignment of the major political parties away from nationwide membership toward purely sectional membership (Kansas-Nebraska Bill)

27. Orderly control of the freedmen (Underground Railway)

28. Interstate Commerce Act (Wabash v. Illinois)

29. The rise of McKinley to the presidency (Marcus Hanna)

30. Pure Food & Drug Act and Meat Inspection Act (Muckrakers)

31. Sherman Anti-trust Act (Clayton Anti-trust Act)

32. Reciprocity (Pan-Americanism)

33.-42.
Match the items in Column II *with those in Column I.*

COLUMN I	COLUMN II
A. Shiloh	33. Manassas
B. Wilderness Campaign	34. Seven Days' Battles
C. 1st Bull Run	35. General Pope
D. Antietam	36. General Pemberton
E. Chickamauga	37. Pittsburg Landing
F. Cemetery Ridge	38. General Meade
G. Peninsular Campaign	39. Sharpsburg
H. From Atlanta to the sea	40. General Pickett
I. Defeated at 2nd Bull Run	41. General Sherman
J. Surrendered Vicksburg	42. Cold Harbor
K. Defeated Lee at Gettysburg	
L. Fredericksburg	

43.-52.
A surplus in the treasury during Cleveland's first term and continuing into B. Harrison's administration became a political controversy between the two major parties. Classify each of the following statements as R, D, RD, or X.

R—if the statement expresses a Republican viewpoint

D—if the statement expresses a Democratic viewpoint

RD—if the statement expresses a view held by a majority of the members of both parties x—if the statement does not fit any of the above categories

43. A surplus in the treasury means that the people have been overtaxed.

44. Almost any method of adjusting the tax income would be acceptable, except tampering with the tariff.

45. It would be unwise to use the surplus to pay the public debt.

46. Public funds should be generously spent for Civil War veterans who suffer disabilities connected with their war service, but care should be taken to avoid legislation granting aid to veterans without such disabilities.

47. The claims of old soldiers of the G.A.R. should not be weighed with apothecaries' scales.

48. Putting necessities of life on the free list will raise our standard of living by lowering prices where it will help the poor people most. At the same time it will melt away the surplus.

49. A surplus in the treasury invites extravagance on the part of the government.

50. We are a billion dollar country and the Congress proudly recognizes our wealth by appropriating a billion dollars to make our nation strong with a great fleet, better harbors, and generous treatment of those who offered their lives in the service of their country.

51. The Monitor v. the Merrimac off Hampton Roads in 1862 had clearly announced the end of wooden navies. Nevertheless, the United States had been very slow to rebuild its naval strength.

52. Whether or not the tariff should be used as a method of reducing the surplus was an issue on which both parties were split. A minority faction of Republicans agreed with the stand taken by the Democratic Party and a minority of the Democrats agreed with the position of the Republican Party.

53.-55. Which is the source of the following quotation?

"Corruption dominates the ballot box, the Legislatures, the Congress, and touches even the ermine of the bench. . . . Newspapers are largely subsidized or muzzled, public opinion silenced, business prostrated, homes covered with mortgages, labor impoverished, and the land concentrating in the hands of capitalists. . . . We have witnessed for more than a quarter century the struggles of the two great political parties for power and plunder, while grievous wrongs have been inflicted upon the suffering people."

(a) Communist Party Platform (Earl Browder 1936)
(b) Progressive Party Platform (Henry Wallace 1948)
(c) Progressive Party Platform (T. Roosevelt 1912)
(d) Socialist Party Platform (Eugene Debs 1920)
(e) Populist Party Platform (James Weaver 1892)

(f) Liberal Republican & Democratic Platform (Horace Greeley 1872)
(g) Whig Party Platform (Wm. Harrison 1840)

56.-58. Which of the following statements concerning the situation involving the Hawaiian Islands in the early 1890's are true?

(a) The 2¢ per pound bounty on American sugar had a severely adverse effect upon the Hawaiian economy.
(b) The American minister at Honolulu favored, and U.S. marines aided, the rebellious Hawaiians to overthrow Queen Liliuokalini.
(c) President Harrison refused to use his influence to achieve the annexation of Hawaii by the U.S.
(d) After investigation, President Cleveland approved the annexation of the Hawaiian Islands.
(e) The Hawaiian Islands were eventually annexed by the U.S. as part of the Treaty of Paris of 1898.
(f) The Hawaiian Islands were annexed by the U.S., not by treaty, but by a joint resolution of Congress.

(1) a, b, f   (2) c, d, e   (3) c, d, f   (4) b, d, e   (5) a, c, e

59. "Manifest Destiny" would apply to which one of the following?

(a) Joining in World War I against Germany
(b) Entering upon a program to beat the U.S.S.R. in the race to the moon
(c) Becoming the leading republic of modern times
(d) Expanding westward from the Mississippi River to the Pacific Ocean
(e) Assuming the burden of aiding backward nations

60. The "Open Door" policy refers to which of the following?

(a) A very liberal immigration policy
(b) Reciprocal trade agreements with the European Common Market
(c) Admission of political refugees from any other nation
(d) Equal trade opportunities with other nations in China
(e) Prison reform advocating an expanded parole system

61. "Logrolling" means which of the following?

(a) An agreement by one group of legislators to support or oppose a particular bill in return for support or opposition for another bill.
(b) Arranging to break up a jam of legislation and get action on the more important bills.
(c) Congressmen voting themselves a pay raise.
(d) A president bringing strong political pressure on Congressional leaders in his party to press for the laws he wants.

(e) Giving "spoils" jobs to persons unfit for their duties.

62. "Waving the bloody shirt" means which of the following?

(a) Yellow journalism tending to provoke war
(b) Activities of Congressmen known as "War Hawks" in 1811-'12
(c) Campaign oratory of Radical Republicans in the 1860's and 1870's
(d) Upton Sinclair's lurid, and largely accurate, account of the slaughter houses of the Chicago stock yards
(e) Opposing war on the moral basis that all intentional killing of people by people is murder

63. "Gerrymandering" means which of the following?

(a) Straightening the useless and dangerous curves in major highways
(b) Avoiding some of the meanderings of nagivable rivers by deepening and straightening the channels
(c) Appropriating public funds for unnecessary prospects as a means of winning votes in the area where the money is spent
(d) Attempts of political machines in urban areas to increase their votes by illegal procedures at polling booths
(e) Redistricting of a state unfairly to the advantage of the party in power

64. President Taft had been referred to as a *crown prince* in American politics. Which of the following explains this "title"?

(a) He was a quiet, dignified, deliberate person.
(b) When nominated in 1908 he had the full support of both progressive and conservative factions in the party.
(c) He had filled the post of Secretary of War with competence.
(d) The outgoing president, T. Roosevelt, had recommended Taft as his successor.
(e) Taft soon displayed a forcefulness in leadership that was somewhat of a surprise in a man of quiet manner and judicial mind.

65.-72.
The treaty banning nuclear test explosions anywhere other than underground went into effect October 10th 1963. Classify each of the following statements as O, S, or X.

o—if the statement is opposed to the treaty
s—if the statement supports the treaty
x—if it does neither

65. The treaty, having already been signed by East Germany, tricks the U.S. into an action that may be considered formal recognition by the U.S. of East Germany.

66. The U.S. proposed the same idea to the U.S.S.R. many months ago and no action was taken.
67. It could mark the beginning of the end of the cold war.
68. The U.S.S.R. proposed this treaty now because she has made gains in scientific knowledge by her recent nuclear test blasts in the atmosphere.
69. Both the U.S. and the U.S.S.R. are concerned over the tremendous cost of the race to the moon.
70. The U.S. is able to detect any violation of this treaty and thus does not have to rely upon the integrity of the U.S.S.R.
71. Such a treaty requires the approval of the Senate.
72. There can be no victor in a nuclear war.

73.-82.
Classify each of the following presidents as belonging to type A or type B.

A. Some presidents have had programs which they drove, or tried to, through Congress. They looked upon themselves as representing the people. They interpreted their election to be an order by the people to carry out the program they had favored in their campaign for office. They expected to rule as well as reign.

B. Other presidents saw themselves as the leader of their party. They saw their job to be that of a chief executive to carry out the laws of the land. It was Congress who made policy by passing laws. They willingly kept in the background.

73. Cleveland	**78.** McKinley
74. Coolidge	**79.** F. D. Roosevelt
75. Grant	**80.** T. Roosevelt
76. Hoover	**81.** Truman
77. Jackson	**82.** Van Buren

83.-84.
One item in each group is out of place. It lacks a factor common to all the other items in its group. Select the odd item.

GROUP A	GROUP B
1. A.A.A.	1. 19th Amendment
2. Free Soilers	2. W.C.T.U.
3. Parity	3. Initiative
4. Okies	4. Referendum
5. Soil Bank	5. 17th Amendment
6. Wheat surplus	6. Australian ballot

85.-100. There are sharp differences of opinion over the Korean conflict. Some support President Truman and others General MacArthur. A few basic facts are in the next paragraph.

On January 25, 1950 North Korean armed forces invaded South Korea by crossing the 38th parallel. The U.N. Security Council passed a resolution calling upon the North Korean forces to withdraw to the 38th parallel. The Security Council asked U.N. members to give every assistance in driving the aggressors back to the 38th parallel. The United States and other U.N. members sent forces and supplies for this purpose. The U.N. asked the United States to appoint a commander for all the U.N. forces in Korea. President Truman appointed General MacArthur as chief United Nations commander.

Classify each of the following statements T, M, *or* X.

> T—if the statement supports Truman
> M—if the statement supports MacArthur
> x—if the statement does neither

Be guided by the above paragraph and by your knowledge of the Korean situation.

85. Although the Korean action was large scale and exceedingly hard fighting there was no declaration of war by Congress.

86. Technically the forces opposing North Koreans were U.N. forces, but without the United States no effective U.N. action could have been taken.

87. General MacArthur drove the North Koreans north of the 38th parallel into their own area and then advised President Truman that occupation of North Korea to its northern border, the Yalu River, was the best procedure for settling the Korean problem.

88. A few days before MacArthur gave the President this advice, Mao Tse-tung had stated that his government could not stand idly by while U.N. forces invaded North Korea.

89. MacArthur captured the North Korean capital, Pyongyang, and advanced to within a few miles of the Yalu River.

90. Red Chinese troops in hordes swept across the Yalu and drove the U.N. forces back across the 38th parallel and almost into the sea at the southern tip of the Korean peninsula.

91. With the entrance of massive Red Chinese forces the United States' naval and air units should have carried the fighting to Chinese ports and mainland.

92. The forces under Chiang Kai-shek in Taiwan should have been used as an invading army attacking China and encouraging a revolt of the Chinese people against their communist government.

93. President Truman considered this policy (91 & 92) and completely rejected it.

94. General MacArthur, in writing a letter to Republican minority leader, Congressman Joseph Martin, urging his campaign policies, opposing the President's policies, and containing the phrase, "there is no substitute for victory," was guilty of gross indiscretion and probably insubordination.

95. General Bradley, Chief of Staff, said of the MacArthur policies that they would lead the U.S. into "the wrong war, at the wrong time, in the wrong place, with the wrong enemy."

96. This flare-up between an able and popular general and a president calls to mind the trouble between General McClellan and President Lincoln.

97. Our allies in NATO overwhelmingly approved of limiting the armed conflict to Korea.

98. As soon as the commander of the U.N. forces appointed by him was unwilling to carry out the presidential objectives and policies, there was little President Truman could do other than dismiss MacArthur from his command.

99. The decision to limit the fighting to Korea when the U.S. had atomic bombs and great superiority on the sea and in the air made acceptance of a stalemate without victory a needless humiliation.

100. Driving the combined Chinese and North Korean forces back to the 38th parallel, as was finally done, and making them stay there was not a stalemate; it was a complete victory carrying out precisely the stated objectives of the United Nations.

Test IX

1. Which one of the following statements about the French and Indian War contains the most significance for a history student?

(a) The British navy proved that England was mistress of the seas.
(b) Pitt was one of England's war ministers.
(c) The expulsion of the French from America set the stage for the American Revolution.
(d) Tactics suitable for the wars in Europe were often unsuitable for battles in the American colonies.
(e) As the British demonstrated at Quebec, trying the impossible is sometimes the road to fame.

2.-3. Which *two* of the following statements best explain the reaction of the American colonies to the tax on tea that led to the Boston Tea Party?

(a) Basically the colonials objected to paying taxes levied by Parliament.
(b) Selling British tea only through agents of the East India Tea Company deprived local colonial merchants of business and led them to join the Sons of Liberty in angry protest against the tax.
(c) Since the Boston Massacre a continuous chain of violent outbreaks made the Tea Party an almost predictable occurrence.
(d) England prevented foreign tea from getting into the colonies and the tax made the British tea very costly.
(e) Parliament was trying to rescue the East India Tea Company from bankruptcy at the expense of the colonial housewife.

4.-5. All of the following factors were points of strength for the Americans in the Revolutionary War. Which *two* were more significant than the others?

(a) The leadership of Washington
(b) Better rifles and better riflemen than the British
(c) Valuable fighting experience in the French and Indian War
(d) Defensive fighting allowed us to pick the time and place of many battles
(e) Avoidance of capture and maintenance of the will to resist would bring victory

6.-7.
6. Which of the following battles was won by the British?

7. Which of the following battles is considered the turning point of the war?

(a) Bennington (b) Germantown (c) Princeton
(d) Saratoga (e) Trenton (f) Yorktown

8. Which statement among the following is the most significant? They all are about the Articles of Confederation.

(a) There was neither an effective executive department nor a satisfactory judicial department.
(b) The government told each state how much it should contribute in support of the central government, but had no power to actually collect the amount due.
(c) The Congress had so little power that members of state legislatures enjoyed greater prestige than did members of Congress.
(d) Conditions of interstate and foreign commerce were chaotic because the central government had no power to enforce uniformity.
(e) The many weaknesses written into the Articles of Confederation were not mistakes in the usual sense; they were necessary concessions to state sovereignty in order to have any central government at all. Only through the experience of the Articles of Confederation could the states move into the Constitution of the United States.

9. The qualification a person must meet in order to vote for a United States Senator are determined by which of the following?

(a) The United States Constitution
(b) The federal Congress
(c) The state in which the person lives
(d) The county in which the person lives
(e) The voting district in which the person lives
(f) None of these

10.-12. Which statements are true about the electoral and popular vote for president?

(a) The percentage of the popular vote and the percentage of the electoral vote received by a presidential candidate are about the same.
(b) The difference between the percentage of popular and electoral vote received by a presidential candidate is too great to be considered about the same, but not great enough to be markedly different.
(c) The difference between the percentage of popu-

lar and electoral vote received by a presidential candidate is usually substantial.

(d) With the possible exception of President Washington's elections, the electoral college has never functioned as intended by those who wrote the Constitution.

(e) The Constitution provides for the "unit rule" which gives all of the electoral votes of any state to whichever candidate gets the most popular votes in that state.

(f) While it is theoretically possible for a presidential candidate to get a larger popular vote than his victorious opponent, it has never happened.

(g) The electoral college system of electing a president gives an advantage to the least populous states.

(1) c, d, g   (2) a, d, e   (3) b, d, f, g   (4) a, e, f, g
(5) b, d, e, f, g   (6) b, f, g

13. Every amendment to the Constitution has been *proposed* by which Constitutional procedure?

14. Every amendment to the Constitution but one has been *ratified* by which Constitutional procedure?

15. Only one amendment has been *ratified* by which Constitutional procedure?

16. Quote or paraphrase the 10th Amendment of the Constitution.

17. Give the month and the date for the convening of the new Congress.

18.-27.
The words or phrases in parentheses with each of the following items have a relationship with the item as indicated by A, B, or C. Designate which letter best applies in each case.

> A—to bring into effect, to support, or to make more effective
> B—to bring to an end, to oppose, or to make less effective
> C—neither A nor B apply

18. An unwritten law founded in tradition (Washington and Jefferson refused to run for a third term)
19. The new republics in Latin America (Monroe Doctrine)
20. The McCulloch v. Maryland decision (Civil War in Kansas)
21. Missouri Compromise (Dred Scott Decision)
22. The "Crime of Reconstruction" (Tweed Ring)
23. Cut-throat rate wars (Pooling)
24. Cleveland's support of his party in 1896 (Free Silver at 16 to 1)
25. Clayton-Bulwer Treaty (Hay-Pauncefote Treaty)

26. Investment by American corporations in Latin America (Dollar Diplomacy)
27. Election of President Hayes (Electoral Commission)

28.-37.
Place the following in chronological order.

A. Hawaiian Islands annexed
B. Texas became a state
C. Mexican Cession
D. Virgin Islands purchased
E. Florida purchased
F. Louisana Territory purchased
G. Gadsden Purchase
H. Webster-Ashburton Treaty
I. Oregon boundary dispute settled
J. Alaska purchased

38.-40. In the Dartmouth College Case, the McCulloch v. Maryland Case, and Gibbons v. Ogden Case the Supreme Court declared action by the states involved to be unconstitutional. In each case the decision rested on one of the six situations listed below. Which one for each case?

1. A state law in conflict with a clause of the Constitution
2. A state law in conflict with a treaty
3. A state law in conflict with a federal law
4. A state constitution in conflict with the federal Constitution
5. A state constitution in conflict with a treaty
6. A state constitution in conflict with a federal law

38. Dartmouth College Case
39. McCulloch v. Md.
40. Gibbons v. Ogden

41.-43. Which of the following statements about the Monroe Doctrine are true?

(a) The idea of the doctrine was suggested by George Canning, British foreign secretary.
(b) It was an early indication that the U.S. was abandoning her traditional policy of isolation.
(c) Monroe approved of Canning's suggestion and he also received approval of the idea from the elder statesmen and ex-presidents, John Adams and Thomas Jefferson.
(d) It was Secretary of State John Q. Adams who persuaded Monroe to make the doctrine an exclusively American policy instead of a joint Anglo-American one.
(e) If the Holy Alliance attempted to violate the doctrine, Monroe was sure that the British fleet would oppose such an act.
(f) England was not interested at the time in extending her colonial empire in Latin America.
(g) For more than 35 years the Monroe Doctrine went without significant challenge.

(1) All of them   (2) All but b   (3) All but a & c
(4) All but g   (5) b, d, e, f   (6) a, c, d, e

44. Calhoun, the leading spokesman for the South in its fight against the protective tariffs of 1824, 1828, and 1832 argued that a protective tariff was an unconstitutional tax because it could not, by its very nature, be a tax for any one of the three constitutional purposes listed in Article I, Section 8 of the Constitution. There was room for argument with Calhoun on only one of these three purposes. Which one?

45.-49. *Five* of the following were not in the Jacksonian Era and hence did not play a part in the reforms and advances sometimes included in the term "Jacksonian Democracy." Indicate each of these *five* by letter.

A. King Caucus replaced by nominating conventions
B. Property qualification for voting decreased
C. A. F. of L. organized by Samuel Gompers
D. Spoils System defended as rotation in office
E. Emma Willard founded the first women's college
F. Oberlin was founded as the first co-educational college
G. Debs founded the American Railway Union
H. Mary Lyon founded the college now known as Mt. Holyoke
I. The Grimke sisters preached abolition
J. Frances Wright lectured on women's rights
K. Clara Barton founded the American Red Cross
L. The Mayo brothers advanced the techniques of surgery
M. Lucretia Mott worked for women's rights
N. Garrison founded the *Liberator*
O. Horace Mann organized a school system for Massachusetts
P. Walter Reed controlled Yellow Fever
Q. William Ladd organized an international peace society

50. Name the political party which first stated that it would tolerate slavery in the then slave states, but would oppose its spread into any new areas.

51. Name the Republican candidate for the presidency in 1856.

52.-55. Which *four* of the following have no association with government land policy?

A. Theodore Roosevelt's conference with several governors
B. Compromise of 1850
C. Granger Laws
D. Esch-Cummins Act
E. Northwest Ordinance of 1787
F. Controversy between Pinchot and Ballinger
G. Wagner-Connery Act
H. Building of the Central Pacific and the Union Pacific railroads

I. Controversy between President Cleveland and Governor Altgeld
J. Morrill Act of 1862
K. Newlands Act of 1902
L. Maryland delaying her ratification of the Articles of Confederation
M. Supreme Court Case of U. S. v. La., Texas, Miss., Ala., and Fla.

56.-58. Actual assassination or attempts to assassinate were carried out against all but which *three* of the following presidents?

A. William Harrison
B. Zachary Taylor
C. Abraham Lincoln
D. James Garfield
E. William McKinley
F. Theodore Roosevelt
G. Warren Harding
H. Franklin Roosevelt
I. Harry Truman
J. John Kennedy

59. In which one of the following periods were the Black Codes effective?

A. From the Dred Scott Case to the firing on Ft. Sumter
B. From the Plessy v. Ferguson Case to the Brown v. Topeka Board of Education
C. From the Reconstruction Acts of 1867-'68 to the Hayes-Tilden election
D. From the Kansas-Nebraska Bill to the Dred Scott Case
E. From Appomattox to the Reconstruction Acts of 1867-'68
F. From the first issue of Garrison's Liberator to John Brown at Harper's Ferry

60. Name the cartoonist who created the political zoo; the Tammany tiger, the Democratic donkey, and the Republican elephant.

61.-63. One name in each group is out of place. It lacks a factor common to all the other names in its group. Select the odd name.

GROUP A	GROUP B	GROUP C
1. Charles Guiteau	1. Frances Wright	1. Wm. L. Garrison
2. John Booth	2. William Ladd	2. Harriet B. Stowe
3. Carl Schurz	3. Horace Greeley	3. Wm. H. Seward
4. Leon Czolgosz	4. Samuel Morse	4. James G. Blaine
5. Lee Oswald	5. Henry George	5. John Brown
	6. Jane Addams	6. Henry Clay

64. What event stimulated President Arthur and the Congress to pass the Pendleton Act?

65.-67. Which of the following statements about the Knights of Labor are true?

(a) The membership of the Knights of Labor was an exceedingly heterogeneous group.

(b) It grew very rapidly and faded out of the labor picture almost as quickly as it had developed.

(c) Its program was limited to very practical economic ends such as more pay, shorter hours, and better working conditions.

(d) Samuel Gompers was one of its early leaders.

(e) While its membership included people of many occupations, it was largely restricted to those with highly developed skills and much better pay than the general run of workers.

(f) The Knights of Labor played a prominent part in the Haymarket Riot in Chicago, the planning of a general strike, and the dynamite bombing that killed seven policemen.

(1) a, b   **(2)** a, f   **(3)** All except d   **(4)** All except f
(5) d, e

68. The term, patronage refund, was used in what form of business enterprise?

69. Which of the following statements is the most substantial explanation of the ineffectiveness of the Interstate Commerce Commission during its first two decades?

(a) The commissioners' salaries were too low to attract really competent men.

(b) The provisions of the Interstate Commerce Act were too vaguely worded to permit effective enforcement.

(c) The railroads could challenge in the courts the orders of the Commission before obeying them.

(d) Public opinion did not support the Interstate Commerce Commission.

(e) The Congress refused to appropriate sufficient funds for the Interstate Commerce Commission.

70.-86.
Match the items in Column II *with those of* Column I.

COLUMN I

A. Establishment of the First Bank of the United States
B. Specie Circular
C. Gold Standard Act
D. Whisky Ring
E. Problem of the Surplus
F. Gold content of the dollar cut about 40%
G. Demonetization of Silver
H. Sub-treasury or Independent Treasury System
I. Stay & Tender Laws
J. Bland-Allison Act
K. Wilson-Gorman Tariff
L. Raised Revenue during the Civil War
M. Nicholas Biddle
N. Salmon P. Chase
O. Credit Moblier
P. James Fiske
Q. Woodrow Wilson
R. Reciprocal Tariffs
S. President Harding

COLUMN II

70. "Black Friday"
71. 1863 National Banking Act
72. Mills Bill
73. Van Buren
74. Jackson
75. "Crime of '73"
76. Union & Pacific Railway
77. Federal Reserve System
78. Klondike Gold Rush
79. 2nd Bank of United States
80. "Silver Dick"
81. President Grant
82. F. D. Roosevelt
83. Captain Daniel Shays
84. Led to the 16th Amendment
85. Income Tax
86. Hamilton

87.-90.
Column I *is a list of Supreme Court cases.* Column II *is a list of statements about those cases. Match the statements with the proper case.*

COLUMN I

A. Chisholm v. Georgia
B. Wabash v. Illinois
C. Insular Cases
D. U.S. v. La., Texas, Miss., Ala., & Fla.

COLUMN II

87. A set back for the Grangers
88. Involved the tariff issue
89. Resulted in the 11th Amendment
90. Involved oil

91. *"I preach to you, my countrymen, that our country calls not for a life of ease but for the life of strenuous endeavor. Nothing in this world is worth doing unless it means effort, pain, difficulty. . . . Let us therefore boldly face the life of strife."*

Which of the following presidents is quoted above?

(**A**) Jefferson (**B**) Grant (**C**) McKinley (**D**) Theodore Roosevelt (**E**) Coolidge (**F**) Hoover (**G**) Kennedy

92.-94. Which of the following statements are true in relation to the prohibition amendment?

(**a**) It was proposed and ratified while Wilson was president.

(**b**) A national plebiscite, while many men were in the armed forces overseas, was a factor in the adoption of this amendment.

(**c**) The W.C.T.U.'s efforts to delay the consideration of this amendment were of little avail.

(**d**) The Anti-Saloon League had worked for years to achieve prohibition.

(**e**) Intoxicating liquor was defined by the Volstead Act.

(**f**) President Wilson vetoed the Volstead Act.

(**g**) For the first three to four years the enforcement of prohibition was very satisfactory.

(**1**) All of them (**2**) a, b, c, g (**3**) a, d, e, f (**4**) b, c, d, e, g (**5**) d, e, f, g (**6**) All except b

95.-97. Which of the following statements associated with the early part of World War II are true?

(**a**) The *Greer, Kearny,* and the *Reuben* were American ships that were victims of German U boats.

(**b**) The *Panay* was an American vessel sent to bring U.S. citizens from Tokyo when war seemed imminent.

(**c**) "Peace in our time" is associated with the Munich Conference.

(**d**) Warsaw was the first city to be the victim of the "blitzkrieg."

(**e**) Germany, Italy, & France formed the Axis Powers of World War II.

(**f**) The U.S. transferred 50 "overage" destroyers to the British navy months before Congress declared war.

(**g**) Even though the U.S.S.R. had taken part of Finland and all of Estonia, Latvia, and Lithuania, the United States extended the Lend-Lease program to include the Soviet Union.

(**1**) a, c, e, g (**2**) b, e, f, g (**3**) a, b, c, d (**4**) c, d, e, f (**5**) a, c, d, f, g (**6**) b, c, f, g

98.-100. Which of the following statements about the presidential campaign of 1948 are true?

(**a**) After finishing the balance of F.D.R.'s fourth term, President Truman was a heavy favorite to win the election.

(**b**) The Dixiecrats were a special group of southern Democrats in support of Truman.

(**c**) The Hoovercrats were a special group of southern Democrats who would not support Truman.

(**d**) Henry Wallace broke from the Democratic Party and became a candidate on the Progressive Party ticket.

(**e**) Not only did Truman win the election, but his party made gains in both houses of Congress and picked up most of the governorships.

(**f**) The Democrats lost electoral votes from the states once known as the "solid South."

(**1**) a, b, e (**2**) d, e, f (**3**) c, d, f (**4**) a, d, e (**5**) b, c, d

Test X

1.-5.

Arrange in chronological order.

A. Burning of the *Gaspee* on the Rhode Island coast
B. Stamp Act Congress
C. Declaratory Act
D. Boston Tea Party
E. Boston Massacre

6. In what building were the 1st and 2nd Continental Congresses held?

7. In what city were the 1st and 2nd Continental Congresses held?

8.-17. Citizen Genêt came to the United States to urge our fulfillment of the Treaty of Alliance of 1778. By this treaty the U.S. had guaranteed French possessions in the West Indies against seizure by the British. In return France had guaranteed the independence of the United States against British aggression. This agreement was a "guarantee from the present time and forever."

Under this treaty France gave substantial help to the United States during the Revolutionary War. In 1793 France, which had recently revolted against an absolute monarchy and established a republic, was at war with England and sought help. Some argued that the U.S. was obligated by treaty and by common decency to help France as she had helped us. Others supported President Washington when he issued a proclamation of neutrality.

Classify each of the following statements as F, US, or X.

F—if the statement supports the French view
US—if the statement supports Washington's
X—if the statement does neither

8. There were some very raw edges left by the treaty ending the American Revolution and there was considerable ill feeling in the U.S. toward England.

9. With England and France at war it was obvious that French possessions in the West Indies were in danger of seizure by the British.

10. The French slogan of *liberty, fraternity, equality* and her Declaration of the Rights of Man were inspired by our own beliefs in the natural rights of man and our Declaration of Independence. France freed herself from a king as did the United States. Treaty or no treaty, the situation clearly indicates the action our national honor demands.

11. ". . . from the present time and forever" suggests a long time that certainly includes more than the span between 1778 and 1793.

12. Washington may well have had this treaty in mind when, in his farewell address, he warned against permanent entangling alliances.

13. The treaty was made with King Louis XVI and it became ineffective upon his death, particularly as his death was brought about by those who now sought our aid.

14. The excesses of the Reign of Terror horrified much of the world and turned many nations and peoples against France.

15. To go to war for any reason would so seriously threaten the life of the new United States that the President was duty bound and morally bound to stay neutral. Self-preservation is the first obligation with nations, transcending all others.

16. While Jefferson took a pro-French attitude in 1793, when he was president ten years later he too did his utmost to avoid involvement in Europe's wars.

17. When France aided the United States she did so to gain revenge against England and perhaps to recover some of her North American possessions. She then detested republics and was following exclusively her own national interests. However regrettable, this is the accepted conduct for nations and national self-interest alone should determine our course of action.

18. The number of votes each state has in the Electoral College depends upon what?

19. Give the date and month for the inauguration of the president.

20.-29.
The words or phrases in parentheses with each of the following items have a relationship with the item as indicated by A, B, or C. Designate which letter best applies in each case.

A—to bring into effect, to support, or to make more effective
B—to bring to an end, to oppose, or to make less effective
C—neither A nor B apply

20. Repeal of the Berlin and Milan Decrees (Macon Act)
21. Monroe Doctrine (England's preference for developing trade rather than enlarging her empire in Latin America)

22. Gag Resolution (John Quincy Adams)

23. Fugitive slave law of 1850 ("Uncle Tom's Cabin")

24. Amount of taxes collected from the excise tax on whisky (Whisky Ring)

25. The strength of the Republican Party (Admission of six northwestern states to the Union in 1889 & 1890)

26. Spheres of influence in China (Clipper Ships)

27. Friendly relations between the U.S. and the Latin American republics (Roosevelt corollary to the Monroe Doctrine)

28. Huerta's efforts to maintain his position as president of Mexico (President Wilson)

29. Federal income tax law of 1894 (Supreme Court 5 to 4 decision)

30.-39.

Match the items in Column II *with the names in* Column I.

COLUMN I	COLUMN II
A. Brown, John	30. Sec. of State when U.S. bought Alaska
B. Decatur, Stephen	31. "... *we must marry ourselves to the British fleet and nation.*"
C. Farragut, David	32. Transatlantic cable
D. Hamilton, Alexander	33. Avoid permanent entangling alliances
E. Clay, Henry	34. A few Kentucky riflemen can take Canada
F. Astor, John J.	35. Established fur trade in the Columbia River valley
G. Field, Cyrus	36. Pottawatomie Creek
H. Jefferson, Thomas	37. "*Our country! In her intercourse with foreign nations may she always be right; but our country, right or wrong.*"
I. Slater, Samuel	
J. Monroe, James	
K. Seward, William	38. "*Damn the torpedoes.*"
L. Washington, George	39. Cotton mill at Pawtucket, R.I.

40.-42. *"Our policy in regard to Europe is ... not to interfere in the internal concerns of any of its powers."*

"It is impossible that the allied powers should extend their political system to any portion of either continent without endangering our peace and happiness."

40. Both the above quotations are from what single source?

41. Name the alliance referred to by "allied powers."

42. "Either continent" means what continents?

43.-45. Which of the following statements about the Kansas-Nebraska Bill are true?

(a) It realigned political parties with the result that the two major parties were almost completely sectional (north and south) and their geographical division was based on differences over slavery.

(b) It stimulated a rapid settlement of Kansas.

(c) The Kansas-Nebraska Bill was passed by Congress to meet an explosive situation in the territories which demanded quick legislative action.

(d) The terms of the Kansas-Nebraska Bill were incompatible with those of the Missouri Compromise.

(e) The bill was primarily the work of the "Little Giant," Daniel Webster.

(f) The 40th parallel separated Kansas from Nebraska.

(1) b, c, d   (2) a, b, e, f   (3) b, d, e, f   (4) a, b, d, f   (5) All of them   (6) a, c, e

46. Which one of the following states did *not* secede from the Union before Lincoln's inauguration?

(A) Alabama   (B) Florida   (C) Georgia   (D) Louisiana   (E) Mississippi   (F) South Carolina
(G) Texas   (H) Virginia

47. Name the Grand Sachem of Tammany Hall who was commonly called the "Boss," a term applied later to many others.

48. Which of the following best describes the Credit Moblier?

A. Home loan association to stimulate settlement under the Homestead Act of 1862.

B. The first widespread plan of installment buying.

C. A corporation to finance railroad building.

D. A credit union organized by workingmen.

E. The forerunner of mail order houses such as Montgomery Ward and Sears Roebuck.

F. The mobilizing of credit in order to alleviate the effects of the panic and depression of 1873.

49. If two or more railroads agreed to charge the same rates for their services and to divide among them their income according to a prearranged formula, they were engaging in what practice made illegal by the Interstate Commerce Act of 1887?

50. What law of Congress do you associate with the Northern Securities Case?

51. The name Gresham should be associated with which one of the following?

(a) Naval power **(b)** Air power **(c)** The army **(d)** Atomic power **(e)** Monetary problems **(f)** International peace **(g)** Space research

52.-58. Each of the following men favored tariffs primarily for revenue or primarily for protection. If revenue select **R,** and if protective select **P** to correspond with their names.

52. (a) Representative
  Wilson
  (b) Morrill
53. (a) Dingley
  (b) Hawley
54. (a) Smoot
  (b) McCumber
55. (a) Underwood

  (b) Payne
56. (a) Aldrich
  (b) McKinley
57. (a) Gorman
  (b) Cleveland
58. (a) Theodore Roosevelt
  (b) Clay

59.-61. Which of the following statements are true about the American Federation of Labor?

(a) It was founded shortly before the Civil War.
(b) Samuel Gompers was its first president.
(c) John Mitchell and Eugene Debs were prominent leaders in the A. F. of L.
(d) It followed a policy for many decades of nonalliance with any political party.
(e) It has been a craft, rather than an industrial, union.
(f) From the 1880's to World War I it was the largest labor union in the United States.
(g) From McKinley to Hoover the A. F. of L. controlled a bloc of votes that meant the difference between victory and defeat for the two major parties.

COLUMN I

A. McCulloch v. Maryland
B. Munn v. Illinois
C. Northern Securities Case
D. Brown v. Topeka Board of Education

71.-73. Which of the following statements about the Roosevelt Corollary to the Monroe Doctrine are true?

(a) It was first applied to the Dominican Republic.
(b) It served as a foundation for better trade relations with Latin America.
(c) It is a policy which, while under another name, is still in effect today.
(d) It was intended to assure fair treatment for European nations in their dealings with Latin American republics.

(1) b, d, e, f   **(2)** a, b, c, g   **(3)** b, c, f   **(4)** b, c, f, g
(5) b, e, g   **(6)** b only

62. Which of the following occurred last?

A. Adjustment of the Maine-New Brunswick border
B. Acquisition of Texas by the U.S.
C. The Gadsden Purchase
D. The California gold rush
E. Settlement of the Oregon boundary

63.-66. The following items are listed in chronological order.

63. Which one is before the Civil War and closest to it?
64. Which one is before 1900 and closest to it?
65. Which one is before World War I and closest to it?
66. Which one is after World War I and closest to it?

(a) lightning rod
(b) cotton gin
(c) steamboat
(d) locomotive
(e) McCormick Reaper
(f) Colt revolver
(g) telegraph
(h) Otis passenger elevator
(i) Westinghouse air brake
(j) barbed wire
(k) telephone
(l) silent motion pictures
(m) Duryea's gasoline-driven automobile
(n) airplane
(o) X-ray
(p) sound movies (talkies)
(q) television
(r) Sputnik

67.-70.

Column I *is a list of Supreme Court cases.* Column II *is a list of statements about these cases. Match each statement with the proper Supreme Court case.*

COLUMN II

67. This case gave some vitality to the Sherman Anti-trust Act.
68. This case involved a bank.
69. This case hinged on the 14th Amendment.
70. This case involved rates charged for the use of a grain elevator.

(e) It had no application to the South American colonies of British, Dutch, and French Guiana.

(1) a, d, e   **(2)** a, c   **(3)** b, c, d   **(4)** b, d, e   **(5)** b, d

74. Which of the following statements is correct?

(a) The president may do whatever he thinks is right and for the national welfare so long as there is no prohibition in the Constitution or laws to prevent such action.
(b) The president must restrict his official actions

to carrying out powers specifically granted to him in the Constitution.

(c) The president may do whatever the Constitution specifically provides and anything reasonably implied by Constitutional provisions. Any dispute about the implication may be settled in the courts.

(d) In time of war or other major emergencies the president may do as he thinks best, without regard to the Constitution.

(e) Whenever a president is in doubt about the extent of his legal powers he may confer with the Supreme Court for authoritative advice.

75. In the judgment of history which of the following is considered the greatest achievement of Theodore Roosevelt?

(a) Conservation & Reclamation
(b) Panama Canal
(c) Contributions to world peace (Nobel Peace Prize)
(d) His part in the Spanish-American War
(e) His vigorous championship of the people

76.-100.

Match the items in Column II *with the names in* Column I. *Some of the names in* Column I *must be used more than once.*

COLUMN I

A. J. Q. Adams

B. James G. Blaine

C. Cleveland

D. Coolidge

E. Wm. L. Garrison

F. Hoover

G. Jackson

H. Jefferson

I. Lincoln

J. Polk

K. Franklin Roosevelt

L. Theodore Roosevelt

M. Zachary Taylor

N. Truman

O. Vanderbilt

P. Washington

Q. Wendell Willkie

R. Woodrow Wilson

COLUMN II

76. Old Hickory
77. Reannexation of Texas & Reoccupation of Oregon
78. Watchful waiting
79. Rough & Ready
80. Avoid excessive factionalism
81. One World
82. We shall soon see the day when poverty is banished from this nation
83. Monticello
84. I do not choose to run
85. Square Deal
86. Mount Vernon
87. Let error be free so long as reason is free to combat it
88. A house divided against itself cannot stand
89. Made the Monroe Doctrine a purely American one
90. Hermitage
91. New Freedom
92. New Deal
93. Fair Deal
94. The plumed knight
95. A public office is a public trust
96. With malice toward none, with charity for all
97. The public be damned
98. The Constitution is a covenant with death and an agreement with hell
99. We have nothing to fear but fear itself
100. Avoid permanent entangling alliances

ANSWERS to Test I

Page 256

1. (a) D	17. 18	43.-45. a, e, f	71. C
(b) J	18. 14	46. O	72. C
2. (a) P	19. 12	47. H	73. F
(b) B	20. 23	48. C	74. A
3. (a) H	21. 13	49. B	75. D
(b) R	22. C	50. N	76. B
4. (a) L	23. R	51. J	77. E
(b) S	24. F	52. A	78. D
5. (a) E	25. F	53. H	79. O
(b) F	26. R	54. E	80. P
6. (a) M	27. F	55. E	81. D
(b) N	28. F	56. D	82. A
7. (a) G	29. R	57. F	83. M
(b) A	30. R	58. A	84. E
8. (a) O	31. F	59. O	85. L
(b) I	32. R	60. I	86. F
9. (a) C	33. A	61. K	87. B
(b) Q	34. C	62. M	88. G
10. (a) K	35. B	63. L	89.-91. 1
(b) G or N	36. A	64. G	92.-94. 1
11. (a) F	37. A	65. I	95.-97. 5
(b) H	38. B	66. Seward	98.-100. 2
12. (a) Q	39. B	67. B	
(b) L	40. B	68. A	
13.-15. 2	41. C	69. D	
16. House of Rep.	42. A	70. E	

ANSWERS to Test II

Page 261

1.-3. 5	26. A	50. 37th	76. C
4. S	27. A	51. Tex. & Cal.	77. A
5. S	28. C	52. Utah	78.-80. 3
6. X	29. B	53. New Mexico	81. J
7. P	30. A	54. J. Q. Adams	82. L
8. S	31. A	55. B	83. A
9. P	32. A	56. E	84. N
10. P	33. B	57. D	85. B
11. S	34. B	58. A	86. K
12. X	35. C	59. F	87. D
13. X	36. 1850	60. C	88. H
14. Senate	37. 1859	61. S	89. M
15. 14	38. 1808	62. S	90. E
16. 22	39. 1860	63. O	91. C
17. 14	40. 1619	64. O	92. O
18. 20	41. 1831	65. O	93.-95. 4
19. Tenure of Office	42. 1788	66. X	96. E
Act	43. 1820	67. X	97. B
20. Constitution	44. 1858	68. O	98. D
21. Laws made in pursu-	45. 1845	69. O	99. A
ance of the Constitu-	46. 1863	70. S	100. C
tion	47. 1854	71. X	
22. Treaties	48. 1861	72. X	
23.-25. 5	49. 1857	73.-75. 1	

ANSWERS to Test III

Page 265

1.-3. 2	24. B	52. E	78. C
4. S	25. C	53. F	79. B
5. S	26. A	54. A	80. B
6. 2/3	27. A	55. G	81. A
7. 2/3	28. C	56. C	82. B
8. 2/3	29. A	57. C	83. A
9. 2/3	30. A	58. B	84. B
10. 3/4	31. A	59. F	85. C
11. S	32. C	60. J	86. J
12. S	33. A	61. I	87. E
13. S	34. S	62. G	88. M
14. S	35. S	63. E	89. O
15. 2/3	36. O	64. H	90. P
16. 13	37. X	65. D	91. A
17. 100%	38. O	66. A	92. D
18. 33 1/3	39. S	67. e	93. H
19. Vice-President	40. X	68. 6	94. G
20. House of Rep.	41. S	69. 4	95. B
21. The enumeration in the Constitution of certain rights shall not be construed to deny or disparage others retained by the people	42. O	70. e	96. F
	43. S	71. A	97. N
	44. O	72. C	98. L
	45. X	73. B	99. K
	46.-48. 6	74. A	100. Q
	49. Jackson	75. A	
	50. B	76. B	
22.-23. c & e	51. D	77. C	

ANSWERS to Test IV

Page 269

1.-3. 1	31.-35. religion, speech, press, petition, assembly (*in any order*)	56. A	81. D
4. A		57. A	82. C
5. C		58. A	83. B
6. A	36. A	59. N	84. (a) E
7. C	37. A	60. X	(b) L
8. A	38. B	61. X	85. (a) C
9. B	39. C	62. N	(b) B
10. A	40. B	63. N	86. (a) I
11. B	41. A	64. N	(b) J
12. C	42. C	65. X	87. (a) D
13. B	43. B	66.-68. 5	(b) K
14.-16. 4	44. B	69. S	88. (a) A
17. 25	45. B	70. S	(b) F
18. 30	46. G	71. O	89. (a) G
19. 35	47. H	72. X	(b) H
20. 2	48. A	73. O	90. C
21. 6	49. K	74. O	91.-93. 4
22. 16	50. F	75. X	94. C
23. 14	51. L	76. X	95. B
24. 14	52. B	77. O	96. D
25. 11	53. D	78. S	97. A
26.-27. b & d	54. E	79. S	98. E
28.-30. 2	55. C	80. A	99. Europe
			100. U.S.S.R.

ANSWERS to Test V

Page 273

1.-3. 5

4. Local courts with jury trials favored smugglers in spite of evidence.

5. The money deposited as bond could be taken in payment of fines.

6. Local deputies had been too friendly with tax evaders.

7. Faneil Hall

8. Boston

9. E

10. B

11. H

12. F

13. A

14. D

15. G

16. C

17. 15

18. 21

19. 14

20. 19

21.-23. 3

24.-26. 5

27.-29. 1

30. B

31. B

32. C

33. A

34. A

35. B

36. B

37. C

38. A

39. A

40.-42. 6

43.-45. 3

46. H

47. G

48. E

49. A

50. C

51. J

52. K

53. F

54. L

55. I

56. E

57. J

58. C

59. L

60. B

61. F

62. G

63. M

64. (a) II
   (b) I

65. (a) III
   (b) III

66. (a) I
   (b) I

67. (a) IV
   (b) II

68. (a) IV
   (b) III

69. (a) III
   (b) IV

70. (a) II
   (b) I

71. (a) II
   (b) III

72. (a) IV
   (b) III

73. (a) IV
   (b) II

74. (a) II
   (b) II

75. R

76. O

77. M

78. J

79. B

80. F

81. N

82. K

83. G

84. P

85. I

86. D

87. L

88. Q

89. C

90. V

91. A

92. T

93. W

94. U

95. (a) B
   (b) B

96. (a) B
   (b) C

97. (a) A
   (b) B

98. (a) A
   (b) B

99. (a) A
   (b) C

100. (a) A
    (b) B

ANSWERS to Test VI

Page 277

1. (a) W
  (b) U

2. (a) E
  (b) F

3. (a) T
  (b) O

4. (a) C
  (b) M

5. (a) B
  (b) A

6. (a) D
  (b) G

7. (a) P
  (b) L

8. (a) Q
  (b) S

9. (a) R
  (b) V

10. (a) K
   (b) J

11. (a) X
   (b) I

12. (a) H
   (b) N

13. e

14. 1775

15. Maryland

16. Northwest Territory

17. Shays

18. Burgoyne

19. Cornwallis

20. c or (1781-'89)

21. legislative

22. executive

23. judicial

24. revenue or tax

25. Senate

26. b

27.-29. c

30.-31. e & h

32. B

33. C

34. C

35. B

36. B

37. A

38. C

39. B

40. B

41. A

42. CCh

43. X

44. CCh

45. Ch

46. C

47. X

48. Ch

49. C

50. X

51. Ch

52. C

53. Ch

54.-55. e & f

56. 1833

57. 1890

58. 1816

59. 1828

60. 1930

61. 1824

62. 1913

63. (a) J
   (b) A

64. (a) E
   (b) H

65. (a) K
   (b) L

66. (a) C
   (b) D

67. (a) I
   (b) B

68. (a) F
   (b) G

69. X

70. X

71. A

72. A

73. S

74. X

75. S

76. A

77. 5

78. 1

79.-81. 6

82. E

83. D

84. F

85. A

86. B

87. C

88.-90. 5

91. B

92. B

93. D

94. B

95. A

96. A

97. D

98. C

99. B

100. C

ANSWERS to Test VII

Page 281

1.-3. 5	32. B	58. (a) G	77. D
4. X	33. A	(b) K	78. C
5. S	34. C	59. (a) C	79. D
6. S	35. B	(b) S	80. D
7. O	36. C	60. (a) U	81. C
8. X	37. A	(b) E	82. A
9. S	38. A	61. (a) D	83. B
10. O	39. C	(b) J	84. A
11. O	40. K	62. (a) I	85. 3
12. X	41. H	(b) N	86. 6
13. X	42. B	63. (a) P	87. D
14. Independence Hall	43. L	(b) H	88. C
15. Philadelphia	44. A	64. (a) B	89. A
16. 7	45. J	(b) L	90. E
17. 9	46. C	65. (a) O	91. B
18. 14	47. E	(b) M	92. e
19. 10	48. F	66. B	93. B
20. 6	49. G	67. D	94. C
21. d	50.-52. B & D	68. A	95. E
22.-24. c	53.-54. Maryland, Dela-	69. C	96. A
25. F	ware, Kentucky, Mis-	70. A	97. F
26. F	souri *(in any order)*	71. C	98. D
27. X	55. Hayes	72. B	99. a
28. X	56. (a) F	73. A	100. Populist
29. R	(b) Q	74. D	
30. A	57. (a) R	75. A	
31. A	(b) A	76. B	

ANSWERS to Test VIII

Page 285

1.-3. 3	21. republican	47. R	77. A
4. (a) K	22. religious	48. D	78. B
(b) R	23. B	49. D	79. A
5. (a) M	24. C	50. R	80. A
(b) I	25. A	51. X	81. A
6. (a) P	26. A	52. X	82. B
(b) J	27. C	53.-55. e	83. 2
7. (a) A	28. A	56.-58. l	84. 2
(b) G	29. A	59. d	85. X
8. (a) B	30. A	60. d	86. X
(b) Q	31. A	61. a	87. X
9. (a) E	32. A	62. c	88. X
(b) N	33. C	63. e	89. X
10. (a) L	34. G	64. d	90. X
(b) H	35. I	65. O	91. M
11. (a) S	36. J	66. X	92. M
(b) C	37. A	67. S	93. X
12. B	38. K	68. O	94. T
13. B	39. D	69. X	95. T
14. C	40. F	70. S	96. X
15. A	41. H	71. X	97. T
16. B	42. B	72. X	98. T
17. C	43. RD	73. A	99. M
18. A	44. R	74. B	100. T
19. a	45. RD	75. B	
20. a	46. D	76. B	

ANSWERS to Test IX

Page 290

1. c
2.-3. a & b (*any order*)
4.-5. a & e (*any order*)
6. b
7. d
8. e
9. c
10.-12. 1
13. ⅔ vote of each House of Congress
14. by legislature of ¾ of the states
15. by conventions held in ¾ of the states
16. The powers not delegated to the U.S. by the Constitution, nor prohibited by it to the states, are reserved to the states respectively, or to the people.
17. January 3rd

18. A
19. A
20. C
21. B
22. C
23. B
24. B
25. B
26. A
27. A
28. F
29. E
30. H
31. B
32. I
33. C
34. G
35. J
36. A
37. D
38. 1
39. 3
40. 1

41.-43. 2
44. provide for the general welfare
45.-49. C-G-K-L-P (*in any order*)
50. Free Soil
51. Fremont
52.-55. C-D-G-I (*in any order*)
56.-58. A-B-G (*in any order*)
59. E
60. Nast
61. 3
62. 4
63. 4
64. Assassination of Garfield
65.-67. 1
68. Cooperative
69. c
70. P
71. N

72. E
73. H
74. B
75. G
76. O
77. Q
78. C
79. M
80. J
81. D
82. F
83. I
84. K
85. L
86. A
87. B
88. C
89. A
90. D
91. D
92.-94. 3
95.-97. 5
98.-100. 2

ANSWERS to Test X

Page 295

1. B
2. C
3. E
4. A
5. D
6. Carpenters Hall
7. Philadelphia
8. X
9. F
10. F
11. F
12. X
13. US
14. X
15. US
16. X
17. US
18. Number of members it has in Congress
19. 20th Jan.
20. A
21. A
22. B
23. C
24. B
25. A
26. C

27. B
28. B
29. B
30. K
31. H
32. G
33. L
34. E
35. F
36. A
37. B
38. C
39. I
40. Monroe Doctrine
41. Holy Alliance
42. No. & So. Amer.
43.-45. 4
46. H
47. Tweed
48. C
49. pooling
50. Sherman Anti-trust Act
51. e
52. (a) R
    (b) P

53. (a) P
    (b) P
54. (a) P
    (b) P
55. (a) R
    (b) R
56. (a) P
    (b) P
57. (a) P
    (b) R
58. (a) P
    (b) P
59.-61. 1
62. C
63. h
64. m
65. o
66. p
67. C
68. A
69. D
70. B
71.-73. 1
74. c
75. a

76. G
77. J
78. R
79. M
80. P
81. Q
82. F
83. H
84. D
85. L
86. P
87. H
88. I
89. A
90. G
91. R
92. K
93. N
94. B
95. C
96. I
97. O
98. E
99. K
100. P

The Declaration of Independence[†]

In Congress, July 4, 1776

THE UNANIMOUS DECLARATION OF THE THIRTEEN UNITED STATES OF AMERICA

When, in the Course of human events, it becomes necessary for one people to dissolve the political bands which have connected them with another, and to assume among the powers of the earth, the separate and equal station to which the Laws of Nature and of Nature's God entitle them, a decent respect to the opinions of mankind requires that they should declare the causes which impel them to the separation.

We hold these truths to be self-evident, that all men are created equal, that they are endowed by their Creator with certain unalienable Rights, that among these, are Life, Liberty, and the pursuit of Happiness. That, to secure these rights, Governments are instituted among Men, deriving their just powers from the consent of the governed, that, whenever any Form of Government becomes destructive of these ends, it is the Right of the People to alter or to abolish it, and to institute new Government, laying its foundation on such principles, and organizing its powers in such form, as to them shall seem most likely to effect their Safety and Happiness. Prudence, indeed, will dictate that Governments long established, should not be changed for light and transient causes; and, accordingly, all experience hath shewn, that mankind are more disposed to suffer, while evils are sufferable, than to right themselves by abolishing the forms to which they are accustomed. But, when a long train of abuses and usurpations, pursuing invariably the same Object, evinces a design to reduce them under absolute Despotism, it is their right, it is their duty, to throw off such Government and to provide new Guards for their future security.—Such has been the patient sufferance of these Colonies; and such is now the necessity which constrains them to alter their former Systems of Government. The history of the present King of Great Britain is a history of repeated injuries and usurpations, all having in direct object the estab-

---

† *Spelling and capitalization follow the parchment copy.*

lishment of an absolute Tyranny over these States. To prove this, let Facts be submitted to a candid world.—

He has refused his Assent to Laws the most wholesome and necessary for the public good.

He has forbidden his Governors to pass Laws of immediate and pressing importance, unless suspended in their operation till his Assent should be obtained; and when so suspended, he has utterly neglected to attend to them.

He has refused to pass other laws for the accommodation of large districts of people, unless those people would relinquish the right of Representation in the Legislature; a right inestimable to them and formidable to tyrants only.

He has called together legislative bodies at places unusual, uncomfortable, and distant from the depository of their public Records, for the sole purpose of fatiguing them into compliance with his measures.

He has dissolved Representative Houses repeatedly, for opposing with manly firmness his invasions on the rights of the people.

He has refused for a long time, after such dissolutions, to cause others to be elected; whereby the Legislative powers, incapable of Annihilation, have returned to the People at large for their exercise; the State remaining, in the meantime, exposed to all the dangers of invasion from without, and convulsions within.

He has endeavored to prevent the population of these States; for that purpose, obstructing the Laws for Naturalization of Foreigners; refusing to pass others to encourage their migrations hither, and raising the conditions of new Appropriations of Lands.

He has obstructed the Administration of Justice, by refusing his Assent to Laws for establishing Judiciary powers.

He has made Judges dependent on his Will alone, for the tenure of their offices, and the amount and payment of their salaries.

He has erected a multitude of New Offices, and sent hither swarms of Officers to harass our people, and eat out their substance.

He has kept among us, in times of peace, Standing Armies, without the Consent of our legislatures.

He has affected to render the Military independent of, and superior to, the Civil power.

He has combined, with others, to subject us to a jurisdiction foreign to our constitution, and unacknowledged by our laws; giving his Assent to their Acts of pretended Legislation:

For quartering large bodies of armed troops among us:

For protecting them by a mock Trial, from punishment, for any Murders which they should commit on the Inhabitants of these States:

For cutting off our Trade with all parts of the world:

For imposing Taxes on us without our Consent:

For depriving us, in many cases, of the benefits of Trial by Jury:

For transporting us beyond Seas to be tried for pretended offenses:

For abolishing the free System of English Laws in a neighboring Province, establishing therein an Arbitrary government, and enlarging its Boundaries, so as to render it at once an example and fit instrument for introducing the same absolute rule into these Colonies:

For taking away our Charters, abolishing our most valuable Laws, and altering, fundamentally, the Forms of our Governments:

For suspending our own Legislatures, and declaring themselves invested with power to legislate for us in all cases whatsoever.

He has abdicated Government here, by declaring us out of his Protection, and waging War against us.

He has plundered our seas, ravaged our Coasts, burnt our towns, and destroyed the lives our our people.

He is, at this time, transporting large Armies of foreign Mercenaries to compleat the works of death, desolation, and tyranny, already begun with circumstances of Cruelty & perfidy scarcely paralleled in the most barbarous ages, and totally unworthy the Head of a civilized nation.

He has constrained our fellow Citizens, taken Captive on the high Seas, to bear Arms against their Country, to become the executioners of their friends and Brethren, or to fall themselves by their Hands.

He has excited domestic insurrections amongst us, and has endeavored to bring on the inhabitants of our frontiers, the merciless Indian Savages, whose known rule of warfare, is an undistinguished destruction of all ages, sexes and conditions.

In every stage of these Oppressions, We have Petitioned for Redress, in the most humble terms; our repeated Petitions have been answered only by repeated injury. A Prince, whose character is thus marked by every act which may define a Tyrant, is unfit to be the ruler of a free people.

Nor have we been wanting in attentions to our British brethren. We have warned them, from time to time, of attempts made by their legislature to extend an unwarrantable jurisdiction over us. We have reminded them of the circumstances of our emigration and settlement here. We have appealed to their native justice and magnanimity, and we have conjured them by the ties of our common kindred to disavow these usurpations, which would inevitably interrupt our connections and correspondence. They too have been deaf to the voice of justice and of consanguinity. We must, therefore, acquiesce in the necessity, which denounces our Separation, and hold them, as we hold the rest of mankind, Enemies in War, in Peace Friends.

We, therefore, the Representatives of the united States of America, in General Congress, Assembled, appealing to the Supreme Judge of the world for the rectitude of our intentions, do, in the Name, and by Authority of the good People of these Colonies, solemnly publish and declare, That these United Colonies are, and of Right ought to be, Free and Independent States; that they are Absolved from all Allegiance to the British Crown, and that all political connection between them and the State of Great Britain is, and ought to be, totally dissolved: and that, as Free and Independent States, they have full Power to levy War, conclude Peace, contract Alliances, establish Commerce, and to do all other Acts and Things which Independent States may of right do. And, for the support of this Declaration, with a firm reliance on the protection of divine Providence, we mutually pledge to each other our Lives, our Fortunes, and our sacred Honor.

The foregoing Declaration was, by order of Congress, engrossed, and signed by the following members:

John Hancock

NEW HAMPSHIRE
 Josiah Bartlett
 William Whipple
 Matthew Thornton
MASSACHUSETTS BAY
 Samuel Adams
 John Adams
 Robert Treat Paine
 Elbridge Gerry
RHODE ISLAND
 Stephen Hopkins
 William Ellery
CONNECTICUT
 Roger Sherman
 Samuel Huntington
 William Williams
 Oliver Wolcott
NEW YORK
 William Floyd
 Philip Livingston
 Francis Lewis
 Lewis Morris
NEW JERSEY
 Richard Stockton
 John Witherspoon

Francis Hopkinson
John Hart
Abraham Clark
PENNSYLVANIA
 Robert Morris
 Benjamin Rush
 Benjamin Franklin
 John Morton
 George Clymer
 James Smith
 George Taylor
 James Wilson
 George Ross
DELAWARE
 Caesar Rodney
 George Read
 Thomas M'Kean
MARYLAND
 Samuel Chase
 William Paca
 Thomas Stone
 Charles Carroll, of Carrollton
VIRGINIA
 George Wythe
 Richard Henry Lee

Thomas Jefferson
Benjamin Harrison
Thomas Nelson, Jr.
Francis Lightfoot Lee
Carter Braxton

NORTH CAROLINA
  William Hooper
  Joseph Hewes
  John Penn

SOUTH CAROLINA
  Edward Rutledge
  Thomas Heyward, Jr.
  Thomas Lynch, Jr.
  Arthur Middleton

GEORGIA
  Button Gwinnett
  Lyman Hall
  George Walton

RESOLVED, That copies of the Declaration be sent to the several assemblies, conventions, and committees, or councils of safety, and to the several commanding officers of the continental troops; that it be proclaimed in each of the united States, at the head of the army.

The Constitution of the United States†

We the People of the United States, in Order to form a more perfect Union, establish Justice, insure domestic Tranquility, provide for the common defence, promote the general Welfare, and secure the Blessings of Liberty to ourselves and our Posterity, do ordain and establish this CONSTITUTION for the United States of America.

ARTICLE. I.

Section. 1. All legislative Powers herein granted shall be vested in a Congress of the United States, which shall consist of a Senate and House of Representatives.

Section. 2. The House of Representatives shall be composed of Members chosen every second Year by the People of the several States, and the Electors in each State shall have the Qualifications requisite for Electors of the most numerous Branch of the State Legislature.

No Person shall be a Representative who shall not have attained to the Age of twenty-five Years, and been seven Years a Citizen of the United States, and who shall not, when elected, be an Inhabitant of that State in which he shall be chosen.

[Representatives and direct Taxes shall be apportioned among the several States which may be included within this Union, according to their respective Numbers, which shall be determined by adding to the whole Number of free Persons, including those bound to Service for a Term of Years, and excluding Indians not taxed, three fifths of all other Persons.] ‡ The actual Enumeration shall be made within three Years after the first Meeting of the Congress of the United States, and within every subsequent Term of ten Years, in such Manner as they shall by Law direct. The Number of Representatives shall not exceed one for every thirty Thousand, but each State shall have at Least one Representa-

---

† *This text of the Constitution follows the engrossed copy signed by Gen. Washington and the deputies from 12 States. The superior number preceding the paragraphs designates the number of the clause; it was not in the original.*
‡ *Changed by section 2 of the 14th Amendment.*

tive; and until such enumeration shall be made, the State of New Hampshire shall be entitled to chuse three, Massachusetts eight, Rhode-Island and Providence Plantations one, Connecticut five, New-York six, New Jersey four, Pennsylvania eight, Delaware one, Maryland six, Virginia ten, North Carolina five, South Carolina five, and Georgia three.

When vacancies happen in the Representation from any State, the Executive Authority thereof shall issue Writs of Election to fill such Vacancies.

The House of Representatives shall chuse their Speaker and other Officers; and shall have the sole Power of Impeachment.

Section. 3. The Senate of the United States shall be composed of two Senators from each State, [chosen by the Legislature thereof,] † for six Years; and each Senator shall have one Vote.

Immediately after they shall be assembled in Consequence of the first Election, they shall be divided as equally as may be into three Classes. The Seats of the Senators of the first Class shall be vacated at the Expiration of the second Year, of the second Class at the Expiration of the fourth Year, and of the third Class at the Expiration of the sixth Year, so that one-third may be chosen every second Year; [and if Vacancies happen by Resignation, or otherwise, during the Recess of the Legislature of any State, the Executive thereof may make temporary Appointments until the next Meeting of the Legislature, which shall then fill such Vacancies].‡

No Person shall be a Senator who shall not have attained to the Age of thirty Years, and been nine Years a Citizen of the United States, and who shall not, when elected, be an Inhabitant of that State for which he shall be chosen.

The Vice President of the United States shall be President of the Senate, but shall have no vote, unless they be equally divided.

The Senate shall chuse their other Officers, and also a President pro tempore, in the absence of the Vice President, or when he shall exercise the Office of President of the United States.

The Senate shall have the sole Power to try all Impeachments. When sitting for that purpose, they shall be on Oath or Affirmation. When the President of the United States is tried, the Chief Justice shall preside: And no person shall be convicted without the Concurrence of two thirds of the Members present.

Judgment in Cases of Impeachment shall not extend further than to removal from Office, and disqualification to hold and enjoy any Office of honor, Trust, or Profit under the United States: but the Party convicted shall nevertheless be liable and subject to Indictment, Trial, Judgment, and Punishment, according to Law.

Section. 4. The Times, Places and Manner of holding Elections for Senators and Representatives, shall be prescribed in each State by the Legislature thereof;

---

† *Changed by section 1 of the 17th Amendment.*
‡ *Changed by clause 2 of the 17th Amendment.*

but the Congress may at any time by Law make or alter such Regulations; except as to the Places of Chusing Senators.

The Congress shall assemble at least once in every Year, and such Meeting shall [be on the first Monday in December,] † unless they shall by Law appoint a different Day.

Section. 5. Each House shall be the Judge of the Elections, Returns and Qualifications of its own Members, and a Majority of each shall constitute a Quorum to do Business; but a small number may adjourn from day to day, and may be authorized to compel the Attendance of absent Members, in such Manner, and under such Penalties, as each House may provide.

Each House may determine the Rules of its Proceedings, punish its Members for disorderly Behavior, and, with the Concurrence of two thirds, expel a Member.

Each House shall keep a Journal of its Proceedings, and from time to time publish the same, excepting such Parts as may in their Judgment require Secrecy; and the Yeas and Nays of the Members of either House on any question shall, at the Desire of one fifth of those Present, be entered on the Journal.

Neither House, during the Session of Congress, shall, without the Consent of the other, adjourn for more than three days, nor to any other Place than that in which the two Houses shall be sitting.

Section. 6. The Senators and Representatives shall receive a Compensation for their Services, to be ascertained by Law, and paid out of the Treasury of the United States. They shall in all Cases, except Treason, Felony, and Breach of the Peace, be privileged from Arrest during their Attendance at the Session of their respective Houses, and in going to and returning from the same; and for any Speech or Debate in either House, they shall not be questioned in any other Place.

No Senator or Representative shall, during the Time for which he was elected, be appointed to any civil Office under the Authority of the United States, which shall have been created, or the Emoluments whereof shall have been increased, during such time; and no Person holding any Office under the United States shall be a Member of either House during his continuance in Office.

Section. 7. All Bills for raising Revenue shall originate in the House of Representatives; but the Senate may propose or concur with Amendments on other bills.

Every Bill which shall have passed the House of Representatives and the Senate, shall, before it become a law, be presented to the President of the United States; If he approve he shall sign it, but if not he shall return it, with his Objections, to that House in which it shall have originated, who shall enter the Objections at large on their Journal, and proceed to reconsider it. If after such Reconsideration two thirds of that House shall agree to pass the bill, it shall be sent, together with the objections, to the other House, by which it shall likewise be reconsidered, and if approved by two thirds of that House, it shall become a

† *Changed by section 2 of the 20th Amendment.*

Law. But in all such Cases the Votes of both Houses shall be determined by Yeas and Nays, and the Names of the Persons voting for and against the Bill shall be entered on the Journal of each House respectively. If any Bill shall not be returned by the President within ten Days (Sundays excepted) after it shall have been presented to him, the Same shall be a Law, in like Manner as if he had signed it, unless the Congress by their Adjournment prevent its Return, in which Case it shall not be a Law.

Every Order, Resolution, or Vote to which the Concurrence of the Senate and House of Representatives may be necessary (except on a question of Adjournment) shall be presented to the President of the United States; and before the Same shall take Effect, shall be approved by him, or being disapproved by him, shall be repassed by two thirds of the senate and House of Representatives, according to the Rules and Limitations prescribed in the Case of a Bill.

Section. 8. The Congress shall have Power To lay and collect Taxes, Duties, Imposts and Excises, to pay the Debts and provide for the common Defence and general Welfare of the United States; but all Duties, Imposts and Excises shall be uniform throughout the United States;

To borrow money on the credit of the United States;

To regulate Commerce with foreign Nations, and among the several States, and with the Indian Tribes;

To establish an uniform Rule of Naturalization, and uniform Laws on the subject of Bankruptcies throughout the United States;

To coin Money, regulate the Value thereof, and of foreign Coin, and fix the Standard of Weights and Measures;

To provide for the Punishment of counterfeiting the Securities and current Coin of the United States;

To establish Post Offices and post Roads;

To promote the Progress of Science and useful Arts, by securing for limited Times to Authors and Inventors the exclusive Right to their respective Writings and Discoveries;

To constitute Tribunals inferior to the Supreme Court;

To define and punish Piracies and Felonies committed on the high Seas, and Offenses against the Law of Nations;

To declare War, grant Letters of Marque and Reprisal, and make Rules concerning Captures on Land and Water;

To raise and support Armies, but no Appropriation of Money to that Use shall be for a longer Term than two Years;

To provide and maintain a Navy;

To make Rules for the Government and Regulation of the land and naval forces;

To provide for calling forth the Militia to execute the Laws of the Union, suppress Insurrections and repel Invasions;

To provide for organizing, arming, and disciplining the Militia, and for governing such Part of them as may be employed in the Service of the United States, reserving to the States respectively, the Appointment of the Officers, and the Authority of training the Militia according to the discipline prescribed by Congress;

To exercise exclusive Legislation in all Cases whatsoever, over such District (not exceeding ten Miles square) as may, by Cession of particular States, and the acceptance of Congress, become the Seat of the Government of the United States, and to exercise like Authority over all Places purchased by the Consent of the Legislature of the State in which the Same shall be, for the Erection of Forts, Magazines, Arsenals, dock-Yards, and other needful Buildings;—And

To make all Laws which shall be necessary and proper for carrying into Execution the foregoing Powers, and all other Powers vested by this Constitution in the Government of the United States, or in any Department or Officer thereof.

Section. 9. The Migration or Importation of such Persons as any of the States now existing shall think proper to admit, shall not be prohibited by the Congress prior to the Year one thousand eight hundred and eight, but a tax or duty may be imposed on such Importation, not exceeding ten dollars for each Person.

The privilege of the Writ of Habeas Corpus shall not be suspended, unless when in Cases of Rebellion or Invasion the public Safety may require it.

No Bill of Attainder or ex post facto Law shall be passed.

† No capitation, or other direct, Tax shall be laid unless in Proportion to the Census or Enumeration herein before directed to be taken.

No Tax or Duty shall be laid on Articles exported from any State.

No Preference shall be given by any Regulation of Commerce or Revenue to the Ports of one State over those of another: nor shall Vessels bound to, or from, one State, be obliged to enter, clear, or pay Duties in another.

No Money shall be drawn from the Treasury, but in Consequence of Appropriations made by Law; and a regular Statement and Account of the Receipts and Expenditures of all public Money shall be published from time to time.

No Title of Nobility shall be granted by the United States: And no Person holding any Office of Profit or Trust under them, shall, without the Consent of the Congress, accept of any present, Emolument, Office, or Title, of any kind whatever, from any King, Prince, or foreign State.

Section. 10. No State shall enter into any Treaty, Alliance, or Confederation; grant Letters of Marque and Reprisal; coin Money; emit Bills of Credit; make any Thing but gold and silver Coin or Tender in Payment of Debts; pass any Bill of Attainder, ex post facto Law, or Law impairing the Obligation of Contracts, or grant any Title of Nobility.

No State shall, without the Consent of the Congress, lay any Imposts or Duties on Imports or Exports, except what may be absolutely necessary for executing its

---

† *See also the 16th Amendment.*

inspection Laws: and the net Produce of all Duties and Imposts, laid by any State on Imports or Exports, shall be for the Use of the Treasury of the United States; and all such Laws shall be subject to the Revision and Control of the Congress.

No State shall, without the Consent of Congress, lay any duty of Tonnage, keep Troops, or Ships of War in time of Peace, enter into any Agreement or Compact with another State, or with a foreign Power, or engage in War, unless actually invaded, or in such imminent Danger as will not admit of delay.

ARTICLE. II.

Section. 1. The executive Power shall be vested in a President of the United States of America. He shall hold his Office during the Term of four years, and, together with the Vice-President, chosen for the same Term, be elected, as follows:

Each State shall appoint, in such Manner as the Legislature thereof may direct, a Number of Electors, equal to the whole Number of Senators and Representatives to which the State may be entitled in the Congress: but no Senator or Representative, or Person holding an Office of Trust or Profit under the United States, shall be appointed an Elector.

[The Electors shall meet in their respective States, and vote by Ballot for two persons, of whom one at least shall not be an Inhabitant of the same State with themselves. And they shall make a List of all the Persons voted for, and of the Number of Votes for each; which List they shall sign and certify, and transmit sealed to the Seat of the Government of the United States, directed to the President of the Senate. The President of the Senate shall, in the Presence of the Senate and House of Representatives, open all the Certificates, and the Votes shall then be counted. The Person having the greatest Number of Votes shall be the President, if such Number be a Majority of the whole Number of Electors appointed; and if there be more than one who have such Majority, and have an equal Number of Votes, then the House of Representatives shall immediately chuse by Ballot one of them for President; and if no Person have a Majority, then from the five highest on the List the said House shall in like Manner chuse the President. But in chusing the President, the Votes shall be taken by States, the Representation from each State having one Vote; a quorum for this Purpose shall consist of a Member or Members from two-thirds of the States, and a Majority of all the States shall be necessary to a Choice. In every Case, after the Choice of the President, the Person having the greatest Number of Votes of the Electors shall be the Vice President. But if there should remain two or more who have equal votes, the Senate shall chuse from them by Ballot the Vice-President.] †

The Congress may determine the Time of chusing the Electors, and the Day

---

† *Superseded by the 12th Amendment.*

on which they shall give their Votes; which Day shall be the same throughout the United States.

No person except a natural-born Citizen, or a Citizen of the United States, at the time of the Adoption of this Constitution, shall be eligible to the Office of President; neither shall any Person be eligible to that Office who shall not have attained to the Age of thirty-five years, and been fourteen Years a Resident within the United States.

In Case of the Removal of the President from Office, or of his Death, Resignation, or Inability to discharge the Powers and Duties of the said Office, the same shall devolve on the Vice President, and the Congress may by Law provide for the Case of Removal, Death, Resignation, or Inability, both of the President and Vice President, declaring what Officer shall then act as President, and such Officer shall act accordingly, until the disability be removed, or a President shall be elected.

The President shall, at stated Times, receive for his Services a Compensation, which shall neither be increased nor diminished during the Period for which he shall have been elected, and he shall not receive within that Period any other Emolument from the United States, or any of them.

Before he enter on the execution of his Office, he shall take the following Oath or Affirmation:—"I do solemnly swear (or affirm) that I will faithfully execute the Office of President of the United States, and will, to the best of my Ability, preserve, protect, and defend the Constitution of the United States."

Section. 2. The President shall be Commander in Chief of the Army and Navy of the United States, and of the Militia of the several States, when called into the actual Service of the United States; he may require the Opinion, in writing, of the principal Officer in each of the executive Departments, upon any subject relating to the Duties of their respective Offices, and he shall have Power to Grant Reprieves and Pardons for Offenses against the United States, except in Cases of Impeachment.

He shall have Power, by and with the Advice and Consent of the Senate, to make Treaties, provided two thirds of the Senators present concur; and he shall nominate, and by and with the Advice and Consent of the Senate, shall appoint Ambassadors, other public Ministers and Consuls, Judges of the supreme Court, and all other Officers of the United States, whose Appointments are not herein otherwise provided for, and which shall be established by Law: but the Congress may by Law vest the Appointment of such inferior Officers, as they think proper, in the President alone, in the Courts of Law, or in the Heads of Departments.

The President shall have Power to fill up all Vacancies that may happen during the Recess of the Senate, by granting Commissions which shall expire at the End of their next Session.

Section. 3. He shall from time to time give to the Congress Information of the State of the Union, and recommend to their Consideration such Measures as he shall judge necessary and expedient; he may, on extraordinary occasions, convene both Houses, or either of them, and in Case of Disagreement between them, with respect to the Time of Adjournment, he may adjourn them to such Time as he shall think proper; he shall receive Ambassadors and other public Ministers; he shall take Care that the Laws be faithfully executed, and shall Commission all the Officers of the United States.

Section. 4. The President, Vice President and all civil Officers of the United States, shall be removed from Office on Impeachment for, and Conviction of, Treason, Bribery, or other high Crimes and Misdemeanors.

ARTICLE. III.

Section. 1. The judicial Power of the United States, shall be vested in one supreme Court, and in such inferior Courts as the Congress may from time to time ordain and establish. The Judges, both of the supreme and inferior Courts, shall hold their Offices during good Behaviour, and shall, at stated Times, receive for their Services, a Compensation, which shall not be diminished during their Continuance in Office.

Section. 2. The judicial Power shall extend to all Cases, in Law and Equity, arising under this Constitution, the Laws of the United States, and Treaties made, or which shall be made, under their Authority;—to all Cases affecting ambassadors, other public ministers and consuls;—to all cases of admiralty and maritime Jurisdiction;—to Controversies to which the United States shall be a Party;—to Controversies between two or more States; between a State and Citizens of another State;†—between Citizens of different States,—between Citizens of the same State claiming Lands under Grants of different States, and between a State, or the Citizens thereof, and foreign States, Citizens or Subjects.

In all Cases affecting Ambassadors, other public Ministers and Consuls, and those in which a State shall be Party, the supreme Court shall have original Jurisdiction. In all the other Cases before mentioned, the supreme Court shall have appellate Jurisdiction, both as to Law and Fact, with such Exceptions, and under such Regulations as the Congress shall make.

The trial of all Crimes, except in Cases of Impeachment, shall be by Jury; and such Trial shall be held in the State where the said Crimes shall have been committed; but when not committed within any State, the Trial shall be at such Place or Places as the Congress may by Law have directed.

Section. 3. Treason against the United States, shall consist only in levying War against them, or in adhering to their Enemies, giving them Aid and Comfort. No Person shall be convicted of Treason unless on the Testimony of two Witnesses to the same overt Act, or on Confession in open Court.

The Congress shall have power to declare the Punishment of Treason, but

---

† *Restricted by the 11th Amendment.*

no Attainder of Treason shall work Corruption of Blood, or Forfeiture except during the Life of the Person attainted.

ARTICLE. IV.

Section. 1. Full Faith and Credit shall be given in each State to the public Acts, Records, and judicial Proceedings of every other State. And the Congress may by general Laws prescribe the Manner in which such Acts, Records and Proceedings shall be proved, and the Effect thereof.

Section. 2. The Citizens of each State shall be entitled to all Privileges and Immunities of Citizens in the several States.

A Person charged in any State with Treason, Felony, or other Crime, who shall flee from Justice, and be found in another State, shall on demand of the executive Authority of the State from which he fled, be delivered up, to be removed to the State having Jurisdiction of the crime.

[No Person held to Service or Labour in one State, under the Laws thereof, escaping into another, shall, in Consequence of any Law or Regulation therein, be discharged from such Service or Labour, but shall be delivered up on Claim of the Party to whom such Service or Labour may be due.] †

Section. 3. New States may be admitted by the Congress into this Union; but no new State shall be formed or erected within the Jurisdiction of any other State; nor any State be Formed by the Junction of two or more States, or parts of States, without the Consent of the Legislatures of the States concerned as well as of the Congress.

The Congress shall have Power to dispose of and make all needful Rules and Regulations respecting the Territory or other Property belonging to the United States; and nothing in this Constitution shall be so construed as to Prejudice any Claims of the United States, or of any particular State.

Section. 4. The United States shall guarantee to every State in this Union a Republican Form of Government, and shall protect each of them against Invasion; and on Application of the Legislature, or of the Executive (when the Legislature cannot be convened) against domestic Violence.

ARTICLE. V.

The Congress, whenever two-thirds of both Houses shall deem it necessary, shall propose Amendments to this Constitution, or, on the Application of the Legislatures of two-thirds of the several States, shall call a Convention for proposing Amendments, which, in either Case, shall be valid to all Intents and Purposes, as part of this Constitution, when ratified by the Legislatures of three-

---

† *Superseded by the 13th Amendment.*

fourths of the several States, or by Conventions in three-fourths thereof, as the one or the other Mode of Ratification may be proposed by the Congress; Provided, [that no Amendment which may be made prior to the Year One thousand eight hundred and eight shall in any Manner affect the first and fourth Clauses in the Ninth Section of the first Article; and] † that no State, without its Consent, shall be deprived of its equal Suffrage in the Senate.

ARTICLE. VI.

All Debts contracted and Engagements entered into, before the Adoption of this Constitution, shall be as valid against the United States under this Constitution, as under the Confederation. This Constitution, and the Laws of the United States which shall be made in Pursuance thereof; and all Treaties made, or which shall be made, under the Authority of the United States, shall be the supreme Law of the Land; and the Judges in every State shall be bound thereby, any Thing in the Constitution or Laws of any State to the Contrary notwithstanding.

The Senators and Representatives before mentioned, and the Members of the several State Legislatures, and all executive and judicial officers, both of the United States and of the several States, shall be bound by Oath or Affirmation to support this Constitution; but no religious Test shall ever be required as a qualification to any Office or public Trust under the United States.

ARTICLE. VII.

The Ratification of the Conventions of nine States shall be sufficient for the Establishment of this Constitution between the States so ratifying the same.

Done in Convention by the Unanimous Consent of the States present the Seventeenth Day of September in the Year of our Lord one thousand seven hundred and Eighty seven, and of the Independence of the United States of America the Twelfth. In Witness whereof We have hereunto subscribed our Names.

---

† *Obsolete.*

Articles in Addition to, and Amendment of, the Constitution of the United states of America, Proposed by Congress, and Ratified by the Legislatures of the Several States, Pursuant to the Fifth Article of the Original Constitution†

ARTICLE [I] ‡

Congress shall make no law respecting an establishment of religion, or prohibiting the free exercise thereof; or abridging the freedom of speech, or of the press; or the right of the people peaceably to assemble, and to petition the Government for a redress of grievances.

ARTICLE [II]

A well regulated Militia, being necessary to the security of a free State, the right of the people to keep and bear Arms shall not be infringed.

ARTICLE [III]

No Soldier, shall, in time of peace, be quartered in any house, without the consent of the Owner, nor in time of war, but in a manner to be prescribed by law.

ARTICLE [IV]

The right of the people to be secure in their persons, houses, papers, and effects, against unreasonable searches and seizures, shall not be violated, and no Warrants shall issue, but upon probable cause, supported by Oath or affirmation, and particularly describing the place to be searched, and the persons or things to be seized.

ARTICLE [V]

No person shall be held to answer for a capital or otherwise infamous crime, unless on a presentment or indictment of a Grand Jury, except in cases arising in the land or naval forces, or in the Militia, when in actual service in time of War or public danger; nor shall any person be subject for the same offence to

---

† *This heading appears only in the joint resolution submitting the first ten amendments.*
‡ *Only the 13th, 14th, 15th, and 16th articles of amendment had numbers assigned to them at the time of ratification.*

be twice put in jeopardy of life or limb; nor shall be compelled in any criminal case to be a witness against himself, nor be deprived of life, liberty, or property, without due process of law; nor shall private property be taken for public use, without just compensation.

ARTICLE [VI]

In all criminal prosecutions, the accused shall enjoy the right to a speedy and public trial, by an impartial jury of the State and district wherein the crime shall have been committed, which district shall have been previously ascertained by law, and to be informed of the nature and cause of the accusations; to be confronted with the witnesses against him; to have compulsory process for obtaining witnesses in his favor, and to have the Assistance of Counsel for his defence.

ARTICLE [VII]

In suits at common law, where the value in controversy shall exceed twenty dollars, the right of trial by jury shall be preserved, and no fact tried by a jury, shall be otherwise reexamined in any Court of the United States, than according to the rules of the common law.

ARTICLE [VIII]

Excessive bail shall not be required, nor excessive fines imposed, nor cruel and unusual punishments inflicted.

ARTICLE [IX]

The enumeration in the Constitution, of certain rights, shall not be construed to deny or disparage others retained by the people.

ARTICLE [X]

The powers not delegated to the United States by the Constitution, nor prohibited by it to the States, are reserved to the States respectively, or to the people.

(Amendments I–X, in force 1791.)

ARTICLE [XI] †

The Judicial power of the United States shall not be construed to extend to any suit in law or equity, commenced or prosecuted against one of the

---

† *Adopted in 1798.*

United States by Citizens of another State, or by Citizens or Subjects of any Foreign State.

ARTICLE [XII] †

The Electors shall meet in their respective States and vote by ballot for President and Vice-President, one of whom, at least, shall not be an inhabitant of the same State with themselves; they shall name in their ballots the person voted for as President, and in distinct ballots the person voted for as Vice-President, and they shall make distinct lists of all persons voted for as President, and of all persons voted for as Vice-President, and of the number of votes for each, which lists they shall sign and certify, and transmit sealed to the seat of the government of the United States, directed to the President of the Senate;—The President of the Senate shall, in the presence of the Senate and House of Representatives, open all the certificates and the votes shall then be counted;—The person having the greatest number of votes for President, shall be the President, if such number be a majority of the whole number of Electors appointed; and of no person have such majority, then from the persons having the highest numbers not exceeding three on the list of those voted for as President, the House of Representatives shall choose immediately, by ballot, the President. But in choosing the President, the votes shall be taken by states, the representation from each state having one vote; a quorum for this purpose shall consist of a member or members from two-thirds of the states, and a majority of all the states shall be necessary to a choice. [And if the House of Representatives shall not choose a President whenever the right of choice shall devolve upon them, before the fourth day of March next following, then the Vice-President shall act as President, as in the case of the death or other constitutional disability of the President.] ‡ The person having the greatest number of votes as Vice-President, shall be the Vice-President, if such number be a majority of the whole number of Electors appointed, and if no person have a majority, then from the two highest numbers on the list, the Senate shall choose the Vice-President; a quorum for the purpose shall consist of two-thirds of the whole number of Senators, and a majority of the whole number shall be necessary to a choice. But no person constitutionally ineligible to the office of President shall be eligible to that of Vice-President of the United States.

ARTICLE XIII *

Section 1. Neither slavery nor involuntary servitude, except as a punishment for crime whereof the party shall have been duly convicted, shall exist within the United States, or any place subject to their jurisdiction.

---

† *Adopted in 1804.*
‡ *Superseded by section 3 of the 20th Amendment.*
* *Adopted in 1865.*

Section 2. Congress shall have power to enforce this article by appropriate legislation.

ARTICLE XIV †

Section 1. All persons born or naturalized in the United States, and subject to the jurisdiction thereof, are citizens of the United States and of the State wherein they reside. No State shall make or enforce any law which shall abridge the privileges or immunities of citizens of the United States; nor shall any State deprive any person of life, liberty, or property, without due process of law; nor deny to any person within its jurisdiction the equal protection of the laws.

Section 2. Representatives shall be apportioned among the several States according to their respective numbers, counting the whole number of persons in each State, excluding Indians not taxed. But when the right to vote at any election for the choice of electors for President and Vice-President of the United States, Representatives in Congress, the Executive and Judicial officers of a State, or the members of the Legislature thereof, is denied to any of the male inhabitants of such State, being twenty-one years of age, and citizens of the United States, or in any way abridged, except for participation in rebellion, or other crime, the basis of representation therein shall be reduced in the proportion which the number of such male citizens shall bear to the whole number of male citizens twenty-one years of age in such State.

Section 3. No person shall be a Senator or Representative in Congress, or elector of President and Vice-President, or hold any office, civil or military, under the United States, or under any State, who, having previously taken an oath, as a member of Congress, or as an officer of the United States, or as a member of any State legislature, or as an executive or judicial officer of any State, to support the Constitution of the United States, shall have engaged in insurrection or rebellion against the same, or given aid or comfort to the enemies thereof. But Congress may by a vote of two-thirds of each House, remove such disability.

Section 4. The validity of the public debt of the United States, authorized by law, including debts incurred for payment of pensions and bounties for services in suppressing insurrection or rebellion, shall not be questioned. But neither the United States nor any State shall assume or pay any debt or obligation incurred in aid of insurrection or rebellion against the United States, or any claim for the loss or emancipation of any slave; but all such debts, obligations, and claims shall be held illegal and void.

Section 5. The Congress shall have the power to enforce, by appropriate legislation, the provisions of this article.

---

† *Adopted in 1868.*

ARTICLE XV †

Section 1. The right of citizens of the United States to vote shall not be denied or abridged by the United States or by any State on account of race, color, or previous condition of servitude—

Section 2. The Congress shall have power to enforce this article by appropriate legislation.

ARTICLE XVI ‡

The Congress shall have power to lay and collect taxes on incomes, from whatever source derived, without apportionment among the several States, and without regard to any census or enumeration.

ARTICLE [XVII] *

The Senate of the United States shall be composed of two senators from each State, elected by the people thereof, for six years; and each senator shall have one vote. The electors in each State shall have the qualifications requisite for electors of the most numerous branch of the State legislature.

When vacancies happen in the representation of any State in the Senate, the executive authority of such State shall issue writs of election to fill such vacancies: *Provided,* That the legislature of any State may empower the executive thereof to make temporary appointments until the people fill the vacancies by election as the legislature may direct.

This amendment shall not be so construed as to affect the election or term of any Senator chosen before it becomes valid as part of the Constitution.

[ARTICLE [XVIII] **

[*Section 1.* After one year from the ratification of this article, the manufacture, sale, or transportation of intoxicating liquors within, the importation thereof into, or the exportation thereof from the United States and all territory subject to the jurisdiction thereof for beverage purposes is hereby prohibited.

[*Section 2.* The Congress and the several States shall have concurrent power to enforce this article by appropriate legislation.

[*Section 3.* This article shall be inoperative unless it shall have been ratified as an amendment to the Constitution by the legislatures of the several States, as

---

† *Proclaimed March 30, 1870.*
‡ *Adopted in 1913.*
* *Adopted in 1913.*
** *Adopted in 1919.*

provided in the Constitution, within seven years from the date of the submission hereof to the States by the Congress.] †

ARTICLE [XIX] ‡

The right of citizens of the United States to vote shall not be denied or abridged by the United States or by any State on account of sex.

Congress shall have power to enforce this article by appropriate legislation.

ARTICLE [XX] *

Section 1. The terms of the President and Vice President shall end at noon on the 20th day of January, and the terms of Senators and Representatives at noon on the 3d day of January, of the years in which such terms would have ended if this article had not been ratified; and the terms of their successors shall then begin.

Section 2. The Congress shall assemble at least once in every year, and such meeting shall begin at noon on the 3d day of January, unless they shall by law appoint a different day.

Section 3. If, at the time fixed for the beginning of the term of the President, the President elect shall have died, the Vice President elect shall become President. If a President shall not have been chosen before the time fixed for the beginning of his term, or if the President elect shall have failed to qualify, then the Vice President elect shall act as President until a President shall have qualified; and the Congress may by law provide for the case wherein neither a President elect nor a Vice President elect shall have qualified, declaring who shall then act as President, or the manner in which one who is to act shall be selected, and such person shall act accordingly until a President or Vice President shall have qualified.

Section 4. The Congress may by law provide for the case of the death of any of the persons from which the House of Representatives may choose a President whenever the right of choice shall have devolved upon them, and for the case of the death of any of the persons from whom the Senate may choose a Vice President whenever the right of choice shall have devolved upon them.

Section 5. Sections 1 and 2 shall take effect on the 15th day of October following the ratification of this article.

Section 6. This article shall be inoperative unless it shall have been ratified as an amendment to the Constitution by the legislatures of three-fourths of the several States within seven years from the date of its submission.

ARTICLE [XXI] **

Section 1. The Eighteenth Article of amendment to the Constitution of the United States is hereby repealed.

Section 2. The transportation or importation into any State, Territory, or

---

† *Repealed by section 1 of the 21st Amendment.* ‡ *Adopted in 1920.*
* *Adopted in 1933.* ** *Adopted in 1933.*

possession of the United States for delivery or use therein of intoxicating liquors in violation of the laws thereof, is hereby prohibited.

Section 3. This article shall be inoperative unless it shall have been ratified as an amendment to the Constitution by conventions in the several States, as provided in the Constitution, within seven years from the date of the submission thereof to the States by the Congress.

ARTICLE [XXII] †

Section 1. No person shall be elected to the office of the President more than twice, and no person who has held the office of President, or acted as President, for more than two years of a term to which some other person was elected President shall be elected to the office of the President more than once. But this article shall not apply to any person holding the office of President when this Article was proposed by the Congress, and shall not prevent any person who may be holding the office of President, or acting as President, during the term within which this Article becomes operative from holding the office of President or acting as President during the remainder of such term.

Section 2. This article shall be inoperative unless it shall have been ratified as an amendment to the Constitution by the legislatures of three-fourths of the several States within seven years from the date of its submission to the States by the Congress.

ARTICLE [XXIII] ‡

Section 1. The District constituting the seat of Government of the United States shall appoint in such manner as the Congress may direct:

A number of electors of President and Vice President equal to the whole number of Senators and Representatives in Congress to which the District would be entitled if it were a State, but in no event more than the least populous State; they shall be in addition to those appointed by the States, but they shall be considered, for the purposes of the election of President and Vice President, to be electors appointed by a State; and they shall meet in the District and perform such duties as provided by the twelfth article of amendment.

Section 2. The Congress shall have power to enforce this article by appropriate legislation.

ARTICLE [XXIV] *

Section 1. The right of citizens of the United States to vote in any primary or other election for President or Vice President, for electors for President or Vice President, or for Senator or Representative in Congress, shall not be denied or abridged by the United States or any State by reason of failure to pay any poll tax or other tax.

Section 2. The Congress shall have power to enforce this article by appropriate legislation.

---

† *Adopted in 1951.* ‡ *Adopted in 1961.* **Adopted in 1964.*

Index

NOTES

NOTES

NOTES

NOTES